SOMETHING ABOUT THE AUTHOR®

Something about
the Author *was named
an* **"Outstanding
Reference Source,"**
*the highest honor given
by the American
Library Association
Reference and Adult
Services Division.*

ISSN 0276-816X

something ABOUT the AUTHOR®

**Facts and Pictures about Authors
and Illustrators of Books for Young People**

volume 230

GALE
CENGAGE Learning™

Detroit • New York • San Francisco • New Haven, Conn • Waterville, Maine • London

GALE
CENGAGE Learning

Something about the Author, Volume 230

Project Editor: Lisa Kumar

Permissions: Leitha Etheridge-Sims

Imaging and Multimedia: Leitha Etheridge-Sims, John Watkins

Composition and Electronic Capture: Amy Darga

Manufacturing: Rhonda Dover

Product Manager: Mary Onorato

For product information and technology assistance, contact us at
Gale Customer Support, 1-800-877-4253.
For permission to use material from this text or product,
submit all requests online at **www.cengage.com/permissions.**
Further permissions questions can be emailed to
permissionrequest@cengage.com

Gale, Cengage Learning
27500 Drake Rd.
Farmington Hills, MI, 48331-3535

LIBRARY OF CONGRESS CATALOG CARD NUMBER 62-52046

ISBN-13: 978-1-4144-6133-5
ISBN-10: 1-4144-6133-X

ISSN 0276-816X

This title is also available as an e-book.
ISBN-13: 978-1-4144-6462-6
ISBN-10: 1-4144-6462-2
Contact your Gale, Cengage Learning sales representative for ordering information.

Printed in Mexico
1 2 3 4 5 6 7 15 14 13 12 11

Contents

Authors in Forthcoming Volumes

Below are some of the authors and illustrators that will be featured in upcoming volumes of *SATA*. These include new entries on the swiftly rising stars of the field, as well as completely revised and updated entries (indicated with *) on some of the most notable and best-loved creators of books for children.

Tristan Bancks ▮ Although Bancks has acted in television since his teen years and produced several short films, his largest fan following in his native Australia has come through his writing. His "Mac Slater" books for middle graders include *The Rules of Cool* and *I Heart NY,* which were released to U.S. readers as *Mac Slater Hunts the Cool* and *Mac Slater vs. the City* respectively. An advocate of reading and storytelling, he is also the author of chapter books and young adult fiction.

Christopher Cardinale ▮ An artist whose work is an outgrowth of his concern over social inequality, Cardinale has worked with communities as a muralist in the United States as well as in Greece and Mexico, and his illustrations have appeared in counterculture periodicals such as *Punk Planet* and *World War 3*. His greatest exposure as an artist has come from his work on *Mr. Mendoza's Paintbrush,* a graphic novel based on a short story by Mexican poet Alberto Luis Urrea.

Stephen Emond ▮ Emond, a Connecticut native, first made a name for himself as a college student when he beat out artists in prestigious art education programs and won publisher Andrew Mc-Meel's nationwide Strip Search talent contest for emerging cartoonists. His passion for cartooning took shape in high school, and his innovative adult work includes the "Emo Boy" comic as well as the YA novels *Happyface* and *Winter Town,* both of which feature a mix of visual and verbal storytelling.

*Sally Hewitt ▮ A former teacher in her native England, Hewitt now specializes in writing nonfiction books for young children. A prolific author who has been praised for her ability to weave facts into an interesting text, her published books include *Mr. Goon Flies to the Moon, All Kinds of Habitats,* and numerous titles in the "It's Science!," "Now I Know," "Amazing Science," "I Can Remember," "Starters," and "Green Team" reader series.

Dick Houston ▮ Houston grew up in the Midwest but fulfilled his dream of living in the wild after a move to Africa. In his job as a safari leader and conservationist, he has led journeys across the Sahara Desert, through rain forests, and into the African bush, where his concern over the continent's threatened wildlife prompted him to help found the conservation nonprofit Elefence International. He was inspired to write his first children's book, *Bulu: African Wonder Dog,* while visiting Zambia's South Luangwa National Park and learning the story of a remarkable Jack Russell terrier.

*Rukhsana Khan ▮ A Pakistan-born Canadian writer and storyteller, Khan draws on her experiences living within two very different cultures in her award-winning picture books for children. In *King of the Skies, Ruler of the Courtyard, Big Red Lollipop,* and *The Roses in My Carpets* she introduces young children who cope with the universal problems of growing up while also living within a Muslim culture that is very different from that experienced by Khan's Canadian and American readers.

*Carolyn Mackler ▮ Mackler writes young adult novels about ordinary girls who feel awkward about themselves and are trying to find a place in their world. In addition to writing popular novels with eye catching, quirky titles that include *Love and Other Four Letter Words, The Earth, My Butt, and Other Big Round Things, Vegan Virgin Valentine,* and *Guyaholic: A Story of Finding, Flirting, Forgetting ... and the Boy Who Changes Everything,* she has also published short stories and articles in a variety of popular teen magazines.

*Gary Paulsen ▮ In lean prose that critics have cited for containing echoes of novelist Ernest Hemingway, Paulsen creates powerful young adult fiction, often setting his stories in wilderness or rural areas and featuring teenagers who arrive at self awareness by way of experiences in nature—through challenging tests of their own survival instincts—or through the ministrations of understanding adults. His honors include the Margaret A. Edwards Award for lifetime achievement in writing books for teens as well as Newbery Medal Honor Book citations for his novels *Dogsong, Hatchet,* and *The Winter Room.*

*Alice Schertle ▮ Schertle is the author of dozens of engaging stories for younger children, including *William and Grandpa, Down the Road,* and the award-winning *We.* Although several of her picture books deal with family situations—in *Maisie* she profiles a loving grandmother and *Down the Road* follows a girl on her first solo trip to the grocery store—she has also crafted poetry collections and original nursery rhymes.

Lee Wildish ▮ Wildish began his creative career as a graphic designer and worked in several different areas before turning to book illustration. Working as a studio manager for a printer and newspaper allowed him to experience the commercial side of being an artist, and during his five year stint creating art and designs for a greeting card company he was able to follow his concepts from start to finish. As a freelance illustrator, his work has been a natural fit for children's books, and it has been paired with texts by authors ranging from Shutta Crum and Kes Gray to Steve Smallman and Marilyn Singer.

Introduction

Something about the Author (*SATA*) is an ongoing reference series that examines the lives and works of authors and illustrators of books for children. *SATA* includes not only well-known writers and artists but also less prominent individuals whose works are just coming to be recognized. This series is often the only readily available information source on emerging authors and illustrators. You'll find *SATA* informative and entertaining, whether you are a student, a librarian, an English teacher, a parent, or simply an adult who enjoys children's literature.

What's Inside *SATA*

SATA provides detailed information about authors and illustrators who span the full time range of children's literature, from early figures like John Newbery and L. Frank Baum to contemporary figures like Judy Blume and Richard Peck. Authors in the series represent primarily English-speaking countries, particularly the United States, Canada, and the United Kingdom. Also included, however, are authors from around the world whose works are available in English translation. The writings represented in *SATA* include those created intentionally for children and young adults as well as those written for a general audience and known to interest younger readers. These writings cover the entire spectrum of children's literature, including picture books, humor, folk and fairy tales, animal stories, mystery and adventure, science fiction and fantasy, historical fiction, poetry and nonsense verse, drama, biography, and nonfiction. Obituaries are also included in many volumes of *SATA* and are intended not only as death notices but also as concise overviews of people's lives and work. Additionally, each edition features newly revised and updated entries for a selection of *SATA* listees who remain of interest to today's readers and who have been active enough to require extensive revisions of their earlier biographies.

Autobiography Feature

Beginning with Volume 103, many volumes of *SATA* feature one or more specially commissioned autobiographical essays. These unique essays, averaging about ten thousand words in length and illustrated with an abundance of personal photos, present an entertaining and informative first-person perspective on the lives and careers of prominent authors and illustrators profiled in *SATA*.

Two Convenient Indexes

In response to suggestions from librarians, *SATA* indexes no longer appear in every volume but are included in alternate (odd-numbered) volumes of the series, beginning with Volume 57.

SATA continues to include two indexes that cumulate with each alternate volume: the Illustrations Index, arranged by the name of the illustrator, gives the number of the volume and page where the illustrator's work appears in the current volume as well as all preceding volumes in the series; the Author Index gives the number of the volume in which a person's biographical sketch, autobiographical essay, or obituary appears in the current volume as well as all preceding volumes in the series.

These indexes also include references to authors and illustrators who appear in *Gale's Yesterday's Authors of Books for Children, Children's Literature Review,* and *Something about the Author Autobiography Series.*

Easy-to-Use Entry Format

Whether you're already familiar with the *SATA* series or just getting acquainted, you will want to be aware of the kind of information that an entry provides. In every *SATA* entry the editors attempt to give as complete a picture of the person's life and work as possible. A typical entry in *SATA* includes the following clearly labeled information sections:

PERSONAL: date and place of birth and death, parents' names and occupations, name of spouse, date of marriage, names of children, educational institutions attended, degrees received, religious and political affiliations, hobbies and other interests.

ADDRESSES: complete home, office, electronic mail, and agent addresses, whenever available.

CAREER: name of employer, position, and dates for each career post; art exhibitions; military service; memberships and offices held in professional and civic organizations.

MEMBER: professional, civic, and other association memberships and any official posts held.

AWARDS, HONORS: literary and professional awards received.

WRITINGS: title-by-title chronological bibliography of books written and/or illustrated, listed by genre when known; lists of other notable publications, such as plays, screenplays, and periodical contributions.

ADAPTATIONS: a list of films, television programs, plays, CD-ROMs, recordings, and other media presentations that have been adapted from the author's work.

WORK IN PROGRESS: description of projects in progress.

SIDELIGHTS: a biographical portrait of the author or illustrator's development, either directly from the biographee—and often written specifically for the *SATA* entry—or gathered from diaries, letters, interviews, or other published sources.

BIOGRAPHICAL AND CRITICAL SOURCES: cites sources quoted in "Sidelights" along with references for further reading.

EXTENSIVE ILLUSTRATIONS: photographs, movie stills, book illustrations, and other interesting visual materials supplement the text.

How a *SATA* Entry Is Compiled

SATA editors examine a wide variety of published sources to gather information for an entry. Biographical and bibliographic sources are consulted, as are book reviews, feature articles, published interviews, and material sometimes obtained from the biographee's family, publishers, agent, or other associates. Whenever possible, the author or illustrator is sent a copy of the entry to check for accuracy and completeness.

Entries that have not been verified by the biographees or their representatives are marked with an asterisk (*).

Contact the Editor

We encourage our readers to examine the entire *SATA* series. Please write and tell us if we can make *SATA* even more helpful to you. Give your comments and suggestions to the editor:

Editor
Something about the Author
Gale, Cengage Learning
27500 Drake Rd.
Farmington Hills MI 48331-3535

Toll-free: 800-877-GALE
Fax: 248-699-8070

Something about the Author Product Advisory Board

The editors of *Something about the Author* are dedicated to maintaining a high standard of excellence by publishing comprehensive, accurate, and highly readable entries on a wide array of writers for children and young adults. In addition to the quality of the content, the editors take pride in the graphic design of the series, which is intended to be orderly yet inviting, allowing readers to utilize the pages of *SATA* easily and with efficiency. Despite the longevity of the *SATA* print series, and the success of its format, we are mindful that the vitality of a literary reference product is dependent on its ability to serve its users over time. As literature, and attitudes about literature, constantly evolve, so do the reference needs of students, teachers, scholars, journalists, researchers, and book club members. To be certain that we continue to keep pace with the expectations of our customers, the editors of *SATA* listen carefully to their comments regarding the value, utility, and quality of the series. Librarians, who have firsthand knowledge of the needs of library users, are a valuable resource for us. The *Something about the Author* Product Advisory Board, made up of school, public, and academic librarians, is a forum to promote focused feedback about *SATA* on a regular basis. The nine-member advisory board includes the following individuals, whom the editors wish to thank for sharing their expertise:

Eva M. Davis
Director,
Canton Public Library,
Canton, Michigan

Joan B. Eisenberg
Lower School Librarian,
Milton Academy,
Milton, Massachusetts

Francisca Goldsmith
Teen Services Librarian,
Berkeley Public Library,
Berkeley, California

Susan Dove Lempke
Children's Services Supervisor,
Niles Public Library District,
Niles, Illinois

Robyn Lupa
Head of Children's Services,
Jefferson County Public Library,
Lakewood, Colorado

Victor L. Schill
Assistant Branch Librarian/Children's Librarian,
Harris County Public Library/Fairbanks Branch,
Houston, Texas

Caryn Sipos
Community Librarian,
Three Creeks Community Library,
Vancouver, Washington

Steven Weiner
Director,
Maynard Public Library,
Maynard, Massachusetts

SOMETHING ABOUT THE AUTHOR

ADLER, Emily

Personal

Born in New York, NY. *Education:* Macalester College, B.A.; Hunter College, M.A. (theatre).

Addresses

Home—New York, NY. *Agent*—Caren Johnson Literary Agency, 132 E. 43rd St., No. 216, New York, NY 10017.

Career

Playwright and fiction writer. Worked variously as a waitress, bakery clerk, conference organizer, production assistant, and preschool and English-as-a-second language teacher. Artistic director for college theatre; Mixed Blessings Theatre Company, cofounder.

Writings

(With Alex Echevarria) *Sweet 15,* Marshall Cavendish (New York, NY), 2009.

Author plays, including *The Frog in the Flipper, Spiritual Playboy,* and *Andromeda Speaks.*

Biographical and Critical Sources

PERIODICALS

Bulletin of the Center for Children's Books, July-August, 2010, Maggie Hommel, review of *Sweet 15,* p. 469.
School Library Journal, July, 2010, Robin Henry, review of *Sweet 15,* p. 80.

ONLINE

Caren Johnson Literary Agency Web Page, http://www.johnsonliterary.com/ (May 15, 2011).*

*   *   *

al ABDULLAH, Rania 1970-
   (Queen Raina)

Personal

Born August 31, 1970, in Kuwait; immigrated to Jordan, 1990; daughter of a pediatrician; married King Abdullah II ibn Al Hussein, June 10, 1993; children: Crown Prince Hussein, Princess Iman, Princess Salma, Prince Hashem. *Education:* American University in Cairo, B.A. (business administration), 1991. *Religion:* Muslim. *Hobbies and other interests:* Running.

Rania al Abdullah, Queen of Jordan (Uli Deck/DPA/Landov. Reproduced by permission.)

Addresses

Home—Amman, Jordan.

Career

Philanthropist and author. Citibank, Amman, Jordan, former investment banker; Apple Computer, Amman, former member of marketing staff; proclaimed queen of Jordan, March 22, 1999. Participant in international gatherings, including Clinton Global Initiative. Member of board, International Youth Foundation, United Nations Foundation, World Economic Forum, Foundation for International Community Assistance, and Forum of Young Global Leaders; Royal Health Awareness Society, chairperson; established Queen Raina scholarship program.

Awards, Honors

Life Achievement Award, American Osteoporosis Foundation, 2001; James C. Morgan Global Humanitarian Award, 2010; named Dama di Gran Croce, Republic of Italy Order of Merit; named to Royal Norwegian Order of St. Olav; named honorary member of international advisory council, International Center for Research on Women; honorary chairperson of philanthropic organizations, including U.N. Girls' Education Initiative and Operation Smile.

Writings

The King's Gift: A Tribute to His Majesty the Late King Hussein of Jordan (in Arabic), illustrated by Angel Dominguez, Michael O'Mara Books (London, England), 2000.

Eternal Beauty, [Jordan], 2008.

Maha of the Mountains, Global Campaign for Education (Amman, Jordan), 2009.

(With Kelly DiPucchio) *The Sandwich Swap,* illustrated by Tricia Tusa, Disney-Hyperion Books (New York, NY), 2010.

Sidelights

Raina al Abdullah is best known to the world as Queen Raina, wife to Jordan's King Abdullah II ibn al Hussein. Beloved by many around the world for both the example she sets as a mother to her four children and the grace she brings to her office, Queen Raina is also active in the education of future generations of Jordanians through her work promoting computer literacy, consistent teaching standards, and the increased involvement of families, businesses, and communities in the educational process. Her position as queen also allows her to work on the international level, advocating for all children's right to a quality education and also serving as a spokesperson for UNICEF. On an individual level, Queen Raina also shares a lesson in tolerating differences in *The Sandwich Swap,* a picture book coauthored by Kelly DiPucchio and illustrated by Tricia Tusa.

Queen Rania was born in Kuwait to Palestinian parents, and her father supported the family's upper-middle-class lifestyle through his work as a pediatrician. She was educated in a private school where she learned to master English and also gained exposure to non-Muslim culture. Queen Raina was earning her degree in business administration at the American University in Cairo in 1990 when Saddam Hussein invaded Kuwait and her family fled to nearby Jordan. She joined her family after graduation and took a job with Citibank. She was twenty-two and working in the marketing department of Apple Computer's Amman branch when she met Prince Abdullah at a dinner party, and the couple was married eighteen months later. Prince Abdullah expected to continue his career in the Jordanian Army. However, when his father, King Hussein, died five years later he had altered the succession, passing the crown from his brother, the Prince Regent, to his son and making Raina queen.

One of Queen Raina's first published books, a tribute to the late King Hussein, was the children's book *The King's Gift: A Tribute to His Majesty the Late King Hussein of Jordan,* and the proceeds from its sales were donated to a Jordanian children's charity. *Eternal Beauty,* her next book, honors Mother's Day, while *Maha of the Mountains* was written for the 2009 Big Read event and focuses on a child's determination to gain an education.

Queen Raina teams up with Kelly DiPucchio on the friendship story The Sandwich Swap, *featuring artwork by Tricia Tusa.*

Queen Raina's story for her fourth book, *The Sandwich Swap,* is based on a childhood memory. Coauthored by veteran children's-book author DiPucchio, it focuses on the relationship between best friends Lily and Salma when each decides that the other's favorite sandwich is beyond distasteful. Lily loves peanut butter and jelly, just like most everyone else she knows. Salma's hummus-on-pita bread sandwich does not seem normal, and even more not-normal is the fact that Salma finds peanut butter and jelly less than appealing. Fortunately, although their disagreement escalates into a lunchroom brawl, the two friends make up while waiting in the principal's office, and they even trade sandwiches! Writing in *Booklist,* Hazel Rochman called *The Sandwich Swap* a "lively picture book" and praised Tusa for crafting "harmonious" illustrations for the collaborative text. A *Publishers Weekly* critic noted the story's "readily apparent themes of acceptance and sharing," while Marjorie Kehe concluded in her *Christian Science Monitor* review that *The Sandwich Swap* contains "a lesson to remember."

Biographical and Critical Sources

PERIODICALS

Booklist, February 15, 2010, Hazel Rochman, review of *The Sandwich Swap,* p. 81.

Children's Bookwatch, June, 2010, review of *The Sandwich Swap.*

Christian Science Monitor, April 2, 1010, Marjorie Kehe, review of *The Sandwich Swap.*

Harper's Bazaar, March, 2003, Lisa DePaulo, "Up Close with Queen Rania," p. 276.

Middle East, March, 1999, Adel Darwish, "Spotlight on a Queen," p. 7.

People, November 21, 2005, Michelle Tauber, "A Very Modern Queen," p. 110.

Publishers Weekly, March 15, 2010, review of *The Sandwich Swap,* p. 50.

Sunday Times (London, England), May 28, 2006, "Her Majesty Won't Be Wearing a Burqa," p. 5.

Time for Kids, January 11, 2008, Ritu Upadhyay, "A Royal Quest for Peace," p. 7.

Time International, November 13, 2006, Scott MacLeod, "Queen Rania," p. 102.

ONLINE

Campaign for Education Web site, http://www.campaignfor education.org/ (May 15, 2011), "Maha of the Mountains."

Rania al Abdullah Home Page, http://www.queenrania.jo (May 27, 2011).*

*   *   *

AREVAMIRP, Esile
See PRIMAVERA, Elise

B

BACIGALUPI, Paolo 1973-

Personal
Born 1973, in Colorado Springs, CO; married, 1998; wife's name Anjula; children: a son. *Education:* Oberlin College, B.A. (East Asian studies), 1994.

Addresses
Home—Paonia, CO. *Agent*—Martha Millard Literary Agency, 420 Central Park W., No. 5H, New York, NY 10025.

Career
Author and journalist. Worked as a Web developer in Boston, MA, c. 1996; *High Country News* (environmental newspaper), staff writer.

Awards, Honors
Hugo Award for Best Novelette nomination, 2005, for "The People of Sand and Slag," 2006, for "The Calorie Man," 2007, for "Yellow Card Man," 2009, for "The Gambler"; Nebula Award for Best Novelette nomination, 2006, for "The People of Sand and Slag," 2010, for "The Gambler," 2011 for *The Alchemist;* Theodore Sturgeon Award, 2006, for "The Calorie Man"; *Locus* Award for Best Collection, 2008, for *Pump Six, and Other Stories;* Hugo Award for Best Novel, Nebula Award, Compton Crook Award, Locus Award for Best First Novel, and John W. Campbell Memorial Award, all 2010, all for *The Windup Girl;* National Book Award nomination, 2010, and Michael L. Printz Award for Best Young-Adult Novel, and Andre Norton Award for Young-Adult Science Fiction and Fantasy, both 2011, all for *Ship Breaker.*

Writings
Pump Six, and Other Stories, Night Shade Books (San Francisco, CA), 2008.

The Windup Girl, Night Shade Books (San Francisco, CA), 2009.
Ship Breaker, Little, Brown (New York, NY), 2010.
(With J.K. Drummond) *The Alchemist,* Subterranean Press (Burton, MI), 2011.

Contributor of short fiction and essays to periodicals, including *Albuquerque Journal, Asimov's Science Fiction, High Country News, Idaho Statesman, Magazine of Fantasy and Science Fiction, Salt Lake Tribune,* and *Salon.com.* Work included in anthology *Year's Best SF 14,* edited by David G. Hartwell and Kathryn Cramer, EOS (New York, NY), 2009.

Author's works have been translated into several languages, including Czech and German.

Adaptations
The Windup Girl was adapted for audiobook, read by Jonathan Davis, Audible, Inc., 2009.

Sidelights
Focusing on "biopunk" science fiction as well as fantasy, Paolo Bacigalupi draws readers into imagined near-future worlds in which industrialized human society's abuse of Earth's resources has led to environmental degradation. Describing Bacigalupi's fiction, *Progressive* writer Laura Paskus noted that he starts with "real environmental crises and then extrapolates into a grotesque future. Trained hunters track down women who defy programs designed to prevent anyone from bearing children in an overcrowded world. A new breed of humans emerges as a result of the vast quantities of PCBs and phthalates we today pump into our bodies. In secret, farmers and geneticists preserve heirloom plants, which have tastes and textures foreign to human tongues." His focus on environmental subjects that make headlines renders Bacigalupi's fiction—including *Pump Six, and Other Stories,* the fantasy novela *The Alchemist,* and his novels *The Windup Girl* and *Ship Breaker*—both prescient and frightening.

Raised by free-spirited parents in a commune and then on an apple orchard in rural Colorado, Bacigalupi loved reading fantasy and science fiction while growing up; *Red Planet, Starship Troopers,* and other Robert A. Heinlein novels as well as J.R.R. Tolkien's *The Hobbit* were among his favorites. He eventually attended Oberlin College where he majored in East Asian studies with a focus on the Chinese language. Traveling also added to Bacigalupi's knowledge, and he spent time in China as well as in Hong Kong, Laos, Malaysia, Singapore, and Thailand. He started writing his own stories while living in Boston and working as a Web developer. As he recalled to *Wired Science* online interviewer Damon Gambuto, at work "all of these marketing people would be coming into my cubicle—it was very Dilbert—they all said the exact same things, they all had the same exact anecdotes no matter what company was coming in. It was really sort of soul killing, and so I actually started writing science fiction around that time. Something to do on the weekends."

Writing mixed with travel over the next few years, as Bacigalupi gradually worked his way west to his native Colorado. Several failed attempts at novels prompted

Cover of Paolo Bacigalupi's award-winning science-fiction novel **Ship Breaker,** *which features cover art by Bob Warner.* (Cover art by Bob Warner. Copyright © by Hachette Book Group USA. All rights reserved. Reproduced by permission.)

him to turn to shorter fiction, and in 1999 his first published short story, "Pocketful of Dharma," resulted in a phone call from noted sci-fi writer Harlan Ellison. Ellison gave the young writer some constructive advice, leading Bacigalupi to produce several other stories before turning back to novel-length fiction. Reviewing *Pump Six, and Other Stories,* which collects "The Calorie Man," "The People of Sand and Slag," "The Tamarisk Hunter," and seven other early works, Regina Schroeder noted in *Booklist* that the author "makes no secret of his social attitudes, but he handles political commentary with grace and packs a lot of thought into quite a small space." A *Publishers Weekly* critic hailed the anthology, writing that Bacigalupi's "stellar" work "displays the astute social commentary and consciousness-altering power of the very best short form science fiction."

Like his short fiction, Bacigalupi's first novel, *The Windup Girl,* is written for adults and explores complex themes such as the unintended consequences of bioengineering in a future world where sea levels are rising and technology has reversed due to the lack of fossil fuels. Engineered foods have brought with them new diseases, while other scientific advances have resulted in genetically engineered humans able to survive these new conditions. As food becomes scarce and elephant-like megodonts serve as society's engine through their energy-intensive labor, the calorie becomes society's new rate of exchange. Set in Thailand, *The Windup Girl* finds calorie hunter Anderson Lake tasked with locating new sources of food energy for his employer, AgriGen. His relationships with Jaidee, a government representative charged with enforcing environmental regulations, and Emiko, an engineered "human" that is being brutally treated, play out in what *School Library Journal* critic Karen E. Brooks-Reese described as a "highly nuanced, violent, and grim novel" featuring a "complex plot and equally complex characters." "East meets West in a clash of cultures brilliantly portrayed in razor-sharp images, tension-building pacing, and sharply etched characters," wrote Jackie Cassada in her review of *The Windup Girl* for *Library Journal.* In the novel "Bacigalupi's near future is terrifying, astonishing, and brilliantly brought to vibrant life," asserted *Booklist* contributor Regina Schroeder.

In *Ship Breaker* Bacigalupi writes for a teen audience. Like *The Windup Girl,* his setting is a near future in which Earth's environment has been degraded. Nailer lives on the Gulf coast of the United States, where he and friend Pima scavenge copper wire from the rusting hulks of oil tankers that now litter the local beaches. When the two teens discover the wreck of a luxury ship, they also find young survivor: a woman passenger named Nita who is still alive, but barely. While Nailer knows that the salvage from this ship would bring in enough money to improve his life and that of Pima, he also knows that his drug-addicted father will stop at nothing to gain control over the find, and possibly harm Nita as well. "Although Bacigalupi's future earth [in

Ship Breaker] is brilliantly imagined and its genesis anchored in contemporary issues, it is secondary to the memorable characters," wrote *Booklist* critic Lynn Rutan, the critic predicting that the "captivating" novel "is sure to win [its author] teen fans." While a *Publishers Weekly* critic noted the story's coming-of-age themes, *Ship Breaker* also deals with "rampant class disparity on individual and international levels," according to the reviewer, and Cynthia K. Ritter concluded in *Horn Book* that Bacigalupi's "thriller will grab and keep readers' attentions as Nailer and Nita 'crew up' in their fight to survive."

As he has expanded his audience from adults to include teens and his medium from the short story to the novel, Bacigalupi has received increasing critical praise. However, the literary honors that have come his way—the Theodore Sturgeon Award, the John W. Campbell Memorial Award, a *Locus* award, a Nebula, and a Hugo—have been unexpected byproducts of his decision to become a writer. "I don't really understand how or why my writing actually resonates with other people," he noted in a *Locus* interview. "It all seems faintly mysterious. I know what I'm trying to write, but the alchemy that happens between the reader and my writing is extraordinary."

Biographical and Critical Sources

PERIODICALS

Booklist, March 15, 2008, Regina Schroeder, review of *Pump Six, and Other Stories,* p. 37; October 15, 2009, Regina Schroeder, review of *The Windup Girl,* p. 32; May 15, 2010, Lynn Rutan, review of *Ship Breaker,* p. 50.

Denver Post, May 30, 2010, Clay Evans, interview with Bacigalupi, p. 11.

Horn Book, July-August, 2010, Cynthia K. Ritter, review of *Ship Breaker,* p. 98.

Library Journal, September 15, 2009, Jackie Cassada, review of *The Windup Girl,* p. 52.

Locus, July, 2007, interview with Bacigalupi.

Progressive, November, 2009, Laura Paskus, "Bacigalupi's World," p. 38.

Publishers Weekly, February 11, 2008, review of *Pump Six, and Other Stories,* p. 54; August 24, 2009, review of *The Windup Girl,* p. 48; April 19, 2010, review of *Ship Breaker,* p. 54; November 8, 2010, review of *The Alchemist,* p. 47.

School Library Journal, December, 2009, Karen E. Brooks-Reese, review of *The Windup Girl,* p. 144; June, 2010, Hayden Bass, review of *Ship Breaker,* p. 94.

ONLINE

Paolo Bacigalupi Home Page, http://windupstories.com (May 27, 2011).

Wired Science Web site, http://www.pbs.org/kcet/wired science/blogs/ (January 25, 2008), Damon Gambuto, interview with Bacigalupi.*

*   *   *

BEAKY, Suzanne 1971-

Personal

Born 1971, in OH; married. *Education:* Columbus College of Art and Design, degree (illustration).

Addresses

Home—Kirksville, MO. *Agent*—Liz Sanders Agency, liz@lizsanders.com. *E-mail*—suzanne@suzannebeaky.com.

Career

Illustrator.

Member

Society of Children's Book Writers and Illustrators (Missouri chapter).

Awards, Honors

Durham (NC) Arts Council Emerging Artist Award; Ellen Dolan Memorial Mentorship Award, Society of Children's Book Writers and Illustrators—Missouri.

Illustrator

Laura Manivong, *One Smart Fish,* Children's Press (New York, NY), 2006.

Greg Owens, *Rupert the Wrong-word Pirate,* Kindermusik International (Greensboro, NC), 2006.

Barbie H. Schwaeber, editor, *She'll Be Comin' 'round the Mountain* (with CD), Soundprints (Norwalk, CT), 2007.

Lauren Barnholdt, *Hailey Twitch Is Not a Snitch,* Sourcebooks Jabberwocky (Naperville, IL), 2010.

Lauren Barnholdt, *Hailey Twitch and the Great Teacher Switch,* Sourcebooks Jabberwocky (Naperville, IL), 2011.

Lauren Barnholdt, *Hailey Twitch and the Campground Itch,* Sourcebooks Jabberwocky (Naperville, IL), 2011.

Linda Lodding, *The Busy Life of Ernestine Buckmeister,* Flashlight Press (New York, NY), 2011.

Books featuring Beaky's art have been translated into French.

Biographical and Critical Sources

PERIODICALS

Booklist, July 1, 2010, Julie Cummins, review of *Hailey Twitch Is Not a Snitch,* p. 60; February 15, 2011, Julie Cummins, review of *Hailey Twitch and the Great Teacher Switch,* p. 76.

ONLINE

Suzanne Beaky Home Page, http://www.suzannebeaky.com
(May 27, 2011).*

*　　*　　*

BERNADETTE
See WATTS, Bernadette

*　　*　　*

BILDNER, Phil

Personal

Born in Jericho, NY. *Education:* Johns Hopkins University, bachelor's degree (political science); New York University School of Law, J.D., 1990; Long Island University, master's degree (elementary education). *Hobbies and other interests:* Tennis, softball, snowboarding, video games.

Addresses

Home—Brooklyn, NY. *Agent*—Jennifer Flannery, Flannery Literary, 1140 Wickfield Ct., Naperville, IL 60563-3300. *E-mail*—phil@philbildner.com.

Career

Writer, educator, and attorney. Admitted to the bars of the State of New York and the State of New Jersey; New York City Public Schools, New York, NY, elementary and middle-school teacher, 1994-2005; full-time writer, 2006—. NOLA Tree (nonprofit service organization), cofounder, 2007, and co-executive director. Presenter at schools.

Awards, Honors

Texas Bluebonnet Award, 2004, for *Shoeless Joe and Black Betsy.*

Writings

PICTURE BOOKS

Shoeless Joe and Black Betsy, illustrated by C.F. Payne, Simon & Schuster (New York, NY), 2002.
Twenty-one Elephants, illustrated by LeUyen Pham, Simon & Schuster (New York, NY), 2004.
The Shot Heard 'round the World, illustrated by C.F. Payne, Simon & Schuster (New York, NY), 2005.
The Greatest Game Every Played: A Football Story, illustrated by Zachary Pullen, Putnam (New York, NY), 2006.

Phil Bildner (Copyright © 2005. Photo courtesy of Phil Bildner.)

Turkey Bowl, illustrated by C.F. Payne, Simon & Schuster Books for Young Readers (New York, NY), 2008.
The Hallelujah Flight, illustrated by John Holyfield, G.P. Putnam's Sons (New York, NY), 2010.
The Unforgettable Season: The Story of Joe DiMaggio, Ted Williams, and the Record-setting Summer of '41, illustrated by S.D. Schindler, G.P. Putnam's Sons (New York, NY), 2011.

YOUNG-ADULT NOVELS

Playing the Field, Simon & Schuster (New York, NY), 2006.
Busted, Simon & Schuster (New York, NY), 2007.

"BARNSTORMERS"/"SLUGGERS" CHAPTER-BOOK SERIES; ILLUSTRATED BY LOREN LONG

Game 1: Porkopolis, Simon & Schuster (New York, NY), 2007, published as *Magic in the Outfield,* 2009.
Game 2: The River City, Simon & Schuster (New York, NY), 2007, published as *Horsin' Around,* 2009.
Game 3: The Windy City, Simon & Schuster Books for Young Readers (New York, NY), 2008, published as *Great Balls of Fire,* 2009.
Water, Water Everywhere, Simon & Schuster Books for Young Readers (New York, NY), 2009.
Blastin' the Blues, Simon & Schuster Books for Young Readers (New York, NY), 2010.
Home of the Brave, Simon & Schuster Books for Young Readers (New York, NY), 2010.

Sidelights

A lawyer turned teacher turned author, Phil Bildner has published both picture books and novels for various reading levels that feature sports-related themes. Best known for his "Sluggers" chapter-book series, which is coauthored and illustrated by Loren Long, Bildner also creates large-format books for younger children that pair engaging illustrations with true-life stories drawn from the history of his favorite sports: baseball and football. His sports-centered picture books include *The*

Unforgettable Season: The Story of Joe DiMaggio, Ted Williams, and the Record-setting Summer of '41, The Shot Heard 'round the World, and *Shoeless Joe and Black Betsy,* the last which earned its author the prestigious Texas Bluebonnet Award.

Born in Jericho, New York, a Long Island suburb, Bildner graduated from Johns Hopkins University and attended the New York University School of Law before working briefly at a Manhattan law firm. After deciding to change careers, he returned to school and earned his master's degree in elementary education before landing his first teaching job at a public school in the South Bronx. A lack of school-district resources forced Bildner to develop innovative teaching methods; he often incorporated music into his lesson plans, drawing the attention of recording artists such as the Dave Matthews Band and The Fugees, who visited his classroom.

Bildner made the leap to published author in 2002 with *Shoeless Joe and Black Betsy,* "an amusing picture-book tall tale," according to *Booklist* contributor Bill Ott. The work concerns baseball great Joe Jackson, who turns to batsmith Charlie Ferguson when his performance slumps at the plate. Charlie makes a special bat, nicknamed Black Betsy, that carries Joe to the major leagues. "The repetition and wry humor of the exchanges between the two superstitious characters pull the legend out of the story," noted *School Library Journal* critic Wendy Lukehart, and a reviewer in *Publishers Weekly* stated that the author "hits a home run here, zeroing in on the bat as just the right lens through which to view his picture book biography."

In *The Shot Heard 'round the World* Bildner chronicles the stirring 1951 pennant race between the New York Giants and the Brooklyn Dodgers. Told from the perspective of a young Dodgers' fan, the work takes readers through one of the most exciting seasons of the sport's Golden Age, "with the text showing how baseball in the pre-television era was a community passion, shared on front stoops and around radios," observed *Booklist* reviewer Ott. "Bildner captures the spirit of Brooklyn in 1951," noted a critic in *Kirkus Reviews* of the author's depiction of the thrilling playoff series between the two teams. The series ended with Bobby Thomson's famous home run. Known as "the shot heard around the world," it propelled the Giants into the World Series.

Illustrated by S.D. Schindler, *The Unforgettable Season* takes readers back a decade earlier in time. In the spring of 1941, the game of baseball introduced two of its most-beloved players: New York Yankee Joe DiMaggio and Boston Red Sox player Ted Williams. For DiMaggio, 1941 was the year he set his amazing fifty-six-game hitting streak, while Williams risked his almost-perfect 4.00 batting average to play the final game of the season. Describing the book as a "warm tribute" to great American athletes, Marilyn Taniguchi added in her *School Library Journal* appraisal of *The Unforget-*

table Season that "even non-sports fans will appreciate how Bildner and Schindler weave period details into this engaging account."

Bildner looks at another landmark sporting event in *The Greatest Game Every Played: A Football Story.* "Deftly blending surefire ingredients—nostalgia, father-son bonding, and on-field action," according to a *Publishers Weekly* contributor, "Bildner's story tells of the 1958 NFL championship game" in which the Baltimore Colts defeated the New York Giants in a sudden-death overtime thriller. Reviewing *The Greatest Game Ever Played, Booklist* Ilene Cooper praised "Bildner's lively text, which brings to light some great football history to share across generations." Football is also the focus of *Turkey Bowl,* in which eight-year-old Ethan looks forward to finally being old enough to participate in his family's traditional Thanksgiving Day football game. When the region is buried by a huge snowfall on Thanksgiving morning, Ethan and his friends find a way to continue the tradition anyway, their resourcefulness captured in C.F. Payne's colorful paintings. "Perfect for reading aloud," according to *School Library Journal* critic Marge Loch-Wouters, *Turkey Bowl* features a "lively story [that] will resonate year-round with sports fans."

Bildner turns from sports to other subjects in several of his stories for young children. A young girl's fascination with the Brooklyn Bridge is the focus of *Twenty-one Elephants,* in which Hannah is determined to walk across the recently completed Brooklyn Bridge even though her skeptical father does not trust the river-spanning structure. After a visit to the circus, where Hannah spies a group of performing elephants, she approaches P.T. Barnum with an unusual request. Bildner and illustrator LeUyen Pham "deftly juggle fact and fiction in this charming tale, which celebrates a child's imagination and faith," wrote a *Publishers Weekly* critic.

Featuring illustrations by John Holyfield, *The Hallelujah Flight* also takes readers into the past. In the story the year is 1932 and African-American pilot James Banning is joined by his young mechanic Thomas Allen on a flight from Los Angeles, California, to Long Island, New York. The first transatlantic flight by an African American, the journey lasted three weeks, and Banning and Allen encountered adventures as well as racial prejudice on their 3,300-mile trip to a hero's welcome in Harlem. *The Hallelujah Flight* "is exciting and fast paced, and the writing is upbeat and inviting," asserted Anne Chapman in her *School Library Journal* review, and a *Kirkus Reviews* writer cited Holyfield's "gorgeous oil paintings" and Bildner's use of "imagined dialogue" in his "briskly told" tale. The book's "story of the pilots' bonding is as memorable as the breakthrough flight," according to *Booklist* critic Hazel Rochman, and a *Publishers Weekly* reviewer asserted that "Holyfield's . . . stylized paintings help this saga get off the ground effortlessly."

Bildner's picture books include **The Hallelujah Flight,** *a true story of early aviation that features artwork by John Holyfield.* (Illustration copyright © 2010 by John Holyfield. Reproduced with permission of G.P. Putnam's Sons, a division of Penguin Books for Young Readers, a member of Penguin Group (USA) Inc., 345 Hudson St., New York, NY 10014. All rights reserved.)

Coauthored and illustrated by Long, Bildner's "Sluggers" series began as the three-book "Barnstormers: Tales of the Travelin' Nine" saga but was expanded due to the coauthors' enthusiasm for their characters. First published as *Game One: Porkopolis, Magic in the Outfield* is set in 1899, and introduces recently orphaned Griffith, Ruby, and Graham Payne. Together with their widowed mom, the siblings join wheelchair-bound Uncle Owen and the Travelin' Nine, a baseball team whose players—friends of their late father—are veterans of the Spanish-American War. As the children soon learn, a well-worn baseball given to them by their uncle has a special power, and Griffith, Ruby, and Graham must learn to harness it while supporting the team in their face off against a local Cincinnati, Ohio team. In *Horsin' Around* (first published as *Game 2: The River City*) the Payne children and their mother continue to support the Travelin' Nine as the team plays off against a strong competitor and Griffith senses the presence of several strange and mysterious individuals, while *Great Balls of Fire/Game 3: The Windy City* finds the children joining the team in Chicago, where Travelin' Niners Crazy Feet, Doc, Tales, and Woody fuel the team to a much-hoped-for victory. The Payne siblings still worry, and they soon learn that their fears have a real face: the greedy sports promoter known as the Chancellor.

In reviewing the first volume in the series, GraceAnne A. DeCandido praised Bildner's "atmospheric" prose, while *School Library Journal* contributor Kim Dare wrote of *Magic in the Outfield* that the story's "level of historical detail is admirable, and Long's dreamy, black-and-white illustrations are breathtaking." The "Sluggers" series continues in *Water, Water Everywhere, Blas-*tin' the Blues, and *Home of the Brave,* all which continue Bildner and Long's old-fashioned, serialized story.

Bildner's young-adult novels include *Playing the Field* and *Busted.* In *Playing the Field* high schooler Darcy Miller, star player on her school's dismal girls' softball team, desperately wants to join the boy's baseball team. When Brandon Basset, the school principal's son, convinces his father that Darcy is a lesbian, the young woman plays along and Mr. Bassett finally allows her on the squad. Reviewing *Playing the Field, Booklist* contributor John Peters called the work a "fearlessly irreverent first novel."

In four interconnected stories, *Busted* examines the motivation of a high-school principal in dealing with natural teen rebelliousness. In *School Library Journal* Carol A. Edwards predicted of *Busted* that "teens who are tired of goody-goodies and morally uplifting endings will enjoy" Bildner's story as an "exception to the rule."

On his home page, Bildner offered some advice for aspiring authors. "When you write, especially when you're first starting out," he stated, "write about what you know, and more importantly, write about what you love. If you're passionate about something, your knowledge and fervor for that subject matter will come across in your written word."

Biographical and Critical Sources

PERIODICALS

Booklist, February 15, 2002, Bill Ott, review of *Shoeless Joe and Black Betsy,* p. 1014; October 1, 2004, Karin Snelson, review of *Twenty-one Elephants,* p. 332; March 1, 2005, Bill Ott, review of *The Shot Heard 'round the World,* p. 1199; April 1, 2006, John Peters, review of *Playing the Field,* p. 31; September 1, 2006, Ilene Cooper, review of *The Greatest Game Ever Played,* p. 117; April 1, 2007, GraceAnne A. DeCandido, review of *Game 1: Porkopolis,* p. 44; September 15, 2008, Ian Chipman, review of *Turkey Bowl,* p. 58; February 1, 2010, Hazel Rochman, review of *The Hallelujah Flight,* p. 62.

Bulletin of the Center for Children's Books, March, 2006, review of *Playing the Field;* March, 2010, Elizabeth Bush, review of *The Halllelujah Flight,* p. 278.

Children's Literature, May, 2006, review of *Playing the Field.*

Kirkus Reviews, December 15, 2001, review of *Shoeless Joe and Black Betsy,* p. 1754; October 1, 2004, review of *Twenty-one Elephants,* p. 956; February 15, 2005, review of *The Shot Heard 'round the World,* p. 226; February 15, 2006, review of *Playing the Field,* p. 177; February 1, 2007, review of *Game 1,* p. 125; July 15, 2007, review of *Busted;* August 15, 2008, review of *Turkey Bowl;* December 1, 2009, review of *The Hallelujah Flight;* February 15, 2010, review of *Blastin' the Blues.*

Kliatt, July, 2007, Myrna Marler, review of *Busted*, p. 8.

Publishers Weekly, January 7, 2002, review of *Shoeless Joe and Black Betsy*, p. 64; December 13, 2004, review of *Twenty-one Elephants*, p. 67; February 7, 2005, review of *The Shot Heard 'round the World*, p. 59; July 24, 2006, review of *The Greatest Game Every Played: A Football Story*, pp. 57-58; February 5, 2007, review of *Game 1*, p. 59; December 21, 2008, review of *The Hallelujah Flight*, p. 60.

School Library Journal, April, 2002, Wendy Lukehart, review of *Shoeless Joe and Black Betsy*, p. 100; November, 2004, Susan Lissim, review of *Twenty-one Elephants*, pp. 90-91; May, 2005, Marilyn Taniguchi, review of *The Shot Heard 'round the World*, p. 77; March, 2006, Michelle Roberts, review of *Playing the Field*, p. 218; April, 2007, Kim Dare, review of *Game 1*, p. 110; August, 2007, Carol A. Edwards, review of *Busted*, p. 110; April, 2008, Diana Pierce, review of *Game 2: The River City*, p. 115; October, 2008, Marge Loch-Wouters, review of *Turkey Bowl*, p. 101; February, 2010, Anne Chapman, review of *The Hallelujah Flight*, p. 75; March, 2011, Marilyn Taniguchi, review of *The Unforgettable Season: The Story of Joe DiMaggio, Ted Williams, and the Record-setting Summer of '41*, p. 140.

ONLINE

Phil Bildner Home Page, http://www.philbildner.com (May 25, 2011).

Phil Bildner Web log, http://philbildner.livejournal.com (May 25, 2011).*

*   *   *

BLAIR, Shannon
See KAYE, Marilyn

*   *   *

BONE, J.
(Jason Bone)

Personal

Born in Canada.

Addresses

Home—Toronto, Ontario, Canada.

Career

Comic book artist and illustrator, beginning early 1990s.

Awards, Honors

Will Eisner Award for Talent Deserving of Wider Recognition nomination, 2001, for "Alison Dare" and "Solar Stella" series.

Illustrator

GRAPHIC NOVELS

Paul Dini, *Mutant Texas: Tales of Sheriff Ida Red* (originally published in comic-book format, beginning 2002), Oni Press (Portland, OR), 2003.

(With Dave Stewart, Darwyn Cooke, and Jeph Loeb) *The Spirit* (originally published in comic-book form, beginning 2007), two volumes, D.C. Comics (New York, NY), 2007–2008.

Illustrator for comic-book series and one-shots, including "Bad Girls," "Batman: The Brave and the Bold," "Billy Batson and the Magic of Shazam!," "D.C. Super Friends," "Gotham Girls," "Jingle Belle," "Justice League," "Madman Atomic Comics," "Mr. Gum," "Solar Stella," "Spider-Man's Tangled Web," "Three Days in Europe," "Retroactive: Wonder Woman—The '70s," "Witchblade Animated," "Wizard," "Wolverine/Doop," "X-Static," and "Yo Gabba Gabba: Comic Book Time!"

"ALISON DARE" GRAPHIC-NOVEL SERIES BY J. TORRES

Alison Dare, Little Miss Adventures (originally published in comic-book form, beginning 2001; also see below), Volume I, Oni Press (Portland, OR), 2002, revised edition, Tundra Books (Toronto, Ontario, Canada), 2010.

Alison Dare, Little Miss Adventures (originally published in comic-book form, beginning 2001; also see below), Volume II, Oni Press (Portland, OR), 2005.

Alison Dare and the Heart of the Maiden (originally published in comic-book form, beginning 2002), Tundra Books (Toronto, Ontario, Canada), 2010.

Sidelights

Based in Toronto, J. Bone is a Canadian comic-book artist and illustrator who is best known as the illustrator of the popular "Alison Dare" comic-book series, a series by J. Bone that has been collected and reprinted in book form. A prolific sequential artist whose work has earned him recognition from the Will Eisner Awards committee, Bone has also gained a following through his work on D.C. Comics' "The Spirit" series as well as on story arc featuring Batman, Wonder Woman, Wolverine, and the members of the Justice League. Appraising the 2007 return of the classic 1940s crime buster the Spirit, Gordon Flagg noted in *Booklist* that Bone's illustrations for Darwyn Cooke's storyline feature a "visual approach [that], like ["Spirit" creator Will] Eisner's, pleasingly balances the cartoony and the illustrative."

Bone developed the visual image of the fictitious Alison Dare independently, but she remained a character without a story until he met Torres during a comic-book convention held their shared home city of Toronto. The two men began a creative collaboration that included several short works, and their attention eventually turned to Dare. Using Bone's sketches of the character, Torres crafted Alison's backstory and several storylines, or arcs, that drew on his childhood love of "Nancy Drew" and "Hardy Boys" novels and the 1960s Saturday-morning television cartoon series *Johnny Quest.*

When readers first meet her in the graphic-novel collection *Alison Dare, Little Miss Adventures,* twelve-year-old Alison is attending Catholic boarding school while her mom, archaeologist Dr. Alice Dare, is working on a dig in Egypt and her superhero-cum-librarian dad is saving the world from evil in his guise as the Blue Scarab. As if that is not enough, her uncle is an international spy. Fortunately for Alison, adventure finds her in the form of a genie who grants her wish to spirit the girl and her two best friends away to Egypt to visit her mom. A family reunion, a stolen mummy, and the machinations of the evil Baron von Baron ultimately play out with what a *Publishers Weekly* critic described as "charm and freshness," while important details are added in Bone's "fluid, confident" black-and-white drawings.

J. Bone created the artwork for J. Torres' comic-book series, which has been collected as **Alison Dare, Little Miss Adventures**. (Illustration copyright © 2010 by J. Bone. Reproduced by permission of Tundra Books.)

Biographical and Critical Sources

PERIODICALS

Booklist, October 1, 2007, Gordon Flagg, review of *The Spirit,* p. 43.

Kirkus Reviews, April 15, 2010, review of *Alison Dare and the Heart of the Maiden.*

Library Media Connection, April, 2003, review of *Alison Dare: Little Miss Adventures,* p. 18.

Publishers Weekly, June 14, 2010, review of *Alison Dare: Little Miss Adventures,* p. 55.

School Library Journal, September, 2010, Sarah Provence, review of *Alison Dare: Little Miss Adventures,* p. 180.

Voice of Youth Advocates, August, 2003, review of *Mutant, Texas: Tales of Sheriff Ida Red,* p. 214.

ONLINE

Bildungsroman Web log, http://slayground.livejournal.com/ (June 18, 2010), interview with Bone and J. Torres.

J. Bone Web log, http://gobukan.blogspot.com (May 15, 2011).*

*   *   *

BONE, Jason
See BONE, J.

*   *   *

BREWER, Paul 1950-

Personal

Born 1950, in CA; married Kathleen Krull (an author), October 31, 1989; children: Jacqui, Melanie. *Education:* University of California—San Diego, certificate (graphic communication), 1993.

Addresses

Home—San Diego, CA. *E-mail*—pbrewer@san.rr.com.

Career

Children's author and illustrator. Worked variously as a salesman, grape stomper, drummer, truck driver and forklift operator, picture framer, cabinetmaker, and boat builder. Discusses career in children's books at schools and libraries.

Awards, Honors

(With Kathleen Krull) One Hundred Titles for Reading and Sharing selection, New York Public Library, 2008, for *Fartiste.*

Writings

SELF-ILLUSTRATED

(Compiler) *The Grossest Joke Book Ever,* Avon Books (New York, NY), 1997.

(Compiler) *You Must Be Joking!: Lots of Cool Jokes, Plus 17 1/2 Tips for Remembering, Telling, and Making Up Your Own Jokes,* foreword by wife, Kathleen Krull, Cricket Books (Chicago, IL), 2003.

(Compiler) *You Must Be Joking, Two!: Even Cooler Jokes, Plus 11 1/2 Tips for Laughing Yourself into Your Own Stand-up Comedy Routine,* Cricket Books (Chicago, IL), 2007.

ILLUSTRATOR

Alden Nusser, *French Fries up Your Nose: 208 Ways to Annoy People,* Avon Books (New York, NY), 1996.

Kathleen Krull, *Clip, Clip, Clip: Three Stories about Hair,* Holiday House (New York, NY), 2002.

Kathleen Krull, *How to Trick or Treat in Outer Space,* Holiday House (New York, NY), 2004.

ILLUSTRATOR; "ROBERT" READER SERIES BY BARBARA SEULING

Oh No, It's Robert, Front Street/Cricket Books (Chicago, IL), 1999.

Robert and the Attack of the Giant Tarantula, Scholastic, Inc. (New York, NY), 2001.

Robert and the Snake Escape, Cricket Books (Chicago, IL), 2001.

Robert and the Great Pepperoni, Cricket Books (Chicago, IL), 2001.

Robert and the Sneaker Snobs, Cricket Books (Chicago, IL), 2002.

Robert and the Instant Millionaire Show, Cricket Books (Chicago, IL), 2002.

Robert and the Three Wishes, Cricket Books (Chicago, IL), 2002.

Robert and the Hairy Disaster, Cricket Books (Chicago, IL), 2002.

Robert and the Scariest Night, Cricket Books (Chicago, IL), 2002.

Robert and the Back-to School Special, Cricket Books (Chicago, IL), 2002.

Robert and the Weird and Wacky Facts, Cricket Books (Chicago, IL), 2002.

Robert and the Clickety-clackety Teeth, Cricket Books (Chicago, IL), 2003.

Robert and the Troublesome Tuba, Cricket Books (Chicago, IL), 2003.

Robert and the Class President, Cricket Books (Chicago, IL), 2003.

Robert and the Chocolate-covered Worms, Cricket Books (Chicago, IL), 2003.

Robert and the Embarassing Secret, Cricket Books (Chicago, IL), 2003.

Robert and the Great Escape, Cricket Books (Chicago, IL), 2003.

Robert and the Lemming Problem, Cricket Books (Chicago, IL), 2003.

Robert Takes a Stand, Cricket Books (Chicago, IL), 2004.

Tripple Rotten Day, Cricket Books (Chicago, IL), 2004.

Robert Computer Hogs, Cricket Books (Chicago, IL), 2004.

Robert and the Eggheads, Cricket Books (Chicago, IL), 2004.

Robert and the Stolen Bike, Cricket Books (Chicago, IL), 2005.

Robert Finds a Way, Cricket Books (Chicago, IL), 2005.

Robert and the Practical Jokes, Cricket Books (Chicago, IL), 2006.

Robert and the Happy Endings, Cricket Books (Chicago, IL), 2007.

Robert Goes to Camp, Cricket Books (Chicago, IL), 2007.

OTHER

(With Kathleen Krull) *Fartiste: An Explosively Funny, Mostly True Story,* illustrated by Boris Kulikov, Simon & Schuster Books for Young Readers (New York, NY), 2008.

(With Kathleen Krull) *Lincoln Tells a Joke: How Laughter Saved the President (and the Country),* illustrated by Stacy Innerst, Harcourt Children's (Boston, MA), 2010.

(With Kathleen Krull) *The Beatles: They Were Fab—They Were Funny,* illustrated by Stacy Innerst, Harcourt Children's (Boston, MA), 2012.

Sidelights

Author and illustrator Paul Brewer found publishing success as the direct result of a preteen's single-minded talent for being annoying and his willingness to share that talent with others. Alden Nusser, the author of Brewer's first illustration project, was twelve years old when he produced his magnum opus, *French Fries up Your Nose: 208 Ways to Annoy People.* Just starting his freelance art career when he accepted the job of illustrating this comedic masterwork, Brewer knew that he had found his niche: making readers laugh. This goal has inspired his own self-illustrated books *The Grossest Joke Book Ever, You Must Be Joking!: Lots of Cool Jokes,, Plus 17 1/2 Tips for Remembering, Telling, and Making Up Your Own Jokes,* and *You Must Be Joking, Two!: Even Cooler Jokes, Plus 11 1/2 Tips for Laughing Yourself into Your Own Stand-up Comedy Routine,* all geared for middle-grade readers. Describing *You Must Be Joking!* as "a primer for budding comedians," Ilene Cooper added in her *Booklist* review that Brewer's "sprightly ink-and-wash illustrations extend the fun," and *School Library Journal* contributor Cynde Suite dubbed the work "a gem among joke books."

Brewer spent several years experimenting with different types of jobs—from grape stomper and boat builder to drummer in a rock band—and his varied experiences

Paul Brewer's illustration projects include Robert and the Great Pepperoni, *part of an easy-reader series by Barbara Seuling.* (Cricket Books, 2001. Illustration copyright © 2001 by Paul Brewer. Reproduced by permission of Carus Publishing Company.)

brought him in touch with a wide range of people and places. When he finally decided that he wanted to work as an artist, he enrolled at the University of California at San Diego, completing his coursework in 1993 and beginning his illustration career shortly thereafter. In addition to creating and illustrating his joke books, Brewer was assigned to create art for *Oh, No, It's Robert,* a boy-friendly beginning reader by Barbara Seuling. When the book became popular, it provided both author and illustrator with a steady stream of "Robert" stories until Seuling ended the series almost a decade later with *Robert Goes to Camp.* Reviewing *Oh, No, It's Robert,* which finds Seuling's young hero struggling with schoolwork, a *Publishers Weekly* contributor maintained that here Brewer's "quirky pen-and-ink illustrations heighten the volume's comic aspects" in a story that features a "likeable and well-intentioned hero." Appraising another series volume, *Robert and the Great Escape,* Cooper maintained that the artist's "cartoon-style illustrations add a slight edge to [the story's] rather predictable events," while in *School Library Journal* Shelley B. Sutherland wrote that "they add an offbeat goofiness that complements the story."

Several of Brewer's illustration assignments have teamed him up with his wife, author Kathleen Krull, whose *Clip, Clip, Clip: Three Stories about Hair* and *How to Trick or Treat in Outer Space* both feature his colorful cartoon art. According to *School Library Journal* reviewer Jody McCoy, *Clip, Clip, Clip* benefits from colored-pencil "illustrations [that] enhance and occasionally surpass the text with great wit" and comic-book-bright colors.

Brewer has also joined Krull as coauthor of *Fartiste: An Explosively Funny, Mostly True Story,* a picture-book illustrated by Boris Kulikov. As a child growing up in the late 1800s, Joseph Pujol amused himself and others by learning to "toot" on demand. Years later, in an effort to support his large family, Pujol turned this questionable talent into performance art and eventually gained fame on the stage of Paris's famed Moulin Rouge. Noting the story's "well-rhymed couplets," *School Library Journal* reviewer Catherine Threadgill added that Brewer and Krull's "gleefully tasteless tale reads easily," while a *Kirkus Reviews* critic deemed *Fartiste* "a total blast." Krull and Brewer have also collaborated on *Lincoln Tells a Joke,* a portrait of U.S. President Abraham Lincoln that focuses on the solemn-looking man's ability to use humor to cope with both personal difficulties and national crises. The sixteenth president "is portrayed as an accessible, endearing, and sympathetic figure," according to *School Library Journal* critic Jody Kopple, while *Horn Book* critic Betty Carter noted the book's reference to Lincoln's "love of language, grammar, and elocution."

One of the reasons why Brewer focuses on jokes in his books for children is his belief that humor is natural for children and a great way to convince even reluctant

Brewer teams up with wife, Kathleen Krull, and creates the art for their collaborative story in Lincoln Tells a Joke: How Laughter Saved the President (and the Country). (Illustration copyright © 2010 by Stacy Innerst. Reproduced by permission of Houghton Mifflin Harcourt.)

readers to dive into a book. "Telling jokes can hone a child's verbal skill (which later in life could lead to public speaking skill)," he asserted on his home page. "Few things boost a kid's self-esteem like telling a joke (or a funny story) successfully. Kids who like telling jokes are more likely to take other risks—acting, debating, sports, the possibilities are endless—because they're less afraid to try new things."

Biographical and Critical Sources

PERIODICALS

Booklist, July, 1999, Kay Weisman, review of *Oh No, It's Robert,* p. 1947; April 1, 2002, Todd Morning, review of *Robert and the Weird and Wacky Facts,* p. 1329; January 1, 2003, Carolyn Phelan, review of *Robert and the Back-to-School Special,* p. 893; April 1, 2003, Shelle Rosenfeld, review of *Robert and the Leming Problem,* p. 1398; February 1, 2004, Ilene Cooper, review of *You Must Be Joking!: Lots of Cool Jokes,, Plus 17 1/2 Tips for Remembering, Telling, and Making Up Your Own Jokes,* p. 969; December 1, 2003, Ilene Cooper, review of *Robert and the Great Escape,* p. 669; April 1, 2004, Jennifer Locke, review of *Robert Takes a Stand,* p. 1364; January 1, 2007, Carolyn Phelan, review of *Robert and the Happy Endings,* p. 81; May 1, 2006, Carolyn Phelan, review of *Robert and the Practical Jokes,* p. 82; August 1, 2008, Ilene Cooper, review of *Fartiste: An Explosively Funny, Mostly True Story,* p. 75; February 15, 2010, Andrew Medlar, review of *Lincoln Tells a Joke: How Laughter Saved the President (and the Country),* p. 73.

Horn Book, January-February, 2002, Betty Carter, review of *Robert and the Great Pepperoni,* p. 83; July-August, 2002, Betty Carter, review of *Robert and the Weird and Wacky Facts,* p. 471; July-August, 2004, Betty Carter, review of *Robert Takes a Stand,* p. 460; July-August, 2006, Betty Carter, review of *Robert and the Practical Jokes,* p. 450; September-October, 2008, Christine M. Heppermann, review of *Fartiste,* p. 610; May-June, 2010, Betty Carter, review of *Lincoln Tells a Joke,* p. 109.

Kirkus Reviews, January 15, 2002, review of *Clip Clip Clip: Three Stories about Hair,* p. 106; October 1, 2002, review of *Robert and the Back-to-School Special,* p. 1481; March 1, 2003, review of *Robert and the Lemming Problem,* p. 398.

Publishers Weekly, June 14, 1999, review of *Oh No, It's Robert,* p. 70; February 25, 2002, review of *Clip Clip Clip,* p. 66; August 9, 2004, review of *How to Trick or Treat in Outer Space,* p. 248; June 2, 2008, review of *Fartiste,* p. 46; March 22, 2010, review of *Lincoln Tells a Joke,* p. 69.

School Library Journal, October, 2001, Janie Schomberg, review of *Robert and the Great Pepperoni,* p. 131; March, 2002, Jody McCoy, review of *Clip Clip Clip,* p. 192; July, 2002, John Sigwald, review of *Robert and the Weird and Wacky Facts,* p. 98; December, 2003, Tina Zubak, review of *Robert and the Lemming Problem,* p. 126; January, 2004, Shelley B. Sutherland, review of *Robert and the Great Escape,* p. 106; February, 2004, Cynde Suite, review of *You Must Be Joking!,* p. 127; April, 2004, Andrea Tarr, review of *Robert Takes a Stand,* p. 124; July, 2004, Lisa G. Kropp, review of *Robert and the Back-to-School Special,* p. 44; November, 2004, Catherine Threadgill, review of *How to Trick or Treat in Outer Space,* p. 110; April,, 2005, Robyn Walker, review of *Robert Finds a Way,* p. 112; June, 2005, Steven Engelfried, review of *You Must Be Joking!,* p. 56; March, 2006, Alison Grant, review of *Robert and the Practical Jokes,* p. 202; June, 2007, Michelle Easley Bridges, review of *Robert and the Happy Endings,* p. 123; October, 2007, Jennifer Cogan, review of *Robert Goes to Camp,* p. 128; March, 2008, Carol S. Surges, review of *You Must Be Joking, Two!: Even Cooler Jokes, Plus 11 1/2 Tips for Laughing Yourself into Your Own Stand-Up Comedy Routine,* p. 181; July, 2008, Catherine Threadgill, review of *Fartiste,* p. 89; March, 2010, Jody Kopple, review of *Lincoln Tells a Joke,* p. 142.

ONLINE

Paul Brewer Home Page, http://www.paulbrewer.com (May 27, 2011).*

C

CALDWELL, Ben 1973-

Personal

Born October, 1973; married; children: twin daughters. *Education:* Parsons School of Design, B.F.A. (illustration); Eugene Lang College for Ancient History, degree.

Addresses

Home—NY. *E-mail*—info@daredetectives.com.

Career

Illustrator, animator, and sequential artist. Freelance artist and designer; also worked in toy design.

Awards, Honors

Russ Manning Award for Most Promising Newcomer in Cartooning nomination, 2006, for "Dare Detectives" comic-book series.

Writings

SELF-ILLUSTRATED

Action! Cartooning, Sterling Pub. Co. (New York, NY), 2004.
Fantasy! Cartooning, Sterling Pub. Co. (New York, NY), 2005.
Manga! Cartooning, Sterling Pub. Co. (New York, NY), 2007.

Creator of comic-book series "The Dare Detectives," Dark Horse Comics, beginning 2004.

ILLUSTRATOR

Ralph J. Fletcher, *Tommy Trouble and the Magic Marble,* Henry Holt (New York, NY), 2000.

Nina Jaffe, *Wonder Woman: Amazon Princess* (based on the character by William Moulton Marston), Harper-Festival (New York, NY), 2004.
Nina Jaffe, *Wonder Woman: The Journey Begins* (based on the character by William Moulton Marston), Harper-Festival (New York, NY), 2004.
L.S. Cauldwell, *The Anna-Mae Mysteries: The Golden Treasure,* Star Publisher (Loretto, PA), 2009.

Contributor to comic-book series, including "Justice League Unlimited," "Star Wars: Clone War Adventures," and "Wednesday Comics."

ILLUSTRATOR; "ALL-ACTION CLASSICS" GRAPHIC-NOVEL SERIES

Michael Mucci, *Dracula* (based on the novel by Bram Stoker), Sterling (New York, NY), 2008.
Michael Mucci, *Tom Sawyer* (based on the novel by Mark Twain), Sterling (New York, NY), 2008.
(With Rick Lacy) Michael Mucci, reteller, *The Odyssey* (based on the story by Homer), Sterling (New York, NY), 2010.

Sidelights

Although Ben Caldwell is best known as a cartoonist, he has also designed toys and created images for use in animated films. His illustrations appear on the cover of popular comic books such as "Justice League Unlimited," as well as in the pages of "Star Wars: Clone Wars" and "Wednesday Comics" series installments. Children's books have also provided Caldwell with a creative outlet; his art is a feature of the "All-Action Classics" sequential-art adaptations of literary classics and his self-illustrated "Dare Detectives" comic-book series focuses on former criminal Maria Dare and her ragtag team of sleuths: Toby "The Muscle" Taylor, Sarah "The Princess" Kincaid, and Sarah's sister Jessica, a woman better known as costumed super spy The Vixen. Reviewing Caldwell's first book illustration project, creating art for Ralph Fletcher's beginning reader *Tommy Trouble and the Magic Marble, Booklist* critic Todd

Morning wrote that his black-and-white drawings are a plus; they have an angularity that nicely straddles the line between realism and cartoons."

Developing his talent for drawing while growing up, Caldwell studied illustration at Parsons School of Design and pursued a career in sequential arts. To help other aspiring comics artists, he shares his accumulated knowledge in the books *Fantasy! Cartooning, Action! Cartooning,* and *Manga! Cartooning.* Here Caldwell presents tips on designing characters and props as well as step-by-step diagrams for budding sequential artists. In *Library Journal* Daniel Lombardo praised *Action! Cartooning* as "fun, concise, short on detail, and long on visual impact," while *School Library Journal* critic Steeve Baker noted of *Fantasy! Cartooning* that "Caldwell shows original thinking" in his sketches and exhibits a style that "is exciting, modern, and unique."

Written by Michael Mucci, the "All-Action Classics" series treats young readers to graphic-novel adaptations of some of the best-known adventure stories in Western literature. *Dracula,* the first book in the series, recounts Jonathan Harker's journey to Transylvania, where he meets Count Dracula and tracks the vampiric man back to England. Praising the graphic novel as an excellent vehicle for exposing "reluctant readers to a worthy classic," Tina Coleman added in her *Booklist* review that Caldwell's "beautiful art" for *Dracula* "aptly captures the mood" of Bram Stoker's tale. Mucci takes readers further into the past in *The Odyssey,* which follows the danger-fraught path of the wanderer Odysseus as he slowly makes his way home after fighting in the Trojan War. Caldwell's "colorful artwork skillfully captures the dynamic action" in the time-honored tale, noted *School Library Journal* critic Andrea Lipinski, and Jesse Karp wrote in *Booklist* that the sequential art for *The Odyssey* features "force and vibrant life . . . , and especially comes alive in the weird purple light of the Underworld and in the nightmarish sea creature Scylla." "A brisk, energetic read," according to a *Kirkus Reviews* writer, Mucci's story "is accompanied by boisterous cartoon art in a dazzling array of candy colors."

Biographical and Critical Sources

PERIODICALS

Booklist, August, 2000, Todd Morning, review of *Tommy Trouble and the Magic Marble,* p. 2138; March 15, 2008, Tina Coleman, review of *Dracula,* p. 58; April 15, 2010, Jesse Karp, review of *The Odyssey,* p. 45.

Children's Bookwatch, January, 2009, review of *The Anna-Mae Mysteries: The Golden Treasure.*

Kirkus Reviews, April 15, 2010, review of *The Odyssey.*

Library Journal, July, 2004, Daniel Lombardo, review of *Action! Cartooning,* p. 80.

School Library Journal, September, 2000. Steve Clancy, review of *Tommy Trouble and the Magic Marble,* p. 196; November, 2005, Steev Baker, review of *Fantasy! Cartooning,* p. 154; July, 2010, Andrea Lipinski, review of *The Odyssey,* p. 107.

ONLINE

Ben Caldwell Home Page, http://www.actioncartooning. com/ (May 25, 2011).

Ben Caldwell Web log, http://purgetheory.blogspot.com (May 25, 2011).*

* * *

CARDON, Laurent 1962-

Personal

Born 1962, in Brazil.

Addresses

Home—São Paulo, Brazil. *E-mail*—laurent@citron vache.com.br.

Career

Illustrator and animation artist. Work in animated films include: (as inbetweener) *Asterix and the Big Fight,* 1989; (as layout artist) *The Adventures of Tintin* (television series), 1991-92; (as layout artist) *The Busy World of Richard Scarry* (television series), 1994; (as layout artist) *Orson and Olivia* (television series), 1995; and (as third assistant director) *Acquaria,* 2003. Teacher of film animation.

Writings

SELF-ILLUSTRATED

Calma, Camaleão!, Edicione Ática (São Paulo, Brazil), 2009.

ILLUSTRATOR

Luiz Vilela, *Contos,* Scipione (São Paulo, Brazil), 1986.

William Shakespeare, *Hamlet, Otelo, A Decima segunda Noite, Rei Leer, A Tempestade,* translation by Monica Stahel of an adaptation by Geraldine McCaughrean, Martins Fontes (São Paulo, Brazil), 1994.

William Shakespeare, *Romeu e Julieta, Macbeth, Henrique V., Sonho de uma noite de verao, Julio Cesar* translation by Monica Stahel of an adaptation by Geraldine McCaughrean, Martins Fontes (São Paulo, Brazil), 1994.

(With William E. Jones, Jr.) Rosa Amanda Strausz, *Um nóna cabeça,* Salamandra (Rio de Janeiro, Brazil), 1998.

Rosa Amanda Strausz, *Alecrim* Objectiva (Rio de Janeiro, Brazil), 2003.

Edith Modesto, *Manobra radical*, Edicione Ática (São Paulo, Brazil), 2003.

Ana Maria Machado, *Amigos secretos*, Edicione Ática (São Paulo, Brazil), 2004.

Ana Maria Machado, *De fora da arca*, Edicione Ática (São Paulo, Brazil), 2004.

Genny Baran Nissenbaum, *Que susto!: Um livro para pais e filhos*, Réptil (Rio de Janeiro, Brazil), 2005.

Angela Carneiro and Marcela Calamo, *Rodas, pra que te quero!*, Edicione Ática (São Paulo, Brazil), 2005.

Fanny Abramovich, *Espantoso!*, Edicione Ática (São Paulo, Brasil), 2005.

Tatiana Belinky, *Kanniferstan: conto alemão*, Edicione FTD (São Paulo, Brazil), 2006.

Ana Maria Machado, *Procura-se lobo*, Editora Ática (São Paulo, Brazil), 2006, translated as *Wolf Wanted*, Groundwood Books (Toronto, Ontario, Canada), 2010.

Jules Verne, *A Volta ao mundo em 80 dias*, translated and adapted by Walcyr Carrasco, Edicione FTD (São Paulo, Brazil), 2007.

Jules Verne, *Vinte mil leguas submarinas*, translated and adapted by Walcyr Carrasco, Edicione FTD (São Paulo, Brazil), 2007.

Jules Verne, *Viagem ao centro da terra*, translated and adapted by Walcyr Carrasco, Edicione FTD (São Paulo, Brazil), 2007.

Ze do Caixão, *O livro horripilante de Zé*, Panda Books (São Paulo, Brazil), 2008.

Uma amizade improvável, Edicione Ática, 2008.

Walcyr Carrasco, *Meus dois pais*, Edicione Ática (São Paulo, Brasil), 2009.

Antóni Pogorélski, *A galinha preta; ou, os habitantes do subterraneo*, Edições SM (São Paulo, Brazil), 2010.

Carmen Lucia Campos, *Meu avô Africano*, Panda Books (São Paulo, Brazil), 2010.

Luís Abreu, *Futebol: de pais para filha*, Edicione Ática (São Paulo, Brazil), 2010.

Rosa Amanda Strausz, *Mamãe trouxe um lobo para casa!*, Edicione FTD (São Paulo, Brazil), 2011.

Alexandré Dumas, *Os três mosqueteiros*, retold by Silvana Salerno, Edicione DCL (Brazil), 2011.

Stella Maris Rexende, *A mocinha do mercado central*, Globo (Brazil), 2011.

Also illustrator of *Macaco como homem*, by Wilhelm Hauff, Scipione (São Paulo, Brazil); *Lilliput de Sorvete e Chocolate*, by Hermes Bernardi Jr., Larousse; *A coleção de bruxas do meu pai*, by Rosa Amanda Strausz, Edicione FTD (São Paulo, Brazil); *De mãos atadas*, by Álvaro Cardoso Gomes, Edicione Ática (São Paulo, Brazil); *Muito além dos sues sonhos*; and *O anjo rouco*.

Biographical and Critical Sources

PERIODICALS

Booklist, April 15, 2010, Carolyn Phelan, review of *Wolf Wanted*, p. 54.

Publishers Weekly, March 29, 2010, review of *Wolf Wanted*, p. 56.

School Library Journal, May, 2010, Maryann H. Owen, review of *Wolf Wanted*, p. 88.

ONLINE

Laurent Cardon Home Page, http://www.citronvache.com.br (February 27, 2011).

Estadão Online, http://www.estado.com/br/ (September 14, 2009), Alessandra da Mata, interview with Cardon (in Portuguese).

*   *   *

CHANDLER, Kristen

Personal

Born in MI; married; children: four. *Education:* University of Utah, M.F.A. (creative writing), 1990. *Hobbies and other interests:* Distance running, fishing, rowing, hiking, skiing, horseback riding, observing wildlife.

Addresses

Home—Salt Lake City, UT.

Career

Author and journalist. Worked variously as a ranch hand, waitress, salesperson, ice-cream-store manager, and secretary; freelance writer. Brigham Young University, teacher of expository writing and instructor in environmental subjects. Presenter at schools; speaker at conferences.

Awards, Honors

YALSA/American Library Association "Hidden Gem" selection, 2010, for *Wolves, Boys, and Other Things That Might Kill Me*.

Writings

Wolves, Boys, and Other Things That Might Kill Me, Viking (New York, NY), 2010.
Girls Don't Fly, 2012.

Sidelights

With her colorful resumé—everything from ranch hand and journalist to store manager and waitress—Kristin Chandler has a wealth of experiences to draw on in her writing. Chandler shares these experiences in her debut young-adult novel, *Wolves, Boys, and Other Things That Might Kill Me*, as well as in her second second novel, *Girls Don't Fly*, the story of an adventurous teen who uses an opportunity to work in the Galapogos as a way to reshape her world.

Inspired by the childhood vacations Chandler spent with her family, touring the West and visiting places like Yellowstone, *Wolves, Boys, and Other Things That Might Kill Me* takes readers to Montana, where sixteen-year-old KJ Carson helps her father with his work as a sportsman's guide. Wolves have recently been reintroduced to nearby Yellowstone after being totally eradicated from that region decades before by hunters. When she sees the behavior of these creatures in the wild she teams up with fellow student Virgil to write a column about the wolves for her school journalism class. Unfortunately, many adults in KJ's ranching town are upset at the wolves' return; they remember losing livestock to stealthy wolf packs. Although KJ hopes that "Wolf Notes" will bring her closer to Virgil, who she likes, she unwittingly touches off a firestorm of controversy that threatens not only her friend but her family as well.

Describing *Wolves, Boys, and Other Things That Might Kill Me* as "a classic coming-of-age tale," Samantha Larsen Hastings added in *School Library Journal* that

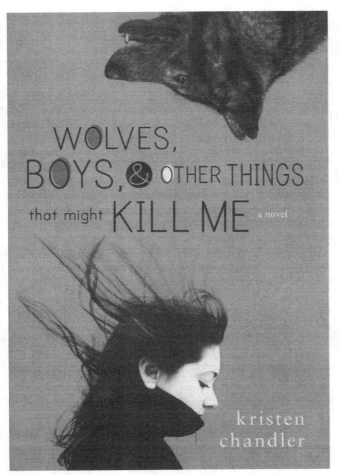

Cover of Kristen Chandler's young-adult novel Wolves, Boys, and Other Things That Might Kill Me, *in which a teen's relationships are complicated by her environmental interests.* (Cover photographs by Bob Elsdale/Getty Images (wolf) and Christopher Wilson/Gallery Stock (girl). Reproduced by permission of Viking Children's Books, a division of Penguin Books for Young Readers, a member of Penguin Group (USA) Inc., 345 Hudson St., New York, NY 10014. All rights reserved.)

Chandler's fact-filled novel is "beautifully written and thought-provoking." Protagonist KJ "is a spitfire," maintained a *Publishers Weekly* critic, and in her "lively drama" the author "writes persuasively about the great outdoors, small-town . . . politics, and young love." "Relieved that the novel bucks the supernatural trend by focusing on real-life wolves rather than werewolves, *Booklist* contributor Kimberly Garnick recommended the story to the many teens interested "in conservation and ecology," and in *Horn Book* Tanya D. Auger asserted that "Chandler's feisty protagonist is fun to follow."

Although Chandler hopes that *Wolves, Boys, and Other Things That Might Kill Me* will give readers a fuller appreciation for wolves, she cautions that the creatures are still wild and unpredictable. "I don't want the reader to anthropomorphize the wolves," she commented to *Salt Lake Tribune* interviewer Ben Fullerton. "It's a temptation, but that can have some devastating consequences. Throughout the book, KJ writes about what she likes and admires about the wolves. She admires them for traits that are fierce and courageous, but when you try to transcribe that to a whole personality, you make a pretty good leap. I think it disrespects animals to say they're people, and vice versa. It's going to Switzerland and saying, 'It's just like Utah.' We should love them for being different. By the same token, I spent a lot of time studying wolves and it has taught me a lot about people. I've gone through a lot of the same experiences as the main characters."

Biographical and Critical Sources

PERIODICALS

Booklist, June 1, 2010, Kimberly Garnick, review of *Wolves, Boys, and Other Things That Might Kill Me,* p. 61.

Bulletin of the Center for Children's Books, July-August, 2010, Kate Quealy-Gainer, review of *Wolves, Boys, and Other Things That Might Kill Me,* p. 476.

Horn Book, July-August, 2010, Tanya D. Auger, review of *Wolves, Boys, and Other Things That Might Kill Me,* p. 102.

Publishers Weekly, May 24, 2010, review of *Wolves, Boys, and Other Things That Might Kill Me,* p. 54.

Salt Lake Tribune, May 13, 2010, Ben Fullerton, interview with Chandler.

School Library Journal, June, 2010, Samantha Larsen Hastings, review of *Wolves, Boys, and Other Things That Might Kill Me,* p. 98.

ONLINE

Kristen Chandler Home Page, http://www.krischandler stories.com (May 27, 2011).*

COLE, Stephen 1971-
(Steve Cole)

Personal

Born 1971, in Bedfordshire, England; married; wife's name Jill; has children. *Education:* University of East Anglia, B.A. (English literature and film studies).

Addresses

Home—Aylesbury, Buckinghamshire, England.

Career

Writer. British Broadcasting Corporation, London, England, editor and writer of children's magazines for four years, commissioning editor of science-fiction titles for BBC Worldwide, beginning 1997, creative editor of pre-teen titles; Ladybird Books, London, managing editor; Simon & Schuster, London, senior editor, then consulting editor, 2001; Rocket Editorial Ltd., founder, beginning 2002.

Writings

FOR CHILDREN

Cars on Mars (pop-up book), illustrated by Louise Gardner, Levinson (London, England), 1997.
Mucky Martians (pop-up book), illustrated by Louise Gardner, Levinson (London, England), 1997.
Alien Olympics (pop-up book), illustrated by Louise Gardner, Levinson (London, England), 1997.
(Adaptor) *My Dad Is an Armed Robber!* (based on the *Microsoap* television series), BBC Books (London, England), 1999.
(Adaptor) *Lodgers from Hell* (based on the *Microsoap* television series), BBC Books (London, England), 1999.
Walking with Beasts: Survival! (based on the television series), BBC Books (London, England), 2001.
Ace Lightning: Official Guide Book (based on the television series), BBC Books (London, England), 2002.
(With Chris Bentley and Graham Bleathman) *Classic Thunderbirds Secret Files: The Inside Story of International Rescue*, Carleton (London, England), 2003.
Shrek: The Essential Guide (based on the animated film), Dorling Kindersley (London, England), 2004, new edition, 2007.
Madagascar: The Essential Guide (based on the animated film), Dorling Kindersley (London, England), 2005.
Thieves like Us, Bloomsbury Children's Books (New York, NY), 2006.
Thieves Till We Die, Bloomsbury Children's Books (New York, NY), 2007.
The Aztec Code, Bloomsbury (London, England), 2007.
The Bloodline Cipher, Bloomsbury (London, England), 2008.

Genie Us, illustrated by Linda Chapman, Red Fox (London, England), 2008, published as *Be a Genie in Six Easy Steps,* HarperCollins (New York, NY), 2009.
Genie and the Phoenix, illustrated by Linda Chapman, Red Fox (London, England), 2009.

Author of other books for children, including film and television adaptations and spin-offs.

ADAPTOR; "DR. WHO" NOVEL SERIES; BASED ON THE TELEVISION SERIES

(Editor) *Short Trips: A Collection of Short Stories* (short stories), BBC Books (London, England), 1998.
(Editor) *More Short Trips* (short stories), BBC Books (London, England), 1999.
(With Natalie Dallaire) *Parallel 59*, BBC Books (London, England), 2000.
(Editor with Jacqueline Rayner) *Short Trips and Side Steps*, BBC Books (London, England), 2000.
The Ancestor Cell, BBC Books (London, England), 2000.
The Shadow in the Glass, BBC Books (London, England), 2001.
Vanishing Point, BBC Books (London, England), 2002.
Timeless, BBC Books (London, England), 2003.
The Monsters Inside, BBC Books (London, England), 2005.
To the Slaughter, BBC Books (London, England), 2005.
The Sycorax, BBC Books (London, England), 2006.
The Art of Destruction, BBC Books (London, England), 2006.
The Feast of the Drowned, BBC Books (London, England), 2006.
Dr. Who: Quiz Book 2, BBC Books (London, England), 2006.
Sting of the Zygons, BBC Books (London, England), 2007.
Dr. Who: Quiz Book 3, BBC Books (London, England), 2007.
Dr. Who: Quiz Book 4, BBC Books (London, England), 2008.
The Vampire of Paris, BBC Books (London, England), 2009.

ADAPTOR; "ADVENTURES OF MR BEAN" SERIES; BASED ON THE TELEVISION SERIES

Bear Essentials, Carleton (London, England), 2002.
No Pets, Carleton (London, England), 2002.
The Great Outdoors, Carleton (London, England), 2002.
Bean's Bounty, Carleton (London, England), 2002.

"WERELING" NOVEL TRILOGY

Wounded, Bloomsbury (London, England), 2003, Razorbill (New York, NY), 2005.
Prey, Bloomsbury (London, England), 2004, Razorbill (New York, NY), 2005.
Resurrection, Bloomsbury (London, England), 2004, Razorbill (New York, NY), 2005.

"ONE WEIRD DAY AT FREEKHAM HIGH" SERIES

Thumb, Oxford University Press (Oxford, England), 2005.
Sock, Oxford University Press (Oxford, England), 2005.
Ouch!, Oxford University Press (Oxford, England), 2005.
Pigeon, Oxford University Press (Oxford, England), 2006.

"ASTROSAURS" CHAPTER-BOOK SERIES; UNDER NAME STEVE COLE

The Hatching Horror, illustrated by Charlie Fowkes, Red Fox (London, England), 2005, published in *Megabookasaurus!,* 2009.
The Seas of Doom, illustrated by Woody Fox, Red Fox (London, England), 2005.
The Mind-Swap Menace, illustrated by Woody Fox, Red Fox (London, England), 2005, published in *Megabookasaurus!,* 2009.
Teeth of the T-Rex, illustrated by Woody Fox, Red Fox (London, England), 2005, published in *Megabookasaurus!,* 2009.
Riddle of the Raptors, illustrated by Charlie Fowkes, Red Fox (London, England), 2005.
The Space Ghost, illustrated by Woody Fox, Red Fox (London, England), 2006.
The Terror-bird Trap, illustrated by Woody Fox, Red Fox (London, England), 2006.
The Skies of Fear, illustrated by Woody Fox, Red Fox (London, England), 2006.
Day of the Dino-droids, illustrated by Woody Fox, Red Fox (London, England), 2006.
The Star Pirates, illustrated by Woody Fox, Red Fox (London, England), 2007.
The Planet of Peril, illustrated by Woody Fox, Red Fox (London, England), 2007.
Teeth of the T-Rex, illustrated by Woody Fox, Red Fox (London, England), 2007.
The Claws of Christmas, illustrated by Woody Fox, Red Fox (London, England), 2007.
The Sun-Snatchers, illustrated by Woody Fox, Red Fox (London, England), 2008.
Revenge of the Fang, illustrated by Woody Fox, Red Fox (London, England), 2008.
Terror Underground, illustrated by Woody Fox, Red Fox (London, England), 2008.
Contest Carnage!, illustrated by Woody Fox, Red Fox (London, England), 2008.
Destination: Danger!, illustrated by Woody Fox, Red Fox (London, England), 2008.
The Space Ghosts, illustrated by Woody Fox, Red Fox (London, England), 2009.
The Dreams of Dread, illustrated by Woody Fox, Red Fox (London, England), 2009.
Deadly Drama!, illustrated by Woody Fox, Red Fox (London, England), 2009.
Jungle Horror!, illustrated by Woody Fox, Red Fox (London, England), 2009.
Christmas Crisis!, illustrated by Woody Fox, Red Fox (London, England), 2009.
The Carnivore Curse, illustrated by Woody Fox, Red Fox (London, England), 2009.

Megabookasaurus!, illustrated by Charlie Fowkes and Woody Fox, Red Fox (London, England), 2009.

"COWS IN ACTION" SERIES

The Ter-moo-nators, illustrated by Woody Fox, Red Fox (London, England), 2007.
The Moo-my's Curse, illustrated by Woody Fox, Red Fox (London, England), 2007.
The Roman Moo-stery, illustrated by Woody Fox, Red Fox (London, England), 2007.
World War Moo, illustrated by Woody Fox, Red Fox (London, England), 2008.
The Wild West Moo-nster, illustrated by Woody Fox, Red Fox (London, England), 2008.
The Battle for Christmoos, illustrated by Woody Fox, Red Fox (London, England), 2008.
The Udderly Moovellous Joke Book, illustrated by Woody Fox, Red Fox (London, England), 2009.
The Pirate Moo-tiny, illustrated by Woody Fox, Red Fox (London, England), 2009.
The Moo-gic of Merlin, illustrated by Woody Fox, Red Fox (London, England), 2009.

"THE HUNTING" SERIES; UNDER NAME STEVE COLE

Z. Rex, Philomel Books (New York, NY), 2009.
Z. Raptor, Philomel Books (New York, NY), 2011.

OTHER

Professor Bernice Summerfield and the Gods of the Underworld (adult novel), Big Finish (Maidenhead, England), 2001.

Sidelights

A children's book author and the founder of Rocket Editorial Ltd., Stephen Cole is the talent behind the popular "Wereling" trilogy, which includes the novels *Wounded, Prey,* and *Resurrection.* Cole established himself as an editor and writer in the London publishing industry by holding a series of posts at BBC Books that involved merchandising the popular television series *Dr. Who.* As a writer for children, Cole began creating television tie-in books such as the "Alien Pop-ups" books *Cars on Mars* and *Mucky Martians,* as well as novel-length adaptations of *Dr. Who* that include *The Sycorax, The Art of Destruction,* and *The Vampire of Paris.* In an interview for the Bloomsbury Web site, he admitted: "I've always loved writing, and always wanted to do it for a living. I just love to write anything, from novels to articles to songs to puzzles to emails!"

Cole's "Wereling" series opens with *Wounded,* which follows seventeen-year-old Kate Folan and sixteen-year-old Tom Anderson as they work out their feelings for each other even as a dark secret keeps them apart. Kate hails from a family of werewolves, although she will not undergo the wolfen transformation unless she mates with a werewolf male. When her family finds and rescues Tom, a mortal teen who was wounded during an accident in the woods, Kate fall for him, and the eventual realization that Kate's family has "turned" Tom comes as a shock to both teens. While Tom is none too happy to discover that he is now a werewolf, Kate is thrown into an emotional tailspin. Rather than either ignoring their growing feelings for each other or succumbing to their supernatural fate, Kate and Tom decide to search for a third option: a cure.

As the "Wereling" trilogy continues, Kate and Tom's joint quest leads them far beyond the desire to consummate their relationship. Ultimately, through the course of *Prey* and *Resurrection,* they learn of the growing power of the lupine community. When a sixteenth-century corpse is unearthed in a German peat bog and rumored to be that of the first-ever werewolf, lupine powers amass even further, forcing the teens to join the struggle to end a revolution that threatens all human life on Earth.

Cover of Stephen Cole's exciting middle-grade novel Z-Rex, *featuring artwork by Cliff Nielsen.* (Illustration copyright © 2009 by Cliff Nielsen. Reproduced by permission of Philomel Books, a division of Penguin Books for Young Readers, a member of Penguin Group (USA) Inc., 345 Hudson St., New York, NY 10014. All rights reserved.)

Praising the first volume in the "Wereling" trilogy, *School Library Journal* contributor Anna M. Nelson wrote that Cole injects *Wounded* with "fast-paced action, horror, intrigue, plot twists, and a touch of romance" to create a mix "sure to please horror fans." In *Kliatt* Joseph DeMarco praised *Wounded* as "a solid read" that contains enough entertainment "to please even tough customers."

Geared for slightly younger readers, Cole's "Astrosaurs" series presents the author's own whimsical theories regarding the fate of Earth's dinosaurs: they constructed space ships and fled the planet prior to the arrival of a deadly meteor. The series follows Captain Teggs, an astrosaur who commandeers the DSS *Sauropod* through space with the help of crewmates Arx, Gypsy, and Iggy. In *Riddle of the Raptors* Teggs and his crew escort several talented athletes to the Great Dinosaur Games, where they plan to represent the Vegetarian sector. When meat-eating raptor thugs raid the spaceship and kidnap two of these athletes, Teggs and his crew are left to locate them and get them to the games on time. *The Hatching Horror,* another book in the popular series, finds Teggs aiding a group of dinos in colonizing a new but unexplored planet where avoiding a clan of egg-eating oviraptors seems to be the biggest challenge. Featuring entertaining illustrations by Charlie Fowkes, Cole's "Astrosaurs" books have a special appeal for reluctant readers due to what *School Library Journal* contributor Mara Alpert described as their "goofy line drawings, fast-paced plot, and general silliness." "Corny is the operative word here," concluded a *Publishers Weekly* critic, recommending *Riddle of the Raptors* for upper-elementary-grade readers "with a fondness for dinosaurs—and silliness."

Also geared for preteens, Cole's novel *Z. Rex* starts off his "The Hunting" series, which focuses on a teen whose computer programmer father has created Ultra Reality, the ultimate video game. Thirteen-year-old Adam Adlar worries when his dad does not return from a business meeting. The meeting was arranged to discuss Ultra Reality, Mr. Adlar's brainchild and a system in which gaming action is directed by players' thoughts rather than through manual controls. When mysterious strangers begin appearing, the teen knows that something is wrong, and as Adam attempts to locate his father and put an end to the plot that a bio-tech company has hatched, he is aided by Z. Rex, a giant tyrannosaurus rex that, created in the company's lab, has the power of speech and the ability to camouflage in addition to sporting a nasty set of teeth and claws. In *Z. Raptor* Adam and his dad are reunited, just in time to face the band of raging raptors that are inhabiting a remote prison island. Reviewing *Z. Rex* in *Booklist,* John Peters enhanced the story's popularity among boys by describing Adam's adventure as "a gory and spectacularly destructive escapade that runs from New Mexico to Edinburgh, [Scotland]." A *Kirkus Reviews* writer also enjoyed Cole's "well-told" story, concluding that its mix of a "fast pace, lots of action, and plenty of unanswered questions" will pull readers in to the "The Hunting" series.

Cole turns to slightly older readers in the companion novels *Thieves like Us* and *Thieves Till We Die,* which focus on a group of teenage misfits whose criminal talents have made them prime candidates for the notorious operation headed by eccentric billionaire Nathaniel Coldhardt. Jonah is a computer hacker; Patch can pick locks; Motti is a master of everything electrical; Tye has an unerring knack for telling and spotting lies; and the suave and beguiling Con is the ultimate salesman. Hired by Coldhardt, the group hides out in their high-tech underground home until they are called on to acquire the ancient artifact for their boss. In *Thieves like Us* Jonah overcomes his moral qualms when he realizes that through crime he can tap his true hacking potential. After joining the group, he travels with the team to Egypt where the goal is to acquire an ancient key that Coldhart believes will grant immortality. The adventure continues in *Thieves till We Die,* as Jonah, Con, Patch, Motti, and Tye travel south to Mexico, hoping to discover the location of an Aztec temple (and its riches) before its power is tapped by a cult determined to cause the end of the world.

Recommending *Thieves like Us* for fans of Eoin Colfer's "Artemis Fowl" novels, Nancy Kim added in *Booklist* that Cole's story is fueled by "fast action, cool gadgets, and clever problem-solving." "Paced like an adventure film," *Thieves like Us* is "replete with hypnotism, Egyptian gods and snakes," noted a *Kirkus Reviews* writer, while *School Library Journal* critic Lori E. Donovan noted the appeal of both *Thieves like Us* and *Thieves till We Die* for reluctant readers. Another *Kirkus Reviews* writer dubbed *Thieves till We Die* "snaky, fun, action-packed adventure," while in *Booklist* Gillian Engberg praised "the central cast of death-defying teen savants," who are bound by their shared understanding "that home is wherever they are, together."

Biographical and Critical Sources

PERIODICALS

Booklist, April 1, 2006, Nancy Kim, review of *Thieves like Us,* p. 31; May 1, 2007, Gillian Engberg, review of *Thieves till We Die,* p. 44; August 1, 2009, John Peters, review of *Z. Rex,* p. 72.

Kirkus Reviews, May, 2005, Joseph DeMarco, review of *Wounded,* p. 32; March 15, 2006, review of *Thieves like Us,* p. 287; April 15, 2007, review of *Thieves till We Die;* August 15, 2009, review of *Z. Rex.*

Kliatt, May, 2005, Joseph DeMarco, review of *Wounded,* p. 32.

Publishers Weekly, May 29, 2006, review of *Riddle of the Raptors,* p. 59.

School Library Journal, April, 2005, Anna M. Nelson, review of *Wounded,* p. 130; August, 2006, Mara Alpert, review of *Riddle of the Raptors,* p. 76; May, 2007, Lori E. Donovan, review of *Thieves till We Die,* p. 130; October, 2009, Genevieve Gallagher, review of *Z. Rex,* p. 122; December, 2009, Caitlin Augusta, review of *Be a Genie in Six Easy Steps,* p. 108.

Science Fiction Chronicle, June, 2005, Michael Johnson, review of *Prey,* p. 44.

Voice of Youth Advocates, February, 2005, Sherrie Williams, review of *Wounded,* p. 489; October, 2005, review of *Prey,* p. 320; June, 2007, Mary Ann Darby and Katherine Wise, review of *Thieves till We Die,* p. 158; October, 2009, Sherrie Williams, review of *Z. Rex,* p. 328.

ONLINE

Bloomsbury Web site, http://www.bloomsbury.com/ (May 13, 2011), "Stephen Cole."

Wereling Web site, http://www.wereling.com/ (August 20, 2005), interview with Cole.

*   *   *

COLE, Steve
See COLE, Stephen

D-E

DEMEULEMEESTER, Linda 1956-

Personal

Born 1956, in British Columbia, Canada; married John DeMeulemeester; children: two sons. *Education:* Simon Fraser University, B.A.; University of Victoria, certificate in continuing education; University of British Columbia, teaching certificate; Clarion West Writer's Workshop, graduate, 2001.

Addresses

Home—British Columbia, Canada. *E-mail*—grimhill@ shaw.ca.

Career

Educator and author. Teacher and educational program advisor specializing in adult education. Author; presenter at schools.

Member

Children's Writers and Illustrators of British Columbia Society, Science Fiction and Fantasy Writers of America, SF Canada, Writers Union of Canada.

Awards, Honors

Red Cedar Award shortlist, Hackmatack Award shortlist, and Diamond Willow Award shortlist, all 2007, and Great Books selection, Canadian Toy Testing Council, and Silver Birch Award, both 2008, all for *The Secret of Grim Hill;* Silver Birch Award shortlist, 2008, for *The Secret Deepens.*

Writings

"GRIM HILL" NOVEL SERIES

The Secret of Grim Hill, Lobster Press (Montreal, Quebec, Canada), 2007.

The Secret Deepens, Lobster Press (Montreal, Quebec, Canada), 2008.
The Forgotten Secret, Lobster Press (Montreal, Quebec, Canada), 2009.
The Family Secret, Lobster Press (Montreal, Quebec, Canada), 2010.
Forest of Secrets, Lobster Press (Montreal, Quebec, Canada), 2011.

Author's work has been translated into French, Korean, and Spanish.

OTHER

Contributor of short fiction and articles to periodicals, including *Canada's Storyteller, Guideposts, Neo-opsis, ChiZine,* and *Parenting Teens Today,* and to e-zines. Short fiction included in anthology *Wyrd Wravings,* Echelon Press.

Adaptations

The Secret of Grim Hill was adapted as an animated television series by Wizard Hat Productions.

Sidelights

Linda DeMeulemeester worked in the education field as both a teacher and literacy advisor before exploring her longtime interest in becoming a writer. Her first novel-length work, *The Secret of Grim Hill,* was eventually accepted by Montreal's Lobster Press and published in 2007 as the first volume in DeMeulemeester's "Grim Hill" middle-grade novel series. When the novel won the Silver Birch Award given by the Ontario Library Association, she was encouraged and she has since produced several sequels, all of which feature a mix of magic, adventure, and a close family relationship. "I grew up and live in a very rainy place," DeMeulemeester told *SATA.* "The fog and mist that rises from the forest has a mystical and dreamy appearance. Watching my son play soccer on the hill in the middle of the rain forest inspired me to think of Grim Hill and [inspired] the book's overall spookiness."

"Reading has been important to me from that first moment in grade one when I realized I was doing more than sounding out and connecting words: I was reading!,"De Meulemeester explained. "I've always wanted to share reading and that has slowly changed into also wanting to share my writing. I credit my grandmother for guiding me to become a story teller. She used to tell me scary stories and tales from a long time ago. From her I learned that, danger + mystery + adventurous thrills = my favourite kind of books. When I was in grade five my school had a story writing contest, and I was one of the youngest students to enter—and guess what, I won first prize. Okay, there was a huge gap between my first publishing success and when I sold the 'Grim Hill' manuscript."

In *The Secret of Grim Hill* Cat and Sookie Peters have had to undergo some changes since their parents' divorce. Now faced with life at her new middle school, Cat longs instead to attend Grimoire, a nearby private school where she believes she will have a better chance of fitting in. Soon Sookie and her friend uncover a local rumor about Grimoire that leads the three children to suspect that something at the secluded school is out of kilter. Further investigation quickly leads the girls into a mystery where creatures from Celtic myths morph into something far more sinister than sprites and fairies. Calling *The Secret of Grim Hill* "just creepy enough to cast a spell over anyone who reads it," Leslie L. Kennedy added in *Resource Links* that DeMeulemeester's novel features "a protagonist who is self-centred enough to be interesting, a precocious kid sister who deserves her own book and a plot that bubbles along at a magical pace worthy of the best witch's brew and a reader's rapt attention."

DeMeulemeester continues her "Grim Hill" series with *The Secret Deepens,* in which Cat pursues her interest in soccer until Sookie's flirtation with magic gets the younger girl into trouble. An upcoming Valentine's Day dance is Cat's focus in *The Forgotten Secret,* at least until a new girl and her aunt arrive in town and prove to be evil creatures working in tandem to steal the souls of young men in love. Other volumes in the "Grim Hill" series include *The Family Secret* and *Forest of Secrets,* the latter in which Cat and her friends are stalked by kidnappers and little sister Sookie may be the only one able to rescue them. Reviewing *The Family Secret,* in which Cat hopes to accompany Sookie on an exchange program to study in Sweden, a *Kirkus Reviews* writer noted that "the fascinating look at Sweden's history and culture" readers are treated to in DeMeulemeester's "light fantasy" makes the novel "an entertaining and worthwhile read."

Biographical and Critical Sources

PERIODICALS

Kirkus Reviews, April 1, 2010, review of *The Family Secret..*
Library Media Connection, 2009, Terry Day, review of *The Secret Deepens,* p. 72.
Resource Links, June, 2007, Leslie L. Kennedy, review of *The Secret of Grim Hill,* p. 26.

ONLINE

Linda DeMeulemeester Home Page, http://grimhill.com (May 15, 2011).
Lobster Press Web site, http://www.lobsterpress.com/ (May 15, 2011), "Linda DeMeulemeester."
Teen Reads Too Web log, http://trtbookclub.blogspot.com/ (May, 20, 2010), interview with DeMeulemeester.

* * *

DICKINSON, Mary-Anne
See RODDA, Emily

Linda DeMeulemeester's "Grim Hill" middle-grade saga includes **The Family Secret,** *a story featuring artwork by John Shroades.* (Illustration copyright © 2010 by John Shroades. Reproduced by permission of Lobster Press Limited.)

DIZIN, Pascal

Personal

Born in CA. *Education:* School of Visual Arts, B.F.A. (cartooning).

Addresses

Home—New York, NY. *E-mail*—pdizin@gmail.com.

Career

Illustrator and cartoonist.

Awards, Honors

Rhodes Family Award for Outstanding Achievement in Cartooning, School of Visual Arts; Texas Maverick Graphic Novels listee, 2010, for *City of Spies* by Susan Kim and Laurence Klavan.

Illustrator

Susan Kim and Laurence Klavan, *City of Spies* (graphic novel), First Second (New York, NY), 2010.

Contributor of illustrations to *Time Out New York.*

Sidelights

Pascal Dizin grew up in Mendocino, California, where his growing skill as an artist kept pace with his interest in comic books. He moved to the east coast to attend the School of Visual Arts, remaining in New York City after earning his B.F.A. in cartooning and establishing his career. Dizin's first book-length project, creating the art for the graphic novel *City of Spies,* draws on his interest in the comic books of the late 1930s through the 1940s—the so-called Golden Age of Comics—and features the cleanly drawn lines, super-hero cast, and good-versus-evil storyline characteristic of the period.

In *City of Spies* Dizin brings to life Susan Kim and Laurence Klavan's story about Evelyn, a ten year old who finds herself living in New York City during World War II. At first Evelyn spends much of her time drawing, but when she finds a friend in Tony, an neighborhood boy, she channels her imagination to the real world, where Axis spies seem to be lurking all around. After a few misses, the spy-hunting duo discovers an actual Nazi spy. Their efforts to track the man down and convince adults of his evildoing result in a story that a *Publishers Weekly* contributor characterized as "a good old-fashioned adventure . . . and rip-roaring fun."

Dizin's illustrations in *City of Spies* were cited by critics as a high point of the story, the *Publishers Weekly* critic writing that his softly toned sequential "art has a period feel while still looking fresh and kid-friendly." In *Booklist* Jesse Karp referenced the work of noted early-twentieth-century Belgian cartoonist Hergé, whose

Self-portrait by Pascal Dizin (Reproduced by permission.)

use of uniform lines and lack of ink shading set a new standard among comics artists and fans of his long-running "The Adventures of Tintin." "With stupefying precision, Dizin's art channels Hergé's "Tintin" in tone, palette, and with the remarkable expressiveness of the clean, flexible figures," asserted Karp. Praising *City of Spies* as a "complex, well-executed work [that] combines a modern, emotional narrative with a European comic style," Douglas P. Davey added in *School Library Journal* that Dizin's art "is a perfect complement to both the period and feel" of Kim and Klavan's text.

Biographical and Critical Sources

PERIODICALS

Booklist, March 15, 2010, Jesse Karp, review of *City of Spies,* p. 60.
Kirkus Reviews, April 15, 2010, review of *City of Spies.*
Publishers Weekly, April 5, 2010, review of *City of Spies,* p. 64.
School Library Journal, May, 2010, Douglas P. Davey, review of *City of Spies,* p. 141.
Teacher Librarian, October, 2010, Joe Sutliff Sanders, "Experimenting with Format," p. 25.

Dizin's ligne clair artwork is a feature of City of Spies, *a graphic novel by Susan Kim and laurence Klavan.* (Illustration copyright © 2010 by Pascal Dizin. Reproduced by permission of Henry Holt & Company, LLC.)

ONLINE

Pascal Dizin Home Page, http://dizin-art.com (May 27, 2011).

*   *   *

EPSTEIN, Robin

Personal

Born November 15, in PA. *Education:* Princeton University, B.A. (English); Columbia University, M.F.A. (nonfiction writing). *Hobbies and other interests:* Running, yoga, reading, watching television.

Addresses

Home—New York, NY. *E-mail*—robin@godisinthepancakes.com.

Career

Writer and educator. Formerly worked in advertising and as a stand-up comedian in New York, NY; writer for network television and for game shows; currently freelance writer. New York University, member of adjunct faculty.

Writings

FICTION

(With Renée Kaplan) *Shaking Her Assets* (adult novel), Berkeley (New York, NY), 2005.

God Is in the Pancakes, Dial Books for Young Readers (New York, NY), 2010.

"GROOVY GIRLS SLEEPOVER CLUB" CHAPTER-BOOK SERIES

The First Pajama Party: Slumberific Six, Scholastic (New York, NY), 2005.
Pranks a Lot: The Girls vs. the Boys, Scholastic (New York, NY), 2005.
Sleepover Surprise: A Twin-sational Birthday, Scholastic (New York, NY), 2005.
Rock and Roll: Divas Supreme, Scholastic (New York, NY), 2005.
Choose or Lose: How to Pick a Winner, Scholastic (New York, NY), 2005.
The Great Outdoors: Take a Hike, Scholastic (New York, NY), 2005.
Growing up Groovy: An Out-of-This-World Adventure, Scholastic (New York, NY), 2005.
Girls of Summer: Bon Voyage, Scholastic (New York, NY), 2005.

OTHER

(With Paul Mauro and others) *Prints and Impressions,* Scholastic (New York, NY), 2003.
How to Survive the Seemingly Impossible: Juggling, Magic Tricks, Illusions, and Other Feats You Really Can Do, illustrated by Kelly Kennedy, Scholastic (New York, NY), 2004.
(With David Borgenicht) *The Worst-case Scenario Survival Handbook: Junior Edition,* illustrated by Chuck Gonzales, Chronicle Books (San Francisco, CA), 2007.
(With sister Amy Epstein Feldman) *So Sue Me, Jackass!: Avoiding Legal Pitfalls That Can Come Back to Bite You at Work, at Home, and at Play,* Penguin (New York, NY), 2009.
(With David Borgenicht and Ben H. Winters) *The Worst-case Scenario Survival Handbook: Middle School,* illustrated by Chuck Gonzales, Chronicle Books (San Francisco, CA), 2009.
(With David Borgenicht and Nathaniel Marunas) *The Worst-case Scenario Survival Handbook: Gross Junior Edition,* illustrated by Chuck Gonzales, Chronicle Books (San Francisco, CA), 2010.

Contributor to periodicals, including *The Forward, Gear, Glamour, New York Times, Marie Claire, Real Simple,* and *Teen People.* Author of television scripts for series, including *This American Life,* and of video-game scripts.

Sidelights

Robin Epstein has spent much of her career working in television, where she has written for game shows and network programming. Turning to print, Epstein's byline has also appeared in popular periodicals such as *Glamour, Real Simple,* and *Teen People,* as well as in children's books. In her "Groovy Girls" books she chronicles the adventures of preteen BFF's Gwen, Reese, Oki, O'Ryan, Vanessa, and Yvette, while in *God Is in the Pancakes* she presents a thoughtful teen-centered story of budding love and intergenerational friendship. Among Epstein's other books are collaborations with her sister, Amy Epstein Feldman, on *So Sue Me, Jackass!: Avoiding Legal Pitfalls That Can Come Back to Bite You at Work, at Home, and at Play,* and with longtime friend Renée Kaplan as coauthors of the humorous working-girl novel *Shaking Her Assets.* Teaming up with several other writers, she also contributed to the entertainment value of *The Worst-Case Scenario Survival Handbook: Gross Junior Edition,* one of several books inspired by *The Worst-Case Scenario Survival Handbook,* Joshua Piven's 1999 guidebook to the perennially pessimistic.

Raised in Pennsylvania, Epstein attended Princeton University where she majored in English. A move to New York City after graduation led to a dual career in which she performed stand-up comedy by night while working in advertising by day. After earning an M.F.A. in non-fiction writing at Columbia University, Epstein moved to television, traveling to the West coast while working on network television shows and even appearing on air

during a teen game show she scripted for the Oxygen network. In the mid-2000s Epstein began to focus increasingly on books, producing her 'tween-friendly "Groovy Girls" books for Scholastic while also branching out into a number of independent projects. One of these project, the young-adult novel *God Is in the Pancakes,* was released in 2010.

In *God Is in the Pancakes* readers meet fifteen-year-old Grace Manning, who is dealing with a recently run-off dad, a stressed-out mom, and a budding romance with friend Eric when she starts work at a local nursing home. Taking her job seriously, she enjoys the home's residents and makes friends with one in particular. Octogenarian Frank Sands has Lou Gehrig's disease, but he is still able to play poker with Grace and enjoy her sharp, dry wit. However, when Frank feels confident enough in their friendship to ask Grace to help him end his life, the request comes as a shock to the teen. She must not only consider her own values but also look beyond herself and try to empathize with a person in a situation she can only imagine. Writing in *Booklist,* Frances Bradburn praised *God Is in the Pancakes* as a "memorable novel [that] offers food for thought and sustenance for the soul" while also treating teens to an "authentic, breezy read." "Powerful and poignant," according to a *Kirkus Reviews* writer, Epstein's story touches on Grace's feelings of abandonment by God; the author's ability to mix "spot-on adolescent banter" with serious moral questions produces a "stellar" teen novel "which offers neither judgments nor simplistic answers." "Fans of Sarah Dessen and Deb Caletti will rejoice at finding Epstein," concluded Suanne Rouch in her laudatory review of *God Is in the Pancakes* for *School Library Journal.*

Cover of Robin Epstein's young-adult novel **God Is in the Pancakes,** *in which a multigenerational friendship brings with it a difficult choice.* (Dial Books, 2010. Cover photograph by Veer Images. Reproduced by permission of Dial Books for Young Readers, a division of Penguin Books for Young Readers, a member of Penguin Group (USA) Inc., 345 Hudson St., New York, NY 10014. All rights reserved.)

Biographical and Critical Sources

PERIODICALS

Booklist, May 15, 2010, Frances Bradburn, review of *God Is in the Pancakes,* p. 36.
Publishers Weekly, October 29, 2007, review of *Worst-Case Scenario Survival Handbook: Junior Edition,* p. 58; May 10, 2010, review of *God Is in the Pancakes,* p. 46.
School Library Journal, May, 2010, Suanne Roush, review of *God Is in the Pancakes,* p. 112; December, 2010, Vicki Reutter, review of *The Worst-Case Scenario Survival Handbook: Gross Junior Edition,* p. 135.
USA Today, August 20, 2009, Bob Minzesheimer, review of *The Worst-Case Scenario Survival Handbook: Middle School,* p. 7.

ONLINE

Robin Epstein Home Page, http://godisinthepancakes.com (May 27, 2011).
Shaking Her Assets Web log, http://robinandrenee.blogspot.com (May 27, 2011).

F

FAUST, Anke 1971-

Personal
Born 1971, in Brilon, Germany. *Education:* Certificate (illustration), 1990.

Addresses
Home—Sörgenloch, Germany. *E-mail*—post@anke-faust.de.

Career
Illustrator of books for children. Ravensburger Verlag, Ravensburg, Germany, former textbook illustrator; freelance illustrator, beginning 1996. Presenter at schools and workshops.

Awards, Honors
Stiftung Buchkunst honor, 1997, for *Kinder laßt uns Kasperle spielen* by Heinrich M. Denneborg and Sylvia Gut, 1999, for *Der Aufstand der Zauberhasen* by Ariel Dorfman; Deutscher Jugendliteraturpreis, 2005, for *Ein Schaf fürs Leben* by Maritgen Matter; Eulenspiegel Bilderbuchpreis nomination, 2010, for *Das grüne Küken* by Adele Sansone.

Writings

SELF-ILLUSTRATED

Engel und anderes Geflügel 12, Rowohlt Taschenbuch (Reinbek, Germany), 2005.
Lina quasselt, Nord Süd (Zurich, Switzerland), 2011.

ILLUSTRATOR

Heinrich M. Denneborg and Sylvia Gut, *Kinder laßt uns Kasperle spielen,* Ravensburger (Ravensburg, Germany), 1996.

Dieter Dambach, *Cartoons, witze, Scherzfragen,* Ravensburger (Ravensburg, Germany), 1997.
Nicholaus Lens, *999 Schülerwitze,* Ravensburger (Ravensburg, Germany), 1997.
Anne M.G. Schmidt, *Wiplala zaubert weiter,* Fischer Schnatzinzel (Frankfurt am Main, Germany), 1998.
Jörn Peter Dirx, *Schon gehört?,* Ravensburger (Ravensburg, Germany), 1998.
Monika Wild, *Was steht mitten in Paris?,* Ravensburger (Ravensburg, Germany), 1998.
Ariel Dorfman, *Der Aufstand der Zauberhasen,* translated from the Spanish by Gertraud Strohm-Katzer, Fischer-Taschenbuch (Frankfurt am Main, Germany), 1998.
Maritgen Matter, *Ein Schaf fürs Leben,* Oetinger (Hamburg, Germany), 2003.
Philip Keifer, *Von Mäusen und Moneten: mein kleines Buch vom Geld,* Coppenrath (Münster, Germany), 2003.
Christa Wißkirchen, *Bühne frei!: lustige Kindersketsche für Schulfeste, Familienfeiern und Co.,* Coppenrath (Münster, Germany), 2004.
Dieter Dambach, *Ferien, Spass und gute Laune,* Ravensburger (Ravensburg, Germany), 2005.
Hjördis Fremjen, *Sensationelle Witze,* Ravensburger (Ravensburg, Germany), 2005.
Marianne Liobl, *Piratenstarker Party-Spass,* Coppenrath (Münster, Germany), 2005.
(With Jutta Knipping) Insa Bauer, *Spuk am Geistersee,* Bondolino (Bindlach, Germany), 2006.
Susanne Tommes, *Rauf aufs Fahrrad!: Wichtiges für Radfahrer,* Coppenrath (Münster, Germany), 2007.
Paul Maar, *Der tätowierte Hund,* Oetinger (Hamburg, Germany), 2007.
Anne Maar, *Applaus für Caruso,* Tulipan (Berlin, Germany), 2009.
Adele Sansone, *Das grüne Küken,* new edition, NordSüd (Zürich, Switzerland), 2010, translation published as *The Little Green Goose,* North-South (New York, NY), 2011.

Books illustrated by Faust have been translated into Catalan, Danish, French, Galacian, Korean, Spanish, and Swedish.

Biographical and Critical Sources

PERIODICALS

Kirkus Reviews, April 1, 2010, review of *The Little Green Goose.*

ONLINE

Anke Faust Home Page, http://www.anke-faust.de (February 27, 2011).*

*   *   *

FINCHLER, Judy 1943-

Personal

Born March 28, 1943, in Paterson, NJ; daughter of Sidney (a postal worker) and Harriet (a teacher) Gold; married Jerome Finchler (an accountant), August 11, 1963; children: Todd, Lauren Finchler Fitch. *Education:* Montclair State University, B.A., 1964; William Paterson College of New Jersey, elementary school certification; Kean College of New Jersey, teacher-librarian certification. *Politics:* "Independent." *Religion:* Jewish.

Addresses

Home—Parsippany, NJ. *E-mail*—finchler@hotmail.com.

Career

Educator, librarian, and author. Teacher in Paterson, NJ, public schools, 1964-67; supplemental instructor in Parsippany, NJ, 1977-81; Paterson Board of Education, teacher, 1981-86, teacher-librarian, beginning 1986; retired. Presenter at schools.

Member

National Education Association, New Jersey Education Association, Paterson Educational Association.

Awards, Honors

Outstanding Service Award, Department of Instructional Services, Paterson Public Schools, 1994.

Writings

Miss Malarkey Doesn't Live in Room 10, illustrated by Kevin O'Malley, Walker & Co. (New York, NY), 1995.
Miss Malarkey Won't Be in Today, illustrated by Kevin O'Malley, Walker & Co. (New York, NY), 2000.
Testing Miss Malarkey, illustrated by Kevin O'Malley, Walker & Co. (New York, NY), 2000.

Judy Finchler (Reproduced by permission.)

You're a Good Sport, Miss Malarkey, illustrated by Kevin O'Malley, Walker & Co. (New York, NY), 2002.
Miss Malarkey's Field Trip, illustrated by Kevin O'Malley, Walker & Co. (New York, NY), 2004.
(With Kevin O'Malley) *Miss Malarkey Leaves No Reader Behind,* illustrated by Kevin O'Malley, Walker & Co. (New York, NY), 2006.
(With Kevin O'Malley) *Congratulations, Miss Malarkey!,* illustrated by O'Malley, Walker & Co. (New York, NY), 2009.

Sidelights

Judy Finchler began her writing career in 1995 while also working as a teacher and librarian in her home state of New Jersey. Following the traditional writer's dictum of "write what you know," Finchler's humorous stories follow the misadventures of a third-grade teacher and her class. Illustrated by artist Kevin O'Malley, the humorous stories in Finchler's books touch on subjects most elementary-grade children can relate to, from standardized testing to team sports to the mix of confusion and hijinks that can occur when an untested substitute teacher heads the classroom. Geared for children in grades two through five, the "Miss Malarkey" books also lure less-enthusiastic readers through Finchler's use of puns and other wordplay throughout her easy-reading stories.

In *Miss Malarkey Doesn't Live in Room 10* a young boy describes how his idealistic view of his teacher's life outside of school is brought down to earth after she moves into the same apartment building where his family lives. "Finchler's lively story destroys a typical misconception in wonderfully comic fashion, with an unnamed narrator trying to fit his teacher's after-hours life neatly into his own childhood frame of reference," noted

Booklist reviewer Stephanie Zvirin. *School Library Journal* contributor Virginia Opocensky also offered a favorable assessment of *Miss Malarkey Doesn't Live in Room 10,* calling Finchler's story "an entertaining romp that's sure to elicit lots of chuckles."

Finchler continues to highlight the humor to be found in a child's perception of his or her teacher in several other books featuring Miss Malarkey. The likeable teacher finds herself battling both unruly and disinterested parents in her role as school soccer coach in *You're a Good Sport, Miss Malarkey,* while in *Miss Malarkey Won't Be in Today* a succession of unpopular substitutes strike out after Miss Malarkey comes down with the flu. A class outing to a local science center provides the setting for *Miss Malarkey's Field Trip,* which a *Kirkus Reviews* writer characterized as a "spot-on slice of school life." Citing O'Malley's "lively" ink-and-marker illustrations for *You're a Good Sport, Miss Malarkey,* Shelley Townsend-Hudson added in her *School Library Journal* review that the upbeat art "leavens a story about a subject[—the lack of sportsmanship in school athletic competition—]of increasing concern to both parents and kids."

Finchler is aided in writing duties by her illustrator in *Miss Malarkey Leaves No Readers Behind,* as Principal Wiggins' rash promise to dye his hair purple inspires the students to take on the challenge of the Everybody Reads in America program, although certain reluctant readers are given extra encouragement by Miss Malarkey. *Testing Miss Malarkey* finds both students and teachers stressing out while anticipating the upcoming season of standardized testing, while the collaborative story by Finchler and O'Malley in *Congratulations, Miss Malarkey* finds the teacher's announcement of her upcoming marriage sparking rumors and worries that she may abandon her class. Reviewing *Miss Malarkey Leaves No Readers Behind* for *School Library Journal,* Rebecca Sheridan noted that Finchler and O'Malley's story "will resonate with those who choose math, video games, and sports over books," while its "expressive" cartoon illustrations "lend humor and credibility" to the tale. The roller-coaster of emotions that a teacher's upcoming marriage engenders "is both very real and rarely seen in books for this age," noted a *Kirkus Reviews* writer in appraising *Congratulations, Miss Malarkey!,* and Finchler's "surprisingly sarcastic" text in *Testing Miss Malarkey* contributes to the book's mix of "silly humor and joyful, creative illustrations," according to *Booklist* contributor Marta Segal.

"I've always loved writing," Finchler once told *SATA.* "Whether in a story, poem, letter, or even a grant proposal, words have always been my dearest friends. Finding the best word, the most appropriate phrase, arranging, rearranging, and expressing my ideas are all deeply satisfying. The experience of seeing my words in print in bookstores and libraries has greatly surpassed even what I envisioned it to be.

"As a lover of the written word, I am also a reader. It's hard to identify where one skill ends and the other begins. That is what I tried to develop in my students: reading is so much more than what you have to do in school. A book is a lifelong companion that will enrich your life. The words you read become a part of you and will in some way be given back in what you write."

Biographical and Critical Sources

PERIODICALS

Booklist, November 15, 1995, Stephanie Zvirin and Kevin O'Malley, review of *Miss Malarkey Doesn't Live in Room 10,* p. 563; September 1, 1998, April Judge, review of *Miss Malarkey Won't Be In Today,* p. 126; October 1, 2000, Marta Segal, review of *Testing Miss Malarkey,* p. 345; October 15, 2002, Shelley Townsend-Hudson, review of *You're a Good Sport, Miss Malarkey,* p. 411; September 15, 2004, Ilene Cooper, review of *Miss Malarkey's Field Trip,* p. 248; July 1, 2006, Carolyn Phelan, review of *Miss Malarkey Leaves No Reader Behind,* p. 65.

Children's Bookwatch, October, 2009, review of *Congratulations, Miss Malarkey!*

Kirkus Reviews, August 1, 2002, review of *You're A Good Sport, Miss Malarkey,* p. 1128; July 1, 2004, review of *Miss Malarkey's Field Trip,* p. 628; June 1, 2006, review of *Miss Malarkey Leaves No Reader Behind,* p. 571; June 15, 2009, review of *Congratulations, Miss Malarkey!*

New York Times Book Review, March 11, 2001, review of *Testing Miss Malarkey,* p. 26.

Publishers Weekly, August 4, 1995, review of *Miss Malarkey Doesn't Live in Room 10,* p. 83; September 14, 1998, review of *Miss Malarkey Won't Be in Today,* p. 68; August 21, 2000, review of *The Return of Miss Malarkey,* p. 75; October 7, 2002, review of *You're a Good Sport, Miss Malarkey,* p. 75; June 7, 2009, review of *Congratulations, Miss Malarkey!,* p. 51.

School Library Journal, December, 1995, Virginia Opocensky, review of *Miss Malarkey Doesn't Live in Room 10,* p. 80; October, 2000, Kate McClelland, review of *Testing Miss Malarkey,* p. 124; October, 2002, Grace Oliff, review of *You're a Good Sport, Miss Malarkey,* p. 105; April, 2004, review of *Testing Miss Malarkey,* p. 27; November, 2004, Grace Oliff, review of *Miss Malarkey's Field Trip,* p. 103; August, 2006, Rebecca Sheridan, review of *Miss Malarkey Leaves No Reader Behind,* p. 81; August, 2009, Mary Hazelton, review of *Congratulations, Miss Malarkey!,* p. 75.

ONLINE

Montville Patch Online, http://montville.patch.com/ (October 15, 2010), Nate Adams, "Child Author Brings 'Malarkey' to Library."*

FRIEDMAN, Hal

Personal

Married; wife's name Sophie; children: Cory, Jessie.

Addresses

Home—Northern NJ.

Career

Author and copywriter. J. Walter Thompson (advertising agency), New York, NY, former copywriter; creative director.

Writings

ADULT NOVELS

Tunnel, Morrow (New York, NY), 1979.
A Hunting We Will Go, HarperCollins (New York, NY), 1998.
Over the Edge, HarperCollins (New York, NY), 1998.

OTHER

(With James Patterson) *Against Medical Advice: A True Story* (also see below), Little, Brown (New York, NY), 2008.

(With James Paterson) *Med Head: My Knock-down, Drag-out, Drugged-up Battle with My Brain* (for young adults; adaptation of *Against Medical Advice*), Little, Brown (New York, NY), 2010.

Biographical and Critical Sources

PERIODICALS

Booklist, March 1, 1998, Wes Lukowsky, review of *A Hunting We Will Go,* p. 1097.
New York Times, November 1, 1998, Marjorie Kaufman, "Lots of People Take His Word for It."
Publishers Weekly, February 2, 1998, review of *A Hunting We Will Go,* p. 78; September 28, 1998, review of *Over the Edge,* p. 74.
Voice of Youth Advocates, June, 2010, Ann Reddy Damo, review of *Med-Head: My Knock-down, Drag-out, Drugged-up Battle with My Brain,* p. 177.

ONLINE

Teenreads.com, http://www.teenreads.com/ (April, 2010), interview with Friedman.*

G

GIBBS, Stuart 1969-

Personal

Born 1969, in Philadelphia, PA; married; wife's name Suzanne; children: Dashiell, Violet. *Education:* University of Pennsylvania, degree, 1991. *Hobbies and other interests:* Travel, skiing, hiking.

Addresses

Home—Los Angeles, CA. *Agent*—ICM, 10250 Constellation Blvd., Los Angeles, CA 90067. *E-mail*—stuart. gibbs@rocketmail.com.

Career

Author and screenwriter. Writer of feature films, television movies, and television pilots. Formerly worked in a zoo.

Writings

Belly Up, Simon & Schuster Books for Young Readers (New York, NY), 2010.
The Last Musketeer, HarperCollins Books for Young Readers (New York, NY), 2011.
Spy School, Simon & Schuster Books for Young Readers (New York, NY), 2012.

Author of scripts for film and television, including *See Spot Run, Parental Guidance,* and *Repli-Kate.* Contributor to animated films *Anastasia, Mickey's Three Musketeers,* and television's *Open Season* series.

Sidelights

Stuart Gibbs works in Los Angeles, where several of his scripts for film and television have been produced. Inspired by the many changes wrought on his life by parenthood, as well as by his own memories of working

Stuart Gibbs (Photograph by Jane Gibbs. Reproduced by permission.)

in a zoo, Gibbs took time away from screenwriting to craft a humorous novel for middle graders that was published in 2010 as *Belly Up.* Due to the success of his first novel—and the fact that it was more fun to write than a screenplay—Gibbs has continued to focus on young-adult fiction. His second novel, *The Last Musketeer* the first of a trilogy about the Three Musketeers as teenagers, was scheduled to be joined by *Spy School,* Gibbs' comic tale of a preteen who is recruited to the C.I.A.'s top-secret Academy of Espionage.

Set in the hill country near San Antonio, Texas, where its author spent his childhood, *Belly Up* finds twelve-year-old Theodore "Teddy" Roosevelt Fitzroy perplexed by the death of Henry Hippo, the mascot of the Fun-Jungle zoo and theme park where Teddy's parents live and work as animal researchers. Although the zoo's public relations staff quickly issues a statement saying that the hippo died of natural causes, the preteen is sure there is more to Henry's passing. Turning sleuth, Teddy teams up with friend Summer McCraken and investigates, learning that the real Henry Hippo was actually not at all lovable. The more the duo digs, the more suspects they find, among them the zoo's head of operations and FunJungle's billionaire owner J.J. McCraken (who also happens to be Summer's dad). Others with a motive to do the hippo in include one of Henry's victims: a midget clown with a hippo-sized grudge.

Praising *Belly Up* as "an auspicious debut," Michael Cart added in *Booklist* that Gibbs' well-plotted and "fast-paced story . . . deftly mixes humor and suspense." "Dense with animal trivia, *Belly Up* will suit attentive readers who love mystery and random facts," predicted Caitlin Augusta in *School Library Journal*, the critic also commending the author's ability to present "issues of animal welfare . . . without being preachy." According to Augusta, the "motley cast of characters" in *Belly Up* "holds its own with quirky personalities and memorable details." In *Kirkus Reviews* a critic gave a nod to "screenwriter Gibbs," noting that he "combines details of the inner workings of zoos with some over-the-top action" to produce "an entertaining read."

Biographical and Critical Sources

PERIODICALS

Booklist, May 1, 2010, Michael Cart, review of *Belly Up,* p. 50.
Kirkus Reviews, April 15, 2010, review of *Belly Up.*
Library Media Connection, October, 2010, Anne Bozievich, review of *Belly Up,* p. 73.
School Library Journal, May, 2010, Caitlin Augusta, review of *Belly Up,* p. 112.

ONLINE

Simon & Schuster Web site, http://authors.simonand schuster.net/ (May 15, 2011), interview with Gibbs.
Stuart Gibbs Home Page, http://stuartgibbs.com (May 20, 2011).

*   *   *

GONZALES, Chuck

Personal

Male. *Education:* Earned college degree.

Chuck Gonzales (Photograph by Barry Rice. Reproduced by permission.)

Addresses

Home—New York, NY. *Agent*—Illo Reps, New York, NY. *E-mail*—chuck@chuckgonzales.com.

Career

Illustrator.

Illustrator

David Borgenicht and Robin Epstein, *The Worst-case Scenario Survival Handbook: Junior Edition,* Chronicle Books (San Francisco, CA), 2007.
David Borgenicht and Justin Heimberg, *The Worst-case Scenario Survival Handbook: Extreme Junior Edition,* Chronicle Books (San Francisco, CA), 2008.
Rick Adams, *36 1/2 Reasons to Laugh: A Slice of Life,* foreword by Doug Savant, Chronicle Books (San Francisco, CA), 2009.
David Borgenicht, Ben H. Winters, and Robin Epstein, *The Worst-case Scenario Survival Handbook: Middle School,* Chronicle Books (San Francisco, CA), 2009.
David Borgenicht, Nathaniel Marunas, and Robin Epstein, *The Worst-case Scenario Survival Handbook: Gross Junior Edition,* Chronicle Books (San Francisco, CA), 2010.
David Borgenicht and Justin Heimberg, *The Worst-case Scenario Survival Handbook: Weird Junior Edition,* Chronicle Books (San Francisco, CA), 2010.

Illustrator of "PSS! Plus+books" educational series, for Price Stern Sloan (New York, NY), 2008. Contributor to periodicals, including *Adweek, Cosmopolitan, Entertainment Weekly, Interior Design, New York Times, Tiger Beat, Wall Street Journal,* and *Weekly Reader.*

ILLUSTRATOR; "PRINCESS POWER" SERIES BY SUZANNE WILLIAMS

The Perfectly Proper Prince, HarperTrophy (New York, NY), 2006.
The Charmingly Clever Cousin, HarperTrophy (New York, NY), 2006.
The Awfully Angry Ogre, HarperTrophy (New York, NY), 2007.

The Stubbornly Secretive Servant, HarperTrophy (New York, NY), 2007.

The Mysterious, Mournful Maiden, HarperTrophy (New York, NY), 2007.

The Gigantic, Genuine Genie, HarperTrophy (New York, NY), 2007.

Biographical and Critical Sources

PERIODICALS

Publishers Weekly, October 29, 2007, review of *The Worst-case Scenario Survival Handbook: Junior Edition,* p. 58.

School Library Journal, January, 2007, Elaine Lesh Morgan, review of *The Charmingly Clever Cousin,* p. 110; November, 2010, Esther Keller, review of *The Worst-case Scenario Survival Handbook: Weird Junior Edition,* p. 136; December, 2010, Vicki Reutter, review of *The Worst-case Scenario Survival Handbook: Gross Junior Edition,* p. 135.

USA Today, August 20, 2009, Bob Minzesheimer, review of *The Worst-case Scenario Survival Handbook: Middle School,* p. 7.

ONLINE

Chuck Gonzales Home Page, http://www.chuckgonzales.com (February 27, 2011).

HarperCollins Publishers Web site, http://www.harpercollins.com/ (May 15, 2011), "Chuck Gonzales."*

*　　*　　*

GRANT, Katie
See GRANT, K.M.

*　　*　　*

GRANT, K.M. 1958-
(Katie Grant)

Personal

Born October 6, 1958, in Cliviger, Lancashire, England; daughter of Simon (a government official) and Mary Towneley; married William Couper Grant, 1985; children: three. *Education:* Glasgow University, degree (medieval history). *Hobbies and other interests:* Playing piano, learning the Russian language.

Addresses

Home—Glasgow, Scotland.

Career

Writer and broadcaster. Broadcast and print journalist, beginning 1997; freelance writer beginning 2002. Presenter at schools and writing workshops.

Writings

How the Hangman Lost His Heart, Puffin Books (London, England), 2006, Walker & Co. (New York, NY), 2007.

Belle's Song, Walker Books for Young Readers (New York, NY), 2011.

Contributor to periodicals, including *Scotsman, History Today, Scottish Daily Mail,* and *Spectator.*

"DE GRANVILLE" NOVEL TRILOGY

Blood Red Horse, Puffin Books (London, England), 2004, Walker & Co. (New York, NY), 2005.

Green Jasper, Walker & Co. (New York, NY), 2006.

Blaze of Silver, Walker & Co. (New York, NY), 2006.

"PERFECT FIRE" NOVEL TRILOGY

Blue Flame, Walker & Co. (New York, NY), 2008.

White Heat, Walker & Co. (New York, NY), 2009.

Paradise Red, Walker & Co. (New York, NY), 2010.

Adaptations

The novels in the "de Granville" trilogy were adapted as audiobooks, Recorded Books, 2005-07.

Sidelights

A journalist who is based in Scotland, K.M. Grant is also the author of a number of works of historical fiction, including the novels in her critically acclaimed "De Granville" and "Perfect Fire" trilogies. A student of medieval history, Grant transports readers back to that colorful era, both in her "de Granville" novels, and in the "Perfect Fire" books, which take place during the crusades, as King Richard the Lionheart marshaled Christians throughout Britain to travel to the Holy Land and battle Muslim leader Saladin. In addition to series fiction, Grant has also written standalone novels, among them *How the Hangman Lost His Heart* and *Belle's Song,* the latter in which a young woman meets the scribe to the English poet Chaucer and makes a pilgrimage to Canterbury to pray for her father's healing.

Growing up as one of seven children, Grant developed an interest in history after hearing tales about her ancestor, Colonel Francis Towneley, "the last man in Britain to be hanged, drawn and quartered," as the author explained on her home page. According to Grant, Towneley was executed for his faith at Kennington Common in 1746. He "was my most romantic ancestor and it was his life, but, more particularly, his death, that taught me from an early age that history was not only exotic and thrilling but also full of gruesome details useful for frightening visitors my six siblings and I particularly disliked," she noted. Grant, who has studied medieval history at Glasgow University, now works as a freelance journalist and broadcaster in her native Scotland.

Grant's debut novel, *Blood Red Horse,* is the first installment in her "de Granville Trilogy." It centers around thirteen-year-old William de Granville, William's older brother Gavin, and an orphaned young woman named Ellie. Although Ellie has been promised to Gavin in marriage, she feels a greater affinity for William, a gifted horseman. When the brothers and their father join King Richard the Lionheart on his crusade against Muslim leader Saladin, William chooses Hosanna, a small, blood-red stallion, as his first warhorse. Once they reach the Holy Land, "Hosanna overcomes mistreatment, attack and injury to inspire both William and Saladin's assistant Kamil, into whose hands the horse briefly falls," noted a critic in *Kirkus Reviews.* According to Jennifer Mattson in *Booklist, Blood Red Horse* "transcends boundaries of gender and genre, with something to offer fans of equestrian fare, historical fiction, and battlefield drama alike."

Romance and political intrigue are at the heart of *Green Jasper,* book two of the "de Granville Trilogy." Having returned to England, battle-scarred Gavin is now lord of the manor. He is also still betrothed to Ellie, but their wedding ceremony is disrupted by Constable de Scabious, a follower of Prince John now that John has usurped the throne in King Richard's absence. When Ellie is abducted by de Scabious, William counsels Gavin to mount a rescue effort, causing a rift with his more cautious sibling. "Grant balances simplistic elements with unsentimental explorations of medieval conflicts between romantic love, brotherly loyalty, and political fealty," observed Mattson, and *Horn Book* reviewer Vicky Smith called the author's "renderings of characters and their motivations" in *Green Jasper* "both completely recognizable and in keeping with the times."

The "de Granville Trilogy" concludes in *Blaze of Silver,* which concerns the efforts of William and Kamil to win the freedom of King Richard, who has been imprisoned in Austria. Praised by *Booklist* reviewer Michael Cart as a novel "as cinematically fast paced and horsecentric as its predecessors," *Blaze of Silver* follows William as he attempts to ransom the king. The love of Hosanna has strengthened the friendship between William and Kamil, but Richard's captor plans a diabolical revenge that threatens both this friendship and the men's very lives. Grant's quickly paced tale "will keep readers moving from one betrayal to the next," predicted Melissa Moore in her *School Library Review* of the concluding "de Granville" novel.

In Grant's "Perfect Fire Trilogy" the year is 1241 and the setting is the kingdom of Occitania in southern France. In *Blue Flame* readers are drawn into another medieval battle: the war between Catholics and Cathars, the latter a sect that believed in dual and dueling gods: Rex Mundi, the malicious creator of the harsh physical plane versus a spiritual god of peace. Considered heretics, the Cathars were ultimately targeted by Catholic kings during what became known as the Albigensian Crusade. In Grant's novel the Catharite Occitanian

knights are sworn guardians of the Blue Flame, which is said to have been lit at the moment of Christ's death. Parsifal, the son of a knight, became the flame's keeper four decades ago, but the solitary task drove him to madness. Now the battle between religious factions threatens the love between Raimon, a Catharite weaver's son, and the high-born Yolanda, niece of a powerful Catholic. As the inquisitions begin and Raimon is labeled a heretic, he is chosen by the Blue Flame to defend his people in a story that "anchors [the] . . . tangled religious and territorial conflicts" of thirteenth-century Occitania "with the story of two young lovers," according to *Booklist* critic Krista Hutley. "Grant knows how to write a love story with subtlety and naturalness, picking up those minute hopes and embarrassments that pave the way from friendship to romance," wrote Anita L. Burkam in her *Horn Book* review of *Blue Flame,* while a *Kirkus Reviews* writer cited Grant for including "impeccably researched details [that] reveal a deep appreciation for the region and its culture."

The "Perfect Fire" saga continues in *White Heat,* as Raimon joins the flame's keeper, Sir Parsifal, to lead the Occitanians in their fight to survive the harsh inquisition. Although Yolanda has been told that her beloved is dead, she continues to resist the attentions of Sir Hugh des Arcis, a Catholic and friend of her uncle, her resolve supported by loyal servant Laila. When a fanatical Cathar known as the White Wolf begins to take control of the heretical faction, Occitania becomes even more chaotic. Now the question becomes whether his love will survive the ravages of a siege, her enforced betrothal to Raimon's enemy, and the growing divisions within Occitania that threatens families, friends, and communities. Grant's story reaches a thrilling conclusion in *Paradise Red,* as Raimon's effort to regain the Blue Flame becomes a race against time when he learns of Sir Hugh's plan to take the flame by storm. Praising *White Heat* as "a thrilling trip back in time," Burkham also cited the story's "thorough scholarship" for allowing readers to experience "an immersion into medieval sights, sounds, and points of view," while *School Library Journal* contributor Heather M. Campbell praised Grant's "gift for description" and her ability to flesh out secondary characters who add "ambivalence about which side is in the right." Reviewing *Paradise Red* for *School Librarian,* Janet Sumner also noted the author's care in realistically portraying this tumultuous historical epoch, writing that, "far from being a sanitized modern version of medieval France," the "Perfect Fire" saga plays out in "harsh reality, both in the sense of how life was and in the cruelties experienced by the characters."

While her series fiction reflects her deep understanding of medieval history, Grant's colorful family history inspired her novel *How the Hangman Lost His Heart,* which was deemed a "clever and entertaining historical black comedy" by London *Sunday Times* contributor Nicolette Jones. Set in eighteenth-century Scotland, the story follows Alice de Granville, the niece of Stuart sympathizer Francis Towneley, as she attempts to re-unite the disembodied head of her beloved uncle with his corpse. "Help comes from two unlikely, but gallant sources—brave [hangman] Dan Skinslicer . . . and the dashing Captain Ffrench of the King's Dragoons," noted Kathryn Ross in her review of the novel for the *Scotsman*. Deeming *How the Hangman Lost His Heart* "a smart, breezy caper," *Horn Book* critic Claire E. Gross cited in particular the story's "quirky" minor players, who are "products of their time . . . , uncompromising in their differences, and refreshingly individual." In *School Library Journal* Corinda J. Humphreys recommended Grant's novel to teens in search of "a rousing read with historical overtones," while *Booklist* critic Michael Cart dubbed *How the Hangman Lost His Heart* an "action-filled adventure" with a "reader-grabbing premise."

"History is glorious," Grant noted on her home page, reflecting on her choice to create historical fiction. "You can tell it straight; you can make it frilly; you can speed it up; you can slow it down; you can twist it; you can dance with it; you can throw it up in the air and see where it lands. My family has a long history, and perhaps that's why to me history has never been a matter of dusty dates and events long past, but has always been a pulsating, insistent force, sometimes comforting, sometimes alarming; sometimes tragic, sometimes funny; sometimes tragically funny, sometimes funnily tragic. Whatever, it's always alive."

Biographical and Critical Sources

PERIODICALS

Booklist, April 1, 2005, Jennifer Mattson, review of *Blood Red Horse*, p. 1359; May 1, 2006, Jennifer Mattson, review of *Green Jasper*, p. 80; February 1, 2007, Michael Cart, review of *Blaze of Silver*, p. 42; November 15, 2007, Michael Cart, review of *How the Hangman Lost His Heart*, p. 37; October 15, 2008, Krista Hutley, review of *Blue Flame*, p. 40; March 15, 2010, Krista Hutley, review of *White Heat*, p. 45.

Bulletin of the Center for Children's Books, May, 2005, review of *Blood Red Horse*, p. 385.

History Today, December, 2005, K.M. Grant, "My Head Start with History," p. 70.

Horn Book, May-June, 2006, Vicky Smith, review of *Green Jasper,* p. 317; January-February, 2008, Claire E. Gross, review of *How the Hangman Lost His Heart,* p. 86; November-December, 2008, Anita L. Burkam, review of *Blue Flame,* p. 704; November-December, 2009, Anita L. Burkam, review of *White Heat,* p. 672.

Kirkus Reviews, March 1, 2005, review of *Blood Red Horse,* p. 287; October 15, 2008, review of *Blue Flame;* September 15, 2009, review of *White Heat.*

Observer (London, England), July 23, 2006, Carole Cadwalladr, review of *How the Hangman Lost His Heart,* p. 385.

School Librarian, summer, 2010, Janet Sumner, review of *Paradise Red,* p. 110.

School Library Journal, May, 2005, Denise Moore, review of *Blood Red Horse,* p. 128; June, 2006, Denise Moore, review of *Green Jasper,* p. 156; May, 2007, Melissa Moore, review of *Blaze of Silver,* p. 132; December, 2007, Corinda J. Humphrey, review of *How the Hangman Lost His Heart,* p. 130; December, 2008, Heather M. Campbell, review of *Blue Flame,* p. 124; January, 2010, Heather M. Campbell, review of *White Heat,* p. 102.

Scotsman, July 1, 2006, Kathryn Ross, review of *How the Hangman Lost His Heart.*

Sunday Times (London, England), May 7, 2006, Nicolette Jones, review of *How the Hangman Lost His Heart.*

ONLINE

K.M. Grant Home Page, http://kmgrant.org (May 15, 2011).

Puffin Web site, http://www.puffin.co.uk/ (May 15, 2011), "K.M. Grant."*

H

HARRIS, Stephen 1959-

Personal

Born 1959, in Melbourne, Victoria, Australia. *Education:* Attended Victorian College of Arts.

Addresses

Home—Australia.

Career

Writer. Australian Broadcasting Corporation, radio producer and presenter; freelance writer.

Awards, Honors

Notable Book selection, Children's Book Council of Australia, 2009, for *Ballroom Bonanza.*

Writings

(With Nina Rycroft) *Ballroom Bonanza: A Hidden Pictures ABC Book,* illustrated by Rycroft, Working Title Press (Kingswood, South Australia, Australia), 2009, Abrams Books for Young Readers (New York, NY), 2010.

Biographical and Critical Sources

PERIODICALS

School Library Journal, June, 2010, Stacy Dillon, review of *Ballroom Bonanza: A Hidden Pictures ABC Book,* p. 83.*

*   *   *

HEALEY, Karen 1981-

Personal

Born, 1981, in Whangarei, New Zealand; daughter of teachers. *Education:* University of Canterbury (Christchurch, New Zealand), B.A. (English and classics), M.A.; University of Melbourne, pursuing Ph.D. *Hobbies and other interests:* Baking, reading.

Addresses

Home—Melbourne, Victoria, Australia. *Agent*—Barry Goldblat Agency, 320 7th Ave., No. 266, Brooklyn, NY 11215. *E-mail*—karen@karenhealey.com.

Career

Author. Formerly worked in a book store; taught English in Japan for two years.

Member

Science Fiction and Fantasy Association of New Zealand.

Awards, Honors

Aurealis Award for Best Young-Adult Novel, 2010, and *New Zealand Post* Children's Book Awards finalist, William C. Morris Award finalist, American Library Association (ALA), ALA Best Books for Young Adults selection, and Sir Julius Vogel Award for Best New Talent, Science Fiction and Fantasy Association of New Zealand, all 2011, all for *Guardian of the Dead.*

Writings

Guardian of the Dead, Little, Brown (New York, NY), 2010.
The Shattering, Little, Brown (New York, NY), 2011.

Author of column "Girls Read Comics (and They're Pissed)" for Girl-Wonder.org.

Adaptations

Guardian of the Dead was adapted for audiobook, Recorded Books, 2010.

Sidelights

Setting her first novel in her native New Zealand, Karen Healey won the attention of local reviewers who commended her use of well-researched mythology from the country's indigenous Maori, as well as other immigrant groups, in a story geared for teen readers. That novel, *Guardian of the Dead,* mixes ancient myths with a present-day romance, resulting in a book that *Booklist* critic Daniel Kraus recommended as "a breath of fresh air after all the vampires, demons, and fairies" appearing in current young-adult fiction.

In *Guardian of the Dead* Ellie Spencer is seventeen years old and spending a year at a boarding school while her parents take a long vacation. Although she finds a best friend in classmate Kevin, Ellie wants to make the most of her relative independence, and when a college theatrical group needs to choreograph a fight scene for an upcoming performance of Shakespeare's *Midsummer Night's Dream* she has the Tae kwon do training to take on the task. As Ellie becomes more involved with the college play, she recognizes that there is something intense going on between the two leading actors: the beautiful but aloof Reka and the totally handsome Mark, the latter whom she quickly falls for. Soon the pressures of schoolwork are replaced by Ellie's worry that something looms on the horizon: something dark and sinister that has lain in wait for a long time.

Describing Healey's story as a "surprising blend of magical realism and ancient Maori mythology," a *Publishers Weekly* critic added in a review of *Guardian of the Dead* that the author's "prose is skilled and her characters well formed." In *School Library Journal* Eric Norton commended the author for weaving Greek myths into her plot, noting that *Guardian of the Dead* "starts off fast and strong and just builds from there," while Deirdre F. Haker observed in her *Horn Book* review that the "permutations and surprises of plot" in Healey's fiction debut "make it a quick, sometimes fascinating read."

Healey spent several years living in Japan as an English teacher, and she credits this experience as valuable to her work as a writer. "If you're a member of the dominant culture where you live, see if you can spend some time in a place where you are not, ideally where the main language is not one you grew up speaking," she noted on her home page. "Your horizons will expand immeasurably, as will the attention you pay to communication and nuance."

Biographical and Critical Sources

PERIODICALS

Booklist, March 15, 2010, Daniel Kraus, review of *Guardian of the Dead,* p. 38.

Horn Book, July-August, 2010, Deirdre F. Baker, review of *Guardian of the Dead,* p. 110.

Publishers Weekly, March 29, 2010, review of *Guardian of the Dead,* p. 60.

School Library Journal, May, 2010, Eric Norton, review of *Guardian of the Dead,* p. 116.

Voice of Youth Advocates, June, 2010, Nancy K. Wallace and Hannah Forrester, review of *Guardian of the Dead,* p. 155.

ONLINE

Karen Healey Home Page, http://www.karenhealey.com (May 15, 2011).

Karen Healey Web log, http://karenhealey.livejournal.com (May 15, 2011).*

Cover of Karen Healey's young-adult novel Guardian of the Dead, *in which a New Zealand teen confronts an ancient evil.* (Little, Brown & Company, 2010. Cover photographs by Shutterstock. Reproduced by permission of Hachette Book Group USA.)

*　　*　　*

HORNUNG, Phyllis
See PEACOCK, Phyllis Hornung

HOROWITZ, Eli

Personal

Born in VA. *Education:* Yale University, earned degree (philosophy).

Addresses

Home—San Francisco, CA. *Office*—McSweeney's Publishing, 849 Valencia St., San Francisco, CA 94111.

Career

Publishing executive, editor, book designer, and author. McSweeney's (publisher), San Francisco, CA, managing editor, beginning c. 2002. Formerly worked as a carpenter. Guest at festivals and conferences.

Writings

(Editor with Ted Thompson) *Noisy Outlaws, Unfriendly Blobs, and Some Other Things That Aren't as Scary, Maybe, Depending on How You Feel about Lost Lands, Stray Cellphones, Creatures from the Sky, Parents Who Disappear in Peru, a Man Named Lars Farf, and One Other Story We Couldn't Quite Finish, So Maybe You Could Help Us Out,* introduction by Lemony Snicket, McSweeney's Books (San Francisco, CA), 2005.

(Editor with Nick Hornby) *The United States of McSweeney's,* McSweeney's Books (San Francisco, CA), 2009.

(With Roger Bennett) *Everything You Know Is Pong: How Mighty Table Tennis Shapes Our World,* HarperCollins (New York, NY), 2010.

(With Mac Barnett) *The Clock without a Face,* illustrated by Scott Teplin and Adam Rex, McSweeney's Books (San Francisco, CA), 2010.

Biographical and Critical Sources

PERIODICALS

Financial Times, June 21, 2008, Mary Cregan, "How to Judge a Book by Its Cover," p. 20.

Guardian, (London, England) November 21, 2009, review of *The United States of McSweeney's,* p. 10.

Kirkus Reviews, April 15, 2010, review of *The Clock without a Face.*

Los Angeles Times, April 27, 2008, interview with Horowitz.

Publishers Weekly, April 26, 2010, review of *The Clock without a Face,* p. 108.*

J

JAVAHERBIN, Mina

Personal
Born in Iran; married; children: two. *Education:* Degree (architecture).

Addresses
Home—San Clemente, CA.

Career
Architect and author. Presenter at schools.

Member
Society of Children's Book Writers and Illustrators.

Awards, Honors
One Hundred Children's Books to Read and Share inclusion, New York Public Library, and *Smithsonian* magazine Notable Book selection, both 2010, and Notable Book for a Global Society selection, International Reading Association, 2011, all for *Goal!*

Writings

Goal!, illustrated by A.G. Ford, Candlewick Press (Somerville, MA), 2010.
The Secret Message, illustrated by Bruce Whatley, Disney/Hyperion Books (New York, NY), 2010.

Sidelights
As an immigrant and world traveler who has followed soccer's growing popularity around the world, Mina Javaherbin quickly recognized the way that the shared excitement for the sport unites people from different countries, cultures, and faiths. Javaherbin captures this power in her first book for children, *Goal!,* which features art-work by A.J. Ford and was described by *Booklist* critic Gillian Engberg as a "heart-tugging picture book" in which her "poetic text" shares a "lyrical story."

Goal! is set in a shantytown in South Africa, where Ajani works hard at his reading. When his teacher announces that he is the best reader in his class, Ajani earns a brand-new soccer ball for his success. There are no playing fields, so he and his friends take to the streets, positioning the buckets that they use as goals and enjoying their game while one of their numbers keeps watch for local bullies. Ultimately, the bullies do come, but the quick-thinking Ajani show that spelling is

Mina Javaherbin's story **Goal!** *comes to life in high-energy artwork by* ***A.G. Ford.*** (Illustration copyright © 2010 by A.G. Ford. Reproduced by permission of Candlewick Press, Somerville, MA.)

not his only talent when he finds a way to keep the came going. Together with Ford's "dramatically lit" paintings, Javaherbin "crisply relays a simple story that should strike a chord with a wide range of readers," predicted a *Publishers Weekly* critic, and Blair Christolon wrote in *School Library Journal* that "the camaraderie" of the story's young characters "is evident."

Featuring colorful artwork by Bruce Whatley, *The Secret Message* also has roots in its author's life experience. In this case, Javaherbin's story is based on "The Parrot and the Merchant," a traditional story by thirteenth-century Persian poet Jalaledin Rumi that her father would sometimes retell at bed-time. In the story, a successful merchant promise to bring presents back to his family when he returns from a trip to India. He promises to do the same for his caged parrot, whose song and beauty have attracted several customers. When the parrot requests a special gift, the merchant complies, not knowing where his generosity will lead. Citing Whatley's humorous artwork for *The Secret Message*, Susan Scheps added in her *School Library Journal* review that Javaherbin's tale "offers an interesting twist" that will likely inspire story-hour discussions "on the meaning of freedom."

Biographical and Critical Sources

PERIODICALS

Booklist, March 1, 2010, Gillian Engberg, review of *Goal!,* p. 77.
New York Times Book Review, June 20, 2010, Julie Just, review of *Goal!,* p. 13.
Publishers Weekly, March 15, 2010, review of *Goal!,* p. 52; September 13, 2010, review of *The Secret Message,* p. 43.
School Library Journal, February, 2010, Blair Christolon, review of *Goal!,* p. 88; December, 2010, Susan Scheps, review of *The Secret Message,* p. 94.

ONLINE

Mina Javaherbin Home Page, http://minajavaherbin.com (May 27, 2011).
Mina Javaherbin Web log, http://minajavaherbin.tumblr.com (May 27, 2011).
Seven Impossible Things before Breakfast Web log (May 4, 2010), interview with Javaherbin.

*   *   *

JOHNSON, Jen Cullerton 1972-

Personal

Born 1972, in Chicago, IL; married; has children. *Education:* Attended Indiana University Bloomington, Dominican University, and University of Chicago; University of New Orleans, MFA (nonfiction writing); Loyola University of Chicago, M.Ed. (curriculum development).

Addresses

Home—Chicago, IL. *E-mail*—jencullertonjohnson@gmail.com.

Career

Educator, author, and urban environmentalist. Teacher in Chicago, IL, public and charter schools, including Simpson Academy; St. Augustine College, Chicago, instructor in writing composition. Switchback Books, member of board. Presenter at schools and workshops.

Member

Society of Children's Book Writers and Illustrators (Illinois chapter), Illinois Reading Council.

Awards, Honors

B. Brooks State of Illinois Poetry Award; Illinois Arts Council fellowship award, 2005; Notable Children's Books designation, *Smithsonian* magazine, Amelia Bloomer Project selection, American Library Association Feminist Task Force, both 2010, and Green Earth Honor Book designation, Newton Marasco Foundation, and Notable Books for a Global Society listee, International Reading Association, both 2011, and Access Africa Children's Book Award, all for *Seeds of Change.*

Writings

Seeds of Change: Planting a Path to Peace, illustrated by Sonia Lynn Sadler, Lee & Low Books (New York, NY), 2010.

Contributor of poetry and short fiction to periodicals, including *Pedestal Magazine,* and to anthology *Kiss Me Goodnight: Stories and Poems by Women Who Were Girls When Their Mothers Died,* edited by Ann Murphy O'Fallon and Margaret Noonan Vaillancourt, Syren Books (Minneapolis, MN), 2005. Translator of Latin-American poetry.

Sidelights

A teacher and workshop leaders as well as a self-styled urban environmentalist, Chicago native Jen Cullerton Johnson has worked with young people in many parts of the world, from cities such as Los Angeles, California, and Buenos Aires, Argentina, to rural areas of Japan and South America. In addition to teaching, Johnson has also developed her skill as a writer, publishing poems and short fiction and also writing grants for educational institutions. Winner of several awards—including the Coretta Scott King/John Steptoe Award for New Talent for its illustrator, Sonia Lynn Sadler—the picture book *Seeds of Change: Planting a Path to Peace,* marked Johnson's debut as a children's author.

In *Seeds of Change* Johnson introduces young children to the work of Wangari Maathai, a Kenyan environmentalist and activist on behalf of African women. Edu-

Seeds of Change, *Jen Cullerton Johnson's story about a Nobel-prize winning environmentalist, comes to life in Sonia Lynn Saddler's colorful art.* (Illustration copyright © 2010 by Sonia Lynn Sadler. Reproduced by permission of Lee & Low Books, Inc.)

cated in the United States, where she studied biology, Maathai eventually returned to Africa, and her work establishing the Green Belt Movement there earned her a Nobel Peace Prize in 2004. In addition to inspiring the people of Kenya to replant thousands of tree seedings to rebuild a landscape lost to development and coffee plantations, she also advocated for women's rights and was even jailed for her efforts.

"What drew me to Wangari was how she spoke to so many different kinds of people from poor women to presidents," Johnson told *Cynsations* online interviewer Cynthia Leitich Smith. In writing *Seeds of Change* "I wanted readers to 'hear Wangari,'" Johnson added. "I decided I would take every opportunity to use Wangari's own words, so when the book is read, it feels as if Wangari Maathai is the room since the words came from her." According to the author, "One of our jobs as writers is to inspire readers with our words, but sometimes inspiration fades or is forgotten, therefore, our words must also move readers to action, be it to plant seed or be nicer to their neighbor."

Enriched by Sadler's "batik-style illustrations, which feature what Carol S. Surges described in *School Library Journal* as "vivid colors [that] sparkle from within the thick white outlines," *Seeds of Change* presents Maathai's story from her early childhood through her receipt of the Nobel prize. According to a *Kirkus Reviews* writer, "Johnson sows her narrative with botanical metaphors" as well as including many quotes from her subject's own autobiographical writings, capturing

the woman's setbacks and accomplishments in a story that is both "idealized and inspiring." While noting the many books for children that have been based on the Green Belt Movement and its founder, a *Publishers Weekly* contributor wrote that *Seeds of Change* "provides older children with a more thorough investigation of Maathai's life." In *Booklist* Gillian Engberg suggested that Johnson's book "complements, rather than duplicates," the books that have been written about this "inspiring activist and her powerful message."

"I live in an urban environment where skyscrapers hem in nature," Johnson commented to *SATA*. "Animals dwell in cages at the zoos. Gardens and greenery thrive in manicured parks. Buoys block off Lake Michigan. Even the stars disappear under the brightness of streetlights. The hours I spend inside my house on the computer surpass the time I spend outside.

"When I began researching and writing *Seeds of Change* . . . I wasn't a Greenie. In fact, my contributions to saving the planet rested on turning off lights, recycling, and an occasional bike-to-work day. Nature, I felt belonged to another world, a world separated from mine.

"At first, what drew me to writing about Maathai's life for children was not the fact that she planted thirty million trees in Kenya but her persistence to find solutions for difficult problems. How do you conquer poverty without destroying the land? How do you preserve the land without disempowering the poor? Wangari took these two complicated issues, poverty and the environment, and found her own answer. She taught poor women a very specific skill; how to plant a tree. By doing so the women planted trees all over Kenya, creating what looked like green belts across the land. The powerful image of green growing again in Kenya gave birth to the name Greenbelt Movement. A movement, I might add, that thrives today as an international organization for the environment and the rights of the disempowered.

"When I stared the research for *Seeds of Change* there were only a few academic journals about Maathai and the Greenbelt Movement. I drew heavily on her biography, *Unbowed*. Wangari spoke to many different kinds of people, from poor women to presidents and from school children to ambassadors. Her words inspired all around her to action. You can feel her persistence and commitment in her speeches. Her words moved me from a passive watcher to an active doer. When she said 'Hajabee, Let's work together,' I understood it didn't just mean turning off a light or recycling a water bottle but being aware of my actions and how my actions impact the world around me.

"Whenever I go on a school visit or do a reading or presentation I make sure that after *Seeds of Change* is read, the students or the audience has a chance to make a connection between themselves and nature. Sometimes we plants trees, other times seeds, but each time there is a connection to reading and doing. People need to dig in the dirt, roll a seed between their fingers, touch the leaves of different plants so that they know that Wangari's experience of embracing nature and caring for the environment can also be part of their own experience.

"The urgency, the nowness of environment issues is upon us. There is no escape, either we find solutions like Wangari did with the Greenbelt Movement or cease to exist. One of our jobs as writers is to inspire reader with our words, but sometimes inspiration fades or is forgotten, therefore, our words must also move readers to action, be it to plant seed or be nicer to their neighbor. I think environmental books for children are doing just that: inspiring and moving readers to action. I am very grateful *Seeds of Change* is part of the genre. I hope new writers push ahead and continue to explore how our nature world and our human place in it is both one of many, and many for the good of all."

Biographical and Critical Sources

PERIODICALS

Booklist, June 1, 2010, Gillian Engberg, review of *Seeds of Change: Planting a Path to Peace,* p. 98.
Children's Bookwatch, July, 2010, review of *Seeds of Change.*
Kirkus Reviews, April 15, 2010, review of *Seeds of Change.*
Publishers Weekly, April 12, 2010, review of *Seeds of Change,* p. 49.
School Library Journal, April, 2010, Carol S. Surges, review of *Seeds of Change,* p. 146.

ONLINE

Cynsations Web log, http://cynthialeitichsmith.blogspot. com/ (November 23, 2010), Cynthia Leitich Smith, interview with Johnson.
Jen Cullerton Johnson Home Page, http://www.jencul lertonjohnson.com (February 27, 2011).
Jen Cullerton Johnson Web log, http://seedsofchange. tumblr.com (May 15, 2011).

* * *

JOHNSON, Steve 1960-

Personal

Born 1960, in MN; married Lou Fancher (a writer and illustrator); children: Nicholas. *Education:* School of Associated Arts (St. Paul, MN), B.F.A.

Addresses

Home—Moraga, CA. *E-mail*—steve@johnsonandfan cher.com.

Career

Commercial artist and illustrator. Freelance illustrator, with wife, Lou Fancher, beginning 1986; pre-production set and character designer for animated films, including *Toy Story,* 1995, and *A Bug's Life,* 1998.

Awards, Honors

(All with Lou Fancher) International Reading Association Children's Book Award, 1989, for *No Star Nights* by Anna Smucker; Minnesota Book Award for Children's Books, 1992, for *The Salamander Room,* by Anne Mazer; gold medal, Society of Illustrators, 1993, for *Up North at the Cabin* by Marsha Wilson Chall; Minnesota Book Award for Children's Books finalist, 1993, for *Up North at the Cabin,* 1996, for *Cat You'd Better Come Home* by Garrison Keillor, 1997, for *My Many Colored Days* by Dr. Seuss, 1998, for *The Lost and Found House* by Michael Cadnum, 1999, for *Coppelia* by Margot Fonteyn, 2002, for both *The Day Ocean Came to Visit* by Diane Wolkstein and *Silver Seeds* by Paul Paolilli and Dan Brewer; Nestlé Children's Book Prize shortlist, 2005, for *The Dancing Tiger* by Malachy Doyle; Image Award nomination, National Association for the Advancement of Colored People, 2009, for *Amazing Peace* by Maya Angelou.

Illustrator

WITH WIFE, LOU FANCHER

Anna Smucker, *No Star Nights,* Knopf (New York, NY), 1989.
Douglas Hill, *Penelope's Pendant,* Doubleday (New York, NY), 1990.
Anne Mazer, *The Salamander Room,* Knopf (New York, NY), 1991.
Jon Scieszka, *The Frog Prince Continued,* Viking (New York, NY), 1991.
Marsha Wilson Chall, *Up North at the Cabin,* Lothrop, Lee & Shephard (New York, NY), 1992.
B.G. Hennessy, *The First Night,* Viking (New York, NY), 1993.
Sarah S. Kilborne, *Peach and Blue,* Knopf (New York, NY), 1994.
Garrison Keillor, *Cat, You Better Come Home,* Viking (New York, NY), 1995.
Dr. Seuss (pseudonym of Theodore Geisel), *My Many Colored Days,* Knopf (New York, NY), 1996.
Michael Cadnum, *The Lost and Found House,* Viking (New York, NY), 1997.
Margot Fonteyn, *Coppélia,* Harcourt Brace (San Francisco, CA), 1998.
Lou Fancher, *The Quest for the One Big Thing,* Disney Press (New York, NY), 1998.
Craig Kee Strete, *The Lost Boy and the Monster,* Putnam's (New York, NY), 1999.
Janet Schulman, adaptor, *Felix Salten's Bambi,* Atheneum (New York, NY), 1999.

Lois Duncan, *I Walk at Night,* Viking (New York, NY), 2000.

Alice Hoffman, *Horsefly,* Hyperion (New York, NY), 2000.

Paul Paolilli and Dan Brewer, *Silver Seeds: A Book of Nature Poems,* Viking (New York, NY), 2001.

Diane Wolkstein, *The Day Ocean Came to Visit,* Harcourt (San Diego, CA), 2001.

Margaret Wise Brown, *Robin's Room,* Hyperion (New York, NY), 2002.

Louise Erdrich, *The Range Eternal,* Hyperion (New York, NY), 2002.

Mary Pope Osborne, *New York's Bravest,* Knopf (New York, NY), 2002.

Lou Fancher, adapter, *The Velveteen Rabbit; or, How Toys Become Real* (based on the story by Margery Williams), Atheneum (New York, NY), 2002.

Mavis Jukes, *You're a Bear,* Knopf (New York, NY), 2003.

Kathleen Krull, *The Boy on Fairfield Street: How Ted Geisel Grew up to Become Dr. Seuss,* Random House (New York, NY), 2004.

Dori Chaconas, *Momma, Will You?,* Penguin (New York, NY), 2004.

H.L. Panahi, *Bebop Express,* Laura Geringer Books (New York, NY), 2005.

Malachy Doyle, *The Dancing Tiger,* Simon & Schuster (New York, NY), 2005.

Karen Hill, *All God's Creatures,* Little Simon (New York, NY), 2005.

Lou Fancher, *Star Climbing,* Laura Geringer Books (New York, NY), 2006.

Dan Gutman, *Casey Back at Bat,* HarperCollins (New York, NY), 2007.

Margie Palatini, *The Cheese,* Katherine Tegen Books (New York, NY), 2007.

Diane Wright Landolf, *What a Good Big Brother!,* Random House (New York, NY), 2008.

Warren Hanson, *Bugtown Boogie,* Laura Geringer Books (New York, NY), 2008.

Stephen Mitchell, reteller, *The Ugly Duckling,* Candlewick Press (New York, NY), 2008.

Maya Angelou, *Amazing Peace: A Christmas Poem,* Random House (New York, NY), 2008.

Marcus Hummon, *Anytime, Anywhere: A Little Boy's Prayer,* Atheneum Books for Young Readers (New York, NY), 2009.

Kenneth Oppel, *The King's Taster,* HarperCollins (New York, NY), 2009.

Kathleen Krull, *A Boy Named FDR: How Franklin D. Roosevelt Grew up to Change America,* Knopf (New York, NY), 2010.

Michael McGowan, *Sunday Is for God,* Schwartz & Wade Books (New York, NY), 2010.

Kathleen Krull, *Jim Henson: The Guy Who Played with Puppets,* Random House Children's Books (New York, NY), 2011.

Sidelights

Together with his wife, Lou Fancher, Steve Johnson is a noted illustrator whose work has been paired with picture-book text by authors ranging from Kathleen Krull, Maya Angelou, and Malachy Doyle to Jon Scieszka and the pseudonymous Dr. Seuss. Husband and wife collaborate at all stages of their creative endeavor, from the initial conception and sketching through finished drawings and design and finally painting. Selected to illustrate Theodore Geisel's *My Many Colored Days,* a manuscript that remained unillustrated and unpublished at the death of one of the most beloved of all writers for children, Johnson and Fancher have also illustrated Krull's picture-book biography *The Boy on Fairfield Street: How Ted Geisel Grew up to Become Dr. Seuss.* In addition to their work in book illustration, the couple has also created art for posters, business publications, commercial advertising, and periodicals and have worked on the creative team that produced the animated films *Toy Story* and *A Bug's Life.*

Johnson and Fancher are noted for their versatility. In *I Walk at Night* by Lois Duncan, for example their use of unusual media—string and oil paints—prompted a *Publishers Weekly* critic to write that the "twilight tones" and textured surface in their images creates an "overall effect [that] is dreamy and atmospheric, and makes for grand bedtime fare." In their illustrations for Alice Hoffman's *Horsefly* they use color to "chart the emotional movement" of Hoffman's story about a girl who loses her fear of horses during a magical flight, creating what *Booklist* reviewer Connie Fletcher described as "rich artwork" that ranges from "dark and angular . . . to brightly glowing."

Brought to life in colorful cartoon art, Margie Palatini's *The Cheese* sways to the melody of "The Farmer in the

New York's Bravest, *a story by Mary Pope Osborne, comes to life in* **Steve Johnson and Lou Fancher's dramatic paintings.** (Illustration © 2002 by Steve Johnson and Lou Fancher. Used by permission of Alfred A. Knopf, an imprint of Random House Children's Books, a division of Random House, Inc.)

Dell" while Fancher and Johnson "pump up the humor" in their art, according to a *Publishers Weekly* contributor. In *School Library Journal,* Susan Moorhead praised the "funny and expressive" animal cast of *The Cheese,* while a perusal of Warren Hanson's *Bugtown Boogie* prompted Kirsten Cutler to remark in the same periodical that "vibrant hues and frenetic energy suffuse the artwork" of Johnson and Fancher. A more traditional approach is in order when dealing with literary classics, and in a review of Stephen Mitchell's retelling of Hans Christian Andersen's *The Ugly Duckling,* a *Kirkus Reviews* writer asserted that the couple's textured images are "spectacular."

A tale of sibling bonding, Diane Wright Landolf's *What a Good Big Brother!* concerns a boy's imaginative efforts to soothe his troubled infant sister. "Johnson and Fancher's mixed-media collages shimmer with vivid colors and warm emotions," Martha Simpson wrote in her *School Library Journal* appraisal of Landolf's story, and a *Publishers Weekly* critic deemed the "use of life-size-and-larger scale" by the husband-and-wife team "riveting." In Canadian author Kenneth Oppel's *The King's Taster,* Max the dog joins forces with the royal cook to concoct a new menu for a finicky monarch. Fancher and Johnson's pictures for Oppel's story "are deliciously capricious with clever collage details," Julie Cummins stated in her *Booklist* review, while in *School Library Journal* Laura Lutz praised the couple's "rich and textured art."

Several of the books featuring Johnson and Fancher's art are grounded in history. Framed as the story of volunteer firefighter Moses Humphreys, who worked in nineteenth-century New York City and saved countless lives before losing his own, Mary Pope Osborne's *New York's Bravest* is also a timely tribute to the firefighters who lost their lives at "Ground Zero" on September 11, 2001. As a *Publishers Weekly* contributor noted, the couple's oil paintings here combine with Osborne's text to "carefully and respectfully balance" the historic and mythic elements of Humphreys' life and produce "a loving tribute" to heroic firefighters everywhere.

Working with author Dan Gutman on *Casey Back at Bat,* a new version of the American saga immortalized in Ernest Thayer's 1888 poem "Casey at the Bat," the couple created a mix of past and present that continues to draw young readers while honoring the era in which the poem was written. In *Booklist,* GraceAnne A. DeCandido wrote of Johnson and Fancher that "the fab team . . . makes wonderful, nineteenth-century-inspired paintings" that reflect the mood of Gutman's nostalgic tale through "their amber glow, Victorian colors, and newsprint shadows."

Angelou's *Amazing Peace: A Christmas Poem* presents a picture-book version of the anti-war poem she composed for the 2005 White House Christmas tree-lighting ceremony. In sharing Angelou's verses with the picture-book set, Johnson and Fancher's mixed-media illustra-

Kenneth Oppel's story in **The King's Taster** *gets an added dose of whimsy from Fancher and Johnson's art.* (Illustration copyright © 2009 by Steve Johnson and Lou Fancher. Reproduced with permission of HarperCollins Children's Books, a division of HarperCollins Publishers.)

tions "reflect the sentiments of the poem while also telling their own story," as Kristen McKulski asserted in her *Booklist* review of *Amazing Peace.*

Biographical and Critical Sources

PERIODICALS

Booklist, November 1, 1996, Hazel Rochman, review of *My Many Colored Days,* p. 510; October 15, 1998, Carolyn Phelan, review of *Copélia,* p. 416; December 1, 2000, Connie Fletcher, review of *Horsefly,* p. 721; April 15, 2002, Kay Weisman, review of *Robin's Room,* p. 1406; July, 2002, Ilene Cooper, review of *New York's Finest,* p. 1847; December 1, 2003, Louise Brueggemann, review of *You're a Bear,* p. 684; February 15, 2006, Carolyn Phelan, review of *Star Climbing,* p. 101; January 1, 2007, GraceAnne A. DeCandido, review of *Casey Back at Bat,* p. 114; November 15, 2008, Kristen McKulski, review of *Amazing Peace: A Christmas Poem,* p. 41; February 1, 2009, Hazel Rochman, review of *What a Good Big Brother!,* p. 47; March 15, 2009, Julie Cummins, review of *The King's Taster,* p. 61; April 15, 2009, Ilene Cooper, review of *Anytime, Anywhere: A Little Boy's Prayer,* p. 45.

Bulletin of the Center for Children's Books, March, 2004, Krista Hutley, review of *The Boy on Fairfield Street: How Ted Geisel Grew up to Become Dr. Seuss,* p. 284.

Horn Book, November-December, 1993, Mary M. Burns, review of *The First Night,* p. 724; November-December, 2002, Roger Sutton, review of *New York's Bravest,* p. 737; May-June, 2007, Miriam Lang Budin, review of *Casey Back at Bat,* p. 265; January-February, 2008, Deirdre F. Baker, review of *The Ugly Duckling,* p. 67; July-August, 2009, Joanna Rudge Long, review of *The King's Taster,* p. 413.

Kirkus Reviews, July 1, 2002, review of *New York's Bravest,* p. 951; August 15, 2002, review of *The Range Eternal,* p. 1222; September 15, 2002, review of *The Velveteen Rabbit,* p. 1389; December 15, 2003, review of *The Boy on Fairfield Street,* p. 1451; April 15, 2005, review of *The Dancing Tiger,* p. 472; June 1, 2005, review of *Bebop Express,* p. 642; February 15, 2006, review of *Star Climbing,* p. 182; November 15, 2007, review of *The Ugly Duckling;* November 1, 2008, review of *Amazing Peace.*

New York Times Book Review, November 21, 1999, Elizabeth Spires, review of *Bambi.*

Publishers Weekly, September 20, 1993, review of *The First Night,* p. 37; November 7, 1994, review of *Peach and Blue,* p. 77; May 8, 1995, review of *Cat, You Better Come Home,* p. 294; October 13, 1997, review of *The Lost and Found House,* p. 74; November 16, 1998, review of *The Quest for the One Big Thing,* p. 77; January 10, 2000, review of *I Walk at Night,* p. 67; August 13, 2001, review of *The Day Ocean Came to Visit,* p. 311; May 20, 2002, review of *Robin's Room,* p. 65; June 24, 2002, review of *New York's*

Johnson's many collaborations with his wife include creating art for Stephen Mitchell's retelling of **The Ugly Duckling.** (Illustration copyright © 2008 by Steve Johnson and Lou Fancher. Reproduced by permission of Candlewick Press, Somerville, MA.)

Bravest, p. 56; September 9, 2002, review of *The Range Eternal,* p. 67; January 23, 2006, review of *Star Climbing,* p. 206; April 2, 2007, review of *The Cheese,* p. 55; January 21, 2008, review of *The Ugly Duckling,* p. 170; November 24, 2008, review of *What a Good Big Brother!,* p. 57; December 8, 2008, review of *Anytime, Anywhere,* p. 57.

School Library Journal, April, 1999, review of *The Quest for the One Big Thing,* p. 94; August, 2001, Margaret A. Chang, review of *The Day Ocean Came to Visit,* p. 174; October, 2002, Susan Oliver, review of *The Range Eternal,* p. 104; December, 2003, Laura Scott, review of *You're a Bear,* p. 118; January, 2004, Anne Chapman Callaghan, review of *The Boy on Fairfield Street,* p. 119; November, 2004, Rebecca Sheridan, review of *Momma, Will You?,* p. 94; July, 2005, Grace Oliff, review of *The Dancing Tiger,* p. 88; April, 2006, Susan Weitz, review of *Star Climbing,* p. 105; January, 2007, Marilyn Taniguchi, review of *Casey Back at Bat,* p. 94; June, 2007, Susan Moorhead, review of *The Cheese,* p. 119; January, 2008, Kirsten Cutler, review of *The Ugly Duckling,* p. 80; July, 2008, Kirsten Cutler, review of *Bugtown Boogie,* p. 74; February, 2009, Martha Simpson, review of *What a Good Big Brother!,* p. 76; June, 2009, Laura Lutz, review of *The King's Taster,* p. 97; January, 2010, Lisa Egly Lehmuller, review of *Sunday Is for God,* p. 77.

ONLINE

BWI Titletales Web site, http://bwibooks.com/ (April 1, 2011), interview with Lou Fancher and Johnson.

Lou Fancher and Steve Johnson Home Page, http://www.johnsonandfancher.com (April 1, 2011).*

* * *

JOSEPH, Patrick
See O'MALLEY, Kevin

* * *

JUÁREZ, Fernando
(Fernando López Juárez)

Personal

Born in Spain; married; children: one daughter. *Education:* Ramón Falcón art school (Lugo, Spain), degree, c. 1995.

Addresses

Home—Madrid, Spain. *E-mail*—fernandolopezjuarez@gmail.com.

Career

Illustrator and visual development artist. Bren Entertainment, junior artist, 2000-04; Ilion (animation studio), Madrid, Spain, currently art director. Freelance illustrator, beginning 2003. Illustrator for animated films, including *Planet 51.*

Illustrator

Kitty Richards, *Twisted Tales* ("Phonics Comics" series; graphic-novel reader), Volume 7, Innovative Kids (Norwalk, CT), 2006.

Walter Staib and Jennifer Fox, *A Feast of Freedom: Tasty Tidbits from the City Tavern,* Running Press Kids (Philadelphia, PA), 2010.

Biographical and Critical Sources

PERIODICALS

Kirkus Reviews, April 15, 2010, review of *A Feast of Freedom: Tasty Tidbits from the City Tavern.*

Publishers Weekly, April 26, 2010, review of *A Feast of Freedom,* p. 107.

School Library Journal, September, 2006, Sadie Mattox, review of *Twisted Tales,* p. 238; August, 2010, Carol S. Surges, review of *A Feast of Freedom,* p. 122.

ONLINE

Fernando Juárez Home Page, http://www.fernandojuarez illustrator.blogspot.com (May 15, 2011).

Illustrationweb Web site, http://illustrationweb.blogspot. com/ (May 15, 2011), "Fernando Juárez."*

*   *   *

JUÁREZ, Fernando López
    See JUÁREZ, Fernando

K

KAYE, Marilyn 1949-
(Shannon Blair)

Personal

Born July 19, 1949, in New Britain, CT; daughter of Harold Stanley (a microbiologist) and Annette Kaye. *Education:* Emory University, B.A., 1967, M.L.S., 1974; University of Chicago, Ph.D., 1983. *Politics:* "Liberal Democrat." *Religion:* Jewish. *Hobbies and other interests:* Learning French, travel.

Addresses

Home—Paris, France. *Agent*—Penny Holroyde, Caroline Sheldon Literary Agency, 71 Hillgate Place, London W8 7SS, England. *E-mail*—mjk719@gmail.com.

Career

Author and educator. Library Quarterly, Chicago, IL, editorial assistant, 1977-79; University of South Carolina, Columbia, instructor in library science, 1980-82; St. John's University, Jamaica, NY, instructor, 1982-86, associate professor of library and information science, 1986-2005.

Awards, Honors

Children's Books of the Year designation, Child Study Association of America, 1985, for *Will You Cross Me?;* Children's Choice designation, International Reading Association/Children's Book Council, 1986, for *Wrong Kind of Boy;* Quick Picks for Reluctant Young-Adult Readers, Young Adult Library Services Association (YALSA)/ American Library Association, 1999, for both *The Vanishing* and *Amy, Number Seven.*

Writings

JUVENILE FICTION

Will You Cross Me?, illustrated by Ned Delaney, Harper (New York, NY), 1985.

Marilyn Kaye (Photograph by Muriel Berthelot. Reproduced by permission.)

Baby Fozzie Is Afraid of the Dark, Weekly Reader (Columbus, OH), 1986.
The Best Baby-Sitter in the World, Scholastic (New York, NY), 1987.
Zoobille Zoo: Big Mess, illustrated by Carol Hudson, Scholastic (New York, NY), 1987.

Miss Piggy and the Big Gorilla, Scholastic (New York, NY), 1988.

What a Teddy Bear Needs, Ladybird (London, England), 1989.

Gonzo the Great, Scholastic (New York, NY), 1989.

The Real Tooth Fairy, illustrated by Helen Cogancherry, Harcourt (New York, NY), 1990.

Attitude, Fawcett (New York, NY), 1990.

The Atonement of Mindy Wise, Harcourt (New York, NY), 1991, published as *Mindy Wise,* Avon (New York, NY), 1993.

A Day with No Math, illustrated by Tim Bowers, Harcourt (New York, NY), 1992.

Disney's The Little Mermaid: The Same Old Song, illustrated by Fred Marvin, Disney Press (New York, NY), 1992.

Disney's The Little Mermaid: Reflections of Arsulu, illustrated by Marvin, Disney Press (New York, NY), 1992.

Runaway, Harper (New York, NY), 1992.

Choose Me, Harper (New York, NY), 1992.

Real Heroes, Harcourt (New York, NY), 1993.

Dream Lover, Troll (Metuchen, NJ), 1995.

Scandal in Paradise, Troll (Metuchen, NJ), 1996.

Trouble in Paradise, Troll (Metuchen, NJ), 1996.

Stranger in Paradise, Troll (Metuchen, NJ), 1997.

The Case of the Haunted Maze, HarperEntertainment (New York, NY), 2004.

Penelope (novelization; based on a screenplay by Leslie Caveny), St. Martin's Griffin (New York, NY), 2007.

Demon Chick, Henry Holt (New York, NY), 2009.

UNDER PSEUDONYM SHANNON BLAIR; TEEN ROMANCE NOVELS

Call Me Beautiful, Bantam (New York, NY), 1984.

Starstruck, Bantam (New York, NY), 1985.

Wrong Kind of Boy, Bantam (New York, NY), 1985.

Kiss and Tell, Bantam (New York, NY), 1985.

"OUT OF THIS WORLD" NOVEL SERIES

Max on Earth, Simon & Schuster (New York, NY), 1986.

Max in Love, Simon & Schuster (New York, NY), 1986.

Max on Fire, Simon & Schuster (New York, NY), 1986.

Max Flips Out, Simon & Schuster (New York, NY), 1986.

Max Goes Bad, Penguin (London, England), 1989.

Max All Over, Penguin (London, England), 1989.

"SISTERS" NOVEL SERIES

Phoebe, Harcourt (New York, NY), 1987

Daphne, Harcourt (New York, NY), 1987.

Cassie, Harcourt (New York, NY), 1987.

Lydia, Harcourt (New York, NY), 1987.

A Friend like Phoebe, Harcourt (New York, NY), 1989.

"CAMP SUNNYSIDE FRIENDS" NOVEL SERIES

No Boys Allowed, Avon (New York, NY), 1989.

Cabin Six Plays Cupid, Avon (New York, NY), 1989.

Color War, Avon (New York, NY), 1989.

New Girl in Cabin Six, Avon (New York, NY), 1989.

Looking for Trouble, Avon (New York, NY), 1990.

Katie Steals the Show, Avon (New York, NY), 1990.

A Witch in Cabin Six, Avon (New York, NY), 1990.

Too Many Counselors, Avon (New York, NY), 1990.

The New-and-Improved Sarah, Avon (New York, NY), 1990.

Christmas Reunion, Avon (New York, NY), 1990.

Erin and the Movie Star, Avon (New York, NY), 1991.

The Problem with Parents, Avon (New York, NY), 1991.

The Tennis Trap, Avon (New York, NY), 1991.

Big Sister Blues, Avon (New York, NY), 1991.

Megan's Ghost, Avon (New York, NY), 1991.

Christmas Break, Avon (New York, NY), 1991.

Happily Ever After, Avon (New York, NY), 1992.

Camp Spaghetti, Avon (New York, NY), 1992.

Balancing Act, Avon (New York, NY), 1992.

School Daze, Avon (New York, NY), 1992.

The Spirit of Sunnyside, Avon (New York, NY), 1992.

"THREE OF A KIND" NOVEL SERIES

With Friends like These, Who Needs Enemies?, Harper (New York, NY), 1990.

Home's a Nice Place to Visit, but I Wouldn't Want to Live There, Harper (New York, NY), 1990.

Will the Real Becka Morgan Please Stand Up?, Harper (New York, NY), 1991.

Two's Company, Four's a Crowd, Harper (New York, NY), 1991.

Cat Morgan, Working Girl, Harper (New York, NY), 1991.

101 Ways to Win Homecoming Queen, Harper (New York, NY), 1991.

"VIDEO HIGH" NOVEL SERIES

Modern Love, Kensington (New York, NY), 1994.

The High Life, Kensington (New York, NY), 1994.

Date Is a Four-Letter Word, Kensington (New York, NY), 1994.

The Body Beautiful, Kensington (New York, NY), 1994.

The Colors of the Heart, Kensington (New York, NY), 1994.

Checking Out, Kensington (New York, NY), 1994.

Groupies, Kensington (New York, NY), 1995.

Secrets and Lies, Kensington (New York, NY), 1995.

"AFTER-SCHOOL CLUB" NOVEL SERIES

Jill's Happy Un-Birthday, Pocket Books (New York, NY), 1997.

Valentine's Day Surprise, Pocket Books (New York, NY), 1997.

Teammates, Pocket Books (New York, NY), 1997.

"LAST ON EARTH" SERIES

The Vanishing, Avon (New York, NY), 1998.

The Convergence, Avon (New York, NY), 1998.

The Return, Avon (New York, NY), 1999.

"REPLICA" NOVEL SERIES

Amy, Number Seven, Bantam (New York, NY), 1998.

Pursuing Amy: Who Can You Trust?, Bantam (New York, NY), 1998.

Another Amy, Bantam (New York, NY), 1998.

Perfect Girls, Bantam (New York, NY), 1999.

Secret Clique, Bantam (New York, NY), 1999.

And the Two Shall Meet, Bantam (New York, NY), 1999.

The Best of the Best, Bantam (New York, NY), 1999.

Mystery Mother, Bantam (New York, NY), 1999.

The Fever, Bantam (New York, NY), 1999.

Ice Cold, Bantam (New York, NY), 2000.

Lucky Thirteen, Bantam (New York, NY), 2000.

In Search of Andy, Bantam (New York, NY), 2000.

The Substitute, Bantam (New York, NY), 2000.

The Beginning, Bantam (New York, NY), 2000.

Transformation, Bantam (New York, NY), 2000.

Happy Birthday, Dear Amy, Bantam (New York, NY), 2001.

Missing Pieces, Bantam (New York, NY), 2001.

Return of the Perfect Girls, Bantam (New York, NY), 2001.

Dreamcrusher, Bantam (New York, NY), 2001.

Like Father, like Son, Bantam (New York, NY), 2001.

Virtual Amy, Bantam (New York, NY), 2001.

All about Andy, Bantam (New York, NY), 2002.

War of the Clones, Bantam (New York, NY), 2002.

Amy, on Her Own, Bantam (New York, NY), 2002.

"REPLICA: PLAGUE TRILOGY" NOVEL SERIES

Play, Bantam (New York, NY), 2002.

Rewind, Bantam (New York, NY), 2002.

Fast Forward, Bantam (New York, NY), 2002.

"GIFTED" NOVEL SERIES

Out of Sight, Out of Mind, Kingfisher (New York, NY), 2009.

Better Late than Never, Kingfisher (New York, NY), 2009.

Here Today, Gone Tomorrow, Kingfisher (New York, NY), 2009.

Finder's Keepers, Kingfisher (New York, NY), 2010.

Now You See Me, Kingfisher (New York, NY), 2010.

Speak No Evil, Kingfisher (New York, NY), 2010.

OTHER

(Co-editor, with Betsy Hearne) *Celebrating Children's Books: Essays on Children's Literature in Honor of Zena Sutherland,* Lothrop (Boston, MA), 1981.

Contributor to other teen novel series. Editor, *Top of the News* (journal of the Association of Library Service to Children and Young Adult Services), 1982-85. Contributor of articles and reviews to library journals and newspapers.

Author's work has been translated into several languages, including Danish, Finnish, French, German, Korean, Portuguese, Russian, Spanish, and Swedish.

Sidelights

In addition to teaching library science on the college level, Marilyn Kaye has established a career writing popular novels for teen and preteen readers. In series such as "Sisters," "Replica," and "Three of a Kind" Kaye places average adolescents in situations that test their characters and their ability to act independently of fads and the whims of their friends. In addition to novels for middle-grade and high-school readers, she has also authored picture books and beginning readers and has promoted quality literature for children through her work as a librarian and magazine essayist. "I suppose, in a way, there's something all my books have in common," Kaye once told *SATA,* "and that's the fact that every feeling I've written about, I've experienced. And I think that feelings—motives, reactions, responses, concerns—these are the core to any work of fiction."

Born in 1949 in central Connecticut, Kaye started writing as soon as she "could make words out of letters and sentences out of words," as she later recalled. While

Cover of Kaye's science-fiction novel Amy, Number Seven, *the first book in her "Replica" series.* (Cover art © 1998 by Craig White. Reproduced by permission of Bantam Books, a division of Random House, Inc.)

she dreamed about being a famous writer someday, she also dreamed about being a ballet dancer, a rock 'n' roll musician, and even an airline stewardess. As Kaye grew older and began comparing her work to that of the writers she was required to study in school, she began to have second thoughts about writing as a career. "I couldn't really imagine anyone other than parents, teachers, and best friends wanting to read what I wrote," she reasoned. Making a practical decision, she opted to pour her energies into other areas, and ultimately earned a master's degree in library science from Emory University.

Working for several years as a children's librarian, and eventually as a college instructor, Kay finally had reason to rethink her decision not to write for publication. "I knew I belonged in the world of children, books, and libraries, but something was missing," as she later explained. "I had been working on an article about the revival of teenage romances, and thinking about how much I'd enjoyed books like that when I was young. At the same time, a friend told me about an experience her teenage daughter was encountering. And all of a sudden, I knew I had a story to write." Publishing her first book, *Call Me Beautiful,* under the pseudonym Shannon Blair, Kaye was encouraged in her decision to resume her childhood passion, and after a few more books she dropped the pseudonym and stepped forth as a full-fledged children's writer.

Early in her prolific career, Kaye expanded her interests from teen romance. An early picture-book effort, *Will You Cross Me?,* describes young New York City residents Sam and Joe and their efforts to play baseball together. The boys live across the street from each other, but neither is allowed to cross the street on his own. *School Library Journal* contributor Nancy Palmer described the book as "simply worded and amusingly spun out," while a critic for *Kirkus Reviews* dubbed *Will You Cross Me?* a "lightly laughable contretemps." Another book for the on-the-way-to-reading set, *The Real Tooth Fairy,* finds young Elise one tooth shy of a full set and feigning sleep in order to be awake for her first visit from the tooth fairy. "A charming explanation for one of childhood's smaller mysteries" was the summation provided by Joan McGrath in *School Library Journal,* while Deborah Stevenson wrote in her *Bulletin of the Center for Children's Books* review that *The Real Tooth Fairy* "offers a wise and loving celebration of a low-profile childhood heroine in the dual incarnation of radiant tooth fairy and sleepy parent."

Although Kay has written several other picture books, she most frequently chooses older teens as her intended audience. Her young-adult novel *The Atonement of Mindy Wise,* in which a fourteen-year-old girl reviews a years' worth of transgressions on the Jewish holy day of Yom Kippur, was dubbed "entertaining reading" with a "light touch of comedy" by *Booklist* contributor Stephanie Zvirin. Mindy lists a host of "not-nice" things—from betraying a confidence to gossiping and

deceiving a parent—in order to gain acceptance from the most popular clique in her new school, but as Zvirin observed, Kaye's readers soon see beyond the teen's guilt as Mindy learns "that popularity isn't as important as being yourself." "Kids will see their own mistakes in Mindy's sins," agreed Roger Sutton in his review of *The Atonement of Mindy Wise* for the *Bulletin of the Center for Children's Books,* "and will appreciate the chance to relish them from a distance."

In addition to adopting a male protagonist in *Real Heroes,* Kaye also tackles some difficult topics, including AIDS, homosexuality, and parental abandonment. Twelve-year-old Kevin is not having a good year; his mother has left his police-officer father and the family home, and a rumor is spreading through school that one of the boy's favorite teachers has just tested positive for HIV, the virus that causes AIDS. Even more distressing to Kevin is the fact that his own dad is behind the move to have this teacher fired. Citing the father-son connection as primary in the novel, Stevenson added in her *Bulletin of the Center for Children's Books* reviewthat "the characters of faithful but confused Kevin and his proud, hurt, and frightened father are well-depicted, as is the changing relationship between the two." "Kaye

A teen finds out that her politician mom has surrendered her to a fate worse than death in Kaye's wry teen novel **Demon Chick.** *(Cover photography by Walter Lockwood/Corbis. Courtesy of Henry Holt & Company, LLC.)*

offers a dramatic account of the social and psychological effects of the AIDS threat," wrote a *Publishers Weekly* critic, the reviewer calling *Real Heroes* "highly readable . . . [and] moving as well as convincing."

Unlike *Real Heroes,* most of Kaye's books feature girls as central characters, and such is the case with *Demon Chick.* A stand-alone novel featuring an imaginative mix of horror and comedy, Kaye's story here finds Jessica Hunsucker in for a rude awakening on the morning of her sixteenth birthday. Although the girl had always known her widowed politician mom to be self-serving, the woman has actually sold the soul of her firstborn child to the devil in exchange for high vote-counts in the polls. Fortunately, Jess's stay in Hell is made more tolerable by a demon named Brad, and soon the two are hatching conspiracies of their own in an "imaginative and satirical" story that *Booklist* critic Shauna Yusko praised for its "wry wit." In her review of *Demon Chick* for *School Library Journal,* Melyssa Malinowski had a similar assessment, predicting that readers of Kaye's fast-paced tale "will cheer [Jessica and Brad] . . . on as they attempt to save the world and work through their rocky relationship," while *Horn Book* critic Rachel L. Smith noted that Jessica's "wry observations and dialogue keep the narrative snappy."

Many of Kaye's written works are organized into multi-volume series, and she has also contributed to larger series. Her "Out of This World" books feature a teen named Max who hails from another planet and tries to fit in among a group of U.S. teens, while "Three of a Kind" consists of six novels about orphans Josie, Becka, and Cat after they become sisters through adoption. Her "Last on Earth" books, which include *The Vanishing, The Convergence,* and *The Return,* follow a group of high schoolers who wind up being the only ones remaining on Earth after an alien race conquers and transports the planet's human inhabitants elsewhere.

Kaye's "Sisters" series, divided into four volumes named after each of the four sisters it focuses on, provides teen readers with differing perspectives on the sometimes questionable actions, choices, and attitudes of teen girls. Thirteen-year-old Cassie Gray cares only about being popular, which translates into an overwhelming preoccupation with clothes, boys, and money and results in a shoplifting incident. Lydia Gray is Cassie's opposite; older, she is a feminist and an intellectual who attempts to make changes in school traditions—until those changes begin to hurt others in her family. Phoebe Gray, the youngest, develops more slowly, both physically and emotionally, than her peers. Returning to school after summer camp, she finds herself left behind as her friends become more interested in makeup and boys, and so withdraws into the library. An attempt by a group of parents to remove certain books they deem "unsuitable" from the school shelves raises Phoebe's mettle, and she ultimately makes her mark on middle-school society by founding a student group protesting censorship. In *Daphne* readers are introduced to the seventh-grade sister as she tries to shake her reputation as the "shy one."

Reviewing Kaye's "Sisters" series for *School Librarian,* Teresa Scragg noted that "the girls are very different in character which gives the author scope to develop many themes and raise several issues of interest to teenage readers." While noting that the novels are "sometimes simplistic," Betsy Hearne maintained in her *Bulletin of the Center for Children's Books* review of both *Cassie* and *Lydia* that Kaye's novel quartet "offer[s] young readers a stepping stone between formula series and more complex fiction."

Featuring a sci-fi bent, Kaye's long-running "Replica" series begins with *Amy, Number Seven.* Seventh-grader Amy Candler seems to be living a pretty normal life until a class assignment to write an autobiography leads her to realize that she knows very little about her past. This, combined with her suspicion that she is being followed by strange men and is able to do things that other people cannot, prompts Amy to quiz her mother regarding her background. At first Mom is evasive, but finally the truth outs, and it involves everything from secret government experiments and test-tube babies to a whole tribe of identical "Amy's" who have been farmed out to adoptive families throughout the country. *Amy, Number Seven* is a "page-turner, perfect for light escapist reading," according to *School Library Journal* contributor Jacqueline Rose, and in *Booklist* Helen Rosenberg predicted that Kaye's readers will "like the outcome, which is satisfying yet open-ended enough to leave them anxious" for future installments. The "Replica" series continues in stories such as *The Best of the Best,* in which an eight-year-old genius is threatening as well as annoying, as well as *Pursuing Amy: Who Can You Trust?, Dreamcrusher,* and *Like Father, like Son.* The series concludes with *Amy, on Her Own,* which find the oft-replicated teen experiencing what it really means—and feels like—to be human. As *Booklist* reviewer Chris Sherman asserted in an appraisal of *Pursuing Amy,* Kaye's high-tension "Replica" books are "guaranteed to hook hard-core nonreaders."

In her "Gifted" series Kaye explores another popular teen genre: the supernatural. Each of the novels, which include *Out of Sight, Out of Mind, Better Late than Never,* and *Here Today, Gone Tomorrow,* focuses on one member of a school's eighth-grade "gifted" class. These students are not gifted in the usual way, however: each possesses a special psychic power that creates problems in her everyday world. In *Here Today, Gone Tomorrow,* for example, Emily experiences visions that, while hazy, often prove to be prophetic although they do not make sense at the time, while in *Better Late than Never* Amanda is able to take over the physical bodies of anyone who inspires her pity and compassion. Other gifted girls in the class include mind-reader Jenna and Tracey, a middle grader with the handy ability to become invisible to others. Reviewing *Here Today, Gone Tomorrow* in *School Library Journal,* Shari Fesko predicted a large audience for the "Gifted" novels and noted that "even minor characters are given depth through Kaye's descriptive text." Also praising Kaye's stories, Emily Chomomaz wrote in the same periodical that the books will likely inspire the interest of reluctant readers, and *Booklist* critic Cindy Welch recommended *Out of Sight, Out of Mind* for featuring an "easy" text salted with "a hint of romance, and mild tension."

While Kaye has shown herself to be a prolific author, she still finds challenges in her chosen career. "Writing is enormously difficult for me," she once explained. "Each type of book I've attempted . . . has presented its own uniquely agonizing problems and challenges which I'm never quite sure I can meet. For me, writing is not a means of baring my soul or articulating personal angst. I want to tell stories, and as I write, I envision readers, and what they might want to hear." Asked why she became a writer of children's books, Kaye responds: "The child in me is close to the surface, and she knows all the best stories."

Biographical and Critical Sources

PERIODICALS

Booklist, June 15, 1991, Stephanie Zvirin, review of *The Atonement of Mindy Wise,* p. 1955; October 15, 1998, Helen Rosenberg, review of *Amy, Number Seven,* p. 412; January 1, 1999, Chris Sherman, review of *Pursuing Amy: Who Can You Trust?,* p. 857; May 15, 2009, Cindy Welch, review of *Out of Sight, Out of Mind,* p. 56; August 1, 2009, Shauna Yusko, review of *Demon Chick,* p. 55; November 1, 2009, Cindy Welch, review of *Here Today, Gone Tomorrow,* p. 45.

Bulletin of the Center for Children's Books, December, 1987, Betsy Hearne, reviews of *Cassie* and *Lydia,* both p. 67; October, 1990, Deborah Stevenson, review of *The Real Tooth Fairy,* p. 33; July, 1991, Roger Sutton, review of *The Atonement of Mindy Wise,* pp. 265-266; May, 1993, Deborah Stevenson, review of *Real Heroes,* pp. 285-286.

Horn Book, September-October, 2009, Rachel L. Smith, review of *Demon Chick,* p. 565.

Kirkus Reviews, March 1, 1985, review of *Will You Cross Me?,* p. 110; August 15, 2009, review of *Demon Chick.*

Publishers Weekly, April 26, 1993, review of *Real Heroes,* p. 80; October 12, 1998, review of *Amy, Number Seven,* p. 77.

School Library Journal, May, 1985, Nancy Palmer, review of *Will You Cross Me?,* p. 106; October, 1990, Joan McGrath, review of *The Real Tooth Fairy,* p. 95; October, 1998, Jacqueline Rose, review of *Amy, Number Seven,* p. 136; June, 2009, Emily Chornomaz, review of *Out of Sight, Out of Mind,* p. 128; October, 2009, Shari Fesko, review of *Here Today, Gone Tomorrow,* p. 128; October, 2009, Melyssa Malinowski, review of *Demon Chick,* p. 128.

School Librarian, May, 1989, Teresa Scragg, reviews of *Phoebe, Daphne, Cassie,* and *Lydia,* all pp. 73-74.

ONLINE

Fantastic Fiction Web site, http://www.fantasticfiction.co.uk/ (May 15, 2011), "Marilyn Kaye."

Macmillan Web site, http://us.macmillan.com/ (May 15, 2011), "Marilyn Kaye."

School Library Journal Online, http://www.schoollibraryjournal.com/slj/ (June 8, 2009), Lauren Barack, "Marilyn Kaye: Gifted and Talented."

*   *   *

KELLY, Tara

Personal

Born in CA. *Education:* University of California at Santa Cruz, B.A. (film and digital media), 2004.

Addresses

Home—Portland, OR. *Agent*—Jennifer Laughran, Andrea Brown Literary Agency, jennl@andreabrownlit.com. *E-mail*—contact@thetaratracks.com.

Career

Musician, author, and Web designer. Has worked as a graphic artist and art teacher.

Writings

Harmonic Feedback, Henry Holt (New York, NY), 2010.
Amplified, Henry Holt (New York, NY), 2011.

Sidelights

Raised in the San Francisco Bay Area, Tara Kelly now lives in Portland, Oregon, where she works as a musician and author in addition to exploring other creative career opportunities. Kelly graduated with a degree leading to a career in film and digital media, then realized that a job in music, while just as difficult to establish, would ultimately be more fulfilling. While making her mark on the local Portland music scene, she has worked a variety of jobs and also found the time to return to the fiction-writing she enjoyed prior to college. Kelly's varied experiences in pursuing her own dreams ultimately inspired her first two novels for young adults: *Harmonic Feedback* and *Amplified,* the latter which finds a seventeen year old homeless as she arrives in Santa Cruz in pursuit of a music career.

Harmonic Feedback introduces sixteen-year-old Drea, whose interest in music and sound design is thwarted by the girl's diagnoses of Asperger's, a mild form of autism that prevents her from correctly interpreting body language, facial expressions, and the emotional nuances in verbal conversations. Drea and her single mother have just moved to western Washington, where the teen is relieved to find kindred spirits Naomi and Justin. After the three new friends decide to form a band, clashes in musical taste punctuate Drea's relationship with Justin, threatening not only to end her chance of performing with other musicians but also to derail a budding romance. *Harmonic Feedback* provides "a strong, authentic sense of Drea's inner life and daily struggles," asserted *Booklist* contributor Gillian Engberg, the critic adding that Kelly's novel features a "sobering, tragic ending" and a message that will resonate with teens.

Biographical and Critical Sources

PERIODICALS

Booklist, June 1, 2010, Gillian Engberg, review of *Harmonic Feedback,* p. 53.

Cover of Tara Kelly's young-adult novel Harmonic Feedback, *in which an autistic teen finds a bridge to "normal" through love of music.*
(Henry Holt & Company, 2010. Cover photograph by Rich Deas. Courtesy of Henry Holt & Company, LLC.)

Bulletin of the Center for Children's Books, July-August, 2010, Karen Coats, review of *Harmonic Feedback,* p. 487.
School Library Journal, August, 2010, Alison Follos, review of *Harmonic Feedback,* p. 104.

ONLINE

Tara Kelly Home Page, http://thetaratracks.com (May 27, 2011).*

* * *

KITANIDIS, Phoebe 1977-

Personal

Born 1977, in Athens, Greece; immigrated to United States; partner's name Robert. *Education:* University of California at Berkeley, B.A. (rhetoric); San Jose University, M.A. (communication studies), 2004. *Hobbies and other interests:* Travel, endurance sports.

Addresses

Home—Seattle, WA.

Career

Author and educator. Former language arts teacher; worked in high-tech industry; freelance writer, beginning 2004. Presenter at writing workshops.

Member

Science Fiction Writers of America, Pacific Northwest Writer's Association.

Writings

(Editor) *Fab Girls' Guide to Friendship Hardship,* Discovery Girls Inc. (San Jose, CA), 2007.
Whisper, Balzer + Bray (New York, NY), 2010.

Contributor to periodicals, including *Discovery Girls.*

Sidelights

A well-traveled author—she attended five elementary schools due to her family's many relocations—Phoebe Kitanidis finally settled in coastal California where she worked as a teacher and earned a master's degree in communications studies. A move further up the coast, to Seattle, Washington, was the result of Kitanidis's decision to take a gamble and embark on a career as a writer. Her focus on teen readers proved to be a fit with *Discovery Girls* magazine, where she contributed articles, and also led to her editorship of *Fab Girls' Guide to Friendship Hardship,* a teen relationship guide. Her first novel, *Whisper,* was published in 2010.

Joy Stefani, the fifteen-year-old protagonist of *Whisper,* has had the ability to "hear" the thoughts of other people since she was a child. Together with her mom and older sister Jessica, with whom she shares this aptitude, Joy taps into other's thoughts and dose things to make them happy. However, the thoughts she now hears are not just the light, trifling ruminations that drift through people's minds; sometimes she can sense the intense, passionate, critical, and even frightening thoughts that emanate from deep in their subconscious. Joy's new ability comes at a cost—debilitating headaches—and as she she copes with it she also copes with everyday issues concerning school and friends. Then there are her worries about Jessica's drug use and unexplained resentments. And what is up with Jessica's boyfriend's brother Jamie, who seems to possess the same mind-reading power? While citing the novel's characteristic coming-of-age themes, Jennifer Miskec added in her *School Library Journal* review that *Whisper* benefits from its author's "intriguing constructions of Joy's powers, unexpected plot moves, and strong characterizations." With its intimate first-person narration, Kitanidis's fiction debut "will strike a chord" with fans of supernatural fiction, predicted a *Kirkus Reviews* writer, and a *Publishers Weekly* contributor dubbed *Whisper* a "paranormal version of *The Breakfast Club*" in which "Joy's narrative voice is appealing."

Biographical and Critical Sources

PERIODICALS

Kirkus Reviews, April 15, 2010, review of *Whisper.*
Publishers Weekly, May 10, 2010, review of *Whisper,* p. 46.
School Library Journal, June, 2010, Jennifer Miskec, review of *Whisper,* p. 106.

ONLINE

HarperCollins Web site, http://www.harpercollins.com/ (May 15, 2011), "Phoebe Kitanidis."
Seattle Examiner Online, http://www.examiner.com/ (December 23, 2009), Caren Gussoff, interview with Kitanidis.*

*   *   *

KLINGER, Shula

Personal

Born in St. Albans, Hertfordshire, England; immigrated to Canada, 1997; married; husband's name Graham; children: Benjamin. *Education:* Ph.D. (education), 2001. *Hobbies and other interests:* Reading, swimming, yoga, baking, walking in the forest.

Addresses

Home—North Vancouver, British Columbia, Canada.

Career

Author and illustrator. Worked for a school board in British Columbia, Canada, until 2008.

Writings

The Kingdom of Strange, Marshall Cavendish (New York, NY), 2008.

Contributor of articles to periodicals in United States, Canada, and the United Kingdom; contributor to programming for Canadian Broadcasting Corporation Radio.

ILLUSTRATOR

Beverly Patt, *Best Friends Forever: A World War II Scrapbook,* Marshall Cavendish Children (New York, NY), 2010.

Sidelights

Shula Klinger was born in England but moved to Canada while earning an advanced degree in education and decided to adopt British Columbia as her new home. Hosting writing workshops and a writing form for preteen writers provided the inspiration for Klinger's first novel, *The Kingdom of Strange.* In addition to her writing, she is also an artist who has created the illustrations for Beverly Patt's *Best Friends Forever: A*

Shula Klinger's illustration assignments include creating the unique illustrations for Beverly Patt's "Best Friends Forever: A World War II Scrapbook. (Illustration copyright © 2010 by Shula Klinger. Reproduced by permission of Marshall Cavendish Children.)

World War II Scrapbook. A story about Dottie and Louise, fourteen-year-old best friends who are pulled apart by the government-run internment of Japanese Americans during wartime, *Best Friends Forever* was recommended by *School Library Journal* critic Emma Burkhart as "a heartwarming tale of friendship" and "a wonderful access point for learning more about World War II and Japanese internment."

Fourteen-year-old Thisbe is Klinger's focus in *The Kingdom of Strange.* In addition to her love of swimming and reading, Thisbe loves to write and she is determined to become a novelist. When she joins a school writing project, the ninth grader develops an e-mail correspondence with a student at another school who is know to Thisbe only under her online name Iphis. Right now is an apportune time for a new confidante: Thisbe's two best friends are pursuing interests that she does not share and the adults in her family have never understood her passion for writing. Iphis understands and comments on her enthusiasms, however, and soon the two e-mail pen pals are sharing all sorts of things, that is, until Thisbe makes an unfortunate discovery that causes her to see the people in her life through a different and more mature lens. *The Kingdom of Strange* is composed primarily of e-mails between Thisbe and Iphis, and Teresa Hughes predicted in *Resource Links* that "young readers will really like the chat-line format" of the novel. Multigenerational elements are also present, Hughes added, noting that Thisbe's custodial "Granny Ed plays an important part" in helping the teen "discover . . . the true meaning of friendship." Klinger also

salts *The Kingdom of Strange* with useful tips and advice for future novelists, prompting *Booklist* critic John Peters to predict that readers "will identify with Thisbe's steady determination to be a writer and benefit from her exercises and not-quite-lectures."

Biographical and Critical Sources

PERIODICALS

Booklist, May 1, 2008, John Peters, review of *The Kingdom of Strange,* p. 79; April 15, 2010, Hazel Rochman, review of *Best Friends Forever: A World War II Scrapbook,* p. 55.

Bulletin of the Center for Children's Books, July-August, 2010, Elizabeth Bush, review of *Best Friends Forever,* p. 497.

Publishers Weekly, May 3, 2010, review of *Best Friends Forever,* p. 50.

Resource Links, October, 2008, review of *The Kingdom of Strange,* p. 20.

School Library Journal, April, 2010, Emma Burkhart, review of *Best Friends Forever,* p. 166.

Voice of Youth Advocates, June, 2008, Kelly Czarnecki, review of *The Kingdom of Strange,* p. 145; April, 2010, Kelly Czarnecki, review of *Best Friends Forever,* p. 61.

ONLINE

Shula Klinger Home Page, http://www.shulaklinger.com (February 27, 2011).*

L

LELOUP, Geneviève

Personal

Born in Belgium; immigrated to United States, 1992. *Education:* École de Recherche Graphique (Brussels, Belgium), B.F.A. (silkscreen printing, animation, and fine art), 1986. *Hobbies and other interests:* Playing music, cooking, travelling.

Addresses

Home and office—Alulu Studio, Brooklyn, NY. *Agent*—Michèle Manasse, New Hope, PA; mmanasse@new-work.com. *E-mail*—alulu@mac.com.

Career

Illustrator and textile designer. Cofounder of greeting-card and paper-product company in Brussels, Belgium, c. late 1980s; freelance textile designer and illustrator, beginning 1992. Commercial clients include American Red Cross, Citibank. Continental Airlines, L.L. Bean, Macy's, Nordstrom, Old Navy, The Gap, and Victoria's Secret.

Illustrator

Sarah Albee, *Super Me!,* Golden Books (New York, NY), 1999.

Carol Pugliano-Martin, *Seasons,* Golden Books (New York, NY), 2002.

Jean Reidy, *Too Pickley!,* Bloomsbury Children's Books (New York, NY), 2010.

Jean Reidy, *Too Purpley!,* Bloomsbury (New York, NY), 2010.

Jean Reidy, *Too Princessy!,* Bloomsbury (New York, NY), 2012.

Contributor to periodicals, including *Profiles, Redbook, Wall Street Journal Europe,* and *Washington Post.*

Sidelights

With her background in textile design, Geneviève Leloup has a talent for combining color and pattern that has also found a home in children's picture books. The Belgian-born Leloup uses vibrant color and stylized shape. Although demand for her work has prompted her to develop a digital component to her portfolio, Leloup has also continued to cultivate her characteristic hand-rendered line style, and her images can be found in advertising and corporate publications, on greeting cards, and in the pages of children's books that include *Super Me!* by Sarah Albee, *Seasons* by Carol Pugliano-Martin, and several humorous picture books by Jean Reidy.

In 1986, after Leloup completed her fine-arts degree at Brussels' École de Recherche Graphique, she cofounded a design company and created art for unique greeting cards and other paper products. She moved to the United States in the early 1990s, where her child-friendly textile designs quickly found a market. Her first illustration project, *Super Me!,* was published in 1999.

Befitting the book's storyline, Leloup weaves textile design into her digital illustrations for Reidy's *Too Purpley!,* the saga of a little girl who cannot find anything to wear in her own closet. With every ensemble she selects, the girl finds some problem, be it color, pattern, or texture. Ultimately, however, readers learn that the child's ultimate goal is comfort in a story that Elaine Lesh Morgan praised in *School Library Journal* for its combination of "descriptive words, . . . great colors and patterns, and a charming protagonist." The story's "whimsical watercolors highlight the absurdity of her [costume] choices," asserted Kay Weisman in *Booklist,* and a *Publishers Weekly* critic noted that "Leloup's persnickety toddler looks like a paper doll" with "an awesome collection of outfits."

While *Too Purpley!* is geared for little girls, Reidy treats little boys to an equally amusing story in *Too Pickley!* Here a young lad is very hungry but also very discriminating: every time a new food is put on his plate, the boy dismisses it as too one thing or the other. "Leloup's bright, digitally mastered illustration" match "the comic pace of Reidy's bouncy rhymes," wrote Martha Simpson in her *School Library Journal* review of *Too Pickley!*, and in *Booklist* Randall Enos asserted that the artist's "irascible illustrations . . . on brilliantly colored pages vividly show the amusing antics" of Reidy's ultra-discriminating young hero.

Biographical and Critical Sources

PERIODICALS

Booklist, January 1, 2010, Kay Weisman, review of *Too Purpley!,* p. 100; May 1, 2010, Randall Enos, review of *Too Pickley!,* p. 92.
Children's Bookwatch, July, 2010, review of *Too Purpley!;* October, 2010, review of *Too Pickley!*
Kirkus Reviews, January 1, 2010, review of *Too Purpley!*
Publishers Weekly, January 11, 2010, review of *Too Purpley!,* p. 46.
School Library Journal, January, 2010, Elaine Lesh Morgan, review of *Too Purpley!,* p. 81; July, 2010, Martha Simpson, review of *Too Pickley!,* p. 69.

ONLINE

Geneviève Leloup Home Page, http://www.alulustudio.com (May 15, 2011).
New-Work Illustration Web site, http://www.new-work. com/ (May 15, 2011), "Geneviève Leloup."

*   *   *

LEVEEN, Tom

Personal

Born in Scottsdale, AZ; married; wife's name Joy. *Education:* Scottsdale Community College, A.A.; attended Arizona State University.

Addresses

Home—AZ. *Agent*—Andrea Brown Literary Agency, CA. *E-mail*—tom@tomleveen.com.

Career

Author and theatre director. Worked as an actor and director, beginning 1988; Is What It Is Theatre, Scottsdale, AZ, cofounder and artistic director, 1995-2006; Chyro Arts Venue (nonprofit visual and performing venue), Scottsdale, cofounder and artistic director, 2007-10. Worked variously in a library and as an editor and business writer. Presenter at schools and conferences.

Awards, Honors

Quick Picks nomination, American Library Association, 2011, for *Party.*

Tom Leveen (Photograph by John Groseclose. Reproduced by permission.)

Writings

Party, Random House (New York, NY), 2010.
Zero, Random House (New York, NY), 2012.

Sidelights

Tom Leveen has spent much of his adult career in the theatre, organizing and directing stage productions in his home city of Scottsdale, Arizona. Leveen was inspired to write his first young-adult novel, *Party,* through his work with young actors as well as by memories of what life was like during his own teenage years.

Party is set in Santa Barbara, California, at that glorious time of year when classes have ended, final exams have decided one's academic fate for better or for worse, and weeks of summer stretch out ahead. For Morrigan, Josh, Ashley, Max, Azize, Beckett, and five other teens, attendance at a celebratory bash distills into eleven unique experiences as alcohol and abandon, sex and romance, frustrations and jealousies, racism and resentments, and other factors spin the evening out of control. As each teen shares his or her perspective on the night in one of eleven chapters, weighty issues are also addressed: morality and religion, the inevitability of war, and apprehensions about the future. The characters' "yearning to connect . . . shines through their pained actions, awkward slang, and . . . profanity," observed *Booklist* reviewer Miriam Aronin, the critic recommending *Party* for older, more sophisticated teen readers. "Plot twists" and "cliffhangers" fuel Leveen's narrative as readers come to know each character through the eyes of others, wrote a *Publishers Weekly* contributor. In *School Library Journal* Nora G. Murphy praised

Party as "a quick and entertaining read" in which the unraveling of the characters' interwoven viewpoints adds "depth to the story."

Leveen discussed his work writing for teens with *Phoenix New Times* online interviewer Claire Lawton. "The easiest thing about writing a YA novel is the nostalgia and escape of writing them . . .," the author explained. "I personally had a great time in high school, even when I said I was miserable, and it's so much fun to go back to that time and make different (fictional) decisions than the ones I made, and see how things might've turned out. . . . It all changes and grows into its own story eventually, but the roots are generally buried in my experiences and relationships I had as a teen. Plus," he added, "I get to dress my characters much better than I dressed; there's no such thing as cystic acne; there's always a snappy comeback; and every so often, talking to the cute girl works out."

"The best part of my job as a YA novelist is meeting with students," Leveen told *SATA*. "I don't talk too much about my books necessarily when I do school visits; I'm much more interested in making sure students know they can accomplish anything, and to not let anyone tell them otherwise."

Biographical and Critical Sources

PERIODICALS

Booklist, May 1, 2010, Miriam Aronin, review of *Party,* p. 78.
Bulletin of the Center for Children's Books, July-August, 2010, April Spisak, review of *Party,* p. 489.
Publishers Weekly, March 22, 2010, review of *Party,* p. 72.
School Library Journal, April, 2010, Nora G. Murphy, review of *Party,* p. 162.

ONLINE

Class of 2K10 Web site, http://www.classof2k10.com/ (May 15, 2011), "Tom Leveen."
Phoenix New Times Online, http://blobs.phoenixnewtimes.com/ (July 27, 2010), Claire Lawton, "100 Creatives: Tom Leveen."
Tom Leveen Home Page, http://www.tomleveen.com (May 15, 2011).

*   *   *

LOWRY, Lois 1937-

Personal

Born March 20, 1937, in Honolulu, HI; daughter of Robert E. (an army dentist) and Katharine Hammersberg; married Donald Grey Lowry (an attorney), June 11, 1956 (divorced, 1977); married Martin Small (died May 17, 2011); children: Alix, Grey (deceased), Kristin, Benjamin. *Education:* Attended Brown University, 1954-56; University of Southern Maine, B.A., 1972; graduate study. *Religion:* Episcopalian. *Hobbies and other interests:* Knitting, gardening, reading, spending time with her grandchildren.

Addresses

Home—Cambridge, MA; ME. *Agent*—Phyllis Westberg, Harold Ober Associates, 425 Madison Ave., New York, NY 10017. *E-mail*—info@loislowry.com.

Career

Children's book author. Worked as a photographer and journalist, beginning 1972; freelance writer, beginning mid-1970s.

Member

Society of Children's Book Writers and Illustrators, PEN New England, PEN American Center, Authors Guild, Authors League of America, MacDowell Colony (fellow).

Cover of Leveen's debut young-adult novel Party, *which follows a single evening from the perspective of several teens.* (Random House Children's Book, 2010. Reproduced by permission of Random House Children's Books, a division of Random House, Inc.)

Lois Lowry (Reproduced by permission.)

Awards, Honors

Children's Literature Award, International Reading Association (IRA), Notable Book designation, American Library Association (ALA), and MA and CA state children's choice awards, all 1978, all for *A Summer to Die;* Children's Book of the Year citation, Child Study Association of America, and ALA Notable Book designation, both 1979, both for *Anastasia Krupnik;* ALA Notable Book designation, 1980, and International Board on Books for Young People Honor List citation, 1982, both for *Autumn Street;* ALA Notable Book designation, 1981, and American Book Award nomination in juvenile paperback category, 1983, both for *Anastasia Again!;* ALA Notable Book designation, 1983, for *The One-Hundredth Thing about Caroline;* Children's Book of the Year designation, Child Study Association of America, 1986, for *Us and Uncle Fraud;* New Jersey State Children's Choice selection, 1986, for *Anastasia, Ask Your Analyst; Boston Globe/Horn Book* Award, Golden Kite Award, Society of Children's Book Writers and Illustrators, and Child Study Award, Children's Book Committee of Bank Street College, all 1987, all for *Rabble Starkey;* Christopher Award, 1988; Newbery Medal, ALA, National Jewish Book Award, and Sidney Taylor Award, National Jewish Libraries, all 1990, all for *Number the Stars;* Newbery Medal, 1994, for *The Giver;* Children's Choice citation, IRA/Children's Book Council, 1997, for *See You Around, Sam!;* Rhode Island Children's Book Award, 2002, for *Gooney Bird Greene;* Hope S. Dean Memorial Award, 2003; Margaret A. Edwards Award, 2007; May Hill Arbuthnot Honor Lecturer, 2011.

Writings

JUVENILE NOVELS

A Summer to Die, illustrated by Jenni Oliver, Houghton Mifflin (Boston, MA), 1977, reprinted, Delacorte (New York, NY), 2007.

Find a Stranger, Say Goodbye, Houghton Mifflin (Boston, MA), 1978.

Autumn Street, Houghton Mifflin (Boston, MA), 1979.

Taking Care of Terrific, Houghton Mifflin (Boston, MA), 1983.

Us and Uncle Fraud, Houghton Mifflin (Boston, MA), 1984.

The One Hundredth Thing about Caroline, Houghton Mifflin (Boston, MA), 1985.

Switcharound (sequel to *The One Hundredth Thing about Caroline*), Houghton Mifflin (Boston, MA), 1985.

Rabble Starkey, Houghton Mifflin (Boston, MA), 1987.

Number the Stars, Houghton Mifflin (Boston, MA), 1989, reprinted, Yearling (New York, NY), 2005.

Your Move, J.P.! (sequel to *Switcharound*), Houghton Mifflin (Boston, MA), 1990.

The Giver (first volume in "Giver" trilogy), Houghton Mifflin (Boston, MA), 1993.

Stay!: Keeper's Story, illustrated by True Kelley, Houghton Mifflin (Boston, MA), 1997.

Looking Back: A Book of Memories, Houghton Mifflin (Boston, MA), 1998.

Gathering Blue (second volume in "Giver" trilogy), Houghton Mifflin (Boston, MA), 2000.

The Silent Boy, Houghton Mifflin (Boston, MA), 2003.

The Messenger (third volume in "Giver" trilogy), Houghton Mifflin (Boston, MA), 2004.

Gossamer, Houghton Mifflin (Boston, MA), 2006.

(Self-illustrated) *The Willoughbys,* Houghton Mifflin (Boston, MA), 2008.

Crow Call (picture book), illustrated by Bagram Ibatoulline, Scholastic Press (New York, NY), 2009.

The Birthday Ball, illustrated by Jules Feiffer, Houghton Mifflin Books for Children (Boston, MA), 2010.

Bless This Mouse (picture book), illustrated by Eric Rohmann, Houghton Mifflin Books for Children (New York, NY), 2011.

Like the Willow Tree: The Diary of Lydia Amelia Pierce ("Dear America" series), Scholastic (New York, NY), 2011.

"ANASTASIA" CHAPTER-BOOK SERIES

Anastasia Krupnik, Houghton Mifflin (Boston, MA), 1979.

Anastasia Again!, illustrated by Diane deGroat, Houghton Mifflin (Boston, MA), 1981.

Anastasia at Your Service, illustrated by Diane deGroat, Houghton Mifflin (Boston, MA), 1982.

Anastasia, Ask Your Analyst, Houghton Mifflin (Boston, MA), 1984.

Anastasia on Her Own, Houghton Mifflin (Boston, MA), 1985.

Anastasia Has the Answers, Houghton Mifflin (Boston, MA), 1986.

Anastasia's Chosen Career, Houghton Mifflin (Boston, MA), 1987.

Anastasia at This Address, Houghton Mifflin (Boston, MA), 1991.

Anastasia, Absolutely, Houghton Mifflin (Boston, MA), 1995.

"SAM" BEGINNING READER SERIES

All about Sam, illustrated by Diane deGroat, Houghton Mifflin (Boston, MA), 1988.

Attaboy, Sam!, illustrated by Diane deGroat, Houghton Mifflin (Boston, MA), 1992.

See You Around, Sam!, Houghton Mifflin (Boston, MA), 1996.

Zooman Sam, Houghton Mifflin (Boston, MA), 1999.

"GOONEY BIRD GREENE" CHAPTER-BOOK SERIES

Gooney Bird Greene, illustrated by Middy Thomas, Houghton Mifflin (Boston, MA), 2002.

Gooney Bird and the Room Mother, illustrated by Middy Thomas, Houghton Mifflin (Boston, MA), 2005.

Gooney the Fabulous, illustrated by Middy Thomas, Houghton Mifflin (Boston, MA), 2007.

Gooney Bird Is So Absurd, illustrated by Middy Thomas, Houghton Mifflin Harcourt (Boston, MA), 2009.

OTHER

Black American Literature (textbook), J. Weston Walsh (Portland, ME), 1973.

Literature of the American Revolution (textbook), J. Weston Walsh (Portland, ME), 1974.

(Photographer) Frederick H. Lewis, *Here in Kennebunkport,* Durrell (Kennebunkport, ME), 1978.

(Author of introduction) *Dear Author: Students Write about the Books That Changed Their Lives,* Conari Press, 1998.

(And photographer) *Looking Back: A Book of Memories* (autobiography), Houghton Mifflin (Boston, MA), 1998.

(Editor) *Shining On: Eleven Star Authors' Illuminating Stories,* Delacorte (New York, NY), 2007.

Contributor of stories, articles, and photographs to periodicals, including *Redbook, Yankee,* and *Down East.*

Adaptations

Find a Stranger, Say Goodbye was adapted as the *Afterschool Special* television film "I Don't Know Who I Am," produced 1980. *Taking Care of Terrific* was adapted as a segment of the television series *Wonderworks,* 1988. *Anastasia at Your Service* was adapted as an audiobook for Learning Library, 1984. *Anastasia Krupnik* was adapted as a filmstrip, Cheshire, 1987. *Gooney Bird Greene and Her True-Life Adventures,* a dramatization by Kent R. Brown, was adapted from *Gooney Bird Greene* and published by Dramatic Publishing, 2005. *The Giver* was adapted as a film by Todd Alcott and directed by Vadim Perelman for Twentieth Century-Fox, c. 2007, and as an opera by Minnesota Opera/Lyric Opera of Kansas City, 2012. Several of Lowry's novels have been adapted as audiobooks by Listening Library.

Sidelights

Lois Lowry, an award-winning author of stories for younger readers, is perhaps best known for her Newbery Medal-winning novels *Number the Stars* and *The Giver,* the latter part of a futuristic novel trilogy that also includes *Gathering Blue* and *Messenger.* Never one to shy from controversy in her stories for older children, Lowry has dealt with topics ranging from the death of a sibling to the Nazi occupation of Denmark to futuristic dystopian societies. Turning to lighter fare, she also shares the humorous antics of a rebellious preteen named Anastasia Krupnik in a series of chapter books and charms younger audiences with picture books such as *Crow Call* and *The Birthday Ball.* Although Lowry's books explore a variety of settings and characters, readers can distill a single unifying theme: "the importance of human connections," as the author wrote on her home page.

In 1937, the year Lowry was born, her father, a military dentist and career army officer, was stationed at Schofield Barracks near Pearl Harbor in Honolulu, Hawai'i. The family separated with the onset of World War II: Lowry's father serving out his tour of duty while Lowry's mother took the children to live with her own family in the Amish country of Pennsylvania. "I remember all these relatively normal Christmases with trees, presents, turkeys, and carols, except that they had this enormous hole in them because there was never any father figure," the author recalled in an interview for *Authors and Artists for Young Adults.* This deep sense of loss is "probably why I've written a terrific father figure into all of my books—sort of a fantasy of mine while growing up." Her grandmother was not especially fond of children, but her grandfather adored her, and Lowry escaped the absolute trauma of war under the shelter of his affection. Much later, Lowry's wartime experience inspired her fourth novel, *Autumn Street.*

Lowry began her career as a journalist and photographer; she was encouraged to write for children by a New York City editor who was impressed by an article she had submitted to the popular women's magazine *Redbook.* In her first novel, *A Summer to Die,* Lowry portrays an adolescent's effort to deal with her older sister's illness and eventual death. When the Chalmers family moves to the country for the summer, thirteen-year-old Meg and fifteen-year-old Molly are forced to share a room. Already jealous of her older sister, Meg becomes increasingly argumentative and resentful when Molly's recurring nosebleeds demand much of her parents' attention. As her sister's condition deteriorates,

Meg realizes that Molly is slowly dying of leukemia. For friendship, she turns to Will Banks, an elderly neighbor who encourages the teen's interest in photography, and tp Ben and Maria, a hippie couple who invites Meg to photograph the birth of their child.

A Summer to Die was well received by critics. Lowry's "story captures the mysteries of living and dying without manipulating the reader's emotions, providing understanding and a comforting sense of completion," observed Linda R. Silver in her review of the novel for *School Library Journal*. In fact, Lowry's tale of Meg and Molly was drawn from life; her older sister, Helen, died of cancer when Lowry was twenty-five years old. Despite its inspiration, the author explained that "very little of [*A Summer to Die*] was factual, except the emotions." Even so, "when my mother read the book she recognized the characters as my sister and me," Lowry added. "She knew that the circumstances in the book were very different, but the characters had great veracity for her."

"Until I was about twelve I thought my parents were terrific, wise, wonderful, beautiful, loving, and well-dressed," Lowry once confessed. "By age twelve and a half they turned into stupid, boring people with whom I did not want to be seen in public. . . . That happens to all kids, and to the kids in my books as well." These same childhood memories, combined with Lowry's own experiences as a parent, inspired her most popular character: Anastasia Krupnik, the spunky, rebellious, and irreverent star of *Anastasia, Ask Your Analyst!*, *Anastasia on Her Own,* and *Anastasia at Your Service,* among other. In *Anastasia Krupnik* the ten-year-old heroine faces numerous comic crises, including a crush on a boy who is continually dribbling an imaginary basketball, and the coming arrival of a new sibling. With the passing of each crisis Anastasia gains new insight into herself, and by the book's close she is prepared to move on to a new level of maturity. "Anastasia's feelings and discoveries should be familiar to anyone who has ever been ten," noted Brad Owens in the *Christian Science Monitor,* "and . . . Lowry has a sensitive way of taking problems seriously without ever being shallow or leaning too far over into despair."

The broad audience appeal sparked by the first "Anastasia" book prompted Lowry to write several other novels following the coming of age of her diminutive heroine. In *Anastasia at Your Service* Anastasia is now twelve years old and tackling a summer job working as a maid to a rich, elderly woman. When the woman turns out to be a classmate's grandmother, the girl must deal with the embarrassment of working for the family of a well-to-do peer. "Despite differences the girls become friends; and with the help of Anastasia's precocious brother Sam, they generate a plot that is rich, inviting, and very funny," noted Barbara Elleman in a *Booklist* review of *Anastasia at Your Service.*

Anastasia appears in several more titles, among them *Anastasia Has the Answers, Anastasia's Chosen Career,* and *Anastasia Again!* As a lovestruck thirteen year old

plying the personal ads, she generates confusion in *Anastasia at This Address,* showcasing what a *Publishers Weekly* reviewer described as her "headstrong, inventive, endearing in irrepressible" self, while her unwitting tampering of the U.S. mail in *Anastasia Absolutely* prompts a "moral crisis" that results in what *Horn Book* reviewer Maeve Visser Knoth predicted would be "light, satisfying reading" for Anastasia's many fans.

While the final book in the "Anastasia" series, *Anastasia Absolutely,* was published in 1995, Lowry turned her focus to the girl's little brother, producing a second series that includes *Attaboy Sam!, See You around, Sam!,* and *Zooman Sam.* In *Zooman Sam* Sam is on the cusp of learning to read. Acquiring the skill will allow him to be someone special, he believes: specifically, the Chief of Wonderfulness. To help him along, his mother crafts a special "Zooman Sam" jumpsuit for Sam to

Cover of Lowry's award-winning novel The Giver, *featuring an illustration by Cliff Neilsen* (Jacket cover copyright © 1999 by Laurel-Leaf. Used by permission of Laurel-Leaf, an imprint of Random House Children's Books, division of Random House, Inc.)

dress up in during Future Job Day at nursery school. With dreams of being a zookeeper, a special job indeed in a room full of children dreaming of more mundane occupations, Sam feels honored when his teacher lets him stand at the head of the circle and tell about a different zoo animal each day for six weeks. With his budding reading skills, Sam is delighted to take on the task and enjoys the attention that comes with it. "Lowry gets everything about Sam just right," wrote Stephanie Zvirin in *Booklist,* while *Horn Book* reviewer Roger Sutton observed that the author "spins interesting variations on her theme," and wraps the book up with "a swell . . . surprise."

Again directed for younger readers, the title character in Lowry's chapter book *Gooney Bird Greene* is the newest arrival to the second grade and the most eccentric person the other students have ever seen. Leaning toward flamboyant dress—a pair of cowboy boots and pajamas one day, a polka-dot shirt and tutu the next—Gooney Bird is also a master storyteller in a small package. She delights in relating tales such as her "absolutely true" adventures of how she flew in from China on a flying carpet, how she got her "diamond earrings" (actually gumball machine trinkets) from a noble prince, and how she earned her oddball name. Encouraged in these tall tales by her teacher, Mrs. Pidgeon, Gooney Bird spins out her imaginative saga, prompting her fellow students to create and tell their own stories. In the process, the entire class—and the book's reader—learns important lessons in storytelling and constructing a compelling and believable narrative. GraceAnne A. De-Candido, writing in *Booklist,* called *Gooney Bird Greene* a "laugh-out-loud" story that serves as "quite a debut" for its young heroine. The book's message and the "cleverly titled stories could spark children's interest in writing their own stories," wrote Janet B. Bair in *School Library Journal.* Peter D. Sieruta, reviewing Lowry's story for *Horn Book,* observed that Gooney Bird is "not always convincing as a character, but she's a fine storyteller, and her message to her classmates—that they, too, have stories to share—is a good one."

Like Anastasia before her, Gooney Bird reappears in several other titles. Still impressing members of Mrs. Pidgeon's second-grade class with her storytelling, she also rises to the challenge of improving her vocabulary in *Gooney Bird and the Room Mother,* arranging a special treat for the school's Thanksgiving celebration as well. Gooney morphs from raconteur to moralist in *Gooney the Fabulous* when her teacher asks each student to write a story inspired by a reading of Aesop's fables, while in *Gooney Bird Is So Absurd* the girl uses whimsy to combat a creative crisis in poetry class, and ultimately shares the loss of a beloved teacher. Reviewing *Gooney Bird and the Room Mother,* Kristine M. Casper dubbed the book "a fast-paced read" in her *School Library Journal* review, adding that Lowry's efforts to encourage vocabulary-building are effectively integrated into the story. Hazel Rochman wrote in *Booklist* that Mrs. Pidgeon's Thanksgiving Day lessons

Cover of Lowry's chapter book **Gooney Bird Greene,** *featuring an illustration by Middy Thomas.* (Cover art © 2002 by Middy Thomas. Used by permission of Random House Children's Books, a division of Random House, Inc.)

"are fun" and that Lowry's story "builds to a tense, beautiful climax." Once more "Gooney takes the lead," announced Ilene Cooper in a *Booklist* review of *Gooney the Fabulous,* the critic adding that the author "nicely individualizes her characters and gets readers interested" in Gooney and her second-grade world. "Few beginning chapter books have the [emotional] range" of *Gooney Bird Is So Absurd,* concluded Carolyn Phelan in the same periodical, "and few writers could manage it with such finesse."

Although her "Anastasia" and "Gooney Bird Greene" stories have been popular lighthearted fare, much of Lowry's success as a novelist has come through her willingness to explore challenging and sometimes controversial teen-oriented topics. For example, she documents an adopted child's search for her biological mother in *Find a Stranger, Say Goodbye.* Although neither Lowry nor any of her children are adopted, she recognized that the subject was an important one that, at the time, was given scant attention. "Maybe it's because of having watched my own kids go through the torture of becoming adults . . . that I think those kinds of issues are important and it's important to deal with them in a sensitive and compassionate way," the author once noted.

Based on a factual account, the novel *Number the Stars* is set against the backdrop of Nazi-occupied Denmark and was the first of Lowry's books to receive the Newbery honor. In the story, ten-year-old Annemarie Johansen and her family are drawn into the war-resistance movement. As narrated by Annemarie, the book follows the family's efforts to shuttle Jews from Denmark into neutral Sweden during World War II, an activity that helped ensure the survival of nearly all of Denmark's Jewish population. The book "avoids explicit description of the horrors of war, yet manages to convey without oversimplification the sorrow felt by so many people who were forced to flee their homeland," wrote a *Children's Literature Review* critic. As quoted in *School Library Journal,* Newbery Awards Committee chair Caroline Ward commented that in *Number the Stars* "Lowry creates suspense and tension without wavering from the viewpoint of Annemarie, a child who shows the true meaning of courage."

Lowry received a second Newbery medal for her 1993 novel *The Giver,* which posits a futuristic utopia wherein every aspect of life—birth, death, families, career choices, emotions, even the weather—is strictly controlled in order to create a safe and comfortable community where humans need not fear violence. Living in this community, twelve-year-old Jonas has reached an important rite of passage: the ceremony in which all children turning thirteen are assigned a life's vocation. Although he is passed over during the ceremony, Jonas is ultimately selected for a unique position: he is to become the new Receiver, a prestigious and powerful person charged with holding all the memories of the community. During his apprenticeship to the current Receiver, an elderly man whom Jonas calls The Giver, the boy learnings all the memories, emotions, and knowledge that the community has given up in favor of peace. At first, these memories are pleasant: images of snow, colors, feelings of love. Then Jonas encounters the darker aspects of human experience—war, death, and pain—and discovers that elderly or infirm community members who are traditionally "Released" are actually being euthanized. This discovery leads the boy to escape from the community with his young foster brother Gabriel.

Lowry ends *The Giver* with an interestingly ambiguous ending in which readers are left unsure of the boys' fate. In a companion novel, *Gathering Blue,* she describes a technologically primitive world in which, as she states in her author's note, "disorder, savagery, and self-interest" rule. As in *The Giver,* a child is chosen to play a special role in the society in *Gathering Blue,* and that child is Kira. Born with a twisted leg—a condition that would normally have resulted in her being put to death as a baby—Kira was somehow allowed to live. Now a talented seamstress, she is chosen to be The Threader, a person whose duty it is to create the robe of The Singer. This garment depicts the history of the world and is used in the society's annual ritual of the Gathering. As The Threader, Kira begins to learn the dark secrets prompting her society's rules and must this knowledge forces her to make a life-altering choice.

Many reviewers praised both *The Giver* and *Gathering Blue* for their sensitive handling of serious themes, a *Publishers Weekly* reviewer hailing the latter novel as a "dark, prophetic tale with a strong medieval flavor." Kay Bowes, writing in *Book Report,* called that same novel "thought-provoking" and "challenging," while a *Horn Book* writer wrote that *Gathering Blue* "shares the thematic concerns of *The Giver* . . . [but] adds a layer of questions about the importance of art in creating and, more ominously, controlling community." Ellen Fader, writing in *School Library Journal,* concluded that with *Gathering Blue* "Lowry has once again created a fully-realized world," predicting that "readers won't forget these memorable characters or their struggles in an inhospitable world."

Messenger continues the story begun in *The Giver* and *Gathering Blue.* Entering the forest sanctuary of "The Village" as a young refugee, Matty has come to love his new home and he respects the community's shared

Cover of Lowry's Holocaust novel **Number the Stars,** *featuring a photograph by the author.* (Bantam Doubleday Dell Books for Young Readers, 1998. Cover photograph by Lois Lowry. Used by permission of Random House Children's Books, a division of Random House, Inc.)

Cover of Lowry's provocative dystopian novel **Gathering Blue,** *a companion story to* **The Giver.** (Copyright © 2000 by Lois Lowry. Reproduced by permission of Houghton Mifflin Harcourt Publishing. All rights reserved.)

values. Now a teen, he has been guided toward adulthood by a blind man named Seer. Increasingly politically aware as he matures, Matty senses that a change has come over those in The Village whom he once respected. Rather than welcoming newcomers, most in the community have become greedy, jealous, and unwilling to share their good fortune. Instead, they are now determined to wall themselves off from the rest of the world. A young man named Leader, guide of The Village (in fact, Jonas from *The Giver*), is also concerned about this change. When Village members vote to prohibit the influx of outsiders, Matty is sent by Leader to find Seer's daughter Kira (from *Gathering Blue*). Making his way through the harsh forest environment outside the Village, the teen hopes to reunite Kira with her father before the opportunity is lost forever. Although Kira is lame and the journey to Seer is arduous, she selflessly refuses to take advantage of Matty's skill as a healer because each use of this power seems to cause Matty harm.

Calling *Messenger* "simply and beautifully written" in her review for the *New York Times Book Review*, Rochman noted the book's position as the third volume in Lowry's loosely knit trilogy. In rereading both *The Giver*

and *Gathering Blue,* she observed that these two volumes contain "unresolved endings." "While *Messenger* may tie the three stories together just a little too neatly," Rochman noted, "it is still far from a sweet resolution. Up to the last anguished page, Lois Lowry shows how hard it is to build community," leaving readers with the same frustration that her main characters experience. "Lowry's many fans will welcome this return to the fascinating world she has created," wrote Paula Rohrlick in a *Kliatt* review of *Messenger,* the critic also citing "the provocative issues she raises" in the suspenseful novel. "Lowry's skillful writing imbues the story with a strong sense of foreboding," concluded Marie Orlando in a review of the novel for *School Library Journal,* while a *Kirkus Reviews* critic predicted that "readers will be absorbed in thought and wonder long after" the final page of *Messenger* is turned.

In *The Silent Boy* Lowry again takes up a solemn theme, introducing Katy Thatcher, Kate's physician father, and their life in a small New England town during the early part of the twentieth century. Peggy Stoltz, a local farm girl hired to help in the Thatcher home, is Katy's close friend. Peggy has a brother named Jacob as well as a sister, Nell, who works in the home next to the Thatchers'. Jacob, considered an "imbecile" or "touched in the head," is a gentle thirteen year old who never speaks but has a profound ability to handle and communicate with animals. After Katy knits together a tenuous friendship with Jacob, she begins to sense the wonder in his affinity with animals. Meanwhile, the girl is dealing with her upcoming seventh birthday, and with the arrival of a new sibling. Nell also expects a baby, the result of a relationship with her employers' son. Ultimately, things come to a head after Jacob disappears with Nell's unwanted and unnamed infant and the baby then turns up dead. Katy cannot believe that the sensitive and gentle Jacob could commit an act of murder, even one that, in his mind, may have been completely acceptable or even desirable. Jacob is eventually incarcerated in an asylum, leaving Katy haunted by the tragedy of his life. "Lowry's graceful, lively prose is dense with historical details," remarked Gillian Engberg in a *Booklist* review of *The Silent Boy.* Ellen Fader, writing in *School Library Journal,* noted of the novel that "Lowry excels in developing strong and unique characters and in showing Katy's life in a small town that changes around her as the first telephones and automobiles arrive." The novel's storyline "balances humor and generosity with the obstacles and injustice of Katy's world," a *Publishers Weekly* reviewer wrote, while a *Kirkus Reviews* writer deemed *The Silent Boy* "a tragedy deftly foreshadowed."

While *The Giver* and its sequels were classified by several reviewers as science fiction, in her novel *Gossamer* Lowry steps clearly into the realm of fantasy. Dubbed "spellbinding" by a *Publishers Weekly* contributor, the story introduces Littlest One, a young creature who, as a member of a race of dream givers, is learning to practice her ancestral art. In touching the objects that make up a certain human's day, dream givers collect threads of memories, sounds, and images, using these to weave together the dreams that fill the minds of the sleeping. Working with experienced teacher Thin Elderly, Littlest is assigned to practice her art in the home of an elderly foster mother, where she comes in contact with John, the woman's troubled young charge. As her skills develop, the dream giver creates images that reflect the healthy relationship developing between John and his foster mother, but as part of her work she must also fight off the efforts of the Sinisteeds, who view John as the perfect vehicle for their horrific nightmares. Reviewing *Gossamer*, the *Publishers Weekly* contributor cited Lowry for her "exquisite, at times mesmerizing writing," while Lauralyn Persson wrote in *School Library Journal* that the author's "carefully plotted fantasy has inner logic and conviction." Noting that *Gossamer* is "written with Lowry's characteristic elegance and economy, and with her usual attentiveness to the internal consistency of her imaginary world," James Hynes concluded in his *New York Times Book Review* appraisal that the novel is "enormously entertaining and . . . very moving."

A humorous mock-melodrama in the tradition of writers such as Edward Gorey and Lemony Snicket, *The Willoughbys* takes readers to the home of a family whose four children—Timothy, Jane, and twins Barnaby A and Barnaby B—are as equally interested in being without parents as their parents are in being without children. As readers quickly learn, the Willoughby children are justified in wishing to be orphaned: their parents are truly uncaring and unparentlike. When Mom and Dad leave on a vacation, they try to sell their home with the children still in it. As the story's odd sequence of events plays out, traditional plot devices such as a foundling infant left on the children's doorstep add to the humor of Lowry's nostalgic story. A "lollipop of witty metafiction," according to *Horn Book* contributor Sarah Ellis, *The Willoughbys* is chock full of Gothic-novel conventions; for example, "the glossary of terms such as 'lugubrious' and 'obsequious' at the end of the book is absolutely choice," according to *School Library Journal* critic Tim Wadhams. Although the novel marks a distinct change of pace for its author, "readers who are willing to give themselves up entirely to the shy foolishness will relish [her] . . . sparkling smart satire," asserted a *Kirkus Reviews* writer, and Phelan remarked of *The Willoughbys* that the story's "sly humor and . . . deadpan zaniness give literary conventions an ironic twist, with hilarious results."

Another lighthearted novel, *The Birthday Ball,* teams Lowry with noted illustrator Jules Feiffer in a story about a princess faced with the choice of a suitor. Soon-to-be-sixteen year old Princess Patricia Priscilla (Pat for short) views her upcoming birthday ball with concern, knowing that none of the three suitors who desire her hand ranks as a Prince Charming. Determined to have one last experience of freedom, Princess Pat trades places with a palace maid and tries to fit in as a new

Lowry teams up with cartoonist Jules Feiffer on the young-adult novel **The Birthday Ball** (Illustration copyright © 2010 by Jules Feiffer. Reproduced by permission of Houghton Mifflin Harcourt Publishing Company. All rights reserved.)

student at the local school. In addition to making friends among classmates who do not know she is a member of royalty, Pat also discovers what may be true love in the person of the attractive young schoolteacher. Praising *The Birthday Ball* for its "wonderfully swirly, evocative, [and] energetic" cartoon illustrations, Geri Diorio added in *School Library Journal* that Lowry's text serves up "a captivating but gentle fairy tale with memorable characters." In *Booklist* Phelan noted the author's "dry wit" and "idiosyncratic" cast, adding that the "neatly constructed plot" of *The Birthday Ball* contains "plot twists [that] bring a few surprises." The author exhibits a "knack for cleverly turning familiar stories on their heels," according to a *Publishers Weekly* contributor, and in the *New York Times Book Review* Krystyna Poray Goddu observed that Lowry's "lighthearted concoction" is filled "with wordplay and alliteration," and introduces "a strong-minded, warm and intelligent girl."

Lowry's experiences as a grandmother have inspired her to create the picture books *Crow Call* and *Bless This Mouse*, the latter illustrated by Eric Rohmann. Nostalgic paintings by Bagram Ibatoulline bring to life the story in *Crow Call,* which captures a memory from the author's childhood. Lizzie is nine years old and excited to have her father back from World War II. Father and daughter have been separated so long that they hardly know each other, and both try hard to please the other. During a morning helping her father hunt the crows that seem bent on destroying their fields of ripening crops the two build a special bond, as Lizzie represses her apprehension about shooting the rapacious creatures and her father respects her unspoken wishes and never fires his gun. "Remarkable, atmospheric illustrations reveal the subdued, cool autumn colors of crunchy dried grass, softly hued sky, and dark leafless trees," wrote Maryann H. Owen, appraising Ibatoulline's artwork in her *School Library Journal* review. In *Crow Call* "Lowry offers a story where the specific becomes universal," noted Ilene Cooper in *Booklist,* and a *Publishers Weekly* contributor deemed the tale "a loving representation of a relationship between parent and child, and an elegy to a less ironic era." "Beautifully written," according to a *Kirkus Reviews* writer, *Crow Call* "reads much like a traditional short story," gradually unfolding in a "narrative [that is] . . . dense with sensory details."

As Lowry's career has stretched through the years from parenthood to grandparenthood, she has collected experiences ranging from joyful to tragic, and she sifts through this lifetime of remembrances in *Looking Back: A Book of Memories.* Resembling a conversation with a friend, the book is "much more intimate and personal than many traditional memoirs," according to *School Library Journal* contributor Barbara Scotto, while a *Publishers Weekly* reviewer noted that "a compelling and inspirational portrait of the author emerges from these vivid snapshots of life's joyful, sad, and surprising moments."

"I tend to see the world of children as fraught with pitfalls and dangers and at the same time blessed by innocence and unfettered expectations," Lowry told an *Instructor* interviewer, while discussing her approach to writing for children. "Often we are unaware of, or deluded about, the real world of children. Too many adults look back through rose-tinted glasses to a sunlit place of unmitigated happiness. Kids, on the other hand, know what it's really like; they understand the cruelties that children inflict on one another and the hypocrisies that adults practice. Literature for the young has to address these things, I think, or risk being dishonest. A surprising number of adults prefer the dishonest literature, that which pretends a pain-free past."

Biographical and Critical Sources

BOOKS

American Women Writers, 2nd edition, St. James Press (Detroit, MI), 2000.

Authors and Artists for Young Adults, Volume 32, Gale (Detroit, MI), 2000.
Beacham's Guide to Literature for Young Adults, Beacham Publishing (Osprey, FL), 1990, Volume 4, 1990, Volume 6, 1994.
Chaston, Joel D., *Lois Lowry,* Twayne (New York, NY), 1997.
Children's Literature Review, Gale (Detroit, MI), Volume 6, 1984, Volume 46, 1997, Volume 72, pp. 192-206.
Dictionary of Literary Biography, Volume 52: *American Writers for Children since 1960: Fiction,* Gale (Detroit, MI), 1987, pp. 249-261.
Green, Carol Hurd, and Mary Grimley Mason, editors, *American Women Writers,* Volume 5, Continuum Publishing (New York, NY), 1994.
Lowry, Lois, *Looking Back: A Book of Memories,* Houghton Mifflin (Boston, MA), 1998.
St. James Guide to Young-Adult Writers, 2nd edition, St. James Press (Detroit, MI), 1999.
Silvey, Anita, editor, *Children's Books and Their Creators,* Houghton Mifflin (Boston, MA), 1995.
Something about the Author Autobiography Series, Volume 3, Gale (Detroit, MI), 1986, pp. 131-146.

PERIODICALS

Book, May-June, 2003, review of *Gooney Bird Greene,* p. 31.
Booklist, October 15, 1979, Barbara Elleman, review of *Anastasia Krupnik,* p. 354; September 1, 1982, Barbara Elleman, review of *Anastasia at Your Service,* p. 46; September 1, 1987, review of *Anastasia's Chosen Career,* pp. 66-67; March 1, 1990, Ilene Cooper, review of *Your Move, J.P.!,* p. 1345; April 1, 1991, Stephanie Zvirin, review of *Anastasia at This Address,* p. 1564; October 1, 1995, Carolyn Phelan, review of *Anastasia, Absolutely,* p. 761; November 1, 1997, Ellen Mandel, review of *Stay!: Keeper's Story,* p. 472; November 1, 1998, Carolyn Phelan, review of *Looking Back,* p. 490; July, 1, 1999, Stephanie Zvirin, review of *Zooman Sam,* p. 1947; September 15, 1999, review of *Looking Back,* p. 254; June 1, 2000, Ilene Cooper, review of *Gathering Blue,* p. 1896; September 1, 2002, GraceAnne A. DeCandido, review of *Gooney Bird Greene,* p. 125; April 15, 2003, Gillian Engberg, review of *The Silent Boy,* p. 1462; February 15, 2004, Hazel Rochman, review of *Messenger,* p. 1056; March 1, 2005, Hazel Rochman, review of *Gooney Bird and the Room Mother,* p. 1197; February 15, 2006, Hazel Rochman, review of *Gossamer,* p. 99; January 1, 2007, Ilene Cooper, review of *Gooney the Fabulous,* p. 81; June 1, 2007, Kathleen Isaacs, review of *Shining On: Eleven Star Authors' Illuminating Stories,* p. 62; February 15, 2008, Carolyn Phelan, review of *The Willoughbys,* p. 81; February 1, 2009, Carolyn Phelan, review of *Gooney Bird Is So Absurd,* p. 43; October 15, 2009, Ilene Cooper, review of *Crow Call,* p. 50; March 1, 2010, Carolyn Phelan, review of *The Birthday Ball,* p. 72.
Book Report, May, 1999, review of *Looking Back,* p. 73; January 2001, Kay Bowes, review of *Gathering Blue,* p. 58.

Books for Keeps, January, 2002, review of *Gathering Blue,* p. 26.

Bulletin of the Center for Children's Books, January, 1980, Zena Sutherland, review of *Anastasia Krupnik,* p. 99; May, 1984, Zena Sutherland, review of *Anastasia, Ask Your Analyst,* p. 169; March, 1990, Ruth Ann Smith, review of *Your Move, J.P.!,* p. 169; September, 1995, Deborah Stevenson, review of *Anastasia, Absolutely,* pp. 20-21; January, 1998, Janice Del Negro, review of *Stay!,* p. 165; January, 1999, Janice Del Negro, review of *Looking Back,* p. 174; September, 1999, review of *Zooman Sam,* p. 21; June, 2004, Krista Hutley, review of *Messenger,* p. 427; July-August, 2006, April Spisak, review of *Gossamer,* p. 507.

Catholic Library World, September, 1999, review of *See You Around, Sam,* p. 33.

Childhood Education (annual), 2010, Terre Sychterz, review of *Crow Call,* p. 337.

Children's Bookwatch, March, 1999, review of *Looking Back,* p. 6; December, 1999, review of *Zooman Sam,* p. 4; March, 2001, review of *Looking Back,* p. 8.

Children's Literature (annual), 2004, Don Latham, "Discipline and Its Discontents: A Foucauldian Reading of 'The Giver,'" pp. 134-151.

Christian Science Monitor, January 14, 1980, Brad Owens, review of *Anastasia Krupnik,* p. B6; March 1, 1985, Lyn Littlfield Hoopes, review of *Us and Uncle Fraud,* p. 65; May 1, 1987, Betsy Hearne, "Families Shaped by Love, Not Convention," pp. B3-B4.

Five Owls, September-October, 1993, Gary D. Schmidt, review of *The Giver,* pp. 14-15; March, 2001, review of *Gathering Blue,* p. 92.

Horn Book, August, 1977, Mary M. Burns, review of *A Summer to Die,* p. 451; December, 1979, Ann A. Flowers, review of *Anastasia Krupnik,* p. 663; October, 1981, Mary M. Burns, review of *Anastasia Again!,* pp. 535-536; September-October, 1985, Ann A. Flowers, review of *Anastasia on Her Own,* pp. 556-557; May-June, 1986, Mary M. Burns, review of *Anastasia Has the Answers,* pp. 327-328; July-August, 1987, Ann A. Flowers, review of *Rabble Starkey,* pp. 463-465; May-June, 1989, Mary M. Burns, review of *Number the Stars,* p. 371; March-April, 1990, Ethel R. Twitchell, review of *Your Move, J.P.!,* pp. 201-202; July-August, 1990, Shirley Haley-James, "Lois Lowry"; November-December, 1993, Patty Campbell, "The Sand in the Oyster," pp. 717-721; July-August, 1994, Lois Lowry, "Newbery Medal Acceptance," pp. 414-422, and Walter Lorraine, "Lois Lowry," pp. 423-426; November-December, 1995, Maeve Visser Knoth, review of *Anastasia, Absolutely,* p. 761; September-October, 1996, Roger Sutton, review of *See You Around, Sam!,* p. 597; January-February, 1998, Roger Sutton, review of *Stay!,* pp. 76-77; January, 1999, Peter D. Sieruta, review of *Looking Back,* p. 87; September, 1999, Roger Sutton, review of *Zooman Sam,* p. 613; September, 2000, Roger Sutton, review of *Gathering Blue,* p. 573; September-October, 2002, Peter D. Sieruta, review of *Gooney Bird Greene,* pp. 575-577; May-June, 2004, Betty Carter, review of *Messenger,* p. 332; July-August, 2006, review of *Gossamer,* p. 446; March-April, 2008, Sarah Ellis, review

of *The Willoughbys,* p. 217; May-June, 2009, Robin L. Smith, review of *Gooney Bird Is So Absurd,* p. 320; March-April, 2010 Christine M. Heppermann, review of *The Birthday Ball,* p. 64; March-April, 2010, "May Hill Arbuthnot Honor Lecture," p. 98.

Instructor, May, 1999, reviews of *The Give,* and *See You Around, Sam,* both p. 16; May, 2001, review of *The Giver,* p. 37; March-April 2008, interview with Lowry, p. 72.

Journal of Adolescent and Adult Literacy, September, 2004, Lori Atkins Goodson, review of *The Silent Boy,* p. 75, and Jo Ann Yazzie, review of *Messenger,* p. 80.

Junior Bookshelf, August, 1979, Mary Hobbs, review of *A Summer to Die,* pp. 224-225.

Kirkus Reviews, April 1, 1986, review of *Anastasia Has the Answers,* pp. 546-547; March 1, 1987, review of *Rabble Starkey,* p. 374; March 15, 1991, review of *Anastasia at This Address,* p. 396; March 1, 1993, review of *The Giver,* p. 301; October 15, 1997, review of *Stay!,* p. 1584; July 15, 1999, review of *Zooman Sam,* p. 1135; March 15, 2003, review of *The Silent Boy,* p. 472; April 1, 2004, review of *Messenger,* p. 333; April 1, 2005, review of *Gooney Bird and the Room Mother,* p. 420; March 1, 2006, review of *Gossamer,* p. 235; April 1, 2007, review of *Gooney the Fabulous;* April 15, 2007, review of *Shining On;* February 15, 2008, review of *The Willoughbys;* September 15, 2009, review of *Crow Call.*

Kliatt, March, 2004, Paula Rohrlick, review of *Messenger,* p. 12; July, 2007, Joanna Solomon, review of *Shining On,* p. 36.

New York Times Book Review, May 21, 1989, Edith Milton, "Escape from Copenhagen," p. 32; October 31, 1993, Karen Ray, review of *The Giver,* p. 26; January 14, 1996, Michael Cart, review of *Anastasia, Absolutely,* p. 23; October 15, 1998, review of *Looking Back,* p. 1534; November 19, 2003, Elizabeth Spires, review of *Gathering Blue,* p. 57; May 16, 2004, Hazel Rochman, "Something's Rotten in Utopia," p. 17; May 14, 2006, James Hynes, review of *Gossamer,* p. 21; June 20, 2010, Krystyna Poray Goddu, review of *The Birthday Ball,* p. 12.

Observer (London, England), October 21, 2001, review of *Gathering Blue,* p. 16.

Publishers Weekly, February 21, 1986, interview with Lowry, pp. 152-153; November 8, 1985, review of *Switcharound,* p. 60; March 15, 1991, review of *Anastasia at This Address,* p. 58; July 28, 1997, review of *Stay!,* p. 75; August 24, 1998, review of *Looking Back,* p. 58; April 5, 1999, review of *Stay!,* p. 243; September 13, 1999, review of *Zooman Sam,* p. 85; July 31, 2000, review of *Gathering Blue,* p. 96; March 24, 2003, review of *The Silent Boy,* p. 76, and Ingrid Roper, interview with Lowry, p. 77; March 6, 2006, review of *Gossamer,* p. 74; February 4, 2008, Lemony Snicket, review of *The Willoughbys,* p. 57; September 28, 2009, review of *Crow Call,* p. 64; February 15, 2010, review of *The Birthday Ball,* p. 131.

Reading Teacher, March, 2001, review of *Gathering Blue,* p. 638.

School Library Journal, May, 1977, Linda R. Silver, review of *A Summer to Die,* pp. 62-63; April, 1980,

Marilyn Singer, review of *Autumn Street,* pp. 125-126; October, 1981, Marilyn Kaye, review of *Anastasia Again!,* p. 144; October, 1983, Kathleen Brachmann, review of *The One Hundredth Thing about Caroline,* p. 160; February, 1986, Maria B. Salvadore, review of *Switcharound,* p. 87; September, 1987, Dudley B. Carlson, review of *Anastasia's Chosen Career,* p. 180; August, 1988, Trev Jones, review of *All about Sam,* p. 96; March, 1989, Louise L. Sherman, review of *Number the Stars,* p. 177; May, 1992, Marcia Hupp, review of *Attaboy, Sam!,* p. 114; October, 1996, Starr LaTronica, review of *See You Around, Sam!,* p. 102; October, 1997, Eva Mitnick, review of *Stay!,* p. 134; September, 1998, Barbara Scotto, review of *Looking Back,* p. 221; September, 1999, review of *Zooman Sam,* p. 193; August 2000, Ellen Fader, review of *Gathering Blue,* p. 186; November, 2002, Janet B. Bair, review of *Gooney Bird Greene,* pp. 129-130; April, 2003, Ellen Fader, review of *The Silent Boy,* pp. 164-165; April, 2004, Marie Orlando, review of *Messenger,* p. 50; May, 2005, Kristine M. Casper, review of *Gooney Bird and the Room Mother,* p. 90; May, 2006, Lauralyn Persson, review of *Gossamer,* p. 132; March, 2007, Julie Roach, review of *Gooney the Fabulous,* p. 176; April, 2007, Nancy P. Reeder, review of *Shining On,* p. 140; June, 2007, Anita Silvey, "The Unpredictable Lois Lowry" (interview), p. 38; April, 2008, Tim Wadham, review of *The Willoughbys,* p. 144; March, 2009, Bethany A. Lafferty, review of *Gooney Bird Is So Absurd,* p. 121; October, 2009, Maryann H. Owen, review of *Crow Call,* p. 98; March, 2010, Geri Diorio, review of *The Birthday Ball,* p. 162.

Voice of Youth Advocates, April, 1999, review of *Looking Back,* p. 76; April, 2001, review of *Gathering Blue,* p. 12; February, 2005, review of *Messenger,* p. 443.

ONLINE

Books 'n' Bytes Web site, http://www.booksnbytes.com/ (May 28, 2003), Harriet Klausner, review of *Gathering Blue.*

Lois Lowry Home Page, http://www.loislowry.com (May 20, 2011).

Lois Lowry Web log, http://loislowry.typepad.com (May 20, 2011).

Rambles Online, http://www.rambles.net/ (May 28, 2003), Donna Scanlon, review of *Gathering Blue.*

OTHER

Good Conversation!: A Talk with Lois Lowry (video), Tim Podell Productions, 2002.

*　　*　　*

LUM, Bernice

Personal

Born in Toronto, Ontario, Canada. *Education:* Sheridan College, B.F.A. (graphic design), 1984.

Addresses

Home—Toronto, Ontario, Canada. *Agent*—Marilyn Malin, 5/33 Ferncroft Av., London NW3 7PG, England. *E-mail*—bernice@bernicelum.com.

Career

Illustrator. Worked variously as a designer and bicycle courier; freelance illustrator in England, 1988-90, and Canada, beginning 1997. *Exhibitions:* Work included in exhibitions at Ogilvy & Mathers Gallery, Toronto, Ontario, Canada, 2002; John Steinberg & Associates, Toronto, 2003-04; Drake Hotel, Toronto, 2004; X-Space Gallery, Toronto, 2005; Omy Gallery, Toronto, 2006; and Spin Gallery, Toronto, 2006.

Awards, Honors

Association of Illustrators UK honourable mention designation, 1996, and Children's Book of the Year shortlist, 1997, both for "Stanley the Dog" series; New Brunswick Early Childhood Literary Award, 1999, for *Pippin Takes a Bath* by K.V. Johansen; Best Children's Book of the Year, Bank Street College of Education, 2003, for *My Pet Hamster* by Anne Rockwell; Portfolio.com gold, silver, bronze, and merit awards, all 2004, gold award and three merit awards, all 2005, and silver award and two merit awards, all 2006.

Writings

SELF-ILLUSTRATED; "STANLEY THE DOG" SERIES

If I Had a Dog, Bloomsbury Children's Books (London, England), 1995.

If My Dog Had a Job, Bloomsbury Children's Books (London, England), 1995.

If My Dog Went on Holiday, Bloomsbury Children's Books (London, England), 1995.

If My Dog Could Drive, Bloomsbury Children's Books (London, England), 1995.

ILLUSTRATOR

Kate Lum, *Stanley's No-Hic! Machine,* Bloomsbury Children's Books (London, England), 1997.

Vic Parker, *Funny Bunny's Funny Day,* Hodder Children's (London, England), 1997.

K.V. Johansen, *Pippin Takes a Bath,* Kids Can Press (Toronto, Ontario, Canada), 1999.

K.V. Johansen, *Pippin and the Bones,* Kids Can Press (Toronto, Ontario, Canada), 2000.

Nicky Farthing, reteller, *The Knock-out Story of David and Goliath,* Lion Children's (London, England), 2000.

K.V. Johansen, *Pippin and Pudding,* Kids Can Press (Toronto, Ontario, Canada), 2001.

Anne Rockwell, *My Pet Hamster,* HarperCollins (New York, NY), 2002.

Stuart J. Murphy, *Three Little Firefighters,* HarperCollins (New York, NY), 2003.

Stuart J. Murphy, *Mighty Maddie,* HarperCollins (New York, NY), 2004.

Anne Adeney, *Whoops!,* 2004.

Ellen Warwick, *Stuff for Your Space,* Kids Can Press (Toronto, Ontario, Canada), 2004.

Ellen Warwick, *Stuff to Hold Your Stuff,* Kids Can Press (Toronto, Ontario, Canada), 2004.

Ellen Warwick, *In-Jean-uity,* Kids Can Press (Toronto, Ontario, Canada), 2006.

Andrew Fusik Peters, *Spies Unlimited: A Secret Stash of Poems, Jokes, Riddles, and Plots,* Oxford University Press (Oxford, England), 2006.

Andrew Delahunty, *Oxford First Dictionary,* Oxford University Press (Oxford, England), 2007.

Nancy Krulik, *Fire Alarm!,* Scholastic, Inc. (New York, NY), 2009.

Nancy Krulik, *First Day,* Scholastic, Inc. (New York, NY), 2009.

Kathleen Fraser, Laura Fraser, and Mary Fraser, *The 175 Best Camp Games: A Handbook for Leaders,* Boston Mills Press (New York, NY), 2009.

Books featuring Lum's art have been translated into French.

ILLUSTRATOR; "TWO BOLD BABIES" SERIES

Anne Liens, *Hey Look!,* Bloomsbury Children's Books (London, England), 1996.

Anne Liens, *Hey Listen!,* Bloomsbury Children's Books (London, England), 1996.

Anne Liens, *What's That Smell?,* Bloomsbury Children's Books (London, England), 1996.

Anne Liens, *Feel This!,* Bloomsbury Children's Books (London, England), 1996.

ILLUSTRATOR; "RUBY ROGERS" CHAPTER-BOOK SERIES

Sue Limb, *Ruby Rogers Is a Waste of Space,* Bloomsbury (London, England), 2006.

Sue Limb, *Yeah, Whatever . . . ,* Bloomsbury (London, England), 2006.

Sue Limb, *In Your Dreams,* Bloomsbury (London, England), 2008.

Sue Limb, *Party Pooper,* Bloomsbury (London, England), 2008.

Sue Limb, *Tell Me about It,* Bloomsbury (London, England), 2008.

Sue Limb, *Would You Believe It?,* Bloomsbury (London, England), 2008.

Sue Limb, *Get Me out of Here!,* Bloomsbury (London, England), 2008.

Sue Limb, *Who Are You Looking At?,* Bloomsbury (London, England), 2008.

Sidelights

Illustrator Beatrice Lum was born in Canada but worked in the United Kingdom for several years while she was establishing her career as a children's book author and

illustrator. Since releasing her entertaining "Stanley the Dog" picture books—*If I Had a Dog, If My Dog Had a Job, If My Dog Went on Holiday,* and *If My Dog Could Drive*—in the mid-1990s, Lum has focused exclusively on creating artwork for stories by other writers, such as K.V. Johansen, Sue Limb, Stuart J. Murphy, Anne Rockwell, Nancy Krulik, and Kathleen Fraser. In addition to fictional stories, she also crafts the artwork for several how-to books by Ellen Warwick, among them *Stuff for Your Space* and *Stuff to Hold Your Stuff. In-Jean-uity,* another book by Warwick, guides creative teens in the art of recrafting worn-out denim jeans into wearable art, and here Lum's "bright, colorful, and exciting" illustrations are a highlight, according to *Resource Links* critic Heather Empey.

Lum was born and raised in Toronto, Ontario, and earned a design degree at Sheridan College. In 1988,

Bernice Lum creates the creative cartoon art for Ellen Warwick's crafty teen guidebook **In-Jean-uity.** (Illustration copyright © 2006 by Bernice Lum. Reproduced by permission of Kids Can Press Ltd., Toronto.)

after freelancing for local design firms for four years, she moved to London and expanded her client base. The rise of computer-assisted graphics changed Lum's prospects in the field, however, and she was eventually faced with a decision: either go digital or find another market for her art. She worked as a bike courier while scouting out other options, and she found those in the picture-book field.

In her first illustration project, Lum teamed up with Johansen to produce the first of three stories featuring a yellow-furred puppy and its human friend Mabel. In *Pippin Takes a Bath* the dog is cleaned up after a day of outdoor play, while a search outside yields a surprise in *Pippin and the Bones*. Pippin the dog meets Pudding the cat in *Pippin and Pudding,* as the friendly puppy befriends a lost kitten and brings it home to Mabel. Reviewing this third book in the series, Judy Cottrell wrote in *Resource Links* that Lum's "watercolor and marker" art "aptly captures the essence and emotions" in Johansen's story, while Shelley Townsend-Hudson remarked on the engaging pairing of "cheery, cartoonlike illustrations and . . . chatty prose" in her *Booklist* review of *Pippin Takes a Bath.*

Another early work, *Stanley's No-Hic! Machine,* allowed Lum to collaborate with her sister in law, Canadian children's author Kate Lum, while her work with Murphy on the picture books *Three Little Firefighters* and *Mighty Maddie* help introduce math concepts to young readers. Her "childlike line drawings with bright colors give readers a sense of action" to *Mighty Maddie,* making it an "appealing book," according to *School Library Journal* critic Erlene Bishop Killeen. Another picture-book project, *My Pet Hamster,* pairs Lum's cartoon art with Rockwell's text describing the steps required to love and care for a tiny household pet. Citing the artist's "large, bold illustrations" for *My Pet Ham-*

ster, Pamela K. Bomboy added in *School Library Journal* that Lum's depiction of the roly-poly hamster is "adorable" and rendered in an engagingly naïf fashion.

Biographical and Critical Sources

PERIODICALS

Booklist, November 15, 1999, Shelley Townsend-Hudson, review of *Pippin Takes a Bath,* p. 636; August, 2000, Susan Dove Lempke, review of *Pippin and the Bones,* p. 2147; June 1, 2006, Stephanie Zvirin, review of *In-Jean-uity,* p. 66; December 15, 2006, Stephanie Zvirin, review of *Stuff to Hold Your Stuff,* p. 53.

Publishers Weekly, August 23, 1999, review of *Pippin Takes a Bath,* p. 57.

School Library Journal, August, 2000, Elaine Lesh Morgan, review of *Pippin and the Bones,* p. 158; December, 2002, Pamela K. Bomboy, review of *My Pet Hamster,* p. 128; January, 2004, Lynda Ritterman, review of *Three Little Firefighters,* p. 120; April, 2004, Augusta R. Malvagno, review of *Stuff for Your Space,* p. 181; October, 2004, Erlene Bishop Killeen, review of *Mighty Maddie,* p. 146; June, 2006, Cynde Suite, review of *In-Jean-uity,* p. 188; March, 2007, G. Alyssa Parkinson, review of *Stuff to Hold Your Stuff,* p. 236.

Resource Links, February, 2000, review of *Pippin Takes a Bath,* p. 4; June, 2000, review of *Pippin and the Bones,* p. 3; April, 2001, Judy Cottrell, review of *Pippin and Pudding,* p. 4; June, 2006, Heather Empey, review of *In-Jean-uity,* p. 20; February, 2007, Claire Hazzard, review of *Stuff to Hold Your Stuff,* p. 27.

ONLINE

Bernice Lum Home Page, http://www.bernicelum.com (February 27, 2011).*

M

MARTON, Jirina 1946-

Personal

Born April 19, 1946, in Liberec, Czechoslovakia (now Czech Republic); immigrated to Canada, 1985; married; children: Michèle. *Education:* School of Applied Arts (Prague, Czechoslovakia), degree (wood sculpture), 1964.

Addresses

Home—Colbourne, Ontario, Canada. *E-mail*—jmarton1@sympatico.ca.

Career

Author and illustrator of children's books. Worked variously as a flower vendor, cleaning lady, factory worker, graphic designer, assistant seamstress, painter, picture framer, and gallery guide, 1964-79; Atelier Y. Agam, Paris, France, painter, 1979-80; Librairie Larousse, Paris, layout artist and designer, 1980-85; freelance illustrator and writer, beginning 1985. Scene painter and designer for *Brundibar* (children's opera), produced in Toronto, Ontario, Canada, 1996. *Exhibitions:* Work exhibited in Europe, Canada, and Japan.

Member

Canadian Society of Children's Authors, Illustrators, and Performers, Writers' Union of Canada, Bureau des Regroupement des Artistes Visuel de l'Ontario (BRAVO-SUD).

Awards, Honors

Grand prize, Itabashi Picture Book Contest, 1995, for *Flowers for Mom;* Amelia Howard-Gibbon Award finalist, Canadian Association of Children's Librarians, 1997, for *Lady Kaguya's Secret;* Governor General's Award for Children's Literature—Illustration (English language) finalist, 2007, for *Arctic Adventures* by Raquel Rivera, and award, 2009, for *Bella's Tree* by Janet Russell.

Jirina Marton (Reproduced by permission.)

Writings

SELF-ILLUSTRATED

Flores para Mamá, Annick Press (Toronto, Ontario, Canada), 1983, translation published as *Flowers for Mom,* 1991.

L'eau (wordless), Bohem Press (Zurich, Switzerland), 1986.

La ville grise (Japanese translation), Gakken (Tokyo, Japan), 1986.

Midnight Visit at Molly's House, Annick Press (Toronto, Ontario, Canada), 1988.

I'll Do It Myself, Annick Press (Toronto, Ontario, Canada), 1989.

Mitzy (in Japanese), Gakken (Tokyo, Japan), 1990.

Amelia's Celebration, Annick Press (Toronto, Ontario, Canada), 1992.

You Can Go Home Again, Annick Press (Toronto, Ontario, Canada), 1994.

(Reteller) *Lady Kaguya's Secret: A Japanese Tale,* Annick Press (Toronto, Ontario, Canada), 1997.

Author's work has been translated into Spanish.

ILLUSTRATOR

Allen Morgan, *Nicole's Boat: A Good-night Story,* Annick Press (Toronto, Ontario, Canada), 1986.

Emil Genouvrier, *Petit Benjamin* (in Japanese), Gakken (Tokyo, Japan), 1986.

Joan Buchanan, *Nothing Else but Yams for Supper!,* Black Moss Press (Windsor, Ontario, Canada), 1988.

Patricia Quinlan, *Kevin's Magic Ring,* Black Moss Press (Windsor, Ontario, Canada), 1989.

Patricia Quinlan, *Emma's Sea Journey,* Annick Press (Windsor, Ontario, Canada), 1991.

Maryke Barnes, *Setting Wonder Free,* Annick Press (Toronto, Ontario, Canada), 1992.

Vera Eizenberger, *The Little Plane Goes on a Journey,* Gakken (Tokyo, Japan), 1999.

Bob Barton, reteller *The Bear Says North: Tales from Northern Lands,* Groundwood Books (Toronto, Ontario, Canada), 2003.

Janet Russell, *Bella's Tree,* Groundwood Books (Toronto, Ontario, Canada), 2007.

Raquel Rivera, *Arctic Adventures: Tales from the Lives of Inuit Artists,* Groundwood Books (Toronto, Ontario, Canada), 2007.

Jean E. Pendziwol, *Marja's Skis,* Groundwood Books (Toronto, Ontario, Canada), 2007.

ILLUSTRATOR; "ADVENTURES OF FERGIE THE FROG" SERIES

Nancy Cocks, *Fergie Tries to Fly,* Novalis (Ottawa, Ontario, Canada), 2002.

Nancy Cocks, *Where, Oh Where, Is Fergie?,* Novalis (Ottawa, Ontario, Canada), 2002.

Nancy Cocks, *Nobody Loves Fergie,* Novalis (Ottawa, Ontario, Canada), 2002.

Nancy Cocks, *Fergie Counts His Blessings,* Novalis (Ottawa, Ontario, Canada), 2002.

Nancy Cocks, *Fergie Goes to Grandma's,* Novalis (Ottawa, Ontario, Canada), 2002.

Nancy Cocks, *Fergie Has a Birthday Party,* Novalis (Ottawa, Ontario, Canada), 2002.

Nancy Cocks, *Fergie Cleans Up,* Novalis (Ottawa, Ontario, Canada), 2002.

Nancy Cocks, *You Can Count on Fergie,* Novalis (Ottawa, Ontario, Canada), 2002.

Sidelights

Canadian-based author and illustrator Jirina Marton trained in her native Czechoslovakia by studying wood sculpture. A move to France allowed Marton to pursue painting in Paris and also gain experience as a layout artist while working for Librairie Larousse, a major French publisher. Soon after she immigrated to Canada in 1985, she was awarded a job illustrating Allen Morgan's picture book *Nicole's Boat: A Good-night Story,* and this work introduced her at to Canadian publishers. In the years since, Marton has continued to experiment with different media, moving from oil pastels to acrylic and then to water color, and she has created original, self-illustrated stories in addition to crafting artwork for text by such authors as Patricia Quinlan, Jean E. Pendziwol, Janet Russell, Bob Barton, and Nancy Cocks. In 2009 Marton won the Governor General's Award for children's book illustrations for her work on *Bella's Tree,* a story by Russell that captures a girl's search for the perfect Christmas tree for her grandmother in austere oil pastel art. Reviewing the award-winning picture book, *School Library Journal* critic Eva Mitnick cited Marton's "full-page, almost-impressionistic oil pastel illustrations" as "evocative."

Marton has long been attracted to art. "At the age of two and a half, I accomplished my first art work," she once recalled to *SATA.* "I was painting on the freshly painted kitchen wall. Up to the present day I remember the pleasure and emotions when applying the colors to the wet wall. I wasn't thinking about becoming an artist. I didn't need to, as, at this particular moment, I was an

Marton's self-illustrated picture books include the family-centered story in You Can Go Home Again. (Illustration copyright © 1994 by Jirina Marton. Reproduced by permission of Annick Press Ltd. All rights reserved.)

artist." While Marton was happy with her artwork, her mother had a different opinion. "She, instead of appreciating my artwork, called the painter to cover it with several layers of paint. After this painful experience, I started to investigate other fields for my future career." "I decided to be a prima ballerina, so my mother took me to a ballet school," she continued. "The teacher, after observing my natural dancing ability, told my mother not to bring me any more, that it would be lost time. Even this experience didn't put down my *esprit*. At the age of five, I couldn't decide whether to be an opera singer, like my mother, or a violinist. This dilemma was resolved when I spent a month in hospital. I loved it so much that I wanted to be a doctor. Then I wanted to be an actor, an Indian, a teacher, and, back to square one, an artist."

Eventually, Marton returned to art and she studied wood sculpture at the School of Applied Arts in Prague, Czechoslovakia (now the Czech Republic). Work at a range of jobs would follow: "flower vendor, cleaning lady, workwoman in a factory, graphic designer, assistant seamstress, painter, picture framer, and guide in a gallery, to name a few. Then, one day, a friend asked me, 'Why don't you illustrate children's books?' And the biggest passion of my life was born."

Marton's first illustration project, *Nicole's Boat,* came about when an editor at Annick Press saw her work and suggested that she do the pictures for Morgan's tale. In *Nicole's Boat,* a father tells his daughter a bedtime story to settle her down to sleep. This "delightful tale," according to Patricia Fry in the *Canadian Review of Materials,* benefits from Marton's "certain whimsy and a richness of incidental detail in each picture." Fry went on to predict that *Nicole's Boat* will appeal to all fathers who fulfill bedtime-read-aloud duties for their children.

Midnight Visit at Molly's House, Marton's first English-language story, describes the night when the moon decides to descend to Earth's surface and go exploring. The picture book won praise for the excellence of Marton's text and illustrations, Pamela Miller Ness writing in *School Library Journal* that the author/illustrator "captures the magical imagination and curiosity of a child's fantasy world, while very gently sharing some adult philosophy." Writing in *Canadian Children's Literature,* Bernard Schwartz chose *Midnight Visit at Molly's House* as one of three Canadian children's books from the 1980s that especially exemplify "high quality text and illustration."

Marton also won praise for *I'll Do It Myself,* an original self-illustrated story that captures preschoolers' determined attempts to gain independence over their environment. Writing in *Canadian Children's Literature,* Allan Sheldon commended the work as a "very satisfying book" in which Marton "blend[s] extraordinarily delicate, filmy, sensuous textures . . . with a like pattern of delicate repetition in the text." The critic also noted that *I'll Do It Myself* contains "one of the most arresting set of endpapers in recent memory": a dream sequence featuring pink elephants.

Originally published in Spanish, Marton's story in *Flowers for Mom* focuses on a young boy's attempt to deliver a bouquet of flowers to his mother. *Canadian Review of Materials* reviewer Brenda Partridge praised the "colourful, childlike illustrations" in this picture book, while *Books in Canada* critic Rhea Tregebov dubbed Marton's illustrations "lovely." In *Amelia's Celebration,* another original, self-illustrated story by Marton, a girl who has been refused permission to stay up for her mother's birthday party manages to create her own adventure and celebration by slipping out of the house and spying on the grownups. After the party is over, Amelia is discovered and assured that *next time* she will be allowed to stay up. In *Quill & Quire* Anne Gilmore praised Marton's illustrations for *Amelia's Celebration,* writing that they "beautifully capture the quality of the night and the dreaminess of an outdoor evening party." *Canadian Review of Materials* contributor Partridge also commented favorably, noting that Marton's picture book benefits from both "rich descriptive passages" and a "narrative that flows easily."

In *You Can Go Home Again* Marton supports another strong story with evocative illustrations. Entranced by

Cover of **Lady Kaguya's Secret,** ***a story adapted from the Japanese and illustrated by Marton.*** (Illustration copyright © 1997 by Jirina Marton. Reproduced by permission of Annick Press.)

her mother's stories about her childhood in Prague, Annie convinces her parents to return to their homeland in hopes of finding some ebony elephants that her mother remembers playing with before the war. *Quill & Quire* reviewer Joanne Findon warmly commended this "lovely story" for its "spare text" and "wistful paintings," all of which "will appeal to a diverse audience of children—and to their parents as well." Noting that the "motif of the elephants provides both a focal point and a satisfying conclusion to the story," Marion Scott recommended *You Can Go Home Again* in *Canadian Review of Materials* for "serious consideration for libraries serving communities with a large multicultural element."

Lady Kaguya's Secret: A Japanese Tale retells a tenth-century Japanese story about the immortal Moon Princess's ill-fated love for a mortal emperor. When a poor bamboo-cutter finds a tiny baby girl hidden in the trunk of a glowing tree, he and his wife raise the child as their own, and she grows into a beautiful poetess beloved by all and courted by many noble suitors. On the day the emperor himself announces that he will marry her, Lady Kaguya must reveal her secret: that she is destined to return to the moon. When the heartbroken emperor pours an elixir into a fire burning at the summit of Mount Fuji, the smoke reaches Lady Kaguya and reminds her of her human love. To insure the accuracy of the book's illustrations, Marton traveled to Japan and did extensive research on Japanese art, creating an unusual story about the powerful bonds of love and the strong links between past and present. According to Mariella Bertelli in *Resource Links,* the book's illustrations "are powerfully composed, presenting contrasting images." "Marton's softly muted oil pastels add to the emotional intensity and mystery of the story," claimed *Booklist* critic Karen Morgan, while Adrienne Kertzer noted in a review for *Canadian Ethnic Studies* that "the book itself is an artwork with a careful aesthetic balance between illustration and prose."

Other more-recent illustration projects include Pendziwol's *Marja's Skis,* which a *Children's Bookwatch* critic dubbed "a heartwarming story that celebrates Scandinavian heritage." The story is set in a logging town where a Finnish girl—the youngest in her family—determines to overcome her fear and learn to ski. "Marton's naive oil pastel illustrations have a softly focused, ethereal quality," wrote Linda Ludke in *School Library Journal,* while *Resource Links* contributor Tanya Boudreau maintained that the artist's "soft touch, her choice of colours and her attention to historic detail give the setting and characters" a in Pendziwol's story "a look from the past."

Another illustration assignment, Raquel Rivera's *Arctic Adventures: Tales from the Lives of Inuit Artists,* introduces four true-life native artisans. Reviewing this work, *Booklist* critic Hazel Rochman maintained that Marton's "beautiful illustrations in colored pencil and mixed me-

Marton's art for Raquel Rivera's **Arctic Adventures** *introduces children to the unique culture of Inuit and other northern peoples.* (Illustration copyright © 2007 by Jirina Marton. Reproduced by permission of Groundwood Books.)

dia show the individual people and creatures in the Arctic landscape close up, sometimes with an edge of magical realism."

Biographical and Critical Sources

PERIODICALS

Booklist, January 1, 1998, Karen Morgan, review of *Lady Kaguya's Secret: A Japanese Tale,* p. 805; July 1, 2007, Hazel Rochman, review of *Arctic Adventures: Tales from the Lives of Inuit Artists,* p. 52; December 1, 2007, Shelle Rosenfeld, review of *Marja's Skis,* p. 49.

Books for Young People, April, 1988, review of *Midnight Visit at Molly's House,* pp. 14, 19.

Books in Canada, August-September, 1988, review of *Midnight Visit at Molly's House,* p. 36; September, 1991, Rhea Tregebov, review of *Flowers for Mom,* pp. 52-53; August, 2001, "Four Czech Chicks," pp. 27-29.

Canadian Children's Literature (annual), number 60, 1990, Bernard Schwartz, review of *Midnight Visit at Molly's House,* pp. 135-137; number 61, 1991, Allan Sheldon, review of *I'll Do It Myself,* pp. 96-99; number 67, 1992, review of *Flowers for Mom,* p. 107; number 72, 1993, review of *Amelia's Celebration,* pp. 61-62.

Canadian Ethnic Studies, Volume 27, number 1, 1995, review of *You Can Go Home Again,* pp. 181-183; spring, 1998, Adrienne Kertzer, review of *Lady Kaguya's Secret,* pp. 175-176.

Canadian Review of Materials, November, 1986, Patricia Fry, review of *Nicole's Boat: A Good-night Story;* September, 1988, review of *Midnight Visit at Molly's House,* p. 182; December, 1989, review of *I'll Do It Myself,* p. 267; September, 1991, Brenda Partridge, review of *Flowers for Mom,* p. 231; May, 1992, Brenda Partridge, review of *Amelia's Celebration,* p. 160; October, 1994, Marion Scott, review of *You Can Go Home Again,* p. 184.

Children's Bookwatch, January, 2008, review of *Marja's Skis.*

Horn Book, November-December, 2003, Christine M. Heppermann, review of *The Bear Says North: Tales from Northern Lands,* p. 758.

Kirkus Reviews, September 15, 2009, review of *Bella's Tree.*

Publishers Weekly, December 8, 1997, review of *Lady Kaguya's Secret,* p. 72.

Quill & Quire, August, 1989, review of *I'll Do It Myself,* p. 14; March, 1992, Anne Gilmore, review of *Amelia's Celebration,* p. 66; August, 1994, Joanne Findon, review of *You Can Go Home Again,* p. 34; September, 1997, review of *Lady Kaguya's Secret,* p. 74.

Resource Links, February, 1998, Mariella Bertelli, review of *Lady Kaguya's Secret,* p. 103; April, 2000, review of *Nicole's Boat,* p. 5; October, 2007, Heather Empey, review of *Arctic Adventures,* p. 24; December, 2007, Tanya Boudreau, review of *Marja's Skis,* p. 9; February, 2010, Anne Burke, review of *Bella's Tree,* p. 6.

School Librarian, fall, 1998, Jane Doonan, review of *Lady Kaguya's Secret,* p. 147.

School Library Journal, May, 1987, Lorraine Douglas, review of *Nicole's Boat,* p. 90; November, 1988, Pamela Miller Ness, review of *Midnight Visit at Molly's House,* p. 94; November, 1994, review of *You Can Go Home Again,* pp. 84-85; February, 1998, Angela J. Reynolds, review of *Lady Kaguya's Secret,* pp. 100-101; October, 2007, Linda Ludke, review of *Marja's Skis,* p. 125; October, 2009, Eva Mitnick, review of *Bella's Tree,* p. 83.

ONLINE

Annick Press Web Site, http://www.annickpress.com/ (August 13, 2003), "Jirina Marton."

Canadian Broadcasting Corporation Books Web site, http://www.cbc.ca/books/ (November 17, 2009), interview with Marton.*

*   *   *

MATSON, Morgan

Personal

Female. *Education:* New School, M.F.A. (writing for children).

Addresses

Home—Venice, CA. *E-mail*—morgan@morganmatson.com.

Career

Author and editor. Scholastic, Inc., New York, NY, assistant editor, c. 2008.

Writings

Amy and Roger's Epic Detour, Simon & Schuster Books for Young Readers (New York, NY), 2010.

Sidelights

Morgan Matson found a publisher for her first young-adult novel, *Amy and Roger's Epic Detour,* while working as an assistant editor at New York City's Scholastic Press. An imaginative story that draws on Matson's own cross-country road trips, the novel quilts a patchwork of notes (some scrawled on napkins and sales re-

Cover of Morgan Matson's humorous middle-grade novel **Amy and Roger's Epic Detour.** (Simon & Schuster/BFYR, 2010. Cover photograph by Image Source/Getty Images.)

ceipts), letters, and e-mails into a story about a teen's break with childhood and willingness to make the most of a future in a new place.

When readers meet Amy Curry in *Amy and Roger's Epic Detour,* the high-school junior is dealing with the recent death of her dad in an automobile accident that she feels was her fault. More upheaval comes when Amy's mother decides to cope with her own grief and help erase sad memories by leaving the West coast and moving to Connecticut. Rather than make the cross-country flight, the teen decides to give herself time to deal with this transition by taking to the highway. The only problem is that she has refused to drive since the accident. Fortunately, her mother's friend's son Roger is willing to come along as chauffer as he is heading for a rendezvous with his father in Pennsylvania. With the passing miles, Amy begins to mellow in her resentment of her traveling companion, and his sincere friendship helps her come to terms with the fact that her childhood has ended and that she has the power to craft her own future. Noting the "budding romance" that also makes its way into Amy's summer journey, a *Publishers Weekly* critic dubbed *Amy and Roger's Epic Detour* "a near perfect summer read that should leave readers with a thirst for travel and romance."

Biographical and Critical Sources

PERIODICALS

Publishers Weekly, May 10, 2010, review of *Amy and Roger's Epic Detour,* p. 47.
School Library Journal, June, 2010, Amy Pickett, review of *Amy and Roger's Epic Tour,* p. 112.

ONLINE

Simon & Schuster Web site, http://authors.simonand schuster.com/ (May 15, 2011), "Morgan Matson."*

* * *

McGRATH, Barbara Barbieri 1953-

Personal

Born September 29, 1953, in Wellesley, MA; daughter of Albert and Dorothy Barbieri; married William M. McGrath, April 16, 1978; children: Emily M., William Louis. *Education:* Laseil College, B.A. *Religion:* Roman Catholic. *Hobbies and other interests:* Surfcasting, SCUBA diving, collecting "sea-pottery."

Addresses

Home and office—7 Jennings Pond Rd., Natick, MA 01760. *Agent*—Sharon Kelleher, Kelleher Agency, MA, sharon@kelleheragency.com. *E-mail*—authorvisits@aol.com.

Barbara B. McGrath (Reproduced by permission.)

Career

Writer and educator. Preschool teacher for sixteen years; freelance writer. Presenter at schools.

Member

Society of Children's Book Writers and Illustrators.

Awards, Honors

Teachers' Choice Award, 1994, and Pick of the List citation, American Bookseller's Association, both for *The M&M's Brand Chocolate Candies Counting Book;* Oppenheim Gold Award, 2010, for *Teddy Bear Counting.*

Writings

The M&M's Brand Chocolate Candies Counting Book, Charlesbridge (Watertown, MA), 1994.
More M&M's Math, Scholastic (New York, NY), 1998.
The Cheerios Counting Book, Scholastic (New York, NY), 1998.
Pepperidge Farm Goldfish Counting Board Book, Scholastic (New York, NY), 1998.
Hershey's Kisses: Counting Board Book, Corp Board Books, 1998.
The Baseball Counting Book, Scholastic (New York, NY), 1999.

The Cheerios Counting Book: 1, 2, 3 (board book), illustrated by Frank Mazolla, Cartwheel Books (New York, NY), 2000.

Skittles Riddles Math, Charlesbridge (Watertown, MA), 2000.

The M&M's Brand Valentine Book, Charlesbridge (Watertown, MA), 2000.

Necco Sweethearts Be My Valentine Book, HarperFestival (New York, NY), 2000.

Kellogg's Froot Loops! Counting Fun Book, Mariposa, 2000.

Pepperidge Farm Goldfish Counting Fun Book, HarperFestival (New York, NY), 2000.

The M&M's Brand Halloween Treat Book, Charlesbridge (Watertown, MA), 2000.

The M&M's Brand Christmas Gift Book, Charlesbridge (Watertown, MA), 2000.

Kellogg's Froot Loops Color Fun Book, HarperFestival (New York, NY), 2001.

The M&M's Brand Birthday Book, Charlesbridge (Watertown, MA), 2001.

The M&M's Brand Easter Egg Hunt, Charlesbridge (Watertown, MA), 2001

The M&M's Brand Color Pattern Book, illustrated by Roger Glass, Charlesbridge (Watertown, MA), 2002.

The M&M's Brand All-American Parade Book, illustrated by Peggy Tagel, Charlesbridge (Watertown, MA), 2003.

I Love Words, Charlesbridge (Watertown, MA), 2003.

The M&M's Count-to-One Hundred Book, Charlesbridge (Watertown, MA), 2003.

(With Peter Alderman) *Soccer Counts!,* illustrated by Paul Estrada, Charlesbridge (Watertown, MA), 2003.

Echoing the story of the Little Red Hen, McGrath's* The Little Green Witch *features colorful artwork by Martha Alexander. (Illustration copyright © 2005 by Martha Alexander. Reproduced by with permission of Charlesbridge Publishing, Inc. All rights reserved.)

The M&M's Brand Addition Book, Charlesbridge (Watertown, MA), 2004.

M&M's Count around the Circle, Charlesbridge (Watertown, MA), 2004.

The Little Green Witch, illustrated by Martha Alexander, Charlesbridge (Watertown, MA), 2005.

The M&M's Brand Subtraction Book, Charlesbridge (Watertown, MA), 2005.

(Compiler) *The Storm: Students of Biloxi, Mississippi Remember Hurricane Katrina,* Charlesbridge (Watertown, MA), 2006.

The Little Red Elf, illustrated by Rosalinde Bonnet, Charlesbridge (Watertown, MA), 2009.

Teddy Bear Counting, illustrated by Tim Nihoff, Charlesbridge (Watertown, MA), 2010.

Teddy Bear Math, illustrated by Tim Nihoff, Charlesbridge (Watertown, MA), 2011.

Contributor to local newspapers.

Some of McGrath's titles have been published in bilingual English/Spanish editions.

Sidelights

Barbara Barbieri McGrath studied early education in college, and her books reflect both her sense of fun and her desire to help young learners grasp concepts such as counting, addition, subtraction, and colors. Her unique concept book *The M&M's Brand Chocolate Candies Counting Book* was considered such a valuable addition to educational titles that it was selected for a Teacher's Choice award. Often incorporating popular candies and cereals into their text, McGrath's math books endeavor to make learning math skills fun for young readers. She also shows her talent for spinning an entertaining story in picture books such as *The Little Green Witch* and *The Little Green Elf,* and she chronicles a contemporary tragedy in *The Storm: Students of Biloxi, Mississippi Remember Hurricane Katrina.*

Although McGrath has crafted many of her counting books using M&M's chocolate candies, other stories incorporate diminutive delicacies such as Cheerios, Goldfish crackers, and Froot Loops cereal. Of *The Cheerios Counting Book,* Hazel Rochman noted in *Booklist* that, "as young preschoolers munch and play and tally, they will find a delicious world they recognize in a book." Like candy, teddy bears are attractive to very young children, and McGrath taps that attraction in both *Teddy Bear Counting* and *Teddy Bear Math,* both of which feature colorful artwork by Tim Nihoff.

Sports become McGrath's vehicle for teaching in *The Baseball Counting Book,* which incorporates rhyme and rhythm as well as baseball themes to teach numbers one through twenty. "The book is full of counting opportunities and is a springboard for many other learning experiences," wrote AnneMarie Hornyak in *Teaching Children Mathematics.* A collaboration with Peter Alderman, McGrath's *Soccer Counts!* teaches counting drills and the history of soccer at the same time. "This soccer-centered counting book is sure to be a winner with fans young and old," assured a *Kirkus Reviews* contributor in a review of the same book. Noting that the reading level may provide few challenges for beginning soccer players, *School Library Journal* critic Blair Christolon suggested that English-as-a-second-language "students may be the best audience for this mixture." As Sarah Olague wrote in *Teaching Children Mathematics,* "both teachers and their students will learn a lot about soccer from this book."

Although most of her books are nonfiction, McGrath retells the story of "The Little Red Hen" with a new cast of characters in both *The Little Green Witch* and *The Little Red Elf.* In the first book, a friendly young witch asks for help in making a pumpkin pie, but friends Ghost, Bat, and Gremlin are all too busy to help, while the star of *The Little Red Elf* confronts a host of tasks—growing a Christmas tree, crafting children's toys, and baking holiday cookies—but Reindeer, Penguin, and Winter Hare only volunteer when there are presents to open. Both stories follow the traditional tale of the little red hen, but they serve up an additional twist at the end "that will make readers laugh out loud," promised Susan Weitz in her *School Library Journal* review of *The Little Green Witch.* Praising *The Little Red Elf* for its "funny asides," Eva Mitnick recommended McGrath's story as "that rare beast: an endearing holiday book without a hint of treacle."

Another change of pace, *The Storm* was inspired by McGrath's trip south to the area where Hurricane Katrina hit in August of 2005, an area that included coastal Mississippi. Working with the teachers and students of

A companion volume to **The Little Green Witch, The Little Red Elf** *gives McGrath another chance to riff on a traditional childhood story.*
(Illustration copyright © 2010 by Rosalinde Bonnet. Reproduced by permission of Charlesbridge Publishing.)

the Biloxi, Mississippi, Public Schools, she crafted a chronicle of the storm's coming as well as its aftermath in *The Storm,* and a portion of book-sale proceeds benefitted Biloxi school. In drawings and paintings as well as in stories, over ninety of the city's young residents, from kindergarten through high school. "Readers will be moved by images and descriptions that students share," noted *School Library Journal* contributor Maura Bresnahan, the critic adding that *The Storm* "emphasizes the resilience of children and the healing powers of art." Some "sharings. . . . are touching and some are even funny, but all are extremely honest," asserted Terre Sychterz in her *Childhood Education* review, and a *New York Times Book Review* contributor dubbed the illustrations in *The Storm* "just as eloquent" as the text.

McGrath once told *SATA:* "I taught preschool for sixteen years while writing public-interest articles for local newspapers. Then I focused on making learning fun—using a 'fun' subject to make the lesson memorable. I use brand-name products to teach hands-on lessons."

Biographical and Critical Sources

PERIODICALS

Arts & Activities, October, 2007, Jerome J. Hausman, review of *The Storm: Students of Biloxi, Mississippi Remember Hurricane Katrina,* p. 14.

Booklist, October 1, 1998, Hazel Rochman, review of *The Cheerios Counting Book,* p. 333; February 15, 1999, Kathy Broderick, review of *The Baseball Counting Book,* p. 1072.

Canadian Review of Materials, May 21, 1999, review of *The Cheerios Counting Book.*

Childhood Education (annual), 2007, Terre Sychterz, review of *The Storm,* p. 328.

Horn Book, November-December, 2009, Kitty Flynn, review of *The Little Red Elf,* p. 645.

Kirkus Reviews, June 15, 2003, review of *Soccer Counts!,* p. 861; June 15, 2005, review of *The Little Green Witch,* p. 687; September 15, 2009, review of *The Little Red Elf;* January 15, 2010, review of *Teddy Bear Counting.*

Publishers Weekly, June 6, 1994, review of *The M&M's Brand Chocolate Candies Counting Book,* p. 64; November 16, 1998, review of *More M&M's Brand Chocolate Candies Math,* p. 77; April 24, 2000, review of *The Cheerios Counting Book,* p. 92; December 11, 2000, "Volumes of Valentines," p. 86; June 25, 2001, review of *Kellogg's Froot Loops Color Fun Book,* p. 75; February 11, 2002, review of *The M&M's Brand Color Pattern Book,* p. 189; August 11, 2003, review of *The M&M's Count-to-One Hundred Book,* p. 281; October 26, 2009, review of *The Little Red Elf,* p. 54.

New York Times Book Review, September 10, 2006, review of *The Storm,* p. 19.

School Library Journal, April, 2001, Ilene Abramson, review of *Skittles Riddles Math,* p. 132; September, 2003, Blair Christolon, review of *Soccer Counts!,* p. 202; January, 2004, Tali Balas, review of *I Love Words,* p. 120; August, 2005, Susan Weitz, review of *The Little Green Witch,* p. 100; December, 2006, Maura Bresnahan, review of *The Storm,* p. 165; October, 2009, Eva Mitnick, review of *The Little Red Elf,* p. 82.

Science Books & Film, November, 2003, review of *The M&M's Count to One Hundred Book,* p. 273; July-August, 2005, Charles Mercer, review of *The M&M's Subtraction Book,* p. 168.

Teaching Children Mathematics, December, 1999, Anne-Marie Hornyak, review of *The Baseball Counting Book,* p. 266; September, 2004, Sarah Olague, review of *Soccer Counts!,* p. 110.

ONLINE

Barbara McGrath Home Page, http://www.barbara mcgrath.com (May 20, 2011).*

* * *

MIDDLETON, Charlotte

Personal

Born in England. *Education:* Cambridge School of Art, B.F.A. (illustration).

Addresses

Home—England. *Agent*—Celia Catchpole, 56 Gilpin Ave., East Sheen, London SW14 8QY, England. *E-mail*—Charlottemiddleton_illustrator@yahoo.co.uk.

Career

Illustrator and author of children's books.

Writings

SELF-ILLUSTRATED

Tabitha's Terrifically Tough Tooth, David & Charles Children's Books (London, England), 1999, Phyllis Fogelman Books (New York, NY), 2001.

Do You Still Love Me?, Gullane Children's (London, England), 2002, Candlewick Press (Cambridge, MA), 2003.

Enrico Starts School, Dial Books for Young Readers (New York, NY), 2004.

Not Old Enough, Gullane Children's (London, England), 2005.

Christopher Nibble, Oxford University Press (Oxford, England), 2009, published as *Nibbles: A Green Tale,* Marshall Cavendish (New York, NY), 2010.

Christopher's Caterpillars, Oxford University Press (Oxford, England), 2011.

ILLUSTRATOR

Carrie Weston, *Lucky Socks,* Gullane Children's Books (London, England), 2001, Phyllis Fogelman Books (New York, NY), 2002.

Kate Petty, *Made with Love: How Babies Are Made,* Macmillan Children's Books (London, England), 2003.

Angela McAllister, *Monster Pet!,* Margaret K. McElderry Books (New York, NY), 2005, published as *Monster!,* Simon & Schuster (London, England), 2005.

Betsy Franco, *Summer Beat,* Margaret K. McElderry Books (New York, NY), 2007.

Sheila M. Bird, *A Windy Day,* Gullane Children's (London, England), 2007.

ILLUSTRATOR; "FRANGIPANI FAIRIES" SERIES BY TITANIA HARDY

The Sunlight Fairy, Simon & Schuster (New York, NY), 2007.

The Sunrise Fairy, Simon & Schuster (New York, NY), 2008.

The Sunset Fairy, Simon & Schuster (New York, NY), 2008.

OTHER

Staying at Nan's (reader; bound with *A Swimmer's Day*), illustrated by Lisa Smith, Nelson Thornes (Cheltenham, England), 2003.

Sidelights

Charlotte Middleton's colorful picture-book illustrations meld engaging line drawings of dot-eyed characters with various collage patterns, all to good effect. In addition to pairing her artwork with original stories in picture books such as *Tabitha's Terrifically Tough Tooth, Enrico Starts School, Do You Still Love Me?,* and *Christopher Nibble,* the British-born Middleton also brings to life stories by a range of authors that include Betsy Franco, Titania Hardy, and Angela McAllister. Reviewing *Summer Beat,* a rhyming story by Franco, Gloria Koster noted in *School Library Journal* that although the "plot is thin," Middleton's "charming depictions of children and pets amid bursts of vibrant color adds to the seasonal celebration," while a *Kirkus Reviews* writer noted that the book's large-format "mixed-media spreads have a freshness that matches this singular time of year."

Middleton developed a passion for drawing as a child, and she eventually earned a degree in illustration at the Cambridge School of Art. Like many illustrators, she crafted an original self-illustrated story to showcase her capabilities to publishers, and in 1999 that story, *Tabitha's Terrifically Tough Tooth,* was released. As its title suggests, a little girl with a loose tooth is excited about the arrival of the tooth fairy, but when the tooth appears stuck Tabitha seeks advice from her father so

that she can be visited by the tiny tooth-collector. "Middleton's bright, clean collages and spare, direct words will delight" young children, according to *Booklist* critic Helen Rosenberg, and a *Publishers Weekly* critic observed that the author/artist's "cartoony style masks its own sophistication with childlike touches." Middleton's "understated yet focused text captures the desire, determination, and disappointment that can surround" the anticipation of a childhood watershed, according to *School Library Journal* contributor Martha Topol, and her "illustrations add . . . pizzazz."

Another important moment of childhood is the focus of *Enrico Starts School,* which introduces a shy young cat who is worried that starting school will mean the end of favorite games and worries over the lack of friends. Fortunately, Emilio decides to make the best of things and he starts to speak up in class. With Middleton's "all-feline cast," the book's "whimsical blend of sophisticated and childlike" art pair with a story that celebrates a preschooler's "ultimate success," according to *Booklist* contributor Shelle Rosenfeld. A *Publishers Weekly* critic cited the sophistication of the artwork in *Enrico Starts School,* writing that the author/illustrator "achieves an effective visual and emotional counterpoint by combining bright, saturated colors with a poignantly scraggly ink line" that "conveys Enrico's vulnerability."

A dog stands in for a young child in Middleton's *Do You Still Love Me?* as a young pup named Dudley enjoys peaceful days with his loving human companion, Anna. Dudley's secure position as favored pet is threat-

Charlotte Middleton's engaging illustrations pair with an equally engaging story about a hungry guinea pig in her picture book **Nibbles: A Green Tale.** (Illustration copyright © 2010 by Charlotte Middleton. Reproduced by Marshall Cavendish Children.)

ened, however, when Pequito the chameleon joins the family and starts to command much of Anna's attention. Even Anna's friends spend their time looking at the little amphibian rather than at the listless dog. When Pequito goes missing, however, Dudley puts aside his jealousy to help search for the creature, earning a new kind of attention in the process. *Do You Still Love Me?* was described by *School Library Journal* critic Jody McCoy as an "engaging bit of biblio-therapy [that] is perfect for any small folk facing change," and a *Publishers Weekly* critic asserted that "Middleton's high sense of style gives the story a fresh, understated sweetness." "The old new-sibling/pet-in-the-house formula is given an original twist," noted a *Kirkus Reviews* writer, while in *Booklist* Gillian Engberg wrote that the author/illustrator opts for a brief text, "letting her brightly hued, uncluttered collages really tell the story."

While *Enrico Starts School* and *Do You Still Love Me?* cast critters in the part of the young child at the center of her story, Middleton's *Nibbles: A Green Tale* stars a guinea pig that acts like a guinea pig—in fact, the book's star was inspired by the pets Middleton cared for as a child. First published in England as *Christopher Nibble*, *Nibbles* follows a dandelion-loving guinea pig in a dandelion-loving town who worries when all the dandelions have been eaten up and the guinea pigs must resort to less-tender greens such as cabbage leaves. Then Nibbles discovers a lone dandelion growing near his home, and when the plant's bright yellow flower is transformed to a fluffy white seedhead he takes steps to ensure that the treasured plant will soon regrow. *Nibbles* serves as an effective introduction to "gardening or plant conservation," according to Catherine Callegari, the *School Library Journal* contributor adding that "Middleton's tale of overconsuming and scarcity is direct but not preachy." In *Booklist* Diane Foote reached a similar conclusion, writing that the book's "lesson about ecological sustainability is [served up] in a palatable package" that finds the engagingly drawn Nibbles confronting "situations with which kids will relate."

Biographical and Critical Sources

PERIODICALS

Booklist, April 15, 2001, Helen Rosenberg, review of *Tabitha's Terrifically Tough Tooth,* p. 1566; February 15, 2002, Gillian Engberg, review of *Lucky Socks,* p. 1023; September 1, 2003, Gillian Engberg, review of *Do You Still Love Me?,* p. 130; September 1, 2004, Shelle Rosenfeld, review of *Enrico Starts School,* p. 134; May 15, 2007, Carolyn Phelan, review of *Summer Beat,* p. 53; May 1, 2010, Diane Foote, review of *Nibbles: A Green Tale,* p. 91.

Children's Bookwatch, September, 2010, review of *Nibbles.*

Kirkus Reviews, January 1, 2002, review of *Lucky Socks,* p. 53; June 15, 2003, review of *Do You Still Love Me?,* p. 862; June 15, 2004, review of *Enrico Starts School,* p. 579; May 1, 2007, review of *Summer Beat.*

Publishers Weekly, July 17, 2000, review of *Tabitha's Terrifically Tough Tooth,* p. 163; November 26, 2001, review of *Lucky Socks,* p. 61; July 7, 2003, review of *Do You Still Love Me?,* p. 70; June 28, 2004, review of *Enrico Starts School,* p. 49.

School Library Journal, June, 2001, Martha Topol, review of *Tabitha's Terrifically Tough Tooth,* p. 126; March, 2002, Wanda Meyers-Hines, review of *Lucky Socks,* p. 206; September, 2003, Jody McCoy, review of *Do You Still Love Me?,* p. 184; July, 2004, Grace Oliff, review of *Enrico Starts School,* p. 82; July, 2005, Shawn Brommer, review of *Monster Pet!,* p. 78; May, 2007, Gloria Koster, review of *Summer Beat,* p. 91; Mary, 2010, Catherine Callegari, review of *Nibbles,* p. 88.

Teacher Librarian, December, 2003, Ruth Cox, review of *Do You Still Love Me?,* p. 10.

ONLINE

Celia Catchpole Web site, http://www.celiacatchploe.co.uk/ (May 20, 2011), "Charlotte Middleton."

Charlotte Middleton Home Page, http://www.charlotte middleton.com (May 20, 2011).*

* * *

MOLNAR, Haya Leah 1951(?)-

Personal

Born c. 1951, in Bucharest, Romania; immigrated to United States at age 13; married. *Religion:* Jewish.

Addresses

Home—New York, NY. *Agent*—Leigh Feldman, DVF Literary Agents, 236 W. 26th St., Ste. 802, New York, NY 10001.

Career

Writer. Former advertising copywriter and creative director; currently full-time writer.

Awards, Honors

National Jewish Book Award, 2010, and Sydney Taylor Awards Notable Book for Teenagers designation, 2011, both for *Under a Red Sky;* numerous awards for copywriting.

Writings

Under a Red Sky: Memoir of a Childhood in Communist Romania, Farrar, Straus & Giroux (New York, NY), 2010.

Sidelights

Born in Romania, Haya Leah Molnar grew up in a close-knit, tumultuous, and multigenerational family where stories held hints of a hidden history and reading allowed her an escape into a quieter world. Life's realities began to crystallize for her at age seven when she learned that she was Jewish and that the Bulgaria she was living in did not make life easy for Jews. A few years later, Molnar and her family—the Zimmermans—left for the United States and the freedoms of a society unhindered by the proscriptions of communism. Despite the challenge of learning a new language, Molnar quickly adapted to her new home and ultimately established a successful career in the advertising industry. By day she would write advertising copy, but her free time was often spent writing poems and short stories. Eventually, Molnar distilled her early experiences into the National Jewish Book Award-winning *Under a Red Sky: Memoir of a Childhood in Communist Romania,* which a *Publishers Weekly* critic dubbed "an impressive debut."

Although Molnar did not learn so until later, her parents—Mr. Zimmerman was a filmmaker and Mrs. Zimmerman had once danced the ballet—survived the Holocaust only to wind up in communist Romania, where hatred of the Jews continued after the close of World War II. To allow their daughter to experience a relatively normal childhood, they never revealed her heritage. Young Eva's childhood was enriched by the presence of several extended relatives, each of whom she paints in her memoir as a unique individual who had an impact upon her. Efforts to portray a life of scarcity and oppression as carefree ended when Eva discovered the truth at age seven and at this point her family determined to escape an increasingly dangerous situation. Ultimately, although separately, Molnar family members managed to gain the permission required in order to immigrate.

Praising *Under a Red Sky* for its "unsentimental, present-tense narrative voice," a *Publishers Weekly* reviewer added that Molnar's memoir is particularly valuable for its depiction of her "personal awakening to her Jewish identity" as well as for its presentation of a child's perspective on adult behavior. According to *Booklist* critic Lynn Rutan, "a vivid story emerges" in Molnar's narrative, her observations "ranging from funny, tender moments of family life to the horrific revelations of the Romanian holocaust, about which little has been written." In addition to its evocative narrative and vividly told family histories, *Under a Red Sky* includes sufficient "history and background . . . to help today's readers understand the context" of the Zimmerman family's plight "without detracting from the story."

Biographical and Critical Sources

BOOKS

Molnar, Haya Leah, *Under a Red Sky: Memoir of a Childhood in Communist Romania,* Farrar, Straus & Giroux (New York, NY), 2010.

PERIODICALS

Booklist, February 15, 2010, Lynn Rutan, review of *Under a Red Sky: Memoir of a Childhood in Communist Romania,* p. 47.
Publishers Weekly, March 29, 2010, review of *Under a Red Sky,* p. 61.
School Library Journal, May, 2010, Nancy Silverrod, review of *Under a Red Sky,* p. 134.
Voice of Youth Advocates, June, 2010, Laura Lehner, review of *Under a Red Sky,* p. 157.

ONLINE

Haya Leah Molnar Home Page, http://hayaleahmolnar. com (May 27, 2011).*

N

NAPOLI, Donna Jo 1948-

Personal

Born February 28, 1948, in Miami, FL; daughter of Vincent Robert and Helen Gloria Napoli; married, December 29, 1968; children: five. *Education:* Harvard University, B.A., 1970, Ph.D., 1973.

Addresses

Home—PA. *Office*—Linguistics Dept., Swarthmore College, Swarthmore, PA 19081. *Agent*—Barry Furrow, Drexel University Earle Mack School of Law, Philadelphia, PA 19104. *E-mail*—dnapoli1@swarthmore.edu.

Career

Author and educator. Smith College, Northampton, MA, lecturer in philosophy and Italian, 1973-74; University of North Carolina, Chapel Hill, lecturer in mathematics and Italian, 1974-75; Georgetown University, Washington, DC, assistant professor of linguistics, 1975-80; University of Michigan, Ann Arbor, professor of linguistics, 1980-87; Swarthmore College, Swarthmore, PA, professor of linguistics, 1987—.

Member

Society of Children's Book Writers and Illustrators, Authors Guild, Authors League of America, Linguistic Society of America, Società linguistica italiana.

Awards, Honors

One Hundred Titles for Reading and Sharing selection, New York Public Library, 1992, Children's Book of the Year selection, Bank Street Child Study Children's Book Committee, 1993, and M. Jerry Weiss Book Award, New Jersey Reading Association, 1996, all for *The Prince of the Pond*; Best Book for Young Adults selection, American Library Association (ALA)/Young Adult Library Services Association (YALSA), 1994, for *The Magic Circle*; Children's Books of the Year selection,

Donna Jo Napoli (Courtesy of Donna Jo Napoli.)

Bank Street Child Study Children's Book Committee, 1995, for *When the Water Closes over My Head*, 1996, for *Jimmy, the Pickpocket of the Palace*; Leeway Foundation Prize for excellence in fiction, 1995; Pick of the Lists selection, American Booksellers Association (ABA), New York Public Library Books for the Teen Age designation, and YALSA Best of selection, all 1996, all for *Zel*; ABA Pick of the Lists selection, and ALA Best Books for Young Adults designation, both 1996, both for *Song of the Magdalene*; Hall of Fame Sports Book for Kids selection, Free Library of Philadelphia, 1996, for *Soccer Shock*; Keystone State Reading Association Young-Adult Book Award nomination, 1994, for *Shark Shock*; Outstanding Merit designation, Bank Street College of Education/Children's Book Council (CBC), 1995, for *Jimmy, the Pickpocket of the*

Palace; Notable Children's Trade Book in the Field of Social Studies selection, National Council for Social Studies/CBC, Carolyn W. Field Honor Book designation, ALA Best Books selection, Golden Kite Award, Society of Children's Book Writers and Illustrators, Sydney Taylor Book Award, National Association of Jewish Libraries, and Best Books for the Teen Age selection, all 1998, all for *Stones in Water*; Drexel University and Free Library of Philadelphia Children's Literature Citation, 1998; Best Books selection, New York Public Library, 1998, for *For the Love of Venice*; ALA Best Books selection, and Best Books selection, New York Public Library, both both 1998, both for *Sirena*; Best Books for the Teen Age selection, and Carolyn W. Field Honor Book designation, both 1999, both for *Spinners*; Notable Books selection, *Smithsonian* magazine, 1999, for *Crazy Jack*; Carolyn W. Field Honor Book selection, 2000, for *Beast;* Bank Street College of Education Best Books listee, 2001, for *Three Days*; Pick of the Lists selection, ABA, Children's Book Sense 76 List inclusion, and Best Children's Books selection, New York Public Library, all 2001, and Kentucky Bluegrass Award, all for *Albert*; Oppenheim Toy Portfolio Best Book designation, and Bank Street College of Education Best Books of the Year designation, both 2002, both for *Flamingo Dream*; Nevada Young Readers Award, 2002, for *Daughter of Venice*; ALA Best Book for Young Adults selection, Golden Kite Honor Book designation, and Books for the Teen Age designation, all 2003, all for *Breath;* Books for the Teen Age designation, 2003, for *The Great God Pan*; Parents Choice Silver Honor Award, 2004, for *North*; ALA Best Books for Young Adults designation, 2004, for *Bound*; Parent's Choice Silver Honor Award, Sydney Taylor Honor Book, and Sons of Italy National Book Club selection, all for *The King of Mulberry Street*; Bank Street College of Education Best Books of the Year designation, 2006, for *Sly the Sleuth and the Pet Mysteries* and *Sly the Sleuth and the Sports Mysteries*; Carolyn W. Field Honor Book designation, 2006, for *Fire in the Hills*; Books for the Teen Age designation, 2007, for *Hush*; Literary Lights for Children Award, Boston Public Library, 2007; Parent's Choice Gold Award, 2009, for *Alligator Bayou*; grants and fellowships in linguistics from National Science Foundation, National Endowment for the Humanities, Mellon Foundation, and Sloan Foundation.

Writings

PICTURE BOOKS

The Hero of Barletta, illustrated by Dana Gustafson, Carolrhoda Books (Minneapolis, MN), 1988.

Albert, illustrated by Jim LaMarche, Harcourt (New York, NY), 2001.

(With Richard Tchen) *How Hungry Are You?,* illustrated by Amy Walrod, Atheneum (New York, NY), 2001.

(With Marie Kane) *Rocky: The Cat Who Barks,* illustrated by Tamara Petrosino, Dutton (New York, NY), 2002.

Flamingo Dream, illustrated by Cathie Felstead, Greenwillow (New York, NY), 2002.

(With Shelagh Johnston) *Hotel Jungle,* illustrated by Kenneth J. Spengler, Mondo (New York, NY), 2004.

Pink Magic, illustrated by Chad Cameron, Clarion Books (New York, NY), 2005.

(With Eva Furrow) *Bobby the Bold,* illustrated by Ard Hoyt, Dial Books for Young Readers (New York, NY), 2006.

The Wishing Club: A Story about Fractions, illustrated by Anna Currey, Henry Holt (New York, NY), 2007.

Corkscrew Counts: A Story about Multiplication, illustrated by Anna Currey, Henry Holt (New York, NY), 2008.

(With Elena Furrow) *Ready to Dream,* illustrated by Bronwyn Bancroft, Bloomsbury (New York, NY), 2009.

The Earth Shook: A Persian Tale, illustrated by Gabi Swiatkowska, Hyperion (New York, NY), 2009.

(With Doreen DeLuca) *Handy Stories to Read and Sign,* illustrated by Maureen Klusza, Gallaudet University Press (Washington, DC), 2009.

Mama Mitti: Wangari Maathai and the Trees of Kenya, illustrated by Kadir Nelson, Simon & Schuster (New York, NY), 2010.

MIDDLE-GRADE NOVELS

Soccer Shock, illustrated by Meredith Johnson, Dutton (New York, NY), 1991.

The Prince of the Pond: Otherwise Known as De Fawg Pin, illustrated by Judith Byron Schachner, Dutton (New York, NY), 1992.

When the Water Closes over My Head, illustrated by Nancy Poydar, Dutton (New York, NY), 1994.

Shark Shock, Dutton (New York, NY), 1994.

Jimmy, the Pickpocket of the Palace, illustrated by Judith Byron Schachner, Dutton (New York, NY), 1995.

The Bravest Thing, Dutton (New York, NY), 1995.

Trouble on the Tracks, Scholastic (New York, NY), 1997.

On Guard, Dutton (New York, NY), 1997.

Changing Tunes, Dutton (New York, NY), 1998.

Shelley Shock, Dutton (New York, NY), 2000.

Three Days, Dutton (New York, NY), 2001.

Gracie: The Pixie of the Puddle, Dutton Children's Books (New York, NY), 2004.

(With Robert Furrow) *Sly the Sleuth and the Pet Mysteries,* illustrated by Heather Maione, Dial Books for Young Readers (New York, NY), 2005.

Ugly, illustrated by Lita Judge, Hyperion Books for Children (New York, NY), 2006.

(With Robert Furrow) *Sly the Sleuth and the Sports Mysteries,* Dial Books for Young Readers (New York, NY), 2006.

(With Robert Furrow) *Sly the Sleuth and the Food Mysteries,* illustrated by Heather Maione, Dial Books for Young Readers (New York, NY), 2007.

Mogo, the Third Warthog, illustrated by Lita Judge, Hyperion Books for Children (New York, NY), 2008.

(With Robert Furrow) *Sly the Sleuth and the Code Mysteries*, Dial Books for Young Readers (New York, NY), 2009.

YOUNG-ADULT NOVELS

The Magic Circle, Dutton (New York, NY), 1993.
Zel, Dutton (New York, NY), 1996.
Song of the Magdalene, Scholastic (New York, NY), 1996.
Stones in Water, Dutton (New York, NY), 1997.
For the Love of Venice, Delacorte (New York, NY), 1998.
Sirena, Scholastic (New York, NY), 1998.
Crazy Jack, Delacorte (New York, NY), 1999.
(With Richard Tchen) *Spinners*, Dutton (New York, NY), 1999.
Beast, Atheneum (New York, NY), 2000.
Daughter of Venice, Delacorte (New York, NY), 2002.
The Great God Pan, Wendy Lamb Books (New York, NY), 2003.
Breath, Simon & Schuster (New York, NY), 2003.
North, Greenwillow Books (New York, NY), 2004.
Bound, Atheneum Books for Young Readers (New York, NY), 2004.
The King of Mulberry Street, Wendy Lamb Books (New York, NY), 2005.
Fire in the Hills (sequel to *Stones in Water*), Dutton Children's Books (New York, NY), 2006.
Hush: An Irish Princess' Tale, Atheneum Books for Young Readers (New York, NY), 2007.
The Smile, Dutton Children's Books (New York, NY), 2008.
Alligator Bayou, Delacorte (New York, NY), 2009.
The Wager, Henry Holt (New York, NY), 2010.

"ANGELWINGS" CHAPTER-BOOK SERIES

Friends Everywhere, illustrated by Lauren Klementz-Harte, Aladdin (New York, NY), 1999.
Little Creatures, illustrated by Lauren Klementz-Harte, Aladdin (New York, NY), 1999.
On Her Own, illustrated by Lauren Klementz-Harte, Aladdin (New York, NY), 1999.
One Leap Forward, illustrated by Lauren Klementz-Harte, Aladdin (New York, NY), 1999.
No Fair!, illustrated by Lauren Klementz-Harte, Aladdin (New York, NY, 2000.
Playing Games, illustrated by Lauren Klementz-Harte, Aladdin (New York, NY), 2000.
Lies and Lemons, illustrated by Lauren Klementz-Harte, Aladdin (New York, NY), 2000.
Running Away, illustrated by Lauren Klementz-Harte, Aladdin (New York, NY), 2000.
April Flowers, illustrated by Lauren Klementz-Harte, Aladdin (New York, NY), 2000.
Partners, illustrated by Lauren Klementz-Harte, Aladdin (New York, NY), 2000.
Left Out, illustrated by Lauren Klementz-Harte, Aladdin (New York, NY), 2000.
Give and Take, illustrated by Lauren Klementz-Harte, Aladdin (New York, NY), 2000.

Know-It-All, illustrated by Lauren Klementz-Harte, Aladdin (New York, NY), 2000.
Happy Holidays, illustrated by Lauren Klementz-Harte, Aladdin (New York, NY), 2000.
New Voices, illustrated by Lauren Klementz-Harte, Aladdin (New York, NY), 2000.
Hang in There, illustrated by Lauren Klementz-Harte, Aladdin (New York, NY), 2001.

OTHER

(Editor) *Elements of Tone, Stress, and Intonation*, Georgetown University Press (Washington, DC), 1978.
(With Emily Rando) *Syntactic Argumentation*, Georgetown University Press (Washington, DC), 1979.
(Editor with William Cressey) *Linguistic Symposium on Romance Languages: 9*, Georgetown University Press (Washington, DC), 1981.
Predication Theory: A Case Study for Indexing Theory, Cambridge University Press (New York, NY), 1989.
(Editor with Judy Anne Kegl) *Bridges between Psychology and Linguistics: A Swarthmore Festschrift for Lila Gleitman*, L. Erlbaum (Mahwah, NJ), 1991.
Syntax: Theory and Problems, Oxford University Press (New York, NY), 1993.
(With Stuart Davis) *Phonological Factors in Historical Change: The Passage of the Latin Second Conjugation into Romance*, Rosenberg & Sellier, 1994.
Linguistics: Theory and Problems, Oxford University Press (New York, NY), 1996.
Language Matters: A Guide to Everyday Questions about Language, Oxford University Press (New York, NY), 2003.
(With Marina Nespor) *L'animale parlante: Introduzione allo studio del linguaggio*, Carocci (Rome, Italy), 2004.
(Editor) *Signs and Voices: Deaf Culture, Identity, Language, and Arts*, Gallaudet University Press (Washington, DC), 2008.
(Coeditor) *Access: Multiple Avenues for Deaf People*, Gallaudet University Press (Washington, DC), 2008.

Contributor to and coeditor of poetry books, including *The Linguistic Muse, Meliglossa, Lingua Franca, Tongue's Palatte*, and *Speaking in Tongues*. Author of numerous professional articles on linguistics. Contributor of short fiction to anthologies compiled and illustrated by Diane Goode, Dutton, 1992, 1997. Contributor of poem to *On Her Way*, Dutton 2004, and of short story to *First Kiss (Then Tell)*, Bloomsbury, 2008.

Napoli's books have been translated into Chinese, Danish, Dutch, Farsi, German, Greek, Hebrew, Italian, Japanese, Korean, Polish, Portuguese, Spanish, and Thai.

Sidelights

A professor of linguistics at Swarthmore College, Donna Jo Napoli has a passion for language that can be seen in her novels for young adults and middle-grade readers. Exploring topics ranging from sports to sharks to fairy tales, Napoli employs both humor and skillful prose to craft stories of hope and inspiration. Noting that her books for young readers "can be broadly divided into two types: contemporary realistic novels and fairy-tale retellings," an essayist in the *St. James Guide to Young Adult Writers* praised the author's "strong points" as her ability to create "genuine, believable characters" and equally believable plots. As the interpreter of stories culled from myth, legend, and biblical sources, Napoli has "forged a brilliant writing career out of making readers see compellingly different interpretations of mythic figures," as *Booklist* GraceAnne A. DeCandido noted in a review of Napoli's novel *Sirena*.

Described as "a gifted author" by a *Kirkus Reviews* critic, Napoli did not plan on becoming a writer. Instead, she received her undergraduate degree in math, pursued Romance languages for her doctorate, and became a professor of linguistics in 1984, after holding several other academic positions. *The Hero of Barletta*, an adaptation of a traditional Italian tale, became her first book for young readers and was published in 1988.

Soccer Shock, Napoli's first original tale for young readers, focuses on a sport popular with her own children. In the story, ten-year-old Adam discovers that he has magic freckles that can both see and talk, and he decides to use this secret to help him earn a place on the school soccer team. "The freckles really steal the show here," commented a *Kirkus Reviews* critic, the reviewer describing *Soccer Shock* as "a well-written story with an affectionate, tolerant cast." Denise Krell, writing in *School Library Journal,* decided that, even with such a "fantastic twist," Napoli's "lighthearted novel succeeds with genuine characters in a believable setting."

A sequel to *Soccer Shock, Shark Shock,* finds Adam a year older and still in communication with his freckles as he also befriends a blind boy during his summer vacation at the beach. While commenting that Napoli's idea of talking freckles "stretches credibility to the breaking point," Maggie McEwen concluded in her *School Library Journal* review of *Shark Shock* that "this light read will appeal to children who have an appreciation for the absurd." Another book in the series, *Shelley Shock,* focuses on Adam and his talking freckles as they have to contend with a girl who makes the soccer team. Here the freckles, through some bad advice, end up creating more problems than they solve for the preteen boy.

Also for middle-grader readers, *The Prince of the Pond: Otherwise Known as De Fawg Pin* employs the fairy tale frog-prince motif, but with a unique twist. A prince is turned into a frog by a hag and is then taken under the protective arm of Jade, a female frog who teaches him the ropes in the pond. Blessed with a prodigious number of spawn, the sensitive frog-prince determines to raise some of them personally. Yet when a human rincess passes by, the frog-prince leaps up to kiss her on the cheek, and becomes a prince, leaving Jade and

their offspring behind. "The frog prince motif has inspired many books," noted *Booklist* reviewer Carolyn Phelan, "but few as original as this novel." Betsy Hearne, writing in the *Bulletin of the Center for Children's Books,* commented both on the point of view—the story is told by Jade, the female frog—and the story's willingness to deal with loss, and concluded that *The Prince of the Pond* is "an animal fantasy that fairy tale readers will relish." A *Kirkus Reviews* critic wrote that Napoli did her research well, citing the book for having an "astonishing amount of in-depth natural history cleverly embedded in its endearing, screwball charm."

To please fans of *The Prince of the Pond* who were curious to know what became of the frog family, Napoli wrote a sequel: *Jimmy, the Pickpocket of the Palace.* Attempting to save his pond from the miserable hag, a young offspring of the prince is transformed into a human and does not care much for the change. Jimmy inevitably ends up working in the palace where he encounters his now-human father. "This successful successor is certain to satisfy old fans and win new friends to the frog prince and his brood," predicted a *Kirkus Reviews* contributor. The third book in the series, *Gracie: The Pixie of the Puddle,* offers a new take on the original story as Jimmy the frog is befriended by a friendly fellow amphibian. When Jimmy once again takes human form during a visit with his regal father, friend Gracie hops after him, dutifully rescuing her shape-shifting acquaintance when Jimmy is trapped in the palace by those hoping he will lead them to a magic ring. In *Booklist* Julie Cummins dubbed *Gracie* a "convincing, funny and cunning tale," while *School Library Journal* critic Miriam Lang Budin praised the book as "a lighthearted fantasy" full of "broadly drawn" fairy-tale characters.

Napoli's young-adult novel *The Magic Circle* serves as a prequel to the well-known fairy tale "Hansel and Gretel." The witch in this version is a good-hearted healer who is cursed by evil spirits with a hunger for children. She moves to the woods so that she will not be tempted, but then one day two succulent children appear on her doorstep. "Napoli flexes her proven talent for unexpected viewpoints, builds strong pace with compressed vigor, and evokes powerful sensory images," noted Betsy Hearne in a review of *The Magic Circle* for the *Bulletin of the Center for Children's Books.* Lisa Dennis, writing in *School Library Journal,* cited the novel's "strongly medieval flavor" and concluded that "Napoli's writing and the clarity of her vision make this. . . . brilliantly conceived and beautifully executed novel . . . sure to be appreciated by thoughtful readers."

Napoli spins a new version of the Rapunzel story in *Zel.* Told alternately from the point of view of Zel as she is held in the tower, the count who wants to save her, and Zel's witch mother, the novel plunges into the psychology of its characters. "The genius of the novel lies not just in the details but in its breadth of vision," noted a contributor to *Publishers Weekly*. "Its shiveringly romantic conclusion will leave readers spellbound." In a *Horn Book* review of *Zel*, Roger Sutton commented that, while the early chapters are a bit of a "wander," the novel ultimately "transforms myth without flippancy, honoring the power of its roots."

Crazy Jack envisions a somewhat darker version of the "Jack and the Beanstalk" tale. In Napoli's retelling nine-year-old Jack is left orphaned after his father gambles away the family farm and then falls off a cliff to his death while trying to rob a wealthy giant. For the next seven years, Jack is obsessed with climbing the cliff that took his father's life. The boy's strange behavior seems like madness to his widowed mother, especially when he claims to have acquired magic beans that will aid him in reaching the cliff's summit—and the home of the murderous giant. Noting that Jack's ascent of the beanstalk and stealing a hen that lays golden eggs "can be interpreted as hallucination," *Kliatt* contributor Claire Rosser explained that Napoli enhances the traditional tale with "modern psychological interpretations," including addictive behavior. Readers "with some basic understanding of the subconscious, will marvel at the neatness of Napoli's narrative" and its "subtle twists of interpretation," Rosser asserted.

Spinners presents the character of Rumpelstiltskin within what Rosser described as "a morality tale of the crippling reality of greed and vengeance." In the story, a young woman named Saskia was raised in a troubled home and now finds solace in spinning wool and other fibers into beautiful yarns. Into her life comes an embittered tailor named Rumpelstiltskin. Once passionately in love with Saskia's mother, who died in childbirth, the tailor is in fact the young woman's father. Greedy for family but unable to love his daughter, Rumpelstiltskin attempts to claim Saskia's child in the hopes that through that child the old man can gain the family he feels was stolen from him. "The novel's emotional content is a stirring mixture of unwise entanglements, foolish father figures, and broken promises," commented Janice M. Del Negro in the *Bulletin of the Center for Children's Books*. "Watching how the tale is unraveled and rewoven is half the fun" of reading Napoli's fairy-tale adaptations, according to Booklist contributor Chris Sherman in his review of *Spinners*.

The Cinderella story shows off its Chinese origins in Napoli's *Bound*, while in *Breath* she retells the mysterious origin of the Pied Piper legend. Set in the fourteenth century, *Bound* finds a young girl named Xing Xing worried over the pain suffered by stepsister Wei Ping. The older girl is enduring the custom of footbinding, and Xing Xing's journey involves a search for soothing medicine. *Breath*, set a century earlier in time, centers on the village of Hamlyn and a sickly, twelve-year-old boy named Salz. Raised by a coven of Christian witches, Salz attempts to discover the cause of a mysterious plague that strikes his town even as the healthy children are removed from the village by a car-

ing piper. *Bound* serves as "both an adventure and a coming-of-age story that will have readers racing to the finish," observed a *Publishers Weekly* critic, while in *Booklist* Gillian Engberg wrote that Napoli's "haunting, sometimes violent tale amplifies themes from well-known Western Cinderella stories" and poses provocative questions about the meaning of the traditional "happily ever after" fairy-tale ending. In *Kirkus Reviews* a reviewer noted of *Breath* that Napoli's "compelling mystery . . . and fully realized characters bring life to the legend," and *Horn Book* critic Susan P. Bloom observed that the author uses "the immediacy of the present tense, with short, clipped sentences," to accent "the edginess of her gruesome tale." In *Booklist*, Michael Cart also noted the darkness of Napoli's retelling. However, the critic added, "history buffs . . . and Napoli fans will find [*Breath*] . . . unarguably artful in its unsparing vision of a pre-Enlightenment Europe."

Another story with traditional roots, *Hush: An Irish Princess' Tale,* is based on Iceland's Laxdaela saga and takes place in the tenth story. The spoiled fifteen-year-old daughter of an Irish king lives in a country constantly under attack by the Vikings. The princess learns that those who toil as slaves can be as strong as kings after she is captured by Russian slavers and feigns muteness in order to survive her ordeal. "Napoli's descriptions are saturated with details, which, while slowing the story, make events seem extraordinarily real," wrote *Booklist* critic Lynn Rutan. Noting that the novel provides a history of the woman immortalized in the Icelandic saga, a *Publishers Weekly* critic praised *Hush* as a "powerful survival story" combining the taut plot and high tension of a popular thriller. *Beast* uncovers the Persian roots of the Beauty and the Beast story and recounts the tale from princely Beast's point of view. Based on a poem by nineteenth-century writer Charles Lamb, *Beast* is "an intriguing and deeply affecting story, and the exotic Persian aspect adds to its flavor," according to *Kliatt* critic Paula Rohrlick.

The Wager introduces readers to a traditional fairy tale from Sicily. Don Giovanni, who had been wealthy, is robbed of his livelihood by a tidal wave. Down on his luck and wandering as a vagrant, the man is approached by the devil, who promises him riches if he agrees to complete a small challenge: he cannot change his clothes, comb his hair, shave, or bathe for three years, three months, and three days. Taking the devil up on the bargain, Don Giovanni gains a truly new perspective on those who are covered in filth and who must live among vermin. *School Library Journal* reviewer Leah Krippner wrote that Napoli's "marvelous story is well told, and the rich, sophisticated language" she employs "will grip skilled readers." According to Engberg, the "vivid descriptions" can be "stomach-churning," but that the fantastic elements heighten the themes of "the importance of appearance, what it means to be civilized, and the line between human and beast." As a

Kirkus Reviews contributor concluded, "No hero ever deserved a happy ending or a bath more."

In addition to fantasies, Napoli has authored several works of realistic fiction. *When the Water Closes over My Head* tells how nine-year-old Mikey is continually confronted with his fear of drowning, but he eventually surmounts this phobia in what a *Kirkus Reviews* writer described as "a funny, easily read story that boys and girls should take to like ducks to water." In *Booklist,* Hazel Rochman drew attention to Napoli's technique of "tightly structured, cinematic episodes" in which her dialogue captures the "daily tangle of close relationships." Rochman concluded of *When the Water Closes over My Head* that "kids will want more stories about this family."

Having overcome his fear of drowning, fourth-grader Mikey returns in *On Guard,* this time to confront anxieties of another sort. The second of four children, Mikey fears that he will not be special enough in any one way to distinguish himself among his siblings. He discovers the sport of fencing and determines to win the medal his teacher awards weekly to a student who has impressed her with a particular skill, accomplishment, or quality. "Napoli is excellent at depicting Mikey's general tendency towards uncertainty, his frustration at his lack of family stardom, and his passionate attachment to his new field," wrote *Bulletin of the Center for Children's Books* reviewer Deborah Stevenson. "Especially with its lure of an offbeat and glamorous sport, this will please many young readers."

In *The Bravest Thing* ten-year-old Laurel has to face the death of her newborn bunnies, an aunt sick with cancer, and her own diagnosis of scoliosis. "Despite the multitude of hard knocks, this is not a problem novel," noted a *Publishers Weekly* critic. "Napoli . . . inspires the reader to believe that obstacles, no matter how daunting, can be made smaller through courage." Another work of nonfiction focusing on modern young people, *Changing Tunes* finds ten-year-old Eileen dismayed to find that her parents' divorce has disrupted her formerly comfortable home, and even her beloved piano is now gone. Ashamed to tell her friends or teachers that her home has been disrupted, she goes in secret to the school's auditorium to practice on the piano. There she meets a sympathetic janitor named Mr. Poole who helps Eileen see that "she can't control the family she was born into," according to a *Kirkus Reviews* contributor. "Napoli's characterizations are well-rounded," added Del Negro, calling *Changing Tunes* a "low-key, gently evolving narrative of a young girl's emotional maturation."

North focuses on Alvin, a black preteen who is inspired by his study of the life of African-American Arctic explorer Matthew Henson. When the boy's mother arranges for his trips to and from his Washington, DC, middle school, Alvin decided to follow in his hero's footsteps. Showing amazing resourcefulness, he runs away to the frozen north, where he grows in confidence while facing a range of challenges. Along with its engaging story, *North* includes "lots of interesting information about Henson and Inuit culture, and important messages about the value of cultural diversity," according to *School Library Journal* critic Connie Tyrrell. Napoli's novel treats readers to "a journey they won't soon forget," according to Phelan, and Rohrlick predicted that the "bravery" of *North*'s young hero, together with "the exotic setting, . . . will draw readers into this unusual adventure story."

Napoli has also written historical fiction for young people. *Song of the Magdalene,* set in ancient Israel, constructs an account of the life of biblical figure Mary Magdalene from a troubled youth as the daughter of a wealthy Jewish widower in the town of Magdala to her experiences as a helper of Jesus. *Voice of Youth Advocates* contributor Libby Bergstrom asserted that "the power of Napoli's investigation into the human psyche will draw YA readers into this book; . . . 'Mary' is a character they will not soon forget." In *Booklist,* Ilene Cooper commented that Napoli's "lyrical writing and layered characterizations" make *Song of the Magdalene* an enjoyable read for a "sophisticated audience."

Stones in Water takes place in Italy during the World War II era and focuses on children living in Nazi concentration camps. Inspired by true events, the novel recounts how thirteen-year-old Roberto, his brother, and his Jewish friend, are taken by German soldiers in a surprise roundup of slave laborers. The boys are unable to tell their distraught parents what has happened to them. Ultimately, Roberto escapes from his Munich work camp, flees through the Soviet Union, and joins a partisan group. In what *Voice of Youth Advocates* contributor Janet Mura called a "harrowing tale of inhumanity, strength, and friendship," Napoli describes the hardships the boys face as some live while others perish. "The honest, understated tone of the narrative . . . makes Napoli's message of the strength which hope and friendship and compassion can impart all the more impressive," wrote an essayist in the *St. James Guide to Young-Adult Writers.* Calling *Stones in Water* "an affecting coming-of-age novel with a vivid and undeniable message about the human costs of war," *Horn Book* reviewer Kitty Flynn added that "Napoli's detailed and gripping descriptions bring the incomprehensible tragedy to life for readers."

Roberto's adventures continue in *Fire in the Hills,* which takes place a year after the action in *Stones in Water.* Returning to Italy in the company of U.S. soldiers charged with invading Sicily, the young teen takes two years to cross the war-torn country to reach his Venice home. Doing what he must in order to survive—including working as a translator for a German soldier—Roberto eventually joins the resistance to fight Italy's Nazi occupation, and he finds romance amid the chaos of wartime. Noting that little has been written describing the role of Italian partisans, Claire Rosser maintained in *Kliatt* that *Fire in the Hills* "makes the actual history vividly real to modern-day readers." *School Library Journal* critic Rita Soltan observed that "Roberto's humanity and strength of character overshadow the brutality" of war, and she dubbed *Fire in the Hills* "powerful World War II literature."

Other stories that take place in Italy include *For the Love of Venice, Daughter of Venice,* and *Three Days.* The first finds an American teen spending the summer in Venice while his father works on a civil-engineering project. Romance soon enters the picture in the form of a pretty Italian teen, but the relationship becomes complicated when the girl's radical politics are revealed. Citing as the novel's strongest attribute Napoli's ability to portray "Venice with loving detail," *School Library Journal* contributor Jennifer A. Fakolt wrote that *For the Love of Venice* "offers a unique slant on contemporary politics and perspectives couched in an exotic romance."

Drawing readers back in time to the sixteenth century, *Daughter of Venice* focuses on fourteen-year-old Donata Mocenigo, who desires to break free of the future desired for a younger daughter born to a family of wealth and station: an adulthood spent in a convent or spent caring for elderly relatives. Disguising herself as a boy, Donata escapes from her home and ultimately finds romance with a Jewish teen who teaches her to read, but whose faith makes him an unsuitable suitor. Praising Napoli for avoiding "the easy anachronism," a *Kirkus Reviews* critic explained that the novel's heroine abides by the dictums of her family and polite society and searches for "a solution to her unhappiness that . . . remains essentially true to her culture and its restrictions." Praising *Daughter of Venice* as "engrossing and exotic," Lisa Prolman observed in *School Library Journal* that, "while a current trend in historical fiction presents a girl with modern sensibilities chafing under the strict rules of a [former] time, nothing about Donata seems forced."

The immigrant experience of Italian Jews, such as Napoli's own grandfather, is the focus of *The King of Mulberry Street,* which takes place in the 1890s. Nine-year-old Beniamino is smuggled onto a ship traveling from Napoli, Italy, to Manhattan, where he must survive, alone. Praised by a *Kirkus Reviews* writer as a "powerfully vivid story" fueled by "the immediacy of Napoli's always-immaculate prose," the novel follows the boy's adventures as he begins a new life as a street urchin in New York City's Five Points neighborhood. With its focus on the challenges faced by young immigrants, *The King of Mulberry Street* "may well offer readers insight into how their own families found their way here—or send them in search of those stories," maintained a *Publishers Weekly* critic. "Napoli is an expert at gripping readers' emotions," observed *School Library Journal* contributor Barbara Scotto, and in *The King of Mulberry Street* "she does [so] with consummate skill."

Immigrants are also the main characters of *Alligator Bayou,* a fictional version of the tragic 1899 lynching of five Sicilian immigrants in Louisiana. Although the immigrants are legally segregated from all of their neighbors—both blacks, and whites—the family befriends members of the African-American community. These friendships lead to the white community taking out violent retribution on the Italians for breaking the law. "Napoli's skillful pacing and fascinating detail combine in a gripping story that sheds cold, new light" on both that era of history in the South and on prejudice against members of different races and national origins, according to Engberg. As Ginny Gustin noted in *School Library Journal,* "Historical events are smoothly integrated with vivid everyday details, strong characterizations, and genuine-sounding dialogue" in *Alligator Bayou,* and a *Publishers Weekly* critic wrote that Napoli's "protagonists are convincingly vulnerable, and the violent climax will ensure that readers remember her message."

Napoli also uses her talent for storytelling in picture books such as *Flamingo Dream, Pink Magic, The Wishing Club: A Story about Fractions,* and *Bobby the Bold.* Based on a tragedy in Napoli's own family, *Flamingo Dream* relays a poignant story about a girl's experiences before and after the death of her fun-loving father to cancer. Their mutual love of all things flamingo is a strong bond between father and daughter, and in Napoli's story the bright pink image reflects the love between the two. In *Horn Book* Kitty Flynn called *Flamingo Dream* "touching" and "unembellished," and a *Kirkus Reviews* critic wrote that the "wonderful collage" pictures by Cathie Felstead "echo the honesty and realism" of Napoli's "wrenching, powerful" story.

In *Ugly* Napoli collaborates with artist Lita Judge to present a retelling of Hans Christian Andersen's "The Ugly Duckling." Transporting the story to Tasmania, she introduces a little creature that hatches out differently than his all-black siblings. Eventually driven from the duck colony, Ugly searches for true friends, meeting a variety of unusual animals in the process. Finally, he discovers his true identity as an Australian black swan in a story featuring "lush . . . details of the natural world . . . and an elegant use of language," according to *School Library Journal* contributor Susan Hepler. "Trust Napoli to work her usual alchemy and make a fabulous coming-of-age story from the bare outline of the reassuring ugly-duckling trope," announced a *Kirkus Reviews* writer in a laudatory review of *Ugly.* Another transported tale, *Mogo the Third Warthog,* presents Napoli's retelling of the "Three Little Pigs" set on the vast grasslands of Africa. As the little warthog tells his story, "Mogo's first-person narration will keep young readers . . . on edge," according to a *Kirkus Reviews* writer.

Kenya is the setting for a picture book based on the true story of Nobel Peace Prize winner Wangari Maathai: *Mama Miti: Wangari Maathai and the Trees of Kenya.* Instead of approaching the tale like a biography, however, Napoli uses a style more like a folktale to present Maathai's work planting trees to improve Kenya. The result is "a vivid portrait of the community from which Maathai's tree-planting mission grows," according to a contributor to *Publishers Weekly.* Engberg praised *Mama Miti* as a "moving tribute," and a *Kirkus Reveiws* contributor dubbed it, "in a word, stunning."

The Earth Shook is another story inspired by true events, although it goes even further into folktale. In 2003, an earthquake shook Bam, Iran, and many children were left orphaned. Now Parisa is the only person left in her town, and she tries to befriend those animals that remain. A *Kirkus Reviews* contributor complimented the book's "poetic text," writing of *The Earth Shook* that "it's refreshing to find a story that juxtaposes our species' finer qualities with its more monstrous ones."

Along with her stories and novels for children, Napoli is a prolific writer in her academic field. Her linguistics work and children's writing intersected with *Handy Stories to Read and Sign,* a book in both English and American Sign Language. "Writing is like a disease for me," Napoli told Monika Schroder in *Booklist.* "I am obsessed with it."

Biographical and Critical Sources

BOOKS

Contemporary Literature Review, Volume 51, Gale (Detroit, MI), 1999, pp. 152-168.
St. James Guide to Young-Adult Writers, 2nd edition, St. James Press (Detroit, MI), 1999.

PERIODICALS

Booklist, January 15, 1993, Carolyn Phelan, review of *The Prince of the Pond: Otherwise Known as De Fawg Pin,* p. 909; July, 1993, Sally Estes, review of *The Magic Circle,* p. 1957; January 1, 1994, Hazel Rochman, review of *When the Water Closes over My Head,* p. 827; October 15, 1994, Frances Bradburn, review of *Shark Shock,* p. 427; March 15, 1995, Ilene Cooper, review of *Jimmy, the Pickpocket of the Palace,* p. 1331; October 1, 1997, Hazel Rochman, review of *Stones in Water,* p. 333; May 1, 1998, Ilene Cooper, review of *For the Love of Venice,* p. 1512; May 15, 1998, John Peters, review of *Changing Tunes,* p. 1627; September 15, 1998, GraceAnne A. DeCandido, review of *Sirena,* p. 221; October 1, 1998, Ilene Cooper, review of *Song of the Magdalene,* p. 341; September 1, 1999, Chris Sherman, review of *Spinners,* p. 124; October 1, 1999, Kay Weisman, review of *Crazy Jack,* p. 355; September 15, 2000, Sally Estes, review of *Beast,* p. 233, and Ellen Mandel, review of *Shelley Shock,* p. 242; September 15, 2001, Michael Cart, review of *How Hungry Are You?,* p. 233; October 1,

2001, GraceAnne A. DeCandido, review of *Three Days,* p. 312; January 1, 2002, Whitney Scott, review of *Beast,* p. 876; March 1, 2002, Lauren Peterson, review of *Rocky, the Cat Who Barks,* p. 1143; April 15, 2002, Ilene Cooper, review of *Flamingo Dream,* p. 1498; April 15, 2003, GraceAnne A. DeCandido, review of *The Great God Pan,* p. 1464; September 15, 2003, Michael Cart, review of *Breath,* p. 232; March 1, 2004, Carolyn Phelan, review of *North,* p. 1190; April 15, 2004, Julie Cummins, review of *Gracie: The Pixie of the Puddle,* p. 1457; December 1, 2004, Gillian Engberg, review of *Bound,* p. 652; August, 2005, Hazel Rochman, review of *The King of Mulberry Street,* p. 1966; September 15, 2005, Carolyn Phelan, review of *Pink Magic,* p. 74; April 1, 2006, Michael Cart, review of *Bobby the Bold,* p. 49; June 1, 2007, Hazel Rochman, review of *The Wishing Club: A Story about Fractions,* p. 87; November 1, 2007, Lynn Rutan, review of *Hush: An Irish Princess' Tale,* p. 40; February 15, 2009, Gillian Engberg, review of *Alligator Bayou,* p. 69; May 1, 2010, Gillian Engberg, review of *The Wager,* p. 79; June 1, 2010, Monika Schroeder, "'I Write Because I Have To': The Books of Donna Jo Napoli," p. S35.
Book Report, March, 2001, Suzanne Manczuk, review of *Beast,* p. 59.
Bulletin of the Center for Children's Books, January, 1993, Betsy Hearne, review of *The Prince of the Pond,* p. 153; April, 1993, Betsy Hearne, review of *The Magic Circle,* p. 260; February, 1997, Deborah Stevenson, review of *On Guard,* p. 217; February, 1998, Betsy Hearne, review of *Stones in Water,* p. 214; September, 1998, Janice M. Del Negro, review of *Changing Tunes,* pp. 24-25; December, 1998, Janice M. Del Negro, review of *Sirena,* p. 140; September, 1999, Janice M. Del Negro, review of *Spinners,* pp. 25-26; December, 1999, Janice M. Del Negro, review of *Crazy Jack,* pp. 119-120; July, 2002, review of *Daughter of Venice,* p. 413; July, 2003, review of *The Great God Pan,* p. 456; October, 2003, Janice Del Negro, review of *Breath,* p. 72; June, 2004, Deborah Stevenson, review of *North,* p. 430; July-August, 2004, Janice Del Negro, review of *Gracie,* p. 2004; January, 2005, Timnah Card, review of *Bound,* p. 222.
Horn Book, September-October, 1996, Roger Sutton, review of *Zel,* p. 603; January-February, 1998, Kitty Flynn, review of *Stones in Water,* p. 77; January, 2000, review of *Crazy Jack,* p. 80; September, 2000, review of *Beast,* p. 577; January, 2001, Donna Jo Napoli, "What's Math Got to Do with It?," p. 61; March, 2001, Christine Heppermann, "Angel Wings and Hard Knocks," p. 239; September, 2001, review of *Three Days,* p. 590; March-April, 2002, Anita L. Burkam, review of *Daughter of Venice,* p. 216; July-August, 2002, Kitty Flynn, review of *Flamingo Dreams,* p. 450; January-February, 2004, Susan P. Bloom, review of *Breath,* p. 85; November-December, 2005, Kathleen Isaacs, review of *The King of Mulberry Street,* p. 721.
Kirkus Reviews, September 15, 1991, review of *Soccer Shock,* p. 1225; October 1, 1992, review of *The Prince of the Pond,* p. 1259; January 1, 1994, review of *When the Water Closes over My Head,* p. 72; May 1, 1995,

review of *Jimmy, the Pickpocket of the Palace*; May 15, 1998, review of *Changing Tunes*, p. 741; September 15, 1998, review of *Sirena*, p. 1386; February 15, 2001, review of *Albert*, p. 263; December 15, 2001, reviews of *Rocky, the Cat Who Barks* and *Daughter of Venice*, both p. 1761; March 15, 2002, review of *Flamingo Dream*, p. 421; May 1, 2003, review of *The Great God Pan*, p. 681; October 15, 2003, review of *Breath*, p. 1274; May 1, 2004, review of *North*, p. 446; May 15, 2004, review of *Gracie*, p. 495; November 1, 2004, review of *Bound*, p. 1046; August 15, 2005, review of *Pink Magic*, p. 1085; October 1, 2005, review of *The King of Mulberry Street*, p. 1085; December 15, 2005, review of *Ugly*, p. 1326; April 15, 2006, review of *Bobby the Bold*, p. 412; July 15, 2006, review of *Fire in the Hills*, p. 727; June 15, 2007, review of *The Wishing Club*; October 1, 2007, review of *Hush*; June 1, 2008, review of *Mogo, the Third Warthog*; February 15, 2009, review of *Alligator Bayou*; July 15, 2009, review of *The Earth Shook*; December 1, 2009, review of *Mama Miti*; April 15, 2010, review of *The Wager.*

Kliatt, May, 1998, review of *For the Love of Venice*, p. 7; September, 1999, review of *Crazy Jack*, p. 12; November, 1999, review of *Spinners*, p. 12; May, 2002, Claire Rosser, review of *Daughter of Venice*, p. 12; July, 2003, review of *The Great God Pan*, p. 15; November, 2003, Paula Rorhlick, review of *Breath*, p. 8; July, 2004, Claire Rosser, review of *Song of the Magdalene*, p. 22; July, 2004, Paula Rohrlick, review of *North*, p. 10; November, 2004, Janice Flint-Ferguson, review of *Bound*, p. 10; September, 2005, Paula Rohrlick, review of *Breath*, p. 22; July, 2006, Claire Rosser, review of *Fire in the Hills*, p. 10.

Library Journal, September 1, 1994, Nancy Dice, review of *The Magic Circle*, p. 244.

Los Angeles Times Book Review, April 8, 2001, review of *Albert*, p. 6.

New York Times Book Review, February 11, 2001, review of *Beast*, p. 26.

Publishers Weekly, November 16, 1992, review of *The Prince of the Pond*, p. 64; June 14, 1993, review of *The Magic Circle*, p. 73; February 21, 1994, review of *When the Water Closes over My Head*, p. 255; October 30, 1995, review of *The Bravest Thing*, p. 62; June 17, 1996, review of *Zel*, p. 66; November 4, 1996, review of *Song of the Magdalene*, p. 77; March 23, 1998, review of *For the Love of Venice*, p. 101; June 15, 1998, review of *Changing Tunes*, p. 60; November 2, 1998, review of *Sirena*, p. 84; July 19, 1999, review of *Spinners*, p. 196; November 1, 1999, reviews of *Friends Everywhere*, p. 84, and *Crazy Jack*, p. 85; November 8, 1999, review of *Stones in Water*, p. 71; November 6, 2000, review of *Beast*, p. 92; March 5, 2001, review of *Albert*, p. 78; August 20, 2001, review of *How Hungry Are You?*, p. 80; February 18, 2002, review of *Daughter of Venice*, p. 97; March 11, 2002, review of *Flamingo Dream*, p. 72;

May 26, 2003, review of *The Great God Pan*, p. 71; April 5, 2004, review of *North*, p. 62; November 8, 2004, review of *Bound*, p. 57; December 19, 2005, review of *The King of Mulberry Street*, p. 65; February 6, 2006, review of *Ugly*, p. 70; October 1, 2007, review of *Hush*, p. 85; February 2, 2009, review of *Alligator Bayou*, p. 50; December 7, 2009, review of *Mama Miti*, p. 46.

School Library Journal, August, 1988, Nancy A. Gifford, review of *The Hero of Barletta*, p. 84; April, 1992, Denise Krell, review of *Soccer Shock*, p. 118; October, 1992, John Peters, review of *The Prince of the Pond*, p. 118; August, 1993, Lisa Dennis, review of *The Magic Circle*, p. 186; March, 1994, Carol Schene, review of *When the Water Closes over My Head*, p. 223; January, 1995, Maggie McEwen, review of *Shark Shock*, p. 109; November, 1997, Marilyn Payne Phillips, review of *Stones in Water*, p. 122; June, 1998, Jennifer A. Fakolt, review of *For the Love of Venice*, p. 148; July, 2000, Sheila Brown, review of *Crazy Jack*, p. 56; October, 2000, Sharon Grover, review of *Beast*, p. 168; November, 2000, Elaine E. Knight, review of *Shelley Shock*, p. 160; May, 2001, Wendy Lukehart, review of *Albert*, p. 130; August, 2001, B. Allison Gray, review of *Three Days*, p. 186; September, 2001, Barbara Wysocki, review of *Beast*, p. 76; October, 2001, Piper L. Nyman, review of *How Hungry Are You?*, p. 126; March, 2002, Lisa Prolman, reviews of *Rocky, the Cat Who Barks*, p. 198, and *Daughter of Venice*, p. 236; May, 2002, Wendy Lukehart, review of *Flamingo Dream*, p. 124; May, 2004, Connie Tyrrell, review of *North*, p. 156; June, 2004, Miriam Lang Budin, review of *Gracie*, p. 116; November, 2004, Barbara Scotto, review of *Bound*, p. 150; September, 2005, Rachel G. Payne, review of *Pink Magic*, p. 183; October, 2005, Barbara Scotto, review of *The King of Mulberry Street*, p. 168; March, 2006, Susan Hepler, review of *Ugly*, p. 199; May, 2006, Diane Eddington, review of *Sly the Sleuth and the Sports Mysteries*, p. 96; September, 2006, Rita Soltan, review of *Fire in the Hills*, p. 214; September, 2007, Mary Jean Smith, review of *The Wishing Club*, p. 172; December, 2007, Cheri Dobbs, review of *Hush*, p. 138; May, 2009, Ginny Gustin, review of *Alligator Bayou*, p. 116; October, 2009, Susan Scheps, review of *The Earth Shook*, p. 99; May, 2010, Leah Krippner, review of *The Wager*, p. 120.

Voice of Youth Advocates, February, 1997, Libby Bergstrom, review of *Song of the Magdalene*, p. 331; February, 1998, Janet Mura, review of *Stones in Water*, pp. 387-388.

ONLINE

Donna Jo Napoli Home Page, http://www.donnajonapoli. com (April 15, 2011).

Swarthmore College Web site, http://www.swarthmore.edu/ (March, 2005), Donna Jo Napoli, "Inside Iran."

Autobiography Feature

Donna Jo Napoli

Napoli contributed the following updated autobiographical essay in 2010:

Several things have shaped me as a writer. One is that I've always felt like an outsider. Another is that I take myself totally seriously. Another is that I have the ability to focus for long periods of time—indeed, I'm obsessive. I would guess that anyone who is reading this is reading in order to know about what events in my life led me to become the kind of writer I am—that is, what events led me to have these characteristics. I don't really believe that coherent explanations for character traits are easily found in tracing events. Nevertheless, I'll let you be the judge.

I have scattered memories of early childhood. I sat on the floor and watched my big brother practice piano in one house we lived in. He was a genius in my eyes. Music got in me then and it stayed. I was a baby in that house, I'm sure. We lived in lots of houses. My father was a contractor and when he would finish building a batch of houses, we would move into the one that hadn't yet sold. We'd stay there until it sold or the bank repossessed it. A few times we moved into apartments. And the last house I lived in with my childhood family was an old Spanish stucco house, the only house we lived in that my father hadn't built. By the time I was thirteen years old, I had lived in thirteen different places. But from that point until I left home at age eighteen, we stayed in that one house.

I was born in Miami, Florida, on February 28, 1948. And sometimes I was sure I could smell the ocean in the wind. When I used to go back to visit as an adult, all I could smell was car gas fumes. But when I was small, Miami wasn't so populated, and there were lots of stands of trees and open spaces. I liked to climb trees. And I liked to wander. I'd cut off palm fronds and attach a string and have my own bow. And I'd use little sticks for arrows. I'd go on adventures, ready to defend myself against anything.

Most of these adventures were alone. My first grade report card is full of comments by the teacher urging my mother to get me to speak more. I was the youngest of four children and it seemed to me that everyone was brilliant and vibrant and had so many interesting things going on in their lives. I was content just to be among them. But my mother must have taken the teacher's advice, because in second grade I got in trouble a few

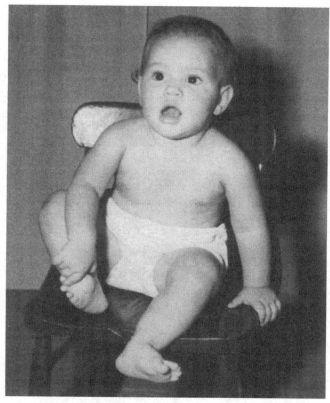

The author, about nine months old (Courtesy of Donna Jo Napoli.)

times for talking in class. I remember that teacher. She struck me as unkind. I was convinced she didn't like me. Once I wrote her a note. It went:

> Dear Mrs. Lorem,
> I hate you.
>   Love,
>   Donna Jo

Mrs. Lorem called in my mother about this letter. My mother hated to go to any meeting of any sort. In fact, there were lots of things I couldn't join as a kid because my mother wouldn't go to sign me up—like Brownies. Oh, how I wanted to be a Brownie. Anyway, my mother, touchingly decked out in a nice dress with a terribly uncomfortable girdle underneath—all this to try to overcome her reticence—went and talked to Mrs. Lorem. I sat in the car and waited for her. On the way home, my mother said to me, "Next time don't sign *love*." I think my mother's sense of being an outsider and her unwillingness to face certain aspects of the world seeped into me. I tend to hate meetings, too. I never go to optional ones.

I was slow to learn to read. I was lousy at recess, because the balls always seemed to hit me in the face, so I'd shut my eyes and scrunch over whenever it was time to play. I never managed to notice things in time. My siblings were always pointing out things and, by the time I'd look, they'd say, "You missed it again." Later when I studied Deaf culture and language in America, I was reminded of that feeling I had of missing the boat all the time—a feeling captured in the Deaf phrase "TRAIN GO SORRY." I also wasn't terribly good at making friends. About the time I'd manage to find someone nice in my neighborhood, we'd move and I'd be the new kid on the block again. I only had to change schools once, though. So I did know people at school. But when I was a child, parents didn't chauffeur their children. If I was to get to another child's house, I was to do it on my own steam—on my feet or on my bike. So I didn't play much with friends outside school. All of these things added together gave me the sensation of traveling through life alone, bumping along on my bike, enjoying what was becoming a rich inner life.

First Holy Communion, age seven, Coral Gables, Florida (Courtesy of Donna Jo Napoli.)

My bike. Oh, I remember my first bike. We were poor and lots of times I was given things that were too big for me. The idea was that they'd last me longer that way, as I grew into them. That's how it was with the bike. I couldn't reach the pedals at first. But I was determined, and I wound up riding it with just the tips of my toes touching. I was in third grade. It was wonderful freedom. I could go all over the place. So now my wanderings got wider, and I was late to supper more and more often. My mother hated that. She bought me a watch once, but I promptly lost it. I had no sense of time and I had very little sense of the value of possessions. I lost a lot of things.

But I found a lot of things, too. Mainly animals. I had a way of coming across stray cats and luring them home with me. I'd dress them up in doll clothes and push them around in a stroller and cuddle them for hours. My mother didn't appreciate the strays. We never kept them long. I also nursed many a hurt bird. Most of them died in shoeboxes. And I had various collections of lizards and snakes.

Sometime in second grade I learned to read. That was a miracle. I couldn't get enough of it. I went to the school library and checked out two books every week (the maximum allowed). And I'd always finish within a couple of days. Pretty soon I got the librarian to allow me to return the books midweek and check out two new ones. We had no books in our house. None whatsoever. We had no magazines. My father read the newspaper. I'm not sure I ever saw my mother read at all. My older siblings had school books. And I had the never-ending library.

I'd take a book and climb a tree and read for hours. Or I'd squirrel away behind the couch and read with a flashlight all day long. My mother used to say I'd ruin my eyes. She used to tell me to go play like other kids. Later, when I was a teen, she worried I'd be too bookish to ever find a husband. I never listened to her. I just put my face into the book and let my mind travel. I wanted a husband—oh, yes—but priorities had to be acknowledged, and my first priority was to find myself.

I liked to hide behind the couch. From my perspective my parents seemed to fight a lot in those days, and I felt safe behind the couch. I also felt safe at school. School was my haven—no one shouted and there were so many books.

*

In fourth grade I had a dreadful experience that still makes me tremble. It was the second week of school and I was in reading class. We had special teachers for reading according to our levels. Of course by that time I was an ace reader, so I was in the advanced group. The reading teacher gave us our first test of the year. But instead of handing us a mimeographed test, she wrote the test on the blackboard. I couldn't read it. I leaned forward. I squinted. I got up out of my seat and walked forward. Mrs. Sap (yup, that was her real name) told me to sit down. So I asked the kid in front of me what the test said. And Mrs. Sap made me leave the room. She said I had cheated. And she sent a note home with me. I was mortified.

My mother knew I wasn't the sort to cheat. I was a spacey, happy child. And there was no one putting any pressure on me to do well at anything. There was no reason for me to cheat. So she took me to the optometrist. Dr. Koblenz asked me which line on the chart was the lowest that I could read. I said, "What chart?" It turned out I was profoundly myopic. Dr. Koblenz said he was amazed I hadn't been killed crossing the street.

I'd had lots of eye tests in school. I feared them. All the children would line up and read the chart at recess. The physical education teacher would call out, "Line five— left to right," or "Line six—right to left," and each child would read off the letters. I'd always wait until close to the end and I'd memorize the letters of each line, forward and backward, so that when it was my turn I could say the letters right. I wasn't trying to fool anyone. I simply didn't know what was going on. I thought the job was to say letters in some magic order and somehow other kids knew how to do that, and I didn't. So I merely learned from them—memorized their answers. I wasn't what you'd call a "with-it" kid; I had no idea what was up.

My glasses changed my life. I could see the balls at recess and pretty soon I could catch them some of the time. I could see where I was going on my bike and I started visiting friends' houses. I felt confident and happy. But my eyes kept getting worse rapidly, and so when I was twelve years old I was given hard contact lenses. This was in 1960, years before contact lenses were popular. The idea was that the hard lenses would shape my corneas and keep my myopia from progressing. I was already legally blind, but I was functionally just as visually able as anyone else, all because of my contacts. I don't know if the contacts did the job they were supposed to do or whether my eyes had already hit bottom, but my eyes didn't get worse, and I can still see today, though at age sixty I gave up my contacts and now wear only glasses.

I went into early adolescence pretty blithely, enjoying all the sights, even going to some parties, beginning to enjoy a changing body. Then lightning struck—my father had a major disaster: he was arrested. In a flamboyant way—it was first page news in the *Miami Herald*; it was on the TV nightly news. While I said before that we were poor, the story isn't really all that simple. Sometimes my father would sell houses and he'd have money. We'd enjoy a period of prosperity. I even got to go to summer camp. And my father bought me a piano one Christmas (I don't know what happened to the piano I remember from my earliest days). But the money

never lasted. My father was a poor businessman and generous to a fault. He'd give the shirt off his back if someone asked—and it seemed that someone was always asking. And he was addicted to gambling. He was also an insulin-dependent diabetic, and I believe that a lot of his very drastic mood swings and rather erratic behavior were due to chemical imbalances that he couldn't control. It all added up to terrific unevenness in the experiences of each of my siblings. I don't know how my siblings looked at our childhood. But I remember being constantly worried about money (among other things; still today I am an expert worrier). I never liked it when someone bought me something, because I was worried that would mean that something we truly needed couldn't be bought. My next older sister was pretty and my mother used to buy her nice clothes now and then. My mother just assumed I'd want the same sort of thing. But it distressed me when she'd buy me something nice. And I never took care of it—grass stains were the rule in all my clothes. Mamma would lament that I was such a tomboy, but I never changed my behavior. So she stopped buying me nice clothes pretty quick.

Despite all this financial insecurity, we lived primarily in middle-class neighborhoods and I went to middle-class schools. So when my father got arrested, it was a foreign experience and total humiliation for all of us. All my siblings had already left home. My next older sister got married at sixteen, so she was just recently out of the house. I faced it alone in that sense.

I was in junior high. The timing couldn't have been worse. Anyone's junior-high experience is at least partially the pits no matter what. But mine was a good sixteen feet under the bottom of the pit. I broke off with the sweet young boy I'd been flirting with. I stopped going around with any of my girlfriends. I applied myself to my schoolwork, delighting in memorizing zillions of Latin verb inflections, reveling in algebra. I became the home-economics whiz, making all my own clothes, cooking meals, and baking pies. I was busy and tough, and nothing, but nothing, was going to hurt me ever. When I graduated from ninth grade I won the award for best student in home economics, in Latin, and in mathematics.

In the meantime, my father was fighting the charges. I didn't inform myself properly about the whole thing—it was his mess, not mine—but I knew it had something to do with theft. And I reevaluated a lot of my home life up to that point; in some ways I started to feel that I shouldn't have been surprised by his arrest. I now looked at the men my father spent time with in new ways. I reviled them. But I never reviled my father. It was a time of great confusion and loss.

He didn't go to jail until I was well into high school. By that time I was barreling along like a runaway train. I became treasurer of the sophomore class, the junior class, and then the student council. (And don't think I wasn't aware of the irony of my father's daughter being entrusted with the money.) I was president of the French club and vice president of the state Latin club and on the math team. And I discovered dance. Like I said, music entered my bones very young. But I seemed to have a deaf ear to tune. Way back in second grade Mrs. Lorem had told me to stand silent and just mouth the words at the Christmas concert. And in ninth grade when I joined the chorus, I realized that Mrs. Lorem's advice had been very good. But when music came on, I just had to respond. In tenth grade I found the appropriate way: the high school's dance teacher introduced me to modern dance and jazz. I was hooked. I danced whenever I could. My friend Vicki Green and I would dance at school events—sometimes to a band that a young man I was dating played the saxophone in.

*

The end of senior year was hard for me. My father came home from prison and he was a shadow of himself. He'd always been noisy and full of energy. My siblings fought with him terribly through adolescence. But I remember fighting with him only once. I expect that was because his own problems pretty much ab-

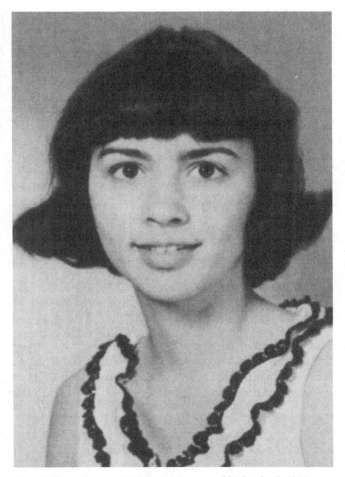

Elected "best all around" in her senior year of high school, 1966 (Courtesy of Donna Jo Napoli.)

sorbed him by the time I hit adolescence. And my mother was more of a hands-off parent, anyway. Now and then my brother would snarl at me, though I knew it was out of concern for my well-being. He was a teacher in my high school and he would assume that teacherly way with me. Now and then my oldest sister would engage me in conversation. She was teaching English at the University of Miami, and she was into discussion. Boy, did we have some long discussions—I remember going to school bleary-eyed the day after one of our late night discussions. She, also, wanted to help me stay on target. But mainly I got to grow up pretty much by myself—a fact I am grateful for.

Really, though, I wasn't on my own. My family was Catholic in name. When I was little, they took me to church and I had my First Holy Communion. All the other children in the family quit going to church before the onset of adolescence. In fact, quitting church was sort of a mark of maturity. I remember my brother once telling me when I was twelve that the only reason I still went to church was that I wasn't willing to grow up. Whatever, I went to church faithfully and I was confirmed. From an early age I rode my bike there alone. When I got older, I made friends with a priest who had a lot of big crooked teeth and wasn't very smart but was extremely good-natured. We would talk about right and wrong, good and evil. When the hormones of adolescence turned on for me, this priest helped me to find my path without turning to sex. But as I read more and as I found myself an outsider, I began to question everything. One day when I was sixteen, I went to confession and told my priest that I didn't believe in the infallibility of the pope. We had a small debate right there in the confessional. And he lost his temper. I think he felt personally betrayed by me, after all our heartfelt conversations. He told me that I wasn't Catholic as long as I felt that way and that I should leave the Church and not come back until I could repent and accept the pope in all his holiness. I left in tears. I never went back.

But the Church was with me, inside me. The rules of the Church are what guided my daily behavior for years. I was a do-gooder. I loved causes. I was constantly pointing out injustices in school policy and trying to get them changed. I worked painting houses and collecting food and clothes for poor people (and this was long before such things were fashionable). I was a crusader. And, quite frankly, I worked to keep myself focused on issues outside the family because home life then was terrible. My mother was miserably lonely and worked hard all day at the laundromat, and often we didn't have a decent meal at night. I was no moral support to her at all. I kept to myself; I was absorbed in a world she was no part of. I still feel guilty for that period—for the way in which I was willing to look at other people's problems and try to help them but was unwilling to look at my mother's problems and try to help her. I realized then, as I do every day of my life, how very hard it is to be a good person.

Rehearsing the part of the Lion in "Androcles and the Lion" at Radcliffe, 1967 (Courtesy of Donna Jo Napoli.)

All these things were going on inside me when my father came home in spring of senior year. I had already been accepted to colleges. I picked Radcliffe College because the catalogue had a whole-page photo of a modern dance class and none of the other catalogues I looked at did that. Radcliffe offered me a full scholarship plus money to buy books and to come home once a year to visit my family. I wanted to go there. My father was afraid. My father, who had always seemed so powerful to me, was afraid. He didn't want me so far from home. He worried I'd be lost up in Boston. And he worried that the family would feel the loss of my help, for I used to help out at the laudromat on the weekends and I worked as a cashier at a grocery store. Plus he didn't understand why a girl needed that kind of education.

All of this was somewhat inconsistent and odd. My oldest sister put herself through college and through a master's program. My brother went to college with my sister's help and then he went through a master's program. Only my next older sister had stopped her education (though she later picked it up and went to nursing school). But, in fact, all my siblings had had rocky situations in their educations at one time or another—all of them had dropped out in one way or another at some point. It's just that eventually they found their way back to school. So in a very real sense my family valued education. Still, my father was in a weakened state—and he didn't want me leaving the family.

But I did. Radcliffe was the official name of the women's college of Harvard University (there's debate about what Radcliffe is today, but that's what it was then). So I went off to Harvard in fall of 1966—and that was another turning point in my life. The world of ideas that I had yearned for in the books I read and that I'd gotten a hint of in my high school honors classes opened up to me at last. I majored in mathematics, which I'd been good at in high school, but which I found I wasn't very good at in college. Still, there was much about it I loved—the elegance of a clean proof, the fact that something could actually be right or wrong, the glorious consistency. And it was sort of fun being one of only a handful of women to major in it. Sometimes I even enjoyed the feeling of anger and in-your-face rebellion I'd get when a male professor (all my mathematics professors were men) would treat me like I didn't deserve to be in the classroom. The fighter inside me got stronger and stronger.

My junior year I took an Italian language class quite by chance. All my grandparents had come to America from Italy, so I knew in some sense I was Italian. And my mother's mother, who spent many years with us at the end of her life, never did learn English. (Actually, that grandmother was born in Alexandria, Egypt, but she was raised in Italy and her culture and language were Italian.) We ate a lot of pasta and cannoli on holidays. Still, my Italianness had been a minor part of my identity while growing up. In college, however, I found that everyone tagged people ethnically. I was tagged Italian. So when I stumbled into that Italian language class, I half expected to find myself at home. I wasn't. Standard Italian was pretty different from what my grandmother spoke—and I couldn't remember much of what my grandmother spoke, anyway. But something of her lingered in me, because my first-year Italian teacher put a lot of effort into trying to drum out my southern Italian accent. Today I'd give anything to have that back. I speak Italian like a (messed up) schoolbook. I'd love to speak it with my grandmother's Calabrese tongue, instead.

The combination of mathematics and Italian (plus I took German freshman year and I'd had years of French and Latin in high school) should have told me I was heading for linguistics. But I didn't know what linguistics was. It was just a word to me, even though my roommate majored in it. In fact, I think it may have been a desire not to compete with my beloved Emily that kept me from looking more into linguistics. So I graduated college in mathematics and went to graduate school in Romance languages and literatures. The first semester of graduate school I took a course on Old Provençal (an old Romance language spoken in the southeast of France) taught by a linguist. And I realized I was a linguist. I switched immediately to a program in Romance linguistics and that's what I got my Ph.D. in.

Academics wasn't the only part of my education years, though, or even the most important part. I met my future husband October 2nd of my freshman year. I realized immediately that I wanted to know him better. But he didn't notice me. It took a lot of effort on my part to get him to see I was there. I even took a fatally boring history course just so I could sit near him and draw romantically explicit pictures in his notebook. That did the trick: we had our first date on February 17th, our first kiss, and after that we just moved ahead together. We got married during my junior year, on his Christmas furlough from the army. He had joined the reserves because the Vietnam War was in full swing and his lottery number was four—which meant he'd get drafted for sure. He had several months away at boot camp, then several years of weekend training. He was a government major and a photographer and a kid who came to Harvard on a huge scholarship and looked around with as much awe as I did. He'd spent the first twelve years of his life in South Dakota, with no hot water in the house and an outhouse out back. Then he'd moved to Iowa and lived in a tiny house on the wrong side of the tracks. His parents were old and poor. He was radically left wing and radically anticlerical and wonderfully sweet. And we resonated in ways that still continue to surprise and comfort me. We've been married forty-two years and I love him more all the time.

Another major part of my life was dance. I went to classes in the morning, ate a huge lunch, and then danced all afternoon, every afternoon. I took modern dance and jazz from Claire Mallardi, whom I remember with so much love that the image of her standing in front of us urging us to stretch our toes out as far as we could—then demanding we stretch them another inch farther—brings tears to my eyes. I performed in dance concerts and once in a musical (I was the lion in the biblical Androcles story). I felt completely free when I danced. Completely whole and good. I didn't really think about what the life of a dancer meant, but when Claire offered me a summer dance scholarship at Connecticut College, I was delighted. Then another dancer came up to me and told me she was on partial scholarship and wanted to go to that summer program and needed the dance scholarship to do it. I stood there silent. This woman had assumed I was another rich Cliffey. I didn't disabuse her. I asked myself whether I really wanted dance as a career—and I came to no conclusion. But I did know that being away from my husband for a whole summer would be painful. I gave up the dance scholarship, though I continued to dance in Boston.

The third major part of my nonacademic life was the need to help others—to try to pay back what was being given to me every day of my life. I discovered the Boston City Missionary Society and I worked in their summer camps in New Hampshire, with kids who were wards of the state of Massachusetts. The summer after I graduated from college I worked for the city of Seattle, Washington, as a counselor for teens in the Neighbor-

hood Youth Corps. It was my job to try to keep these teens in school, both by negotiating whatever problems they had with their summer employers and by convincing their families that the long-term benefits of staying in school would outweigh the immediate benefits of their dropping out of high school and working full time. My teens were from racial minorities, mainly Native Americans, and full of challenge. I was passionately in love with them. But, as with dance, I realized that social work couldn't be a career for me. Being passionately in love with the people you are supposed to help, especially when their problems are enormous, leads to constant inner turmoil. At the end of the day I was a limp rag. I couldn't have survived that life. So I was indeed lucky that I soon discovered linguistics—which gave me all the intellectual challenge I craved and still left me enough soul to have a loving personal life.

None of this related to writing as a career. Once in college, though, I took an expository writing class. It was a required course. We wrote mainly essays. But one assignment was to write a fictional dialogue. I wrote about a young woman and a young man discussing whether or not to go off for the weekend together. I wrote it from the woman's point of view, giving her thoughts as well as her words. All we got of the man was his words. She was a virgin and she was debating all those thou-

Napoli and her husband in Los Angeles, 1970 (Courtesy of Donna Jo Napoli.)

sands of issues we all have to debate when we decide how to live our sexual lives. The teacher of that class called me up at my dorm. I'd never been called by a teacher at Harvard before. I'd hardly ever even gone to office hours, except to get a registration card signed or something administrative like that. But he called me up and told me I should become a writer. I was momentarily dazzled. But I quickly decided never to take another writing class. I didn't want to be the proverbial starving writer. I wanted to earn money and never have to make my family move and never have to make my children worry about whether there would be food on the table. I was practical. Still, that man's words stuck in my brain, so that I remember them clearly even today.

*

My husband's and my lives twisted around each other, sometimes comfortably and sometimes painfully, for many years. He went to law school and I went to graduate school. Then he clerked for a judge in Boston and finally took a job as a litigator in a city law firm. I got my Ph.D. in 1973 and spent a postdoctoral year in linguistics at MIT while I worked part-time teaching Italian language (in the Italian department) and theoretical syntax (in the philosophy department) at Smith College. That year I also got pregnant. The pregnancy marked a major change in our relationship. We were both hardheaded and we both needed a lot of growing up in order to give of ourselves in the ways that marriage demands. Please don't misunderstand me: young people can have good marriages—they can know themselves well and choose wisely and be kind to one another. So I'm not knocking young love. But we weren't among those blessed marriages. We didn't know ourselves well enough and we weren't kind. We thought more than once of splitting up and going our separate ways through life—and sometimes we did more than just think about it. But getting pregnant was a decision to commit ourselves to each other no matter what. For many people getting married may be that commitment. But for us it was the involvement of another life—of the innocent life of our first child—that was the crucial moment.

When our first daughter was three weeks old, my husband quit his law firm job—a job that had turned ever more demanding, calling for late night work and weekend work—and took a job teaching at the law school of the University of North Carolina in Chapel Hill. I got a part-time job there. And my job is worth noting, because it put together weird things about me. I taught an advanced language course in the Italian department; I taught a linguistics course on the history of Italian in the Italian department; and I taught a course on the linguistic analysis of the metrics of poetry in the mathematics department.

That last one was a bit of a stretch. But the chair of mathematics, Fred Stone, was a remarkable man. His faculty wanted to know what all the fuss was about this

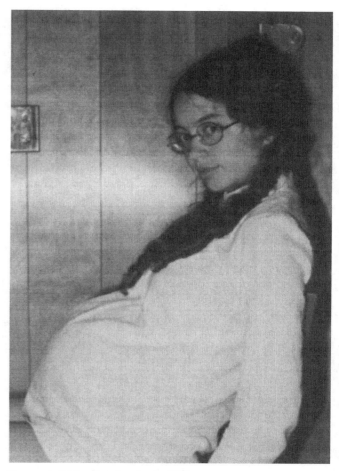

Pregnant with her first daugher in 1974 (Courtesy of Donna Jo Napoli.)

fellow Noam Chomsky who did syntax at MIT—and I'd just come from a year of working at MIT and I loved this fellow Chomsky. So he let me teach a course on poetry to the mathematics students for pay and in return I taught a weekly seminar on theoretical syntax to the mathematics faculty for free. It was great fun.

That was a wonderful year. Our daughter started out fabulous—a marvel—and just got better and better. I kept her with me all the time except when I was teaching, when I'd pass her into my husband's hands. Sometimes I even taught the mathematics faculty seminar with my daughter strapped to my chest. She was my little friend and I didn't want to let go of her ever.

I wrote a lot of poems that year, partly inspired by the course I was teaching in the math department but mostly inspired by my daily life. It became habit. Ever since then I've written poetry whenever I feel the extremes—euphoria or fundamental need or misery. I don't consider myself a poet. While the act of writing fiction makes one a fiction writer, I don't believe the act of writing poetry makes one a poet. There's a certain mindset to poets—a certain mode of translating reality—that can't be turned off or on, it's just there. I write poetry as an exercise sometimes and as a release sometimes, but my natural mode is fiction. Nevertheless, over my career thus far I've contributed to several volumes of poetry by linguists and co-edited five of them.

*

The next year, summer of 1975, we moved to Washington, DC. My husband kept teaching law, now at American University, and I took a job teaching linguistics at Georgetown University. We lived in a neighborhood of the District called Mount Pleasant. In those days the neighborhood was mainly African American, with considerable numbers of refugees from San Salvador, scattered handfuls of Koreans, and a few white people—mostly gay couples. We lived in a row house with a tiny front yard and we dug a sandbox that almost filled the yard. Beside the sand box there was just enough room for a full-sized teepee. Children up and down our block played in that yard with our children. Once our neighbor said that a photo of kids playing in our sandbox could be used for a UNICEF poster. I was very proud of that fact.

We lived there five years and had two more children, both sons. But we also had sadness. I had a miscarriage between my daughter and my first son. For many people a miscarriage is no big deal. I've known women who have taken such things in stride. But I didn't. I wanted that baby very much. And, though he never even breathed, though I never even felt him kick inside me, I loved him and I missed him when he gave up residence in my body. I grieved for him. My grief was compounded by the fact that our doctor and our friends kept saying miscarriages were ordinary things and we should move on and get pregnant again and just forget about it. Everyone wanted to leave it behind—as though that baby had never existed. Even my husband felt that way. We became estranged emotionally. And I sought comfort in writing letters to a friend.

I wrote those letters every day. Sometimes twice a day. Sometimes three times. I was obsessed. I wrote about the baby I lost, and about growing up in my unruly family, and about the hard times in my marriage, and about my personal failures and hopes and dreams. I wrote out my heart. Eventually, I came to terms with the loss of that baby. And I even got pregnant again. And then my first son was born, and I was happy with my two wonderful healthy children. But my friend, the one I'd been writing to, did a miraculous thing for me: he saved my letters. He handed them to me in a big box. He said. "Look, you've written a novel."

He was wrong. Letters to a friend are not a novel. Epistolary novels, of which there are many terrific ones, are carefully shaped. But I didn't know my friend was wrong. I thought I'd written something that had form. And I realized that I loved to write. Writing transported and absorbed me. It allowed me to say things I didn't dare say in person. It allowed me to be eloquent, when in person I am a mouse. And, as I looked at those let-ters, I realized it allowed me to be whoever I wanted to be, for some of those letters didn't sound like me—they sounded at once much stronger and wiser and much more vulnerable and lost than I really was.

That was the start of my writing career—right there in that miscarriage and those letters. I hope no one else starts like that, but that was my start.

By that time storytelling was a major part of my day. I'd sit with my family and we'd go around the circle telling stories. Sometimes we'd tell old favorites, like "Cinderella," varying it by telling it from different points of view. Other times we'd tell stories about things that had really happened to us that day. We lived near the National Zoo, and we went there several times a week—so animals found their way into many of these realistic stories. Still other times we'd just make up outlandish things, sometimes spinning out a single story over weeks (a specialty of my husband's).

And I wrote down the stories I told. Being completely naive about how these things worked, I sent my stories to New York publishers. That's how I began my collection of letters of rejection.

*

In 1980, after five years in Washington, DC, we moved to Ann Arbor, Michigan, where my husband worked for the law school of the University of Detroit and I worked for the linguistics department of the University of Michigan. Moving was culture shock: we went from a multiracial lower-class inner-city neighborhood to a white small city. We tried to ease the shock for our oldest child, the only one who had yet gone to school, by moving to the neighborhood of the elementary school that had the best racial mix: Angell Elementary. However, once we got to town we found out that our own neighborhood was white and that the racial mix in the school was due to the fact that children were bused in from graduate student housing. So our poor daughter couldn't play with most of her friends after school, because she had no way to get to their homes. Still, she made a lot of friends from all over the world, and she still writes to one in Japan.

We had two more children during our Michigan years: another daughter and then our third son. My husband and I kept up our habit of passing the preschoolers back and forth between us, though the juggling act got more and more precarious. We never used day care. We never used babysitters unless it was at night and the littlest ones were already asleep. I savored their day-by-day changes way too much to ever leave them for long. I recognize how lucky I was to be able to do this. It was only the combination of two academic schedules that allowed the luxury. But I am quite sure that if we hadn't both been academics, I would have withdrawn from a career for those years. Child-rearing is, without a doubt, the most important responsibility and privilege I've had

Napoli and children at the beach in Forte dei Marmi, Italy, 1983 (Courtesy of Donna Jo Napoli.)

or will ever have. And it goes by so quickly. Even a six year old has a world view—a set of internalized parameters—and a need to go off without being fettered by large protective hands. Opening my hands and letting them go, one by one, was harder to learn than holding them close and whispering sweet somethings. But my first child was a formidable teacher. Indeed, all my children are fiercely independent. By the age of four, all of them could make a nutritionally balanced meal. You may laugh. But when a four year old sets the table and puts a cup of yogurt in front of everyone and a bowl of cut fruit and some nice dark bread ripped into hand-sized chunks, a mother's heart melts. Or mine did. The only thing I don't seem to have managed to teach them on the domestic side is how to do laundry. But that may be because laundry to me means the dreaded laudromat of my high-school years—so I've never really felt comfortable about them doing it. I was the laundry fairy of our house during the years our children were home.

Through it all I wrote stories and sent them out. My collection of rejection letters got so big that my husband once said we could wallpaper our house with them—and that Michigan house was like a big old barn. I had hundreds of letters of rejection.

While my writing life wasn't going well at all, my professional life finally got stable and my family life got very secure. I had been denied early tenure at Georgetown University on the grounds that I was the only untenured member in my department and the new president of the University, Father Healy, refused to have any fully tenured departments. This was despite the fact that I'd published strongly and my teaching evaluations were superb. Being very dumb about political things, I fought the tenure decision—actually having an argu-

ment with Father Healy himself. I believe the man had difficulty understanding why a woman needed tenure in any case. He kept reminding me that my husband had a good job and I was a mother. My arguing only resulted in people who had supported me before suddenly saying I was acting uncollegial. So I left and tried my luck at Michigan. I worked my way through the ranks in record time, becoming a full professor in 1984 at the age of only thirty-six. That's because I published so much—dozens of articles and several books. People often commented on how prolific I was. They thought I was completely committed to the field of linguistics.

In fact, I am committed to linguistics. It is a wonderful discipline—it opens your head and, therefore, your heart. But that commitment was not the reason for my heavy publishing. Rather, I'm a writer—I was then and I have been since 1975. I wrote more in linguistics than most other scholars my age because I simply loved the act of writing itself—not because I was any more scholarly than others. I loved shaping the arguments on paper. I loved leading my reader through to the conclusion.

My family thrived in this period. My husband took an interest in health law and blossomed as a scholar. My oldest child was a whirlwind of activity, trying to turn our house into a center for the arts with her piano, violin, and flute playing as well as her ceramics and painting and dancing. She danced the role of Fritz in *The Nutcracker* with the Pittsburgh Ballet before an audience of a thousand, night after night. She was wonderful. My oldest son became a maniac bike rider and soccer player, breaking many things around the house as his ball ricocheted here and there. He also took piano and violin lessons and then picked up trumpet. And he spent zillions of hours making model cars and airplanes—

completing a 1,000-piece model at the age of only five. The three little ones were all happy and jabbering away. The five of them fueled my writing with their spirits.

*

Eventually I sold a story to Carolrhoda Books of Minneapolis: *The Hero of Barletta* (which didn't come out until 1988, though it was accepted in 1984). It was a retelling of a traditional joke-story I heard in Italy one summer. We spent most of our summers in Italy in those days because my linguistic research was on Italian syntax. We had a rule that we followed ever after—and that was that we could go anywhere we wanted in the summers, anywhere at all in the whole world, so long as the summer paid for itself. As a result, I've taught classes and given lectures throughout Europe and in Australia and South Africa and China, as has my husband. The whole family has a wanderlust. Four of my children worked in Europe during one or more of their teen summers. And one of them has lived and worked in Europe for several years now.

I felt happy to sell that first story, but I also felt rather strange: the message seemed to be that I could tell traditional stories, but not stories I made up from scratch. It was a mixed message.

The family in Venice, 1988 (Courtesy of Donna Jo Napoli.)

We moved to Swarthmore, Pennsylvania, in 1987, and that's where we've been ever since. The move here was again because of trouble at my job. An English professor who was lethally ignorant about linguistics was put in charge of the linguistics program at the University of Michigan. He told me I had to revise the content of my classes, and when I argued with him, he threatened to spank me. I will never cease to be sickened by the sexism I have encountered in academia. I came as close to hating that man as I have ever come to hating anyone. I left. I left a fabulous university that I loved so very much, as well as lots of friends and great colleagues, because a man threatened to spank me. It's the sort of humiliation no one should have to endure.

Life seemed to expand for many years. My husband taught at a law school in Delaware, where he became the director of the Health Law Center and then added on directorship of the school's graduate programs. Eventually he moved to a law school in Philadelphia, but kept doing work in health law. Our oldest daughter kept up her role as humanist, but added the role of scientist. She taught neighborhood kids in piano, violin, and flute throughout high school, but her heart was captured by a great chemistry teacher. She majored in the studio arts at Duke University as a premed student, graduated with distinction, then went to Temple University School of Medicine, where she specialized in medical care of the urban underserved, and is now a primary-care physician. Our oldest son also mixed the arts and science. He taught neighborhood kids trumpet while he was in high school and he was an amateur competitive ballroom dancer in college. But science won as his career, too. He got a Ph.D. in chemistry from Harvard and then went to Harvard Law School. He's now a chemistry patent lawyer.

Our middle son was a bit of a wild man in many ways. He seemed to love every new thing he encountered. While his big sister and big brother were into sports in high school pretty strongly, joining the varsity teams, and his big brother also did crew and soccer in college, our middle son did some sports in that way (wrestling and baseball), but he also got into fencing in a shockingly serious way and became a nationally ranked foil fencer. When he was sixteen he was the National Champion in Foil Fencing in Division II of the USA. He decided to go to Stanford University precisely because he wanted to work with that fencing coach. He did a special major through the Department of Geology, and eventually moved into sculpture and then into lamp design. He supported himself as an artist for many years, living sometimes in Italy and sometimes in New York, but then got involved with a nonprofit social action group and turned from his design work to nonprofit organizational work, mostly in London. He's now getting a master's degree in human tights at a European program.

Our younger daughter loved music, the way all her older siblings did, and she was also into animals. She raised dozens of rabbits in elementary school. Then she got into theater in high school and was in several plays. At Harvard she continued that drama work, but also took art courses and won the Silk Screen award her freshman year. But, like her two oldest siblings, science won in the end. She majored in biology and went to the University of Pennsylvania's School of Veterinary Medicine, then did an internship and now works at a veterinary hospital where she is doing graduate study as well as clinic work.

And our youngest son, well, he seemed to be our only laid-back child. He played so many instruments, including cello and piano, but the trumpet was his love and he continued playing it and also singing at weekly concerts throughout his four years at Harvard. He also did soccer, and skateboarding, and just generally seemed to enjoy life, never getting too passionate about anything. Then he found birding. That did it. He learned to recognize birds by sight and sound. He can take you on a walk you'll never forget, making you notice so many things for the first time. He majored in math in college, then worked in the ornithology department of a museum, and eventually found his way back to academia. He's now a Ph.D. student in mathematical biology.

So that's what happened to them over the following two decades. As for me, I teach linguistics at Swarthmore College, a small college with dedicated students who I admire to the point of adoration. For every hour I put into them, they put in ten hours and come back with the most challenging questions I've ever faced. I think I have a job in heaven.

For several years I carefully divided my time between writings in linguistics and fiction writing. But in 1990, when I finally found a New York publisher that would buy my work, I started spending a little more time on fiction. Then my writing life snowballed and I couldn't write things fast enough. I had so many stories in my head and editors seem to want to publish them. So for maybe fifteen years I spent considerably more time on fiction than on linguistics. Then I had a shift back. . . but I'll talk about that later.

*

The story of my first novel, *Soccer Shock,* is an interesting one. I found myself a New York agent and I sent her that manuscript. She loved it. But then a man in her firm who had experience with children's fiction read it and said that it would never work because the idea of talking freckles was too dopey (his word) for any child to ever swallow. My agent advised me to drop the freckles. My children voted to keep the freckles. I didn't know what to do. Then my middle son spoke up strongly. He said that only a top-notch fantasy writer could advise me properly and he knew just who I should ask: Lloyd Alexander. My son's fifth grade class had visited Lloyd's home that fall and my son felt he knew Lloyd personally. I, actually, had met Lloyd, because

I'd invited him to speak to a class of mine at Swarthmore College, but I didn't consider him a friend. Nevertheless, I telephoned him and said that his good friend, my son, had suggested I call, and I explained the problem. I said, "Should I drop the freckles?" He said, "How can I know without seeing the manuscript? So send me the manuscript." Lloyd Alexander was perhaps the most generous-spirited human being I've ever had the privilege of knowing. I popped the manuscript in the mail that day. Three days later he called me and said, "Don't drop the freckles. Drop your agent."

And so I sent *Soccer Shock* to Dutton Children's Books and in fall, 1990, Lucia Monfried, the editor-in-chief, bought it (it came out in 1991). That was the beginning of a wonderful relationship and several novels. All my children had played soccer at one time or another, but it was my oldest son who coached me through that book. The sequel to it, *Shark Shock* (1994), is also partly due to my oldest son. One summer we were at a beach in North Carolina and we made the mistake of watching the movie *Jaws*. Our son became terrified of sharks, and that terror was used in *Shark Shock*. The blind character in that book, Seth, came right out of the fears I had when I was twelve of going blind myself.

These two books wound up forming a trilogy with *Shelley Shock* (2000), a story of a girl who wants to be on the soccer team that has so far only allowed boys. It was influenced by my oldest daughter, who met exactly that situation when we moved to Michigan, and who broke the gender barrier by joining that team. The name Shelley came from my good friend, Shelley Nixon, who is also a writer (she wrote *From Where I Sit*—a fabulous book) and whose spirit of independence is infused in the character of Shelley.

My second novel, *The Prince of the Pond: Otherwise Known as De Fawg Pin* (1992), grew directly out of all those nights of storytelling with the family when my children were very young. It was also influenced by a short poem by Joanne Casullo, a poet from Nebraska who spent a year in Ann Arbor. But mostly this story came into my head because of the kind of childhood I had. Though I was a loved child, I was never taken seriously. When I had a success, the most anyone ever did was pat me briefly on the head. When I had a problem, people would look at me as though I had to be crazy—for what could be so bad in my little life? The family problems were so huge that my own life within it was dwarfed. The only one who took me seriously, as a result, was me. So that's what I do—I take just about everything seriously. And when I write for children, I am dead serious. If you sit back and think seriously about the frog prince story even just for a moment, you will realize that without a frog to help this prince through the ordeal, he would have been snake meat fast. That's the truth, right? So Jade had to exist. There's no way around that. In some ways I think I don't really write fiction—I just give the true story, at least when it comes to fairy tales. The sequel, *Jimmy, the Pickpocket of the Palace* (1995), was written because so many children asked me what happened to the frog family left behind in the pond. They were right: the story wasn't finished. And it still wasn't finished after the second book. So I wound up making a trilogy, closing it with *Gracie, the Pixie of the Puddle* (2004), finally giving some closure to Jade.

I should point out that while I have done two trilogies that just happened to grow on their own, this is not the normal way to do trilogies, and I believe it is not the best way to do them. Rather, planning out a series makes much more sense. I have done two sets of real series since then—planned-out series—and they seem more cohesive to me than those original two trilogies.

My third novel was *The Magic Circle* (1993). The motive for this novel came from a question my younger daughter asked when she was ten years old: "'Why are there so many wicked witches and evil stepmothers in fairy tales, but no wicked warlocks and evil stepfathers?" My little feminist heart beat hard and I flipped the pages of my mind through all the fairy tales I knew, looking for the worst woman character I could find. There she was: the witch in the story of Hansel and Gretel. Nothing could be worse than wanting to eat human children. So I had her—my protagonist—and my job was to try to figure out why she did everything she did. I began with an exploration of cannibalism—which led me to witchcraft—which led me to Reformation Germany at the start of the 1600s. The basic issue of this tale is the question: how much are you willing to give up in order to be a decent person? It's a question I've grappled with my whole life. The Ugly One in *The Magic Circle* does a better job at answering it than I have ever managed to do. While there is no sequel to this novel, it is became the first in a string of dark fairy tales that is still, I hope, playing out. My second dark fairy tale, *Zel,* based on the Rapunzel story, came out in 1996, and it was followed by *Spinners* (coauthored with Richard Tchen), the Rumpelstiltskin story, and *Crazy Jack,* the Jack and the Beanstalk story, both in 1999. Then came *Beast* (Beauty and the Beast) in 2000, *Breath* (the Pied Piper legend) in 2003, *Bound* (Cinderella) in 2004, and *The Wager* (based on the Sicilian fairy tale of Don Giovanni di Fortuna) in 2010. Closely related in style and theme is *Hush: An Irish Princess Tale,* which came out in 2007 and which takes a very minor character from one of the Icelandic sagas and builds up a back story for her.

Napoli in her laundry room/study, 1993 (Courtesy of Donna Jo Napoli.)

I chose each of these tales largely because the plot line made my skin crawl in one way or another. *The Wager,* in particular, got to me because of the graphic renderings of the underbelly of poverty—something I will always be grateful to my editor, Reka Simonsen, for not sanitizing out. People sometimes think that it's an easy life to be homeless—it's a lazy life. Nothing could be further from the truth.

My mode of working on fairy tales is to go back to the earliest example I can find of the tale and see what I can mine from it. Often the early versions are quite short—a page or two. They amount to not much more than a plot line, and usually a rather disconnected one. This sends me straight to the library to find books about the time and place the story is set in. I'll read about the political history, economic development, culture and customs, flora and fauna, essentially anything I can get my hands on. I also head to the Internet and try to see if I can find images of old paintings done in that time and place, or photographs of the countryside. The Internet also often allows me access to snatches of music typical of the time and place that I might otherwise have a very hard time tracking down. Because the college I work at subscribes to many major online journals, I can also locate plenty of reliable information via the Internet.

I love doing the research for a book. I'm convinced that we are, to a large extent, products of the world we live in. That goes even for iconoclasts, since they are somewhat defined in chosen contrast to that world. If I were to pick you up and plop you down in Downpatrick, Ireland, in 900, and if you could magically overcome the language barrier so that you understood what the people around you were saying and they understood you, you'd still find that in so many ways you didn't understand their world. What made them laugh or cry, what made them confused, the explanations they gave for the natural phenomena they observed, the problems they saw in life and the solutions they were able to entertain—all those things and more might very well feel inexplicable to you. So when I write a story, I try hard to ground the character in the setting, and to give readers enough entry into that setting that they can make sense of the character in her world. My goal is to pick you up plop you down in another world, but to hold your hand every moment you're there.

While I love these fantasy based tales, I also enjoy writing realistic novels. My first totally realistic novel, *When the Water Closes over My Head* (1994), goes back to my oldest son again—with his terrific fear of drowning, as well as of many other things. He was born with an overdeveloped sense of mortality—something his youngest brother seems to share, but which the other three—the intrepid ones—can't begin to understand. The family in that novel is loosely based on an early stage of my family—right down to the grandparents in Iowa. The friends of the family are based on our friends

in Iowa. The sequel to it, *On Guard,* deals with the same character as he learns how to fence. My middle son coached me through this one, of course. It came out in 1997.

Another realistic novel came out in 1995: *The Bravest Thing.* This is the story of a girl who wants to become a veterinarian, so she raises rabbits. The soul of my younger daughter pervades the story, and she, in fact, did the illustrations in the book. This book is very dear to me because the aunt in the book has cancer and my own sister was dying of cancer when I was writing it. At times I could hardly bear some of the scenes. I would put the manuscript away and just cry.

I've written several other contemporary realistic novels. *Trouble on the Tracks* came out in 1997. It's the adventure of a thirteen-year-old boy and his little sister, both Americans, who travel alone on an overnight train within Australia. They get involved with a bird-napping ring and wind up thrown off the train. This story grew out of personal experience. My family spent the summer of 1992 in Australia and we took a train called The Ghan from Adelaide to Alice Springs (the opposite direction of the children's travels in the novel). One of the things I found most amazing in Australia was the great number of spectacularly colorful birds. Many of them are protected species, so it's illegal to export them. But sometimes bird-nappers capture them and sneak them out of the country to sell to rich people all around the world. That summer a large bird-napping ring was busted up, scattering the seeds for my novel.

The next realistic novel was *Changing Tunes* (1998), about a girl whose parents get divorced and who, besides losing her father from the household, loses the piano, which is hugely important to her. This book happened because my oldest son had three best friends, and all their families went through divorces when they were in middle school. I wanted to write about the mixture of feelings I sensed them going through, but I didn't want to invade their privacy. So I wrote about a girl, instead, and I put her in fifth grade, and I entirely made up the events that happened to her; it was only the emotions that belonged to my son's friends.

Another one is *For the Love of Venice* (1998), which has as its setting the political controversy within the city of Venice over the building of the sea wall to stop the flooding. Since our family has spent many summers in Venice, I was close to this issue. Then there's *Three Days* (2001), about an American girl traveling with her American daddy in Italy, when he has a heart attack and dies. He manages to pull off the road safely, but she's alone and in shock. Two men pick her up and. . . Well, you need to read it. That story grew out of a real event, too. An Italian girl was traveling with her Italian daddy several years before that and he died. It was hours before anyone stopped to pick up this grieving child by the side of the road. The story of that girl, only six years old if I remember right, became nationally

The author with her familiy at her twenty-fifth college reunion at Harvard, 1995 (Courtesy of Donna Jo Napoli.)

known. People were so upset that no one had stopped to help her for so long. Letters to the editor in major newspapers all over the country asked what had become of the Italian soul. It was a moment of national identity crisis, as I saw it. And it shook me to the core, because our family had traveled a lot in places where if a child wound up alone, it could be seriously dangerous. That little girl's experience was my worst nightmare. I tucked it away in the back of my head because I wasn't willing to face it. But when my youngest child became a teenager, I dragged it out of my memory and turned it into a story.

My only other contemporary realistic novel is *North* (2004), about a boy in Washington, DC, whose greatest hero is Matthew Henson, and who winds up running away from home and heading north, like Henson did. He doesn't make it all the way to the pole, but he does get past the Arctic Circle. My family lived in Washington, in this boy's neighborhood (Mt. Pleasant) for five years, and my oldest daughter had a friend whose mother was what I considered overly protective. I wondered what was going to happen between him and his mom when he hit puberty. Hence, the book.

I've also written historical fiction that isn't fantasy. In fact, my first such book marked a major change in my writing career. That career had been moving along relatively smoothly, with me working with a single editor at a single publishing house, Dutton. I even won a nice award for excellence in fiction writing from the Leeway Foundation in 1995 and I received a summer grant from the American Association of University Women in 1995 to do the social-science research that gave the background for my story *Zel*. Some of my books had gotten starred reviews and been nominated for awards and put on special reading lists. So things had been wonderful.

However, in the fall of 1995 I had a difficult decision to make. There is no single age that I write for, nor is there any single style or genre that I stick to. That means that it's fairly unlikely that there would exist a single publisher who would find all my manuscripts publishable within their vision of how their publishing house worked. And in 1995, I was faced with the choice of either burying a manuscript that Dutton did not want to publish, or going with another publishing house on it. It was frightening to think of doing a novel without Lucia Monfried as my editing partner. She is ideal and our working relationship to this day is an author's dream. I present her with first drafts (not always—sometimes my first drafts are just too dreadful to inflict on her—but now and then I do, and she'll actually take the time to read a very first draft) and she tells me whether she's interested in seeing a second draft or not. If she gives it the go ahead, I revise and get feedback from others. My family gives feedback on the very first draft, of course. But that's not all. I corner children in grocery stores and on street corners and I ask them if they'll read my manuscripts. I send out e-mail pleas to my college community, seeking child readers. And much of the time they agree. So I get feedback from virtual strangers. Then I rewrite and send the manuscript back to Lucia. She gives big bold criticisms at this point—things like "make it tighter," "bring it to a higher peak," "use this character or dump him," big things like that. I rewrite and then I read to classes. I have teachers from preschool through high school who are kind enough to allow me to come into their classrooms and read day after day and gather comments from their students. Then I rewrite again and send the manuscript back to Lucia. At this point she usually makes specific comments chapter by chapter. And I revise, getting more comments from friends that I rope into reading my manuscripts. And Lucia might make more comments. And I revise. Eventually Lucia says it's ready. With that kind of support, you can imagine, perhaps, how very hard it was for me to think of striking out without her.

Furthermore, I was truly shaken in my own evaluation of the manuscript. When someone you respect and love feels a manuscript is not suitable for the profile of their publishing house for whatever reason, it gives pause for thought. I was panic-stricken. So I called Lloyd Alexander again—my mentor in moments of total loss. And Lloyd gave me solid-gold advice. He told me that I should write whatever I needed to write—whether it be light mysteries or dark gothic tales or slapstick comedy or heartfelt contemporary stories or even erotica. He said my soul as a writer belonged to me. And he told me that I should listen to myself—that I should give credence to my inner voice and put that story before the public if I believed in it.

I wasn't really sure I believed in the manuscript any more, but I was so upset by the whole turn of events that I knew something inside me would burst if I didn't act. So I decided to give it a try, and thus began my relationship with Brenda Bowen, then editor-in-chief at Scholastic. My first novel edited by Brenda came out in 1996: *Song of the Magdalene*. Set in the town of Magdala in the Palestine of the first century, the story shows the life of a girl from the age of ten to eighteen. The research for this book took most of a year, and a lot of my misery over the loss of my baby is built into the center of this story. But a lot of my childhood joy in religion is also woven into the book. My oldest daughter drew the beautiful map in the book, which makes it that much more special to me. (She went on to do maps in several other books of mine, as well. Remember, she

was the studio arts major.) And it was my younger daughter's love of Mary Magdalene, from having seen the musical *Jesus Christ, Superstar,* that led me to write it in the first place. My mother said this was the best story I'd ever written. She died in 2002, and she read everything I wrote. This book tells a story of many kinds of love, with particular attention to the loves between women—and it certainly is connected to the women I have loved. It's dedicated to my sister Marie, the sibling I was closest to growing up.

Working with Brenda Bowen was a good experience, a really good experience. We went on to do five more young-adult novels, three younger novels, and two picture books. We also did a series of sixteen chapter books, the "Angelwings" books, from 1999 through 2001. She has since left editing—which is a great loss to writers—but she's now an agent, and I can't imagine a better one. She represents me on that part of my work that my husband doesn't feel comfortable handling.

One of my favorite experiences regarding editing was working with Brenda on *Sirena* (1998). Set in ancient Greece, it essentially tells the story of the Trojan War from the point of view of a mermaid. I love the classical myths, and I was delighted to do another in 2003: *The Great God Pan.* This is the story of the goat-god Pan falling in love with the princess Iphigenia, daughter of the great Agamemnon, and my editor on it is another great in children's literature, Wendy Lamb. Wendy has her own imprint at Random House and I've been lucky enough to do a string of novels with her. She has eclectic taste, of course, but what she's worked on with me mostly is historical fiction. Since she seems to have real insight into Italian matters, we've focused together on Italy or Italian-Americans in most of our work together. She edited *Daughter of Venice* (2002), which is about a girl from a noble family in 1592 Venice who wants an education. I'm astonished and enormously pleased to say that the book is carried at the Doge's Palace museum, right there in the heart of Venice.

Wendy also edited *The King of Mulberry Street* (2005), about an Italian boy whose mother puts him on a cargo ship as a stowaway and he winds up on the streets of New York all alone in 1892. That story is to some extent based on the life of my paternal grandfather, if the stories my parents told me were true. Through working on that book Wendy taught me so much about how to sift through facts, using only those that make the story move forward and changing any that, by their transformation, could make a better story. The most recent one we did was *Alligator Bayou* (2009), about a group of Sicilian immigrants in Tallulah, Louisiana, who got lynched in 1899 largely for economic reasons; their friendship with the African-American population was seen as a threat to the plantation system. This was a painful book to write because I grew so fond of the characters as I explored them through various scenes, all the while knowing they had to die. Again, Wendy taught me so much, this time mostly about timing and rhythm. We worked on the last few chapters, the ones that had to go at breakneck speed, for months and months.

Some of my other historical fiction books also centered on Italy or Italians. *Stones in Water* (1997) and the sequel, *Fire in the Hills* (2006), look at the path a Venetian boy takes through World War II. With other Italian boys, he is essentially kidnapped by the Germans and has to work for the war effort in Germany, Poland, and Ukraine, before he runs away. That takes about six months, and it fills the first book. Then he has to make it back home to Venice, and that takes about three years, since Italy changed sides in the war and the north was occupied by the Germans. He has to go through many hardships before he finally finds himself on the bridge back out to Venice. A third book, *The Smile* (2008), is about the young woman who sat for the portrait known as the "Mona Lisa." The story starts in 1492 in Florence, Italy. She's only thirteen then. And it goes on until she's twenty-four, and a mother. All these books were edited by Lucia, and I hope we'll do more.

It may seem odd to you, my reader, that I talk about editors at all. But writing is a pretty scary business. I sit in a room all alone all day long simply typing. I don't really have anyone to bounce ideas off as I'm going. Some writers do—they like to work out their stories in detail before they start writing. But I prefer to discover my story as I'm writing it. So I'm very much alone. That means that when I finally show a draft to someone, whatever they say feels like it's right—it's sacred—it's almost the word of God. I find myself trusting my editors implicitly. They are my partners. And I've been lucky enough never to be let down by them.

So in this regard I must mention another couple of editors. I've written two middle grade humorous novels that are based on fairy tales: *Ugly* (2006), which is the Ugly Duckling tale, and *Mogo, the Third Warthog* (2008), which is the story of the three little pigs. Both are in the vein of the frog prince trilogy: lots of information about natural history, yet classic fairy tales. These are among my favorite types of books to write because they don't give me nightmares, unlike some of my dark fairy tales and some of my historical fiction. Brenda Bowen was the editor who bought both of these, but she left and they were put into the hands of Namrata Tripathi, who has a wonderful eye both for editing and for picking the right illustrator for the words. Nami also edited a picture book of mine that I'll talk about later, and she and I are now working on another picture book, *The Crossing,* which I hope will come out in 2011.

*

It took me forever (or so it seemed) to sell my first picture book. Maybe because I am not a visually oriented person and I didn't understand for the longest time what a giant role illustrations play in picture books. I knew very well that illustrations were delightful. I was lucky enough to have Judy Schachner as the illustrator on my froggy trilogy. But those were novels, and in novels the illustrations mainly support the writing. So I didn't really get it. In picture books the illustrations build up the world that you cannot build up with words, because you have so few words to work with—perhaps 1200, not many more. One of the things that I find amazing about editors is that they have the skill to take a manuscript of just words and figure out which illustrator could build a satisfying world to set those words in—and most of them, at least in my experience, do it very well. But Nami is among the best.

Another uncanny editor in that respect is Paula Wiseman. She edited my first picture book, *Albert* (2001), which was, by the way, rejected by I think twenty-six editors before Paula took it, and then went on to do very well, getting starred reviews and other honors and winning the Kentucky Bluegrass Award. This was a really tough book to illustrate, because it's about a man who puts his hand through the iron grillwork over his window and winds up with birds building a nest in it. He has to stand there while the eggs mature and hatch, and until the last fledgling leaves the nest. So the whole story takes place in one spot. The canonical picture book moves you through a variety of locales, each offering lots of opportunities for illustrators. The classic *Good Night Moon,* written by Margaret Wise Brown and illustrated by Clement Hurd, is the gigantic exception—normally a story that takes place in just one spot doesn't allow for satisfying illustrations. Paula was a genius in choosing Jim LaMarche as illustrator, because Jim LaMarche is a genius at using varieties of perspectives and playing with nuances in facial expressions. I am incredibly lucky, because I've been paired with him again on a book called *Sand* (or that's its working title at this point), which will come out with Hyperion when Jim finishes his part.

Paula also edited my most recent picture book, *Mama Miti: Wangari Maathai and the Trees of Kenya* (2010), where she enlisted Kadir Nelson as illustrator—another brilliant choice. This book is about how a single woman in Kenya managed to get the entire Greenbelt movement started, in large part through encouraging women to plant trees. How much can you do with a book about planting trees? But Kadir had no trouble producing a profusion of colors and designs—and expressive faces and hands—that never makes you feel like you're dealing with just one kind of tree. I marvel at him. And it was Paula who knew the right match of illustrator to manuscript. I hope I get the chance to work with her again.

So at this moment Paula serves as bookends to my picture books. There are a dozen other picture books between those bookends. Some of them are with coauthors. I never intended to write fiction with anyone else. As a linguist, I prefer to work with a coauthor because we each bring different strengths to the work and we have each other to bounce our ideas off of. Theoretical linguistics is a field that proceeds largely via argumentation, so this works beautifully. But fiction didn't strike me as the kind of work that people could easily collaborate on. Then my sister Marie got sick, and in the last stages of her cancer, we sometimes told stories to distract her from the pain. One of those stories was about her dog Rocky, who had to go live with her daughter because she couldn't take care of him anymore. I wrote it up, and Marie and I together refined the words. It was published as *Rocky: The Cat Who Barks* in 2002. Marie died in 1996, so she never saw the book, but she at least knew it would get published; she knew she'd be a published author, which made her smile.

I've gone on to write a picture book with each of my daughters. *Bobby the Bold* (2006) is about a bonobo, a type of ape, who can do some American Sign Language signs. I wrote it with my veterinarian daughter, who as a teenager worked one summer in the London zoo and got to know bonobos. *Ready to Dream* (2009) is about a little girl who travels to Australia with her mother and fancies herself to be an artist. She meets an Aboriginal artist and her whole picture of what art is develops from one that is product-oriented to one that is process-oriented. This one I did with my older daughter, the studio arts major in college. And I've done one picture book with a dear friend, *Hotel Jungle* (2004), about a hotel in Africa that is taken over by baboons, and another picture book with another dear friend, that I'll talk about below.

I've also worked with a mathematician friend on two mathematics tales, *How Hungry Are You?* (2001) and *Corkscrew Counts* (2008). I love doing math tales. It's fun to take some abstract concept, like fractions, and try to find a fun story that not only gets across the concept, but uses the concept in some heart-warming way (or at least that's how I think about it). To myself, I call these stories "math with a heart." I've done another one by myself, *The Wishing Club* (2007), and I hope to do many more.

Two other picture books I've written alone are based on family events. My nephew was killed and he left behind a young son and a pregnant wife. The son came to stay with us soon after the death, and I wanted to read him books about the death of a parent to help him. But I couldn't find appropriate picture books. At that point the books available were either too abstract (about leaves changing color) or too metaphorical (about a chair now being empty) for his particular needs. There were plenty of books on the death of a grandparent— but he needed one about a parent. So I wrote one, *Flamingo Dream* (2002), which still makes me cry when I open it. But that's what my grand-nephew needed and what he deserved: something that would allow him to face how profound his loss and grief were. This is not a

book for all kids—but it serves those who need it, and it's a recommended book for children dealing with grief. I also wrote a happy book influenced by family: *Pink Magic* (2005). This is about a boy who loves pink and who desperately wants to receive something in the mail, and the way his sister winds up helping him. It's a sweet story and it could well have been rendered saccharin by the wrong illustrations. But the illustrator, Chad Cameron, decided to go jazzy—and, as a result, the book is just so much fun. Generally, it is unusual for picture books to be translated into other languages because esthetic preferences regarding illustrations vary from country to country. Only three of my picture books have been translated—two into Korean, and this one into Brazilian Portuguese, and a fourth is about to be translated into Japanese. I am convinced it is the illustrations that made *Pink Magic* appeal to a non-American market. The kids are remarkably un-pinpointable with respect to their race or ethnicity. Boy would I love to do another book with Chad Cameron.

One of my best experiences as a writer relates to another picture book. When my novel, *Beast,* came out, I got an e-mail from an Iranian editor-translator telling me that his publishing house had decided to translate the book (which is set largely in 1500 Persia) into Farsi. Because the United States has no diplomatic relations with Iran, he said they were simply going to "steal" the book—I'd get no money. And he asked me whether I therefore wanted nothing to do with him, or if, instead, I'd be willing to answer any questions he came up with as he was translating. I was thrilled at the idea that Iranians might read my story and I was gratified that all my long, long research on Persia had resulted in a book about their own country that they actually wanted. So I jumped at the chance. That translator, Elvand Hossein Ebrahimi, became a dear friend. The book came out in Iran and was well received. In 2005 I visited Iran for ten days as a guest of the Ministry of Islamic Culture and Guidance, and Elvand took me to many places, tourist spots, of course, but also schools and day-care centers. You can read about my experience on the Swarthmore Web site. The Internet article tells how I visited a day care center in Bam, the site of a devastating earthquake. After that visit, I talked with Iranian writers and they fed me lots of Iranian folk literature. So I wrote a story about an earthquake, which is infused with allusions to well-known Iranian literature of the past and present. It came out in 2009: *The Earth Shook: A Persian Tale.* Again, the illustrator, Gabi Swiatkowska, did a superb job—and it was the editor Nami Tripathi who chose her. The money I've made from that book so far has gone to UNICEF, earmarked for the day care center in Bam.

Among the remaining books on my list is a series of four chapter books that I've done with my youngest son: *Sly the Sleuth and the Pet Mysteries* (2005), *Sly the Sleuth and the Sports Mysteries* (2006), *Sly the Sleuth and the Food Mysteries* (2007), and *Sly the Sleuth and the Code Mysteries* (2009). I used the term "chapter books" earlier without defining it (my "Angelwings" series is also chapter books). Chapter books are books for new readers who have better skills than early-reader books require but are not necessarily ready for full-fledged novels. So typically the chapters are quite short. And typically the whole book runs to under 100 pages, often only 60 or so. My son and I decided to aim for not just the second/third-grade crowd, but also for older children who are still struggling with learning to read in English, maybe because of some learning problem, maybe because English is a second language. So the humor in those books stretches upward, and a teen could easily enjoy reading them. The publishing house decided to give quite young illustrations to the books, however—and, while we enjoy the illustrations, that pretty much pulled the rug out from under our hopes for reaching that older readership. It's a pity. But publishing houses have to think of the bottom line: money. The biggest market for the books is elementary school, so they made the illustrations appeal to those readers.

An interesting fact about writing is that writers have little control and rarely much input at all on questions beyond the words in the manuscript. Illustrations, covers, even titles often are imposed. For the most part I've been phenomenally lucky with regard to these issues, but I do wish my son and I had prevailed on the question of how to pitch the "Sly the Sleuth" series.

*

And this, finally, brings me back to linguistics, my other love. In the fall of 1993, a student of mine wrote her senior thesis on literacy questions with respect to deaf and hard-of-hearing children. Since I had to guide her through this, I had to read everything she read. By the end of the semester, a fire had been built under me. I was reading about Deaf culture and sign language as much and as fast as I could. And I've kept doing that ever since. This new passion has reconnected me with my love of linguistics. These days I'm spending more and more time writing linguistics articles in which I analyze the structure of sign languages and on doing activism work for Deaf rights, which involves both organizing conferences and writing articles for journals (about rights with respect to language choice and usage). Together with a friend who is a certified translator and who has worked in education, I've coauthored the book *Handy Stories to Read and Sign* (2009), with accompanying DVD. These are stories are presented in both English and ASL on the same page and in the DVD. They offer a new method of teaching reading to children whose major language is a sign language. I would love to do more such stories, but we need to see how effective these first stories are.

Besides all these books for children and young adults, however, I write adult novels. Brenda Bowen is my agent, and I recently gave her the first manuscript. That is not the first adult story I've written; I've been writing them for years without any success in selling them. But that is the first one I've asked her to try to sell for me. Now I wait to see. But in the meantime, I keep writing. That's what it means to be a writer—you just write, whether you get published or not.

So far I haven't published anything that is too close to autobiographical. Certain parts of my life still hurt to tell about. Writing this autobiographical essay has been painful in many ways. But I might well try such a novel—who knows? People often ask me where the ideas for my stories come from. While I'm not sure that I always know where a story comes from, I can say that I never have trouble coming up with ideas and I have difficulty understanding how anyone could have that trouble. My own life so far has not been glamorous or easy or extraordinary. Yet it has led me to constantly look around and reevaluate. And it has brought me in contact with interesting places and people. I believe that if you keep your eyes and ears and mind and heart open, you will find plenty to write about—more than anyone could ever write in a lifetime.

People often ask me if I write with a goal in mind—if I write in order to teach a moral or preach. I don't. Even in my math tales, I write from my heart and gut. So it's not surprising that a lot of my views on life are discernible in my books. But I never set out to convince people of a particular point. And I deeply resent children's books that do that. Writers for children are in a particularly responsible position. Children have a tendency to believe what they read. They look to books for truth and knowledge and guidance. For that reason alone, writers have to be strict with themselves. We cannot indulge in our favorite diatribes. We must be honest and fair at all times. We offer—we don't persuade. And anyone who stands on a soapbox before children is abusing power.

That doesn't mean, however, that I feel comfortable presenting everything objectively to children. I don't. The world is full of beauty and evil, and we are all part of both. Children know this from a very early age. They take in information, they try to understand. But their understanding is delicate and fragmented, and if it is ever to become strong and whole, it needs to be nurtured along. When I write for children, I do not hesitate to present them with the sadness of mortality and the horrors of wickedness—but I always also try to leave them with a sense of hope, with the sense that whether or not they can change the problems in life, they can find a way to live decently and joyfully. Hope is an internal matter. I strive to cultivate it in my readers. Children offer fertile ground.

People often ask me if I like being a writer. I love being a writer. But I didn't always love it. All those years of collecting letters of rejection were hard on me. One of the sad things about American society is our attitude toward the arts. When a child writes a poem, we praise

Napoli, on a boat going from Napoli to Capri in 2007; behind her is Mt. Vesuvius (Courtesy of Donna Jo Napoli.)

lavishly. But when an adult writes a poem, we might receive it politely, but in our hearts we suspect the person is deluded. Unless someone's work is published or bought, we have trouble respecting it. We raise art onto a pedestal and we treat the artist as a genius. All of this is detrimental to our spirits and to the life of art in our country. Writing doesn't just burst from our foreheads like the birth of a goddess. Writing takes a lot of hard work. It took me years to learn the discipline necessary for following my characters and not imposing some truth from the real world around me into the truth of the fictional world on paper. It took me years to learn not to try to show off—to understand that any word, any turn of phrase, that draws attention to itself and away from the story is counterproductive. And I'm still relearning these lessons and more every day. Maybe that's why I love writing—because it keeps me learning, it keeps my head running. And I have advice for writers out there. In the immediately preceding sentence I almost wrote "for would-be writers" rather than "for writers," but there are no would-be writers. If you write, you are a writer. If you want to write and you don't, you aren't a writer. Writing is like a disease—you don't choose it, it seizes you. It claws into your chest and rips

out your heart. You feel incomplete if you aren't working on a story. You write just as you would breathe. So if you are a writer, you have all my sympathy, but also all my encouragement. Write as much as you can, as often as you can, and you will get better and better and better.

There are four rules I like to give to young writers when I go on school visits. One is to write what you know about. That doesn't mean you should write only about yourself or your school or your country or your race. It means you should do research, serious research, and then write. And the lovely freebie that comes along is that you'll know more about this great big wonderful world.

A second rule is to write about something important. That doesn't mean you should write about a death in the family or a wedding or a birth—the canonical important things. It means you should search your heart for what really matters to you and use those feelings in your story. A child who isn't invited to a birthday party she really wants to go to can suffer deeply. A child who finally makes the soccer team can rejoice ecstatically.

These are important things, these moments of daily life.

A third rule is to use good language. Here's where I part from many school teachers. But I believe in my approach. The standard for what's good language in contemporary fiction should be your ear. If your ear says it's natural, go with it. That doesn't mean all your characters have to talk the way you talk. Listen to the people around you. Grandparents speak differently from parents, who speak differently from teens, who speak differently from eight year olds, who laugh with delight at the speech of two year olds. Revel in those differences. Pay attention to regional talk, ethnic talk. Pay attention to how people change their phrasing in formal situations.

The standard for historical fiction—and I include certain ways of telling fairy tales and myths in here—is different. Here you have to guess a little bit. Certainly if you're writing about medieval times, you cannot write the way the people spoke, both because you don't know how they spoke and because your reader would never understand it even if you presented it accurately. So what do you do? In these situations I use whatever mechanisms I can think of to give a sense of distance in time (and often of place). I choose vocabulary that isn't all that common. I don't use contractions (notice how "I am tired" is more formal than "I'm tired"). I sneak in archaisms like the word "whom." These things can help.

My fourth rule isn't really mine. I learned it from the inimitable Katherine Paterson, who I love dearly. Katherine says, "Write what only you can write." To me this means that every time you write a scene, walk around it. Look at it from every perspective. Find a perspective that makes your heart beat wildly—that's the perspective to tell it from. If you can't find that perspective, then cut that scene. You probably don't need it. You must care desperately about what you write in order to have a chance of making your reader care about it. So bring all the knowledge you have the world, of the way people behave, of what truly matters or truly is trivial, and let that inform the stories that you write.

Napoli with her grandchildren, August 2010 (Courtesy of Donna Jo Napoli.)

The stories around about you—they are fiction—but you must be there as you write them.

Let me end this with another question people often ask me: what are my plans as a writer now? To this I have a few things to say. One is that I've got things already in the works that I hope will come out soon, some of which I mentioned earlier. Another one is a picture book with my youngest son called *In the Garden.* I don't know when the illustrator will finish. And one is a novel for middle grade called *Lights on the Nile,* which Jordan Brown is editing. I worked with him on an earlier YA, and he's beautifully detailed in his criticisms (he doesn't pull any punches), but also consistently encouraging—a winning combination. We are in the middle of editing that book right now.

Also, I'm presently working on new projects. *National Geographic* just asked me to do a book of Greek myths—not a novel, but a collection of short stories.

Another is that the spectacular illustrator David Wiesner came to me last year with a pile of art work and asked me if I saw a story that might pull it together. After getting over the shock of such an honor and staring at the art for several months, I wrote a draft of a story, and now we are doing a graphic novel together. Both of these projects carry me into new areas, both scare me, and both thrill me. I hope they really happen.

Beyond that, I have little idea of what I'll do. The adult story that Brenda will try to sell has a character that grew very dear to me, and I'd love to write more stories about him. But I've got so many stories at different stages now—some partly in the computer, some totally in my head. I work on them often, but almost in a haphazard way, picking up whatever I'm driven to pick up on a given day and working till I finish a draft, then picking up something else at random. Where I will go next, I don't know. But I yearn to get there. I trust my heart to lead me.

O

O'MALLEY, Kevin 1961-
(Patrick Joseph)

Personal

Born 1961; married; wife's name Dana; children: Connor, Noah.

Addresses

Home and office—Baltimore, MD. *Agent*—Melissa Turk, 9 Babbling Brook Ln., Suffern, NY 10901. *E-mail*—komalley@comcast.net.

Career

Author and illustrator. Presenter at schools.

Writings

SELF-ILLUSTRATED

Froggie Went a'Courtin', Stewart, Tabori & Chang (New York, NY), 1992.

Let's Sing about America, Troll Associates (Mahwah, NJ), 1993.

Who Killed Cock Robin?, Lothrop, Lee & Shepard (New York, NY), 1993.

The Box, Stewart, Tabori & Chang (New York, NY), 1993.

There Was a Crooked Man, Little Simon (New York, NY), 1995.

Roller Coaster, Lothrop, Lee & Shepard (New York, NY), 1995.

Carl Caught a Flying Fish, Simon & Schuster Books for Young Readers (New York, NY), 1996.

Velcome, Walker & Company (New York, NY), 1997.

Leo Cockroach—Toy Tester, Walker & Company (New York, NY), 1999.

My Lucky Hat, Mondo Publishing (New York, NY), 1999.

Bud, Walker & Company (New York, NY), 2000.

Humpty Dumpty Egg-Splodes, Walker & Company (New York, NY), 2001.

Little Buggy, Harcourt (San Diego, CA), 2002.

Mount Olympus Basketball, Walker & Company (New York, NY), 2003.

Little Buggy Runs Away, Gulliver Books (San Diego, CA), 2003.

Straight to the Pole, Walker & Company (New York, NY), 2003.

Lucky Leaf, Walker & Company (New York, NY), 2004.

(Co-illustrated with Carol Heyer and Scott Goto) *Once upon a Cool Motorcycle Dude,* Walker & Company (New York, NY), 2005.

Gimme Cracked Corn and I Will Share, Walker & Company (New York, NY), 2007.

Backpack Stories, Albert Whitman (Morton Grove, IL), 2009.

Animal Crackers Fly the Coop, Walker & Company (New York, NY), 2010.

(Co-illustrator with Carol Heyer and Scott Goto) *Once upon a Royal Superbaby,* Walker & Company (New York, NY), 2010.

The Great Race, Walker Books for Young Readers (New York, NY), 2011.

ILLUSTRATOR

Joanne Oppenheim, *Row, Row, Row Your Boa,* Bantam (New York, NY), 1993.

John Schindel, *What's for Lunch?,* Lothrop, Lee & Shepard (New York, NY), 1994.

Ellen B. Jackson, *Cinder Edna,* Lothrop, Lee & Shepard (New York, NY), 1994.

JoAnn Vandine, *Run! Run!,* Mondo (Greenvale, NY), 1995.

Stuart J. Murphy, *Too Many Kangaroo Things to Do!,* HarperCollins (New York, NY), 1996.

Robert Kraus, *Big Squeak, Little Squeak,* Orchard Books (New York, NY), 1996.

David A. Adler, *Chanukah in Chelm,* Lothrop, Lee & Shepard (New York, NY), 1997.

Dan Harder, *Colliding with Chris,* Hyperion Books for Children (New York, NY), 1997.

Phyllis Root, *Rosie's Fiddle,* Lothrop, Lee & Shepard (New York, NY), 1997.

Jonathan London, *The Candystore Man,* Lothrop, Lee & Shepard (New York, NY), 1998.

Franklyn Mansfield Branley, *The Planets in Our Solar System,* HarperCollins (New York, NY), 1998.

Betty Ren Wright, *Pet Detectives!,* BridgeWater Books (Mahwah, NJ), 1999.

Michael O. Tunnell, *Halloween Pie,* Lothrop, Lee & Shepard (New York, NY), 1999.

Debbie Dadey, *King of the Kooties,* Walker & Company (New York, NY), 1999.

Stuart J. Murphy, *Jump, Kangaroo, Jump,* HarperCollins (New York, NY), 1999.

Ellen A. Kelley, *The Lucky Lizard,* Dutton Children's Books (New York, NY), 2000.

Joseph E. Wallace, *Big and Noisy Simon,* Hyperion Books for Children (New York, NY), 2001.

Stuart J. Murphy, *Dinosaur Deals,* HarperCollins (New York, NY), 2001.

John W. Stewigh, *Making Plum Jam,* Hyperion Books for Children (New York, NY), 2002.

Gordon Snell, *Twelve Days: A Christmas Countdown,* HarperCollins (New York, NY), 2002.

Denise Brennan-Nelson, *Someday Is Not a Day of the Week,* Sleeping Bear Press (Chelsea, MI), 2005.

Susan Pearson, *Slugs in Love,* Marshall Cavendish (New York, NY), 2006.

Marjorie Dennis Murray, *Hippo Goes Bananas!,* Marshall Cavendish (New York, NY), 2006.

Paul Many, *Dad's Bald Head,* Walker & Company (New York, NY), 2007.

Phyllis Root, *Paula Bunyan,* Farrar, Straus & Giroux (New York, NY), 2009.

Ellen Javernick, *The Birthday Pet,* Marshall Cavendish Children (New York, NY), 2009.

Georgia Bragg, *How They Croaked: The Awful Ends of the Awfully Famous,* Walker & Company (New York, NY), 2011.

Helen Ketteman, *If Beaver Had a Fever,* Marshall Cavendish Children (New York, NY), 2011.

ILLUSTRATOR; "MISS MALARKEY" SERIES BY JUDY FINCHLER

Miss Malarkey Doesn't Live in Room 10, Walker & Company (New York, NY), 1995.

Testing Miss Malarkey, Walker & Company (New York, NY), 2000.

Miss Malarkey Won't Be in Today, Walker & Company (New York, NY), 2000.

You're a Good Sport, Miss Malarkey, Walker & Company (New York, NY), 2002.

Miss Malarkey's Field Trip, Walker & Company (New York, NY), 2004.

(And coauthor) *Miss Malarkey Leaves No Reader Behind,* Walker & Company (New York, NY), 2006.

(And coauthor) *Congratulations, Miss Malarkey!,* Walker & Co. (New York, NY), 2009.

ILLUSTRATOR UNDER NAME PATRICK JOSEPH

Kathryn Heling, *Mouse Makes Magic: A Phonics Reader,* Random House (New York, NY), 2002.

Kevin O'Malley's illustration projects include creating the artwork for Phyllis Root's **Rosie's Fiddle.** (Illustration © 1995 by Kevin O'Malley. Reproduced by permission of HarperCollins Publishers.)

Kathryn Heling, *Mouse Makes Words: A Phonics Reader,* Random House (New York, NY), 2002.

Kathryn Heling, *Mouse's Hide-and-Seek Words: A Phonics Reader,* Random House (New York, NY), 2003.

OTHER

(With Patrick O'Brien) *Captain Raptor and the Moon Mystery,* illustrated by O'Brien, Walker & Company (New York, NY), 2005.

(With Patrick O'Brien) *Captain Raptor and the Space Pirates,* illustrated by O'Brien, Walker & Company (New York, NY), 2007.

Sidelights

Baltimore, Maryland-based author and illustrator Kevin O'Malley began drawing as a child, inspired by the illustrations in Maurice Sendak's groundbreaking children's book *Where the Wild Things Are.* A prolific author and artist who utilizes a variety of mediums and styles in his illustrations, O'Malley has contributed artwork to books by writers such as Michael O. Tunnell, Phyllis Root, Gordon Snell, and Paul Many, as well as to books by Judy Finchler, author of the "Miss Malarkey" stories. As an author, he also creates original self-illustrated stories such as *Straight to the Pole, Lucky Leaf, Gimme Cracked Corn and I Will Share,* and *Animal Crackers Fly the Coop,* all of which pair his characteristic colorful art with stories filled with humor and leading to upbeat endings. In the words of Janice M. Del Negro, writing in the *Bulletin of the Center for Children's Books,* "O'Malley infuses his mixed-media images with an inherent liveliness and raucous personality that demand attention."

Described as a "simple story" about forgiveness by *Booklist* reviewer Gillian Engberg, *Little Buggy Runs Away* finds a young beetle known as Little Buggy determined to run away from home after a fight with Big Buggy. Despite the help of two friendly ants, the outside world—and a scary lightning storm—proves too intimidating for the creature, and Little Buggy eventually learns to put his small disagreement into perspective in order to return home. "Children will easily recognize the bugs' roiling emotions, which O'Malley expertly captures in his characters' faces," commented Engberg, "and the supporting cast's humorous asides, printed in dialogue bubbles, will elicit some giggles." "O'Malley's wise decision to start the story after Little Buggy has run away allows youngsters to identify with the diminutive hero's feelings rather than his circumstances," noted a *Publishers Weekly* critic, and that the author/illustrator's "slick visuals, broad humor and . . . warm-hearted portrayal of helpful friends" make Little Buggy a likeable hero for the read-aloud crowd.

A lesson in stick-to-it-iveness illustrated in comic-book fashion, complete with dialogue balloons and digitized color blocks, O'Malley's *Lucky Leaf* finds a young video gamester shooed out of doors on a fall day by his parents. Accompanied by the family dog, the boy soon links up with a group of friends who have met the same fate. After a period of boredom, the group decides that a lone leaf hanging in an otherwise barren tree will bring good luck to whichever boy catches it when it falls. Noting that "there's more going on in the pictures than O'Malley's text would indicate," a *Kirkus Reviews* contributor wrote that video-game fans will "feel right at home in the comic-book format." Predicting that the book's graphic design will attract even reluctant readers, a *Publishers Weekly* reviewer concluded that with *Lucky Leaf* "O'Malley delivers another triumph for the kids who have to be dragged kicking and screaming away from their action figures and video games."

O'Malley's pun-filled *Gimme Cracked Corn and I Will Share* centers on the efforts of Chicken to locate a barn that houses buried treasure: cracked corn. With his friend George the rooster, Chicken undertakes a journey that requires her to cross a road, evade a hawk, and bargain with a great pink pig. *Gimme Cracked Corn and I Will Share* garnered praise for both its text and its illustrations. "Much of the art has the look of woodcuts, with an appealing heft and depth to it," noted Ilene Cooper in her *Booklist* review of O'Malley's tale. The author/illustrator "hatches every fowl joke and riddle and then some," stated a critic in *Kirkus Reviews,* and Betty Carter remarked in *Horn Book* that the book's "corny story will tickle many a funny bone, eggsactly its intention."

Readers return to the farmyard in *Animal Crackers Fly the Coop,* O'Malley's offbeat version of the Grimm Brothers' classic story about the Bremen town musicians. After Hen decides to travel to the big city and fulfill her dream of becoming a comedienne, she is joined by a cat, a dog, and a cow. When they encounter a gang of ne'er-do-wells along the way, the animals take advantage of their audience, and their noisy comedy act receives an unexpected reception. In *Booklist* Andrew Medlar noted the humor in the book's "nonstop comedic wordplay and puns," as well as O'Malley's "distinctive" multimedia illustrations. In *School Library Journal* Barbara Elleman dubbed *Animal Crackers Fly the Coop* "clever, well executed, and loaded with laughs," and commended the author/artist for creating a four-star animal cast "with a flair for witticisms and bad jokes."

O'Malley employs a graphic-novel format in the four tales he includes in *Backpack Stories,* which follows the relation of four young students and their carryalls. In one story the author/illustrator postulates the early history of the shoulder pouch as it extended from caveman days through the classical world of the ancients. A boy uses his backpack to transport a questionably science experiment in another tale, while a girl is transformed by her school book-bag into a superhero in yet another. The final story, "Day of the Living Backpack," spoofs the horror genre in describing a sinister satchel that takes on a life of its own. In *Booklist* Medlar called *Backpack Stories* "an imaginative look at the secret

O'Malley teams up with author David A. Adler on the holiday-themed picture book Chanukah. (Illustration copyright 1997 by Kevin O'Malley. Reproduced by permission of HarperCollins Publishers.)

lives and power of these [ubiquitous] carryalls," and a *Publishers Weekly* critic observed that O'Malley "make[s] good use of puns and tropes from comic books, TV, and movies." *Backpack Stories* features an engaging "combination of silliness and colorfully graphic comic-book-style illustrations," according to *School Library Journal* critic Maura Bresnahan, and a *Kirkus Reviews* writer deemed the work a "pleasing diversion for anyone who's ever lugged a zillion-pound backpack."

An intrepid dinosaur from Planet Jurassica leads a mission into space in *Captain Raptor and the Moon Mystery,* one of a pair of books O'Malley has created with fellow author/illustrator Patrick O'Brien. After spotting a bright flash on Eon, Captain Raptor and his reptilian crew board his ship, the *Megatooth,* to investigate and soon find themselves battling a giant octopus and laser-equipped astronauts. According to a *Publishers Weekly* critic, the coauthors "gamely alternate . . . between

hysteria-tinged suspense . . . and gallantry . . ., with plenty of time out for pyrotechnics." A contributor in *Kirkus Reviews* also complimented the story, praising O'Brien's detailed illustrations and predicting that young readers "will roar with approval." In a companion volume, *Captain Raptor and the Space Pirates,* captain and crew must track down the scalawags who stole precious jewels from Jurassica. "Few readers—reluctant or otherwise—will be able to resist this clever mix of dinosaurs, pirates, and science fiction," observed Mary Jean Smith in her *School Library Journal* review of O'Malley and O'Brien's second picture-book collaboration.

O'Malley also shares illustration duties on the picture books *Once upon a Cool Motorcycle Dude* and *Once upon a Royal Superbaby,* both which feature the work of artists Carol Heyer and Scott Goto. Each story is recounted from the divergent perspectives of a boy and a girl, gaining humor from misunderstandings, assumptions, and the personal commentary of the dual storytellers. In *Once upon a Royal Superbaby,* for example, the story of a young princess grows to involve a motorcycle-riding, dragon-slaying monarch, a queen who loves shopping, a royal infant who may or may not be sweet in nature, and an exciting kidnaping by a giant cyclops. Readers of all ages "will find much to enjoy in this amusing take on the creative process," concluded Laura Tillotson in her *Booklist* review of *Once upon a Royal Superbaby.*

In addition to his self-illustrated titles, O'Malley provides artwork for books by other writers. A long-running collaboration with Finchler has resulted a the popular series of beginning readers about Miss Malarkey, a spunky elementary-school teacher. In *Testing Miss Malarkey* the educator prepares her students for a battery of standardized tests as the school community becomes increasingly frazzled, and she gamely takes on coaching duties for a youth soccer team in *You're a Good Sport, Miss Malarkey.* "O'Malley's colorful cartoons extend the slapstick, over-the-top humor" in *Testing Miss Malarkey,* Kate McClelland remarked in *School Library Journal,* while the story in *You're a Good Sport, Miss Malarkey* "is well served by O'Malley's lively illustrations," as *Booklist* critic Shelley Townsend-Hudson

Ellen Jackson's fractured fairy tale **Cinder Edna** *gets an added dose of whimsy from O'Malley's detailed line-and-color art.* (Illustration copyright © 1994 by Kevin O'Malley. All rights reserved. Used by permission of HarperCollins Children's Books, a division of HarperCollins Publishers.)

observed. The concluding volume of the series, *Congratulations, Miss Malarkey!,* is coauthored by O'Malley and Finchler and finds the beloved teacher ready to get married and change her name. Predicting that the humorous story "will be a hit" with early-elementary-grade students, Mary Hazelton added in *School Library Journal* that O'Malley's "cartoon illustrations drawn with markers and colored pencils round out the humor" and feature "a variety of layouts and changes in perspective."

Slugs in Love, a work by Susan Pearson, follows the budding romance between a pair of slimy creatures. Though shy Marylou piques Herbie's interest with her wonderful love letters, his efforts to respond always fail to catch her attention until he devises a clever solution to his problem. "Bright, clear cartoon artwork provides a slug's-eye view of the garden and its inhabitants," wrote *School Library Journal* reviewer Amanda Moss, and a *Publishers Weekly* contributor noted that O'Malley "endows the community of slugs with a variety of expressions both whimsical and witty." In Paul Many's *Dad's Bald Head,* a young boy learns to accept his father's strange new appearance. "The calm, smiling figures in O'Malley's pictures echo Many's laid-back tone," a *Kirkus Reviews* contributor remarked, and Rachel G. Payne observed in *School Library Journal* that O'Malley's illustrations "are animated and mesh well with the buoyant text."

Another illustration project, Ellen Javernick's *The Birthday Pet,* features a rhyming text that follows the loving efforts of each member of Danny's misguided family to give the boy the best possible pet for his birthday. "While Javernick's verses are simple yet clever, it is O'Malley's energetic drawings that make the book shine," asserted *School Library Journal* contributor Martha Simpson, and a *Kirkus Reviews* writer cited the book's "expressive, action-packed illustrations." Phyllis Root's retelling of a well-known American tall tale in *Paula Bunyan* also benefits from O'Malley's art, which Carolyn Phelan characterized in *Booklist* as "cartoon-like ink drawings" that incorporate "exaggerated facial expressions." The artist's "white-framed, woodcutlike pictures, heavily outlined with intricate line shading," feature "sweeping panoramic views," according to *School Library Journal* critic Marianne Saccardi, while Jerry Griswold wrote in his *New York Times Book Review* of *Paula Bunyan* that the book represents "a happy pairing of writer and artist."

Although he notes that the career of an illustrator can be difficult at times, O'Malley derives great pleasure from his work. As he told *Underdown.org* interviewer Anna Olswanger, "I would love to do this forever because when I get calls or letters from kids who say, 'I am this person,' or, 'I love that book,' that's the reward. That's the payoff."

Biographical and Critical Sources

PERIODICALS

Booklist, September 1, 1998, April Judge, review of *Miss Malarkey Won't Be in Today,* p. 126; October 1, 2000, Marta Segal, review of *Testing Miss Malarkey,* p. 345; October 15, 2002, Shelley Townsend-Hudson, review of *You're a Good Sport, Miss Malarkey,* p. 411; May 1, 2003, Gillian Engberg, review of *Mount Olympus Basketball,* p. 1594; November 15, 2003, Gillian Engberg, review of *Little Buggy Runs Away,* p. 602; September 15, 2004, Ilene Cooper, review of *Miss Malarkey's Field Trip,* p. 248; July 1, 2006, Carolyn Phelan, review of *Miss Malarkey Leaves No Reader Behind,* p. 65; September 1, 2007, Todd Morning, review of *Captain Raptor and the Space Pirates,* p. 124; December 1, 2007, Ilene Cooper, review of *Gimme Cracked Corn and I Will Share,* p. 47; March 1, 2009, Carolyn Phelan, review of *Paula Bunyan,* p. 53; April 1, 2009, Shelle Rosenfeld, review of *The Birthday Pet,* p. 42; September 15, 2009, Andrew Medlar, review of *Backpack Stories,* p. 54; February 15, 2010, Andrew Medlar, review of *Animal Crackers Fly the Coop,* p. 79; November 1, 2010, Laura Tillotson, review of *Once upon a Royal Super Baby,* p. 74.

Bulletin of the Center for Children's Books, March, 2000, Janice M. Del Negro, "True Blue: Kevin O'Malley."

Childhood Education, summer, 2003, Amy Livengood, review of *You're a Good Sport, Miss Malarkey,* p. 245.

Children's Bookwatch, October, 2009, review of *Congratulations, Miss Malarkey!,*

Horn Book, January-February, 2008, Betty Carter, review of *Gimme Cracked Corn and I Will Share,* p. 77; March-April, 2010, Betty Carter, review of *Animal Crackers Fly the Coop,* p. 48.

Kirkus Reviews, August 1, 2002, review of *You're a Good Sport, Miss Malarkey,* p. 1128; August 15, 2003, review of *Little Buggy Runs Away,* p. 1077; October 1, 2003, review of *Straight to the Pole,* p. 1228; July 1, 2004, review of *Miss Malarkey's Field Trip,* p. 628; August 15, 2004, review of *Lucky Leaf,* p. 810; March 1, 2005, review of *Captain Raptor and the Moon Mystery,* p. 293; April 15, 2007, review of *Dad's Bald Head;* August 1, 2007, reviews of *Gimme Cracked Corn and I Will Share* and *Captain Raptor and the Space Pirates;* February 1, 2009, review of *The Birthday Pet;* June 15, 2009, review of *Congratulations, Miss Malarkey!;* July 15, 2009, review of *Backpack Stories;* March 1, 2010, review of *Animal Crackers Fly the Coop.*

New York Times Book Review, May 31, 2009, Jerry Griswold, review of *Paula Bunyan,* p. 18.

Publishers Weekly, September 14, 1998, review of *Miss Malarkey Won't Be in Today,* p. 68; October 27, 2003, review of *Little Buggy Runs Away,* p. 67; November 3, 2003, review of *Straight to the Pole,* p. 73; October 4, 2004, review of *Lucky Leaf,* p. 87; March 7, 2005, review of *Captain Raptor and the Moon Mystery,* p. 68; December 4, 2006, review of *Slugs in Love,* p. 58; July 16, 2007, review of *Gimme Cracked Corn and I Will Share,* p. 164; September 3, 2007, review of *Captain Raptor and the Space Pirates,* p. 61; September 21, 2009, review of *Backpack Stories,* p. 58.

School Library Journal, October, 2000, Kate McClelland, review of *Testing Miss Malarkey,* p. 124; May, 2003, Marge Loch-Wouters, review of *Mount Olympus Basketball,* p. 126; November, 2003, Joy Fleishhacker, review of *Straight to the Pole,* and Grace Oliff, review of *Little Buggy Runs Away,* p. 112; March, 2004, Andrew Medlar, review of *Mount Olympus Basketball,* p. 67; November, 2004, Grace Oliff, review of *Miss Malarkey's Field Trip,* p. 103; August, 2006, Rebecca Sheridan, review of *Miss Malarkey Leaves No Reader Behind,* p. 81; March, 2007, Amanda Moss, review of *Slugs in Love,* p. 184; June, 2007, Rachel G. Payne, review of *Dad's Bald Head,* p. 115; September, 2007, Mary Jean Smith, review of *Captain Raptor and the Space Pirates,* p. 224; August, 2007, Carolyn Janssen, review of *Gimme Cracked Corn and I Will Share,* p. 88; September, 2007, Mary Jean Smith, review of *Captain Raptor and the Space Pirates,* p. 224; March, 2009, Martha Simpson, review of *The Birthday Pet,* p. 117, and Marianne Saccardi, review of *Paula Bunyan,* p. 126; August, 2009, Mary Hazelton, review of *Congratulations, Miss Malarkey!,* p. 75; September, 2009, Maura Bresnahan, review of *Backpack Stories,* p. 130; February, 2010, Barbara Elleman, review of *Animal Crackers Fly the Coop,* p. 91; September, 2010, Kim T. Ha, review of *Once upon a Royal Superbaby,* p. 132.

ONLINE

Kevin O'Malley Home Page, http://www.booksbyomalley.com (May 15, 2011).

Underdown.org, http://www.underdown.org/ (August 1, 2008), Anna Olswanger, interview with O'Malley.*

* * *

OBERDIECK, Bernhard 1949-

Personal

Born February 24, 1949, in Oerlinghausen, Westfalen, Germany; married; children: two sons. *Education:* Institute of Applied Art (Bielefeld, Germany), degree (graphic arts), 1975.

Addresses

Home—Ramerberg, Germany *E-mail*—info@kinderbuchillustration.com.

Career

Illustrator and author of children's books. Freelance illustrator, beginning c. 1990.

Member

Society of Children's Book Writers and Illustrators.

Writings

SELF-ILLUSTRATED

Das kleine Buch der Stille, Ars-Edition (Munich, Germany), 1983, reprinted, 2000.

Die kleine Freude an kleinen Dingen, Ars-Edition (Munich, Germany), 1984.

Das kleine Buch vom einfachen Leben, Ars-Edition (Munich, Germany), 1984.

Begleit mich zu den Feldern, Ars-Edition (Munich, Germany), 1985.

(With Luise Griebler) *Die Erde ist dein Haus, der Himmel ein Fenster*, 1986.

Herzlichen Glückwunsch zum Geburtstag, Ars-Edition (Munich, Germany), 1987.

Was machst du, kleine Katze?, Loewe (Bindlach, Germany), 2003.

Was machst du, kleines Küken?, Loewe (Bindlach, Germany), 2003.

Was machst du, kleine Maus?, Loewe (Bindlach, Germany), 2005.

Was machst du, kleine Ente?, Loewe (Bindlach, Germany), 2005.

Was machst du, kleiner Hund?, Loewe (Bindlach, Germany), 2005.

Was machst du, kleines Kaninchen?, Loewe (Bindlach, Germany), 2005.

Halloween und Kürbisgeist, Patmos (Düsseldorf, Germany), 2005.

Lieber Osterhase, kommst du bald?, Patmos (Düsseldorf, Germany), 2006.

Alle Jahre wieder, F.X. Schmid (Ravensburg, Germany), 2006.

Der Sandmann ist da! (with CD), Ars-Edition (Munich, Germany), 2006.

Alle meine Entchen, Ars-Edition (Munich, Germany), 2006.

De Samichlaus und s'Christchind, Baumgartner (Affoltern am Albis, Switzerland), 2008.

Alle meine Entchen, Ars-Edition (Munich, Germany), 2008.

Mein allererster Märchenschatz, Ars-Edition (Munich, Germany), 2009.

ILLUSTRATOR

Brigitte März, *Von Gänsen, Schafen, Bäumen, Ähren und was sie Gutes uns bescheren*, Fabula-Verlag (Bad Aibling, Germany), 1981.

Hans Baumann, *Wie kommt die Katze auf das Dach?*, Thienemann (Stuttgart, Germany), 1983.

Anne Pernack, *Vom Zauber des Liedes*, Ars-Edition (Munich, Germany), 1985.

Gabriele Munzert, *Nepomuk im Lande Verkehrt*, Ellermann (Munich, Germany), 1985.

Gina Ruck-Pauquèt, *Strubbelhund Emilio*, Loewe (Bindlach, Germany), 1987.

Christian Bienieck, *Knusper, knusper Mäuschen*, Ellermann (Munich, Germany), 1990.

Tilde Michels, *Ich schenk dir einen Riesenschirm*, Sauerländer (Aarau, Switzerland), 1990.

Justine Rendal, *The Dancing Cat*, Simon & Schuster Books for Young Readers (New York, NY), 1991.

Katharine Ross, adaptor, *The Ugly Duckling*, Random House (New York, NY), 1991.

Jurij Brezan, *Die Geschichte von der Arche Noah*, Maier (Ravensburg, Germany), 1992.

Sigrid Heuck, *Eulengespenst und Mäusespuk: eine Spukgeschichte*, Thienemann (Stuttgart, Germany), 1992, translated as *A Ghost in the Castle*, Annick Press (Toronto, Ontario, Canada), 1994.

Ingrid Uebe, *Tinas Tannenbaum*, Benziger (Würzburg, Germany), 1993.

Rolf Isau, *Der Drache Gertrud*, Thienemann (Stuttgart, Germany), 1994.

Michael Ende, *Lirum, larum, Willi Warum*, Thienemann (Stuttgart, Germany), 1995.

Michael Ende, *Der Teddy und die Tiere*, Thienemann (Stuttgart, Germany), 1993.

Heinz Janisch, *Sarah und der Wundervogel*, Betz (Vienna, Austria), 1996.

Ursel Scheffler, *Das alte Karussell*, Thienemann (Stuttgart, Germany), 1996.

Ingrid Uebe, *Max mit der Mütze*, Bücherbär (Würzburg, Germany), 1998.

Marilyn Barrett, *Ein Garten für die Seele*, Scherz (Bern, Switzerland), 1998.

Angelika Glitz, *Meist ist Bert ein toller Hecht*, Betz (Vienna, Austria), 1998.

Hans Baumann, *Wie kommt die Katze auf das Dach?*, Schauenburg (Nürnberg, Germany), 2000.

Manfred Mai, *Kleiner Bär ganz grooooß!*, Ravensburger (Ravensburg, Germany), 2000.

Barbara Cratzius, *Das bärige Spiel-und Bastelbuch fürs ganze Jahr*, Ars-Edition (Munich, Germany), 2000.

Kristina Filthaut, *Es tanzt ein Bi-Ba-Butzemann*, 2000.

Wilhelm and Jacob Grimm, *Die Bremer Stadtmusikanten*, Ars-Edition (Munich, Germany), 2002.

Udo Weigelt, *Zwei Eulen und die kluge dicke Maus*, Nord-Süd (Gossau, Switzerland), 2002.

Gerdt von Bassewitz, *Peterchens Mondfahrt*, Ars-Edition (Munich, Germany), 2002.

Ulrich Maske and Constanze Schargan, *Ri, ra, rutsch*, Ars-Edition (Munich, Germany), 2003.

Wilhelm and Jacob Grimm, *Die allerschönsten Märchen*, Ars-Edition (Munich, Germany), 2004.

Sabine Hirler, *Arche Noah*, Ars-Edition (Munich, Germany), 2005.

Wilhelm and Jacob Grimm, *Die allerliebsten Märchen*, Ars-Edition (Munich, Germany), 2005.

(With Denis Gordeev) Stephanie True Peters, *A Princess Primer*, Dutton (New York, NY), 2006.

Christa Wißkirchen, *Der Osterhas auf Reisen*, Coppenrath (Münster, Germany), 2006.

Norbert Landa, *Delfingeschichten*, RM-Buch-und-Medien-Vertrieb (Rheda-Wiedenbrück, Germany), 2007.

Christa Wißkirchen, *Als das Christkind auf die Erde kam*, Coppenrath (Münster, Germany), 2007.

Hans Christian Andersen, *The Princess and the Pea*, retold by John Cech, Sterling (New York, NY), 2007.

Beat Widmer and Christine Grossenbacher, *Die Abenteuer von Schnäddi-&-Höppi,* Schnäddi-&-Höppi (Winterthur, Switzerland), 2008.

Juliane Sophie Kayser, *Malchen und die vergessene Zeit,* Wellhöfer (Mannheim, Germany), 2009.

Wilhelm and Jacob Grimm, *Das große Märchenbuch,* Nelson (Hamburg, Germany), 2009.

Wilhelm and Jacob Grimm, *Mein Grimm-Märchenbuch,* Ars-Edition (Munich, Germany), 2010.

John Cech, reteller, *Puss in Boots,* Sterling (New York, NY), 2010.

Books featuring Oberdiek's artwork have been translated into Portuguese, Spanish, and Swedish.

Biographical and Critical Sources

PERIODICALS

Booklist, February 1, 2010, Shelle Rosenfeld, review of *Puss in Boots,* p. 52.

Kirkus Reviews, May 15, 2007, review of *The Princess and the Pea.*

School Library Journal, September, 2007, Kirsten Cutler, review of *The Princess and the Pea,* p. 156; June, 2010, Miriam Lang Budin, review of *Puss in Boots,* p. 87.

ONLINE

Bernhard Oberdieck Home Page, http://www.kinderbuch illustration.com (May 27, 2011).*

*   *   *

OERTEL, Andreas 1966-

Personal

Born 1966, in Germany; immigrated to Manitoba, Canada. *Education:* University of Winnipeg, degree. *Hobbies and other interests:* Archaeology.

Addresses

Home—Lac du Bonnet, Manitoba, Canada.

Career

Author for children.

Writings

"ARCHAEOLOJESTERS" FANTASY SERIES

The Archaeolojesters, Lobster Press (Montreal, Quebec, Canada), 2010.

Pillars of Time, Lobster Press (Montreal, Quebec, Canada), 2010.

Trouble at Impact Lake, Lobster Press (Montreal, Quebec, Canada), 2011.

Biographical and Critical Sources

PERIODICALS

Kirkus Reviews, April 1, 2010, review of *The Archaeolojesters;* October 1, 2010, review of *Pillars of Time;* April 15, 2011, review of *Trouble at Impact Lake.*

School Library Journal, April, 2010, Cheryl Ashton, review of *The Archaeolojesters,* p. 164.

ONLINE

Andrea Oertel Home Page, http://www.andreasoertel.com (May 15, 2011).

Lobster Press Web site, http://www.lobsterpress.com/ (May 15, 2011), interview with Oertel.*

P-Q

PAILLOT, Jim

Personal

Married; children: two. *Education:* College degree. *Hobbies and other interests:* Hiking, biking, collecting robots.

Addresses

Home—Gilbert, AZ. *E-mail*—jim@jimpaillot.com.

Career

Illustrator, designer, and author. Assisted design of Port Discovery for Children's Museum, Baltimore, MD. Presenter at schools.

Awards, Honors

Roald Dahl Funny Prize, 2009, for *Stinking Rich and Just Plain Stinky* by Philip Ardagh.

Writings

SELF-ILLUSTRATED

Create Your Own Slimy, Gooey Gunk: Packed with Recipes for Making Your Own Dinosaur Snot, Martian Melt, Fake Barf, and Loads of Other Disgusting Stuff!, Walter Foster Pub. (Laguna Hills, CA), 2001.
Life's Least Important Questions, Sterling Pub. (New York, NY), 2002.
Jim Moskowitz and Casey Carle, *Bubbleology: A Hands-on Science Kit*, Innovative Kids, 2003.

ILLUSTRATOR

Chris Tait, *How to . . . Be a Kid*, Sterling Pub. Co. (New York, NY), 2003.

Steve Metzger, *The Great Turkey Race*, Scholastic (New York, NY), 2006.
Trudi Trueit, *No Girls Allowed (Dogs Okay)* ("Secrets of a Lab Rat" series), Aladdin (New York, NY), 2010.
Jeff Dinardo, *Attack of the Bully Bug*, Red Chair Press, 2011.

ILLUSTRATOR; "MY WEIRD SCHOOL" SERIES BY DAN GUTMAN, EXCEPT WHERE NOTED

Miss Daisy Is Crazy!, HarperTrophy (New York, NY), 2004.
Mr. Klutz Is Nuts!, HarperTrophy (New York, NY), 2004.
Mrs. Roopy Is Loopy!, HarperCollins (New York, NY), 2004.
Miss Lazar Is Bizarre!, HarperCollins (New York, NY), 2005.
Miss Small Is off the Wall!, HarperTrophy (New York, NY), 2005.
Mr. Hynde Is out of His Mind!, HarperTrophy (New York, NY), 2005.
Mrs. Cooney Is Loony!, HarperTrophy (New York, NY), 2005.
Ms. Hannah Is Bananas!, HarperCollins (New York, NY), 2005.
Ms. LaGrange Is Strange!, HarperCollins (New York, NY), 2005.
Miss Holly Is Too Jolly!, HarperTrophy (New York, NY), 2006.
Mr. Docker Is off His Rocker!, HarperCollins (New York, NY), 2006.
Mrs. Kormel Is Not Normal!, HarperCollins (New York, NY), 2006.
Mrs. Patty Is Batty!, HarperTrophy (New York, NY), 2006.
Ms. Todd Is Odd!, HarperCollins (New York, NY), 2006.
Dr. Carbles Is Losing His Marbles!, HarperTrophy (New York, NY), 2007.
Miss Suki Is Kooky!, HarperTrophy (New York, NY), 2007.
Mr. Louie Is Screwy!, HarperCollins (New York, NY), 2007.
Mr. Macky Is Wacky!, HarperTrophy (New York, NY), 2007.

Mrs. Yonkers Is Bonkers!, HarperCollins (New York, NY), 2007.

Ms. Coco Is Loco!, HarperTrophy (New York, NY), 2007.

Ms. Krup Cracks Me Up!, HarperTrophy (New York, NY), 2008.

Officer Spence Makes No Sense!, HarperTrophy (New York, NY), 2009.

Miss Child Has Gone Wild!, HarperCollins (New York, NY), 2011.

Ms. Leakey Is Freaky!, HarperCollins (New York, NY), 2011.

ILLUSTRATOR; "MY WEIRD SCHOOL DAZE" SERIES BY DAN GUTMAN

Mrs. Dole Is out of Control!, HarperTrophy (New York, NY), 2008.

Mr. Sunny Is Funny!, HarperTrophy (New York, NY), 2008.

Mr. Granite Is from Another Planet!, HarperTrophy (New York, NY), 2008.

Coach Hyatt Is a Riot!, HarperCollins (New York, NY), 2009.

Officer Spence Makes No Sense!, HarperCollins (New York, NY), 2009.

Mrs. Jafee Is Daffy!, HarperCollins (New York, NY), 2009.

Dr. Brad Has Gone Mad!, HarperCollins (New York, NY), 2009.

Miss Laney Is Zany!, HarperCollins (New York, NY), 2010.

Mrs. Lizzy Is Dizzy!, HarperCollins (New York, NY), 2010.

Miss Mary Is Scary!, HarperCollins (New York, NY), 2010.

Mr. Tony Is Full of Baloney!, HarperCollins (New York, NY), 2010.

ILLUSTRATOR; "SECRETS OF A LAB RAT" CHAPTER-BOOK SERIES BY TRUDI TRUEIT

No Girls Allowed (Dogs Okay), Aladdin (New York, NY), 2010.

Mom, There's a Dinosaur in Beeson's Lake, Aladdin (New York, NY), 2010.

Scab for Treasurer?, Aladdin (New York, NY), 2011.

ILLUSTRATOR; "GRUBTOWN TALES" CHAPTER-BOOK SERIES BY PHILIP ARDAGH

Stinking Rich and Just Plain Stinky, Faber & Faber (London, England), 2009.

The Year That It Rained Cows, Faber & Faber (London, England), 2009.

The Far from Great Escape, Faber & Faber (London, England), 2009.

Sidelights

Although he has created graphic images for businesses ranging from Coca Cola and Nickelodeon to Walt Disney Imagineering, Arizona-based artist Jim Paillot is best known as the illustrator of Dan Gutman's popular

"My Weird School" and "My Weird School Daze" beginning chapter-book series. His animated color illustrations as well as his humorous line drawings have also appeared in many other books that have particular appeal for elementary-aged boys, such as Trudi Trueit's "Secrets of a Lab Rat" series and Philip Ardagh's humorous "Grubtown Tales" stories. Citing the "kooky black-and-white cartoon illustrations" for "My Weird School Daze" installment *Coach Hyatt Is a Riot!,* Elaine Lesh Morgan predicted in her *School Library Journal* review that "even the most reluctant reader will be drawn in by the humor and . . . silliness" of the Gutman/Paillot collaboration.

Teaming up with Trueit, Paillot's entertaining art captures the antics of Scab McNally, the fourth-grade star of the "Secrets of a Lab Rat" series. In *No Girls Allowed (Dogs Okay)* the high-spirited nine year old hides his wish for a puppy behind in-school antics that frustrate his teachers. To fund the purchase of a new pet, Scab begins marketing a useful stink spray designed to keep annoying siblings at bay. A classroom incident unleashes the substance, with humorous consequences, and Paillot's quirky cartoons help "extend the outrageous scenes," according to *Booklist* critic Hazel Rochman. Scab returns in *Mom, There's a Dinosaur in Beeson's Lake,* as a reasonable fear of drowning threatens to sink his plans to go fishing with his uncle until the creative fourth grader finds a way to pass a crucial swimming test. In *Scab for Treasurer* a run for school office is required to prove once and for all that competing candidate Missy Malone is actually an invading alien: as Scab reasons, no human fourth grader could possibly know the answer to ALL their teacher's questions. Dubbing *Mom, There's a Dinosaur in Beeson's Lake* "laugh-out-loud" funny, Amanda Moss Struckmeyer also cited Paillot's cartoon art in recommending the book to fans of Dav Pilkey's popular "Captain Underpants" stories. A *Kirkus Reviews* critic wrote that the artist's "angular drawings suit the characters' zany antics" in Trueit's "chuckle-inducing" "Secrets of a Lab Rat" books.

Biographical and Critical Sources

PERIODICALS

Booklist, September 1, 2004, Shelle Rosenfeld, review of *Miss Daisy Is Crazy!,* p. 121; April 1, 2009, Hazel Rochman, review of *No Girls Allowed (Dogs Okay),* p. 40.

Bulletin of the Center for Children's Books, July, 2003, review of *How to Be a Kid,* p. 464; March, 2009, Jeannette Hulick, review of *No Girls Allowed (Dogs Okay),* p. 299.

Kirkus Reviews, June 15, 2004, review of *Miss Daisy Is Crazy!,* p. 577; December 15, 2009, review of *Mom, There's a Dinosaur in Beeson's Lake.*

Publishers Weekly, April 28, 2003, review of *Bubbleology: A Hands-on Science Kit,* p. 72; May 19, 2003, review of *How to . . . Be a Kid,* p. 77; July 19, 2004, review of *Miss Daisy Is Crazy!,* p. 161.

School Library Journal, November, 2004, Kristina Aaronson, review of *Mr. Klutz Is Nuts!,* p. 104; March, 2009, Wendy Woodfill, review of *No Girls Allowed (Dogs Okay),* p. 129; June, 2009, Elaine Lesh Morgan, review of *Coach Hyatt Is a Riot!,* p. 88; May, 2010, Adam Moss Struckmeyer, review of *Mom, There's a Dinosaur in Beeson's Lake,* p. 92; September, 2010, Donna Atmur, review of *Miss Laney Is Zany!,* p. 124.

ONLINE

Jim Paillot Home Page, http://jimpaillot.com (February 27, 2011).*

---

* * *

PEACOCK, Phyllis Hornung 1977-
(Phyllis Hornung)

Personal

Born 1977, in MO; married Chris Peacock. *Education:* Columbus College of Art and Design, B.F.A. (illustration; magna cum laude), 1999. *Hobbies and other interests:* Hiking, reading, anime, visiting bookstores.

Addresses

Home—Plano, TX. *E-mail*—phyllis@phyllishornung peacock.com.

Career

Illustrator.

Awards, Honors

Magazine Merit Award, Society of Children's Book Writers and Illustrators (SCBWI), 2003; SCBWI Letter of Merit, 2008; Learning Teacher's Choice Award for Children's Books, *Science Books & Films* Best Books for Children citation, and ABC Best Books for Children designation, all 2004, all for *What's Your Angle, Pythagoras?* by Julie Ellis.

Illustrator

(As Phyllis Hornung) Angeline Sparagna LoPresti, *A Place for Zero: A Math Adventure,* Charlesbridge (Watertown, MA), 2003.

(As Phyllis Hornung) Bonnie Highsmith Taylor, *Simon Can't Say Hippopotamus,* Mondo (New York, NY), 2003.

(As Phyllis Hornung) Lucy Malka, *The New House,* Mondo (New York, NY), 2004.

(As Phyllis Hornung) Julie Ellis, *What's Your Angle Pythagoras?: A Math Adventure,* Charlesbridge (Watertown, MA), 2004.

(As Phyllis Hornung) Kelly Terwilliger, *Bubbe Isabella and the Sukkot Cake,* Kar-Ben Pub. (Minneapolis, MN), 2005.

Julie Ellis, *Pythagoras and the Ratios: A Math Adventure,* Charlesbridge (Watertown, MA), 2010.

Contributor to periodicals, including *New Moon.*

ILLUSTRATOR; "PRINCESS MADISON" SERIES

(As Phyllis Hornung) Karen Scalf Linamen, *Princess Madison and the Royal Darling Pageant,* Fleming H. Revell (Grand Rapids, MI), 2006.

(As Phyllis Hornung) Karen Scalf Linamen, *Princess Madison and the Whispering Woods,* Fleming H. Revell (Grand Rapids, MI), 2006.

Karen Scalf Linamen, *Princess Madison and the Paisley Puppy,* Fleming H. Revell (Grand Rapids, MI), 2007.

Sidelights

Phyllis Hornung Peacock illustrates books for young readers that range from fiction to nonfiction, although her ability to portray abstract concepts effectively has resulted in her receiving requests to illustrate mathematics-based texts. Beginning with Angeline Sparagna LoPresti's *A Place for Zero: A Math Adventure,* she has also teamed up with author Julie Ellis on the award-winning picture book *What's Your Angle Pythagoras?: A Math Adventure.* Her art has also meshed well with the entertaining storylines in Karen

Phyllis Hornung Peacock's illustration work includes teaming up with Julie Ellis on **Pythagoras and the Ratios: A Math Adventure.** (Illustration copyright © 2010 by Phyllis Hornung Peacock. Reproduced by Charlesbridge Publishing.)

Scalf Linamen's "Princess Madison" series, which include *Princess Madison and the Royal Darling Pageant, Princess Madison and the Whispering Woods,* and *Princess Madison and the Paisley Puppy.* Recommending *Princess Madison and the Paisley Puppy* in *Children's Bookwatch,* a critic added that Peacock's "colorful illustrations boldly display Princess Madison's enthusiasm," while *Princess Madison and the Whispering Woods* was recommended as "ideal for bedtime or storytime reading."

Peacock was raised in St. Louis, Missouri, where she was exposed to technical subjects by her parents, who worked in the accounting and programming fields. In high school she found herself drawn to fantasy art and animation, and she decided to enroll at the Columbus College of Art & Design, where she ultimately majored in illustration, graduating magna cum laude. In order to be available to publishers, Peacock moved to New York City, found a day job working as a secretary, and passed her portfolio among publishers and other clients. In 2001 she relocated to the West coast, and she now bases her freelance career in Texas, working for magazines and trade and educational publishers.

Peacock's first thirty-two-page picture-book-illustration assignment, *A Place for Zero,* helps young children make sense of the abstract concept of zero and infinity. Although Gay Lynn Van Vleck cautioned in her *School Library Journal* review that LoPresti's pun-filled text might be too advanced for beginners, Peacock's "lively, colorful cartoons of legged numbers" are designed to capture the attention of "preschoolers or kindergartners."

In *What's Your Angle, Pythagoras?* Ellis presents what *School Library Journal* contributor Jennifer England described as a "clear and interesting explanation" of the Greek philosopher/mathematician's boyhood trip to Egypt and the experience that led him to develop the geometric theorem that now bears his name. Author and artist reteam in *Pythagoras and the Rations,* in which Ellis explores the mathematics underlying musical notation while also introducing young children to progressive ratios. While England cited Peacock's use of "a warm and clear palette" in her cartoon art for *What's Your Angle, Pythagoras?*, *Pythagoras and the Ratios* inspired Barbara Auerbach to recommend the artist's "acrylic and colored pencil cartoons" for accurately "depict[ing] the clothing and lifestyle" of the ancient world. "The book's educational aspects are fascinating," asserted a *Kirkus Reviews* writer in appraising the second story featuring Pythagoras, and Peacock's "illustration bring these to life."

Biographical and Critical Sources

PERIODICALS

Booklinks, November, 2004, Sheri McDonald and Sally Rasch, review of *What's Your Angle Pythagoras?: A Math Adventure,* p. 13.

Booklist, September 1, 2005, Ilene Cooper, review of *Bubbe Isabella and the Sukkot Cake,* p. 146.
Children's Bookwatch, November, 2006, review of *Princess Madison and the Whispering Woods;* April, 2007, review of *Princess Madison and the Paisley Puppy.*
Kirkus Reviews, December 1, 2009, review of *Pythagoras and the Ratios: A Math Adventure.*
Publishers Weekly, August 2, 2004, review of *What's Your Angle, Pythagoras?,* p. 73.
School Library Journal, October, 2003, Gay Lynn Van Vleck, review of *A Place for Zero: A Math Adventure,* p. 154; October, 2004, Jennifer England, review of *What's Your Angle, Pythagoras?,* p. 140; October, 2005, Rachel Kamin, review of *Bubbe Isabella and the Sukkot Cake,* p. 131; February, 2010, Barbara Auerbach, review of *Pythagoras and the Ratios,* p. 108.
Science Books and Film, November-December, 2004, Charles Mercer, review of *What's Your Angle, Pythagoras?,* p. 265.
Teaching Children Mathematics, April, 2004, review of *A Place for Zero,* p. 430.

ONLINE

Phyllis Hornung Peacock Home Page, http://www.phyllis hornungpeacock.com (May 27, 2011).

* * *

POLAK, Monique 1960-

Personal

Born May 20, 1960, in Montréal, Québec, Canada; daughter of Mazimilien (a criminal court judge) and Celine (a homemaker) Polak; married Chaim Melamed, December 16, 1979 (divorced 1985); married Michael Shenker (a journalist), June 2, 1996; children: (first marriage) Alicia. *Education:* McGill University, B.A. (English literature), 1981; Concordia University, M.A. (English literature), 1984. *Religion:* Jewish.

Addresses

Home—Montréal, Québec, Canada. *Office*—Marianopolis College, 4873 Westmount Ave., Westmount, Québec H3Y 1X9, Canada. *E-mail*—mpolak@videotron.ca.

Career

Educator, journalist, and author. Marianopolis College, Montréal, Québec, Canada, instructor in English and humanities, 1987—. Freelance journalist.

Member

Canadian Society of Children's Authors, Illustrators, and Performers.

Awards, Honors

Our Choice designation, Canadian Children's Book Centre, 2005, for *Flip Turn,* 2006, for *On the Game;* American Library Association Popular Paperback desig-

Monique Polak (Photograph by Studio Iris. Reproduced by permission.)

nation, 2005, for *Home Invasion;* Quebec Writers' Federation Prize for Children's and Young-Adult Literature, 2009, for *What World Is Left.*

Writings

YOUNG-ADULT NOVELS

No More Pranks, Orca Book Publishers (Victoria, British Columbia, Canada), 2004, Orca Book Publishers (Custer, WA), 2005.

On the Game, James Lorimer (Halifax, Nova Scotia, Canada), 2005.

Home Invasion, Orca Book Publishers (Victoria, British Columbia, Canada), 2005.

All In, James Lorimer (Halifax, Nova Scotia, Canada), 2005.

Finding Elmo, Orca Book Publishers (Custer, WA), 2007.

Scarred, James Lorimer (Toronto, Ontario, Canada), 2007.

121 Express, Orca Book Publishers (Custer, WA), 2008.

What World Is Left, Orca Book Publishers (Custer, WA), 2008.

Junkyard Dog, Orca Book Publishers (Custer, WA), 2009.

The Middle of Everywhere, Orca Book Publishers (Custer, WA), 2009.

Miracleville, Orca Book Publishers (Custer, WA), 2011.

OTHER

Flip Turn (middle-grade novel), James Lorimer (Halifax, Nova Scotia, Canada), 2004.

Contributor to Montréal *Gazette.*

Sidelights

In addition to writing novels for middle graders and young adults, Monique Polak teaches English at Montréal's Marianopolis College and also writes for a local newspaper. While many of her stories feature contemporary teens who get into difficulties due to bad choices or external challenges, Polak earned critical praise for *What World Is Left,* an historical novel that earned its author the 2009 Quebec Writers' Federation Prize for Children's and Young-Adult Literature. Asked why she writes for teens, Polak told an Orca Books Web site interviewer: "I write because I'm obsessed with stories—the weirder, the wilder, the more embarrassing, the better!!" "I write for young adults because I think young adults are the most interesting people in the world," she added. "There's so much going on inside their heads. They're questioning themselves and the world around them. When I was a young adult, books helped me make sense of the world. I hope my books can do that for readers, too."

Polak always knew she wanted to grow up and be a writer. "When I was a kid, I used to hide under the dining room table during dinner parties so I could listen in on the adults' conversations," she admitted in her Orca Books online interview. "Nowadays, I no longer lurk under tables, but I still listen in a lot. I've found bathrooms and locker rooms are especially good places to find stories. I pretend to be washing my hands or doing up my shoelaces, when actually I'm doing research for my books." Interestingly, it was during college, while pursuing the English major traditionally sought by aspiring writers, that Polak shifted her focus, away from storytelling. As the author once told *SATA,* "I was good at writing term papers, and eventually a thesis (on Lewis Carroll's "Alice" books), but I was daunted by all the great writers and I began to lose touch with my more creative side."

After college Polak began her academic career. "Though I loved (and still love) working with young people, I felt something was missing," she explained. "So, gradually, I came back to writing. At first, I worked in a journal, then I began selling book reviews and eventually feature stories to the *Gazette,* Montréal's English-language daily. When I finally felt confident enough, I returned to fiction writing."

Polak's first novel, *Flip Turn,* was inspired by actual events and benefits from her background as a journalist. "*Flip Turn* is the story of a competitive swimmer," she explained. "I researched the book by tracking a Montréal area swim team for several months. And on a more personal level, I explored the theme of competition—

something I've grappled with in my own life. A certain amount of competitive instinct serves us well, but too much can break down bonds between people."

Like *Flip Turn, No More Pranks* was inspired by a personal experience, in this case a vacation to coastal Tadoussac, Québec. In the novel, suspension results when a teen impersonates his high-school vice principal on a local radio call-in show. When the boy is shipped off to the Atlantic coast to work for his uncle, who operates whale-watch boat tours, he is able to use his skill for mimicry to help an injured whale and identify the man who has hurt it. Another story featuring undisciplined teens, *121 Express* finds Lucas commuting to school by bus after he moves to a new town. Hoping to trade in his nerdy reputation for popularity, Lucas joins the misbehaving cool kids sitting at the back of the bus by tormenting other nerdy students. When the behavior of these back-of-the-bus rowdies escalates to the point where they put an elderly woman in the hospital, Lucas must rethink his priorities.

Cover of Polak's young-adult novel **No More Pranks**, *which finds a teen forced to resort to hijinks to bring about justice.* (Orca Book Publishers, 2004. Cover designed by Lynne O'Rourke. Cover photograph by Eyewire. Reproduced by permission.)

Featuring urban settings Set in the city and based on contemporary news items, *On the Game* focuses on a juvenile prostitution ring while *All In* explores the issue of teen gambling and addiction at a private school. *Scarred,* a story about a teen girl who deals with emotional problems by cutting herself, "breaks new ground as a novel about self-injury," according to *Resource Links* critic Bonnie Campbell, and Polak's additional themes "of strained familial relations, parents who live vicariously through their children's successes, self-sabotage, and child abuse, all combine to make for compelling reading."

The inspiration for *Home Invasion* came from news articles about a rash of break-ins in Montréal during which the thieves encountered family members at home. The novel also explores a teenager's difficult adjustment to his new stepfather, a plot element that echoed the experiences of Polak's own daughter after the author's remarriage. In the novel Josh dislikes his new stepfather, Clay, and becomes especially resentful when his mother leaves the two men alone for a week. Curious about what life would be like in a traditional two-parent family, the teen hides in a neighbor's home and observes their family time. When he is not caught, Josh continues housebreaking, but things get out of hand when he witnesses an actual home invasion and realizes that he could help bring the perpetrators to justice. Calling *Home Invasion* "a short little book with a lot going on," Sally Tibbetts added in *Kliatt* that "Josh's voice is convincing" and his story "will definitely appeal to YAs, especially reluctant readers."

Animals are central characters in several of Polak's stories. In *Finding Elmo* a fifteen year old is determined to find out who stole a black cockatoo named Elmo from his family's pet store, while a boy's curiosity about a grey-muzzled guard dog living at a local store leads to the discovery of animal mistreatment in *Junkyard Dog*. In focusing on "complex" subjects such as "animal cruelty, bad home situations, [and] alopecia," *Junkyard Dogs* will appeal to students with reading difficulties who "are interested in reading about topics that are serious," according to Alison Edwards in *Resource Links*. "Like many of the Orca books," the critic added, "it would be a good supplement to a human dynamics or even career course and help students who arc dealing with adult situations." In *Booklist* Daniel Kraus wrote that "Polak writes with a nervy confidence" and her attention to detail injects "authenticity" to her "powerful story."

Polak takes readers to northern Québec in *The Middle of Everywhere,* as Toronto teen Noah Thorpe evades local school bullies by moving to the Inuit community of George River where his divorced father now lives. As he becomes familiar with the local native culture, fifteen-year-old Noah learns that challenges exist everywhere, even where life is lived close to nature. "Polak incorporates the customs and language of the Inuit seamlessly into her narrative," wrote Karyn Huenemann in her *Resource Links* review of *The Middle of Every-*

Cover of Polak's young-adult novel **The Middle of Everywhere,** *featuring cover art by Monique Dykstra.* (Orca Book Publishers, 2009. Cover photograph by Monique Dykstra. Reproduced by permission of Orca Book Publishers.)

where, and her narrative lets readers "feel that the world she depicts not only could be, but is, essentially true." "The survival-adventure details will engage reluctant readers," predicted *School Library Journal* critic Vicki Reutter, and Polak also includes "elements of romance when Noah strives to impress an Inuit classmate." According to a *Kirkus Reviews* writer, the author's skill in depicting the strengthening relationship between father and son in *The Middle of Everywhere* serves as "a nice counterpoint to Noah's reaction to this exotic world into which he not only arrives but that he discovers he admires."

The experiences of Polak's mother during World War II inform her award-winning novel *What World Is Left.* While growing up, the author heard little about her mother's wartime experiences, or of the woman's imprisonment in Czechoslovakia's Theresienstadt transit/labor camp and Jewish ghetto. At age eighty, however, the woman finally shared her story, describing her experiences there. To research her novel, Polak visited her mother's childhood home in the Netherlands as well as her Jewish school in Amsterdam. She also toured Theresienstadt, where 140,000 Jews were housed and over 30,000 died before being transported elsewhere.

When readers first meet Anneke Van Raalte in *What World Is Left,* she lives in an upscale home near Amsterdam, where her father works as a cartoonist. Her comfortable life ends in 1942, at age fourteen, when Germany invades Holland and her family is transported to Theresienstadt. Although she experiences the day-to-day deprivations of camp life, Anneke is also aware of Nazi efforts to portray the ghetto as a "show camp" in order to fool the International Red Cross as to their ultimate purpose: eliminating European Jews. When her father is forced to use his artistic talent to create Nazi propaganda, the girl must wrestle with her sense of what is right and how far she will go to preserve her life and the lives of those she loves. Calling *What World Is Left* "often graphic and realistic," Rita Soltan added in *School Library Journal* that Polak's story "raises questions of moral principles and beliefs while it portrays the horrors of the Holocaust." *What World Is Left* is "a candid look at a father's presumed collusion," wrote a *Publishers Weekly* critic, "a perspective rarely seen in YA literature about the Holocaust." For *Booklist* reviewer Hazel Rochman, the main strength of Polak's story is "Anneke's first-person, present-tense voice," and "the details" the teen reveals about her ordeal "are unforgettable."

It took Polak over five years to finds a publisher for her first novel. "Looking back at those years . . . I'm really proud that I didn't give up," she once told *SATA.* "So that's my main advice to aspiring writers: don't ever, ever give up! I kept writing, kept reading, and kept trying to improve my stories and style. And eventually, my efforts paid off." Polak also recommends keeping a daily journal; "I find [it] helps keep my writing muscle limber. In my journal, I write about whatever's on my mind, and that sometimes includes story ideas. Then, on a day when I'm not teaching, I go for a run before I sit down at my computer. For me, running is another good way to get ideas and to think about how I want to tell my stories."

"When I was little, my favourite book was *The Little Engine That Could,*" Polak more-recently told *SATA.* "In many ways, we writers have to be like that little engine, chugging along even when it's an uphill journey. But even if I wanted to, I couldn't stop writing. I write because writing is the most challenging thing I do. I write because writing helps me make sense of difficult situations and feelings. And most of all, I write because I love stories. I often tell my students that to me, the air feels thick with stories. It's our job to find those stories and tell them."

Biographical and Critical Sources

PERIODICALS

Canadian Book Review (annual), 2004, Sylvia Pantaleo, review of *No More Pranks,* p. 518; 2005, Deborah Dowson, review of *Home Invasion,* p. 514, and Dave Jenkinson, review of *On the Game,* p. 515.

Booklist, December 15, 2008, Hazel Rochman, review of *What World Is Left,* p. 51; October 15, 2009, Daniel Krau, review of *Junkyard Dog,* p. 53; November 15, 2009, Shauna Yusko, review of *The Middle of Everywhere,* p. 35.

Kirkus Reviews, September 15, 2009, review of *The Middle of Everywhere.*

Kliatt, January, 2005, Claire Rosser, review of *No More Pranks,* p. 17; January, 2006, Sally Tibbetts, review of *Home Invasion,* p. 17.

Publishers Weekly, October 13, 2008, review of *What World Is Left,* p. 55.

Resource Links, February, 2005, Evette Berry, reviews of *Flip Turn,* p. 20, and *No More Pranks,* p. 39; February, 2006, Heather Empey, review of *Home Invasion,* p. 49, and Evette Berry, review of *On the Game,* p. 50; October, 2006, Meredith Snyder, review of *All In,* p. 40; October, 2007, Bonnie Campbell, review of *Scarred,* p. 38; February, 2008, Angela Thompson, review of *121 Express,* p. 36; October, 2009, review of *Junkyard Dog,* p. 23.

School Library Journal, April, 2009, Rita Soltan, review of *What World Is Left,* p. 140; November, 2009, Vicki Reutter, review of *The Middle of Everywhere,* p. 118.

Voice of Youth Advocates, February, 2006, Teri S. Lesesne, review of *Home Invasion,* p. 491; April, 2009, Alissa Lauzon and Ashley Brown, review of *What World Is Left,* p. 56.

ONLINE

Canadian Children's Book Week Web site, http://www.bookweek.ca/ (November 15, 2006), "Monique Polak."

Monique Polak Home Page, http://moniquepolak.com (May 15, 2011).

Orca Book Publishers Web site, http://www.orcabook.com/ (May 15, 2011), "Monique Polak."

*   *   *

POTTER, Ryan

Personal

Born in MI. *Education:* B.A. (American history); M.A. (American history), 2000.

Addresses

Home—Royal Oak, MI. *Agent*—Jen Rofe, Andrea Brown Literary Agency, jennifer@andreabrownlit.com. *E-mail*—exitstrategy17@gmail.com.

Career

Novelist.

Writings

Exit Strategy, Flux (Woodbury, MN), 2010.

Sidelights

Ryan Potter devoted six years to studying American history and earned an advanced degree in the subject before realizing that sifting through the dusty facts of the past was far less interesting than making up compelling stories about the present. A brief flirtation with screenwriting followed before Potter turned to fiction, and after publishing several short stories he turned to a longer work. He wrote his first novel-length manuscript in the summer of 2005 and then set about finding an agent and a publisher for his manuscript. Demonstrating that Potter may have found his creative niche, that manuscript was published in 2010 as the young-adult novel *Exit Strategy.*

In *Exit Strategy* Potter takes readers to suburban Detroit, where the decaying core of the formerly vibrant city has drained its region of hope for the future. Zach Ramsey, the narrator, lives in Blaine, a fictional blue-collar town that is home to one of the many vehicle assembly plants that fuel southeastern Michigan. Like his friends, Zach watches the adults around him succumb to alcohol, drugs, and other distractions that help them deal with the fear of losing their jobs. Although he is determined to move away after graduation, Zach has one more year of high school to go, and now he wants to make the most of his final summer at home. While spending time with buddy Tank, Zach begins a relationship with Tank's beautiful sister, Sarah. His friend's family soon reveals fatal flaws, however, and Zach finds his confidence in adults severely shaken. Then a discovery about Tank forces Zach to make several crucial choices, choices that could destroy his friend's high-school wrestling career.

In *Kirkus Reviews* a critic deemed *Exit Strategy* "both fast-paced and riveting," and a *Publishers Weekly* critic noted of Potter's story that the "working class setting feels well realized." "Zach promises no happy endings at the outset of his present-tense narrative," wrote John Peters in his *Booklist* review of *Exit Strategy,* but Potter's "decidedly dark comedy" ultimately leaves its young protagonist with possibilities for a better future.

In an online interview with Cynthia Leitich Smith for *Cynsations* online, Potter discusses the challenges of writing about behavior that most parents find problematic. "I think you run into trouble if you start sounding preachy about the dangers of such 'edgy' behavior," he noted. "On the other hand, . . . many teens smoke. Many teens drink. Some kids experiment and decide they'll live without that stuff. Others end up with lifelong habits. These are facts of life." "Teens are smart readers," he added. "What they don't want is a health lesson disguised as a novel. . . . It's the story that counts, so. . . . stay away from the moral bully pulpit. You can teach a lesson, but don't be too blunt about it. It's a fine line."

Cover of Ryan Potter's novel Exit Strategy, *in which a teen becomes trapped by the troubles of friends and family living in a dying town.* (Flux, 2010. Cover photograph by iStockphoto/David Edwards. Reproduced by permission of Llewellyn Publications.)

Biographical and Critical Sources

PERIODICALS

Booklist, February 15, 2010, John Peters, review of *Exit Strategy,* p. 70.
Kirkus Reviews, February 15, 2010, review of *Exit Strategy.*
Publishers Weekly, February 8, 2010, review of *Exit Strategy,* p. 51.
Voice of Youth Advocates, June, 2010, Jan Chapman, review of *Exit Strategy,* p. 158.

ONLINE

Cynsations Web log, http://cynthialeitichsmith.glogspot.com/ (October 20, 2010), Cynthia Leitich Smith, interview with Potter.
Ryan Potter Home Page, http://www.exitstrategy17.com (February 27, 2011).

PRIMAVERA, Elise 1954-
(Esile Arevamirp)

Personal

Born May 19, 1954, in West Long Branch, NJ; daughter of Jerry (a builder) and Corrine (a homemaker) Primavera. *Education:* Moore College of Art, B.F.A., 1976; attended Art Students' League, 1980-84.

Addresses

Home—Red Bank, NJ. *E-mail*—eprimavera@earthlink. net.

Career

Freelance fashion illustrator, 1976-79; freelance children's book illustrator, 1979—.

Awards, Honors

New Jersey Institute of Technology Award, 1983, for *The Bollo Caper* by Art Buchwald, and 1988, for *Christina Katerina and the Time She Quit the Family* by Patricia Lee Gauch; Christopher Award, Oppenheim Toy Portfolio Platinum Award, and Irma S. and James H. Black Book Award, Bank Street College of Education, all 1999, all for *Raising Dragons.*

Writings

SELF-ILLUSTRATED

Basil and Maggie, J.B. Lippincott (Philadephia, PA), 1983.
Ralph's Frozen Tale, Putnam (New York, NY), 1991.
The Three Dots, Putnam (New York, NY), 1993.
Plantpet, Putnam (New York, NY), 1994.
The Secret Order of the Gumm Street Girls (juvenile novel), HarperCollins (New York, NY), 2006.
Thumb Love, Robin Corey Books (New York, NY), 2010.
The House at the End of Ladybug Lane, illustrated by Valeria Docampo, Robin Corey Books (New York, NY), 2012.
Libby of Hi Hopes (juvenile novel), Simon & Schuster (New York, NY), 2012.
Ms. Rapscott's Girls (middle-grade novel), Dial (New York, NY), 2013.

SELF-ILLUSTRATED; "AUNTIE CLAUS" NOVEL SERIES

Auntie Claus, Harcourt (New York, NY), 1999.
Auntie Claus and the Key to Christmas, Harcourt (New York, NY), 2002.
Auntie Claus, Home for the Holidays, Simon & Schuster Books for Young Readers (New York, NY), 2009.

SELF-ILLUSTRATED; "FRED AND ANTHONY" CHAPTER-BOOK SERIES; AS ESILE AREVAMIRP

Fred and Anthony Escape from the Netherworld (graphic novel), Hyperion (New York, NY), 2007.

Fred and Anthony Meet the Demented Super-de-Germ-O Zombie, Hyperion (New York, NY), 2007.

Fred and Anthony Meet the Heine Goblins from the Black Lagoon, Hyperion (New York, NY), 2007.

Fred and Anthony's Horrible, Hideous Back-to-School Thriller, Hyperion (New York, NY), 2008.

"LOUISE THE BIG CHEESE" NOVEL SERIES; ILLUSTRATED BY DIANE GOODE

Louise the Big Cheese: Divine Diva, Simon & Schuster Books for Young Readers (New York, NY), 2009.

Louise the Big Cheese and the La-di-dah Shoes, Simon & Schuster Books for Young Readers (New York, NY), 2010.

Louise the Big Cheese and the Back-to-School Smarty-pants, Simon & Schuster Books for Young Readers (New York, NY), 2011.

Louise the Big Cheese and the Ooh-la-la Charm School, Simon & Schuster Books for Young Readers (New York, NY), 2011.

ILLUSTRATOR

Joyce St. Peter, *Always Abigail,* J.B. Lippincott (Philadelphia, PA), 1981.

Dorothy Crayder, *The Joker and the Swan,* Harper (New York, NY), 1981.

Margaret K. Wetterer, *The Mermaid's Cape,* Atheneum (New York, NY), 1981.

Eila Moorhouse Lewis, *The Snug Little House,* Atheneum (New York, NY), 1981.

Margaret K. Wetterer, *The Giant's Apprentice,* Atheneum (New York, NY), 1982.

Art Buchwald, *The Bollo Caper: A Furry Tale for All Ages,* Putnam (New York, NY), 1983.

Natalie Savage Carlson, *The Surprise in the Mountains,* Harper (New York, NY), 1983.

Delia Ephron, *Santa and Alex,* Little, Brown (Boston, MA), 1983.

Miriam Anne Bourne, *Uncle George Washington and Harriot's Guitar,* Putnam (New York, NY), 1983.

Elaine Moore, *Grandma's House,* Lothrop (New York, NY), 1985.

Margaret Poynter, *What's One More?,* Atheneum (New York, NY), 1985.

Jean Fritz, *Make Way for Sam Houston,* Putnam (New York, NY), 1986.

Jamie Gilson, *Hobie Hanson, You're Weird,* Lothrop (New York, NY), 1987.

Patricia Lee Gauch, *Christina Katerina and the Time She Quit the Family,* Putnam (New York, NY), 1987.

Jamie Gilson, *Double Dog Dare,* Lothrop (New York, NY), 1988.

Elaine Moore, *Grandma's Promise,* Lothrop (New York, NY), 1988.

Jane Yolen, *Best Witches: Poems for Halloween,* Putnam (New York, NY), 1989.

Patricia Lee Gauch, *Christina Katerina and the Great Bear Train,* Putnam (New York, NY), 1990.

Diane Stanley, *Moe the Dog in Tropical Paradise,* Putnam (New York, NY), 1992.

Diane Stanley, *Woe Is Moe,* Putnam (New York, NY), 1995.

Mary-Claire Helldorfer, *Jack, Skinny Bones, and the Golden Pancakes,* Viking (New York, NY), 1996.

Helen Elizabeth Buckley, *Moonlight Kite,* Lothrop (New York, NY), 1997.

Jerdine Nolen, *Raising Dragons,* Silver Whistle (San Diego, CA), 1998.

Adaptations

The Secret Order of the Gumm Street Girls was adapted for audiobook, read by Colleen Delany, HarperChildren's Audio, 2006, and optioned for film by Sony Pictures Animation.

Sidelights

Although she has become well known as the author/ illustrator of the humorous books in the "Louise the Big Cheese," "Auntie Claus," and "Fred and Anthony" books, Elise Primavera began her illustration career creating artwork for picture books that feature stories by such noted authors as Jane Yolen, Natalie Savage Carlson, and Jerdine Nolen—in 2004 she was even asked to illustrate the Christmas Brochure for the White House. Combining soft-edged, brightly colored pastels and subtle charcoal with more-opaque media such as gouache and acrylics, Primavera's illustrations have been praised for their liveliness and imagination, and compared to the work of fellow illustrator Lane Smith. "Primavera's . . . illustrations . . . fairly burst forth from the pages, adding to the exaggerated humor" of Mary-Claire Helldorfer's *Jack, Skinny Bones, and the Golden Pancakes,* in the opinion of *Booklist* contributor Kay Weisman, while a *Publishers Weekly* reviewer noted that the artist's "rip-roaring" and "dynamic spreads heighten the suspense" of the story.

Primavera began her career by producing fashion illustrations, but after several years she began to feel that her creativity was not being challenged. In 1979, she decided to make a change and delve into children's book illustration. As part of her career transition she attended an illustrator's workshop which gave her the confidence she needed. "I felt very encouraged after three weeks," Primavera recalled to Jim Roginski in an interview for *Behind the Covers: Interviews with Authors and Illustrators of Books for Children and Young Adults.* While she had an agent market her fashion-illustration skills, Primavera decided to represent herself as a children's illustrator and walked the streets of New York City with her portfolio. "I saw everybody and anybody who would give me an appointment," the author-illustrator recalled of her first year, "and once I got in the door I'd always ask if there was anyone else that could see me while I was there."

Primavera's first break came when she was hired to create a book jacket for Harper & Row. A picture-book assignment followed a few months later, and by 1981, she

Elise Primavera's illustration projects include the humorous drawings for Patricia Gauch's **Christina and the Time She Quit the Family.** (Illustration copyright © 1987 by Elise Primavera. All rights reserved. Used by permission of G.P. Putnam's Sons, a division of Penguin Books for Young Readers, a member of Penguin Group (USA) Inc., 345 Hudson St., New York, NY 10014. All rights reserved.)

had two illustrated picture books to her credit: Dorothy Crayder's *The Joker and the Swan* and Joyce St. Peter's *Always Abigail.* Two years later, Primavera added "author" to her credits with the publication of *Basil and Maggie,* the story of a young girl who receives an unusual gift of a pony named Basil. Visions of walking away with a blue ribbon at the local horse show vanish into smoke after Basil proves himself less than surefooted next to his sleek thoroughbred competitors, but Maggie falls in love with him anyway in a story that a *Publishers Weekly* contributor called "just the antidote to have on hand when everything goes wrong." Primavera's illustrations were the object of praise as well; *School Library Journal* contributor Roberta Magid commented that the book's "charcoal drawings accentuate the humorous situation."

In another original self-illustrated story, *The Three Dots,* a trio of animals—Sal the moose, Henry the frog, and Margaret the duck—share odd polka-dotted markings and decide to form a musical group and take Manhattan by storm. Citing Primavera's "off-the-wall volume" for its "kicky watercolors" and "hilarious scenes," a *Publishers Weekly* contributor concluded that *The Three Dots* "should get lots of play." While less than enthusiastic about the text, Dot Minzer appreciated the book's "colorful, oversized" pictures. In her *School Library Journal* appraisal of *The Three Dots,* she observed that

Primavera's "spirited and amusing . . . pictures will grab a young audience and bring smiles to their faces."

An animal protagonist is also featured in *Ralph's Frozen Tale,* a picture book that finds Arctic explorer Ralph stuck without a dogsled until he is helped by a polar bear that can speak. "Primavera's swirling blues, greens, purples and whites give depth and beauty to the trackless, snowy wastes traversed by her heroes," noted *School Library Journal* contributor Lisa Dennis in regard to the volume's humorous and highly detailed illustrations. In the intriguingly titled *Plantpet,* Primavera spins the story of a lonely junk collector who discovers a caged plant which, when given suitable care, grows into a leaf-covered gardener. In the process the author/illustrator creates what a *Publishers Weekly* critic characterized as "another quirky tale that celebrates buddydom."

In *Auntie Claus* Primavera introduces the family of a perennially popular character. The older sister to Santa Claus and great aunt to young Christopher and Sophie Kringle, Auntie Claus lives in a penthouse apartment in which every day is decorated as if it was Christmas. Suspicious about her great-aunt's annual disappearance each November, Sophie hides in the woman's luggage and winds up at the North Pole where she is put to work sorting letters for Santa. *Auntie Claus and the Key to Christmas* finds young Christopher skeptical about the existence of Santa Claus. The child is determined to test out his theory that Santa is a fraud by doing everything he can to get on the proverbial list of Bad Boys and Girls until a trip north with Auntie Claus sets the lad straight. *Auntie Claus, Home for the Holidays* finds Santa Claus's older sister staying at home to watch Sophie's performance as the Sugar Plum Fairy in *The Nutcracker.* Her presence in town over the holiday means that she will also host the entire North Pole staff at her penthouse apartment.

Dubbing *Auntie Claus* a "frothy Christmas escapade," Ilene Cooper added in *Booklist* that Primavera's "pictures deftly combine sophistication. . . . with a wildly childlike world view." While reviewers had positive comments about the author/illustrator's lighthearted holiday tales, the artwork in her "Auntie Claus" stories earned her particularly high marks. The acrylic paintings in *Auntie Claus, Home for the Holidays* "fill the city to the brim with holiday energy," noted a *Publishers Weekly* critic, and a *Kirkus Reviews* writer commented that in *Auntie Claus and the Key to Christmas* "Primavera's stylish illustrations in jewel tones are darkly lit with just the right sense of mysterious danger and theatrical suspense for this dramatic tale." "The wordplay and stylish jewel-toned illustrations" in the second "Auntie Claus" book should "appeal to sophisticated adults as well as to kids," predicted Virginia Walter in *School Library Journal,* and Mara Alpert wrote in the same periodical that the artwork in *Auntie Claus, Home for the Holidays* will "reward careful viewers" with "exuberant and stylized" images full of "color and excitement, and interesting details."

Captured in engaging cartoon art by Diane Goode, Primavera's *Louise the Big Cheese: Divine Diva* introduces a little girl who dreams of greatness. When Louise learns that the school play will be *Cinderella* she envisions herself in the title role. Tragedy strikes, however, when her friend Fern is given the lead, and to make matters worse Louise is cast in the role of a lowly mouse. "Primavera's breezy story . . . and Goode's distinctive artwork intermingle wonderfully," wrote Cooper, the *Booklist* critic adding that the story's young heroine "makes a splash as a girl who knows what she wants." A *Publishers Weekly* reviewer commented on the appropriate choice of bubblegum pink in the story's illustrations, noting that it contributes to the "buoyant tale" about a girl with a "larger-than-life outlook." A *Kirkus Reviews* writer predicted that *Louise the Big Cheese* "presents a protagonist with whom many a mini-diva will . . . identify from page one."

Louise returns in *Louise the Big Cheese and the La-di-da Shoes*, *Louise the Big Cheese and the Back-to-School Smarty-pants*, and *Louise the Big Cheese and the Ooh-la-la Charm School*, all illustrated by Goode in tones of candy pink. In *Louise the Big Cheese and the La-di-da Shoes* jealousy again enters the picture when Louise wishes for fancy shoes like the ones Fern gets to wear to school, and the girl's goal of making top grades seems impossible until an easygoing substitute teacher illustrates the value of real achievement in *Louise the Big Cheese and the Back-to-School Smarty-pants*. "With wit and humor," *Louise the Big Cheese and the La-di-da Shoes* illustrates "the importance of friends who

Primavera creates a popular Christmastime character in her book series that begins with **Auntie Claus.** (Illustration copyright © 1999 by Elise Primavera. Reproduced by permission of Houghton Mifflin Company.)

support you through both good and poor fashion choices," quipped a *Kirkus Reviews* writer, while Linda Staskus dubbed the story's young heroine as "a lovable, spunky character with big dreams" in her *School Library Journal* review of the same book. In *Louise the Big Cheese and the Back-to-School Smarty-pants* Primavera shares "a timely message for readers on both side of the [teacher's] desk," noted another *Kirkus Reviews* writer, the critic also praising the combination of Primavera's story and Goode's comic art.

Primavera turns to fantasy in *Fred and Anthony Escape from the Netherworld,* a graphic-novel chapter book that is geared for preteen boys. Ten-year-old best friends Fred and Anthony share a passion for Chex Mix, Pez candies, and B-rated monster movies, and the only thing that motivates them to stray from the television in Fred's basement is the need to earn enough money to pay someone else to do their school homework. Their first employment opportunity turns out to have frightening implications in Primavera's series opener. The boys go in for professional ghost hunting in *Fred and Anthony Meet the Demented Super-de-Germ-O Zombie.* This time a trip into the Netherworld brings them fact to face with a zombie that decides that the world would be better off without a Fred and an Anthony. Other adventures featuring the young slackers include *Fred and Anthony Meet the Heinie Goblins from the Black Lagoon,* as a summer at Camp Plenty Wampum exposes another portal to the Netherworld that causes problems when the camp becomes overrun with some cute but ultimately problematic Heinie Goblins from down under. When their school principal reorganizes fourth grade between a health club and boot camp, the friends quickly realize that visitors from the Netherworld must be at work in *Fred and Anthony's Horrible, Hideous Back-to-School Thriller,* the fourth volume in Primavera's graphic-novel saga. According to a *Kirkus Reviews* writer, Primavera (here writing as Esile Arevamirp) "never lets up on either the laughs or the helter-skelter action" in *Fred and Anthony Escape from the Netherword,* "expertly blending short blocks of text with . . . cartoon panels." Describing Privavera's fourth-grade heroes as "snack-glutton slackers," *School Library Journal* contributor Joanna K. Fabicon added that in *Fred and Anthony Meet the Heine Goblins from the Black Lagoon* Primavera's cartoons "are drawn with a sharp, manic line" and "easy laughs pepper the plot."

With *The Secret Order of the Gumm Street Girls* Primavera announced her step into novel-length fiction; other novels for young readers have also included *Libby of Hi Hopes* and *Ms. Rapscott's Girls.* In *The Secret Order of the Gumm Street Girls* readers are introduced to Ivy Diamond when she and her former-beauty-queen mom move into a house on Gumm Street, in the town of Sherbet. Together with neighboring girls Cat, Franny, and Pru, Ivy is magically transported into a series of fantastical lands where echoes of L. Frank Baum's "Oz" books mix with a modern mystery involving a pair of red shoes, a missing piano teacher, and a mesmerizing cleaning woman who is something other than she

Primavera teams up with author Diane Stanley in the entertaining picture book Moe the Dog in Tropical Paradise, *part of a series featuring a friendly and fun-loving pup.* (Illustration copyright © 1992 by Elise Primavera. Reproduced by permission of G.P. Putnam's Sons, a division of Penguin Books for Young Readers, a member of Penguin Group (USA) Inc., 345 Hudson St., New York, NY 10014. All rights reserved.)

appears. Calling Ivy "a humorous yet disarmingly wise omniscient narrator," a *Publishers Weekly* writer described *The Secret Order of the Gumm Street Girls* as a "postmodern, surreal reworking of" *The Wizard of Oz* in which Primavera's "cheerful pen-and-inks . . . recall the work of [noted cartoonist] Jules Feiffer." A *Kirkus Reviews* writer characterized the novel as "ambitious and good-natured," adding that the author's story is well salted "with satire, invention and silliness à la Baum." "Primavera's illustrations . . . are small artistic gems that unite the text," wrote Lisa Marie Williams, the *School Library Journal* critic adding that *The Secret Order of the Gumm Street Girls* shares "an adventure that will keep readers on the edge of their seats."

In all her illustration projects, whether for her own books or for texts by other authors, Primavera makes it a point to "make the most bizarre thing seem possible and real to the reader," as she told Roginski. "It's sort of like watching a good magician perform: you know he really can't be pulling that rabbit out of the hat, but it all looks so real that for a moment something magical really is happening. This is the response that I try to work for through my illustrations."

She counts among her inspirations the artist-illustrators associated with Howard Pyle and the Brandywine School that developed in and around Chadd's Ford,

Pennsylvania, in the early 1900s. "I especially like N.C. Wyeth, Jessie Willcox Smith, and Charlotte Harding," she commented. Of her own artwork, one of the most memorable projects was creating the illustrations for Jane Yolen's *Best Witches: Poems for Halloween*. "For research, I spent a lot of time in the local costume store," Primavera recalled. "When I actually finished *Best Witches* (nine months later), my studio was crammed with witches' hats, rubber skeletons, fright wigs, plastic frogs, and black hairy spiders. At the time I was selling my house, and I used to love to watch my real estate agent show prospective buyers the studio—I don't think they knew whether to laugh or report me to the local authorities!"

Biographical and Critical Sources

BOOKS

Behind the Covers: Interviews with Authors and Illustrators of Books for Children and Young Adults, Libraries Unlimited (Littleton, CO), 1985, pp. 161-166.

PERIODICALS

Booklist, March 15, 1995, Stephanie Zvirin, review of *Woe Is Moe,* p. 1338; October 15, 1996, Kay Weisman, review of *Jack, Skinny Bones, and the Golden Pancakes,* p. 426; April, 1998, Stephanie Zvirin, review of *Raising Dragons,* p. 1334; September 1, 1999, Ilene Cooper, review of *Auntie Claus,* p. 150; September 15, 2002, Ilene Cooper, review of *Auntie Claus and the Key to Christmas,* p. 246; December 15, 2006, Ilene Cooper, review of *The Secret Order of the Gumm Street Girls,* p. 49; August 1, 2009, Ilene Cooper, review of *Louise the Big Cheese: Divine Diva,* p. 80.

Bulletin of the Center for Children's Books, September, 1994, review of *Plantpet,* p. 24.

Horn Book, March-April, 1998, Susan P. Bloom, review of *Raising Dragons,* p. 217.

Kirkus Reviews, November 15, 1991, review of *Ralph's Frozen Tale,* p. 1474; November 1, 2002, review of *Auntie Claus and the Key to Christmas,* p. 1624; October 1, 2006, review of *The Secret Order of the Gumm Street Girls,* p. 1022; July 1, 2007, review of *Fred and Anthony Escape from the Netherworld;* September 15, 2009, review of *Auntie Claus;* February 15, 2010, review of *Louise the Big Cheese and the La-di-da Shoes;* June 1, 2011, review of *Louise the Big Cheese and the Back-to-School Smarty-pants.*

Kliatt, August 15, 2009, review of *Louise the Big Cheese;* February 15, 2010, review of *Louise the Big Cheese and the La-di-da Shoes;* September 15, 2010, review of *Thumb Love.*

Publishers Weekly, April 29, 1983, review of *Basil and Maggie,* p. 52; October 11, 1991, review of *Ralph's Frozen Tale,* p. 63; October 4, 1993, review of *The Three Dots,* p. 78; August 8, 1994, review of *Plantpet,* p. 434; March 13, 1995, review of *Woe Is Moe,* p. 69; November 11, 1996, review of *Jack, Skinny Bones, and the Golden Pancakes,* p. 73; February 22, 1999, review of *Moe the Dog in Tropical Paradise,* p. 97; September 27, 1999, review of *Auntie Claus,* p. 56; November 13, 2006, review of *The Secret Order of the Gumm Street Girls,* p. 58; September 14, 2009, review of *Louise the Big Cheese: Divine Diva,* p. 47; October 26, 2009, review of *Auntie Claus, Home for the Holidays,* p. 55; October 4, 2010, review of *Thumb Love,* p. 47.

Quill & Quire, November, 1993, review of *The Three Dots,* p. 40.

School Library Journal, May, 1983, Roberta Magid, review of *Basil and Maggie,* p. 65; February, 1992, Lisa Dennis, review of *Ralph's Frozen Tale,* pp. 76-77; January, 1994, Dot Minzer, review of *The Three Dots,* p. 97; November, 1994, Lynn Cockett, review of *Plantpet,* p. 88; June, 1995, Karen James, review of *Woe Is Moe,* p. 96; October, 1996, Lauralyn Persson, review of *Jack, Skinny Bones, and the Golden Pancakes,* p. 96; October, 2002, Virginia Walter, review of *Auntie Claus and the Key to Christmas,* p. 62; December, 2006, Lisa Marie Williams, review of *The Secret Order of the Gumm Street Girls,* p. 152; December, 2007, Elaine E. Knight, review of *Fred and Anthony's Escape from the Netherworld,* p. 98; September, 2008, Joanna K. Fabicon, review of *Fred and Anthony Meet the Heinie Goblins from the Black Lagoon,* p. 157; January, 2009, Jackie Partch, review of *Fred and Anthony's Horrible, Hideous Back-to-School Thriller,* p. 82; September, 2009, Ieva Bates, review of *Louise the Big Cheese: Divine Diva,* p. 131; October, 2009, Mara Alpert, review of *Auntie Claus, Home for the Holidays,* p. 83; February, 2010, Linda Staskus, review of *Louise the Big Cheese and the La-di-da Shoes,* p. 92; October, 2010, Lisa Glasscock, review of *Thumb Love,* p. 92.

ONLINE

Elise Primavera Home Page, http://www.eliseprimavera.com (May 15, 2011).*

*   *   *

QUEEN RAINA
See AL ABDULLAH, Rania

R

RAILSBACK, Lisa

Personal

Born in Moline, IL. *Education:* University of New Mexico, M.A. (playwriting); University of Texas at Austin, M.F.A. (writing). *Hobbies and other interests:* Hiking, travel, wildlife.

Addresses

Home—Austin, TX. *E-mail*—Lisa@Lisarailsback.com.

Career

Playwright and novelist. Jerome fellowship Playwrights' Center, Minneapolis, MN, c.2002; Michener fellow in Writing, University of Texas at Austin; writer in residence at Anderson Center for Interdisciplinary Studies, Red Wing, MN. Involved in animal rescue.

Awards, Honors

Beverly Hills Theatre Guild Award, Best Children's Script designation, Stages Repertory Theatre/Southwest Theatre Association, all c. 2000, all for *Noonie's Masterpiece in Purple;* National Bonderman Playwriting for Youth Award, for *Stone Girls Dreaming;*

Writings

Noonie's Masterpiece in Purple (play; also see below), Dramatic Pub. (Woodstock, IL), 2000.
Betti on the High Wire, Dial Books (New York, NY), 2010.
Noonie's Masterpiece (based on the play *Noonie's Masterpiece in Purple*), illustrated by Sarajo Frieden, Chronicle Books (San Francisco, CA), 2010.

Author of plays, including *Stone Girls Dreaming,* produced in Red Wing, MN, 2005, and published in *Dramatics* magazine, November, 2010; and *Bug Boy Blues,* produced in New York, NY, 2007.

Adaptations

Betti on the High Wire was adapted for audiobook, Random House/Listening Library, 2010.

Sidelights

Lisa Railsback worked as a playwright for several years before earning her M.F.A. in writing at the University of Texas at Austin. From her home in the Lone Star State, Railsback continues to write for both the stage and for young people, and the focus of much of her work is transformation and the creative life. Her plays include *Bug Boy Blues,* an adaptation of Franz Kafka's novel *Metamorphosis* that is geared for young audiences. Another work for the stage, *Noonie's Masterpiece in Purple,* inspired Railsback's first middle-grade novel, *Noonie's Masterpiece,* while her second novel, *Bettie on the High Wire,* was inspired by her travels to Thailand, where she volunteered at a refugee camp for several years.

As Railsback noted on her home page, *Noonie's Masterpiece* stands as "a tribute to any creative person who understands the joy, anguish, and hard labor involved in pursuing the artistic dream." In the story, ten-year-old Noonie Norton lives with her aunt and uncle as well as a cousin, none of whom realize that she is on her way to being a famous abstract painter. In fact, she is ready to be discovered, ready right NOW, but her relatives are unable to see her talent. In fact, Noonie feels invisible now that her mom has died and her archeologist father spends all his time jetting around the world on business. Fortunately, although her relatives do not see her need to be noticed, Noonie's fourth-grade art teacher does. Although her attempt to use art as a vehicle to communicate with her relatives backfires, the girl gets encouragement from a surprising source and ultimately realizes that what her teacher says is true: creative people are the ones who effect change in the world. Noonie's "pain and vulnerability are as evident as her belief in herself as an artist," noted *Booklist* critic Carolyn Phelan, while a *Publishers Weekly* critic described Railsback's story as "a rewarding, if not masterful, pep talk"

Cover of Lisa Railsback's middle-grade novel **Betti on the High Wire,** *which focuses on an orphaned girl who dreams of life in the circus.*
(Jacket cover design by Jennifer Kelly. Reproduced by permission of Penguin Books for Young Readers, a member of Penguin Group (USA) Inc., 345 Hudson Street, New York, NY 10014. All rights reserved.)

on the importance of being true to your creative muse. D. Maria LaRocco observed in *School Library Journal* that the author "maintains the prominent theme of art serving as therapy" in her "lovely, quirky portrait" of the eccentric and spontaneous Nonnie, while a *Kirkus Reviews* writer noted that Railsback's young heroine is "filled with the self-absorption and longing" typical of children her age.

Described by a *Publishers Weekly* contributor as "a poignant comedy rooted in a tragic contemporary reality," *Betti on the High Wire* introduces another ten year old. In this case, Railsback's heroine is ten-year-old Babo, an orphaned daughter of circus performers who is attempting to survive in a war-torn region. Street smart Babo looks after a group of younger children, reassuring them with stories and creating a refuge at the site of the circus where she was raised. When an American couple, the Buckworths, decide to adopt her and take her to their home, Babo (now Betti) is determined to misbehave so that she can return to her homeland. As she helps another young adoptee adjust to his new surroundings, however, the girl begins to question her atti-

tude and slowly starts to warm to her new family and opportunities. "Babo's bravado is endearing," wrote a *Publishers Weekly* contributor in appraising *Betti on the High Wire,* "and her giggle-provoking adventures lighten the story's dark backdrop." In her *School Library Journal* review of Railsback's novel, Deborah Vose noted that the story "captures many aspects of culture dissonance well, and the challenge of bridging two cultures," and "may well resonate with children who have had to adjust to a new situation."

Biographical and Critical Sources

PERIODICALS

Booklist, May 1, 2010, Carolyn Phelan, review of *Noonie's Masterpiece,* p. 87.
Bulletin of the Center for Children's Books, July-August, 2010, Deborah Stevenson, review of *Betti on the High Wire,* p. 498.
Kirkus Reviews, March 1, 2010, review of *Noonie's Masterpiece;* April 15, 2010, review of *Betti on the High Wire.*
New York Times, January 21, 2000, Laurel Graeber, review of *Noonie's Masterpiece in Purple,* p. 48.
Publishers Weekly, April 19, 2010, review of *Noonie's Masterpiece,* p. 53; June 28, 2010, review of *Betti on the High Wire,* p. 127.
School Library Journal, June, 2010, Deborah Vose, review of *Betti on the High Wire,* p. 118; July, 2010, D. Maria LaRocco, review of *Noonie's Masterpiece,* p. 95.

ONLINE

Cynsation Web log, http://cynthialeitichsmith.blogspot.com/ (December 15, 2010), Cynthia Leitich Smith, interview with Railsback.
Lisa Railsback Home Page, http://www.lisarailsback.com (February 27, 2011).*

* * *

RESAU, Laura 1973-

Personal

Born 1973, in Baltimore, MD; married; husband's name Ian; children: one son. *Education:* St. Mary's College, B.A.; University of Arizona, M.A. *Hobbies and other interests:* Hiking, reading, dancing.

Addresses

Home—Fort Collins, CO. *E-mail*—lresau@hotmail.com.

Career

Writer, educator. Previously taught English as a second language (ESL) in Oaxaca, Mexico; Front Range Community College, Fort Collins, CO, cultural anthropology and ESL teacher. Presenter at schools.

Laura Resau (Photograph by Tina Wood. Reproduced by permission.)

Awards, Honors

Parents' Choice Award, Parents' Choice Foundation, 2006, and Colorado Book Award, Américas Award Honorable Mention, Judy Goddard Arizona Young-Adult Book Award, Notable Social Studies Trade Book designation, and Best Book for Young Adults selection, American Library Association (ALA), all c. 2007, all for *What the Moon Saw;* Puffin Foundation grant, Arts Alive fellowship, Barbara Deming Memorial Fund grant, all c. 2006, all for *The Queen of Water;* James Cook Book Award (OH) honorable mention, Colorado Book Award in young-adult category, and Cooperative Children's Book Center's (CCBC) Choice selection, all 2008, and CYBILS Award finalist, Américas Award, International Reading Association Young-Adult Fiction Award, and ALA Best Book for Young Adults designation, all for *Red Glass;* Colorado Book Award, 2009, for *The Indigo Notebook;* Colorado Book Award finalist, Américas Award Commended selection, Bank Street College Best Children's Books of the Year selection, Capitol Choices Noteworthy designation, and CCBC Choices listee, all c. 2010, all for *Star in the Forest;* Colorado Book Award finalist, 2010, for *The Ruby Notebook.*

Writings

What the Moon Saw (for children), Delacorte Press (New York, NY), 2006.

Red Glass, Delacorte Press (New York, NY), 2007.
The Indigo Notebook, Delacorte Press (New York, NY), 2009.
Star in the Forest, illustrated by Gary Blythe, Delacorte Press (New York, NY), 2010.
The Ruby Notebook, Delacorte Press (New York, NY), 2010.
(With Maria Virginia Farinango) *The Queen of Water,* Delacorte Press (New York, NY), 2011.

Contributor of essays on Mexico to *Lonely Planet* and *Travelers' Tales* anthologies, and of children's fiction and creative nonfiction to periodicals including *Cicada, Cricket,* and *Skipping Stones.*

Adaptations

Red Glass was adapted for audiobook, read by Emma Bering, Listening Library, 2009. *The Indigo Notebook* was adapted for audiobook, read by Justine Eyre, Listening Library, 2009.

Sidelights

A teacher on the college level, Laura Resau was inspired to write by her travels in Latin America and Europe as well as her love of storytelling. Since publishing her first novel, *What the Moon Saw,* Resau has continued writing, producing fiction that includes *Star in the Forest*, a story for younger readers, as well as the young-adult novels *Red Glass,* the companion stories *The Indigo Notebook* and *The Ruby Notebook,* and the collaborative novel *The Queen of Water,* which she coauthored with María Virginia Farinango.

Born in Maryland, Resau spent the first decade of her life running and playing in the alleys of Baltimore. When she was eleven years old, her family moved to the suburbs, and Resau became enchanted with the woods, streams, and fields nearby. After graduating from college, she decided to travel and explore other parts of the world. In Oaxaca, Mexico, a small university offered her a job and she spent the next two years meeting people, learning Spanish, and experiencing the culture and stories of the region. Her time in Mexico led Resau to study cultural anthropology at the University of Arizona, where she earned her master's degree.

Resau returned to the United States and began to teach English as a Second Language (ESL) and cultural anthropology at Front Range Community College in Fort Collins, Colorado. Her essays on Mexico have appeared in the anthologies *Lonely Planet* and *Travelers' Tales,* and her creative nonfiction and fiction for children has been published in various periodicals, including *Cricket.* Her first children's book, *What the Moon Saw,* was published in 2006.

In *What the Moon Saw* readers meet Clara Luna, a fourteen-year-old Mexican-American, as she learns about her heritage and how her father came to the United States. In a review for *Kliatt,* Janis Flint-Ferguson described *What the Moon Saw* as "a beautifully told story of finding oneself by holding on to ancient traditions." A contributor for *Kirkus Reviews* also enjoyed the novel, citing the novel as full of "evocative language that is rich in imagery and nuance and speaks to the connections that bind us all."

Like *What the Moon Saw,* Resau's other novels focus on teens with Hispanic roots. For sheltered, sixteen-year-old Sophie, the central character in *Red Glass,* a nighttime phone call draws her into the drama of a Mexican-American family. Called to the hospital, she and her mother and her stepfather meet five-year-old Pablo, the surviving member of a family that attempted to cross the Mexican-American border before succumbing to the elements. The family takes Pablo into their home and Sophie treats him as her little brother. When contact is finally made with the boy's Mexican family, Sophie joins her great aunt Dika and Dika's boyfriend and son to take Pablo south to Guatemala to meet his extended family. On the trip the teen discovers the courage possessed by her fellow passengers, especially Dika, a refuge from war-torn Bosnia. Ultimately Sophie must face her own fears as well in a story that combines "magical elements and coincidence" in a coming-of-age tale that *Booklist* critic Carolyn Phelan recommended

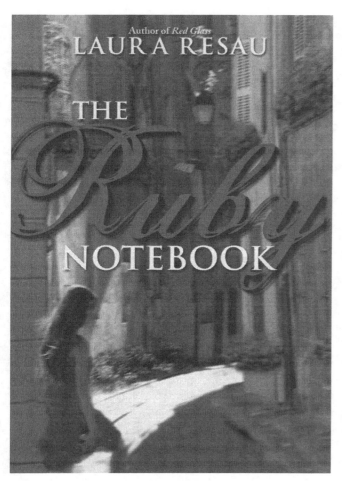

Cover of Resau's young-adult novel The Ruby Notebook, *featuring artwork by Ericka O'Rourke.* (Delacorte Press, 2010. Cover art by Ericka O'Rourke. Reproduced by permission of Random House Children's Books.)

for its "vivid characters, . . . fine imagery, and . . . satisfying story arc." "Suffused with the region's vibrant colors, Resau's . . . memorable novel deftly blends Latin America's richness and mystery with the brutal realities its emigrants carry away," maintained a *Publishers Weekly* contributor, and a *Kirkus Reviews* writer dubbed *Red Glass* "emotionally charged and powerful." Kathleen Isaacs noted in *School Library Journal* that Resau's "love for the culture and physical setting of rural Oaxaca and northern Guatemala is shown in beautiful, descriptive detail."

Resau also addresses the issue of illegal immigration in a story for younger readers. Featuring illustrations by Gary Blythe, *Star in the Forest* captures the emotions of Colorado fifth-grader Zitlally after her father is deported back to Mexico and her mother and sisters worry that they will be next. To escape the worry and tension in her family, the girl finds a hide-out in a field of abandoned auto parts, but she is not the only one to take refuge there. A mongrel dog is also there, chained to a truck, and Zitlally names him Star, believing the dog to be connected in spirit to her father. With her new friend Crystal, she gains the affection of the dog, and trains him. When they arrive one day to find Star gone, the girls begin a search that allows Zitlally to do something to save her father and family as well. *Star in the Forest* is "a well-told and deeply satisfying read," asserted *School Library Journal* critic Kathleen Isaacs, citing Resau's focus "on the developing friendships, both between Zitlally and her previously ignored neighbor, and between the fearful youngster and the dog." For a *Kirkus Reviews* writer, Resau's novel introduces readers to Nahua and Mixtec traditions, "like their belief in animal totems," to produce "a story of friendship that will speak to children of different cultures." In *Booklist,* Hazel Rochman dubbed *Star in the Forest* an "unforgettable narrative of a girl's daily struggle to find a home."

Both *The Indigo Notebook* and *The Ruby Notebook* focus on Zeeta, a fifteen year old who lives a peripatetic life with her mother Layla, an English teacher with a penchant for travel. When readers first meet her in *The Indigo Notebook,* Zeeta is living in the Ecuadorian Andes, where a friendship with American-born Wendell leads to a search for missing parents and a dangerous adventure in which fantasy melds with a budding romance. Zeeta's story continues in *The Ruby Notebook,* where the teen's new temporary home in southern France connects her with a mysterious admirer—her fantôme—and also with Jean-Claude, a handsome street performer who may be pulling her heart away from the soon-to-visit Wendell. Noting the vivid settings, likeable characters, and mystical elements that Resau weaves into Zeeta's initial adventure, *School Library Journal* critic Sue Giffard recommended *The Indigo Notebook* as "an entertaining and suspenseful read," while a *Kirkus Reviews* writer praised the novel as a "remarkably engrossing, layered work" "Although one can guess where the plot is headed, teens will still want to go along for the ride, so enjoyable is the writing," concluded Geri Diorio in her *School Library Journal* review of *The Ruby Notebook,* a novel enriched by Resau's "robust descriptions" and engaging first-person narrative.

Biographical and Critical Sources

PERIODICALS

Booklist, October 15, 2006, Gillian Engberg, review of *What the Moon Saw,* p. 47; September 15, 2007, Carolyn Phelan, review of *Red Glass,* p. 63; November 1, 2009, Carolyn Phelan, review of *The Indigo Notebook,* p. 36.

Children's Bookwatch, December, 2006, review of *What the Moon Saw.*

Horn Book, January-February, 2008, Megan Lynn Isacc, review of *Red Glass,* p. 93; March-April, 2010, Susan Dove Lempke, review of *Star in the Forest,* p. 69.

Kirkus Reviews, September 1, 2006, review of *What the Moon Saw,* p. 912; August 15, 2007, review of *Red Glass;* September 15, 2009, review of *The Indigo Notebook;* March 1, 2010, review of *Star in the Forest.*

Kliatt, September, 2006, Janis Flint-Ferguson, review of *What the Moon Saw,* p. 17.

Publishers Weekly, October 1, 2007, review of *Red Glass,* p. 58.

School Library Journal, September, 2006, Melissa Christy Buron, review of *What the Moon Saw,* p. 217; October, 2006, review of *What the Moon Saw,* p. 50; October, 2007, Kathleen Isaacs, review of *Red Glass,* p. 162; December, 2009, Sue Giffard, review of *The Indigo Notebook,* p. 130; February, 2010, Kathleen Isaacs, review of *Star in the Forest,* p. 122; October, 2010, Geri Diorio, review of *The Ruby Notebook,* p. 124.

ONLINE

Laura Resau Home Page, http://www.lauraresau.com (May 15, 2011).

*   *   *

RICHARDS, Jame

Personal

Married; children: two daughters. *Education:* Wellesley College, B.A.; University of Massachusetts at Dartmouth, M.A.

Addresses

Home—Monroe, CT. *Agent*—Trident Media Group, 41 Madison Ave., Fl. 36, New York, NY 10010. *E-mail*—contact@jamerichards.com.

Career

Author.

Jame Richards (Photograph by Jennifer May. Reproduced by permission.)

Member

Society of Children's Book Writers and Illustrators.

Writings

Three Rivers Rising: A Novel of the Johnstown Flood, Alfred A. Knopf (New York, NY), 2010.

Adaptations

Three Rivers Rising was adapted for audiobook, audible.com and Brilliance Audio, 2010.

Sidelights

History has fascinated Jame Richards since elementary school, and her family's summer trips to museums and sites of historical interest only fueled the fire. Richards taps this interest in her first work for young adults, *Three Rivers Rising: A Novel of the Johnstown Flood,* which Jill Heritage Maza characterized in her *School Library Journal* review as a "gem of a novel-in-verse."

Three Rivers Rising takes readers back to the summer of 1888, as sixteen-year-old Celestia Whitcomb vacations with her family at the exclusive South Fork Fishing and Hunting Club, on the shores of Pennsylvania's Lake Conemaugh. Lake Conemaugh is actually a reservoir, and its waters are held in the Allegheny Mountains by an aging and neglected earthen dam. This summer is special, however, as she now meets Peter, a local working-class teen, and they fall in love. Events abruptly separate them, but they secretly keep their love alive and hope to reunite, despite her father's efforts to push her into an arranged marriage. As readers follow Celestia on her way down the mountain to Johnston to seek out her beloved Richards, they see her intersect with two other young women, as they begin a normal May day in 1889, marveling at the heavy rain and not realizing that they will soon be statistics in one of the most tragic floods in U.S. history.

Creating "strong characters with few words" in *Three Rivers Rising,* Richards "artfully interweaves the lives of these independent thinkers" into the chronicle of a tragedy that unfolds in an account that is "painful and immediate," according to a *Publishers Weekly* critic. The novel's "ability to wear so many hats—-heart-tugging romance, nail-biting suspense novel, and social commentary. . .—more than earns it a place on the shelves of all libraries serving teens," asserted Maza of Richards' poetic chronicle, and in *Booklist* Debbie Carton asserted of *Three Rivers Rising* that the story's "moving" exploration of "class divisions and social mores" is couched in a tale that is both "intensely romantic and polished."

Biographical and Critical Sources

PERIODICALS

Booklist, April 15, 2010, Debbie Carton, review of *Three Rivers Rising: A Novel of the Johnstown Flood,* p. 58.
Bulletin of the Center for Children's Books, May, 2010, Elizabeth Bush, review of *Three Rivers Rising,* p. 396.

Cover of Richard's historical novel **Three Rivers Rising,** *which focuses on the Johnstown Flood tragedy of 1889.* (Cover art copyright © 2010 by Alfred A. Knopf. Reproduced by permission of Random House Children's Books, a division of Random House, Inc.)

Kirkus Reviews, March 15, 2010 review of *Three Rivers Rising.*
Publishers Weekly, March 29, 2010, review of *Three Rivers Rising,* p. 60.
School Library Journal, April, 2010, Jill Heritage Maza, review of *Three Rivers Rising,* p. 166.

ONLINE

Class of 2K10 Web site, http://www.classof2k10.com (May 15, 2011).
Jame Richards Home Page, http://www.jamerichards.com (May 15, 2011).
Jame Richards Web log, http://jamerichards.blogspot.com (May 15, 2011).

*   *   *

ROBERTON, Fiona

Personal

Born in Oxford, England. *Education:* Studied art and design in London, England, and New York, NY.

Addresses

Home—London, England. *E-mail*—design@ilovepork chop.com.

Career

Designer, illustrator, and author.

Awards, Honors

Australian Publishers Association Book Design Award for Best Designed Picture Book, 2010, for *Wanted: The Perfect Pet.*

Writings

Porkchop and Mouse, Penguin (Camberwell, Victoria, Australia), 2007.
Wanted: The Perfect Pet, Penguin Books Australia (Camberwell, Victoria, Australia), 2009, G.P. Putnam's Sons (New York, NY), 2010.
Perfect Present,, 2011.

Sidelights

Designer and illustrator Fiona Roberton lives and works in London, where she has created visual art for clients that have included Warner Brothers and the British Broadcasting Corporation as well as Sony, EMI, American Express, and Goldman Sachs. Roberton's first book for children, *Porkchop and Mouse,* was published in Australia. As she announced, unabashed, on her home page, *Porkchop and Mouse* "was inspired by her love

Fiona Roberton's story of a boy who wishes for a dog comes to life in the spare art in **Wanted: The Perfect Pet.** (Illustration copyright © 2010 by Fiona Roberton. Reproduced by permission of G.P. Putnam's Son, a division of Penguin Books for Young Readers, a member of Penguin Group (USA) Inc., 345 Hudson St., New York, NY 10014. All rights reserved.)

of cakes, holidays, and her inability to share." Her second picture book, *Wanted: The Perfect Pet,* grew out of Roberton's "love of dogs, ducks and disguises."

Henry, the boy readers meet in *Wanted: The Perfect Pet,* has dozens of frogs but wishes for a doggy companion. Consequently, he places an advertisement outlining his requirements for the perfect pet: a waggy tail, long velvety ears, and a warm, wet nose. Although Henry clearly wants a dog, when lonely Duck comes upon Henry's advertisement he decides to respond. In a clever disguise that masks his beak, wings, and webbed feet, Duck waddles to Henry's house, where the two get along well until poor Duck's disguise begins to unravel. Fortunately, Henry is wise enough to realize that Duck's natural attributes are also valuable, and his specifications for the perfect pet are recalibrated to Duck's satisfaction. Rendered in black line with shades of grey, yellow, and green, Roberton's illustrations for *Wanted: The Perfect Pet* are "effective in conveying mood, action, and humor," according to *School Library Journal* contributor Catherine Callegari, and a *Kirkus Reviews* writer asserted that the "fantastic silliness" in the book is ratcheted up by the artist's "simple, even childlike, tongue-in-cheek drawings." *Wanted: The Perfect Pet* "brings a delightful sophistication and a unique twist to the kid-wanting-a-pet theme," according to *Booklist* reviewer Patricia Austin, the critic adding that the picture book may also "ignite discussions about problem solving and being open to the unexpected." Noting the engaging details in Roberton's cartoon art, a *Publishers Weekly* contributor added that the author/artist's verbal "asides are just as funny as the main story" and help make the picture book a "winking blend of whimsy and irony."

Biographical and Critical Sources

PERIODICALS

Booklist, July 1, 2010, Patricia Austin, review of *Wanted: The Perfect Pet,* p. 68.
Kirkus Reviews, April 15, 2010, review of *Wanted: The Perfect Pet.*
Publishers Weekly, April 19, 2010, review of *Wanted: The Perfect Pet,* p. 53.
School Library Journal, July, 2010, Catherine Callegari, review of *Wanted: The Perfect Pet,* p. 69.

ONLINE

Fiona Roberton Home Page, http://www.iloveporkchop. com (February 27, 2011).*

*   *   *

RODDA, Emily 1948-
(Mary-Anne Dickinson, Jennifer Rowe)

Personal

Born Jennifer Rowe, 1948, in New South Wales, Australia; married; children: one daughter, three sons. *Education:* University of Sydney, M.A., 1973. *Hobbies and other interests:* Reading.

Addresses

Home—Sydney, New South Wales, Australia

Career

Full-time writer, beginning 1994. Angus & Robertson (publishers), Sydney, New South Wales, Australia, former editor of children's books; former editor, *Australian Women's Weekly*.

Awards, Honors

Children's Book of the Year selection, Children's Book Council of Australia (CBCA), 1985, for *Something Special*, 1987, for *Pigs Might Fly*, 1989, for *The Best-Kept Secret*, 1991, for *Finders Keepers*, 1994, for *Rowan of Rin*. 1999 (with Craig Smith) for *Bob the Builder and the Elves;* BILBY Award, Ipswich Festival of Children's Literature, 1995, for *Rowan of Rin;* Dromkeen Medal, Courtney Oldmeadow Children's Literature Foundation, 1995, for contributions to Australian children's literature; CBCA Children's Honour Book of the Year selection, 1997, for *Rowan and the Keeper of the Crystal;* Aurealis Award shortlist, 2007, and Patricia Wrightson Prize for Children shortlist, New South Wales Premier's Literary Awards, and CBCA Children's Book of the Year selection shortlist, both 2008, all for *The Key to Rondo;* KOALA Legend Award, 2010; numerous child-selected awards, including YABBA, KOALA, KROC, COOL, and WAYRBA honors.

Writings

Something Special, illustrated by Noela Young, Angus & Robertson (Sydney, New South Wales, Australia), 1984, Holt (New York, NY), 1989.

Pigs Might Fly, illustrated by Noela Young, Angus & Robertson (Sydney, New South Wales, Australia), 1986, published as *The Pigs Are Flying!*, Greenwillow (New York, NY), 1988.

The Best-Kept Secret, illustrated by Noela Young, Angus & Robertson (North Ryde, Australia), 1988, Holt (New York, NY), 1990.

Finders Keepers, illustrated by Noela Young, Omnibus Books (Norwood, South Australia, Australia), 1990, Greenwillow (New York, NY), 1991.

Crumbs!, illustrated by Kerry Argent, Omnibus Books (Norwood, South Australia, Australia), 1990.

The Timekeeper, illustrated by Noela Young, Omnibus Books (Norwood, South Australia, Australia), 1992, Greenwillow (New York, NY), 1993.

Power and Glory, illustrated by Geoff Kelly, Allen & Unwin (St. Leonards, Australia), 1994, Greenwillow (New York, NY), 1996.

Yay!, illustrated by Craig Smith, Omnibus Books (Norwood, South Australia, Australia), 1996, Greenwillow (New York, NY), 1997.

Game Plan, illustrated by Craig Smith, Omnibus Books (Norwood, South Australia, Australia), 1998.

Green Fingers, illustrated by Craig Smith, Omnibus Books (Norwood, South Australia, Australia), 1998.

Where Do You Hide Two Elephants?, illustrated by Andrew McLean, Omnibus Books (Norwood, South Australia, Australia), 1998, Gareth Stevens (Milwaukee, WI), 2001.

Fuzz, the Famous Fly, illustrated by Tom Jellett, Omnibus Books (Norwood, South Australia, Australia), 1999.

The Julia Tapes, Puffin (Ringwood, Australia), 1999.

Bob the Builder and the Elves, illustrated by Craig Smith, ABC Books (Sydney, New South Wales, Australia), 2000, published as *Bob and the House Elves*, illustrated by Tim Archbold, Bloomsbury (London, England), 2001.

Gobbleguts, ABC Books (Sydney, New South Wales, Australia), 2000.

Dog Tales, Omnibus Books (Norwood, South Australia, Australia), 2001.

Squeak Street, illustrated by Andrew McLean, Working Title Press (Kingswood, Australia), 2002.

The Long Way Home, illustrated by Danny Snell, Working Title Press (Kingswood, Australia), 2002.

The Magic Key, illustrated by Raoul Vitale, HarperCollins (New York, NY), 2004.

Tales of Deltora, illustrated by Marc McBride, 2005, Scholastic, Inc. (New York, NY), 2006.

The Unicorn, illustrated by Raoul Vitale, HarperCollins (New York, NY), 2004.

(With Marc McBride) *How to Draw Deltora Monsters*, Scholastic, Inc. (New York, NY), 2005.

The Star Cloak, illustrated by Raoul Vitale, HarperCollins (New York, NY), 2005.

The Water Sprites, illustrated by Raoul Vitale, HarperCollins (New York, NY), 2005.

The Peskie Spell, illustrated by Raoul Vitale, HarperCollins (New York, NY), 2006.

The Rainbow Wand, illustrated by Raoul Vitale, HarperCollins (New York, NY), 2006.

Enter the Realm, illustrated by Raoul Vitale, HarperCollins (New York, NY), 2007.

The Charm Bracelet, illustrated by Raoul Vitale, Spotlight (Edina, MN), 2008.

The Flower Fairies, illustrated by Raoul Vitale, Spotlight (Edina, MN), 2008.

The Last Fairy-apple Tree, illustrated by Raoul Vitale, Spotlight (Edina, MN), 2008.

The Third Wish, illustrated by Raoul Vitale, Spotlight (Edina, MN), 2008.

Bungawitta, illustrated by Craig Smith, 2011.

Editor of anthology *She's Apples: A Collection of Winning Stories for Young Australians*.

"ROWAN OF RIN" SERIES

Rowan of Rin, Omnibus Books (Norwood, South Australia, Australia), 1993, Greenwillow (New York, NY), 2001.

Rowan and the Travellers, Omnibus Books (Norwood, South Australia, Australia), 1994, published as *Rowan and the Travelers*, Greenwillow (New York, NY), 2001.

Rowan and the Keeper of the Crystal, Omnibus Books (Norwood, South Australia, Australia), 1996, Greenwillow (New York, NY), 2002.

Rowan and the Zebak, Omnibus Books (Norwood, South Australia, Australia), 1999, Greenwillow (New York, NY), 2002.

Rowan of the Buckshah, Omnibus Books (Norwood, South Australia, Australia), 2003, published as *Rowan and the Ice Creepers,* Greenwillow (New York, NY), 2004.

"DELTORA QUEST" SERIES

The Forests of Silence, Scholastic (New York, NY), 2000.

The Lake of Tears, Scholastic Australia (Sydney, New South Wales, Australia), 2000, Scholastic (New York, NY), 2001.

City of the Rats, Scholastic Australia (Sydney, New South Wales, Australia), 2000, Scholastic (New York, NY), 2001.

The Shifting Sands, Scholastic Australia (Sydney, New South Wales, Australia), 2000, Scholastic (New York, NY), 2001.

Dread Mountain, Scholastic Australia (Sydney, New South Wales, Australia), 2000, Scholastic (New York, NY), 2001.

The Maze of the Beast, Scholastic Australia (Sydney, New South Wales, Australia), 2000, Scholastic (New York, NY), 2001.

The Valley of the Lost, Scholastic Australia (Sydney, New South Wales, Australia), 2000, Scholastic (New York, NY), 2001.

Return to Del, Scholastic Australia (Sydney, New South Wales, Australia), 2000, Scholastic (New York, NY), 2001.

The Deltora Book of Monsters: By Josef, Palace Librarian in the Reign of King Alton, illustrated by Marc McBride, Scholastic Australia (Sydney, New South Wales, Australia), 2001, Scholastic, Inc. (New York, NY), 2006.

Cavern of the Fear, Scholastic (New York, NY), 2002.

The Isle of Illusion, Scholastic Australia (Sydney, New South Wales, Australia), 2002.

The Shadowlands, Scholastic Australia (Sydney, New South Wales, Australia), 2002.

Dragon's Nest, Scholastic Australia (Sydney, New South Wales, Australia), 2003, Scholastic, Inc., (New York, NY), 2004.

Shadowgate, Scholastic, Inc. (New York, NY), 2004.

Isle of the Dead, Scholastic, Inc. (New York, NY), 2004.

Sister of the South, Scholastic Australia (Sydney, New South Wales, Australia), 2004, Scholastic, Inc. (New York, NY), 2005.

"STORYTELLING CHARMS"/"FAIRY REALM" SERIES

(Under name Mary-Anne Dickinson) *The Charm Bracelet,* Bantam Books (Sydney, New South Wales, Australia), 1994, published under name Emily Rodda, HarperCollins (New York, NY), 2003.

(Under name Mary-Anne Dickinson) *The Flower Fairies,* Bantam Books (Sydney, New South Wales, Australia), 1994, published under name Emily Rodda, HarperCollins (New York, NY), 2003.

(Under name Mary-Anne Dickinson) *The Third Wish,* Bantam Books (Sydney, New South Wales, Australia), 1995, published under name Emily Rodda, HarperCollins (New York, NY), 2003.

(Under name Mary-Anne Dickinson) *The Last Fairy-Apple Tree,* Bantam Books (Sydney, New South Wales, Australia), 1995, published under name Emily Rodda, HarperCollins (New York, NY), 2003.

(Under name Mary-Anne Dickinson) *The Magic Key,* Bantam Books (Sydney, New South Wales, Australia), 1995, published under name Emily Rodda, HarperCollins (New York, NY), 2004.

(Under name Mary-Anne Dickinson) *The Unicorn,* Bantam Books (Sydney, New South Wales, Australia), 1996, published under name Emily Rodda, HarperCollins (New York, NY), 2004.

The Fairy Realm (series omnibus), ABC Books (Sydney, New South Wales, Australia), 2002.

"TEEN POWER INC./RAVEN HILL MYSTERIES" SERIES

The Secret of Banyan Bay, Ashton Scholastic (Sydney, New South Wales, Australia), 1994.

The Sorcerer's Apprentice, Ashton Scholastic (Sydney, New South Wales, Australia), 1994, Scholastic, Inc. (New York, NY), 2005.

The Bad Dog Mystery, Ashton Scholastic (Sydney, New South Wales, Australia), 1994.

Beware the Gingerbread House, Ashton Scholastic (Sydney, New South Wales, Australia), 1994, Scholastic, Inc. (New York, NY), 2005.

Cry of the Cat, Ashton Scholastic (Sydney, New South Wales, Australia), 1994.

The Disappearing TV Star, Ashton Scholastic (Sydney, New South Wales, Australia), 1994.

The Ghost of Raven Hill, Ashton Scholastic (Sydney, New South Wales, Australia), 1994 Scholastic, Inc. (New York, NY), 2005.

Green for Danger, Ashton Scholastic (Sydney, New South Wales, Australia), 1994.

Deep Secrets, Ashton Scholastic (Sydney, New South Wales, Australia), 1994, Scholastic, Inc., (New York, NY), 2006.

Poison Pen, Ashton Scholastic (Sydney, New South Wales, Australia), 1994.

Breaking Point, Ashton Scholastic (Sydney, New South Wales, Australia), 1994.

Nowhere to Run, Ashton Scholastic (Sydney, New South Wales, Australia), 1995.

Crime in the Picture, Ashton Scholastic (Sydney, New South Wales, Australia), 1995.

The Case of Crazy Claude, Ashton Scholastic (Sydney, New South Wales, Australia), 1995.

Fear in Fashion, Ashton Scholastic (Sydney, New South Wales, Australia), 1995.

Dangerous Game, Ashton Scholastic (Sydney, New South Wales, Australia), 1995.

Danger in Rhyme, Ashton Scholastic (Sydney, New South Wales, Australia), 1995.

The Missing Millionaire, Ashton Scholastic (Sydney, New South Wales, Australia), 1995.

Haunted House, Ashton Scholastic (Sydney, New South Wales, Australia), 1995.

Cry Wolf, Ashton Scholastic (Sydney, New South Wales, Australia), 1996.

Photo Finish, Ashton Scholastic (Sydney, New South Wales, Australia), 1996.

Stage Fright, Ashton Scholastic (Sydney, New South Wales, Australia), 1996.

St. Elmo's Fire, Ashton Scholastic (Sydney, New South Wales, Australia), 1996.

Bad Apples, Ashton Scholastic (Sydney, New South Wales, Australia), 1996.

Dirty Tricks, Ashton Scholastic (Sydney, New South Wales, Australia), 1996, Scholastic, Inc. (New York, NY), 2006.

The War of the Work Demons, Ashton Scholastic (Sydney, New South Wales, Australia), 1997.

Hit or Miss, Ashton Scholastic (Sydney, New South Wales, Australia), 1998.

Hot Pursuit, Ashton Scholastic (Sydney, New South Wales, Australia), 1998.

Deep Freeze, Ashton Scholastic (Sydney, New South Wales, Australia), 1999.

The Secret Enemy, Ashton Scholastic (Sydney, New South Wales, Australia), 1999.

Dead End, Ashton Scholastic (Sydney, New South Wales, Australia), 1999, Scholastic, Inc. (New York, NY), 2006.

"RONDO" SERIES

The Key to Rondo, Omnibus Books (Norwood, South Australia, Australia), 2007, Scholastic Press (New York, NY), 2008.

The Wizard of Rondo, Omnibus Books (Malvern, South Australia, Australia), 2008, Scholastic Press (New York, NY), 2009.

The Battle for Rondo, Omnibus Books (Malvern, South Australia, Australia), 2009, Scholastic Press (New York, NY), 2010.

UNDER NAME JENNIFER ROWE

The Commonsense International Cookery Book, Angus & Robertson (Sydney, New South Wales, Australia), 1978.

(Editor) *More Poems to Read to Young Australians,* Royal New South Wales Institute for Deaf and Blind Children (North Rocks, Australia), 1980.

Eating Well in Later Life, Angus & Robertson (Sydney, New South Wales, Australia), 1982.

Grim Pickings, Allen & Unwin (Sydney, New South Wales, Australia), 1988.

Murder by the Book, Allen & Unwin (Sydney, New South Wales, Australia), 1989.

Death in Store, Allen & Unwin (Sydney, New South Wales, Australia), 1991, Doubleday (Garden City, NY), 1993.

The Makeover Murders, Allen & Unwin (St. Leonards, Australia), 1992, Doubleday (Garden City, NY), 1993.

Stranglehold, Allen & Unwin (St. Leonards, Australia), 1993, Bantam (New York, NY), 1995.

(Editor) *Love Lies Bleeding: A Crimes for a Summer Christmas Anthology,* Allen & Unwin (St. Leonards, Australia), 1994.

Lamb to the Slaughter, Bantam (New York, NY), 1996.

Deadline, Allen & Unwin (St. Leonards, Australia), 1997, published as *Suspect,* Ballantine (New York, NY), 1999.

Something Wicked, Ballantine (New York, NY), 1999.

Angela's Mandrake and Other Feisty Fables, Allen & Unwin (St. Leonards, Australia), 2000, published as *Fairy Tales for Grown-Ups,* 2001.

Sidelights

One of Australia's favorite children's authors and a five-time winner of the Children's Book Council of Australia's Children's Book of the Year Award, Emily Rodda has written numerous picture books as well as several series for older readers, most notably the "Rowan of Rin," "Deltora Quest," and "Rondo" books. Rodda's fantasy novels have been consistently praised for featuring carefully drawn imaginary realms where quests are complicated by riddles, magic, and mixed motives. Writing under her real name, Jennifer Rowe, she has also produced adult mysteries as well as cookbooks. This prolific output is particularly remarkable because Rodda did not become a full-time writer until 1994. Before that she held a job as a magazine editor, while raising four small children. "I feel very lucky to have a job I love so much," she noted on her home page.

Emily Rodda's middle-grade novel **The Best-kept Secret** *is brought to life in artwork by Noela Young.* (Avon Camelot, 1988, Angus & Robertson Publishers, 1988. Text copyright © 1988 by Emily Rodda. Illustrations copyright © 1988 by Noela Young. Reproduced by permission of HarperCollins AUS.)

Born in New South Wales, Rodda worked as an editor at both an Australian publishing house and at a woman's magazine before turning her hand to juvenile fiction. She chose her grandmother's maiden name as a pseudonym because at the time of her first publication, her publisher, Angus & Robertson, was also her employer. Rodda's first novel, *Something Special,* was an attempt to document her daughter's growth, and with four children, Rodda had a lot of material at hand for subsequent titles. Aimed at primary graders, *Something Special* tells the story of a little girl, Samantha, who becomes involved in her mother's rummage sale. Set in contemporary times and with a realistic setting, the book nonetheless contains an element of fantasy: Samantha and her friend, Lizzie, become involved with the spirits of the former owners of the clothing donated for the sale. A *Books for Keeps* critic called *Something Special* a "thought-provoking and eerie tale" which "catches quite brilliantly the dash, excitement, and movement of the preparations" for the sale. Writing about the U.S. edition, a *Kirkus Reviews* critic commented that the book offers an "unusual story, beautifully structured and simply but gracefully told," while *School Library Journal* contributor Elisabeth LeBris noted that the book "is told in a light tone with lots of dialogue."

With *Something Special* Rodda won the Australian Children's Book of the Year Award, one of the most prestigious prizes in Australia. The award not only helped sales of the initial title, but also had reviewers and readers alike awaiting a second book. As the author commented in an interview in *Magpies:* "I was astounded and surprised because I hadn't held out the faintest hope of actually winning. . . . As a child I had always wanted to be a writer; now maybe I really was one." Rodda also noted in the interview, however, that "second books are much harder to pull off than first ones."

Rodda's second book, *Pigs Might Fly,* is a lighthearted fantasy that employs mystery and magical travel to another world. Rachel, about age seven, is in bed with a cold and longs for some excitement to break up her boring days. A picture drawn by a sign-painting friend of her father's is meant to cheer Rachel up but leads to much more radical results. The picture shows Rachel riding a unicorn in her pajamas while pigs fly overhead. Soon Rachel finds herself on the unicorn while actual pigs are playing in the sky. Reviewing the U.S. edition, published as *The Pigs Are Flying!,* Karen P. Smith commented in *School Library Journal* that this is "an engaging fantasy for beginning fans of the genre," while Karen Jameyson called the story a "comfortable swirl of suspense, adventure, and amusing characters" in *Horn Book.* A *Books for Keeps* contributor concluded by calling *Pigs Might Fly* a "beautifully unfolded tale from an illuminating, fresh-voiced writer." Award committees reached similar conclusions as reviewers, for this second book also earned a Children's Book of the Year Award from the Children's Book Council of Australia (CBCA).

Rodda stuck with fantasy for her third title, *The Best-Kept Secret,* which features a magical carousel ride. When this carousel comes to town, the residents all find reasons why they should take a ride on it into the future, including young Joanna, who rescues a boy lost in the future. None of the characters who take the magic ride realize that they are at crossroads in their lives; Joanna has just learned she is to become a big sister. Rescuing the young boy in the future, then, is an unconscious acceptance of this new role. Gerald Haigh, reviewing the book in the *Times Educational Supplement,* noted that Rodda's story "is subtle and layered, and pricks at the emotions in all sorts of ways." A *Kirkus Reviews* critic dubbed it a "deceptively simple tale" and a "charmingly original, neatly structured story," while *School Library Journal* contributor Joanne Aswell concluded that *The Best-Kept Secret* is an "amusing, optimistic chapter book fantasy to read alone or aloud."

Rodda's first male protagonist appears in *Finders Keepers,* a longer and more sophisticated juvenile novel. When Patrick takes part in a novel interactive quiz game on his television, he has no idea he will pass through

Cover of Rodda's humorous middle-grade novel **The Timekeeper,** *featuring cover art by Noela Young.* (Omnibus Books, 1992. Cover design copyright © Omnibus Books, 2009. Reproduced by permission of Omnibus Books, a division of Scholastic Australia.)

the "Barrier" separating his reality from the "Other Side," but that in fact is exactly what happens. Patrick becomes a Finder of all those things people misplace day to day. His prize is a computer he has been longing for. As Laurie Copping commented in *Reading Time, Finders Keepers* moves at "a rapid pace, fantasy and reality interchanging so rapidly that sometimes the reader may wonder whether or not they are experiencing the real or the unreal." A *Publishers Weekly* reviewer also noted the "lightning speed" at which Rodda keeps her story going and concluded that the book was "an uncommonly satisfying read."

Patrick reappears in *The Timekeeper,* a sequel to *Finders Keepers,* in which he is once again summoned through the Barrier, this time to prevent the destruction of worlds on both sides. Obstacles make his mission all the harder, and Rodda blends elements of computer technology to create "an action-filled fantasy with warm, believable depictions of family relationships," according to Anne Connor in *School Library Journal.* A *Kirkus Reviews* commentator called *The Timekeeper* an "engaging light fantasy."

Rodda has also used the contemporary world of high tech in other books for young readers, including *Crumbs!* and the picture book *Power and Glory.* The successive competency levels of a video game form the core of the latter title, which Carolyn Phelan dubbed an "unexpected pleasure" in a starred *Booklist* review. John Sigwald, writing in *School Library Journal,* called *Power and Glory* a "big, bold, colorful and cartoony quest for control over electronic nemeses," while a *Kirkus Reviews* contributor noted the "clever analogies" Rodda makes between the witch, goblin, and ogre of the video game and family members of the boy who is playing the game. "Rodda builds up a throbbing rhythm that approximates the intensity of the play," observed a *Publishers Weekly* reviewer of this "rousing" picture book.

Far afield from the techno world of the 1990s are Rodda's series of novels about the adventures of Rowan, two of which have been honored by the CBCA. The first title in the series, *Rowan of Rin,* tells the magical story of the village of Rin, where the locals awake one morning to discover that their source of water, a nearby river, has slowed to a mere trickle. As the days pass, matters get worse and the stream almost totally dries up. The villagers depend on this stream to water their animals, the "bukshah," and these can no longer get enough water. Something must be done. The villagers agree that someone must travel up the Mountain, an eerie and frightening place, to find out what the problem is. The Wise Woman provides the villagers with a map along with a guiding chant, but it is only the boy who tends the bukshah, Rowan, who can figure out the meaning of the map. Rowan sets out on his quest with six others, braving obstacles, including a dragon, until he reaches the top of the Mountain and is able to restore the stream to life. In the process, Rowan also saves the life of his protector, Strong John.

Cover of **Rowan and the Keeper of the Crystal,** *part of a series by* **Rodda that features artwork by Mark Elliott.** (HarperTrophy, 2002. Cover art copyright © 2002 by Mark Elliott. Reproduced by permission of HarperCollins Publishers.)

Horn Book correspondent Karen Jameyson called *Rowan of Rin* a "quest adventure of the highest order" and a "riveting fantasy." Jameyson also noted that Rodda's characters "step off the page as individuals." *Magpies* contributor Joan Zahnleiter commented that the "text is very visual, sparkling with vivid imagery. It would lend itself to an exciting TV production." The "Rowan of Rin" series has become popular worldwide, with Internet chat rooms dedicated to its plots. Throughout the series, Rowan has evolved from a sickly and timid youngster to a careful but courageous lad to whom others look for leadership. In a discussion of *Rowan and the Travelers,* published in Australia as *Rowan and the Travelers,* a *Kirkus Reviews* critic commended Rodda for her novels that "prove . . . that a weak body can hide a hero's heart."

In *Rowan and the Travelers* it falls to Rowan to save his fellow villagers from a strange curse that causes them to fall asleep where they stand. "Once again Rodda's fantasy world, a folkloric Anytime, becomes a vivid reality for readers," commented Kay Weisman in *Booklist.* In *School Library Journal,* Trish Anderson observed that *Rowan and the Travelers* "proves heroism comes in many sizes." *Rowan and the Keeper of the*

Crystal, the third book in the series, finds Rowan in a desperate quest to put together an antidote after his mother is poisoned at the critical moment in which she must choose a new leader for the village. *Horn Book* correspondent Anne St. John wrote that the novel "offers an ideal mix of suspenseful plot, unusual characters, and an engaging hero."

The Zebak are the historic enemies of Rowan's people, and in *Rowan and the Zebak,* the young hero must journey to their land to rescue his kidnapped sister. As with the previous titles in the series, Rowan's success depends upon his courage and upon his ability to understand magic and the enigmatic riddles posed to him by the wise woman Sheba. In her *Booklist* review of the title, Weisman declared that "Rowan's adventures are riveting, with plot twists sufficient to keep the outcome in doubt." Writing in *School Library Journal,* Mara Alpert noted that Rowan "is not the flashiest of heroes, but in each story he grows a little more confident."

While the "Rowan of Rin" series is perhaps better known internationally, Rodda also built an audience for her "Deltora Quest" fantasies, in which three friends—Leif, Jasmine, and Barda—face perils both ordinary and fantastic to retrieve a set of seven precious stones that their people have used to ward off enemies in the past. When the stones are restored to the Belt of Deltora, the land will be freed of the Shadow Lord, a force with evil intentions. In the Australian editions of each "Deltora" novel, the belt appears on the spine of the book, with the stones that have been rescued in each previous volume. In his *Magpies* review of books five to eight in the "Deltora Quest" series, Russ Merrin wrote: "The full series is quite simply, a huge achievement. It is vividly written, rich in detail and highly imaginative in its execution. It melds together well, flows cohesively, and reads easily."

Rodda's "Fairy Realm" series—which she originally published as the "Storytelling Charms" series under the name Mary-Anne Dickinson—is aimed at middle-grade readers having their first taste of fantasy. Jessie, the heroine of these volumes, is an ordinary girl who discovers that her destiny lies equally in the everyday world and in an alternative universe peopled by fairies, elves, trolls, ogres, and other fabulous creatures. In the series debut, *The Charm Bracelet,* Jessie discovers that her grandmother is actually queen of the fairies, and that the two of them must go into the fairy realm to renew its magic and ensure its safety. *Booklist* critic Ellen Mandel suggested that "intergenerational teamwork and a girl's levelheaded thinking combine" in the novel to produce an "exciting fantasy." A *Publishers Weekly* reviewer called *The Charm Bracelet* a "taut, engaging fantasy tale" with "an intriguing plot and appealing characters." According to a *Kirkus Reviews* contributor, "Rodda tells a suspenseful, well-knit tale, enlivened by humor and heroism."

In *The Key to Rondo,* the first volume in Rodda's "Rondo" saga, Leo Ziflak is heir to a music box that has been in his family for generations. The box comes with a set of three rules that must never be broken: wind it no more than three times, never shut it while it is playing, and never move the box until the music has stopped. Although Leo follows these simple directions, problems come when rule-breaking cousin Mimi arrives for a visit and unleashes something evil that has been imprisoned in the paintings that adorn the box. As they search for a way to recapture this creature—a witch called the Blue Queen—Leo discovers that the box also serves a portal to another world. Soon he must venture there, in search of the missing Mimi, even at his own peril. Leo and Mimi's story continues in *The Wizard of Rondo,* as a missing magician and a young man facing an unjust fate both require the help of the young cousins, and the concluding volume, *The Battle for Rondo.* Although "Leo and Mimi's adventure is unpredictable and daring, . . . they learn valuable lessons about greed's harm, working together, and trusting each other," wrote Ashleigh Larsen in her *Kliatt* review of *The Key to Rondo,* and a *Kirkus Reviews* writer recommended the book's setting as "a splendidly vivid world" that is full of "nursery-rhyme references and fairy-tale motifs." "Children will get a thrill from identifying the

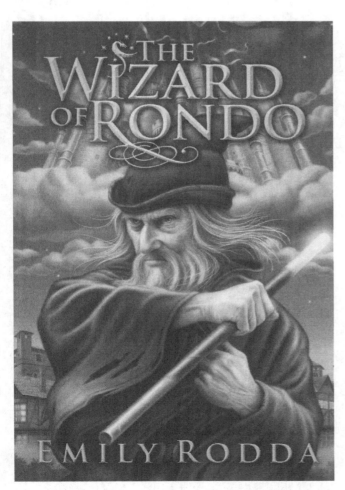

Cover of Rodda's middle-grade adventure The Wizard of Rondo, *featuring artwork by Allen Douglas.* (Scholastic Press, 2008. Cover art by Allen Douglas. Reproduced by permission of Scholastic, Inc.)

familiar tales referenced" in Rodda's fantasy world, predicted Kelly Vikstrom, the *School Library Journal* critic adding of *The Key to Rondo* that the book's "rollicking, action-packed plot moves along quickly and twists keep readers guessing." Appraising *The Wizard of Rondo,* Christi Esterle recommended the story to fans of German writer Cornelia Funke, adding that Rodda's characters "are instantly charming and display a variety of quirks, foibles, and virtues." "Leo and Mimi's second venture into Rondo . . . provides frights, pleasures and as much poignant beauty as the first," asserted a *Kirkus Reviews* writer of Rodda's second "Rondo" fantasy adventure.

Other series by Rodda include the "Teen Power Inc." novels and the award-winning "Rondo" books, the latter which are geared for middle-grade readers. Rodda's contribution to the "Teen Power Inc." adventure/mystery series numbered more than two dozen titles, which were first published in Australia in the 1990s. Series installments *Beware the Gingerbread House, The Sorcerer's Apprentice,* and *The Ghost of Raven Hill* were more-recently repackaged as the "Raven Hill Mysteries," a series which *School Library Journal* critic Elaine E. Knight praised as a mystery series in which "the action is brisk and exciting and the dialogue is lively and occasionally humorous."

Although the first decade of her writing life found Rodda working late at night after her children had gone to bed, she now devotes her days to her craft. In a *Magpies* interview, she described the kind of book she likes to write. "I love things that all tie up and in fact I find things that don't very irritating if they're that type of book," Rodda said. "The kind of book that I regard as an adventure or a fantasy or whatever, I think that deserves a good, neat ending. . . . There's no little clue that doesn't have a meaning. . . . Maybe it's a response to the general messiness of life, but I find it very satisfying."

Biographical and Critical Sources

BOOKS

Children's Literature Review, Volume 23, Gale (Detroit, MI), 1994, pp. 207-213.

PERIODICALS

Booklist, April 15, 1996, Carolyn Phelan, review of *Power and Glory,* p. 1441; November 15, 2001, Kay Weisman, review of *Rowan and the Travelers,* p. 574; January 1, 2002, Kay Weisman, review of *Rowan and the Keeper of the Crystal,* p. 859; March 1, 2002, Kay Weisman, review of *Rowan and the Zebak,* p. 1133; January 1, 2003, Ellen Mandel, review of *The Charm Bracelet,* p. 892; December 15, 2007, Kay Weisman, review of *The Key to Rondo,* p. 47; October 1, 2009, Kay Weisman, review of *The Wizard of Rondo,* p. 38.

Books for Keeps, September, 1986, review of *Something Special,* p. 23; March, 1989, review of *Pigs Might Fly,* p. 18; May, 2001, Annabel Gibb, review of *Bob and the House Elves,* p. 21.

Books for Your Children, spring, 1985, Ron Morton, review of *Something Special,* p. 11.

Horn Book, November-December, 1988, Karen Jameyson, review of *The Pigs Are Flying!,* p. 784; November-December, 1993, Karen Jameyson, review of *Rowan of Rin,* pp. 778-780; September, 2001, Anne St. John, review of *Rowan and the Travelers,* pp. 593-594; March-April, 2002, Anne St. John, review of *Rowan and the Keeper of the Crystal,* pp. 217-218.

Kirkus Reviews, November 1, 1989, review of *Something Special,* p. 1597; May 15, 1990, review of *The Best-Kept Secret,* p. 802; October 1, 1993, review of *The Timekeeper,* p. 1278; February 15, 1996, review of *Power and Glory,* p. 299; October 1, 2001, review of *Rowan and the Travelers,* p. 1432; January 1, 2002, review of *Rowan and the Keeper of the Crystal,* p. 50; May 1, 2002, review of *Rowan and the Zebak,* p. 666; January 1, 2003, review of *The Charm Bracelet,* p. 65; December 15, 2007, review of *The Key to Rondo;* September 1, 2009, review of *The Wizard of Rondo.*

Kliatt, January, 2008, Ashleigh Larsen, review of *The Key to Rondo,* p. 12.

Magpies, July, 1990, "Emily Rodda," pp. 19-21; November, 1993, Joan Zahnleiter, review of *Rowan of Rin,* p. 31; September, 1998, Rayma Turton, review of *Bob the Builder and the Elves,* p. 35; March, 2001, Russ Merrin, reviews of *Dread Mountain, The Maze of the Beast, The Valley of the Lost,* and *Return to Del,* all p. 35.

Publishers Weekly, October 18, 1991, review of *Finders Keepers,* p. 25; May 6, 1996, review of *Power and Glory,* p. 81; February 10, 2003, review of *The Charm Bracelet,* p. 188; February 25, 2008, review of *The Key to Rondo,* p. 79.

Reading Time, number 3, 1987, Howard George, review of *Pigs Might Fly,* p. 66; number 4, 1990, Laurie Copping, review of *Finders Keepers,* p. 25; number 4, 1991, Emily Rodda, "CBCA Acceptance Speech," p. 5.

School Library Journal, September, 1988, Karen P. Smith, review of *The Pigs Are Flying!,* pp. 185-186; January, 1990, Elisabeth LeBris, review of *Something Special,* pp. 106, 108; January, 1991, Joanne Aswell, review of *The Best-Kept Secret,* pp. 79-80; October, 1993, Anne Connor, review of *The Timekeeper,* p. 128; May, 1996, John Sigwald, review of *Power and Glory,* p. 97; January, 2002, Trish Anderson, review of *Rowan and the Travelers,* p. 140; May, 2002, Janet Gillen, review of *Rowan and the Keeper of the Crystal,* p. 160; July, 2002, Mara Alpert, review of *Rowan and the Zebak,* p. 124; August, 2003, Debbie Whitbeck, review of *The Charm Bracelet,* p. 140; April, 2006, Elaine E. Knight, review of *Beware of the Gingerbread House,* p. 147; May, 2006, Charli Osborne, review of *The Sorcerer's Apprentice,* p. 77; April, 2008, Kelly Vikstrom, review of *The Key to Rondo,* p. 147; December, 2009, Christi Esterle, review of *The Wizard of Rondo,* p. 130.

Times Educational Supplement, February 17, 1989, Gerald Haigh, review of *The Best-Kept Secret,* p. B28.

ONLINE

Emily Rodda Home Page, http://www.emilyrodda.com (May 15, 2011).
Scholastic Australia, http://www.scholastic.com.au/ (February 20, 2003), "Emily Rodda."*

*   *   *

RODRIGUEZ, Béatrice 1969-

Personal

Born 1969, in France; married; children: two. *Education:* École d'Arts Decoratifs (Strasbourg), degree.

Addresses

Home—France.

Career

Artist and illustrator.

Writings

SELF-ILLUSTRATED

The Chicken Thief, Enchanted Lion Books (New York, NY), 2010.
Fox and Hen Together, Enchanted Lion Books (New York, NY), 2011.
Treasure Thief, Enchanted Lion Books (New York, NY), 2011.

Author's books have been published in several languages, including French and German.

ILLUSTRATOR

Françoise de Guibert, *Caballos y Ponis/Horses and Ponies,* 2005.

Biographical and Critical Sources

PERIODICALS

Booklist, June 1, 2010, Shelle Rosenfeld, review of *The Chicken Thief,* p. 30.
Chicken's Bookwatch, April, 2010, review of *The Chicken Thief.*
Kirkus Reviews, April 15, 2011, review of *Fox and Hen Together.*

Publishers Weekly, April 19, 2010, review of *The Chicken Thief,* p. 51; November 8, 2010, review of *The Chicken Thief,* p. 31.
School Library Journal, August, 2010, Lauralyn Persson, review of *The Chicken Thief,* p. 84.*

*   *   *

ROTH, R.G.
See ROTH, Robert

*   *   *

ROTH, Rob
See ROTH, Robert

*   *   *

ROTH, Robert 1965-
(R.G. Roth, Rob Roth)

Personal

Born 1965, in NY; married; wife's name Cheryl Marie (an artist); children: two daughters. *Education:* Rhode Island School of Design, B.F.A. (painting).

Addresses

Home—Hudson, OH. *Agent*—Lindgren & Smith, Inc., 676A 9th Ave., New York, NY 10036. *E-mail*—robertroth@roadrunner.com.

Career

Illustrator and fine-art painter. *Exhibitions:* Works exhibited at Bologna Landi Gallery, East Hampton, NY, 1993-94; Grey Gallery, New York, NY, 1993; La Mama La Galleria, New York, NY, 1993; Heckscher Museum, New York, NY, 1995-96; Gorman Gallery, Providence, RI, 2000-01; New York Public Library, 2006; Sherrie Gallery, Columbus, OH, 2007; SecondFloor Gallery, Cleveland, OH, 2007; Kelly Randall Gallery, Cleveland, 2007; SPACES, Cleveland, 2007; and at galleries on Martha's Vineyard. Work included in permanent collections at Ritz Carlton, American Express, the New Yorker, Columbia University, and Northeastern University.

Awards, Honors

Eight awards from Museum of American Illustration; two medals from Heckscher Museum.

Illustrator

Sheron Williams, *And in the Beginning . . . ,* Atheneum (New York, NY), 1992.
(As Rob Roth) Donna Guthrie, *Nobiah's Well: A Modern African Folktale,* Ideals Children's Books (Nashville, TN), 1993.

Arthur A. Levine, *Pearl Moscowitz's Last Stand,* Tambourine Books (New York, NY), 1993.

Laurence Yep, *Tiger Woman,* BridgeWater Books (Mahwah, NJ), 1994.

Kristine L. Franklin, *When the Monkeys Came Back,* Atheneum (New York, NY), 1994.

Burton Albert, *Journey of the Nightly Jaguar: Inspired by an Ancient Mayan Myth,* Atheneum Books for Young Readers (New York, NY), 1996.

Sylvia Rosa-Casanova, *Mama Provi and the Pot of Rice,* Atheneum Books for Young Readers (New York, NY), 1997.

(As Rob Roth) Marguerite W. Davol, *Why Butterflies Go by on Silent Wings,* Orchard Books (New York, NY), 2001.

Tim Myers, *Tanuki's Gift: A Japanese Tale,* Marshall Cavendish (New York, NY), 2003.

(As R.G. Roth) Karen Ehrhardt, *This Jazz Man,* Harcourt (Orlando, FL), 2006.

(As R.G. Roth) Richard Michelson, *Busing Brewster,* Alfred A. Knopf (New York, NY), 2010.

(As R.G. Roth) Leslie Staub, *Everybody Gets the Blues,* Houghton Mifflin Harcourt (Boston, MA), 2012.

Works featured in *Communication Arts* and *Print* magazine.

Adaptations

This Jazz Man was adapted as a CD-with-book package by Live Oak Media, 2010.

Sidelights

Sometimes crediting his illustration work under the name R.G. Roth or Rob Roth, Robert Roth is a fine-art painter who has contributed images to several books for children. Raised on Long Island, Roth attended the Rhode Island School of Design where he worked in acrylics and oilstick and developed a style inspired by the sand, sea, and light of the region where he grew up. Now based in Hudson, Ohio, where he is married to fellow artist Cheryl Marie Roth, he has exhibited his paintings in galleries and museums throughout the northeast, and has earned praise for the colorful abstract illustrations he contributes to stories by such authors as Laurence Yep, Karen Ehrhardt, Richard Michelson, and Leslie Staub. Reviewing Roth's work for *Tanuki's Gift: A Japanese Tale,* a story by Tim Myers about a Buddhist priest who is visited yearly by a lonely wild dog, a *Kirkus Reviews* writer asserted that the book's "collage illustrations, created with painted papers, glow in their simplicity and sunny gold palette," while *School Library Journal* critic Nancy A. Gifford recommended the picture book for its "strong and lasting message."

In Ehrhardt's *This Jazz Man* the author adapts the traditional children's counting song "This Old Man" to reference jazz music, and Roth reinforces Ehrhardt's conceit in his depiction of what *Booklist* contributor Gillian Engberg described as "colorful, mixed-media images . . . that have their own staccato beat" and are "ren-dered in geometric shapes and textured prints." A *Kirkus Reviews* writer noted the artist's use of "interesting shapes and multiple colors," remarking in particular on the "nifty patterned outfits" Roth crafts for the musicians at the center of Ehrhardt's tale. Recommending *This Jazz Man* as "an uptempo introduction for youngest music lovers," a *Publishers Weekly* contributor added that Roth's "candy-colored collages burst from the pages."

Another of Roth's illustration projects to attract critical praise, Michelson's *Busing Brewster,* takes readers back to the 1970s as two African-American brothers are bussed from their inner-city community to a nearby elementary school in a predominately white community. Capturing the efforts of a first grader to find friends among his new classmates, Roth contributes "understated ink, watercolor, and collage illustrations" featuring "expressive body language," according to *Booklist* critic Hazel Rochman, and in *Publishers Weekly* a reviewer praised the "stylized mixed media images" in *Busing Brewster.* Appearing "like an artful interpretation of the era's cartoons," the critic added, Roth's use of angular shapes "underscore the collision of innocence and prejudice, anger and hope" in Michelson's story.

Biographical and Critical Sources

PERIODICALS

American Music Teacher, April-May, 2007, Adrienne Wiley, review of *This Jazz Man,* p. 87.

Booklist, November 15, 2006, Gillian Engberg, review of *This Jazz Man,* p. 53; March 15, 2010, Hazel Rochman, review of *Busing Brewster,* p. 46.

Bulletin of the Center for Children's Books, March, 2007, Elizabeth Bush, review of *This Jazz Man,* p. 289; July-August, 2010, Elizabeth Bush, review of *Busing Brewster,* p. 495.

Childhood Education, summer, 2004, Irene A. Allen, review of *Tanuki's Gift: A Japanese Tale,* p. 214.

Kirkus Reviews, March 15, 2003, review of *Tanuki's Gift,* p. 474; October 15, 2006, review of *This Jazz Man,* p. 1069; April 15, 2010, review of *Busing Brewster.*

New York Times Book Review, September 21, 2003, December 5, 2010, review of *Busing Brewster,* p. 39.

Publishers Weekly, February 10, 2003, review of *Tanuki's Gift,* p. 186; October 23, 2006, review of *This Jazz Man,* p. 48; May 3, 2010, review of *Busing Brewster,* p. 49.

School Library Journal, July, 2003, Nancy A. Gifford, review of *Tanuki's Gift,* p. 115; December, 2006, Judith Constandinides, review of *This Jazz Man,* p. 98; June, 2010, Mary Landrum, review of *Busing Brewster,* p. 80; September, 2010, Mary Landman, review of *This Jazz Man,* p. 68.

ONLINE

Robert Roth Home Page, http://robertrothgallery.com (May 27, 2011).

Robert Roth Web log, http://robertrothpaintings.blogspot.
com (May 27, 2011).*

*　　*　　*

ROWE, Jennifer
See RODDA, Emily

*　　*　　*

ROYSTON, Angela 1945-

Personal

Born 1945, in Yorkshire, England; daughter of Richard
(a chartered accountant) and Chloe Wilkinson; married
1979; children: one son, one daughter. *Ethnicity:*
"White." *Education:* University of Edinburgh, M.A.,
1966. *Politics:* Green Party. *Religion:* "Agnostic." *Hobbies and other interests:* Tennis, walking, travel.

Addresses

Home—London, England. *E-mail*—angela@royston
mail.co.uk.

Career

Writer and editor. Ginn (publisher), London, England,
editor, 1969-73; Macdonald Educational, London, children's nonfiction editor, 1973-78; Grisewood & Dempsey, London, children's nonfiction editor, 1978-82;
freelance writer and editor, 1982—. Writer-in-residence
and presenter at schools.

Member

National Association for Writers in Education, Amnesty
International, Greenpeace.

Writings

FOR CHILDREN

Picture Word Book, illustrated by Colin Maclean, Moira
Maclean, and Liz Graham-Yooll, St. Michael (London, England), 1982.
My First Library Road Travel, Macdonald (London,
England), 1986.
Just Look at Road Transport, Macdonald (London,
England), 1987, published as *Road Transport,* Rourke
Enterprises (Vero Beach, FL), 1988.
Birthday Party ("Stepping Stones 123" series), Warwick
(New York, NY), 1988.
Shopping ("Stepping Stones 123" series), Warwick (New
York, NY), 1988.
My Family ("Stepping Stones 123" series), Warwick (New
York, NY), 1988.

(With Graham Thompson) *Monster Road Builders,* Barron's (New York, NY), 1989.
(With Graham Thompson) *Monster Building Machines,*
Barron's (New York, NY), 1990.
Car: See How It Works ("Tell Me About. . ." series), illustrated by Colin King, Frances Lincoln (London,
England), 1990, published as *My Lift-the-Flap Car
Book,* Barron's (New York, NY), 1991.
(With Terry Pastor) *The A-to-Z Book of Cars,* Barron's
(New York, NY), 1991.
Buildings, Bridges, and Tunnels, Warwick Press (New
York, NY), 1991.
Flowers, Trees, and Other Plants, Warwick Press (New
York, NY), 1991.
The Human Body and How It Works, illustrated by Rob
Shone and Chris Forsey, Warwick Press (New York,
NY), 1991.
People and Places, Warwick (New York, NY), 1991.
The Senses: A Lift-the-Flap Body Book, illustrated by Edwina Riddell, Barron's (Hauppauge, NY), 1993.
Big Machines, illustrated by Terry Pastor, Little, Brown
(Boston, MA), 1994.
(With David Bellamy) *How Green Are You?,* Frances Lincoln (London, England), 1994.
Getting Better, Frances Lincoln (London, England), 1994.
*Whirrs, Watts, and Whooshes: The Stories of 14 Inventions
That Changed the World,* David Bennett Books (London, England), 1994.
Healthy Me (lift-the-flap book), illustrated by Edwina Riddell, Barron's (Hauppauge, NY), 1995.
A First Atlas, Scholastic (New York, NY), 1995.
You and Your Body: 101 Questions and Answers, Facts on
File (New York, NY), 1995.
Where Do Babies Come From?, DK Publishing (New
York, NY), 1996.
(Translator and adaptor, with Ghislaine Nouvion Severs
and others) Christine Lazier, *Wild Animals,* Creative
Education (Mankato, MN), 1997.
One Hundred Greatest Medical Discoveries, Grolier Educational (Danbury, CT), 1997.
One Hundred Greatest Women, Grolier Educational (Danbury, CT), 1997.
Fire Fighters!, DK Publishing (New York, NY), 1998.
Digesting: How We Fuel the Body ("Under the Microscope" series), Grolier Educational (Danbury, CT),
1998.
Truck Trouble ("Eyewitness" series), DK Publishing (New
York, NY), 1998.
Space Shuttle Mission 7, Ginn (New York, NY), 1998.
Transportation ("Environment Starts Here" series),
Raintree-Steck-Vaughn (Austin, TX), 1999.
Recycling ("Environment Starts Here" series), Raintree-Steck-Vaughn (Austin, TX), 1999.
On the Move, Kingfisher (New York, NY), 2000.
Volcanoes, Reader's Digest (Pleasantville, NY), 2000.
Pyramids, Reader's Digest (Pleasantville, NY), 2000.
Mighty Machines: Stories of Machines at Work, Kingfisher
(New York, NY), 2000.
Space Station: Accident on Mir, DK Publishing (New York,
NY), 2000.
Blue Whales ("Amazing Animals" series), Weigl Publishers (Mankato, MN), 2003.

Junior Science Diagrams on File, Volumes 1-2, Facts on File (New York, NY), 2003.

Alligators and Crocodiles ("Amazing Animals" series), Weigl Publishers (Mankato, MN), 2004.

Wolves ("Amazing Animals" series), Smart Apple Media (Mankato, MN), 2004.

How to Get Ahead in Armed and Civilian Forces, Raintree (Oxford, England), 2007.

How to Get Ahead in IT and Administration, Raintree (Oxford, England), 2007.

(With Andy Charman and Jenny Vaughan, *My First Book of Knowledge,* Southwater (London, England), 2007.

Explaining Asthma, Franklin Watts (London, England), 2008, Smart Apple Media (Mankato, MN), 2010.

Explaining Down Syndrome, Franklin Watts (London, England), 2008, Smart Apple Media (Mankato, MN), 2010.

Sustainable Cities ("How Can We Save Our World?" series), Arcturus Pub. (Mankato, MN), 2009.

Sustainable Energy, Arcturus Pub. (Mankato, MN), 2009.

Gun Crimes ("Solve It with Science" series), Franklin Watts (London, England), 2009, Smart Apple Media (Mankato, MN), 2010.

Does It Soak up Water?: All about Absorbent and Waterproof Materials ("All about Materials" series), Franklin Watts (London, England), 2009.

Does It Stay Warm?: All about Heat ("All about Materials" series), Franklin Watts (London, England), 2009.

Astronauts Working in Space, Capstone Press (Mankato, MN), 2010.

Diet ("Being Healthy, Feeling Great" series), PowerKids Press (New York, NY), 2010.

Homes That Move, Capstone Press (Mankato, MN), 2010.

Polar Bears and Their Homes, Capstone Press (Mankato, MN), 2010.

Inventors Who Changed the World, Crabtree (New York, NY), 2010.

Storms, Marshall Cavendish Benchmark (New York, NY), 2010.

Hurricanes, Marshall Cavendish Benchmark (New York, NY), 2011.

Heroes of Medicine and Their Discoveries, Crabtree (New York, NY), 2011.

Space Blog, Crabtree (New York, NY), 2011.

Ancient Greek Adventure, Crabtree (New York, NY), 2011.

"ANIMAL LIFE STORIES" SERIES

The Deer, illustrated by Bernard Robinson, Warwick (New York, NY), 1988.

The Duck, illustrated by Maurice Pledger and Bernard Robinson, Warwick (New York, NY), 1988.

The Fox, illustrated by Bernard Robinson, Warwick (New York, NY), 1988.

The Otter, illustrated by Bernard Robinson, Warwick (New York, NY), 1988.

The Penguin, illustrated by Trevor Boyer, Warwick (New York, NY), 1988.

The Tiger, illustrated by Graham Allen, Warwick (New York, NY), 1988.

The Elephant, illustrated by Bob Bampton, Warwick (New York, NY), 1989.

The Frog, illustrated by Bernard Robinson, Warwick (New York, NY), 1989.

The Hedgehog, illustrated by Maurice Pledger, Warwick (New York, NY), 1989.

The Mouse, illustrated by Maurice Pledger, Warwick (New York, NY), 1989.

The Squirrel, illustrated by Maurice Pledger, Warwick (New York, NY), 1989.

The Whale, illustrated by Jim Channel, Warwick (New York, NY), 1989.

The "Animal Life" books have been translated into Spanish.

"FARM ANIMAL STORIES" SERIES

Cow, illustrated by Bob Bampton, Warwick (New York, NY), 1990.

Goat, illustrated by Eric Robson, Warwick (New York, NY), 1990.

Hen, illustrated by Dave Cook, Warwick (New York, NY), 1990.

Pig, illustrated by Jim Channel, Warwick (New York, NY), 1990.

Pony, illustrated by Bob Bampton, Warwick (New York, NY), 1990.

Sheep, illustrated by Josephine Martin, Warwick (New York, NY), 1990.

"WHAT'S INSIDE" SERIES

Small Animals, DK Books (New York, NY), 1991.

Insects, DK Books (New York, NY), 1991.

Shells, DK Books (New York, NY), 1991.

Toys, DK Books (New York, NY), 1991.

My Body, DK Books (New York, NY), 1991, reprinted, 2008.

Plants, DK Books (New York, NY), 1991.

"EYE OPENER" SERIES

Cars, photographs by Tim Ridley, illustrated by Jane Cradock-Watson and Dave Hopkins, Aladdin Books (New York, NY), 1991.

Diggers and Dump Trucks, photographs by Tim Ridley, illustrated by Jane Cradock-Watson and Dave Hopkins, Aladdin Books (New York, NY), 1991.

Dinosaurs, photographs by Colin Keates, illustrated by Jane Cradock-Watson and Dave Hopkins, Aladdin Books (New York, NY), 1991.

Jungle Animals, photographs by Philip Dowell, Dave King, and Jerry Young, illustrated by Martine Blaney and Dave Hopkins, Aladdin Books (New York, NY), 1991.

Night-Time Animals, photographs by Dave King, illustrated by Jane Cradock-Watson and Dave Hopkins, Aladdin Books (New York, NY), 1992.

Ships and Boats, photographs by Tim Ridley, illustrated by Jane Cradock-Watson and Dave Hopkins, Aladdin Books (New York, NY), 1992.

Planes, Aladdin Books (New York, NY), 1992.

Sea Animals, photographs by Steve Shott, illustrated by Jane Cradock-Watson and Dave Hopkins, Aladdin Books (New York, NY), 1992.

Insects and Crawly Creatures, photographs by Jerry Young, illustrated by Jane Cradock-Watson and Dave Hopkins, Aladdin Books (New York, NY), 1992.

Trains, photographs by Dave King, illustrated by Jane Cradock-Watson and Dave Hopkins, Aladdin Books (New York, NY), 1992.

Birds, photographs by Dave King, illustrated by Jane Cradock-Watson and Dave Hopkins, Aladdin Books (New York, NY), 1992.

Baby Animals, photographs by Steve Shott and Jane Burton, illustrated by Jane Cradock-Watson and Dave Hopkins, Aladdin Books (New York, NY), 1992.

"SEE HOW THEY GROW"/"BABY ANIMALS" SERIES

Puppy, DK Books (New York, NY), 1991.

Chick, photographs by Jane Burton, Lodestar Books (New York, NY), 1991.

Kitten, photographs by Jane Burton, Lodestar Books (New York, NY), 1991, revised, DK Pub. (New York, NY), 2007.

Frog, photographs by Kim Taylor and Jane Burton, Lodestar Books (New York, NY), 1991, revised, DK Pub. (New York, NY), 2007.

Duck, photographs by Barrie Watts, Lodestar Books (New York, NY), 1991, revised, DK Pub. (New York, NY), 2007.

Rabbit, photographs by Barrie Watts, illustrated by Rowan Clifford, Dorling Kindersley (London, England), 1991, published as *Bunny,* Lodestar Books (New York, NY), 1992, revised, DK Pub. (New York, NY), 2007.

Mouse, photographs by Barrie Watts, Lodestar Books (New York, NY), 1992, revised, DK Pub. (New York, NY), 2008.

Lamb, photographs by Gordon Clayton, illustrated by Jane Cradock-Watson, Lodestar Books (New York, NY), 1992, revised, DK Pub. (New York, NY), 2008.

EDITOR; "SCIENCE NATURE GUIDES" SERIES

Wild Flowers of North America, Thunder Bay Press (San Diego, CA), 1994.

Birds of North America, Thunder Bay Press (San Diego, CA), 1994.

Trees of North America, illustrated by David More, Thunder Bay Press (San Diego, CA), 1994.

John Burton, *Mammals of North America,* illustrated by Jim Channell, Thunder Bay Press (San Diego, CA), 1995.

"BODY SYSTEMS" SERIES

(With Jackie Hardie) *Moving,* Rigby Interactive Library (Crystal Lake, IL), 1997.

Reproduction and Birth, Rigby Interactive Library (Crystal Lake, IL), 1997.

Eating and Digestion, Rigby Interactive Library (Crystal Lake, IL), 1997.

Thinking and Feeling, Rigby Interactive Library (Crystal Lake, IL), 1997.

"GEOGRAPHY STARTS HERE" SERIES

Weather around You, Raintree-Steck-Vaughn (Austin, TX), 1998.

Where People Live, Raintree Steck-Vaughn (Austin, TX), 1998.

Maps and Symbols, Raintree-Steck-Vaughn (Austin, TX), 1999.

"FIRST LIBRARY" SERIES

Life Cycle of a Bean, Heinemann Library (Des Plaines, IL), 1998, published as *Life Cycle of a Broad Bean,* Heinemann Library (London, England), 1998, 2nd edition, 2009.

Life Cycle of a Butterfly, Heinemann Library (Des Plaines, IL), 1998, 2nd edition, Heinemann Library (London, England), 2009.

Life Cycle of a Chicken, Heinemann Library (Des Plaines, IL), 1998, 2nd edition, Heinemann Library (London, England), 2009.

Life Cycle of a Frog, Heinemann Library (Des Plaines, IL), 1998, 2nd edition, Heinemann Library (London, England), 2009.

Life Cycle of a Kangaroo, Heinemann Library (Des Plaines, IL), 1998, 2nd edition, Heinemann Library (London, England), 2009.

Life Cycle of a Guinea Pig, Heinemann Library (Des Plaines, IL), 1998, 2nd edition, Heinemann Library (London, England), 2009.

Life Cycle of a Sunflower, Heinemann Library (Des Plaines, IL), 1998, 2nd edition, Heinemann Library (London, England), 2009.

Life Cycle of an Apple, Heinemann Library (Des Plaines, IL), 1998, 2nd edition, Heinemann Library (London, England), 2009.

Life Cycle of an Oak Tree, Heinemann Library (Des Plaines, IL), 2000, 2nd edition, Heinemann Library (London, England), 2009.

Life Cycle of a Dog, Heinemann Library (Des Plaines, IL), 2000, 2nd edition, Heinemann Library (London, England), 2009.

Life Cycle of a Mushroom, Heinemann Library (Des Plaines, IL), 2000, 2nd edition, Heinemann Library (London, England), 2009.

Life Cycle of a Salmon, Heinemann Library (Des Plaines, IL), 2000, 2nd edition, Heinemann Library (London, England), 2009.

"INSIDE AND OUT" SERIES

Stars and Planets, illustrated by Stephen Maturin and Roger Stewart, Heinemann Library (Des Plaines, IL), 1998.

Emergency Rescue, illustrated by Roger Stewart, Heinemann Library (Des Plaines, IL), 1998.

Horses and Ponies, Heinemann Library (Des Plaines, IL), 1998.

Flying Machines, illustrated by Sebastian Quigley, Heinemann Library (Des Plaines, IL), 1998.

Boats and Ships, illustrated by John Downes, Heinemann Library (Des Plaines, IL), 1998.

The Earth, illustrated by Jonathan Adams, Heinemann Library (Des Plaines, IL), 1998.

Cars, illustrated by Roger Stewart, Heinemann Library (Des Plaines, IL), 1998.

Under the Sea, Heinemann Library (Des Plaines, IL), 1998.

Trucks, illustrated by Chris Forsey, Heinemann Library (Des Plaines, IL), 1998.

Pets, Heinemann Library (Des Plaines, IL), 1998.

Tractors, illustrated by Terry Gabbey, Heinemann Library (Des Plaines, IL), 1998.

"PLANTS" SERIES

Plants and Us, Heinemann Library (Des Plaines, IL), 1999.

Strange Plants, Heinemann Library (Des Plaines, IL), 1999.

British Plants, Heinemann Library (Des Plaines, IL), 1999.

Trees, Heinemann Library (Des Plaines, IL), 1999.

Flowers, Fruits, and Seeds, Heinemann Library (Des Plaines, IL), 1999.

How Plants Grow, Heinemann Library (Des Plaines, IL), 1999.

"SAFE AND SOUND" SERIES

Fit and Strong, Heinemann Library (Des Plaines, IL), 1999.

Safety First, Heinemann Library (Des Plaines, IL), 2000.

Clean and Healthy, Heinemann Library (Des Plaines, IL), 2000.

Eat Well, Heinemann Library (Des Plaines, IL), 2000.

A Healthy Body, Heinemann Library (Des Plaines, IL), 2000.

"ON THE MOVE" SERIES

The Digger, Kingfisher (New York, NY), 2000.

The Truck, Kingfisher (New York, NY), 2000.

The Tractor, Kingfisher (New York, NY), 2000.

The Tugboat, Kingfisher (New York, NY), 2000.

The Helicopter, Kingfisher (New York, NY), 2000.

The Jumbo Jet, Kingfisher (New York, NY), 2000.

"LEARN TO SAY NO!" SERIES

Tobacco, Heinemann Library (Chicago, IL), 2000.

Alcohol, Heinemann Library (Chicago, IL), 2000.

Marijuana, Heinemann Library (Chicago, IL), 2000.

Inhalants, Heinemann Library (Chicago, IL), 2000.

"IT'S CATCHING" SERIES

Pink Eye, Heinemann Library (Chicago, IL), 2000.

Warts, Heinemann Library (Chicago, IL), 2000.

Chicken Pox, Heinemann Library (Chicago, IL), 2002.

Colds, Heinemann Library (Chicago, IL), 2002.

Head Lice, Heinemann Library (Chicago, IL), 2002.

"MY WORLD OF SCIENCE" SERIES

Using Electricity, Heinemann Library (Chicago, IL), 2001, revised, Heinemann Library (London, England), 2008.

Solids, Liquids, and Gases, Heinemann Library (Chicago, IL), 2001.

Water, Heinemann Library (Chicago, IL), 2001, revised, Heinemann Library (Oxford, England), 2008.

Sound and Hearing, Heinemann Library (Chicago, IL), 2001, revised, Heinemann Library (Oxford, England), 2008.

Materials, Heinemann Library (Chicago, IL), 2001, revised, Heinemann Library (Oxford, England), 2008.

Magnets, Heinemann Library (Chicago, IL), 2001, revised, Heinemann Library (Oxford, England), 2008.

Light and Dark, Heinemann Library (Chicago, IL), 2001, revised edition, 2008.

Color, Heinemann Library (Chicago, IL), 2001, revised edition, 2008.

Forces and Motion, Heinemann Library (Chicago, IL), 2001, revised edition, 2008.

Hot and Cold, Heinemann Library (Chicago, IL), 2001, revised edition, 2008.

Bendy and Rigid, Heinemann Library (Chicago, IL), 2003, published as *Flexible and Rigid,* 2008.

Conductors and Insulators, Heinemann Library (Chicago, IL), 2003, revised edition, 2008.

Heavy and Light, Heinemann Library (Chicago, IL), 2003, revised, Heinemann Library (Oxford, England), 2008.

Human Growth, Heinemann Library (Chicago, IL), 2003, revised, Heinemann Library (Oxford, England), 2008.

Living and Nonliving, Heinemann Library (Chicago, IL), 2003, revised, Heinemann Library (Oxford, England), 2008.

Magnetic and Non-Magnetic, Heinemann Library (Chicago, IL), 2003, revised edition, 2008.

Natural and Man-Made, Heinemann Library (Chicago, IL), 2003, revised, Heinemann Library (Oxford, England), 2008.

Shiny and Dull, Heinemann Library (Chicago, IL), 2003, revised edition, 2008.

Smooth and Rough, Heinemann Library (Chicago, IL), 2003, revised, Heinemann Library (Oxford, England), 2008.

Soft and Hard, Heinemann Library (Chicago, IL), 2003, revised, Heinemann Library (Oxford, England), 2008.

Transparent and Opaque, Heinemann Library (Chicago, IL), 2003, revised edition, 2008.

"MACHINES IN ACTION" SERIES

Wheels and Cranks, Heinemann Library (Chicago, IL), 2001.

Pulleys and Gears, Heinemann Library (Chicago, IL), 2001.

Springs, Heinemann Library (Chicago, IL), 2001.

Ramps and Wedges, Heinemann Library (Chicago, IL), 2001.

Levers, Heinemann Library (Chicago, IL), 2001.
Screws, Heinemann Library (Chicago, IL), 2001.

"IN TOUCH" SERIES

Internet and E-mail, Heinemann Library (Chicago, IL), 2002.
Post, Heinemann Library (Chicago, IL), 2002.
Telephone and Fax, Heinemann Library (Chicago, IL), 2002.

"LIVING NATURE" SERIES

Amphibians, Chrysalis Education (North Mankato, MN), 2003.
Birds, Chrysalis Education (North Mankato, MN), 2003.
Fish, Chrysalis Education (North Mankato, MN), 2003.
Flowers, Chrysalis Education (North Mankato, MN), 2003.
Insects, Chrysalis Education (North Mankato, MN), 2003.
Mammals, Chrysalis Education (North Mankato, MN), 2003.
Reptiles, Chrysalis Education (North Mankato, MN), 2003.

"BODY NEEDS" SERIES

Vitamins and Minerals for a Healthy Body, Heinemann Library (Chicago, IL), 2003, 2nd edition, Heinemann Library (London, England), 2009.
Water and Fiber for a Healthy Body, Heinemann Library (Chicago, IL), 2003, 2nd edition, Heinemann Library (London, England), 2009.
Proteins for a Healthy Body, Heinemann Library (Chicago, IL), 2003, 2nd edition, Heinemann Library (London, England), 2009.

"EXTREME SURVIVAL" SERIES

Space, Raintree (Chicago, IL), 2003.
Deserts, Raintree (Chicago, IL), 2004.
Mountains, Raintree (Chicago, IL), 2004.

"LOOK AFTER YOURSELF" SERIES

Get Some Exercise!, Heinemann Library (Chicago, IL), 2003.
Get Some Rest!, Heinemann Library (Chicago, IL), 2003.
Healthy Ears and Eyes, Heinemann Library (Chicago, IL), 2003.
Healthy Food, Heinemann Library (Chicago, IL), 2003.
Healthy Hair, Heinemann Library (Chicago, IL), 2003.
Healthy Skin, Heinemann Library (Chicago, IL), 2003.
Healthy Teeth, Heinemann Library (Chicago, IL), 2003.
Keep Healthy!, Heinemann Library (Chicago, IL), 2003.

"STAY HEALTHY"/"BODY MATTERS" SERIES

Why Do Bones Break? and Other Questions about Bones and Muscles, Heinemann Library (Chicago, IL), 2003.
Why Do Bruises Change Color? and Other Questions about Blood, Heinemann Library (Chicago, IL), 2003.
Why Do I Get a Sunburn? and Other Questions about Skin, Heinemann Library (Chicago, IL), 2003.
Why Do I Get a Toothache? and Other Questions about Nerves, Heinemann Library (Chicago, IL), 2003.
Why Do I Sneeze? and Other Questions about Breathing, Heinemann Library (Chicago, IL), 2003.
Why Do I Vomit? and Other Questions about Digestion, Heinemann Library (Chicago, IL), 2003.
Why Do My Eyes Itch? and Other Questions about Allergies, Heinemann Library (Chicago, IL), 2003.
Why Does My Body Smell? and Other Questions about Hygiene, Heinemann Library (Chicago, IL), 2003.
Why Do We Need to Eat?, Heinemann Library (Chicago, IL), 2006.
Why Do We Need to Be Active?, Heinemann Library (Chicago, IL), 2006.
What Should We Eat?, Heinemann Library (Chicago, IL), 2006.

"WHAT'S IT LIKE?"/"IT'S NOT CATCHING" SERIES

Allergies, Heinemann Library (Chicago, IL), 2004.
Asthma, Heinemann Library (Chicago, IL), 2004.
Broken Bones, Heinemann Library (Chicago, IL), 2004.
Bumps and Bruises, Heinemann Library (Chicago, IL), 2004.
Burns and Blisters, Heinemann Library (Chicago, IL), 2004.
Cuts and Grazes, Heinemann Library (Chicago, IL), 2004.
Stings and Bites, Heinemann Library (Chicago, IL), 2004.
Tooth Decay, Heinemann Library (Chicago, IL), 2004.
Using a Wheelchair, Heinemann Library (Chicago, IL), 2005.
Down's Syndrome, Heinemann Library (Chicago, IL), 2005.
Deafness, Heinemann Library (Chicago, IL), 2005.
Cancer, Heinemann Library (Chicago, IL), 2005.
Blindness, Heinemann Library (Chicago, IL), 2005.

"MY AMAZING BODY" SERIES

Breathing, Raintree (Chicago, IL), 2004.
Eating, Raintree (Chicago, IL), 2004.
Growing, Raintree (Chicago, IL), 2004.
Moving, Raintree (Chicago, IL), 2004.
Senses, Raintree (Chicago, IL), 2004.
Staying Healthy, Raintree (Chicago, IL), 2004.

"MY WORLD OF GEOGRAPHY" SERIES

Coasts, Heinemann Library (Oxford, England), 2004, Heinemann Library (Chicago, IL), 2005.
Forests, Heinemann Library (Oxford, England), 2004, Heinemann Library (Chicago, IL), 2005.
Islands, Heinemann Library (Oxford, England), 2004, Heinemann Library (Chicago, IL), 2005.
Deserts, Heinemann Library (Chicago, IL), 2005.
Lakes, Heinemann Library (Chicago, IL), 2005.

Mountains, Heinemann Library (Chicago, IL), 2005.
Oceans, Heinemann Library (Chicago, IL), 2005.
Rivers, Heinemann Library (Chicago, IL), 2005.

"FIVE SENSES" SERIES

Hearing, Chrysalis (North Mankato, MN), 2005.
Touch, Chrysalis (North Mankato, MN), 2005.
Taste, Chrysalis (North Mankato, MN), 2005.
Smell, Chrysalis (North Mankato, MN), 2005.
Sight, Chrysalis (North Mankato, MN), 2005.

"HOW ARE THINGS MADE?" SERIES

How Is Chocolate Made?, Heinemann Library (Chicago, IL), 2005.
How Is a Soccer Ball Made?, Heinemann Library (Chicago, IL), 2005.
How Is a Pencil Made?, Heinemann Library (Chicago, IL), 2005.
How Is a Bicycle Made?, Heinemann Library (Chicago, IL), 2005.
How Is a Book Made?, Heinemann Library (Chicago, IL), 2005.

"MATERIAL DETECTIVES" SERIES

Water: Let's Look at a Puddle, Heinemann Library (Chicago, IL), 2005.
Wood: Let's Look at a Baseball Bat, Heinemann Library (Chicago, IL), 2006.
Soil: Let's Look at a Garden, Heinemann Library (Chicago, IL), 2006.
Rock: Let's Look at Pebbles, Heinemann Library (Chicago, IL), 2006.
Plastic: Let's Look at a Frisbee, Heinemann Library (Chicago, IL), 2006, published as *Let's Look at the Frisbee,* Raintree (Oxford, England), 2006.
Paper: Let's Look at a Comic Book, Heinemann Library (Chicago, IL), 2006.
Metal: Let's Look at a Knife and Fork, Heinemann Library (Chicago, IL), 2006.
Glass: Let's Look at Marbles, Heinemann Library (Chicago, IL), 2006.

The "Material Detectives" books have been translated into Spanish.

"HOW'S YOUR HEALTH?" SERIES

Nits and Head Lice, Franklin Watts (London, England), 2006.
Cuts, Bruises, and Breaks, Franklin Watts (London, England), 2006, Smart Apple Media (Mankato, MN), 2009.
Tooth Decay, Franklin Watts (London, England), 2006, Smart Apple Media (Mankato, MN), 2009.

"RAINTREE FUSION" SERIES

The Life and Times of a Drop of Water: The Water Cycle, Raintree (Chicago, IL), 2006.

The Day the Sun Went Out: The Sun's Energy, illustrated by Darren Lingard, Raintree (Chicago, IL), 2006.
Alien Neighbors?: The Solar System illustrated by Darren Lingard and John Haslam, Raintree (Chicago, IL), 2006, published as *Alien Neighbours?,* Raintree (Oxford, England), 2006.

"YOUR BODY—INSIDE AND OUT" SERIES

Senses, Franklin Watts (London, England), 2007.
Bones and Muscles, Franklin Watts (London, England), 2007, Sea-to-Sea Publications (Mankato, MN), 2011.
Teeth and Hair, Franklin Watts (London, England), 2007, Sea-to-Sea Publications (Mankato, MN), 2011.

"PLANT TOP TENS" SERIES

(With Michael Scott) *Africa's Most Amazing Plants,* Raintree (Chicago, IL), 2008.
(With Michael Scott) *Asia's Most Amazing Plants,* Raintree (Chicago, IL), 2008.
(With Michael Scott) *Australasia's Most Amazing Plants,* Raintree (Chicago, IL), 2008.
(With Michael Scott) *Europe's Most Amazing Plants,* Raintree (Chicago, IL), 2008.
(With Michael Scott) *North America's Most Amazing Plants,* Raintree (Chicago, IL), 2008.
(With Michael Scott) *South America's Most Amazing Plants,* Raintree (Chicago, IL), 2008.

"ECO-ACTION" SERIES

Buildings of the Future, Heinemann Library (Chicago, IL), 2008.
Consumerism of the Future, Heinemann Library (Chicago, IL), 2008.
Travel of the Future, Heinemann Library (Chicago, IL), 2008.

"PROTECT OUR PLANET" SERIES

Disappearing Forests, Heinemann Library (Chicago, IL), 2008.
Disappearing Wildlife, Heinemann Library (Chicago, IL), 2008.
Global Warming, Heinemann Library (Chicago, IL), 2008.
Oceans and Rivers in Danger, Heinemann Library (Chicago, IL), 2008.
Polluted Air, Heinemann Library (Chicago, IL), 2008.

"HEADLINE ISSUES" SERIES

Getting Rid of Waste, Heinemann Library (Chicago, IL), 2008.
Energy for the Future, Heinemann Library (Chicago, IL), 2008.
Climate Change, Heinemann Library (Chicago, IL), 2009.
Animals under Threat, Heinemann Library (Chicago, IL), 2009.

"LOOKING AT" SERIES

Looking at Forces and Motion: How Do Things Move?, Enslow Publishers (Berkeley Heights, NJ), 2008.
Looking at Life Cycles: How Do Plants and Animals Change?, Enslow Publishers (Berkeley Heights, NJ), 2008.
Looking at Weather and Seasons: How Do They Change?, Enslow Publishers (Berkeley Heights, NJ), 2008.

"WILD WEATHER" SERIES

Floods, QEB Pub. (Laguna Hills, CA), 2008.
Hurricanes and Tornadoes, QEB Pub. (Mankato, MN), 2008.

"MY BODY" SERIES

Why Do I Brush My Teeth?, QED (London, England), 2009, QEB Pub. (Irvine, CA), 2009.
Why Do I Wash My Hands?, QEB Pub. (Irvine, CA), 2009.
Why Do I Run?, QEB Pub. (Mankato, MN), 2010.
Why Do I Sleep?, QEB Pub. (Mankato, MN), 2010.

"DISGUSTING BODY FACTS" SERIES

Itches and Scratches, Raintree (Chicago, IL), 2010.
Mites and Bites, Raintree (Chicago, IL), 2010.
Ooze and Goo, Raintree (Chicago, IL), 2010.
Puke and Poo, Raintree (Chicago, IL), 2010, published as *Sick and Poo*, Raintree (Oxford, England), 2010.
Twitches and Sneezes, Raintree (Chicago, IL), 2010.

OTHER

Henry VIII, Pitkin Unichrome (Andover, Hampshire, England), 1999.
The Six Wives of Henry VIII, Pitkin Unichrome (Andover, Hampshire, England), 1999.
Mary Queen of Scots, Pitkin Unichrome (Andover, Hampshire, England), 1999.
Best of York, Pitkin Unichrome (Andover, Hampshire, England), 1999.
Pitkin Guide to the City of York, Pitkin Unichrome (Andover, Hampshire, England), 1999.
(Editor) John McIlwain, *Pitkin Guide to the City of Lincoln*, Pitkin Publishing (Stroud, England), 2007.
(Editor) Annie Bullen, *Pitkin Guide to the City of Oxford*, Pitkin Publishing (Stroud, England), 2007.
(Editor) Annie Bullen, *Pitkin Guide to the City of York*, Pitkin Publishing (Andover, England), 2007.
(Editor) Annie Bullen, *Pitkin Guide to the City of Norwich*, Pitkin Publishing (Andover, England), 2007.
(Editor) Annie Bullen, *Pitkin Guide to the City of Bath*, Pitkin Publishing (Andover, England), 2007.

Sidelights

A prolific writer, Angela Royston is the author of numerous nonfiction books for young readers that focus on science-based topics ranging from the human body to the life cycle of a kangaroo to the functioning of a lever. Hoping to inspire an interest in science on children of all ages, Royston creates books for readers ranging from preschool to the middle grades; as she once told *SATA*, "I very much enjoy the challenge of writing about a wide variety of subjects." In her work as a writer, Royston has taken on subjects as technical as bridge building, global warming, and the process of digestion, translating such processes into age-appropriate language. "I had a broad education," the prolific author explained, "and I feel able to tackle almost any subject, provided I can find good research material."

Born in 1945 in Yorkshire, England, Royston eventually attended the University of Edinburgh where she earned her master's degree in 1966. After graduation, she moved south to London, where she worked as a secretary for two years and then found work as a nonfiction editor for children's books. In 1973 she worked for Macdonald Educational, eventually moving on to Grisewood & Dempsey. Editing for publishers gave Royston an excellent introduction to the process of creating nonfiction books for children, and when she began her family she also began working full time as a freelance writer and editor. With many contacts in the publishing industry, much of Royston's work has been on commissioned books for various series.

Her writing for preschoolers includes both stand-alone books and books divided among various series. *Where Do Babies Come From?* is characteristic Royston, as she "dishes up just the right amount" of information in simplified and concise language, according to a *Publishers Weekly* reviewer. As the same writer further noted, "Royston's matter-of-fact presentation is informative, reassuring and discreet." A contributor for *Kirkus Reviews* called *Where Do Babies Come From?* an "outstanding introduction for preschoolers who are already starting to ask a lot of questions about reproduction," and added that the book's "brief text and stunning full-color photographs provide just enough information to satisfy young questioners." Royston also provides preschoolers with mechanical know-how in both *My Lift-the-Flap Car Book*, which kids "will adore," according to *Booklist* contributor Ilene Cooper, and *Monster Road-Builders*, the latter a look at nine huge machines used in building roads. As *School Library Journal* critic Susan Hepler noted, "Each page features several information-laden sentences," along with double-page spreads of the machine in question.

Royston's series titles for preschoolers include "Stepping Stones 123" and "Farm Animal Stories." Reviewing the six titles in the latter series—*The Cow, The Goat, The Hen, The Pony, The Pig,* and *The Sheep*—Diane Nunn noted in *School Library Journal* that the author's "narration is in simple story form, relating both daily and seasonal activities of the animals from mating behaviors and birth through adulthood." Nunn asserted that the series' "basic facts are accurate," but warned readers to "be aware that these books depict farm animals in an idyllic rural setting that has disappeared in most areas of the [United States]."

The majority of Royston's books for young readers are geared for the five-to-seven-year-old group and include "Eye Openers," "See How They Grow," "Inside and Out," "Animal Life Stories," and "Protect Our Planet," among many others. In "Eye Openers" photographs and drawings blend with a simple text to illustrate and explicate topics ranging from machines such as cars and airplanes to animals such as dinosaurs and birds. Reviewing *Cars, Diggers and Dump Trucks, Dinosaurs,* and *Jungle Animals* in *School Library Journal,* Steven Engelfried called the "Eye Openers" series a "winning visual package" with "just enough [information] to satisfy readers or listeners while they pore over the exciting illustrations." In another round-up review of *Baby Animals, Planes, Sea Animals,* and *Ships and Boats,* Dorcas Hand noted in *School Library Journal* that these are "four pleasing offerings for board-book graduates." Hand also remarked, "Each double-page spread. . . . offers a descriptive paragraph and a large, excellent-quality, full-color photograph of the subject." Reviewing *Baby Animals* and *Sea Animals* in *School Librarian,* Joan Hamilton Jones commented that the series "is de-signed to be both educational and entertaining," and does so "by combining bright photographs with large printed texts." Jones concluded that Royston's texts lead readers "into a world of fascinating information" in these books, while *School Librarian* critic Joan Feltwell praised the series for containing "a feast of fine photographs designed to enthrall and capture the imagination of three-to six-year-olds." *School Library Journal* reviewer Eldon Younce wrote in his review of *Trains* that "young train enthusiasts will find this slim volume right on track."

One of Royston's most-popular series for beginning readers, "See How They Grow," is a group of eight books which focus on various baby animals and show how they develop via an engaging story format. Owen Edwards, reviewing the entire series in *Entertainment Weekly,* commented that virtual reality was still only virtual, "but until the nerds catch up with the need, there are the "See How They Grow" books," which "offer lots of pictures, information—and charm." A critic for *Kirkus Reviews* called *Rabbit,* one of the eight books in the series, "an unusually attractive informational book for the youngest," while *Lamb* and *Mouse* inspired *School Librarian* critic Mary Crawford to characterize the production values of the series as "superb,"

Answering an important question pondered by every sweet tooth, Angela Royston's **How Is Chocolate Made?** *takes readers on a tour of the candy-bar business, from beans to wrapper.* (Heinemann Library, 2005. Cover photograph by Corbis. Reproduced by permission.)

"These books will be popular with a wide range of children as they are both informative and lovely to look at," Crawford concluded.

The "See How They Grow" series shares several qualities with Royston's "First Library" series, which explains the life cycles of various plant and animal species. *Booklist* contributor Carolyn Phelan ranked *Life Cycle of a Bean* as one of several titles in the series that would be "useful for primary classrooms studying individual species or life cycles," while Frances E. Millhouser wrote in *School Library Journal* that *Life Cycle of an Oak Tree* follows the tree's development from acorn to established tree in a "brightly illustrated narrative."

Royston's "Inside and Out" books (first published in England as "A First Look Through") continue this informative look at everyday objects and animals, but with a slightly different twist. The books in this series blend short descriptive paragraphs with acetate double spreads. In "Animal Life Stories" Royston features twelve different creatures: the deer, otter, duck, frog, fox, hedgehog, squirrel, mouse, whale, tiger, elephant, and penguin, in titles named after the animal in question. A writer for *Appraisal* reviewed *The Whale* and dubbed the "Animal Life" series "aptly named" because the "text consists of factual material, but reads like a story" that "would be appropriate for the beginning reader and for reading aloud." Another contributor for *Appraisal* praised Royston's "very readable style" in a collective review of *The Fox, The Duck, The Tiger, The Otter,* and *The Penguin.* "Animals are universally the favorite science subject of the five to eight age group," the same reviewer concluded, and "these colorful, interesting books are recommended to help fill the need."

Royston's beginning-reader series "Plants" features flora rather than fauna, while "Safe and Sound" takes a look at human health and well-being. Reviewing *Flowers, Fruits, and Seeds, How Plants Grow,* and *Strange Plants,* in *School Library Journal,* Katherine Borchert called the three "Plants" books "serviceable additions for collections in need of easy nonfiction." Kit Vaughan, also writing in *School Library Journal,* felt that two titles in the "Safe and Sound Series," *Eat Well* and *A Healthy Body,* "inform and educate readers" through the use of "short sentences and a limited vocabulary."

Royston's titles for DK's "Eyewitness" series are also aimed at beginning readers; *Truck Trouble* follows a driver attempting to make a delivery on a day when nature and his truck seem to be working against him. Susan Dove Lempke commented in *Booklist* on the "little zip of suspense" in the title, as readers wonder if the driver will make his delivery on time. Focusing on smaller, simple contrivances in her "Machines in Action" series, Royston explains how screws, levers, pulleys, and springs make work easier. Reviewing *Screws*

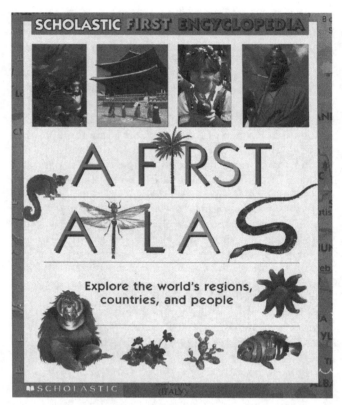

Royston's fact-filled books include Scholastic's well-illustrated **A First Atlas.** (Cover copyright © 1995 by Scholastic Inc. and Two-Can Publishing Ltd. Reproduced by permission.)

and *Springs* for *School Library Journal,* Maren Ostergard considered these books to be "clear introductions to very specific topics."

In addition to series books for young readers, Royston has penned stand-alone books as well as series for middle-grade students. Popular individual titles hereinclude *The A-to-Z Book of Cars* and *100 Greatest Medical Discoveries.* In *The A-to-Z Book of Cars* she presents a "browsing guide to automobiles" that *Booklist* critic Julie Corsaro predicted "is likely to burn rubber in the circulation department" due to its appealing topic. A writer for *Science Books and Films* noted of the same title that it is a "wonderful road book."

Royston covers dozens of medical topics in *100 Greatest Medical Discoveries,* a book that "teems with information by both word and picture," according to a contributor for *Junior Bookshelf.* The same writer remarked that, although the book is aimed at ten to fourteen year olds, it could be "enjoyed by both younger and older groups." Royston's *Big Machines* is a stand-alone title for younger readers that provides "a colorful introduction to nine machines," including the backhoe, street cleaner, and combine, according to Karen Harvey of *Booklist.*

Developed for children with reading difficulties Royston's "First Look At" series focuses on a different animal or plant in every volume. Delvene Barnett, reviewing series installment *Fish* in *School Librarian,* found it "inspiring," and a book that "could also be used with slow learners and older, less-able children."

The "Science Nature Guides" books present introductions to wild flowers, trees, birds, and mammals of Great Britain and of North America in separate editions. Each book includes not only text and illustrations, but also activities, such as making a cast of animal footprints in *Mammals of North America.* Reviewing that title in *School Librarian,* Ann Jenkin concluded that "this book is extremely good value and will be enjoyed by 8 to 12-year-olds at school or at home." Reviewing *The Human Body and How It Works,* a writer for *Appraisal* noted that Royston's book "includes detailed drawings of the human skeleton, of a developing baby, and experiments that are both appropriate for and of interest to elementary children."

In the "Body Matters" and "It's Not Catching" series, Royston answers questions about natural body functions and diseases for young readers. Titles such as *Why Do I Vomit? and Other Questions about Digestion* and *Why Do My Eyes Itch? and Other Questions about Allergies* address common concerns children have, as well as providing information sought by students writing reports about functions of the human body. A reviewer for *School Library Journal* deemed the books in this series "accessible introductions." The "It's Not Catching" series illuminates non-contagious ailments in titles such as *Allergies* and *Tooth Decay.* Reviewing the series installments *Asthma, Broken Bones,* and *Stings and Bites* for *School Library Journal,* Donna Marie Wagner considered them "concise, informative books filled with facts."

Royston's "Look After Yourself" series gives advice to young readers on how to best care for their bodies. "The writing is clear and direct," Joyce Adams Burner wrote of the series in her *School Library Journal* review of both *Get Some Exercise!* and *Get Some Rest!* In a review of *Healthy Hair* and other titles in the series, Kate Kohlbeck noted in the same periodical that "these guides provide the basics."

Also focusing on body functions, Royston's "Disgusting Body Facts" series lures readers in with humor: series installments include the irresistibly titled *Itches and Scratches, Mites and Bites, Ooze and Goo, Puke and Poo,* and *Twitches and Sneezes.* In *Puke and Poo* readers learn the truth about flatulence, vomit, and other activities usually not spoken about. "The chapter headings will have . . . grade-schoolers hooting and jeering," predicted *Booklist* contributor Hazel Rochman, the critic noting the series' planned appeal to reluctant readers.

Royston investigates how common objects are made in the "How Are Things Made?" series, and she looks at materials and substances through household items in the "Material Detectives" series. Describing objects such as marbles or pebbles to illuminate glass and rock,

or considering a puddle to discuss water, the "Material Detectives" series contains such books as *Paper: Let's Look at a Comic Book* and *Metal: Let's Look at a Knife and Fork.* Featuring a different approach, the "How Are Things Made?" series delves into the creation of soccer balls, books, and chocolate. Reviewing *How Is Chocolate Made?* for *Booklist,* Hazel Rochman noted that the title "covers quite a lot in its step-by-step account of the manufacturing process."

Scientific issues of relevance to today's newsreaders are the focus of Royston's timely "Protect Our Planet" and "Eco-Action" series. In *Global Warming,* part of the first-named group, she provides children with an introduction to the theory of climate change, then touches on areas such as shifting weather patterns, polar ice melt, and ways the situation might be offset through alternative energy use. *Oceans and Rivers in Danger* and *Polluted Air* continue what *School Library Journal* critic Eva Elisabeth VonAncken described as the author's examination of the "causes and results of, and possible solutions to, the problem" outlined in the title. "Young readers will come away not frightened, but understanding why they should be concerned," asserted John Peters in his *Booklist* review of *Global Warming.*

Also futuristic in focus, "Eco-Action" titles *Buildings of the Future* and *Consumerism of the Future* use theories of climate change to imagine how changes in human activity might adapt to changing planetary conditions. In both books "Royston does not oversimplify problems but shows what the pitfalls are of many seemingly pro-environmental actions, such as projects that aim to create a reduction in carbon dioxide but do not," noted Judith V. Lechner in *School Library Journal.* Reviewing *Buildings of the Future* in *Science Scope,* Jean Worsley praised the book's format, citing the author's statement of a focused challenge, the many "charts, graphs, and maps . . . found throughout the series," and the inclusion of "questions . . . that will pique readers' curiosity."

Royston has made a winning combination of simplified text along with well-selected illustrations to come up with individual titles and series that both entertain and inform young readers. In doing so, she follows her own golden rule, which she once explained to *SATA.* "I most like to work on books which are 'fun' and always try to find an interesting approach to explaining or describing things. I always become interested in the subjects of the books I work on, and I hope to stimulate that interest in the reader."

Biographical and Critical Sources

PERIODICALS

Appraisal: Science Books for Young People, summer, 1989, review of *The Fox,* p. 82; summer, 1990, review of *The Whale,* pp. 46-47; autumn, 1991, review of *The Human Body and How It Works,* p. 98.

Booklist, September 15, 1991, Ilene Cooper, review of *My Lift-the-Flap Car Book,* p. 154; October 15, 1991, Julie Corsaro, review of *The A-to-Z Car Book,* pp. 434-435; January 1, 1994, review of *My Lift-the-Flap Plane Book,* p. 837; March 15, 1994, Karen Harvey, review of *Big Machines,* p. 1369; April 15, 1998, Carolyn Phelan, review of *Life Cycle of a Bean,* p. 1449; July, 1998, Susan Dove Lempke, reviews of *Fire Fighters* and *Truck Trouble,* both p. 189; September 15, 2005, Hazel Rochman, review of *How Is Chocolate Made?,* p. 68; December 1, 2005, Hazel Rochman, review of *Water: Let's Look at a Puddle,* p. 68; September 1, 2008, John Peters, review of *Global Warming,* p. 102; April 1, 2009, John Peters, review of *Floods,* p. 50; April 1, 2010, Hazel Rochman, review of *Puke and Poo,* p. 68.

Entertainment Weekly, April 10, 1992, Owen Edwards, review of "See How They Grow" series, p. 70.

Junior Bookshelf, August, 1995, review of *100 Greatest Medical Discoveries,* p. 150.

Kirkus Reviews, December 15, 1991, review of *Rabbit,* pp. 1597-1598; May 1, 1996, review of *Where Do Babies Come From?,* p. 692; November 15, 2009, review of *My Body.*

Library Media Connection, November, 2003, review of *Water and Fiber for a Healthy Body,* p. 79.

Magpies, May, 1994, review of *Plane: See How It Works,* p. 37.

Publishers Weekly, May 27, 1996, review of *Where Do Babies Come From?,* p. 78.

School Librarian, August, 1992, Joan Hamilton Jones, review of *Baby Animals* and *Sea Animals,* p. 98; August, 1992, Mary Crawford, reviews of *Lamb* and *Mouse,* both p. 98; November, 1992, Joan Feltwell, review of *Night-Time Animals,* p. 143; November, 1994, Ann Jenkin, review of *Mammals,* p. 158; February, 1997, Delvene Barnett, review of *Fish,* p. 40; spring, 2000, review of *Life Cycle of a Mushroom,* p. 20; summer, 2003, review of *Why Do Bruises Change Color? and Other Questions about Blood,* p. 76; summer, 2010, Godfrey Hall, review of *Wild Weather,* p. 106.

School Library Journal, February, 1990, J.J. Votapka, review of *The Elephant,* p. 85; May, 1990, Susan Hepler, review of *Monster Road Builders,* pp. 100-101; November, 1990, Diane Nunn, review of *The Cow,* p. 107; January, 1992, Steven Engelfried, review of *Cars,* p. 97; October, 1992, Dorcas Hand, review of *Baby Animals,* p. 109; February, 1993, Eldon Younce, review of *Trains,* p. 86; March, 1993, Karey Wehner, review of *Insects and Crawly Creatures,* p. 194; May, 1994, Eldon Younce, review of *Big Machines,* p. 110; November, 1995, John Peters, review of *A First Atlas,* p. 134; May, 1998, Frances E. Millhouser, review of *Under the Sea,* p. 137; February, 1999, Eldon Younce,

reviews of *Life Cycle of a Sunflower* and *Life Cycle of a Chicken,* both p. 101; January, 2000, Katherine Borchert, review of *Flowers, Fruits, and Seeds,* and Kit Vaughan, review of *Eat Well,* both p. 126; April, 2001, Maren Ostergard, reviews of *Screws* and *Springs,* both p. 134; April, 2003, Christine A. Moesch, reviews of *Why Do I Vomit? and Other Questions about Digestion* and *Why Do My Eyes Itch? and Other Questions about Allergies,* both p. 154; July, 2003, Joyce Adams Burner, review of *Where Do Babies Come From?,* p. 78; February, 2004, Joyce Adams Burner, reviews of *Get Some Exercise!* and *Get Some Rest!,* both p. 138; February, 2004, Kate Kohlbeck, reviews of *Healthy Food, Healthy Hair,* and *Healthy Teeth,* all p. 138; April, 2004, reviews of *Why Do I Vomit? and Other Questions about Digestion* and *Why Do My Eyes Itch? and Other Questions about Allergies,* both p. 21; December, 2004, Donna Marie Wagner, reviews of *Asthma, Broken Bones,* and *Stings and Bites,* all p. 137; August, 2005, Christine A. Moesch, reviews of *Cancer, Down's Syndrome,* and *Using a Wheelchair,* all p. 116; August, 2005, Christine A. Moesch, review of *Cancer,* p. 116; May, 2008, Judith V. Lechner, reviews of *Consumerism of the Future* and *Buildings of the Future,* both p. 149; August, 2008, Eva Elisabeth VonAncken, reviews of *Polluted Air* and *Oceans and Rivers in Danger,* both p. 113; December, 2009, Frances E. Millhouser, reviews of *Life Cycle of a Mushroom* and *Life Cycle of an Oak Tree,* both p. 98.

Science Books and Films, June-July, 1991, review of *The A-to-Z Book of Cars,* p. 131; June, 1995, reviews of *The Mouse, The Hedgehog,* and *The Elephant,* all p. 156; August, 1995, review of *You and Your Body: 101 Questions and Answers,* p. 180; September, 1999, review of *Maps and Symbols,* p. 218; January, 2000, reviews of *A Healthy Body* and *Clean and Healthy,* both p. 37; July, 2002, reviews of *Solids, Liquids, and Gases* and *Hot and Cold,* both p. 468; May, 2003, review of *Why Do I Sneeze? and Other Questions about Breathing* p. 132; November, 2003, review of *Wolves,* p. 277.

Science Scope, March, 2008, Jean Worsley, review of *Buildings of the Future,* p. 96; April-May, 2008, Jean Worsley, review of *Consumerism of the Future,* p. 68.

Times Educational Supplement, April 13, 2001, Jon O'Connor, reviews of *Levers, Ramps and Wedges, Springs, Pulleys and Gears, Screws,* and *Wheels and Cranks,* all p. 22.

ONLINE

Angela Royston Home Page, http://www.angelaroyston.com (May 15, 2011).

S

SADLER, Sonia Lynn

Personal
Born in KS. *Education:* Attended Maryland Institute College of Art; Parsons School of Design, B.F.A. (fashion design).

Addresses
Home—Bowie, MD. *E-mail*—lynnartsl@aol.com.

Career
Illustrator, designer, and fashion designer. Sonia Lynn Sadler Arts, founder and designer of greeting cards. *Exhibitions:* Works exhibited at Artcurian Gallery, Brooklyn, NY, and Tina's Gallery, Potomac, MD.

Awards, Honors
Hallmark Golden Key Award for fashion design, Hecht Company; Children's Book of the Year Honor award, African-American Academy of Arts and Letters, 2005, for *Ma Dear's Old Green House* by Denise Lewis Patrick; Notable Children's Books designation, *Smithsonian* magazine, Amelia Bloomer Project selection, American Library Association (ALA) Feminist Task Force, and Green Earth Book Award Honor Book designation, Newton Marasco Foundation, all 2010, and Notable Books for a Global Society listee, International Reading Association, and Coretta Scott King/John Steptoe Award for New Talent, American Library Association, both 2011, all for *Seeds of Change* by Jen Cullerton Johnson.

Illustrator
Denise Lewis Patrick, *Ma Dear's Old Green House,* Just Us Books (East Orange, NJ), 2004.

Jen Cullerton Johnson, *Seeds of Change: Planting a Path to Peace,* Lee & Low Books (New York, NY), 2010.

Sidelights
Sonia Lynn Sadler's vividly colored stylized illustrations are a highlight of Denise Lewis Patrick's *Ma Dear's Old Green House* and Jen Cullerton Johnson' *Seeds of Change: Planting a Path to Peace,* the latter which earned Sadler the American Library Association's coveted Coretta Scott King/John Steptoe Award for New Talent in 2011. Describing herself as a colorist, Sadler noted on her home page that "pattern and color define my work. My interest in color and pattern comes from watching the women in my family work with fabric. They made their own clothes, [and] later these

Sonia Lynn Sadler's illustration projects include creating the colorful artwork for Jen Cullerton Johnson's Seeds of Change. (Illustration copyright © 2010 by Sonia Lynn Sadler. Reproduced by permission of Lee & Low Books, Inc.)

clothes would become colorful prized quilts." "I love to watch children because the things they do inspire me," the artist added.

Because her father was in the military, Sadler traveled to several different countries and attended school in several different states while growing up. Determined to study fine art and illustration, she enrolled at the Maryland Institute College of Art before transferring to the prestigious Parsons School of Design to earn her degree in fashion design. In her career in the fashion industry, Sadler has worked for several top design firms, where her fashion accessories have been featured on publications such as *Women's Wear Daily* and the *New York Times*. As her creative interests have expanded, she has also moved into illustration and produces a line of greeting cards in addition to creating picture-book art.

Sadler's first illustration project, capturing Patrick's fond memories of her grandmother's home in her artwork for *Ma Dear's Old Green House*, drew praise from *Booklist* critic Jennifer Mattson, who noted that the "compelling interpretations of a relatively predictable, nostalgic text augurs the arrival of a promising new talent." Reviewing *Seeds of Change* in *School Library Journal*, Carol S. Surges wrote that Cullerton's picture-book biography of Nobel Prize-winning environmentalist Wangari Maathai pairs an in-depth look at the Kenyan woman who started the Green Belt movement with "batik-style illustrations that fill the pages" with "vivid colors." For *Booklist* critic Gillian Engberg, "Sadler's bright mixed-media art" for the book captures "the presence . . . of a vibrant natural world" while a *Publishers Weekly* contributor noted that in *Seeds of Change* the artist's "highly stylized"scratchboard images distill the African landscape into "elemental shapes" and transform Cullerton's story into "a tropically colored quilt."

Biographical and Critical Sources

PERIODICALS

Booklist, February 1, 2005, Jennifer Mattson, review of *Ma Dear's Old Green House*, p. 978; June 1, 2010, Gillian Engberg, review of *Seeds of Change: Planting a Path to Peace*, p. 98.
Publishers Weekly, April 12, 2010, review of *Seeds of Change*, p. 49.
School Library Journal, January, 2005, Mary N. Oluonye, review of *Ma Dear's Old Green House*, p. 96; April, 2010, Carol S. Surges, review of *Seeds of Change*, p. 146.

ONLINE

Sonia Lynn Sadler Home Page, http://www.sonialynnsadler arts.com (May 27, 2011).*

SANSONE, Adele 1953-

Personal
Born 1953, in Vienna, Austria.

Addresses
Home—Axams, Austria.

Career
Author of books for children. Presenter at schools and festivals.

Awards, Honors
Preis Parole for picture books; Landes Steiermark Kinder-und Jugendliteraturpreis, 2004, for *Hassan*.

Writings

FOR CHILDREN; SELF-ILLUSTRATED

Der kleine Luchs hehrt heim, Tyrolia-Verlag (Innsbruck, Austria), 1995.
Auf Wiedersehen, kleines Murmeltier, Rhätikon Verlag, 1998.
Amelie, Schatten im Dunkel, Rhätikon Verlag, 2001.
Florian lässt sich Zeit: eine Geschichte zum Down Syndrom, Tyrolia-Verlag (Innsbruck, Austria), 2002.
Hassan (chapter bookl), Rhätikon Verlag, 2004.
Amelie, Knödel und Co., Novum-Verlag (Vienna, Austria), 2007.
Amelie und die Stachelritter, Novum-verlag (Vienna, Austria), 2008.
Erster Kuss und Regenguss (chapter book), G & G (Vienna, Austria), 2008.
Diese eine Reise (chapter book), Von-Loeper-Literaturverlag (Karlsruhe, Germany), 2009.

FOR CHILDREN

Das grüne Küken, illustrated by Alan Marks, Neugebauer (Zürich, Austria), 1999, translated by J. Alison James as *The Little Green Goose*, North-South Books (New York, NY), 1999, illustrated by Anke Faust, NordSüd (Zürich, Switzerland), 2010.

ILLUSTRATOR

Ilse Scherr, *Tina Valentina*, Carinthia Verlag (Klagenfurt, Germany), 1999.
Ines A. Kohm, *Die kleine Elfe mit den großen Füßen*, Tosa (Vienna, Austria), 2006.

Sidelights

Adele Sansone is an Austrian-born author and illustrator whose self-illustrated books for children include both picture books and chapter books. Sansone began to write and illustrate stories for very young children in the mid-1990s, and her gently tinted artwork appears alongside her original stories in *Der kleine Luchs hehrt heim, Florian lässt sich Zeit: eine Geschichte zum Down Syndrom,* and three tales featuring an adventurous young girl names Amelie. *Hassan,* Sansone's first novel-length work, was awarded a Landes Steiermark children's book honor in 2004, and her stories have also been recognized by several other awards committees in her native Austria. As an illustrator, she has contributed artwork to Ilse Scherr's *Tina Valentina* and Ines A. Kohm's *Die Kleine Elfe met den großen Füßen.*

Alan Marks creates the engaging watercolor art for German author Adele Sansone's picture book **The Little Green Goose.** (Illustration by Alan Marks. Copyright © 2011 NordSud Verlag AG, CH-8005 Zurich/Schweiz.)

Sansone's **The Little Green Goose** *features artwork by Anke Faust in its 2010 edition.* (Illustration copyright © 2010 by Anke Faust. © 2011 NordSud Verlag AG, CH-8005 Zurich/Schweiz.)

First published in 1999 with illustrations by Alan Marks, Sansone's *Grüne Küken* proved so popular with children that it was quickly translated into several other language, and is known in English as *The Little Green Goose*. A new edition, with colorful collage images by Anke Faust, reintroduced the story to both English-and German-speaking children a little over a decade later. In Sansone's story, Mr. Goose enjoys playing with the barnyard chicks so much that he wishes for a gosling of his very own. When the hens stubbornly refuse to share even one of their many fertilized eggs, the farm dog comes to the rescue. The egg the dog discovers is large and dirty, but the optimistic Goose sets to work keeping it warm. Mr. Goose's efforts are eventually rewarded when he hears a loud crack, and a little green creature emerges from the shell. Although Little Green Goose (actually a baby dinosaur) eventually decides to search for a father who looks more like himself, he ultimately soon returns to Mr. Goose in a story that a *Publishers Weekly* critic noted for its "happy humor."

Biographical and Critical Sources

PERIODICALS

Booklinks, March, 2006, Diane Foote, review of *The Little Green Goose,* p. 51.

Booklist, April 15, 1999, Hazel Rochman, review of *The Little Green Goose,* p. 1538; October 1, 2001, Isabel Schon, review of *The Little Green Goose,* p. 329.

Bulletin of the Center for Children's Books, July, 1999, review of *The Little Green Goose,* p. 399.

Publishers Weekly, April 26, 1999, review of *The Little Green Goose,* p. 82.

School Librarian, winter, 1999, review of *The Little Green Goose,* p. 187.

School Library Journal, September, 1999, Linda Ludke, review of *The Little Green Goose,* p. 203.

Times Educational Supplement, April 30, 1999, review of *The Little Green Goose,* p. 22.

ONLINE

Adele Sansone Home Page, http://www.adele-sansone.com (May 27, 2011).*

*　　*　　*

SCHEFFLER, Axel 1957-

Personal

Born 1957, in Hamburg, Germany; immigrated to England, 1982; partner's name Clementine; has children. *Education:* University of Hamburg, degree; attended Bath Academy of Art, 1985. *Hobbies and other interests:* Walking, cooking, reading, yoga.

Addresses

Home and office—London, England.

Career

Illustrator. Formerly worked in advertising. Judge for Booktrust's Early Years Award; affiliated with National Bookstart Day.

Awards, Honors

Nestlé Smarties' Gold Medal Award for picture books, and Kate Greenaway Medal nomination, both 1999, and Blue Peter Award for Best Book to Read Aloud, and Experian Big-Three Book Prize, both 2000, all for *The Gruffalo* by Julia Donaldson; Kate Greenaway Medal nomination, 2002, for *Monkey Puzzle;* Blue Peter Award for Best Book to Read Aloud, Children's Book Award shortlist, Sheffield Children's Book Award shortlist, and Scottish Children's Book Award, all 2002, all for *Room on the Broom* by Donaldson; W.H. Smith Children's Book of the Year Honor designation, 2005, for *The Gruffalo's Child* by Donaldson; Blue Peter Award for Best Book to Read Aloud, 2005, for *The Snail and the Whale* by Donaldson

Writings

SELF-ILLUSTRATED

(Reteller) *Kleine Schweinerei,* Beltz & Gelberg (Weinheim, Germany), 1994.

(Reteller) *Die drei kleinen Schweinchen und der böse Wolf,* Beltz & Gelberg (Weinheim, Germany), 1994.

Miezekatz, wo gehst du hin?: Kinderreime, Beltz & Gelberg (Weinheim, Germany), 1995.

Die drei Wünsche: nach einem englishcne Märchen, Beltz & Gelberg (Weinheim, Germany), 1995.

Wenn der Bär nach Hause kommt, Beltz & Gelberg (Weinheim, Germany), 1996.

(Reteller) *Proverbs from Far and Wide,* Macmillan (London, England), 1997, published as *Let Sleeping Dogs Lie and Other Proverbs from around the World,* Barron's Educational (Hauppauge, NY), 1997.

Jingle Jangle Jungle, Macmillan (London, England), 2003.

Muddle Farm, Macmillan (London, England), 2004, published as *Muddle Farm: A Magnetic Play Book,* Barrons Educational (Hauppauge, NY), 2007.

Lizzy the Lamb (board book), Campbell (London, England), 2005.

Pip the Puppy (board book), Campbell (London, England), 2005.

Katie the Kitten (board book), Campbell (London, England), 2005.

Freddy the Frog (board book), Campbell (London, England), 2006.

How to Keep a Pet Squirrel, Faber & Faber (London, England), 2010.

SELF-ILLUSTRATED; "PIP AND POSY" BOARD-BOOK SERIES

The Super Scooter, Noisy Crow (London, England), 2011.

The Little Puddle, Noisy Crow (London, England), 2011.

ILLUSTRATOR

Helen Cresswell, *The Piemakers,* Faber & Faber (London, England), 1988.

Bernard McCabe, *The Bottle Rabbit,* Faber & Faber (Boston, MA), 1988.

Bernard McCabe, *Bottle Rabbit and Friends,* Faber & Faber (Boston, MA), 1989.

Jon Blake, *Daley B.,* Walker (London, England), 1992, published as *You're a Hero, Daley B.!,* Candlewick Press (Boston, MA), 1992.

Robert Leeson, *Smark Girls,* Walker (London, England), 1993.

Julia Donaldson, *A Squash and a Squeeze,* Margaret K. McElderry Books (New York, NY), 1993.

Phyllis Root, *Sam Who Was Swallowed by a Shark,* Candlewick Press (Cambridge, MA), 1994, published as *Sam Who Went to See,* Walker Books (London, England), 2005.

Robert Leeson, *The Amazing Adventures of Idle Jack,* Walker (London, England), 1995.

David Henry Wilson, *Do Gerbils Go to Heaven?,* Macmillan (London, England), 1996.

David Henry Wilson, *Do Goldfish Play the Violin?,* Macmillan (London, England), 1996.

David Henry Wilson, *Please Keep off the Dinosaur,* Macmillan (London, England), 1996.

David Henry Wilson, *Never Say Moo to a Bull,* Macmillan (London, England), 1996.

David Henry Wilson, *Can a Spider Learn to Fly?*, Macmillan (London, England), 1996.

David Henry Wilson, *How the Lion Lost His Lunch*, Macmillan (London, England), 1996.

Ian Whybrow, *The Bedtime Bear*, Macmillan (London, England), 1996.

Martine Oborne, *Juice the Pig*, Holt (New York, NY), 1996.

Keto von Waberer, *Vom Gluck, eine Leberwurst zu lieben: und andere kulinarische Glossen*, Kiepenheuer & Witsch, 1996.

Kate Petty, *Sam Plants a Sunflower: A Lift-the-Flap Nature Book with Real Seeds*, Andrews McMeel (Kansas City, MO), 1997.

Kate Petty, *Rosie Plants a Radish: A Lift-the-Flap Nature Book with Real Seeds*, Andrews McMeel (Kansas City, MO), 1997.

Bernard McCabe, *Pongle!: A Week with the Bottle Rabbit*, Fibre & Fibre (Ludlow, England), 1997.

Paul van Loon, *Auch Monster brauchen ein Zuhause*, translated from the Dutch by Mirjam Pressler, Dressler (Hamburg, Germany), 1997.

Robert Leeson, *Lucky Lad!*, Walker (London, England), 1997.

Ian Whybrow, *The Christmas Bear*, Macmillan (London, England), 1998.

Kate Petty, *Ben Plants a Butterfly Garden: A Lift-the-Flap Nature Book with Real Seeds*, Macmillan (London, England), 1998.

Robert Leeson, *Why's the Cow on the Roof?*, Walker (London, England), 1998.

Julia Donaldson, *The Gruffalo*, Dial Books for Young Readers (New York, NY), 1999, tenth anniversary edition, Macmillan Children's (London, England), 2009.

Ian Whybrow, *The Tickle Book*, Macmillan (London, England), 2000.

Julia Donaldson, *Monkey Puzzle*, Dial Books for Young Readers (New York, NY), 2000.

David Henry Wilson, *Never Steal Wheels from a Dog*, Macmillan (London, England), 2001.

Julia Donaldson, *Room on the Broom*, Dial Books for Young Readers (New York, NY), 2001.

Uwe Timm, *Rennschwein Rudi Rüssel*, Nagel & Kimche, 2002.

Julia Donaldson, *The Smartest Giant in Town*, Macmillan Children's (London, England), 2002, published as *The Spiffiest Giant in Town*, Dial Books for Young Readers (New York, NY), 2003.

Toon Tellegen, *Briefe vom Eichhorn an die Amiese*, translated from the Dutch by Mirjam Pressler, DTV Deutscher Taschenbuch (Germany), 2003.

Julia Donaldson, *The Snail and the Whale*, Macmillan Children's Books (London, England), 2003.

Uwe Timm, *Die Zugmaus*, DTV Deustscher Taschenbuch (Germany), 2003.

Nicky Scott, *Reduce, Reuse, Recycle: An Easy Household Guide*, Alison Green (Totnes, England), 2004.

Julia Donaldson, *The Gruffalo's Child*, Macmillan (London, England), 2004, Dial Books for Young Readers (New York, NY), 2005.

Brian Moses, selector, *Monster Poems*, Macmillan (London, England), 2005.

Julia Donaldson, *Charlie Cook's Favorite Book*, Macmillan (London, England), 2005, Dial Books for Young Readers (New York, NY), 2006.

Alison Green, reteller, *Mother Goose's Nursery Rhymes, and How She Came to Tell Them*, Macmillan (London, England), 2007, published as *Mother Goose's Storytime Nursery Rhymes*, Arthur A. Levine Books (New York, NY), 2007, portions published as *Mother Goose's Bedtime Rhymes*, Macmillan (London, England), 2007, *Mother Goose's Playtime Rhymes*, 2008, and *Mother Goose's Action Rhymes*, 2009.

Anna Semlyen, *Cutting Your Car Use: Save Money, Be Healthy, Be Green!*, new edition, Alison Green (Totnes, England), 2007.

Martine Oborne, *Hamilton's Hats*, Macmillan Children's (London, England), 2007.

Julia Donaldson, *Tiddler*, Alison Green (London, England), 2007, published as *The Fish Who Cried Wolf*, Arthur A. Levine Books (New York, NY), 2008.

David Henry Wilson, *Making Mischief with Jeremy James*, Macmillan Children's (London, England), 2008.

Julia Donaldson, *The Gruffalo Pop-up Theatre Book*, Macmillan Children's Books (London, England), 2008.

Julia Donaldson, *Where's My Mom?*, Dial Books for Young Readers (New York, NY), 2008.

Julia Donaldson, Stick Man, Alison Green (London, England), 2008, Arthur A. Levine Books (New York, NY), 2009.

T.S. Eliot, *Old Possum's Book of Practical Cats*, seventieth-anniversary edition, Faber & Faber (London, England), 2009.

Julia Donaldson, *The Snail and the Whale*, Macmillan Children's (London, England), 2009.

Julia Donaldson, *Tabby McTat*, Alison Green (London, England), 2009.

Julia Donaldson, *Zog*, Alison Green (London, England), 2009.

Illustrator of stories by authors in Germany and the Netherlands.

Books featuring Scheffler's art have been translated into over twenty languages, including Danish, Dutch, French, Italian, Spanish, and Welsh.

ILLUSTRATOR; "TALES FROM ACORN WOOD" SERIES

Julia Donaldson, *Rabbit's Nap*, Campbell (London, England), 2000.

Julia Donaldson, *Fox's Sox*, Campbell (London, England), 2000.

Julia Donaldson, *Hide and Seek Pig*, Campbell (London, England), 2000.

Julia Donaldson, *Postman Bear*, Campbell (London, England), 2000.

ILLUSTRATOR; "MY FIRST GRUFFALO" BOARD-BOOK SERIES

Julia Donaldson, *Animal Actions*, Macmillan Children's (London, England), 2011.

Julia Donaldson, *Numbers,* Macmillan Children's (London, England), 2011.

Julia Donaldson, *Colours,* Macmillan Children's (London, England), 2011.

Julia Donaldson, *Opposites,* Macmillan Children's (London, England), 2011.

Sidelights

Axel Scheffler is a German-born illustrator and author whose cartoon-like images have brought to life numerous picture books. Although he has worked with a variety of authors, Scheffler's collaborations with Julia Donaldson have been his most popular and produced *The Gruffalo,* a "verse fable of the brave, clever little mouse who ventures 'a stroll in a deep, dark wood'" that "has the symmetry and simplicity of the perfect story," according to London *Observer* contributor Robert McCrum. First published in 1999, *The Gruffalo* has become something of a modern-day childhood classic and has also sparked a sequel, *The Gruffalo's Child,* as well as the "My First Gruffalo" board-book series. In addition to crafting distinctive artwork for texts by English-language writers such as Jon Blake, Donaldson, Martine Osborne, Paul Shipton, Phyllis Root, and David Henry Wilson, Scheffler has also illustrated German-language versions of popular European tales by authors such as Toon Tellegen, Uwe Timm, and Paul van Loon.

Scheffler immigrated to England in 1982, while in his mid-twenties, and earned a degree from the Bath Academy of Art. After graduating in 1985, he got a job in advertising but quickly turned to book illustration as a

One of Axel Scheffler's many collaborations with Donaldson, **Room on the Broom** *adds humor to a story cast with Halloween characters.* (Illustration copyright © 2001 by Axel Scheffler. Reproduced by permission of Dial Books for Young Readers, a division of Penguin Books for Young Readers, a member of Penguin Group (USA) Inc., 345 Hudson St., New York, NY 10014. All rights reserved.)

Charlie Cook's Favorite Book *is one of several popular collaborations between Scheffler and author Julia Donaldson.* (Illustration copyright © 2005 by Axel Scheffler. All rights reserved. Reproduced by permission of Dial Books for Young Readers, a division of Penguin Books for Young Readers, a member of Penguin Group (USA) Inc., 345 Hudson St., New York, NY 10014. All rights reserved.)

perfect vehicle for his engaging line-and-color art. A prolific artist whose work has appeared in dozens of children's stories, Scheffler was honored by London-based publisher Faber & Faber when he was selected to illustrate the seventieth-anniversary edition of T.S. Eliot's *Old Possum's Book of Practical Cats* for publication in 2009.

While *The Gruffalo* has remained their most popular work, Donaldson and Scheffler have teamed up to produce several other books, among them *Charlie Cook's Favorite Book, Where's My Mom?, The Snail and the Whale, The Fish Who Cried Wolf,* and *Stick Man.* Reviewing *The Snail and the Whale* in *School Library Journal,* Kathleen Kelly MacMillan noted that "the flat, cartoonish look of Scheffler's multimedia illustrations perfectly complements" Donaldson's "rollicking" story about a tiny traveling mollusk. Dubbed by a *Publishers Weekly* critic as "another charmer from the duo behind *The Gruffalo, Charlie Cook's Favorite Book* features what *Booklist* critic Carolyn Phelan described as "amusing"pencil, ink, and color art that "make[s] the most" of the ten different settings and casts of characters in Donaldson's tale.

Published in England as *Tiddler, The Fish Who Cried Wolf* features another engaging mix of story and art as a small fish who tells exaggerated stories finds that his talent for tall-tale-telling comes in handy after he drifts far from his school. Complementing Donaldson's "reader-friendly" rhyming text, Scheffler's "colorful, detailed illustrations feature an endearing cast of undersea denizens," according to Grace Oliff in *School Library Journal.* His "engaging illustrations" for *The Stick Man* help prove "that almost any item can be a character in a children's book," asserted one *Kirkus Reviews* writer, while another concluded of *Where's My Mom?* that "Scheffler's wonderfully colorful pictures" treat readers to "a different take on the lost-child theme."

In addition to his illustration work, Scheffler has also created several self-illustrated stories, among them *Let Sleeping Dogs Lie and Other Proverbs from around the World, Muddle Farm, How to Keep a Pet Squirrel,* and his "Pip and Posy" board books, as well as several fairy-tale retellings that he published in German. Inspired a set of concisely written instructions he discovered in an early-twentieth-century children's encyclopedia, *How to Keep a Pet Squirrel* captures Scheffler's imaginings as to whether a small child could actually keep and house such a quick-moving wild animal. Praising the artwork as "sprightly and full of fun," London *Daily Telegraph* contributor Toby Clements added that the author/illustrator captures the "rather charming instructions" of the original article with his "distinctive" art.

Biographical and Critical Sources

PERIODICALS

Booklist, May 1, 1993, Janice Del Negro, review of *A Squash and a Squeeze,* p. 1602; July, 1997, Michael Cart, review of *Juice the Pig,* p. 1822; July, 1999, Stephanie Zvirin, review of *The Gruffalo,* p. 1950; September 1, 2001, GraceAnne A. DeCandido, review of *Room on the Broom,* p. 120; March 1, 2003, Carolyn Phelan, review of *The Spiffiest Giant in Town,* p. 1201; May 1, 2006, Carolyn Phelan, review of *Charlie Cook's Favorite Book,* p. 88; August 1, 2008, Janice Del Negro, review of *The Fish Who Cried Wolf,* p. 75.

Bookseller, January 20, 2006, Caroline Horn, review of *The Gruffalo,* p. 9.

Children's Bookwatch, February, 2008, review of *Mother Goose's Storytime Nursery Rhymes;* February, 2010, review of *Old Possum's Book of Practical Cats.*

Daily Telegraph (London, England), October 23, 2010, Toby Clements, review of *How to Keep a Pet Squirrel,* p. 26.

Horn Book, January-February, 2005, Jennifer M. Brabander, review of *The Gruffalo's Child,* p. 75; November-December, 2009, Kitty Flynn, review of *Stick Man,* p. 640; January-February, 2010, Joanna Rudge Long, review of *Old Possum's Book of Practical Cats,* p. 98.

Kirkus Reviews, August 1, 2001, review of *Room on the Broom,* p. 1121; January 1, 2003, review of *The Spiffiest Giant in Town,* p. 60; February 15, 2004, review of *The Snail and the Whale,* p. 176; May 1, 2006, review of *Charlie Cook's Favorite Book,* p. 455; January 15, 2008, review of *Where's My Mom?;* April 15, 2008, review of *The Fish Who Cried Wolf;* September 15, 2009, review of *Stick Man.*

Observer (London, England), May 17, 2009, Robert McGrum, "The Giant of Modern Literature? It Has to Be *The Gruffalo,*" p. 24.

Publishers Weekly, June 29, 1992, review of *Daley B.,* p. 61; April 26, 1993, review of *A Squash and a Squeeze,* p. 78; May 30, 1994, review of *Sam Who Was Swallowed by a Shark,* p. 55; June 21, 1999, review of *The Gruffalo,* p. 67; September 10, 2001, review of *Room on the Broom,* p. 92; January 6, 2003, review of *The Spiffiest Giant in Town,* p. 59; February 23, 2004, review of *The Snail and the Whale,* p. 75; December 13, 2004, review of *The Gruffalo's Child,* p. 68; January 10, 2005, review of *The Spiffiest Giant in Town,* p. 58; May 15, 2006, review of *Charlie Cook's Favorite Book,* p. 71; March 3, 2008, review of *Ladybug Girl,* p. 45; March 3, 2008, review of *Where's My Mom?,* p. 45; May 19, 2008, review of *The Fish Who Cried Wolf,* p. 53; September 7, 2009, review of *Stick Man,* p. 43.

School Librarian, spring, 2010, Peter Andrews, review of *Tabby McTat,* p. 27.

School Library Journal, July, 1997, Marsha McGrath, review of *Juice the Pig,* p. 72; September, 2001, Pamela K. Bomboy, review of *Room on the Broom,* p. 187; March, 2003, Bina Williams, review of *The Spiffiest Giant in Town,* p. 191; February, 2004, Kathleen Kelly MacMillan, review of *The Snail and the Whale,* p. 111; March, 2005, Marge Loch-Wouters, review of *The Gruffalo's Child,* p. 170; July, 2006, Jill Heritage Maza, review of *Charlie Cook's Favorite Book,* p. 71; August, 2007, Susan Moorhead, review of *Mother Goose's Storytime Nursery, Rhymes,* p. 98; May, 2008, Julie Roach, review of *Where's My Mom?,* p. 94; June, 2008, Grace Oliff, review of *The Fish Who Cried Wolf,* p. 100; October, 2009, Eva Mitnick, review of *Stick Man,* p. 79; November, 2009, Marilyn Taniguchi, review of *Old Possum's Book of Practical Cats,* p. 130.

ONLINE

Images of Delight Web site, http://www.imagesofdelight.com/ (April 29, 2007), "Axel Scheffler."

London Telegraph Online, http://www.telegraph.co.uk/ (August 25, 2007), Isabel Albiston, interview with Sheffler.*

*   *   *

SCOTT, Jennifer Power 1968-

Personal

Born 1968, in Newfoundland, Canada; married Jeff Scott (a musician); children: one daughter. *Education:* Carleton University (Ottawa, Ontario, Canada), M.A. (journalism).

Addresses

Home—Saint John, New Brunswick, Canada.

Career

Journalist, television producer, author, and singer. Canadian Broadcasting Corporation, former reporter and associate producer; freelance writer and producer of television documentaries for Discovery Channel Canada and elsewhere.

Awards, Honors

Red Maple Award nomination, 2011, for *Green Careers.*

Writings

Green Careers: You Can Make Money and Save the Planet, Lobster Press (Montréal, Québec, Canada), 2010.

Contributor to periodicals, including *Canadian Living.*

Sidelights

Jennifer Power Scott drew on her investigative skills and curiosity as a journalist to write what became her first published book, *Green Careers: You Can Make Money and Save the Planet.* A resident of the Canadian Maritimes—she grew up in Newfoundland before relocating to New Brunswick—Scott began her career as a reporter and producer for the Canadian Broadcasting Corporation. She now works as a freelance writer, penning articles for magazines such as *Canadian Living,* and the television documentaries she has directed and produced have aired on the Discovery Channel Canada and other networks.

Green Careers had its start as an article Scott wrote at the request of a *Canadian Living* editor. After the article was published and came to the attention of the president of Montréal's Lobster Press, a book was born. In *Green Careers* Scott introduces thirty people from around the world who are pursuing careers that respond to Earth's environmental stresses. "I interviewed a pilot who has flown into a hurricane, [Dario Merlo,] a young man who devotes his life to taking care of bonobo apes, and a classical pianist who performed at Carnegie Hall in a dress made of recycled juice pouches!," Scott noted in describing her research on the Lobster Press Web site. "It's amazing how much diverse opportunity is out there right now." Other interviewees included a California architect who specializes in environmentally sound building, a Chicago man who inspires inner-city children with an interest in nature, a British Columbia woman who established children's camps that focus on ecology, a man who brews eco-friendly beer, and another who has found a market for earthworm castings, a valuable fertilizer. These individuals "gave me a great sense of hope for the future," Scott added. "I think we

Cover of Jennifer Power Scott's **Green Careers**, *a guide for eco-minded young capitalists.* (Lobster Press, 2010. Reproduced by permission of Lobster Press Limited.)

are living in an amazing time, a time of fundamental change in the way we live and think. Things often seem bleak on the environmental front, but I believe people like the ones in my book are making the world better. They care about more than making money and living lavishly. They want to make a real difference to other people and to the planet."

In addition to inspiring stories, *Green Careers* included sidebars filled with facts as well as online resources and a list of institutions that offer environmental-based studies. "These inspirational stories are sure to spark interest and creative thinking," predicted Patricia Ann Owens in her review of Scott's book for *School Library Journal.* Reviewing *Green Careers* for *Resource Links,* Angela Thompson noted that, with its "accessible and teen-friendly" language, the book will serve as a "stellar resource" for job seekers.

Biographical and Critical Sources

PERIODICALS

Resource Links, February, 2010, Angela Thompson, review of *Green Careers: You Can Make Money and Save the Planet,* p. 41.
School Library Journal, April, 2010, Patricia Ann Owens, review of *Green Careers,* p. 180.

ONLINE

Lobster Press Web site, http://www.lobsterpress.com/ (May 29, 2011), "Jennifer Power Scott."*

*   *   *

SNYDER, Betsy

Personal

Married 2007; husband's name Jeff. *Education:* Attended college.

Addresses

Home—Cleveland, OH. *Agent*—Lori Nowicki, Painted Words, lori@painted-words.com. *E-mail*—betsy@ betsysnyder.com.

Career

Illustrator, designer, and author of books for children. American Greetings, former staff artist; freelance designer for clients including Target, Nickelodeon, Toys 'R' Us, Starbucks, St. Jude's Hospital, Papyrus, and Peaceable Kingdom Press.

Member

Society of Children's Book Writers and Illustrators.

Awards, Honors

Silver ADDY Award (Cleveland), 2006; Film/Video Silver Telly Award, 2009; Oppenheim Toy Portfolio Gold Seal award, and Cooperative Children's Book Center Choice selection, both 2009, both for *Haiku Baby;* Best Children's Books of the Year selection, Bank Street College of Education, 2011, for *Sweet Dreams Lullaby;* Dr. Toy Best Green Product Award, 2011, for board game Hoot Owl Hoot.

Writings

SELF-ILLUSTRATED

Haiku Baby, Random House Children's Books (New York, NY), 2008.
Have You Ever Tickled a Tiger?, Random House Children's Books (New York, NY), 2009.
Sweet Dreams Lullaby, Random House Children's Books (New York, NY), 2010.

ILLUSTRATOR

Brian P. Cleary, *Peanut Butter and Jellyfishes: A Very Silly Alphabet Book,* Millbrook Press (Minneapolis, MN), 2007.

Betsy Snyder (Reproduced by permission.)

Dianne Ochiltree, *It's a Firefly Night,* NorthWord Books for Young Readers (Minnetonka, MN), 2008.

Lara Bergen, *Don't Throw That Away!: A Lift-the-flap Book about Recycling and Reusing,* Little Simon (New York, NY), 2009.

Lily's Potty, Begin Smart (Maplewood, NJ), 2010.

Pete's Potty, Begin Smart (Maplewood, NJ), 2010.

Work included in *Society of Illustrators Annual,* 2006, 2007.

Sidelights

Betsy Snyder creates colorful artwork that appears on stickers and puzzles, games, gift wrap, and greeting cards in addition to picture books and board books. Beginning her book-illustration career in 2007, she has crafted art that brings to life tales by writers that include Laura Bergen, Dianne Ochiltree, and Brian P. Cleary. With her continued focus on children, Snyder has also created several original self-illustrated stories, among them *Haiku Baby, Have You Ever Tickled a Tiger?,* and *Sweet Dreams Lullaby.* In addition to her work in picture books, she is also the designer of the board game *Hoot Owl Hoot!,* which won a Dr. Toy Best Green Product award in 2011. "Snyder's cheery collages add some oomph to this hunt-for-the-word alphabet book," wrote a *Publishers Weekly* contributor in praise of the artist's first illustration project, Cleary's *Peanut Butter and Jellyfishes: A Very Silly Alphabet Book.*

In *Haiku Baby* Snyder captures the world that an infant experiences, where each bird, leaf, and snowflake is something new to be discovered. Her text, written in the Japanese poetic form called haiku, uses seventeen syllables to crystallize each of these experience and is

paired with Snyder's colorful collage art. In *Have You Ever Tickled a Tiger?* she presents a new version of the classic "pat the bunny" theme, while in *Sweet Dreams Lullaby* a sleeping bunny rabbit shares its dreams of its cozy meadow world, where fluffy dandelions, chirping frogs, fuzzy caterpillars, and bright blue robins eggs all add color, texture, and sound. Praising *Sweet Dreams Lullaby* as "a soothing bedtime story with just the right amount of sweetness," *Booklist* critic Rebecca Wojahn also cited Snyder's "charming collage artwork." "The language is rich and evocative, drawing on listeners' sense of memory," noted Hope Morrison in her review of the same story for the *Bulletin of the Center for Children's Books,* and a *Kirkus Reviews* writer commended Snyder's "digitally produced art" for featuring "a rich, soothing palette befitting the gentle cadence" of her nighttime tale.

Biographical and Critical Sources

PERIODICALS

Booklist, December 15, 2009, Rebecca Wojahn, review of *Sweet Dreams Lullaby,* p. 46.

Bulletin of the Center for Children's Books, February, 2010, Hope Morrison, review of *Sweet Dreams Lullaby,* p. 261.

Kirkus Reviews, December 15, 2009, review of *Sweet Dreams Lullaby.*

Publishers Weekly, April 9, 2007, review of *Peanut Butter and Jellyfishes: A Very Silly Alphabet Book,* p. 52.

School Library Journal, May, 2007, June Wolfe, review of *Peanut Butter and Jellyfishes,* p. 114; February, 2010, Lauralyn Persson, review of *Sweet Dreams Lullaby,* p. 96.

Snyder pairs her colorful art with an engaging bedtime story in **Sweet Dreams Lullaby.** (Illustration copyright © 2010 by Betsy Snyder. Reproduced by permission of Random House Children's Books, a division of Random House, Inc.)

ONLINE

Betsy Snyder Home Page, http://www.betsysnyder.com (May 15, 2011).
Betsy Snyder Web log, http://betsysnyder.blogspot.com (May 15, 2011).
Painted Words Web site, http://www.painted-words.com/ (May 15, 2011), "Betsy Snyder."*

*   *   *

STAMATY, Mark Alan 1947-

Personal

Born August 1, 1947, in Brooklyn, NY; son of Stanley (an artist) and Clara (an artist) Stamaty. *Education:* Cooper Union, B.F.A., 1969.

Addresses

Home—New York, NY. *Agent*—Sheldon Fogelman, 10 E. 40th St., New York, NY 10016. *E-mail*—markstamaty@earthlink.net.

Career

Writer and artist. Formerly worked as a taxi driver, cabana boy at beach club, camp counselor, file clerk, and snack bar attendant. *Time* magazine, New York, NY, political cartoonist, 1994-96. *Exhibitions:* Work included in juried exhibitions, including Boston Printmakers Show, and at American Institute of Graphic Arts, 1975.

Awards, Honors

State Museum of New Jersey's Purchase Award; fine-art awards for etchings; citations from Brooklyn Museum and Brooklyn Public Library, 1973, for *Yellow, Yellow* by Frank Asch, and 1975, for *Who Needs Donuts?*; two gold medals, including 1974, and one silver medal, Society of Illustrators; Premio Satira Politica Forte Dei Marmi (Italy), 2005; Page One Award, Newspaper Guild of New York; Augustus Saint Gaudens Award for Career Achievement in Art, Cooper Union, 2007.

Writings

SELF-ILLUSTRATED; FOR CHILDREN

Who Needs Donuts?, Dial (New York, NY), 1973, reprinted, Alfred A. Knopf (New York, NY), 2003.
Small in the Saddle, Windmill Books (New York, NY), 1975.
Minnie Maloney and Macaroni, Dial (New York, NY), 1976.
Where's My Hippopotamus?, Dial (New York, NY), 1977.
Captain Fiddle's Yo-yo, 1978.

Too Many Time Machines; or, The Incredible Story of How I Went Back in Time, Met Babe Ruth, and Discovered the Secret of Home-Run Hitting, Viking (New York, NY), 1999.
Alia's Mission: Saving the Books of Iraq, Alfred A. Knopf (New York, NY), 2004.
Shake, Rattle, and Turn That Noise Down!: How Elvis Shook Up Music, Me, and Mom, Knopf (New York, NY), 2010.

OTHER

(Illustrator) Frank Asch, *Yellow, Yellow*, McGraw (New York, NY), 1971.
MacDoodle Street (collected comics), introduction by Jules Feiffer, Congdon & Weed (New York, NY), 1980.
Washingtoon (collected comics), Congdon & Weed (New York, NY), 1983.
More Washingtoons (collected comics), Prentice Hall (New York, NY), 1986.

Creator of comic "Washingtoons" for *Village Voice*, then national syndication, 1981, and online comic "Doodlennium" for *Slate*. Creator of "Boox," for *New York Times Book Review*, 2001-03. Contributor to periodicals, including *Austin-American Statesman*, *Boston Globe*, *Esquire*, *Gentleman's Quarterly*, *Harper's*, *New Republic*, *Newsweek*, *New Yorker*, *New York Magazine*, *New York Times Magazine*, *Pittsburgh Post-Gazette*, *Playboy*, *Wall Street Journal*, and *Washington Post Magazine*, sometimes via syndication. Artwork selected for publication in *Communication Arts Annual* and *American Illustration Annual*.

Adaptations

"Washingtoons" inspired a cable television series that aired during the 1980s.

Sidelights

Beginning his career in the mid-1970s as a children's book illustrator, Mark Alan Stamaty eventually turned to cartoons. During the 1980s and 1990s his satirical "MacDoodle Street" and "Washingtoon" strips entertained readers of the *Village Voice* as well as *Time* and other magazines after they went into syndication. Stamaty's first picture book, 1973's *Who Needs Donuts?*, features complex and highly detailed illustrations that have been credited for inspiring the "Where Is Waldo?" phenomenon of more recent year; considered a cult comix classic, it was re-released in a thirtieth-anniversary edition. Other books for children include *Alia's Mission: Saving the Books of Iraq* and *Shake, Rattle, and Turn That Noise Down!: How Elvis Shook up Music, Me, and Mom*, the latter an entertaining memoir of Stamaty's preteen years.

Stamaty was raised in Elberon, New Jersey, in a creative household; his father, Stanley Stamaty, created humor cartoons for a living while his mother, Clara Gee

Mark Alan Stamaty reaches back to his childhood love affair with Elvis Presley in creating his picture book Shake, Rattle, and Turn That Noise Down! (Illustration copyright © 2010 by Mark Alan Stamaty. Reproduced by permission of Alfred A. Knopf, an imprint of Random House Children's Books, a division of Random House, Inc.)

Stamaty, was a painter and illustrator. Not surprisingly, Mark also opted for a career in art and he earned his B.F.A. from New York City's prestigious and highly competitive Cooper Union in 1969. His first illustration project was creating art for Frank Asch's picture book *Yellow, Yellow,* and more book projects followed over the coming years, including *Who Needs Donuts?, Small in the Saddle, Minnie Maloney and Macaroni, Where's My Hippopotamus?,* and *Captain Fiddle's Yo-yo.*

In 1981 Stamaty left children's books and began creating cartoons for the *Village Voice* that featured New York City landmarks; popular with local readers, these large-scale cartoons were also featured on posters. His first comic strip, "MacDoodle Street," came next, followed by "Washingtoons," which focused on politics from a national rather than local level. Based on Stamaty's in-depth research of national politics, "Washingtoons" is memorable for its character Congressman Bob Forehead, who was based on President John F. Kennedy. Eventually syndicated to dozens of newspapers around the United States, "Washingtoons" also became the basis of several book-length comics collections as well as a cable television series.

After chronicling the foibles of local and national politics as well as other current issues for several decades, Stamaty returned to children's fiction with the graphic novel *Alia's Mission.* Based on a true story, *Alia's Mission* focuses on Alia Muhammad Baker, a woman whose passion for books led her to become chief librarian in Basra, Iraq. When she became aware of the imminent invasion of the city in 2003, Baker requested permission to remove prized books from the library for safekeeping. Although the Iraqi government denied her request, she acted anyway, ultimately relocating 30,000 books to the homes of private Iraqi citizens before bombs began falling on Basra. In what a *Publishers Weekly* contributor described as "crisp" ink-and-wash sequential images, Stamaty "effectively captures the danger of the moment" and his "text conveys the intense emotions" of his subject, "from anguish to sorrow to joy." Also commending *Alia's Mission, Booklist* critic Jennifer Mattson compared the book to Art Spiegelman's graphic-novel classic *Maus,* calling Stamaty's work "sophisticated and timely," while a *Kirkus Reviews* writer cited the cartoonist's "straightforward, slightly exaggerated graphic style."

Another book for children, *Shake, Rattle, and Turn That Noise Down!,* takes readers back to the mid-1950s, as eight-year-old Stamaty receives his first radio and discovers the high-energy music that inspired the term "rock and roll." His first '45 purchase, Elvis Presley's "Love Me Tender," shocked his mother when "Hound Dog" proved to be on the "B" side. The woman realizes that she has lost her third-grade son to the rockabilly sound when the young Stamaty pompadours his hair and practices his version of The King in preparation for his school's upcoming talent show. In *Publishers Weekly* a contributor characterized *Shake, Rattle, and Turn That Noise Down!* as a "comic-book-style trip down memory lane" that treats readers to "a pantheon of rock and blues musicians from Bill Haley to Bo Diddley." Stamaty's story will also be helpful to older adults trying to explain their own musical coming of age to today's teens, noted Ian Chipman, the *Booklist* reviewer going on to recommend the full-color graphic-novel/memoir as an aid in "mak[ing] . . . a convincing case that an old, dead singer really was cool."

"I believe in trying to save the earth from pollution and garbage [and] in other things too numerous to name and difficult to explain," Stamaty once commented. "Then, of course, I believe in my art, in self-expression, and in creativity. I hope these things will always be at the center of my life, unless something better comes along. But what I'm doing now gives me considerable joy at times. My motivation is a deep desire to live and feel alive."

Biographical and Critical Sources

PERIODICALS

Booklist, February 1, 2005, Jennifer Mattson, review of *Alia's Mission: Saving the Books of Iraq,* p. 958; November 1, 2009, Ian Chipman, review of *Shake, Rattle, and Turn That Noise Down!: How Elvis Shook up Music, Me, and Mom,* p. 59.

Bulletin of the Center for Children's Books, February, 2005, Elizabeth Bush, review of *Alia's Mission,* p. 266; February, 2010, Elizabeth Bush, review of *Shake, Rattle and Turn That Noise Down!,* p. 262.

Horn Book, March-April, 2005, Susan Dove Lempke, review of *Alia's Mission,* p. 218; March-April, 2010, Roger Sutton, review of *Shake, Rattle, and Turn That Noise Down!,* p. 81.

Kirkus Reviews, January 1, 2005, review of *Alia's Mission,* p. 57; December 1, 2009, review of *Shake, Rattle, and Turn That Noise Down!*

New York Times Book Review, April 9, 2010, Julie Just, review of *Shake, Rattle, and Turn That Noise Down!,* p. 15.

Publishers Weekly, December 8, 2003, review of *Who Needs Donuts?,* p. 63; December 20, 2004, review of *Alia's Mission,* p. 59; December 14, 2009, review of *Shake, Rattle, and Turn That Noise Down!,* p. 57.

School Library Journal, March, 2005, Hillias J. Martin, review of *Alia's Mission,* p. 239; May, 2010, Barbara Elleman, review of *Shake, Rattle, and Turn That Noise Down!,* p. 142.

ONLINE

Mark Alan Stamaty Home Page, http://markstamaty.com (May 21, 2011).*

* * *

SYLVER, Adrienne

Personal

Born in IN; married; husband's name Mike; children: two. *Education:* Ashland College (now Ashland University), B.S.; Ohio University, M.S. (magazine journalism). *Hobbies and other interests:* Reading, traveling, walking, swimming, listening to music, spending time with friends and family.

Addresses

Home—Miami, FL. *Agent*—John Rudolph, Dystel & Goderich; jrudolph@dystel.com. *E-mail*—adsylver@bellsouth.net.

Career

Writer and journalist. Former reporter for daily newspapers, including *Miami News;* Baptist Hospital of Miami (now Baptist Health), public-relations writer beginning c. 1990s. Presenter at schools.

Member

Society of Children's Book Writers and Illustrators (member of Florida chapter).

Writings

Hot Diggity Dog: The History of the Hot Dog, illustrated by Elwood H. Smith, Dutton Children's Books (New York, NY), 2010.

Contributor to periodicals, including *South Florida Parenting.*

Sidelights

Born in Indiana and raised in Ohio, Adrienne Sylver eventually opted for the warmer weather of Florida, where she now makes her home. Sylver channeled her natural curiosity into a career as a journalist, earning both a bachelor's and master's degree in the subject. She worked for a series of ever-larger Florida newspapers before leaving the journalism field for a more-satisfying job in public relations. The instincts that made Sylvera good reporter never left her, however, and an interesting factual tidbit she heard while listening to the radio ultimately led to her first children's book, *Hot Diggity Dog: The History of the Hot Dog.*

In addition to enjoying the humorous artwork by Elwood H. Smith, readers of *Hot Diggity Dog* will come away with a gold-mine of hot-dog-related trivia. From its controversial beginnings (both Germany and Austria claim to have created the popular sausage, but ancient Rome may have developed it first) to its role at the forefront of twentieth-century popular culture—think ballparks, backyard cookouts, the Wienermobile, and the popular hot-dog stand—the hot dog also has regional variants, as Sylver shows in her comprehensive guide. "Fun facts fly fast and furious," noted Daniel Kraus in his *Booklist* review of *Hot Diggity Dog,* the critic adding that the "visual chaos" Smith creates on each page "is intentional and plays into the mustard-stained mitts" of Sylver's hot-dog-loving readership. A *Publishers Weekly* critic dubbed the culinary triviafest "an energetic combination of history and food for thought," while in *School Library Journal* Marge Loch-Wouters recommended *Hot Diggity Dog* as "the perfect browsable title about that quintessential kid food."

"I wasn't one of those kids who knew at the age of four what she wanted to be . . . ," Sylver admitted on her home page in discussing her road to becoming a published writer. "It really wasn't until my junior year [in college], when a teacher suggested I do some freelance pieces for the local newspaper, that I found my niche. I liked interviewing people and writing about them." In addition to enjoying interviews, Sylver also enjoys reading. "By reading, you're also learning the musicality of writing," she maintained, explaining the similarity between reading prose and listening to music. "There is a certain rhythm and style to both, a building of emotion and tension, highs and lows. There's a flow to dialogue. And, for those who really analyze what they read (which, truthfully, is not usually me), there's a lot to be learned about plotting, themes, the bigger picture of a novel."

Biographical and Critical Sources

PERIODICALS

Booklist, April 15, 2010, Daniel Kraus, review of *Hot Diggity Dog: The History of the Hot Dog,* p. 48.

Bulletin of the Center for Children's Books, May, 2010, Deborah Stevenson, review of *Hot Diggity Dog,* p. 402.

Publishers Weekly, May 3, 2010, review of *Hot Diggity Dog,* p. 50.

School Library Journal, June, 2010, Marge Loch-Wouters, review of *Hot Diggity Dog,* p. 91.

ONLINE

Adrienne Sylver Home Page, http://www.adriennesylver. com (May 27, 2011).

Cynsations Web log, http://cynthialeitichsmith.blogspot. com/ (May 13, 2010), Cynthia Leitich Smith, interview with Sylver.*

T

TELLER, Janne 1964-

Personal
Born April 8, 1964, in Copenhagen, Denmark. *Education:* Degree (macroeconomics). *Hobbies and other interests:* Reading, walking, opera, travel, thoughtful conversations with friends.

Addresses
Home—Copenhagen, Denmark. *Agent*—Lars Ringhof Agency, Nybrogade 22, DK-1203, Copenhagen, Denmark. *E-mail*—mail@janneteller.dk.

Career
Economic consultant and author. Consultant in humanitarian and conflict resolution for the European Union and the United Nations in Dar-es-Salaam, Brussels, New York, and in Mozambique, until 1995; consultant. currently freelance writer.

Awards, Honors
Danish Cultural Ministry prize, 2001, and Prix Libbylit (France), 2008, both for *Intet;* Michael L. Printz Honor Book designation, 2011, for *Nothing.*

Writings

FICTION

Odins ø (novel), Forlaget Centrum (Denmark), 1999, translated by Anne Born as *Odin's Island,* 2006.

Intet, Dansklørerforeningens Forlag (Denmark), 2000, translated by Martin Aitken as *Nothing,* Atheneum Books for Young Readers (New York, NY), 2010.

Hvis der var krig i Norden (essay; title means "If Scandinavia Were at War Where Would You Go?), illustrated by Helle Vibeke Jensen, Dansklørerforeningens Forlag (Denmark), 2004.

Kattens tramp (novel), Gyldendal (Copenhagen, Denmark), 2004.

Kom (novel), Gyldendal (Copenhagen, Denmark), 2008.

Author's work has been translated into French, German, Spanish, and Swedish.

OTHER

(Editor with Sven Holm and Thomas Rasmussen) *Skriv din Satan, 25 forfattere om at vøre forfatter* (anthology: title means "Write Your Devil: 25 Writers on Being a Writer"), People's Press (Denmark), 2004.

Contributor of essays and short stories to periodicals, including *Politiken, Corriere della Serra, Danish Teachers, Informacion, Le Monde de l'Education, Lettre Internationale,* and *Strand,* and to anthologies.

Adaptations
Film rights to *Nothing* were sold to Crone Film, for adaptation into an animated movie.

Sidelights
Award-winning Danish writer Janne Teller is know for her existential and often controversial fiction, which includes novels for adults and teens as well as essays and the coauthored writer's anthology *Skriv din Satan, 25 forfattere om at vøre forfatter.* Published in English translation as *Odin's Island, Odins ø* examines political and religious extremism, while *Kattens tramp* tells a love story set in the Balkans during the war-torn 1990. Reviewing *Odins ø* in *World Literature Today,* Lanae Hjortsvang Isaacson described Teller's novel as "an intriguing, often amusing blend of Nordic mythology and poetry, modern love story, biting social satire, political and religious intrigue, and pure fantasy, all woven into an irresistible narrative that makes no claim on reality or social realism but shares a world of mystery and imaginary adventure with the reader."

Born in Copenhagen, Denmark, Teller earned a degree in macroeconomics. During her career she aided the efforts of multinational organizations such as the United Nations and the European Union in resolving conflicts involving humanitarian concerns in countries such as Bangladesh, Mozambique, and Tanzania. In 1995 Teller made the decision to change her focus: she left her work as an economist and channeled her creative talents as a writer. Four years later she published *Odins ø*, and she continues to write, working from her home in Copenhagen as well as from residences in international cities such as New York City and Paris.

Teller's first book for a teen readership, *Intet*, was made available to English-language readers as *Nothing* and features her characteristic focus on existence through its dispassionate narration by a girl named Agnes. The novel's main character is seventh grader Pierre Anthon, who attends Tring School. Shortly after arriving on the first day of class, Pierre gets up from his desk and announces to his classmates that life has no meaning but is only a slow progression toward death. After Pierre walks from the room and out of the building, his classmates follow and find him sitting in a plum tree. Endeavoring to prove to their skeptical friend wrong and that there are reasons to live for, the seventh graders decide to assemble physical objects that prove their point. Each will bring an object that another has chosen, they reason, but this flawed process is quickly distorted as harmful requests are made, feelings are hurt, and revenge becomes the students' primary objective.

Nothing "is horrifying, and draws obvious comparison to William Golding's *Lord of the Flies*," noted Johanna Lewis in *School Library Journal*, the critic citing Agnes's "methodical telling" for helping to "set . . . the shocking events in high relief." "The matter-of-fact, ruthlessly logical amorality of these teens is chilling," wrote a *Kirkus Reviews* writer, although Teller's prose is "gorgeously lyrical . . . and dreadfully bleak." Calling *Nothing* a "haunting novel," a *Publishers Weekly* critic recommended Teller's work to sophisticated teens looking for "a provocative and challenging parable about human instability," while *Booklist* critic Daniel Kraus dubbed Teller's novel "indelible, elusive, and timeless," with "all the marks of a classic." "The terse purposefulness of her prose may put off some readers," Kraus added of *Nothing*, "but that singularity is also what will endure the test of time."

Biographical and Critical Sources

PERIODICALS

Booklist, December 1, 2009, Daniel Kraus, review of *Nothing*, p. 44.
Daily Telegraph (London, England), January 13, 2007, John Courtenay Grimwood, review of *Odin's Island*, p. 28.

Kirkus Reviews, January 15, 2010, review of *Nothing*.
Publishers Weekly, January 4, 2010, review of *Nothing*, p. 48.
School Library Journal, April, 2010, Johanna Lewis, review of *Nothing*, p. 169.
World Literature Today, winter, 2001, Lanae Hjortsvang Isaacson, review of *Odins ø*, p. 154.

ONLINE

Janne Teller Home Page, http://www.janneteller.dk (May 27, 2011).
Simon & Schuster Web site, http://authors.simonand schuster.com/ (May 15, 2011), "Janne Teller."*

*　　　*　　　*

TORRES, J. 1969-
(Joseph Torres)

Personal

Born 1969, in Manila, Philippines; immigrated to Canada; married; children: one son. *Education:* McGill University, degree.

Addresses

Home—Toronto, Ontario, Canada.

Career

Writer and author of television scripts. Former teacher of English as a second language; former staff writer for "Rugrat" syndicated comic strip.

Awards, Honors

Harvey Award nomination, 2001, for "Sidekicks"; Eisner Award nomination for Best Title for Young Readers, 2003, for "Alison Dare"; Shuster Award for Outstanding Canadian Writer, 2006; YALSA/American Library Association Best Graphic Novel selection, 2004, for *Days like This*, and 2010, for *Lola: A Love Story*.

Writings

GRAPHIC NOVELS

Sidekicks: The Transfer Student (originally published in comic-book form, beginning 2002), illustrated by Takeshi Miyazawa, Oni Press (Portland, OR), 2003.
Jason and the Argobots (originally published in comic-book form, beginning 2002), two volumes, illustrated by Mike Norton, Oni Press (Portland, OR), 2003.
Days like This, illustrated by Scott Chantler, Oni Press (Portland, OR), 2002.

(Adaptor) Hong-seok Seo, *Dragon Hunter* (originally published in comic-book form), translated by Hye-Young Im, Volumes 9-15, Tokyopop, 2004–2006.

Scandalous, illustrated by Scott Chantler, Oni Press (Portland, OR), 2004.

Love as a Foreign Language, illustrated by Eric Kim, two volumes, Oni Press (Portland, OR), 2005–2006.

Blinded by the Light, illustrated by Kevin MacKenzie, Scholastic (New York, NY), 2005.

Raven's Secret, illustrated by Kevin MacKenzie, Scholastic (New York, NY), 2005.

(Adaptor) Lee YoungYou, *Moon Boy,* ICE Kunion (Seoul, Korea), 2006.

(With Bill Matheny) *Duty Calls,* illustrated by Christopher Jones and Terry Beatty, D.C. Comics (New York, NY), 2007.

Missing You, illustrated by Eric Kim, Pocket Books (New York, NY), 2007.

(With Tony Bedard) *Green Arrow and Black Canary: Road to the Altar,* illustrated by Paulo Siqueira and others, D.C. Comics (New York, NY), 2008.

Blue Beetle: Reach for the Stars, illustrated by Rafael Albuquerque, David Baldeon, and Freddie Williams II, D.C. Comics (New York, NY), 2008.

Recharge, illustrated by Morgan Luthi, Boom Kids (Los Angeles, CA), 2010.

(With Matt Wayne) *Batman: The Brave and the Bold* (originally published in comic-book form, beginning 2010), illustrated by Andy Suriano, Phil Moy, and Carlo Barberi, D.C. Comics (New York, NY), 2010.

Lola: A Ghost Story, illustrated by Elbert Or, Oni Press (Portland, OR), 2010.

Contributor to comic-book series, including (with Tom Levins) "The CopyBook Tales," (with Levins) "Siren," "Monster Fighters, Inc.," "Noble Causes," "Robo Dojo," "X-Men Unlimited," "X-Men: Ronin," "Black Panther," "Cannon Busters," "The Batman Strikes!," "Ninja Scroll," "The Legion of Super-Heroes in the 31st Century," "Blue Beetkle," "Wonder Woman," "Wonder Girl," "Green Arrow/Black Canary," "Batman: The Brave and the Bold," "Wall-E," "Jinx," and "Life with Archie." Contributor to anthologies *9-11: Artists Respond,* Dark Horse Comics, 2002, and *Avatar: The Last Airbender,* Dark Horse Comics, 2011. Contributor to periodicals, including *Nickelodeon.* Editor for comic books; penciller for comic-book series "Gespenster Geschichten," 1974. Writer for animated comics *Hi Hi Puffy Ami Yumi, Edgar and Ellen,* and *League of Super Evil.*

Author's works have been translated into French.

"ALISON DARE" GRAPHIC-NOVEL SERIES; ILLUSTRATED BY J. BONE

Alison Dare, Little Miss Adventures (originally published in comic-book form, beginning 2001; also see below), Volume I, Oni Press (Portland, OR), 2002, revised edition, Tundra Books (Toronto, Ontario, Canada), 2010.

Alison Dare, Little Miss Adventures (originally published in comic-book form, beginning 2001; also see below), Volume II, Oni Press (Portland, OR), 2005.

Alison Dare and the Heart of the Maiden (originally published in comic-book form, beginning 2002), Tundra Books (Toronto, Ontario, Canada), 2010.

"TEEN TITANS" GRAPHIC-NOVEL SERIES

Teen Titans Go!: Truth, Justice, Pizza? (originally published in comic-book form, beginning 2004), illustrated by Todd Nauck, D.C. Comics (New York, NY), 2004.

Teen Titans Go!: Bring It On! (originally published in comic-book form), illustrated by Todd Nauck and Lary Stucker, D.C. Comics (New York, NY), 2005.

Teen Titans Go!: Ready for Action! (originally published in comic-book form), illustrated by Todd Nauck, D.C. Comics (New York, NY), 2005.

Teen Titans Go!: On the Move! (originally published in comic-book form), illustrated by Sean Galloway, D.C. Comics (New York, NY), 2006.

Teen Titans Spotlight: Wonder Girl, D.C. Comics (New York, NY), 2008.

"DEGRASSI, THE NEXT GENERATION" GRAPHIC NOVEL SERIES; BASED ON THE TELEVISION SERIES

Degrassi, the Next Generation: Extra Credit: Turning Japanese, illustrated by Ed Northcott, Pocket Books (New York, NY), 2006.

Degrassi, the Next Generation: Extra Credit: Suddenly Last Summer, illustrated by Ramón Pérez, Fenn Publishing (Bolton, Ontario, Canada), 2006, Pocket Books (New York, NY), 2007.

Degrassi, the Next Generation: Extra Credit: Safety Dance, illustrated by Steve Rolston, Pocket Books (New York, NY), 2007.

Sidelights

Born in the Philippines but now living and working in Ontario, Canada, J. Torres, is an award-winning author and editor of comic books and graphic novels. Gearing much of his work for younger readers, Torres has produced the popular "Teen Titans Go!" and "Alison Dare" comic-book series, both of which have been collected and published in graphic-novel format. He has alternated his work for younger readers with mainstream comic-book series featuring characters such as Batman, Blue Beetle, and Wonder Woman. His comics have also appeared in child-centered magazines as well as in daily newspapers, and he was one of several staff writers for the "Rugrats" comic strip. "I like writing in different genres," Torres explained to *Publishers Weekly* online interviewer Brigid Alverson. "I like writing for different audiences. I suppose one could say that my work in comics is as eclectic as my tastes and likes in the comics I read. Hopefully, most people are saying the work is good, and that's what all my different books have in common."

Torres was born in Manila and raised in Montréal, Québec, where he attended McGill University. He worked as an ESL instructor before linking up with longtime friend and artist Tim Levins to create several comic-book stories, among them the semi-autobiographical "Copybook Tales" and the three-part "Siren." His popular "Alison Dare" series, a collaboration with sequential artist and fellow Toronto resident J. Bone, is geared for young readers and has been republished as the graphic-novels *Alison Dare, Little Miss Adventures* and *Alison Dare and the Heart of the Maiden.* The series was inspired by Torres' love of early-twentieth-century Belgian cartoonist Hergé's classic comic strip "Tintin" as well as by the "Nancy Drew" and "Hardy Boys" novels and the *Johnny Quest* television cartoon series he remembers watching as a child.

In addition to "Alison Dare," Torres has also written graphic novels such as *Love as a Foreign Language, Days like This,* and *Lola: A Ghost Story,* as well as a comic-book series based on the popular late-'80s-to-early-'90s television series *Degrassi Junior High* and *Degrassi High,* all which are geared for older teens and deal with adolescent issues and interpersonal relationships. *Lola* is set in Torres' native Philippines and focuses on a teenager whose visit to the home of his late grandmother is haunted by dreams, visions, and unsettling memories from early childhood. Set in New York City during the early 1960s, *Days like This* focuses on talented teens whose dreams of becoming the next singing star on A.M. radio are on their way to being realized. Paired with what a *Publishers Weekly* critic described as Scott Chantler's "simple, cute and clean-lined" drawings, Torres crafts a "charming" story that makes *Days like This* "quick entertainment for younger teens." In *Library Journal* Steve Raiteri recommended the same graphic novel for "fans of 'Archie' comics, Trina Robbins' 'Go Girl,' or Sixties pop music," noting that Torres' "simple story packs . . . a wealth of period detail" into the live of its characters.

J. Torres teams up with sequential artist J. Bone to introduce an adventurous preteen heroine in the comic books published in graphic-novel format as **Alison Dare and the Heart of the Maiden.** (Illustration copyright © 2010 by J. Bone. Reproduced by permission of Tundra Books.)

Some of Torres' works for older readers focus on humor, such as "Teen Titans Go!," which D.C. Comics ran for fifty-five issues after fans demanded seven extra installments. In "Sidekicks," which was collected into the graphic novel *Sidekicks: The Transfer Student*, a super-strong teen enrolls in a training academy that teaches her the skills needed to be a superhero sidekick. "Written in the universal language of youth trapped in high-school hell," according to a *Publishers Weekly* critic, *Sidekicks* mixes Takeshi Miyazawa's "ultra-hip" line art with Torres' "heartfelt, smart-ass dialogue" to create "a fluid dance between sweetness and sass."

Biographical and Critical Sources

PERIODICALS

Kirkus Reviews, April 15, 2010, review of *Alison Dare and the Heart of the Maiden.*

Library Journal, September 1, 2003, Steve Raiteri, review of *Days like This,* p. 143.

Library Media Connection, April, 2003, review of *The Collected Alison Dare: Little Miss Adventures,* p. 18; November-December, 2008, Nelda Brangwin, review of *Legion of Super-Heroes in the 31st Century: Tomorrow's Heroes,* p. 81.

Publishers Weekly, June 9, 2003, review of *Sidekicks: The Transfer Student,* p. 38; September 29, 2003, review of *Days like This,* p. 46; June 14, 2010, review of *Alison Dare: Little Miss Adventures,* p. 55.

School Library Journal, May, 2010, Andrea Lipinski, review of *A Ghost Story,* p. 143; September, 2010, Sarah Provence, review of *Alison Dare: Little Miss Adventures,* p. 180.

Teacher Librarian, February, 2005, Michele Gorman, review of *Teen Titans Go! Truth, Justice, Pizza?,* p. 24; February, 2009, Joe Sutliff Sanders, review of *Revising Superheroes,* p. 57.

Voice of Youth Advocates, February, 2007, Kat Kan, review of *Love as a Foreign Language,* p. 517; April, 2010, Lynne Farrell Stover, review of *Lola: A Ghost Story,* p. 76.

ONLINE

Bildungsroman Web log, http://slayground.livejournal.com/ (June 18, 2010), interview with Torres and J. Bone.

J. Torres Home Page, http://www.jtorresonline.com (May 27, 2011).

Publishers Weekly Online, http://www.publishersweekly.com/ (March 22, 2010), Brigid Alverson, interview with Torres.*

* * *

TORRES, Joseph
See TORRES, J.

U-Y

UNZNER, Christa 1958-
(Christa Unzner-Fischer)

Personal

Born March 4, 1958, in Schoneiche, East Germany (now Germany); daughter of Heinz (a graphic artist) and Thea (a graphic artist) Unzner; married Peter Fischer Sternaux (a graphic artist), September 18, 1982 (divorced, 1991); married second husband. *Education:* Attended Berlin School of Advertising and Design, 1976-79. *Hobbies and other interests:* Literature, music, traveling.

Addresses

Home and office—The Hague, Netherlands. *E-mail*—1@christa-unzner.de.

Career

Illustrator of books for children. Dewag Werbung (advertising agency), Berlin, Germany, graphic artist for three years; freelance illustrator, beginning 1982; Nord-Süd Verlag, Gossau, Switzerland, illustrator, beginning 1991. *Exhibitions:* Work included in solo and group exhibitions in Germany, France, Poland, and Czechoslovakia.

Awards, Honors

Wettbewerb award for children's illustrations; Schonste Buchere award.

Writings

SELF-ILLUSTRATED

(Under name Christa Unzner-Fischer) *Im Spielzeugland,* Der Kinderbuchverlag (Berlin, West Germany), 1985.

ILLUSTRATOR; UNDER NAME CHRISTA UNZNER-FISCHER

Jurij Brezan, *Die Reise nach Krakau,* Verlag Neues Leben (Berlin, West Germany), 1982.

Karl Mundstock, *Ali und die Bande vom Lauseplatz,* Der Kinderbuchverlag (Berlin, West Germany), 1982.

Erna Linde and Günter Linde, *Liebe geht durch den Magen,* Verlag Neues Leben (Berlin, West Germany), 1982.

Das Malvenhaus (anthology), Der Kinderbuchverlag (Berlin, West Germany), 1983.

Von Witzbolden, Spaßvögeln und Schelmen (anthology), Verlag Neues Leben (Berlin, West Germany), 1983.

Uta Mauersberger, *Die Geschichte vom Plumpser,* Der Kinderbuchverlag (Berlin, West Germany), 1984.

Arthur Schnitzler, *Therese,* Verlag Neues Leben (Berlin, West Germany), 1985.

Elisabeth Hering, *Kostbarkeiten aus dem deutschen Märchenschatz,* Altberliner (Berlin, Germany), 1985.

Günter Preuss, *Feen sterben nicht,* Der Kinderbuchverlag (Berlin, West Germany), 1985.

Heinrich Hoffmann von Fallersleben, *Kitzlein, Spitzlein und Fritzlein,* Der Kinderbuchverlag (Berlin, West Germany), 1985.

Der Fuchs und die Weintrauben (fable), Altberliner (Berlin, Germany), 1985.

Hanna Kuenzel, *Vom Jörg, der Zahnweh hatte,* Der Kinderbuchverlag (Berlin, West Germany), 1986.

Mein Vater, meine Mutter (anthology), Verlag Neues Leben (Berlin, West Germany), 1986.

Dunkel wars, der Mond schien helle (nursery rhymes), Altberliner (Berlin, West Germany), 1987, reprinted, 2010.

Gerhard Dahne, *Kostbarkeiten aus dem deutschen Sagenschatz,* Altberliner (Berlin, West Germany), 1987.

Daumengroß und starker Hans (fairy tale), Der Kinderbuchverlag (Berlin, West Germany), 1988.

Uta Mauersberger, *Kleine Hexe Annabell,* Der Kinderbuchverlag (Berlin, West Germany), 1988.

Liebeszauber (anthology), Verlag Tribune, 1988.

Reinhard Griebner, *Himmelhochjauchzend Zutodebetrübt,* Der Kinderbuchverlag (Berlin, West Germany), 1989.

Heinz Kahlau, *Die Häsin Paula,* Verlag Junge Welt (Berlin, West Germany), 1989.

Der Mond ist aufgegangen (lullaby), Altberliner (Berlin, West Germany), 1989.

Ruth Zechlin, *Eine Kuh, die saß im Schwalbennest* (lullaby), Verlag Edition Peters (Leipzig, West Germany), 1989.

Leo Lenvers, *Jean-le-Niais,* Edition Nathan (Paris, France), 1990.

Genevieve Laurencin, *Un gros ballon tout petit,* Edition Nathan (Paris, France), 1991.

Barbara Haupt, *Mein Bruder Joscha,* Hoch Verlag (Stuttgart, Germany), 1991.

Gebüder Grimm, *Blanche Neige,* Edition Nathan (Paris, France), 1992.

Anneliese Probst, *Märchen und Sagen aus dem Harz,* Altberliner (Berlin, Germany), 1992.

Anneliese Probst, *Sagen und Märchen aus Thüringen,* Altberliner (Berlin, Germany), 1992.

Joachïm Walter, *Kuddelmuddelkunterbunt und Ausserüberordentlich,* Der Kinderbuchverlag (Berlin, Germany), 1992.

Gerda Marie Scheidl, *Loretta und die kleine Fee,* Nord-Süd (Gossau, Switzerland), 1992, translated by J. Alison James as *Loretta and the Little Fairy,* North-South (New York, NY), 1992.

Hermann Moers, *Annis Traumtanz,* Nord-Süd (Zürich, Switzerland), 1992, translated by Rosemary Lanning as *Annie's Dancing Day,* North-South (New York, NY), 1992.

Ingrid Ostheeren, *Der echte Nikolaus bin ich,* Nord-Süd (Gossau, Switzerland), 1993, translated as *I Am the Real Santa Claus,* North-South (New York, NY), 1993.

Wolfram Hänel, *Waldemar und die weite Welt,* Nord-Süd (Zürich, Switzerland), 1993, translated by Alison James as *The Extraordinary Adventures of an Ordinary Hat,* North-South (New York, NY), 1994.

Andreas Greve, *Kluger kleiner Balthasar,* Nord-Süd (Zürich, Switzerland), 1994, translated as *Balthazar,* North-South (New York, NY), 1994.

Anne Braun, *Wihnachten ist en bald,* Arena Verlag (Würsburg, Germany), 1994.

Ingrid Ostheeren, *Martin hat keine Angst mehr,* Nord-Süd (Zürich, Switzerland), 1994, translated by J. Alison James as *Martin and the Pumpkin Ghost,* North-South (New York, NY), 1994.

ILLUSTRATOR

Alfred Könner, *Der Tanz auf der Trommel: Tiermärchen aus aller Welt,* Alberliner (Berlin, Germany), 1994.

Anneliese Probst, *Sagen und Märchen von der Insel Rügen,* Altberliner (Berlin, Germany), 1994.

Anneliese Probst, *Sagen und Märchen von der Nordsee,* Altberliner (Berlin, Germany), 1994.

Antonie Schneider, *Ich bin der kleine König,* Nord-Süd (Zürich, Switzerland), 1995.

Christa Zeuch, *Kitty kmmt zu spät zur Schule,* Arena Verlag (Würsburg, Germany), 1995.

Wolfram Hänel, *Romeo liebt Julia,* Nord-Süd (Zürich, Switzerland), 1995, translated by Rosemary Lanning as *Jasmine and Rex,* North-South (New York, NY), 1995.

Anneliese Probst, *Sagen und Märchen aus Sachsen,* Altberliner (Berlin, Germany), 1995.

Brigitte Jud, *Gänsebluümchen,* Ensslin-Verlag, 1995.

Jacob and Wilhelm Grimm, *Von Hexen, Feen und allerlei Zaubereien,* retold by Friedl Hofbauer, Annette Betz Verlag (Vienna, Austria), 1995.

Jacob and Wilhelm Grimm, *Von Schelmen und Glückskindern,* retold by Friedl Hofbauer, Annette Betz Verlag (Vienna, Austria), 1996.

Ursel Scheffler, *Der Spion unter dem Dach,* Nord-Süd (Zürich, Switzerland), 1996, translated as *The Spy in the Attic,* North-South (New York, NY), 1996.

Mari Osmundsen, *Das Königreigh Novemberland,* translated from the Norwegian by Dagmar Lendt, Herder (Vienna, Austria), 1996.

Dorothea Lachner, *Das ganz besondere Ostergeschenck,* Nord-Süd (Zürich, Switzerland), 1996, translated by Marianne Martens as *Smoky's Special Easter Present,* North-South (New York, NY), 1996.

Jacob and Wilhelm Grimm, *Tiermärchen,* retold by Friedl Hofbauer, Annette Betz Verlag (Vienna, Austria), 1997.

Eva Polak, *So ist das mit Opa,* Sauerländer (Aarau, Germany), 1997.

Hans Christian Andersen, *Die Schönsten Märchen,* Altberliner (Berlin, Germany), 1997.

Wolfram Hänel, *Anna Nass küsst Alexander!,* Nord-Süd (Zürich, Switzerland), 1997.

Georg Wieghaus, *Indianergeschichten,* Arena Verlag (Würsburg, Germany), 1997.

Dorothea Lachner, *Hexenfest für Merrilu,* Nord-Süd (Zürich, Switzerland), 1997 translated by J. Alison James as *Meredith, the Witch Who Wasn't,* North-South (New York, NY), 1997.

Eva Polak, *Nick steht Kopf,* Sauerländer (Aarau, Germany), 1998.

(With Harald Larisch) Juliane Neuhasen and Brunhild Sprandel, *ABC Reise: Eine Fibel,* Volk & Wissen (Berlin, Germany), 1998.

Virginia Allen Jensen, *Wo steckt der Teppichfelzer?,* Sauerländer (Aarau, Germany), 1998.

Anne Liersch, *Ein Haus für alle,* Nord-Süd (Zürich, Switzerland), 1999, translated by J. Alison James as *A House Is Not a Home,* North-South (New York, NY), 1999.

Allen Kurzweil, Das Geheimnis des Erfinders, Arena Verlag (Würsburg, Germany), 1999.

Ursel Scheffler, *Die Kinder ause der Schneemannstraße,* Kerle Verlag (Freiburg, Germany), 1999.

Ursel Scheffler, *Der Mann mit dem schwarzen Handschuh,* Nord-Süd (Zürich, Switzerland), 1999, translated by Rosemary Lanning as *The Man with the Black Glove,* North-South (New York, NY), 1999.

Gerda Marie Scheidl, *Das meue Schwesterchen,* Nord-Süd (Zürich, Switzerland), 1999, translated as *Tommy's New Sister,* North-South (New York, NY), 1999.

(With Peter Sternaux) Christian Morgenstern, *Morgenstern Kindergedichte,* Annette Betz Verlag (Vienna, Austria), 1999.

Dorothea Lachner, *Zauberspuk bei Merrilu,* Nord-Süd (Zürich, Switzerland), 2000 translated by J. Alison James as *Meredith's Mixed-up Magic,* North-South (New York, NY), 2000.

Anne Liersch, *Nele und Wuschel,* Nord-Süd (Zürich, Switzerland), 2000, translated by J. Alison James as *Nell and Fluffy,* North-South (New York, NY), 2001.

Jacob and Wilhelm Grimm, *Die beliebtesten Märchen der Gebrüder Grimm,* retold by Friedl Hofbauer, Annette Betz Verlag (Vienna, Austria), 2001.

Eva Angerer, *Viel Glück, kleiner Kater,* Nord-Süd (Zürich, Switzerland), 2001.

Miseha Damjan, *Der Clown sagte Nein,* Nord-Süd (Zürich, Switzerland), 2001, translated by Anthea Bell as *The Clown Said No,* North-South (New York, NY), 2001.

Wolfram Hänel, *Weekend with Grandmother,* North-South (New York, NY), 2002.

Udo Weigelt, *Marike wird die Geister los,* Nord-Süd (Zürich, Switzerland), 2002, translated by Marisa Miller as *Miranda's Ghosts,* North-South (New York, NY), 2002.

Jutta Treiber, *Rosa träumt,* Annette Betz Verlag (Vienna, Austria), 2002.

Dorothea Lachner, *Hexenzank mit Merrilu,* Nord-Süd (Gossau, Switzerland), 2003, translated by J. Alison James as *Meredith and Her Magical Book of Spells,* North-South Books (New York, NY), 2003.

Barbara Kinderman, *Romeo und Julia nach William Shakespeare,* Kinderman Verlag (Berlin, Germany), 2003, translated by J. Alison James as *William Shakespeare's Romeo and Juliet,* North-South Books (New York, NY), 2006.

Hans Christian Andersen, *Die Kleine Meerjungfrau,* Arena Verlag (Würsburg, Germany), 2004.

Maria Seidemann, *Was macht der Kater in der Nacht,* Coppenrath (Münster, Germany), 2004.

Sebastian Tonner, *Das Geheimnis der Heiligen Nacht,* Kaufmann Verlag (Berlin, Germany), 2004.

Hans Christian Andersen, *Die Schneeköningin,* Arena Verlag (Würsburg, Germany), 2005.

Gerdt von Bassewitx, reteller, *Peterchens Mondfahrt,* Arena Verlag (Würsburg, Germany), 2005.

Elisabeth Hewson, *Mozart und seine Opern* (with CD), Obv & Hpt., 2005.

Marie-Catherine d'Aulnoy, *Die weiße Katze,* Leiv-Verlag (Leipzig, Germany), 2006.

Barbara Kindermann, adaptor, *Das Käthchen von Heilbronn* (based on the story by Heinrich von Kleist), Kindermann Verlag (Berlin, Germany), 2006.

Simone Linder, *Wasserelfe Aelin,* Minedition (Bargteheide, Germany), 2007, translated as *Aelin the Water Fairy,* Minedition (New York, NY), 2008.

Simone Linder, *Luftelfe Tara,* Minedition (Bargteheide, Germany), 2007, translated as *Tara the Air Fairy,* Minedition (New York, NY), 2008.

Simone Linder, *Erdgono Amar,* Minedition (Bargteheide, Germany), 2007, translated as *Amar the Earth Fairy,* Minedition (New York, NY), 2007.

Die Alpabfahrt, Vaneck Verlag, 2007.

Karma Wilson, *Princess Me,* Margaret K. McElderry Books (New York, NY), 2007.

Ammi-Joan Paquette, *The Tiptoe Guide to Tracking Fairies,* Tanglewood (Terre Haute, IN), 2009.

Regina Fackelmayer, *Ein Weihnachtsbaum für Mia,* Nord-Süd (Gossau, Switzerland), 2009, translated as *The Gifts,* North-South (New York, NY), 2009.

Anna Xiulan Zeeck, *Kuku, König der Tierkreiszeichen,* Desina Verlag (Oldenburg, Germany), 2010.

Elisabeth Zöller and Brigitte Kolloch, *Heute ist alles erlaubt, oder? Kindergeburstag bei Marie und Max,* Kaufmann Verlag (Berlin, Germany), 2011.

Anna Xiulan Zeeck, *Nicki und der kleine chinesische Drache,* Desina Verlag (Oldenburg, Germany), 2011.

Illustrator of translations of English-language classics, including *Tristan and Isolde* and plays by William Shakespeare. Contributor of illustrations to German-language textbooks and reader series.

Books featuring Unzer's work have been translated into several languages, including French, Spanish, and Swedish.

ILLUSTRATOR; "USBORNE YOUNG READING" SERIES

Mary Sebag-Montefiore, adaptor, *Little Women* (based on the story by Louisa May Alcott), Usborne (London, England), 2006.

Karen Ball and Rosie Dickins, *Leonardo da Vinci,* Usborne (London, England), 2007.

Rosie Dickins, *Shakespeare,* Usborne (London, England), 2008.

Conrad Mason, reteller, *Macbeth,* Usborne (London, England), 2008.

Louie Stowell, reteller, *Hamlet,* Usborne (London, England), 2008.

Rosie Dickins, *Twelfth Night,* Usborne (London, England), 2009.

Rosie Dickins, *The Tempest,* Usborne (London, England), 2010.

Sidelights

Born in Germany but now making her home in the Netherlands, Christa Unzner is a prolific illustrator whose books for children are noted for their expressive characters and detailed backgrounds. Since 1995, Unzner (who first published under the name Unzner-Fischer) has illustrated books written by authors ranging from Wolfram Hanel and Udo Weigelt to Dorothea Lachner, Karma Wilson, Anne Liersch, and Regina Fackelmayer.

Raised in Schoeneiche near what was then East Berlin, Unzner "grew up painting and drawing," as she once told *SATA.* "I grew up in . . . a house with a large, beautiful garden. My parents, both graphic artists, gave my brother and me a very creative atmosphere and raised us up to think independently, which wasn't exactly easy, living . . . [in a communist country]. After school I did an apprenticeship as a window decorator and then studied at the School of Advertising and Design in Berlin. I studied there for one year under my father, who has had a very important influence on my life. He was my toughest critic and my strongest supporter. After my studies, I worked for three years in an advertising agency. Advertising didn't really interest me—I always wanted to illustrate picture books. So I started applying to various publishing companies, and since 1982 I have been working as a freelance illustrator.

Although many of Unzner's illustration projects feature texts in German, a large number have also been translated into English. Even William Shakespeare's plays benefit from Unzner's art; in Barbara Kinderman's retelling of *Romeo and Juliet,* for example, the bard's "timeless tale is retold in clear prose" and brought to life in sepia-toned "watercolor-and-pen illustrations [that] are well executed," according to *School Library Journal* contributor Nancy Menaldi-Scanlon.

In Hanel's *Jasmine and Rex,* a chapter-book variation on the Romeo and Juliet story, animals play all the roles in Unzner's "expressive pen-and-ink and watercolor illustrations," according to Linda Wicher in *School Library Journal.* Another story by Hanel, *Weekend with Grandmother,* focuses on a boy's quiet adventures with his grandmother. Here "Unzner's watercolor-over-ink sketches adorn every page and bring warmth and dimension to the story," observed a contributor to *Kirkus Reviews.*

With Lachner, Unzner has produced several gently scary books about Meredith, a very unusual witch. In *Meredith, the Witch Who Wasn't* crafty Meredith likes to make things with her hands, but that does not earn her any points with the other witches. To win their approval, she must learn to cast spells; but despite practicing, her spells never amount to much and she is eventually relieved of her status as witch. Then, one day, an elderly witch visits Meredith's tree house and, seeing how well she has managed to make everything herself,

Christa Unzner creates the detailed multimedia artwork that captures the fanciful nature of Ammi-Joan Paquette's **The Tiptoe Guide to Tracking Fairies.** (Illustration copyright © 2009 by Christa Unzner. Reproduced by permission of Tanglewood Press.)

returns Meredith's powers to her. In *Meredith's Mixed Up Magic* the hapless witch accidentally conjures up an uninvited guest, and the result is humorous mayhem when the two spell-casters square off. Unzner's "art is full of amusing details and captures the action fully," wrote *School Library Journal* reviewer Jeanne Clancy Watkins in a review of *Meredith's Mixed Up Magic,* while *School Library Journal* reviewer Lisa Smith praised *Meredith, the Witch Who Wasn't* as an "upbeat story" in which Unzner's "illustrations . . . are full of humorous details."

Unzner's art is also a feature of Anne Liersch's *A House Is Not a Home,* in which a group of animal friends decides to build a home for the impending winter until Badger steps in and takes charge, alienating everyone with his know-it-all attitude. Although the other animals decide to go off and build the kind of home they want to live in and leave Badger to himself, they welcome him back once he realizes the error of his ways. In Mischa Damjan's *The Clown Said No* the artist captures the energy of a group of circus performers that decides to leave the circus and create its own travelling show. Although maintaining that Damjan's story is "uneven," Amy Lilien-Harper wrote that Unzner's art for *The Clown Said No* features "expressive" animal faces "and the composition works quite well." A generous young girl is the focus of *The Gifts,* a holiday-themed story that was originally published in German as *Ein Weihnachtsbaum für Mia.* Here "Unzner's ethereal illustrations use a softly shaded palette" to evoke the girl's "solitary lifestyle," observed a *Kirkus Reviews* writer, and in *Booklist* Carolyn Phelan enjoyed the "sensitive artwork," noting that its nostalgic quality "includes a delicately spattered effect." Unzner's "soft but light-filled" images "bringing their own magic to the message at the heart of this old-fashioned story," concluded Cynthia Ritter in her *Horn Book* review of *The Gifts.*

In Weigelt's *Miranda's Ghosts* a young girl returning home from a Halloween party decides to give some of the creatures who appear at night in her bedroom a taste of their own medicine. "Unzner's ghosts leer, their eyes pop, and long, fiendishly distorted noses protrude from amorphous expressions," remarked a reviewer for *Publishers Weekly.* Another imaginative girl is the focus of Karma Wilson's *Princess Me,* a "gentle rhyming fantasy" in which "Unzner conjures up a world that's prettily, proudly girly," according to a *Publishers Weekly* contributor. Still another fanciful story, Ammi-Joan Paquette's *The Tiptoe Guide to Tracking Fairies,* finds Unzner crafting multimedia images in which "photographs [are] juxtaposed with cartoonlike drawings of . . . magical creatures," according to *School Library Journal* contributor Linda M. Kenton.

"In the beginning of my career in East Germany, I was very insecure and was constantly looking to find my own personal style," Unzner recalled of her early career. "Later, my work changed dramatically, perhaps because of personal changes in my life, but perhaps also be-cause of political changes [resulting from leaving a communist country]. I no longer work with the pressure of having to be successful, but now I work because of the pleasure I get out of being able to support myself by making beautiful books for children. Perhaps because of this my illustrations have become more lively and my drawings have become much freer and more open."

Biographical and Critical Sources

PERIODICALS

Booklist, September 1, 1997, Julie Corsaro, review of *Meredith, the Witch Who Wasn't,* p. 133, November 1, 1999, Mart Segal, review of *A House Is Not a Home,* p. 539; August 1, 2006, Hazel Rochman, review of *William Shakespeare's Romeo and Juliet,* p. 77; May 1, 2009, Ilene Cooper, review of *The Tiptoe Guide to Tracking Fairies,* p. 90; November 1, 2009, Carolyn Phelan, review of *The Gifts,* p. 52.
Horn Book, November-December, 2009, Cynthia Ritter, review of *The Gifts,* p. 640.
Kirkus Reviews, March 15, 2002, review of *Weekend with Grandmother,* p. 412; September 15, 2009, review of *The Gifts.*
Publishers Weekly, September 23, 2002, review of *Miranda's Ghosts,* p. 72; October 1, 2007, review of *Princess Me,* p. 55; April 13, 2009, review of *The Tiptoe Guide to Tracking Fairies,* p. 48.
School Library Journal, July, 1995, Jeanne Clancy Watkins, review of *You Shall Be King!,* p. 68; January, 1996, Linda Wicher, review of *Jasmine and Rex,* p. 84; September, 1996, Joy Fleishhacker, review of *Smoky's Special Easter Present,* p. 182; November, 1997, Lisa Smith, review of *Meredith, the Witch Who Wasn't,* p. 91; November, 1999, Christine A. Moesch, review of *A House Is Not a Home,* December, 1999, Lisa Smith, review of *The Man with the Black Glove,* p. 112; January, 2001, Jeanne Clancy Watkins, review of *Meredith's Mixed Up Magic,* p. 102; July, 2002, Amy Lilien-Harper, review of *The Clown Said No,* p. 87; February, 2003, Kathleen Kelly MacMillan, review of *Miranda's Ghosts,* p. 124; December, 2006, Nancy Menaldi-Scanlan, review of *William Shakespeare's Romeo and Juliet,* p. 164; January, 2008, Linda M. Kenton, review of *Princess Me,* p. 100; September, 2009, Linda M. Kenton, review of *The Tiptoe Guide to Tracking Fairies,* p. 131.

ONLINE

Christa Unzner Home Page, http://www.christa-unzner.de (May 15, 2011).*

*   *   *

UNZNER-FISCHER, Christa
See UNZNER, Christa

VILLENEUVE, Anne

Personal

Born in Canada. *Education:* College degree.

Addresses

Home—Montréal, Québec, Canada. *E-mail*—anne@
annevilleneuve.com.

Career

Author, illustrator, and graphic designer.

Awards, Honors

Canadian Children's Book Centre Choice designation,
1994, for *Arthur Throws a Tantrum* by Ginette An-
fousse; Mr. Christie Prize, 1998, for *Une gardienne
pour Étienne* by Robert Souliéres; Québec-Wallonie-
Bruxelles prize, Canadian Governor General's Literary
Award, and Christie award finalist, all 2000, all for
L'écharpe rouge; TD/Canadian Children's Literature
Award for French-language work, 2005, for *Le nul et la
chipie* by François Barcelo, 2009, for *Chère Traudie;*
Marcel Couture prize, Alvine Belsile prize finalist, and
Baobab Prize finalist, all 2009, all for *Chère Traudie;*
Communication-Jeunesse Culinar award finalist for chil-
dren's book illustration.

Writings

SELF-ILLUSTRATED

La grattouillette, Les 400 Coups (Laval, Québec, Canada),
1995.
Mariano Otero, Editions Vue sur Mer (Dinard, France),
1996.
Lécharpe rouge, Les 400 Coups (Laval, Québec, Canada),
1999, translated as *The Red Scarf,* Tundra Books
(Plattsburgh, NY), 2010.
Chère Traudi, Les 400 Coups (Montréal, Québec, Canada),
2008.

Author's work has been translated into Spanish.

ILLUSTRATOR

Cécile Gagnon, *Le passager mystérieux,* Ovale (Sillery,
Québec, Canada), 1988.
Ginette Anfousse, *Père d'Arthur,* La Courte Échelle (Mon-
tréal, Québec, Canada), 1989, translated by Sarah
Cummins as *Arthur's Dad,* Formac (Halifax, Nova
Scotia, Canada), 1991.
Linda Brousseau, *Le père de Noélle,* P. Tisseyre (Montréal,
Québec, Canada), 1990.
André Vigeant, *Le bestiaire d'Anaïs,* Boréal (Montréal,
Québec, Canada), 1991.

Jacques Pasquet, *Sans queue ni tête,* Québec Aérique
(Montréal, Québec, Canada), 1991.
Ginette Anfousse, *Les barricades d'Arthur,* La Courte
Échelle (Montréal, Québec, Canada), 1992, translated
by Sarah Cummins as *Arthur Throws a Tantrum,* For-
mac (Halifax, Nova Scotia, Canada), 1993.
Ginette Anfousse, *Le chien d'Arthur,* La Courte Échelle
(Montréal, Québec, Canada), 1993, translated by Sa-
rah Cummins as *Arthur's Puppy Problem,* Formac
(Halifax, Nova Scotia, Canada), 1994.
Marie Cliche, *Zoë, Zut et Zazou,* Héritage (St.-Lambert,
Québec, Canada), 1994.
Linda Bergeron, *Un micro s.v.p.!,* Héritage (St.-Lambert,
Québec, Canada), 1995.
Mireille Villeneuve, *Le petit avion jaune,* Héritage (St.-
Lambert, Québec, Canada), 1995, 2nd edition, 2002.
Linda Bergeron, *Le magasin à surprises,* Héritage (St.-
Lambert, Québec, Canada), 1996.
Sylvie Högue and Giséle Internoscia, *Gros comme la lune,*
Héritage (St.-Lambert, Québec, Canada), 1996.
Carole Tremblay, *Le génie du lavabo,* Dominique et Cie.
(St.-Lambert, Québec, Canada), 1996.
Sylvie Högue and Giséle Internoscia, *Le piége: Percival et
Kit-Kat,* Dominique et Cie. (St.-Lambert, Québec,
Canada), 1997.
Carmen Marois, *L'idée de Saugrenue,* P. Tisseyre (St.-
Lambert, Québec, Canada), 1997.
Marie-Andrée Mativat, *Les patins d'Ariane,* Souliéres (St.-
Lambert, Québec, Canada), 1998.
Mireille Villeneuve, *Léonie déménage,* Dominique et Cie.
(St.-Lambert, Québec, Canada), 1998.
Robert Souliéres, *Une gardienne pour Étienne!: Un conte,*
Les 400 Coups (Laval, Québec, Canada), 1998.
Mireille Villeneuve, *Des amis pour Léonie,* Dominique et
Cie. (St.-Lambert, Québec, Canada), 1998.
Cécile Gagnon, *La rose et le diable,* Souliéres (St.-
Lambert, Québec, Canada), 2000.
(With Michel Grant and Philippe Germain) Michel Brin-
damour, *Les imbattables!,* Didier (Montréal, Québec,
Canada), 2000.
Sylvie Högue and Giséle Internoscia, *La rançon: Percival
et Kit-Kat,* Dominique et Cie. (St.-Lambert, Québec,
Canada), 2000.
Mireille Villeneuve, *L'incroyable invention de Félicio,* Do-
minique et Cie. (St.-Lambert, Québec, Canada), 2000,
translated by David Homel as *Felicio's Incredible In-
vention,* Dominique & Friends (St.-Lambert, Québec,
Canada), 2000, Picture Window Books (Minneapolis,
MN), 2005.
Mireille Villeneuve, *Les mystéres de Félicio,* Dominique et
Cie. (St.-Lambert, Québec, Canada), 2001, translated
as *Mysteries for Felicio,* Dominique & Friends (St.-
Lambert, Québec, Canada), 2001, Picture Window
Books (Minneapolis, MN), 2005.
Mireille Villeneuve, *Félicio et le clown amoureux,* Domin-
ique et Cie. (St.-Lambert, Québec, Canada), 2002,
translated by Carolyn Perkes as *Felicio and the
Lovesick Clown,* Dominique & Friends (St.-Lambert,
Québec, Canada), 2002, published as *A Clown in Love,*
Picture Window Books (Minneapolis, MN), 2005.
Robert Souliéres, *Pas de panique!,* Éditions du Renouveau
pédagogique (Laval, Québec, Canada), 2002.

Carmen Marois, *Beauté monstre,* Souliéres (St.-Lambert, Québec, Canada), 2002.

Carmen Marois, *Le trésor d'Archibald,* Souliéres (St.-Lambert, Québec, Canada), 2002.

Carmen Marois, *Archibald et la reine noire,* Souliéres (St.-Lambert, Québec, Canada), 2003.

Yvon Brochu, *Un amour de prof,* Dominique et Cie. (St.-Lambert, Québec, Canada), 2003.

Bernard Boucher, *Mimi chat: poémes,* Les 400 Coups (Montréal, Québec, Canada), 2004.

François Barcelo, *Le nul et la chipie,* Souliéres (St.-Lambert, Québec, Canada), 2004.

Nathalie Savaria, *Me voilá!: mon album de bébé,* Hurtubise (Montréal, Québec, Canada), 2004.

Jean-Pierre Davidts, *Coup de cochon,* Boréal (Montréal, Québec, Canada), 2005.

François Barcelo, *Le fatigante et le fainéant,* Souliéres (St.-Lambert, Québec, Canada), 2006.

Nathalie Savaria, *Prét pas prét, j'y vaise!: mon album d'enfance de 3 à 6 ans,* Hurtubise (Montréal, Québec, Canada), 2006.

Jean-Pierre Davidts, *Histoire de fous,* Boréal (Montréal, Québec, Canada), 2006.

Andrée Poulin, *Les petites couettes de Babette,* Québec Amérique (Montréal, Québec, Canada), 2006.

Andrée Poulin, *Les cacahouettes de Babette,* Québec Amérique (Montréal, Québec, Canada), 2006.

Jean-Pierre Davidts, *Scandale au palais,* Boréal (Montréal, Québec, Canada), 2007.

Jean-Pierre Davidts, *Kestudi,* Boréal (Montréal, Québec, Canada), 2008.

Andrée Poulin, *Les marionnettes de Babette,* Québec Amérique (Montréal, Québec, Canada), 2008.

Jean-Pierre Davidts, *Zozo,* Boréal (Montréal, Québec, Canada), 2009.

Mireille Villeneuve, *Félicio et le clown a'léole,* Dominique et Cie. (St.-Lambert, Québec, Canada), 2009.

François Barcelo, *Le menteur et la rouspéteuse,* Souliéres (St.-Lambert, Québec, Canada), 2010.

Nathalie Bertrand, *Tom le terrible,* Éditions du Renouveau pédagogique (St.-Laurent, Québec, Canada), 2010.

Linda Bergeron, *Le champion des collections,* Dominique et Cie. (St.-Lambert, Québec, Canada), 2010.

Contributor to periodicals, including *La Presse* and *The Gazette;* contributor to books, including *Fricassées de grimaces: seix histoires drôles et attachantes,* Les 400 Coups (Montréal, Québec, Canada), 2009.

Sidelights

A Canadian artist and illustrator who is based in Québec, Anne Villeneuve has found success as a commercial illustrator as well as gaining fans through her

Anne Villeneuve weaves together a fanciful story and her colorful cartoon art in her award-winning picture book **The Red Scarf.** (Illustration copyright © 2010 by Anne Villeneuve. Reproduced by permission of Tundra Books Inc.)

work in picture books. Her book illustrations have appeared in her own stories, as well as in works by writers such as Carmen Marois, Robert Souliéres, and sister Mireille Villeneuve that are geared for French-language readers. Villeneuve was awarded both a Governor General's Literary Award for children's illustration and a Canadian Children's Literature Award for her original story *L'écharpe rouge*, and she has gained English-language fans since this story was translated as *The Red Scarf*. Another award-winning work by Villeneuve, the evocative *Chère Traudi*, tells the true story of a Dutch man who reflects on his experiences under German occupation during World War II.

"Consistently suprising and irrepressible," in the opinion of *Booklist* critic Randall Enos, *The Red Scarf* is an almost-wordless story that begins as a taxi driving rodent named Turpin discovers that one of his customers has left a red scarf on the passenger seat of his cab. Hoping to track down the scarf's owner, a magician, Turpin tracks the performer to a circus tent and becomes the main actor in a series of amazing acts, including being swallowed by a lion, walking a tightrope, and finding himself serving as the centerpiece of an amazing magical trick. Ultimately, the cabbie learns who the true owner of the scarf is in a picture book that "brims with insouciant charm," according to a *Publishers Weekly* critic. In her cartoon art for the story, Villeneuve "keeps the action at forefront, with minimal backgrounds and energetic compositions," according to *School Library Journal* critic Gay Lynn Van Vleck, and a *Kirkus Reviews* contributor noted that, "from the character design to the hand-lettering," *The Red Scarf* "comes from a place that still appreciates craft."

Biographical and Critical Sources

PERIODICALS

Booklist, January 1, 2010, Randall Enos, review of *The Red Scarf*, p. 98.
Children's Bookwatch, February, 2010, review of *The Red Scarf*.
Kirkus Reviews, January 15, 2010, review of *The Red Scarf*.
Publishers Weekly, January 11, 2010, review of *The Red Scarf*, p. 47.
Resource Links, October, 2004, Odile Rollin, review of *Le nul et la chipie*, p. 50; April, 2007, Jacqueline Girouard, review of *La fatigante et le fainéant*, p. 56; February, 2010, Susan Miller, review of *The Red Scarf*, p. 60.
School Library Journal, January, 2010, Gay Lynn Van Vleck, review of *The Red Scarf*, p. 83.

ONLINE

Anne Villeneuve Home Page, http://www.annevilleneuve. com (May 27, 2011).

Tundra Books Web site, http://www.tundrabooks.com/ (May 20, 2011), "Anne Villeneuve."*

*　　*　　*

WALDRON, Kevin 1979-

Personal

Born 1979, in Dublin, Ireland; immigrated to England; immigrated to United States.

Addresses

Home—New York, NY.

Career

Author and illustrator.

Awards, Honors

Read-It-Again Cambridgeshire Children's Picture Book Award shortlist, 2008, and Opera Prima award, Bologna Children's Book Fair, 2009, both for *Mr. Peek and the Misunderstanding at the Zoo;* Bisto Children's Book of the Year Award shortlist, Children's Books Ireland, 2011, for both *The Owl and the Pussycat* by Edward Lear and *Tiny Little Fly* by Michael Rosen; named among Booktrust Ten Rising Stars of Picture-book Illustration; Bull-Bransom Award, National Museum of Wildlife Art, 2011, for *Tiny Little Fly*.

Writings

SELF-ILLUSTRATED

Mr. Peek and the Misunderstanding at the Zoo, Templar Publishing (Dorking, Surrey, England), 2008, Candlewick Press (Somerville, MA), 2010.

ILLUSTRATOR

Michael Rosen, *Tiny Little Fly,* Candlewick Press (Somerville, MA), 2010.
Edward Lear, *The Owl and the Pussycat,* new edition, Simon & Schuster (London, England), 2010.

Works featuring Waldron's art have been translated into Dutch, German, and Japanese.

Sidelights

Born in Dublin, Ireland, and now making his home in New York City, Kevin Waldron is an artist and author whose first book for children, the quirky *Mr. Peek and the Misunderstanding at the Zoo*, earned him both the attention of critics and an Opera Prima award from a prestigious Italian illustrator's showcase. In addition to his original story, Waldron has also created award-winning art for both Michael Rosen's *Tiny Little Fly* and a new edition of nineteenth-century English nonsense writer Edward Lear's *The Owl and the Pussycat*. He creates his retro-inspired images by beginning with pencil drawings and adding typographical or other design elements and opaque gouache colors before manipulating them on the computer to create an "aged news print" look.

In *Mr. Peek and the Misunderstanding at the Zoo* the titular zookeeper starts off the day by donning the smaller jacket belonging to his son, Jimmy. When the jacket's tightness causes him to believe that he is putting on weight, Mr. Peek begins to loose his good humor, and his negativity is sensed by the animals, all of which take the criticism personally. Fortunately, a chance lunchtime visit by his son, young Jimmy Peak, who is enveloped in a far-too-large-to-be-his coat, sets all in the zoo to rights. Praising the humor in *Mr. Peek and the Misunderstanding at the Zoo*, *Booklist* critic Daniel Kraus added that Waldron's "digital-media artwork has an organic, pencil-scratch feel and uses a flattened perspective to good effect." The mercurial emotions of the story's lanky main character "are contagious," asserted a *Publishers Weekly* critic, and the zookeeper's influence on others "serves as an excellent reminder to practice optimism in words and deeds."

Featuring a text by former British children's laureate Michael Rosen, *Tiny Little Fly* finds a brave and quick-thinking winged insect able to fool a tiger, then an elephant, then a hippopotamus. The large-format picture book was shortlisted for Children's Books Ireland's 2011 Bisto Children's Book of the Year award and also earned Waldron the National Museum of Wildlife Art's annual Bull-Bransom Award. Predicting that Rosen's story will cause young listeners to "giggle in delight," London *Times* critic Amanda Craig added that Waldron's "bright, bold, textured illustrations" of the story's animal characters "climax . . . in a hilarious picture of catastrophe."

Biographical and Critical Sources

PERIODICALS

Booklist, April 1, 2010, Daniel Kraus, review of *Mr. Peek and the Misunderstanding at the Zoo*, p. 47.
Publishers Weekly, April 26, 2010, review of *Mr. Peek and the Misunderstanding at the Zoo*, p. 105.
School Library Journal, May, 2010, Martha Simpson, review of *Mr. Peek and the Misunderstanding at the Zoo*, p. 94.
Times (London, England), November 13, 2010, Amanda Craig, review of *Tiny Little Fly*, p. 12.

ONLINE

Kevin Waldron Home Page, http://www.kevinwaldron.co.uk (May 27, 2011).
National Museum of Wildlife Art Web site, http://www.wildlifeart.org/ (May 15, 2011), "Kevin Waldron."*

*   *   *

Kevin Waldron's stylized retro-inspired art lends a sophisticated air to his story for **Mr. Peek and the Misunderstanding at the Zoo.** (Templar Books, 2010. Illustration copyright © 2010 by Kevin Waldron. Reproduced by permission of Candlewick Press, Somerville, MA.)

WATTS, Bernadette 1942-
(Bernadette)

Personal

Born May 13, 1942, in Northampton, England; daughter of Bert (a surveyor) and Josephine Watts. *Education:* Maidenstone College of Art, diploma (design). *Hobbies and other interests:* Music, films, reading, looking at art, travel.

Addresses

Home—England. *E-mail*—info@bernadettewatts.com.

Career

Illustrator and artist. *Exhibitions:* Work has been exhibited in Bologna, Italy, and London, England, and at the Biennale in Bratislava, Czech Republic.

Awards, Honors

Premio graphico (Bologna, Italy), 1969, for *One's None* by James Reeves; Owl Prize, Shikosha & Maruzen (Tokyo, Japan), 1986, for *The Little Match Girl* by Hans Christian Andersen.

Writings

SELF-ILLUSTRATED

(Under name Bernadette) *Hans the Miller Man*, McGraw, 1969.

(Reteller) Jakob and Wilhelm Grimm, *Jorinda and Jorindel*, World Publishing (London, England), 1970, North-South (New York, NY), 2005.

(Reteller) *Cinderella and the Little Glass Slipper*, Franklin Watts (London, England), 1971.

(Under name Bernadette) *Varenka*, Oxford University Press (London, England), 1971, Putnam (New York, NY), 1972.

(Under name Bernadette) *The Proud Crow*, Albert Whitman (Morton Grove, IL), 1973.

(Under name Bernadette) *David's Waiting Day*, Aardvark (London, England), 1975.

(Under name Bernadette) *The Little Flute Player*, Abelard-Schuman (London, England), 1975, published as *Brigitte and Ferdinand*, Prentice-Hall (New York, NY), 1976.

(Adaptor) Jacob and Wilhelm Grimm, *Snow White*, Faber & Faber (London, England), 1983.

(Reteller) *Goldilocks und die drei Bären*, Nord-Süd (Gossau, Switzerland), 1984, translated as *Goldilocks and the Three Bears*, Abelard/North-South (London, England), 1984.

(Reteller) Jacob and Wilhelm Grimm, *The Elves and the Shoemaker*, North-South (London, England), 1986.

(Under name Bernadette) *St. Francis and the Proud Crow*, Andersen (London, England), 1987.

(Adaptor) Jacob and Wilhelm Grimm, *Snow-White and Rose-Red*, North-South (London, England), 1988.

Tattercoats, North-South (London, England), 1988.

(Reteller) Gerda Marie Scheidle, *Ein Esel geht hach Bethlehem*, Nord-Süd (Gossau, Switzerland), 1988, translated as *The Little Donkey: A Christmas Story*, Abelard/North-South (London, England), 1988.

Hans Millerman, Oxford University Press (London, England), 1989.

(Reteller) Jacob and Wilhelm Grimm, *The Ragamuffins*, North-South (London, England), 1989.

(Adaptor) Hans Christian Andersen, *The Fir Tree*, North-South (London, England), 1990.

(Reteller) *The Wind and the Sun: An Aesop Fable*, North-South (New York, NY), 1992.

(Reteller) *The Brave Little Tailor: A Fairy Tale*, North-South (London, England), 1994.

The Christmas Bird, North-South (New York, NY), 1996.

Harvey Hare: Postman Extraordinaire, North-South (London, England), 1997.

(Reteller) *The Town Mouse and the Country Mouse: An Aesop Fable*, North-South (New York, NY), 1998.

Happy Birthday, Harvey Hare!, North-South (New York, NY), 1998.

Harvey Hare's Christmas, North-South (New York, NY), 1999.

(Reteller) *The Lion and the Mouse: An Aesop Fable*, North-South (New York, NY), 2000.

(And adaptor) Hans Christian Andersen, *The Ugly Duckling*, North South (New York, NY), 2000.

(Reteller) La Fontaine, *The Rich Man and the Shoemaker: A Fable*, North-South Books (New York, NY), 2002.

The Smallest Snowflake, North-South (New York, NY), 2009.

Author's work has been translated into Africaans and Welsh.

ILLUSTRATOR

Alfred, Lord Tennyson, *The Lady of Shalott*, new edition, Dobson Books (London, England), 1966, Franklin Watts (New York, NY), 1968.

Eva Lis Wiorio, *Forbidden Adventure*, Ronald, Whiting & Wheaton (London, England), 1967.

Jacob and Wilhelm Grimm, *Little Red Riding Hood*, Oxford University Press (Oxford, England), 1968, revised with new translation, North-South (New York, NY), 2009.

Rhoda D. Power, *The Big Book of Stories from Many Lands*, Franklin Watts (London, England), 1969.

James Reeves, *One's None: Old Rhymes for New Tongues*, Franklin Watts (London, England), 1969.

Ruth Ainsworth, *Look, Do, and Listen*, Heinemann (London, England), 1969.

Reinhold Ehrhardt, *Kikeri; or, The Proud Red Rooster*, translated from the German, Macdonald (London, England), 1970.

Kathleen Arnott, *Animal Folk Tales from around the World*, Blackie (London, England), 1970, selections published as *Animal Tales from Many Lands* and *The Golden Fish, and Other Stories*, both 1972.

George Mendoza, *The Christmas Tree Alphabet Book*, World Publishing (New York, NY), 1971.

Leonard Wibberley, *Journey to Untor*, Ariel Books (New York, NY), 1971.

Robina Beckles Willson, *The Shell on Your Back: Houses and Homes*, Heinemann (London, England), 1972.

Jacob and Wilhelm Grimm, *Mother Holly*, North-South (London, England), 1972.

Jacob and Wilhem Grimm, *Hansel and Gretel*, translated by J. Dobson, Dobson Books (London, England), 1974.

Jacob and Wilhem Grimm, *Rapunzel*, translated by J. Dobson, Dobson Books (London, England), 1975.

Jacob and Wilhelm Grimm, *Aschenputtel*, Nord-Süd (Monchaltorf, Switzerland), 1977, translation published as *Cinderella*, J. Dent (London, England), 1979.

Margaret Rogers, *Green Is Beautiful*, Andersen Press (London, England), 1977.

Arthur Scholey, *Sallinka and the Golden Bird*, Prentice-Hall (New York, NY), 1978.

Gerda Marie Scheide, *'Tschibi und das große Meer*, Nord-Süd (Monchaltorf, Switzerland), 1979, translated by Gwen Marsh as *Chibby: The Little Fish*, J. Dent (London, England), 1980.

Jacob and Wilhelm Grimm, *Three Tales*, Little, Brown (Boston, MA), 1980.

Patricia Crampton, reteller, *Aesop's Fables*, J. Dent (London, England), 1980.

The Christmas Story (from the New Testament), Abelard (London, England), 1982.

Hans Christian Andersen, *Das kleinie Mädchen mit den Schwefelhölzchen,* Nord-Süd (Mönchaltorf, Germany), 1983, translated as *The Little Match Girl,* Abelard/North-South (London, England), 1983.

Jacob and Wilhelm Grimm, *The Sleeping Beauty,* Abelard/North-South (London, England), 1984.

Gerda Marie Scheidl, *Der kleine Gärtner,* Nord-Süd (Gossau, Switzerland), 1985, translated by Rosemary Lanning as *George's Garden,* Abelard/North-South (London, England), 1986.

Jacob and Wilhelm Grimm, *König Drosselbart,* Nord-Süd (Gossau, Switzerland), 1985, translated by Rosemary Lanning as *King Thrushbeard,* North-South (London, England), 1985.

Brigitte Hanhart, adaptor, *Schuster Martin,* based on a story by Leo Tolstoy, Nord-Süd (Gossau, Switzerland), 1986, translated by Michael Hale as *Shoemaker Martin,* North-South (New York, NY), 1986.

Jock Curle, *The Four Good Friends,* North-South (London, England), 1987.

Hans Christian Andersen, *Die Schneekhönigin,* Nord-Süd (Gossau, Switzerland), 1987, translated and adapted by Anthea Bell as *The Snow Queen: A Fairy Tale,* North-South (London, England), 1987.

Naomi Lewis, reteller, *Thumbelina,* based on the story by Hans Christian Andersen, North-South (London, England), 1990.

Russell Johnson, *The Princess and the Carpenter,* North-South (London, England), 1991.

Russell Johnson, *Trouble at Christmas,* North-South (London, England), 1991.

Christina Rossetti, *Fly Away, Fly Away over the Sea, and Other Poems for Children,* North South (London, England), 1991.

Bernadette Watts creates charming illustration for her woodland story in **Happy Birthday, Harvey Hare!** (North-South Books, 1998. Copyright © 1998 by Bernadette Watts. Reproduced of permission Bernadette Watts.)

Jacob and Wilhelm Grimm, *The Bremen Town Musicians,* translated from the German by Anthea Bell, North-South (New York, NY), 1992.

Jacob and Wilhelm Grimm, *Rumplestiltskin: A Fairy Tale,* translated from the German by Anthea Bell, North-South (New York, NY), 1993.

Gerda Marie Scheidl, *Der Hirsebrei,* Nord-Süd (Gossau, Switzerland), 1994, translated by Rosemary Lanning as *Matthew's Miracle: A Christmas Story,* North-South (London, England), 1994.

Jacob and Wilhelm Grimm, *The Wolf and the Seven Little Kids,* translated from the German by Anthea Bell, North-South (New York, NY), 1995.

Karen Christensen, *Rachel's Roses,* Barefoot Books (Bath, England), 1995.

Jacob and Wilhelm Grimm, *Little Brother and Little Sister,* translated from the German by Anthea Bell, North-South (New York, NY), 1996.

Rosemary Lanning, reteller, *Jona und der grösse Wal,* Nord-Süd (Gossau, Switzerland), 2001, translated as *Jonah and the Whale: A Story from the Bible,* North-South Books (New York, NY), 2001.

Udo Weigelt, *Biber geht fort,* Nord-Süd (Gossau, Switzerland), 2002, translated by Sibylle Kazeroid as *Old Beaver,* North-South Books (New York, NY), 2002.

Brigitte Sidjanski, *Der Fluss,* Minedition, 2008, translation adapted by Watts as *The River,* Minedition (New York, NY), 2008.

Jacob and Wilhelm Grimm, *The Star Child,* translated and adapted by J. Alison James, North-South (New York, NY), 2010.

Sidelights

Compared by many reviewers to celebrated illustrator Brian Wildsmith, British artist Bernadette Watts gives new life to the works of such well-known storytellers as the Brothers Grimm, Hans Christian Andersen, and Aesop through the illustrations she has done for numerous adaptations of classic fairy and folktales. In addition to her career as a professional illustrator of children's books, Watts has also written several of her own stories, among them *Tattercoats, David's Waiting Day,* and several self-illustrated tales featuring the endearing Harvey Hare. In praise of Watts's talent, a *Kirkus Reviews* writer remarked of a reissue of the artist's 1968 *Little Red Riding Hood* that the work "demonstrates her mastery of the picture-book form as she juxtaposes characters across the [two-page spread] . . . at strategic moments, employs fully saturated pages at some turns and spot art at others, all heightening readers' focus and dramatic tension."

Born in Northampton, England, during World War II, Watts loved art as a child, and she eventually trained to become a designer at Maidenstone College of Art. Her skill at capturing animals and nature made her a perfect fit as a picture-book artist; since creating the artwork for a new edition of Alfred, Lord Tennyson's beloved poem "The Lady of Shalott," Watts has concentrated on children's literature: particularly on the classic folk and fairy stories that have captured young imaginations for generations.

In *Tattercoats* Watts tells the story of three farm children who create a scarecrow for their father's field at harvest time. Left to the fall and winter weather before being re outfitted the following spring for a place in the family garden, the lonely scarecrow yearns for news of his owners and inquires of the many animals that inhabit his field during the changing seasons. The scarecrow's sense of isolation is successfully conveyed in Watts's illustrations, according to *School Library Journal* contributor Jane Salters, the critic adding that in *Tattercoats* "the expression of mood through vast space and weather is the book's strength." A *Publishers Weekly* reviewer also praised the book, writing that the "warmth" of Watts's "beautifully done illustrations is matched by a story rich with family love and caring."

In *David's Waiting Day* a young boy anxiously awaits the arrival of a baby sister who is soon to come home from the hospital, while *The Christmas Bird* features a holiday theme. In the latter self-illustrated tale, Watts introduces a young girl named Katya as she hears about the birth of the baby Jesus. Embarking on a quest to bring gifts of a cat, a loaf of bread, and a bird whistle to the newborn, Katya encounters several adventures in a picture book that a *School Library Journal* contributor dubbed a "quiet selection with a seasonal message." Another original self-illustrated story, *The Smallest*

Watts brings to life a holiday story in her nostalgic ink-and-wash art for **The Christmas Bird.** (North-South Books, 1996. Copyright © 1996 by Bernadette Watts. Reproduced by permission of Bernadette Watts.)

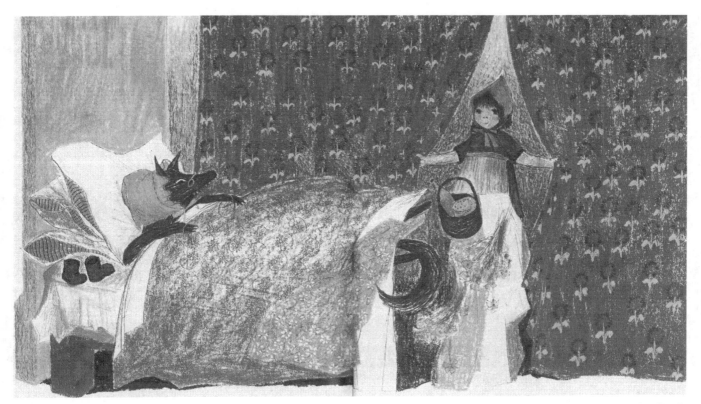

Watts showcases her ability to breathe new life into traditional stories in her artwork for a retelling of the Brothers Grimm's **Little Red Riding Hood.**
(North-South Books, 2009. Illustration copyright © 2009 by Bernadette Watts. © 2011 NordSud Verlag AG, CH-8005 Zurich/Schweiz.)

Snowflake, finds a wistful snowflake gaining its wish to land someplace special when it winds up in the window box of a quaint rural cottage as part of the last snowfall of winter. Calling Watts's tale "as sturdy yet delicate as her artwork," Carolyn Phelan added in *Booklist* that *The Smallest Snowflake* features illustrations "warmed with washes and strokes of color."

One of several stories to feature Watts's original picture-book character, *Harvey Hare, Postman Extraordinaire* "evokes a pastoral world of charm and grace" in its story of a reliable flop-eared mail carrier, according to *Booklist* reviewer Susan Dove Lempke. Calling the same story "an appealing look at the value of doing one's work well," *School Library Journal* contributor Maura Bresnahan had particular praise for Watts's portrayal of the natural surroundings of the postman and his friends. Harvey returns in both *Happy Birthday, Harvey Hare!* and *Harvey Hare's Christmas.*

The works of nineteenth-century German folklorists Jacob and Wilhelm Grimm have been the basis for many of Watts's picture-book illustrations. In *Rapunzel* she uses vibrant shades of pastel and what a *Junior Bookshelf* contributor described as "primitive, child-like figures" to "soften the terror and cruelty" of the Brothers Grimm's story of a beautiful young girl who is locked away in a tall tower by an evil witch. The artist's use of earthy tones gives her rendition of *The Bremen Town Musicians* "an overall feeling of gentleness," while her use of scratchy outlines effectively reflects the person-

alities of the four older animals in this classic Grimm tale, according to *School Library Journal* reviewer Linda Boyles. *The Elves and the Shoemaker,* a classic tale about a poor, hardworking craftsman and his family and the tiny elves that secretly help the couple escape poverty, is presented to young audiences in a manner that "underscores the story's themes of homely virtue and marital union," asserted a *Publishers Weekly* reviewer. Remarking on the re-issuance of *Jorinda and Jorindel,* one of Watts's earliest illustration projects, Mirian Lang Budin wrote in *School Library Journal* that the author/illustrator retells the Grimm Brothers' story "with a grace that is equally reflected in her pen-and-ink illustrations."

The fairy stories of noted storyteller Hans Christian Andersen have also been successfully re-worked for picture books by Watts. In *The Fir Tree,* for example, the illustrator uses diverse media—including water color, chalk, and inked line—in shades of yellow and gold to tell the story of the small tree that realized too late that it had wasted its chance to be happy by spending its days wanting to be something it was not. In *Thumbelina* Watts presents what *Junior Bookshelf* contributor Marcus Crouch described as a "delightful treatment" of the beloved story about a miniature maiden, and while the critic questioned the adaptation of Andersen's sophisticated tales into picture-book format, he concluded that, "if we must have such books let them be Watts.'"

Continuing her work within the pantheon of time-honored children's stories, Watts also breathes new life into *The Wind and the Sun: An Aesop Fable*. This story—which depicts the battle for importance between the sun and the wind as they test their strength upon a poor traveler making his way home in a new red cloak—"is made vividly real in the artist's delightful landscapes in which a never-never-land is invoked with a sure and sensitive touch," according to Crouch. Equally celebratory of the artist's efforts here, *Booklist* critic Leone McDermott deemed *The Wind and the Sun* "a warm rendition of Aesop's fable about the power of gentleness." Turning to a more-recent storyteller, seventeenth-century French fabulist Jean de La Fontaine, *School Library Journal* critic Lauralyn Persson predicted of Watts's illustrations for La Fontaine's *The Rich Man and the Shoemaker: A Fable* that "younger children will love poring over the details; there are plenty of them, yet the pages retain an uncluttered look of simplicity."

Biographical and Critical Sources

PERIODICALS

Booklist, January 15, 1993, Leone McDermott, review of *The Wind and the Sun: An Aesop Fable,* p. 916; March 15, 1997, Susan Dove Lempke, review of *Harvey Hare, Postman Extraordinaire,* p. 1247; October 1, 2002, John Peters, review of *The Rich Man and the Shoemaker: A Fable,* p. 329; April 15, 2005, Jennifer Mattson, review of *Jorinda and Jorindel,* p. 1457; February 15, 2008, Carolyn Phelan, review of *The River,* p. 94; October 15, 2009, Carolyn Phelan, review of *The Smallest Snowflake,* p. 56.
Junior Bookshelf, February, 1976, review of *Rapunzel,* pp. 14-15; August, 1990, Marcus Crouch, review of *Thumbelina,* p. 164; December, 1993, Marcus Crouch, review of *The Wind and the Sun: An Aesop Fable,* p. 237-238.
Kirkus Reviews, April 15, 2005, review of *Jorinda and Jorindel,* p. 474; October 1, 2009, review of *Little Red Riding Hood;* October 15, 2009, review of *The Smallest Snowflake.*
Publishers Weekly, April 28, 1989, review of *Tattercoats,* p. 78; June 27, 1986, review of *The Elves and the Shoemaker,* p. 89; October 19, 2009, review of *The Smallest Snowflake,* p. 50.
School Library Journal, July, 1989, Jane Salier, review of *Tattercoats,* p. 77; July, 1992, Linda Boyles, review of *The Bremen Town Musicians,* p. 68; October, 1996, review of *The Christmas Bird,* p. 42; March, 1997, Maura Bresnahan, review of *Harvey Hare, Postman Extraordinaire,* p. 168; December, 2001, Kathy Piehl, review of *Jonah and the Whale: A Story from the Bible,* p. 124; June, 2002, Maryann H. Owen, review of *Old Beaver,* p. 114; April, 2003, Lauralyn Persson, review of *The Rich Man and the Shoemaker,* p. 156; June, 2005, Miriam Lang, review of *Jorinda and Jorindel,* p. 116; April, 2008, Heidi Estrin, review of *The River,* p. 123; November, 2009, Anne Beier, review of *The Smallest Snowflake,* p. 91; October, 2010, Margaret Bush, review of *The Star Child,* p. 98.

ONLINE

Bernadette Watts Home Page, http://www.bernadettewatts. com (February 27, 2011).*

*   *   *

WESTERFELD, Scott

Personal

Born in TX; married Justine Larbalestier (a researcher and writer).

Addresses

Home—New York, NY; Sydney, New South Wales, Australia. *Agent*—Jill Grinberg, Anderson Grinberg Literary Management, 244 5th Ave., 11th Fl., New York, NY 10001. *E-mail*—scott@scottwesterfeld.com.

Career

Writer. Worked as a composer and media designer; textbook editor, until 1996.

Awards, Honors

Notable First Novel selection, *Locus* magazine, 1997, for *Ploymorph;* Philip K. Dick Award special citation, and *New York Times* Notable Book citation, both 2000, for *Evolution's Darling;* Best Book for Young Adults selection, Young Adult Library Services Association, 2004, and Aurealis Award nomination, both for *Peeps;* New York Public Library Books for the Teen Age selection, and Aurealis Award for Best Young-Adult Novel, both 2004, both for *Midnighters;* Children's Book Council of Australia Best Teen Book of the Year listee, 2004; Aurealis Award, 2010, for *Leviathan.*

Writings

FOR CHILDREN

The Berlin Airlift, Silver Burdett (Englewood Cliffs, NJ), 1989.
Watergate, Silver Burdett (Englewood Cliffs, NJ), 1991.
Blossom vs. the Blasteroid, Scholastic (New York, NY), 2002.
Diamonds Are for Princess, Scholastic (New York, NY), 2002.
Rainy Day Professor, Scholastic (New York, NY), 2002.
So Yesterday, Razorbill (New York, NY), 2004.

Peeps, Razorbill (New York, NY), 2005.

The Last Days (sequel to *Peeps*), Razorbill (New York, NY), 2006.

(Editor) *The World of the Golden Compass: The Otherworldly Ride Continues,* Borders Group (Ann Arbor, MI), 2007.

Bogus to Bubbly: An Insider's Guide to the World of Uglies (also see below), Simon Pulse (New York, NY), 2008.

Short fiction included in anthology *Love Is Hell,* HarperTeen (New York, NY), 2008; and *The Starry Rift: Tales of New Tomorrows,* edited by Jonathan Strahan, Viking (New York, NY), 2008.

"MIDNIGHTERS TRILOGY"

The Secret Hour, Eos (New York, NY), 2004.
Touching Darkness, Eos (New York, NY), 2005.
Blue Noon, Eos (New York, NY), 2005.

"UGLIES TRILOGY"

Uglies, Simon Pulse (New York, NY), 2005.
Pretties, Simon Pulse (New York, NY), 2005.
Specials, Simon Pulse (New York, NY), 2006.
Extras, Simon Pulse (New York, NY), 2007.

"LEVIATHAN TRILOGY"

Leviathan, illustrated by Keith Thompson, Simon Pulse (New York, NY), 2009.

Behemoth, illustrated by Keith Thompson, Simon Pulse (New York, NY), 2010.

Goliath, illustrated by Keith Thompson, Simon Pulse (New York, NY), 2011.

SCIENCE-FICTION NOVELS; FOR ADULTS

Polymorph, Penguin (New York, NY), 1997.
Fine Prey, Penguin (New York, NY), 1998.
Evolution's Darling, Four Walls Eight Windows (New York, NY), 1999.
The Killing of Worlds, Tor (New York, NY), 2003.
The Risen Empire, Tor (New York, NY), 2003.

Also author of short stories.

Adaptations

Film rights to the "Uglies" novels were acquired by Twentieth Century-Fox, 2006. *Leviathan* and *Behemoth* were adapted as audiobooks, Simon & Schuster Audio, 2009, 2010, respectively.

Sidelights

Spending his early career as a musical composer whose works have been performed in dance productions both in the United States and Europe, Scott Westerfeld

moved into writing by working as a textbook editor, ghostwriter, and creator of educational software programs for children. Now, as a fiction writer focused primarily in the science-fiction genre, he pens novels and short stories for both adults and younger readers. Westerfeld's work is characterized as "space opera," which Gerald Jonas defined in the *New York Times* as "far-future narratives that encompass entire galaxies and move confidently among competing planets and cultures, both human and otherwise." In an interview on the Penguin Web site, Westerfeld explained that he is attracted to this form of fiction because it is "a way of writing (and of reading) which utilizes the power of extrapolation. It expands both the real world . . . and the literary. In regular fiction, you might be alienated. In [science fiction] . . . you're an alien."

Westerfeld began his fiction-writing career with the novel *Polymorph,* which explores identity and sexual issues via a title character who is able to change gender and appearance. The plot was inspired by the author's

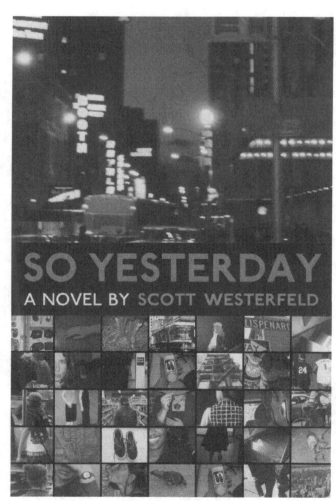

A trend-spotting teen develops a new talent when he and a friend uncover a conspiracy to control the definition of "cool." in Scott Westerfeld's **So Yesterday.** (Jacket photos copyright © 2004 by Lauren Monchik and John Son. Reproduced by permission of Razorbill, a division of Penguin Books for Young Readers, a member of Penguin Group (USA) Inc., 345 Hudson St., New York, NY 10014. All rights reserved.)

move to New York City in the 1980s and his awe at the layers of diversity created through successive waves of immigration and the range in city residents' wealth, values, and cultures. Also for adults, his novel *Evolution's Darling* earned Westerfeld a Philip K. Dick Award special citation as well as Notable Book status from the *New York Times. Evolution's Darling,* which tells the story of an artificial intelligence that evolves into a sentient being through its relationship with a teenage girl, was also praised by Trevor Dodge, who wrote in his review for the *Review of Contemporary Fiction* that the story challenges readers to "ponder if a machine can be made human, and if so, what purpose humanity would serve."

Westerfeld reshapes his sci-fi themes for a younger readership in several trilogies, including "Midnighters," "Uglies," and "Leviathan." His "Midnighters" books take readers into a parallel world where hidden dangers lurk for a group of Midwestern teens. *The Secret Hour,* is the first volume in the "Midnighters" trilogy, focuses on fifteen-year-old Jessica Day, a new student at Oklahoma's Bixby High. While feeling predictably out of place in her new town, and coping, as usual, with a bratty younger sister and flaky parents, Jessica begins to find other things strange. The water tastes a bit off, and her dreams are becoming increasingly vivid and unsettling. Eventually, Jessica bands together with four other students as one of only a few "midnighters": people who, born at the stroke of midnight, have the ability to live in the day's hidden twenty-fifth hour. In this special time she is able to move about in a world where time has temporarily stopped: the only creatures capable of motion are other midnighters and a species of predator known as a darkling. Jessica and her new friends ultimately band together to discover Jessica's special power after it becomes clear that an evil darkling force is bent on her destruction.

Reviewing *The Secret Hour, Kliatt* contributor Michele Winship praised the work as a "unique and fresh fantasy setting," while a *Kirkus* critic dubbed it a "thrilling series starter." In addition to noting what a *Publishers Weekly* reviewer described as the novel's "inventive" plot, critics praised Westerfeld's writing, *School Library Journal* contributor Sharon Grover noting the book's "intriguing characters," "exciting" plot, and "compelling" prose style.

Jessica's story continues in *Touching Darkness* and *Blue Noon,* as the five teens learn that something in Bixby's distant past now threatens the community's present. Discovering her skill as a flame bringer has not been able to end her problems; now Jessica realizes that she is being hunted by humans by day as well as by darklings at night. All five midnighters must now work together to understand and develop their special powers in order to fight this growing dual menace. In *School Library Journal* Sharon Grover cited *Touching Darkness* as "far scarier and much more convincing" than the first novel in the series, while a *Kirkus* critic noted

that Westerfeld's "powerful page-turner is compelling as it pits heroes against unspeakable evil both human and supernatural."

Likening the "Midnighters" novels to a television series, Charles de Lint offered his analysis of the trilogy in the *Magazine of Fantasy and Science Fiction.* "Westerfeld keeps the story going at a good pace and has deepened not only the mythology of the series, but also the characters," de Lint asserted. "Individuals and group dynamics continue to evolve and change, the characters reacting the way real people do, showing petty traits as well as selfless heroics," he added. "And when they change, the changes remain. There aren't any cop-outs or easy answers."

In his "Uglies" novels Westerfeld crafts a near-future world where cosmetic surgery is a required process for everyone at age sixteen in order to live in New Pretty Town. The first novel, *Uglies,* follows soon-to-be sixteen-year-old Tally as she discovers that there are options to the government-sponsored surgery scheduled to make her beautiful and ensure her future in New Pretty Town. At an outpost that is home to a group of renegades called the Smoke, Tally learns that a world in which everyone is equally beautiful has a terrifying down side. Praising *Uglies* in *Kliatt,* Samantha Musher added that Westerfeld "asks engaging questions about the meaning of beauty, individuality, and betrayal" in his story. Comparing Westerfeld's dystopian vision to Aldous Huxley's in *Brave New World,* London *Times* contributor Amanda Craig maintained that Tally's world "is a seeming Utopia resting on ruthless suppression of individual freedom; Scott Westerfeld's vision, portrayed through the dawning consciousness of his heroine, is less literary and more filmic than Huxley's, but thought through with pleasing logic and debated with a sharp wit."

The "Uglies" series continues in *Pretties, Specials,* and *Extras,* as Westerfeld plays out the consequences to residents of his futuristic utopia. In *Pretties* Tally's search for a cure for the mindless life of a New Pretty is derailed when she is drawn in by the lax, partygoing Pretty culture, while *Specials* follows her efforts to turn back the government-mandated program of emotional pacification. The fourth volume in the series, *Extras,* finds fifteen-year-old Anita getting into trouble while attempting to make her reputation as an investigative journalist now that rank is no longer based on beauty in Pretty Town. "Westerfeld excels at creating a futuristic pop culture that feels thrillingly plausible," noted Mattson of the novel, and *Kliatt* critic Samantha Musher called the author "a master world builder," adding that the society in *Extras* has "recognizable analogies to the familiar Internet culture of Facebook and blogging, but he takes them enough steps further to be original."

With *Leviathan* Westerfeld began his "Leviathan Trilogy," which also includes *Behemoth* and *Goliath.* Illustrated by Keith Thompson, the books are geared for

Cover of Westerfeld's sci-fi fantasy novel **The Secret Hour,** *the first volume in his "Midnighters" YA trilogy.* (Jacket art copyright © by Kamil Vojnar. Used by permission of HarperCollins Children's Books, a division of HarperCollins Publishers.)

middle-grade readers. A mix of steampunk, World War I military history, and advances in bioengineering, the "Leviathan" books were inspired by Westerfeld's discovery of Fenton Ash's 1906 sci-fi novel *A Trip to Mars.* "There was a King of Mars, and a Prince of Mars, but typical of books written in that era, no Princess of Mars," the author told *Publishers Weekly* contributor Sue Corbett. "I wanted a story that had the same look and feel, but would appeal to girls, too." In *Leviathan* readers witness the assassination of Archduke Franz Ferdinand that sparked World War I, and then turn to the archduke's orphaned son Prince Alek. A parallel story thread follows British teen Deryn Sharp, who disguises herself as a boy so she can join Great Britain's wartime Air Service. Ultimately, Alek and Deryn meet on opposite sides of a battle between Europe's two competing camps: the militaristic, heavily mechanized Clankers and the airborne Darwinists, who have found a way to bioengineer animals to military uses. The airship *Leviathan* is actually a giant whale that remains buoyed due to the aspiration of hydrogen-breathing microorganisms. Recommending the series for fans of Philip Reeve's *Mortal Engines,* Ian Chipman added in *Booklist* that *Leviathan* features an "ingenious premise"

that is "boosted almost entirely by exciting and sometimes violent fight sequences" and Thompson's "lavish" illustrations. "The protagonists' stories are equally gripping and keep the story moving," a *Publishers Weekly* critic similarly noted, "and Thompson's detail-rich panels bring Westerfeld's unusual creations to life." Reviewing *Behemoth,* which finds Deryn and Alek teaming up to change Europe's course, a *Publishers Weekly* contributor predicted that the book's "exciting and inventive tale of military conflict and wildly reimagined history should captivate a wide range of readers."

In a break from science fiction, Westerfeld has also penned *So Yesterday,* which a *Kirkus Reviews* writer described as a "clever, quirky romp" through the pop culture of New York City. In the book seventeen-year-old Hunter parlays his talent as a trend-spotter into a job with a high-profile clothing manufacturer. Hunter gained his skill after moving to the Big Apple from the Midwest; with few friends and a lot of time on his hands, he channeled his powers of observation about the signals people send through their actions and appearances into a Web log that soon became a popular read in the city. From trend spotter, Hunter must now become a crime stopper after his boss, Mandy, is kidnaped by a radical group determined to steal a new—and very trendy—shoe design.

Praising *So Yesterday,* Gillian Engberg described the book in *Booklist* as a "hip, fascinating thriller [that] aggressively questions consumer culture." The critic also enjoyed Hunter's sometimes cynical, sometimes enlightening narration about modern consumerism and marketing, while the *Kirkus Reviews* critic described him as "a charming narrator with an original take on teen life." Roger Sutton drew comparison's to Westerfeld's science-fiction work, noting in *Horn Book* that while much of *So Yesterday* focuses on Hunter's search for "the Next Cool Thing," the storyline "emanates an attractive edginess and often feels like it's just about to tip into sci-fi territory." In *Kliatt* Winship wrote that Westerfeld manages to inject the latest version of "cool" in "a fast-paced, fun novel that's not afraid to poke fun at our own consumerism while at the same time recognizing that cool rules."

Westerfeld turns to horor in *Peeps* and *The Last Days,* two novels that are set in New York City and focus on rock musician wannabees Moz and Zahler. In *Peeps,* which *Booklist* critic Jennifer Mattson praised as a "smart urbane fantasy," a parasite that is transmitted like an STD causes carriers to become vampires. College freshman Cal Thompson acquires the disease right after he moves to the city from Texas and spends a drunken night with a woman named Morgan. Although he is now a "peep", Cal does not experience all the symptoms of vampirism; still, and his increased night vision makes him the perfect employee of the peep-hunting Night Watch organization. On the hunt for Morgan, Cal falls in love, but his sense of honor forces him to keep his feelings undercover as he tracks down Morgan while also questioning the sudden rapid spread of the parasite in the city. In *The Last Days* Moz meets Pearl, a fellow musician, when she helps him salvage a Stratocaster guitar, and they form a band. Their new singer is a Peep who keeps her vampirism under control, while the band's drummer is able to sense the invisible horrors that are attracted to the band's sound. Describing *Peeps* as "an engaging conspiracy" filled "with provocative facts," a *Publishers Weekly* critic recommended it as "a story to get the brain working." Praising the "engaging" characters and "breezy dialogue" in *The Last Days*, Lynn Rutan added in her *Booklist* review that "Westerfeld continues his captivating, original vision, improving it in this tightly plotted sequel."

Discussing Westerfeld's work within the context of the challenges inherent in writing science fiction, Jonas commented in the *New York Times* that "to master such material and still bring to life characters with recognizable emotions and aspirations is a challenge few writers care to take on. Westerfeld succeeds admirably."

Biographical and Critical Sources

PERIODICALS

Analog Science Fiction, July 6, 2003, Tom Easton, review of *The Risen Empire.*

Booklist, December 1, 1997, John Mort, review of *Polymorph,* p. 612; February 15, 2003, Regina Schroeder, review of *The Risen Empire,* p. 1060; September 15, 2003, Regina Schroeder, review of *The Killing of Worlds,* p. 219; September 15, 2004, Gillian Engberg, review of *So Yesterday,* p. 235; March 15, 2005, Jennifer Mattson, review of *Uglies,* p. 1287; August, 2005, Jennifer Mattson, review of *Peeps,* p. 2019; September 1, 2006, Lynn Rutan, review of *The Last Days,* p. 112; January 1, 2008, Jennifer Mattson, review of *Extras,* p. 58; May 15, 2008, Holly Koelling, review of *The Starry Rift: Tales of New Tomorrows,* p. 58; August 1, 2009, Ian Chipman, review of *Leviathan,* p. 58.

Fantasy and Science Fiction, review of *Polymorph,* p. 46.

Horn Book, January-February, 2005, Roger Sutton, review of *So Yesterday,* p. 101.

Kirkus Reviews, January 15, 2003, review of *The Risen Empire,* p. 118; January 15, 2004, review of *The Secret Hour,* p. 90; August 1, 2004, review of *So Yesterday,* p. 750; February 1, 2005, reviews of *Touching Darkness,* p. 182, and *Uglies,* p. 237.

Kliatt, March, 2004, Michele Winship, review of *The Secret Hour,* p. 16; September, 2004, Michele Winship, review of *So Yesterday,* p. 17; March, 2005, Samantha Musher, review of *Uglies,* p. 29; March, 2006, Michele Winship, review of *Blue Noon,* p. 18; November, 2007, Samantha Musher, review of *Extras,* p. 15.

Library Journal, April 15, 2000, review of *Evolution's Darling,* p. 128; September 15, 2003, Jackie Cassada, review of *The Killing of Worlds,* p. 95.

Magazine of Fantasy and Science Fiction, June, 2006, Charles de Lint, review of "Midnighters Trilogy," p. 29.

New York Times, June 18, 2000, Gerald Jones, review of *Evolution's Darling,* p. 22; April 27, 2003, Gerald Jones, review of *The Risen Empire,* p. 23.

Publishers Weekly, April 17, 2000, review of *Evolution's Darling,* p. 57; January 20, 2003, review of *The Risen Empire,* p. 61; March 22, 2004, review of *The Secret Hour,* p. 87; October 4, 2004, review of *So Yesterday,* p. 89; March 21, 2005, review of *Uglies,* p. 53; October 3, 2005, review of *Peeps,* p. 71; November 17, 2008, review of *Love Is Hell,* p. 59; July 20, 2009, Sue Corbett, "Scott Westerfeld," p. 31; August 24, 2009, review of *Leviathan,* p. 62; September 13, 2010, review of *Behemoth,* p. 46.

Review of Contemporary Fiction, fall, 2000, Trevor Dodge, review of *Evolution's Darling,* p. 151.

School Library Journal, December, 1989, Ann Welton, review of *The Berlin Airlift,* p. 127; July, 2006, Heather M. Campbell, review of *Blue Noon,* p. 114; January, 2008, June H. Keuhn, review of *Extras,* p. 129; June, 2008, Dylan Thomarie, review of *The Starry Rift: Tales of New Tomorrows,* p. 152; September, 2009, Heather M. Campbell, review of *Leviathan,* p. 176; October, 2010, review of *Behemoth,* p. 128.

Science Fiction Chronicle, February-March, 2003, Don D'Ammassa, review of *The Risen Empire,* p. 54; June, 2004, Sharon Grover, review of *The Secret Hour,* p. 152; March, 2005, Sharon Grover, review of *Touching Darkness,* p. 220, and Susan W. Hunter, review of *Uglies,* p. 221.

Times (London, England), January 21, 2006, "Pretty Faces, Hideous Truths," p. 17; November 11, 2006, Amanda Craig, "The Future: Imperfect," p. 15.

ONLINE

Baltimore City Paper Online, http://www.citypaper.com/ (July 12, 2000), Adrienne Martini, review of *Evolution's Darling.*

Penguin Web site, http://www.penguin.com/ (July, 1998), interview with Westerfeld.

Sci-Fi.com, http://www.scifi.com/ (May 8, 2004), Thomas Myer, review of *Polymorph;* Donna McMahon, review of *Fine Prey;* Paul Witcover, reviews of *The Risen Empire* and *Evolution's Darling;* Steven Sawicki, review of short story "Non-Disclosure Agreement."

Scott Westerfeld Home Page, http://www.scottwesterfeld. com (May 15, 2011).*

*   *   *

WIJNGAARD, Juan 1951-

Personal

Born 1951, in Buenos Aires, Argentina; mother an artist; immigrated to Netherlands; immigrated to United States, 1989; married Sharon Berman (a musician and ethnomusicologist); children: five sons. *Education:* Royal College of Art (London, England), degree. *Hobbies and other interests:* Restoring and making hurdy-gurdies, French medieval and folk music, performing Flemish bagpipes.

Addresses

Home—Corrales, NM. *E-mail*—juan@juanwijngaard. com.

Career

Illustrator, musician, and fine-art painter. Worked briefly in an office; illustrator, beginning 1980s; fine-art painter beginning 2003. Luthier; performer with musical groups Blowzabella, c. late 1970s, Stop S'il Vous Plait, and ¡Viva la Pepa!, beginning 2006. *Exhibitions:* Work exhibited internationally, including at Victoria & Albert Museum, London, England; Barbican Centre, London; Centre Pompidou, Paris, France; and throughout United States, including Corrales Bosque Gallery, Corrales, NM.

Awards, Honors

Mother Goose Award, 1981, for *Green Finger House* by Rosemary Harris; Kate Greenaway Medal, 1985, for *Sir Gawain and the Loathly Lady* retold by Selina Hastings; numerous other awards.

Writings

SELF-ILLUSTRATED

Bear, Crown Publishers (New York, NY), 1990.
Cat, Crown Publishers (New York, NY), 1990.
Dog, Crown Publishers (New York, NY), 1990.
Duck, Crown Publishers (New York, NY), 1990.
Buzz! Buzz!, Lodestar Books (New York, NY), 1995.

ILLUSTRATED

Rosemary Harris, *Green Finger House,* Harper & Row (New York, NY), 1981.
Selina Hastings, reteller, *Sir Gawain and the Green Knight,* Lothrop, Lee & Shepard (New York, NY), 1981.
Rosemary Harris, *Janni's Stork,* Harper & Row (New York, NY), 1982.
Dennis Lee, *Jelly Belly,* Harper & Row (New York, NY), 1983.
Selina Hastings, reteller, *Sir Gawain and the Loathly Lady,* Lothrop, Lee & Shepard (New York, NY), 1985.
William Mayne, *The Blemyah Stories,*, 1987.
Sara and Stephen Corrin, *The Faber Book of Favourite Fairy Tales,* Faber & Faber (Boston, MA), 1988.
Jenny Koralek, *Hanukkah: The Festival of Lights,* Walker Books (London, England), 1989.

The Nativity, Lothrop, Lee & Shepard (New York, NY), 1990.
Wendy Cheyette Lewison, *Going to Sleep on the Farm,* Dial Books for Young Readers (New York, NY), 1992.
Jean Van Leeuwen, *Emma Bean,* Dial Books for Young Readers (New York, NY), 1993.
Nathaniel Tripp, *Thunderstorm!,* Dial Books for Young Readers (New York, NY), 1994.
Sonia Levitin, *A Piece of Home,* Dial Books for Young Readers (New York, NY), 1996.
Diane Wolkstein, *Esther's Story,* Morrow Junior Books (New York, NY), 1996.
Berlie Doherty, collector, *Tales of Wonder and Magic,* Candlewick Press (Cambridge, MA), 1997.
Jan Mark, *The Midas Touch,* Candlewick Press (Cambridge, MA), 1999.
John Ruskin, *The King of the Golden River: A Legend of Stiria,* new edition, Candlewick Press (Cambridge, MA), 2000.
Toby Forward, *Shakespeare's Globe: An Interactive Pop-up Theatre,* Candlewick Press (Cambridge, MA), 2005.
Mal Pete and Elspeth Graham, *Cloud Tea Monkeys,* new edition, Candlewick Press (Somerville, MA), 2010.

Sidelights

Born and raised in Buenos Aires, Argentina, award-winning illustrator Juan Wijngaard also resided in the Netherlands, Switzerland, and England before establishing his home in the southwestern United States. Although his passions have been divided between art and music for much of his life, Wijngaard has found his greatest success as a fine-art painter and illustrator, and his works have been exhibited at museums and galleries throughout the world. He began his career in book illustration in the early 1980s, and his detailed paintings have been pared with texts as varied as Toby Forward's *Shakespeare's Globe: An Interactive Pop-up Theatre,* nineteenth-century author John Ruskin's *The King of the Golden River: A Legend of Stiria,* and Sonia Levitin's evocative immigration story *A Piece of Home.* "Wijngaard's . . . realistic watercolor renderings, perceptive and expressive, virtually tell the story on their own," noted a *Publishers Weekly* contributor in appraising Levitin's story of a young boy's journey from Russia to the United States, while in *Booklist* Carolyn Phelan deemed the ingenious *Shakespeare's Globe* to be "beautifully painted." Citing the "superlative, painterly style" of the water-color illustrations in Wendy Cheyette Lewison's *Going to Sleep on the Farm,* a *Publishers Weekly* contributor noted that Winjgaard creates "portraits and landscapes with equal finesse," and his "striking, diverse perspectives of an idyllic farm scene" are enriched by his "keen observation of children's movements."

Wijngaard grew up in a creative household where he was encouraged to draw by his mother, a painter. Although he did not consider himself particularly gifted, the time he invested in drawing, and seeing his persistence translate into improvement, was perhaps more valuable that an artistic gift. As a teenager Wijngaard and his family relocated to the Netherlands, and they also lived in Switzerland for a time. After high school he suffered the monotony of an office job long enough to realize that he wanted to make his career in art. Once again, persistence paid off: after his first two applications were rejected, Wijngaard was admitted into London's Royal College of Art. While in school he discovered a second creative love—medieval folk music—and he has crafted and restored authentic instruments and performed this music since the 1970s. He also earned his first illustration assignment, creating the award-winning art for Rosemary Harris's *Green Finger House* while he was still a student.

In reviews of Wijngaard's contributions to children's literature, most critics have noted his attention to detail and his ability to capture the subtle emotions of a story with his paintbrush. In his work for *Cloud Tea Monkeys,* by Mal Peet and Elspeth Graham, he brings to life a Chinese legend about a poor young girl who is helped in finding a cure for her mother's illness with the help of a band of friendly monkeys. The "simple, elegant, and moving" eloquence in *Cloud Tea Monkeys* "is especially well complemented by Wijngaard's sumptuous illustrations," observed *Booklist* reviewer Ian Chipman,

Juan Wijngaard's illustrations have appeared in books that include Elspeth Graham and Mal Peet's engaging beginning reader Cloud Tea Monkeys. (Illustration copyright © 2010 by Juan Wijngaard. Reproduced by permission of Candlewick Press, Somerville, MA on behalf of Walker Books, London.)

while a *Publishers Weekly* critic wrote that the artist's "formal, expressive ink and gouache illustrations capture every nuance" of the Asian-inspired tale.

Another highly commended illustration project, Diane Wolkstein's *Esther's Story,* brings to life the biblical tale about the woman who braved a king's wrath in order to save the Jewish people. Winjgaard's "beautiful artwork . . . uses Persian costumes and motifs to excellent effect," wrote *Booklist* reviewer Ilene Cooper. The "lavish illustrations and Wolkstein's rendering . . . breathe new humanity into this grand and glorious story," asserted a *Publishers Weekly* reviewer, while in *Horn Book* Mary M. Burns hailed the art in *Esther's Story* as "opulently designed, painstakingly detailed, [and] richly allusive." Wijngaard's "elegant, glowing" images "suggest Persian art while retaining their own integrity in a handsome tribute to female heroism," Burns added.

Although Wijngaard worked in ink and opaque water color early in his illustration career, he has altered both his approach and his style as he has been exposed to different illustration challenges. In 2003 he began working in oils, a shift that brought with it recognition as a fine-art painter. "One of my favourite little pleasures in life is going to my studio with a bag full of new art supplies to play with," Wijngaard commented on the Walker Books Web site. "After illustrating over thirty books, I have started painting for its own sake, using oil paints on canvas. It is very different painting something that has to be seen from across a room, from something you hold in your hand!"

Biographical and Critical Sources

PERIODICALS

Booklist, April 1, 1994, Mary Harris Veeder, review of *Thunderstorm!,* p. 1453; March 15, 1996, Ilene Cooper, review of *Esther's Story,* p. 1264; November 15, 1996, Hazel Rochman, review of *A Piece of Home,* p. 594; May 15, 1999, Julie Corsaro, review of *Tales of Wonder and Magic,* p. 1625; November 15, 1999, Hazel Rochman, review of *The Midas Touch,* p. 631; May 1, 2005, Carolyn Phelan, review of *Shakespeare's Globe: An Interactive Pop-up Theatre,* p. 1581; February 15, 2010, Ian Chipman, review of *Cloud Tea Monkeys,* p. 75.

Horn Book, May-June, 1996, Mary M. Burns, review of *Esther's Story,* p. 354.

Kirkus Reviews, February 15, 2010, review of *Cloud Tea Monkeys.*

New York Times Book Review, October 20, 1985, review of *Sir Gawain and the Loathly Lady;* September 13, 1992, Meg Wolitzer, review of *Going to Sleep on the Farm.*

People, December 13, 1993, Susan Toepfer and Elizabeth Sporkin, review of *Emma Bean,* p. 38.

Publishers Weekly, March 29, 1991, reviews of *Dog, Duck, and Bear,* all p. 92; June 1, 1992, review of *Going to Sleep on the Farm,* p. 60; August 2, 1993, review of *Emma Bean,* p. 79; February 12, 1996, review of *Esther's Story,* p. 72; September 30, 1996, review of *The Nativity,* p. 91; November 18, 1996, review of *A Piece of Home,* p. 74; January 17, 2000, review of *The King of the Golden River: A Legend of Stiria,* p. 58; August 15, 2005, review of *Shakespeare's Globe,* p. 60; January 25, 2010, review of *Cloud Tea Monkeys,* p. 119.

School Librarian, summer, 2010, Anne-Marie Tarter, review of *Cloud Tea Monkeys,* p. 100.

School Library Journal, November, 2005, Nancy Menaldi-Scanlan, review of *Shakespeare's Globe,* p. 159; April, 2010, Miriam Lang Budin, review of *Cloud Tea Monkeys,* p. 136.

Times (London, England), February 28, 2010, Nicolette Jones, review of *Cloud Tea Monkeys,* p. 48.

ONLINE

Juan Wijngaard Home Page, http://juanwijngaard.com (May 27, 2011).

Walker Books Web site, http://www.walker.co.uk/ (May 15, 2011), "Juan Wijngaard."*

*　　*　　*

WILLIAMS, Maiya 1962-

Personal

Born December 18, 1962, in Corvallis, OR; married; children: three. *Education:* Harvard University, degree.

Addresses

Home—Los Angeles, CA. *E-mail*—MaiyaWV@aol.com.

Career

Writer and television producer. Columbia Pictures Television, story editor and consultant, beginning 1986, assistant to director of comedy development, beginning 1992, and supervising producer or co-producer of television series *Roc, The Fresh Prince of Bel-Air, The Wayans Bros.,* and *MADtv;* freelance writer beginning 2004. *Harvard Lampoon,* former editor and vice president.

Awards, Honors

International Reading Association Fiction Award; Southern California Booksellers Association Children's Book Prize.

Writings

The Golden Hour, Amulet Books (New York, NY), 2004.
The Hour of the Cobra (sequel to *The Golden Hour*), Amulet Books (New York, NY), 2006.

Maiya Williams (Photograph by Rich Schmitt. Reproduced by permission.)

The Hour of the Outlaw (sequel to *The Hour of the Cobra*), Amulet Books (New York, NY), 2007.
The Fizzy Whiz Kid, Amulet Books (New York, NY), 2010.

Writer for television series, including *What's Happening Now!,* 1985, *The Redd Foxx Show,* 1986, *Amen,* 1986, *New Attitude,* 1990, *Going Places,* 1990-91, *Roc,* 1992, *The Fresh Prince of Bel-Air,* 1993-95, *The Wayans Bros.,* 1995-99, *The Pjs,* 2000, *MADtv,* 2002-06, *Class of 3000,* 2007, *The Wanda Sykes Show,* 2009-10, and *Futurama,* 2010.

Adaptations

The Golden Hour was adapted for audiobook, read by Kevin R. Free, Recorded Books, 2004.

Sidelights

Maiya Williams has had a long and successful career in television, both as a writer and producer for television shows such as *The Fresh Prince of Bel-Air, MADtv,* and *Roc.* In 2003 Williams also branched out into fiction writing, finding equal success as the author of the middle-grade novel *The Fizzy Whiz Kid* and a time-travel fantasy trilogy that includes *The Golden Hour, The Hour of the Cobra,* and *The Hour of the Outlaw.*

In *The Golden Hour* readers meet Rowan Popplewell and younger sister Nina as they look ahead to spending the summer with eccentric aunts Agatha and Gertrude in the small town of Owatannauk, Maine. Thirteen-year-old Rowan just wants to play video games and avoid remembering that his mom is dead. However, when he and Nina meet neighboring twins Xanthe and Xavier Alexander, he finds that real-life adventures are far more fun than guiding the action of online avatars. When the four children discover that a boarded-up old hotel in town is actually a way-station for time travelers, they ignore the warnings of Agatha and Gertrude to avoid the place. Soon Nina and Rowan find themselves joining the twins in late eighteenth-century Paris, France. The year is 1789, and the country is on the brink of revolution. With Nina lost somewhere in the riotous city, Rowan, Xanthe, and Xavier decide to split up and track her down, hopefully without drawing unwanted attention and winding up in the line forming for a date with Madame Guillotine. Citing the story's "mix of history, adventure, fantasy, and character growth," a *Kirkus Reviews* contributor added that Williams "is reasonably meticulous with historical detail" while also "keeping the story moving." The author "is a talented

Cover of Williams' young-adult novel The Fizzy Whiz Kid, *featuring artwork by Michael Koelsch.* (Amulet Books, 2010. Cover art copyright © 2010 by Michael Koelsch. Reproduced by permission of Harry N. Abrams, Inc.)

visual storyteller," wrote *New York Times Book Review* critic Doug Ward, and in *The Golden Hour* her "descriptions . . . are vivid . . . , her characters real and her settings palpable." "Action-packed and laden with good-natured humor," according to a *Publishers Weekly* critic, *The Golden Hour* "is a journey worth taking."

Rowan and Nina's adventures continue in *The Hour of the Cobra,* as the four children return to the time portal at the abandoned hotel. This time they travel back in time to ancient Egypt, where manuscripts at the Alexandrian library are threatened and must be saved for posterity. Although the rules of time travel are strict—no meddling with the past—Xanthe begins a friendship with Cleopatra and her influence on the future monarch may have history-changing consequences. The wild west of the late 1800s is the place where Rowan, Nina, and the twins find themselves in *The Hour of the Outlaw,* as they deal with the lawlessness and intolerance of desperate people hoping to get rich quick during the California Gold Rush. Meanwhile, while dealing with a mysterious rift in the laws of time travel, the siblings track down teen runaway Balthazar Weber, whose father invented time travel. Noting that Williams includes well-researched details about life in Ptolemaic Egypt to flesh out her story in *The Hour of the Cobra,* Beth L. Meister added in *School Library Journal* that Xanthe and Xavier's "roles in Egypt are limited because they are African American, an unusual touch for a fantasy novel." In *Booklist* Phelan remarked on the "action, reflection, and humor" in *The Hour of the Outlaw,* while Tasha Saecker noted in *School Library Journal* that the humorous perspective of contemporary teens on life in "the Old West gives this book a readability . . . often . . . absent from historical fiction."

Williams turns from time-travel fantasy to humor in *The Fizzy Whiz Kid.* When readers meet Mitch Mathis, the sixth grader has just moved to Hollywood where his entomologist father is studying cockroaches. All his fellow students are involved with the movie business in one way or another, and Mitch yearns to fit in. When he enters a talent search and is hired to act in several commercials for Fizzy Wiz Soda, Mitch quickly becomes caught up in the glamour of the film industry. Although he ignores his old friends in favor of new ones on the film set, his true pals do not fail him when Fizzy Whiz is targeted by a government agency and Mitch becomes the poster boy for unhealthy junk food. "Williams' breezy tale is as addictive and bubbly as a Fizzy Whiz itself," wrote *Booklist* critic Daniel Kraus, "and her experience in the entertainment industry packs real value" into the novel. A *Publishers Weekly* critic dubbed *The Fizzy Whiz Kid* an "effervescent comedy" that "spotlights the unglamorous side of show business," while *School Library Journal* reviewer Terrie Dorio recommended the book as "an entertaining read" for middle graders.

Biographical and Critical Sources

PERIODICALS

Black Issues Book Review, March-April, 2005, Brittainy McCree, review of *The Golden Hour,* p. 16.

Booklist, March 15, 2004, Carolyn Phelan, review of *The Golden Hour,* p. 1307; May 15, 2006, Carolyn Phelan, review of *The Hour of the Cobra,* p. 61; January 1, 2008, Carolyn Phelan, review of *The Hour of the Outlaw,* p. 76; March 1, 2010, Daniel Kraus, review of *The Fizzy Whiz Kid,* p. 70.

Journal of Adolescent & Adult Literacy, April, 2005, Sara Ann Schettler, review of *The Golden Hour,* p. 621.

Kirkus Reviews, February 15, 2004, review of *The Golden Hour,* p. 187; March 15, 2006, review of *The Hour of the Cobra,* p. 303; January 1, 2010, review of *The Fizzy Whiz Kid.*

Kliatt, January, 2005, Sherri Ginsberg, review of *The Golden Hour,* p. 42.

Publishers Weekly, March 22, 2004, review of *The Golden Hour,* p. 86; February 22, 2010, review of *The Fizzy Whiz Kid,* p. 65.

New York Times Book Review, August 8, 2004, Doug Ward, review of *The Golden Hour,* p. 17.

Reading Teacher, November, 2005, Gary Willhite, review of *The Golden Hour,* p. 277.

School Library Journal, April, 2004, Beth L. Meister, review of *The Golden Hour,* p. 163; July, 2006, Beth L. Meister, review of *The Hour of the Cobra,* p. 116; January, 2008, Tasha Saecker, review of *The Hour of the Outlaw,* p. 129; May, 2010, Terrie Dorio, review of *The Fizzy Whiz Kid,* p. 125.

ONLINE

Maiya Williams Home Page, http://www.maiyawilliams.com (May 27, 2011).

*   *   *

WOHNOUTKA, Mike

Personal

Born in Spicer, MN; father an engineer; married; children: Franklin, Olivia. *Education:* Savannah College of Art and Design, B.F.A. (illustration), 1993.

Addresses

Home—Minneapolis, MN. *E-mail*—mwtka@yahoo.com.

Career

Illustrator and fine-art painter. Formerly worked as a designer for a gift company. Presenter at schools. *Exhibitions:* Work included in Original Art Show, Society of Illustrators, New York, NY, 2008.

Awards, Honors

Buckaroo Award nomination, 2001, for *Cowboy Sam and Those Confounded Secrets* by Kitty Griffin and Kathy Combs; Beverly Cleary Children's Choice Award,

Mike Wohnoutka (Reproduced by permission.)

2003, for *Davey's Blue-eyed Frog* by Patricia Harrison Easton; Bank Street College of Education Best Children's Book designation, 2004, for *The Foot-stomping Adventures of Clementine Sweet* by Griffin and Combs, and 2008, for *Jack's House* by Karen Magnuson Beil.

Illustrator

Julie Glass, *Counting Sheep,* Random House (New York, NY), 2000.

David L. Harrison, *Johnny Appleseed: My Story,* Random House (New York, NY), 2001.

Kitty Griffin and Kathy Combs, *Cowboy Sam and Those Confounded Secrets,* Clarion (New York, NY), 2001.

Patricia Harrison Easton, *Davey's Blue-eyed Frog,* Clarion (New York, NY), 2003.

Kitty Griffin and Kathy Combs, *The Foot-stomping Adventures of Clementine Sweet,* Clarion (New York, NY), 2004.

Stephen Krensky, *My Dad Can Do Anything,* Random House (New York, NY), 2004.

This Little Piggy, Kindermusik International (Greensboro, NC), 2005.

Gary Hogg, *Look What the Cat Dragged In!,* Dutton (New York, NY), 2005.

Roni Schotter, *When the Wizzy Foot Goes Walking,* Dutton (New York, NY), 2007.

Karen Magnuson Beil, *Jack's House,* Holiday House (New York, NY), 2008.

Marjorie Blain Parker, *Mama's Little Duckling,* Dutton (New York, NY), 2008.

Constance Van Hoven, *The Twelve Days of Christmas in Minnesota,* Sterling Pub. Co. (New York, NY), 2009.

(With Guy Francis) Tim Kehoe, *The Unusual Mind of Vincent Shadow* (includes notebook), Little, Brown (New York, NY), 2009.

Susanna Leonard Hill, *Can't Sleep without Sheep,* Walker & Co. (New York, NY), 2010.

(With others) Tim Kehoe, *Vincent Shadow: Toy Inventor* (includes notebook), Little, Brown (New York, NY), 2011.

Contributor to periodicals, including *Cricket* and *Spider.*

Sidelights

A graduate of the Savannah College of Art and Design, Minnesota native Mike Wohnoutka now works in advertising and editorial illustration, where his clients include General Mills and *Cricket* magazine. In addition to his work in commercial illustration, Wohnoutka has also provided the artwork for numerous children's books, including *Cowboy Sam and Those Confounded Secrets* by coauthors Kitty Griffin and Kathy Combs, *When the Wizzy Foot Goes Walking* by Roni Schotter, and *Can't Sleep without Sheep* by Susanna Leonard Hill. Reviewing Hill's story about a little girl whose sleeplessness puts demands on a flock of leaping sheep, Kim T. Ha added in *School Library Journal* that Wohnoutka's "charming, rounded illustrations" contribute to a story that "will quickly become a bedtime favorite."

Growing up in Spicer, Minnesota, Wohnoutka was encouraged to draw by his father, who provided his son with extra copies of oversized engineering documents which had printing on only one side. By high school, he was encouraged by his art teacher to consider a career that would allow him to use his talent for drawing, and a scholarship to Georgia-based Savannah College of Art and Design cemented Wohnoutka's choice of vocation.

Wohnoutka's first children's-book project was illustrating *Counting Sheep,* a story by Julie Glass that was published in 2000. When a youngster struggles to fall asleep one night, he begins counting off a series of creatures, including sheep, kangaroos, monkeys, and bees, all of which quickly crowd into his bedroom. The illustrator's "pleasing paintings . . . ably balance [the] fantasy and humor" in Glass's tale, *Booklist* reviewer Carolyn Phelan stated of the picture book. Wohnoutka has also crafted the pictures for David L. Harrison's *Johnny Appleseed: My Story.* In this easy reader, the legendary American tall-tale figure offers his help to a pioneer family and then recounts his life for the children's amusement. Wohnoutka offers "buoyant paintings that capture the beauty of the landscape," Phelan noted of the work.

Set in Dry Gulch, Texas, *Cowboy Sam and Those Confounded Secrets* is a tall tale by Griffin and Combs. The dedicated keeper of the residents' private thoughts,

A loving relationship is captured in Wohnoutka's humorous paintings for Marjorie Blain Parker's **Mama's Little Duckling.** (Illustration copyright © 2008 by Mike Wohnoutka. Reproduced by permission of Dutton Children's Books, a division of Penguin Books for Young Readers, a member of Penguin Group (USA) Inc., 345 Hudson St., New York, NY 10014. All rights reserved.)

Cowboy Sam keeps every secret stashed under his ten-gallon hat. When the hat fills up, however, it begins popping off Sam's head, threatening to spill its contents. Sam tries to weigh down the hat with horseshoes and bags of oats, but to no avail until he concocts the perfect solution to the problem. A *Publishers Weekly* reviewer compared Wohnoutka's illustrations to those of Mark Teague, "particularly in their large-as-life perspectives and round, stylized faces, but the palette here is milder, brushed with the soft colors of the Southwest."

Wohnoutka also collaborates with Griffin and Combs on *The Foot-stomping Adventures of Clementine Sweet,* another humorous tale. Angered that her sixth birthday has been forgotten, Clementine disrupts a family reunion by stomping on the feet of her relatives, which soon becomes her trademark manner of expressing frustration. When a twister threatens her town, the youngster puts her strong legs to work for a good cause. According to *School Library Journal* critic Grace Oliff, Wohnoutka's "acrylic cartoon illustrations" for *The Foot-stomping Adventures of Clementine Sweet* "provide a sunny landscape and a pugnacious heroine seen from a variety of amusing perspectives."

Writer Patricia Harrison Easton is helped by Wohnoutka in putting a visual twist on a familiar tale in her picture-book text for *Davey's Blue-eyed Frog.* After a spell transforms Princess Amelia into a frog, she is discovered by Davey, a youngster who despises the thought of kissing an amphibian and hates Amelia's bossy manner. "Wohnoutka's light, cartoony pencil illustrations keep the story hopping along," remarked a critic in *Kirkus Reviews,* and Phelan observed that in "sympathetic and often amusing depictions of the characters," Wohnoutka's illustrations "enhance the story's child appeal." In Gary Hogg's *Look What the Cat Dragged In!* the members of the Lazybone family bully their frantic feline into completing numerous household chores. When the Lazybones contemplate getting a dog, however, the cat decides to even the score. Wohnoutka's "animated scenes put the right spin on the absurdity," wrote Julie Cummins in her *Booklist* review of Hoggs' humorous picture book.

A work told in verse, Schotter's *When the Wizzy Foot Goes Walking* follows an energetic toddler throughout his day. Writing in *School Library Journal,* Amy Lilien-Harper commented that "Wohnoutka's boldly painted cartoons are full of motion and fit the story well." In *Mama's Little Duckling,* a read-aloud by Marjorie Blain Parker, Mama Quack cautiously watches over her inquisitive youngster, Dandelion Duckling, who loves exploring. When Dandelion alerts its mother to danger, though, the worried mother gains confidence in its abilities. Wohnoutka's illustrations for Parker's text again garnered praise. "Glowing with bold shades of turquoise, orange, gold, and green, the oversize illustrations vibrantly depict" the setting and action of the story, Judith Constantinides remarked in *School Library Journal.*

Wohnoutka's artwork for Roni Schotter's story in When the Wizzy Foot Goes Walking *captures the perspective of a lighthearted child.* (Illustration copyright © 2007 by Mike Wohnoutka. Reproduced by permission of Dutton Children's Books, a division of Penguin Books for Young Readers, a member of Penguin Group (USA) Inc., 345 Hudson St., New York, NY 10014. All rights reserved.)

Other picture-book projects include *Jack's House,* Karen Magnuson Beil's revisioning of the popular cumulative rhyme. In this story, Jack builds his house with the help of Max, a dog with construction expertise and a hard-working crew of other pups. In his illustrations, Wohnoutka appeals to young boys: his busy canine workers use a wide range of tools and machinery in building the home, all while Jack is distracted elsewhere. Adding humor to Beil's story, these images "are . . . full of small details for readers to enjoy," according to *School Library Journal* critic Susan E. Murray, the critic predicting of *Jack's House* that the "beguiling" picture book "will be a hit . . . at storytimes."

"Ever since I can remember I knew I wanted to be an artist," Wohnoutka once told *SATA.* "My dad, who was an engineer at the Highway Department, would bring home reams of paper that had highway plans on one side and were blank on the other. I would be so excited to have all that paper to draw on and would fill each sheet with race cars, snowmobiles, baseball players, super heroes, everything I was interested in. In high school my art teacher, Mr. Chase, encouraged me to pursue art as a career. This, along with a scholarship, led me to the Savannah College of Art and Design in Savannah, Georgia. Since graduating with a B.F.A. in illustration, I have worked with various clients. Even though I was a trouble maker in grade school (principals still make me nervous), I enjoy visiting schools and talking to students about illustrating children's books."

Biographical and Critical Sources

PERIODICALS

Booklist, December 1, 2000, Carolyn Phelan, review of *Counting Sheep,* p. 725; February 1, 2002, Carolyn Phelan, review of *Johnny Appleseed: My Story,* p. 949; March 1, 2003, Carolyn Phelan, review of *Davey's Blue-eyed Frog,* p. 1197; March 1, 2004, Ilene Cooper, review of *The Foot-stomping Adventures of Clementine Sweet,* p. 1204; November 1, 2005, Julie Cummins, review of *Look What the Cat Dragged In!,* p. 52; October 15, 2009, Ian Chipman, review of *The Unusual Mind of Vincent Shadow,* p. 65.

Kirkus Reviews, April 15, 2003, review of *Davey's Blue-eyed Frog,* p. 606; November 1, 2005, review of *Look What the Cat Dragged In!,* p. 1184; July 15, 2007, review of *When the Wizzy Foot Goes Walking;* January 15, 2008, review of *Mama's Little Duckling;* August 15, 2008, review of *Jack's House;* October 1, 2009, review of *The Unusual Mind of Vincent Shadow.*

Publishers Weekly, July 16, 2001, review of *Cowboy Sam and Those Confounded Secrets,* p. 180; January 14, 2008, review of *Mama's Little Duckling,* p. 56; November 2, 2009, review of *The Unusual Mind of Vincent Shadow,* p. 52.

School Library Journal, December, 2001, Shara Alpern, review of *Cowboy Sam and Those Confounded Secrets,* p. 103; July, 2003, Linda B. Zeilstra, review of *Davey's Blue-eyed Frog,* p. 95; March, 2004, Grace Oliff, review of *The Foot-stomping Adventures of Clementine Sweet,* p. 169; February, 2006, Julie Roach, review of *Look What the Cat Dragged In!,* p. 104; August, 2007, Amy Lilien-Harper, review of *When the Wizzy Foot Goes Walking,* p. 90; February, 2008, Judith Constantinides, review of *Mama's Little Duckling,* p. 94; October, 2008, Susan E. Murray, review of *Jack's House,* p. 101; December, 2009, Jeffrey Hastings, review of *The Unusual Mind of Vincent Shadow,* p. 122; September, 2010, Kim T. Ha, review of *Can't Sleep without Sheep,* p. 125.

ONLINE

Children's Literature Network Online, http://www.childrens literaturenetwork.org/ (May 21, 2011), "Mike Wohnoutka."

Mike Wohnoutka Home Page, http://mikewohnoutka.com (May 21, 2011).

*   *   *

YEATES, Thomas 1955-

Personal

Born January 19, 1955; married; has children. *Education:* Joe Kubert School of Art (now the Kubert School), degree.

Addresses

Office—P.O. Box 124, Jenner, CA 95450 *E-mail*—tyeates@arrowflight.com.

Career

Sequential artist and illustrator for comic books and children's books.

Writings

GRAPHIC NOVELS

(With Mark Johnson) Roy Thomas, *The Dragonlance Saga,* TSR (Lake Geneva, WI), 1987.

(With Timothy Truman) Timothy Truman, *Scout: The Four Monsters,* Eclipse Books (Forestville, CA), 1988.

Don McGregor, *Zorro: The Dailies, the First Year,* Image Comics (Orange, CA), 2001.

(With others) Al Williamson, *Hidden Lands,* Dark Horse (Milwaukie, OR), 2004.

(With Cary Nord) Kurt Busiek, *Conan: The Frost Giant and Other Stories* (originally published in comic-book format), Dark Horse Comics (Milwaukie, OR), 2005.

Justine and Ron Fontes, *Atalanta: The Race against Destiny: A Greek Myth,* Graphic Universe (Minneapolis, MN), 2007.

Bob Hughes, *The Outlaw Prince* (based on *The Outlaw of Torn* by Edgar Rich Burroughs), Dark Horse Comics (Milwaukie, OR), 2011.

Contributor to comic-book series for publishers Epic/Marvel, D.C. Comics, Image Comics, and Dark Horse Comics, including "Tarzan," "Conan," "Swamp Thing," "Timespirits," "Universe X," and "Warlord."

GRAPHIC NOVELS; "GRAPHIC MYTHS AND LEGENDS" SERIES

Jef Limke, *King Arthur: Excalibur Unsheathed: An English Legend,* Graphic Universe (Minneapolis, MN), 2007.

Paul D. Storrie, *Robin Hood: Outlaw of Sherwood Forest: An English Legend,* Graphic Universe (Minneapolis, MN), 2007.

Jeff Limke, *Arthur and Lancelot: The Fight for Camelot: An English Legend,* Graphic Universe (Minneapolis, MN), 2008.

Dan Jolley, *Odysseus: Escaping Poseidon's Curse: A Greek Legend,* Graphic Universe (Minneapolis, MN), 2008.

Paul D. Storrie, *Perseus: The Hunt for Medusa's Head: A Greek Myth,* Graphic Universe (Minneapolis, MN), 2008.

Paul D. Storrie, *William Tell: One against an Empire: A Swiss Legend,* Graphic Universe (Minneapolis, MN), 2009.

Sidelights

Through his work as a illustrator for major comic-book publishers such as D.C. Comics, Image Comics, Marvel, and Dark Horse, Thomas Yeates has become known for breathing new life into heroic characters such as Conan the Barbarian, who made his way into comic books in the early twentieth century after being created by nineteenth-century novelist Edgar Rice Burroughs. After studying at the Joe Kubert School of Art, which specializes in cartooning and graphic art, Yeates worked in underground comics, such as Larry Shell's "Alien Encounters" series, before approaching mainstream comic-book publishers. By the 1980s he was freelancing for D.C. Comics, where he worked on "Swamp Thing," and he has also contributed to Marvel's "Universe X" series, among others. Reviewing Yeates' work on Kurt Busiek's "Conan" story arc—collected into graphic-novel form as *Conan: The Frost Giant and Other Stories*—*Library Journal* critic Steve Raiteri wrote that the book's "vivid and realistic artwork, lushly colored, matches the storytelling well."

Yeates' art is noted for its realism and strong use of line, and the artist channels this realism into the work he has done on the "Graphic Myths and Legends" books retelling the stories of several of history's heroes. In *Perseus: The Hunt for Medusa's Head: A Greek Myth* Yeates and writer Paul Storrie "provide . . . a riveting introduction to this demigod's exploits," according to *School Library Journal* critic Joy Fleischhacker, while *Odysseus: Escaping Poseidon's Curse: A Greek Legend* pairs a "brisk narrative" by writer Dan Jolley with Yeates' "vigorous artwork" to tell the story of the famous traveler and warrior as he returns home to Ithaca after fighting in the Trojan War. Yeates returns to ancient myths in illustrating *Atalanta: The Race against Destiny: A Greek Myth,* a standalone graphic novel by husband-and-wife writing team Justine and Ron Fontes that "will win readers with is concise storytelling and energetic artwork," according to Fleishhacker.

Biographical and Critical Sources

PERIODICALS

Booklist, February 15, 2005, Gordon Flagg, review of *Hidden Lands,* p. 1071.

Library Journal, September 15, 2005, Steve Raiteri, review of *Conan: The Frost Giant's Daughter and Other Stories,* p. 53.

School Library Journal, November, 2006, Eric Norton, review of *To the Ends of the Earth: An Egyptian Myth,* p. 167; April, 2009, Joy B. Fleishhacker, "Superheroes of Ancient Greece: Spanning the Centuries in a Single Bound," p. 5.

ONLINE

Thomas Yeates Home Page, http://www.thomasyeates.com (May 27, 2011).*

YOLEN, Jane 1939-

Personal

Born February 11, 1939, in New York, NY; daughter of Will Hyatt (an author and publicist) and Isabelle (a social worker, puzzle-maker, and homemaker) Yolen; married David W. Stemple (a professor of computer science and ornithologist), September 2, 1962 (died of cancer, March, 2006); children: Heidi Elisabeth, Adam Douglas, Jason Frederic. *Education:* Smith College, B.A., 1960; University of Massachusetts, M.Ed., 1976; completed course work for doctorate in children's literature at University of Massachusetts. *Politics:* "Liberal Democrat." *Religion:* Jewish/Quaker. *Hobbies and other interests:* "Folk music and dancing, reading, camping, politics, all things Scottish."

Addresses

Home—Phoenix Farm, 31 School St., Box 27, Hatfield, MA 01038; Wayside, 96 Hepburn Gardens, St. Andrews, Fife KY16 9LN, Scotland. *Agent*—Elizabeth Harding Curtis Brown Ltd., 10 Astor Place, New York, NY 10003.

Career

Saturday Review, New York, NY, production assistant, 1960-61; Gold Medal Books (publishers), New York, NY, assistant editor, 1961-62; Rutledge Books (publishers), New York, NY, associate editor, 1962-63; Alfred A. Knopf, Inc. (publishers), New York, NY, assistant juvenile editor, 1963-65; full-time professional writer, beginning 1965. Editor of imprint Jane Yolen Books for Harcourt Brace Jovanovich, 1988-98. Teacher of writing and lecturer, 1966—; has taught children's literature at Smith College. Chairman of board of library trustees, Hatfield, MA, 1976-83; member of Hatfield Arts Council.

Member

Society of Children's Book Writers and Illustrators (co-founder and member of advisory board, 1974—, and former New England regional advisor), Science Fiction/Fantasy Writers of America (president, 1986-88), Author's Guild, Children's Literature Association (member of board of directors, 1977-79), Science Fiction Poetry Association, National Association for the Preservation and Perpetuation of Storytelling, Western New England Storyteller's Guild (founder), Bay State Writers Guild, Western Massachusetts Illustrators Guild (founder), Smith College Alumnae Association.

Awards, Honors

Boys' Club of America Junior Book Award, 1968, for *The Minstrel and the Mountain;* Lewis Carroll Shelf Award, 1968, for *The Emperor and the Kite,* 1973, for *The Girl Who Loved the Wind;* Best Books of the Year selection, *New York Times,* 1968, for *The Emperor and*

Jane Yolen (Copyright © 2000 by Jason Stemple. Reprinted by permission of Curtis Brown, Ltd. All rights reserved.)

the Kite; American Library Association (ALA) Notable Book designation, 1968, for *World on a String*; Children's Book Showcase selection, Children's Book Council (CBC), 1973, for *The Girl Who Loved the Wind,* and 1976, for *The Little Spotted Fish;* Golden Kite Award, Society of Children's Book Writers and Illustrators (SCBWI), 1974, ALA Notable Book designation, 1975, and National Book Award nomination, 1975, all for *The Girl Who Cried Flowers and Other Tales;* Golden Kite Honor Book designation, 1975, for *The Transfigured Hart,* and 1976, for *The Moon Ribbon and Other Tales;* Christopher Medal, 1978, for *The Seeing Stick,* and 2000, for *How Do Dinosaurs Say Goodnight?;* Children's Choice selection, International Reading Association (IRA)/CBC, 1980, for *Mice on Ice,* and 1983, for *Dragon's Blood;* Parents' LL.D., College of Our Lady of the Elms (Chicopee, MA), 1981, and Smith College, 2003; Choice selections, Parents' Choice Foundation, 1982, for *Dragon's Blood,* 1984, for *The Stone Silenus,* and 1989, for both *Piggins* and *The Three Bears Rhyme Book;* Garden State Children's Book Award, New Jersey Library Association, 1983, for *Commander Toad in Space;* CRABbery Award, Acton (MD) Public Library, 1983, for *Dragon's Blood;* ALA Best Books for Young Adults selection, 1984, for *Heart's Blood;* Mythopoeic Society Fantasy Award, 1984, for *Cards of Grief,* 1993, for *Briar Rose,* 1998, for "Young Merlin" trilogy; Daedelus Award, 1986; *The Lullaby Songbook* and *The Sleeping Beauty* selected among Child Study Association of America's Children's Books of the Year,

1987; World Fantasy Award, 1988, for *Favorite Folktales from around the World;* Parents' Choice Silver Seal award, Jewish Book Council Award, and Sydney Taylor Book Award, Association of Jewish Libraries, all 1988, Judy Lopez Honor Book designation, and Nebula Award finalist, both 1989, and Maude Hart Lovelace Award, 1996, all for *The Devil's Arithmetic;* Kerlan Award, 1988, for "singular achievements in the creation of children's literature"; Golden Sower Award, Nebraska Library Association, 1989, and Charlotte Award, New York State Reading Association, both for *Piggins;* Smith College Medal, 1990; Skylark Award, New England Science Fiction Association, 1990; Regina Medal, 1992, for body of writing; Keene State College Children's Literature Festival award, 1995; *Storytelling World* Award, 1997, for "The World the Devil Made Up"; honorary doctorate, Keene State College, 1998; named Literary Light, Boston Public Library, 1998; Nebula Award for Best Short Story, 1997, for "Sister Emily's Lightship"; Nebula Award for Best Novelette, 1998, for "Lost Girls"; Anna V. Zarrow Award, 1999; Smith College Remarkable Women designation, 1999, and honorary Ph.D., 2003; California Young Reader Medal in Young-Adult Category, 2001, and ALA Best Books and Best Books for Young Adults designations, both 2004, all for *Armageddon Summer;* National Outdoor Book Award, 2002, for *Wild Wings;* National Storytelling Network ORACLE Award, 2003; *Writer* Award, 2004; John Burroughs Society Award, 2010, for *A Mirror to Nature;* Massachusetts Reading Association Award, 2010, for lifetime achievement; Bank Street College of Education Best Books selection, 2010, for both *Come to the Fairie's Ball* and *My Uncle Emily;* named Grand Master, Science Fiction Poetry Association, 2010; (with Andrew Fusek Peters) Oppenheimer Gold Award, 2010, for *Switching on the Moon,* and *All Star;* (with Heidi Stemple) Crystal Kite Award, SCBWI—New England Region, 2010, for *Not All Princesses Dress in Pink. The Emperor and the Kite* was named a Caldecott Medal Honor Book designation, 1968, for illustrations by Ed Young; *Owl Moon* received the Caldecott Medal, 1988, for illustrations by John Schoenherr.

Writings

FOR CHILDREN; PICTURE BOOKS AND FICTION

The Witch Who Wasn't, illustrated by Arnold Roth, Macmillan (New York, NY), 1964.

Gwinellen, the Princess Who Could Not Sleep, illustrated by Ed Renfro, Macmillan (New York, NY), 1965.

The Emperor and the Kite, illustrated by Ed Young, World Publishing (Cleveland, OH), 1967, reprinted, Philomel (New York, NY), 1988.

The Minstrel and the Mountain: A Tale of Peace, illustrated by Anne Rockwell, World Publishing (Cleveland, OH), 1967.

Isabel's Noel, illustrated by Arnold Roth, Funk & Wagnalls (New York, NY), 1967.

Greyling: A Picture Story from the Islands of Shetland, illustrated by William Stobbs, World Publishing (Cleveland, OH), 1968, illustrated by David Ray, Philomel (New York, NY), 1991.

The Longest Name on the Block, illustrated by Peter Madden, Funk & Wagnalls (New York, NY), 1968.

The Wizard of Washington Square, illustrated by Ray Cruz, World Publishing (Cleveland, OH), 1969.

The Inway Investigators; or, The Mystery at McCracken's Place, illustrated by Allan Eitzen, Seabury (New York, NY), 1969.

Hobo Toad and the Motorcycle Gang, illustrated by Emily McCully, World Publishing (Cleveland, OH), 1970.

The Seventh Mandarin, illustrated by Ed Young, Seabury (New York, NY), 1970.

The Bird of Time, illustrated by Mercer Mayer, Crowell (New York, NY), 1971.

The Girl Who Loved the Wind, illustrated by Ed Young, Crowell (New York, NY), 1972.

The Girl Who Cried Flowers and Other Tales, illustrated by David Palladini, Crowell (New York, NY), 1974.

The Boy Who Had Wings, illustrated by Helga Aichinger, Crowell (New York, NY), 1974.

The Adventures of Eeka Mouse, illustrated by Myra McKee, Xerox Education Publications (Middletown, CT), 1974.

The Rainbow Rider, illustrated by Michael Foreman, Crowell (New York, NY), 1974.

The Little Spotted Fish, illustrated by Friso Henstra, Seabury (New York, NY), 1975.

The Transfigured Hart, illustrated by Donna Diamond, Crowell (New York, NY), 1975, reprinted, Harcourt (New York, NY), 1997.

Milkweed Days, photographs by Gabriel Amadeus Cooney, Crowell (New York, NY), 1976.

The Moon Ribbon and Other Tales, illustrated by David Palladini, Crowell (New York, NY), 1976, 1976.

The Seeing Stick, illustrated by Remy Charlip and Demetra Maraslis, Crowell (New York, NY), 1977.

The Sultan's Perfect Tree, illustrated by Barbara Garrison, Parents' Magazine Press (New York, NY), 1977.

The Hundredth Dove and Other Tales, illustrated by David Palladini, Crowell (New York, NY), 1977.

Hannah Dreaming, photographs by Alan R. Epstein, Museum of Fine Art (Springfield, MA), 1977.

The Lady and the Merman, illustrated by Barry Moser, Pennyroyal Press, 1977.

Spider Jane, illustrated by Stefan Bernath, Coward (New York, NY), 1978.

The Simple Prince, illustrated by Jack Kent, Parents' Magazine Press (New York, NY), 1978.

No Bath Tonight, illustrated by Nancy Winslow Parker, Crowell (New York, NY), 1978.

The Mermaid's Three Wisdoms, illustrated by Laura Rader, Collins (New York, NY), 1978.

Dream Weaver and Other Tales, illustrated by Michael Hague, Collins (New York, NY), 1979, published as *Dream Weaver,* 1989.

Spider Jane on the Move, illustrated by Stefan Bernath, Coward (New York, NY), 1980.

Mice on Ice, illustrated by Lawrence DiFiori, Dutton (New York, NY), 1980.

Shirlick Holmes and the Case of the Wandering Wardrobe, illustrated by Anthony Rao, Coward (New York, NY), 1981.

The Acorn Quest, illustrated by Susanna Natti, Harper (New York, NY), 1981.

Brothers of the Wind, illustrated by Barbara Berger, Philomel (New York, NY), 1981.

Sleeping Ugly, illustrated by Diane Stanley, Coward (New York, NY), 1981.

The Boy Who Spoke Chimp, illustrated by David Wiesner, Knopf (New York, NY), 1981.

Uncle Lemon's Spring, illustrated by Glen Rounds, Dutton (New York, NY), 1981.

(Reteller) *The Sleeping Beauty,* illustrated by Ruth Sanderson, Knopf (New York, NY), 1986.

Owl Moon, illustrated by John Schoenherr, Philomel (New York, NY), 1987.

Dove Isabeau, illustrated by Dennis Nolan, Harcourt (New York, NY), 1989.

Baby Bear's Bedtime Book, illustrated by Jane Dyer, Harcourt (New York, NY), 1990.

Sky Dogs, illustrated by Barry Moser, Harcourt (New York, NY), 1990.

(Reteller) *Tam Lin: An Old Ballad,* illustrated by Charles Mikolaycak, Harcourt (New York, NY), 1990.

Elfabet: An ABC of Elves, illustrated by Lauren Mills, Little, Brown (Boston, MA), 1990.

Letting Swift River Go, illustrated by Barbara Cooney, Little, Brown (Boston, MA), 1990.

The Dragon's Boy, Harper (New York, NY), 1990.

Wizard's Hall, Harcourt (New York, NY), 1991.

Hark! A Christmas Sampler, illustrated by Tomie dePaola, music by son, Adam Stemple, Putnam (New York, NY), 1991.

(Reteller) *Wings,* Harcourt (New York, NY), 1991.

All Those Secrets of the World (autobiographical fiction), illustrated by Leslie Baker, Little, Brown (Boston, MA), 1991.

Encounter, illustrated by David Shannon, Harcourt (New York, NY), 1992.

Eeny, Meeny, Miney Mole, illustrated by Kathryn Brown, Harcourt (New York, NY), 1992.

Mouse's Birthday, illustrated by Bruce Degen, Putnam (New York, NY), 1993.

Hands, illustrated by Chi Chung, Sundance Publishing, 1993.

Honkers, illustrated by Leslie Baker, Little, Brown (Boston, MA), 1993.

Travelers Rose, Putnam (New York, NY), 1993.

Beneath the Ghost Moon, illustrated by Laurel Molk, Little, Brown (Boston, MA), 1994.

Grandad Bill's Song, illustrated by Melissa Bay Mathis, Philomel (New York, NY), 1994.

And Twelve Chinese Acrobats (autobiographical fiction), illustrated by Jean Gralley, Philomel (New York, NY), 1994.

Good Griselle, illustrated by David Christiana, Harcourt (New York, NY), 1994.

The Girl in the Golden Bower, illustrated by Jane Dyer, Little, Brown (Boston, MA), 1994.

Old Dame Counterpane, illustrated by Ruth Tietjen Councell, Putnam (New York, NY), 1994.

(Reteller) *Little Mouse and Elephant: A Tale from Turkey,* illustrated by John Segal, Simon & Schuster (New York, NY), 1994.

(Reteller) *The Musicians of Bremen: A Tale from Germany,* illustrated by John Segal, Simon & Schuster (New York, NY), 1994.

The Ballad of the Pirate Queen, illustrated by David Shannon, Harcourt (New York, NY), 1995.

Before the Storm, illustrated by Georgia Pugh, Boyds Mills Press (Honesdale, PA), 1995.

(Reteller) *A Sip of Aesop,* illustrated by Karen Barbour, Blue Sky Press (New York, NY), 1995.

Merlin and the Dragons, illustrated by Ming Li, Dutton (New York, NY), 1995.

The Wild Hunt, illustrated by Francisco Mora, Harcourt (New York, NY), 1995.

(With daughter Heidi E.Y. Stemple) *Meet the Monsters,* illustrated by Patricia Ludlow, Walker (New York, NY), 1996.

Nocturne, illustrated by Anne Hunter, Harcourt (New York, NY), 1997.

Child of Faerie, Child of Earth, illustrated by Jane Dyer, Little, Brown (Boston, MA), 1997.

Miz Berlin Walks, illustrated by Floyd Cooper, Philomel (New York, NY), 1997.

(Reteller) *Once upon a Bedtime Story: Classic Tales,* illustrated by Ruth Tietjen Councell, Putnam (New York, NY), 1997.

The Sea Man, illustrated by Christopher Denise, Putnam (New York, NY), 1997.

Twelve Impossible Things before Breakfast (short stories), Harcourt (New York, NY), 1997.

House, House, photographs by the Howes Brothers and son Jason Stemple, Marshall Cavendish (New York, NY), 1998.

King Long Shanks, illustrated by Victoria Chess, Harcourt (New York, NY), 1998.

(Reteller) *Pegasus, the Flying Horse,* illustrated by Ming Li, Dutton (New York, NY), 1998.

Raising Yoder's Barn, illustrated by Bernie Fuchs, Little, Brown (Boston, MA), 1998.

(Reteller) *Prince of Egypt,* Dutton (New York, NY), 1998.

(With Heidi E.Y. Stemple) *Mary Celeste: An Unsolved Mystery from History,* illustrated by Roger Roth, Simon & Schuster (New York, NY), 1999.

Moonball, illustrated by Greg Couch, Simon & Schuster (New York, NY), 1999.

Off We Go!, illustrated by Laurel Molk, Little, Brown (Boston, MA), 2000.

Harvest Home, illustrated by Greg Shed, Harcourt (San Diego, CA), 2000.

Boots and the Seven Leaguers: A Rock-and-Troll Novel, Harcourt (San Diego, CA), 2000.

(Editor) *Sherwood: Original Stories from the World of Robin Hood,* illustrated by Dennis Nolan, Philomel (New York, NY), 2000.

(Editor, with Heidi E.Y. Stemple, and author of introduction) *Mirror, Mirror: Forty Folktales for Mothers and Daughters to Share,* Viking (New York, NY), 2000.

(With Heidi E.Y. Stemple) *The Wolf Girls: An Unsolved Mystery from History,* illustrated by Roger Roth, Simon & Schuster (New York, NY), 2001.

Welcome to the River of Grass, illustrated by Laura Regan, Putnam (New York, NY), 2001.

The Hurrying Child, illustrated by Stephen T. Johnson, Silver Whistle (San Diego, CA), 2001.

(With Shulamith Oppenheim) *The Fish Prince and Other Stories: Mermen Folk Tales,* illustrated by Paul Hoffman, Interlink (New York, NY), 2001.

Time for Naps, illustrated by Hiroe Nakata, Little Simon (New York, NY), 2002.

(With Robert J. Harris) *Girl in a Cage,* Philomel (New York, NY), 2002.

(Reteller) *The Firebird,* illustrated by Vladimir Vagin, HarperCollins (New York, NY), 2002.

Bedtime for Bunny: A Book to Touch and Feel, illustrated by Lynn Norton Parker, Little Simon (New York, NY), 2002.

Animal Train, illustrated by Doug Cushman, Little Simon (New York, NY), 2002.

Sword of the Rightful King: A Novel of King Arthur, Harcourt (San Diego, CA), 2003.

(With Shulamith Oppenheim) *The Sea King,* illustrated by Stefan Czernecki, Crocodile Books (Brooklyn, NY), 2003.

(With Heidi E.Y. Stemple) *Roanoke, the Lost Colony: An Unsolved Mystery from History,* illustrated by Roger Roth, Simon & Schuster (New York, NY), 2003.

My Brother's Flying Machine: Wilbur, Orville, and Me, illustrated by Jim Burke, Little, Brown (New York, NY), 2003.

Mightier than the Sword: World Folktales for Strong Boys, illustrated by Raul Colón, Harcourt (San Diego, CA), 2003.

Hoptoad, illustrated by Karen Lee Schmidt, Silver Whistle (San Diego, CA), 2003.

The Flying Witch, illustrated by Vladimir Vagin, HarperCollins (New York, NY), 2003.

(With Robert J. Harris) *Prince across the Waters,* Philomel (New York, NY), 2004.

(With Heidi Stemple) *The Barefoot Book of Ballet Stories,* illustrated by Rebecca Guay, Barefoot Books (Cambridge, MA), 2004.

Soft House, illustrated by Wendy Anderson Halperin, Candlewick Press (Cambridge, MA), 2005.

Meow: Cat Stories from around the World, illustrated by Hala Wittwer, HarperCollins (New York, NY), 2005.

Grandma's Hurrying Child, illustrated by Kay Chorao, Harcourt (Orlando, FL), 2005.

Baby Bear's Chairs, illustrated by Melissa Sweet, Harcourt (Orlando, FL), 2005.

(With Adam Stemple) *Apple for the Teacher: Thirty Songs for Singing while You Work,* Harry N. Abrams (New York, NY), 2005.

(Editor) *Trot, Trot to Boston: Lap Songs, Finger Plays, Clapping Games, and Pantomime Rhymes,* illustrated by Will Hillenbrand, musical arrangements by Adam Stemple, Candlewick Press (Cambridge, MA), 2005.

(With Adam Stemple) *Pay the Piper: A Rock 'n' Roll Fairy Tale,* Starscape (New York, NY), 2006.

Baby Bear's Books, illustrated by Melissa Sweet, Harcourt (Orlando, FL), 2006.

Dimity Duck, illustrated by Sebastien Braun, Philomel Books (New York, NY), 2006.

(With Adam Stemple) *Troll Bridge: A Rock 'n' Roll Fairy Tale,* Starscape (New York, NY), 2006.

Baby Bear's Big Dreams, Harcourt (Orlando, FL), 2007.

(With Robert J. Harris) *Rogue's Apprentice,* Philomel Books (New York, NY), 2007.

(With Heidi E.Y. Stemple) *Sleep, Black Bear, Sleep,* illustrated by Brooke Dyer, HarperCollins (New York, NY), 2007.

Johnny Appleseed: The Legend and the Truth, illustrated by Jim Burke, HarperCollins (New York, NY), 2008.

Naming Liberty, illustrated by Jim Burke, Philomel Books (New York, NY), 2008.

Sea Queens: Women Pirates around the World, illustrated by Christine Joy Pratt, Charlesbridge (Watertown, MA), 2008.

My Father Knows the Names of Things, illustrated by Stepháne Jorisch, Simon & Schuster (New York, NY), 2009.

The Scarecrow's Dance, illustrated by Bagram Ibatoulline, Simon & Schuster (New York, NY), 2009.

An Egret's Day, photographs by Jason Stemple, Wordsong (Honesdale, PA), 2009.

Come to the Fairies' Ball, illustrated by Gary Lippincott, Wordsong (Honesdale, PA), 2009.

My Uncle Emily, illustrated by Nancy Carpenter, Philomel Books (New York, NY), 2009.

On the Slant, photographs by Jason Stemple, Richard C. Owen (Katonah, NY), 2009.

(With Heidi E.Y. Stemple) *The Barefoot Book of Dance Stories,* Barefoot Books (Cambridge, MA), 2009.

The Seeing Stick, illustrated by Daniela Jaglenka Terrazzini, RP/Kids (Philadelphia, PA), 2009.

All Star!: Honus Wagner and the Most Famous Baseball Card Ever, illustrated by Jim Burke, Philomel Books (New York, NY), 2010.

Elsie's Bird, illustrated by David Small, Philomel Books (New York, NY), 2010.

Hush, Little Horsie, illustrated by Ruth Sanderson, Random House (New York, NY), 2010.

Lost Boy: The Story of the Man Who Created Peter Pan, illustrated by Steve Adams, Dutton Children's Books (New York, NY), 2010.

(With Heidi E.Y. Stemple) *Not All Princesses Dress in Pink,* illustrated by Anne-Sophie Lanquetin, Simon & Schuster Books for Young Readers (New York, NY), 2010.

(With J. Patrick Lewis) *Self-Portrait with Seven Fingers: The Life of Marc Chagall in Verse,* Creative Editions (Mankato, MN), 2010.

Creepy Monsters, Sleepy Monsters: A Lullaby, illustrated by Kelly Murphy, Candlewick Press (Somerville, MA), 2011.

(Reteller) *Sister Bear: A Norse Tale,* illustrated by Linda Graves, Marshall Cavendish Children's (New York, NY), 2011.

The Day Tiger Rose Said Good-bye, illustrated by Jim LaMarche, Random House Children's Books (New York, NY), 2011.

Waking Dragons, illustrated by Derek Anderson, Simon & Schuster Books for Young Readers (New York, NY), 2012.

"GIANTS" SERIES; PICTURE BOOKS

The Giants Go Camping, illustrated by Tomie DePaola, Seabury (New York, NY), 1979.

The Giants' Farm, illustrated by Tomie DePaola, Seabury (New York, NY), 1997.

"COMMANDER TOAD" SERIES; FICTION; ILLUSTRATED BY BRUCE DEGEN

Commander Toad in Space, Coward (New York, NY), 1980.

Commander Toad and the Planet of the Grapes, Coward (New York, NY), 1982.

Commander Toad and the Big Black Hole, Coward (New York, NY), 1983.

Commander Toad and the Dis-Asteroid, Coward (New York, NY), 1985.

Commander Toad and the Intergalactic Spy, Coward (New York, NY), 1986.

Commander Toad and the Space Pirates, Putnam (New York, NY), 1987.

Commander Toad and the Voyage Home, Putnam (New York, NY), 1998.

"ROBOT AND REBECCA" SERIES; FICTION

The Mystery of the Code-carrying Kids, illustrated by Jurg Obrist, Knopf (New York, NY), 1980, illustrated by Catherine Deeter, Random House (New York, NY), 1980.

The Robot and Rebecca and the Missing Owser, illustrated by Lady McCrady, Knopf (New York, NY), 1981.

"PIGGINS" SERIES; PICTURE BOOKS; ILLUSTRATED BY JANE DYER

Piggins, Harcourt (New York, NY), 1987.

Picnic with Piggins, Harcourt (New York, NY), 1988.

Piggins and the Royal Wedding, Harcourt (New York, NY), 1988.

"YOUNG MERLIN" SERIES; FICTION

Passager, Harcourt (San Diego, CA, 1996.

Hobby, Harcourt (San Diego, CA), 1996.

Merlin, Harcourt (San Diego, CA), 1997.

The Young Merlin Trilogy (includes *Passager, Hobby,* and *Merlin*), Harcourt (Orlando, FL), 2004.

"TARTAN MAGIC" SERIES; FICTION

The Wizard's Map, Harcourt (San Diego, CA), 1998.

The Pictish Child, Harcourt (San Diego, CA), 1999.

The Bagpiper's Ghost, Harcourt (San Diego, CA), 2002.

"YOUNG HEROES" SERIES; FICTION

(With Robert J. Harris) *Odysseus in the Serpent Maze,* HarperCollins (New York, NY), 2001.

(With Robert J. Harris) *Hippolyta and the Curse of the Amazons,* HarperCollins (New York, NY), 2002.

(With Robert J. Harris) *Atalanta and the Arcadian Beast,* HarperCollins (New York, NY), 2003.

(With Robert J. Harris) *Jason and the Gorgon's Blood,* HarperCollins (New York, NY), 2004.

FOR CHILDREN; NONFICTION

Pirates in Petticoats, illustrated by Leonard Vosburgh, McKay (New York, NY), 1963.

World on a String: The Story of Kites, World Publishing (Cleveland, OH), 1968.

Friend: The Story of George Fox and the Quakers, Seabury (New York, NY), 1972, second edition, foreword by Larry Ingle, Wuaker Press of Friends General Conference (Philadelphia, PA), 2006.

(Editor, with Barbara Green) *The Fireside Song Book of Birds and Beasts,* illustrated by Peter Parnall, Simon & Schuster (New York, NY), 1972.

The Wizard Islands, illustrated by Robert Quackenbush, Crowell (New York, NY), 1973.

Ring Out! A Book of Bells, illustrated by Richard Cuffari, Seabury (New York, NY), 1974.

Simple Gifts: The Story of the Shakers, illustrated by Betty Fraser, Viking (New York, NY), 1976.

(Compiler) *Rounds about Rounds,* music by Barbara Green, illustrated by Gail Gibbons, Watts (New York, NY), 1977.

The Lap-Time Song and Play Book, musical arrangements by Adam Stemple, illustrated by Margot Tomes, Harcourt (New York, NY), 1989.

A Letter from Phoenix Farm (autobiography), photographs by Jason Stemple, Richard C. Owen (Katonah, NY), 1992.

Jane Yolen's Songs of Summer, musical arrangements by Adam Stemple, illustrated by Cyd Moore, Boyds Mills Press (Honesdale, PA), 1993.

Welcome to the Green House, illustrated by Laura Regan, Putnam (New York, NY), 1993.

Jane Yolen's Old MacDonald Songbook, illustrated by Rosekrans Hoffman, Boyds Mills Press (Honesdale, PA), 1994.

Sing Noel, musical arrangements by Adam Stemple, illustrated by Nancy Carpenter, Boyds Mills Press (Honesdale, PA), 1996.

Milk and Honey: A Year of Jewish Holidays, illustrations by Louise August, musical arrangements by Adam Stemple, Putnam (New York, NY), 1996.

Welcome to the Sea of Sand, illustrated by Laura Regan, Putnam (New York, NY), 1996.

Welcome to the Ice House, illustrated by Laura Regan, Putnam (New York, NY), 1998.

Tea with an Old Dragon: A Story of Sophia Smith, Founder of Smith College, illustrated by Monica Vachula, Boyds Mills Press (Honesdale, PA), 1998.

The Perfect Wizard: Hans Christian Andersen, illustrated by Dennis Nolan, Dutton (New York, NY), 2004.

"DINOSAURS" PICTURE-BOOK SERIES; ILLUSTRATED BY MARK TEAGUE

How Do Dinosaurs Say Good Night?, Blue Sky Press (New York, NY), 2000.

How Do Dinosaurs Get Well Soon?, Blue Sky Press (New York, NY), 2003.

How Do Dinosaurs Count to Ten?, Blue Sky Press (New York, NY), 2004.

How Do Dinosaurs Clean Their Room?, Blue Sky Press (New York, NY), 2004.

How Do Dinosaurs Eat Their Food?, Blue Sky Press (New York, NY), 2005.

How Do Dinosaurs Learn Their Colors?, Blue Sky Press (New York, NY), 2006.

How Do Dinosaurs Play with Their Friends?, Blue Sky Press (New York, NY), 2006.

How Do Dinosaurs Go to School?, Blue Sky Press (New York, NY), 2007.

How Do Dinosaurs Say I Love You?, Blue Sky Press (New York, NY), 2009.

How Do Dinosaurs Laugh out Loud?, Cartwheel Books (New York, NY), 2010.

How Do Dinosaurs Love Their Cats?, Blue Sky Press (New York, NY), 2010.

How Do Dinosaurs Love Their Dogs?, Blue Sky Press (New York, NY), 2010.

How Do Dinosaurs Say Happy Birthday?, Blue Sky Press (New York, NY), 2011.

FOR CHILDREN; POETRY

See This Little Line?, illustrated by Kathleen Elgin, McKay (New York, NY), 1963.

It All Depends, illustrated by Don Bolognese, Funk & Wagnalls (New York, NY), 1970.

An Invitation to the Butterfly Ball: A Counting Rhyme, illustrated by Jane Breskin Zalben, Parents' Magazine Press (New York, NY), 1976.

All in the Woodland Early: An ABC Book, illustrated by Jane Breskin Zalben, Collins (New York, NY), 1979, reprinted, Caroline House (Honesdale, PA), 1991.

How Beastly!: A Menagerie of Nonsense Poems, illustrated by James Marshall, Philomel (New York, NY), 1980.

Dragon Night and Other Lullabies, illustrated by Demi, Methuen (New York, NY), 1980.

(Editor) *The Lullaby Songbook,* musical arrangements by Adam Stemple, illustrated by Charles Mikolaycak, Harcourt (New York, NY), 1986.

Ring of Earth: A Child's Book of Seasons, illustrated by John Wallner, Harcourt (New York, NY), 1986.

The Three Bears Rhyme Book, illustrated by Jane Dyer, Harcourt (New York, NY), 1987.

Best Witches: Poems for Halloween, illustrated by Elise Primavera, Putnam (New York, NY), 1989.

Bird Watch, illustrated by Ted Lewin, Philomel (New York, NY), 1990.

Dinosaur Dances, illustrated by Bruce Degen, Putnam (New York, NY), 1990.

An Invitation to the Butterfly Ball: A Counting Rhyme, illustrated by Jane Breskin Zalben, Caroline House, 1991.

(Compiler) *Street Rhymes around the World,* Wordsong (Honesdale, PA), 1992.

Jane Yolen's Mother Goose Songbook, musical arrangements by Adam Stemple, illustrated by Rosecrans Hoffman, Boyds Mill Press (Honesdale, PA), 1992.

(Compiler) *Weather Report,* illustrated by Annie Gusman, Boyds Mills Press (Honesdale, PA), 1993.

Mouse's Birthday, illustrated by Bruce Degen, Putnam (New York, NY), 1993.

Raining Cats and Dogs, illustrated by Janet Street, Harcourt (New York, NY), 1993.

What Rhymes with Moon?, illustrated by Ruth Tietjen Councell, Philomel (New York, NY), 1993.

(Editor) *Sleep Rhymes around the World,* Boyds Mills Press (Honesdale, PA), 1993.

(Compiler and contributor) *Alphabestiary: Animal Poems from A to Z,* illustrated by Allan Eitzen, Boyds Mills Press (Honesdale, PA), 1994.

Sacred Places, illustrated by David Shannon, Harcourt (New York, NY), 1994.

Animal Fare: Zoological Nonsense Poems, illustrated by Janet Street, Harcourt (New York, NY), 1994.

The Three Bears Holiday Rhyme Book, illustrated by Jane Dyer, Harcourt (New York, NY), 1995.

(With Nancy Willard) *Among Angels,* illustrated by S. Saelig Gallagher, Harcourt (New York, NY), 1995.

Water Music: Poems for Children, photographs by Jason Stemple, Boyds Mills Press (Honesdale, PA), 1995.

(Compiler) *Mother Earth, Father Sky: Poems of Our Planet,* illustrated by Jennifer Hewitson, Boyds Mills Press (Honesdale, PA), 1996.

O Jerusalem, illustrated by John Thompson, Scholastic (New York, NY), 1996.

Sea Watch: A Book of Poetry, illustrated by Ted Lewin, Putnam (New York, NY), 1996.

(Compiler and contributor) *Sky Scrape/City Scape: Poems of City Life,* illustrated by Ken Condon, Boyds Mills Press (Honesdale, PA), 1996.

(Compiler) *Once upon Ice and Other Frozen Poems,* photographs by Jason Stemple, Boyds Mills Press (Honesdale, PA), 1997.

Snow, Snow: Winter Poems for Children, photographs by Jason Stemple, Wordsong (Honesdale, PA), 1998.

The Originals: Animals That Time Forgot, illustrated by Ted Lewin, Philomel (New York, NY), 1998.

Color Me a Rhyme: Nature Poems for Young People, photographs by Jason Stemple, Boyds Mills Press (Honesdale, PA), 2000.

(With Heidi E.Y. Stemple) *Dear Mother, Dear Daughter: Poems for Young People,* illustrated by Gil Ashby, Boyds Mills Press (Honesdale, PA), 2001.

Wild Wings: Poems for Young People, photographs by Jason Stemple, Boyds Mills Press (Honesdale, PA), 2002.

Horizons: Poems as Far as the Eye Can See, photographs by Jason Stemple, Boyds Mills Press (Honesdale, PA), 2002.

The Radiation Sonnets: For My Love, in Sickness and in Health, Algonquin Books (Chapel Hill, NC), 2003.

Least Things: Poems about Small Natures, photographs by Jason Stemple, Boyds Mills Press (Honesdale, PA), 2003.

Fine Feathered Friends: Poems for Young People, photographs by Jason Stemple, Boyds Mills Press (Honesdale, PA), 2004.

Count Me a Rhyme: Animal Poems by the Numbers, photographs by Jason Stemple, Wordsong Press (Honesdale, PA), 2006.

(Editor, with Andrew Fusek Peters) *Here's a Little Poem: A Very First Book of Poetry,* illustrated by Polly Dunbar, Candlewick Press (Cambridge, MA), 2007.

Shape Me a Rhyme: Nature's Forms in Poetry, photographs by Jason Stemple, Wordsong (Honesdale, PA), 2007.

A Mirror to Nature: Poems about Reflection, photographs by Jason Stemple, Wordsong (Honesdale, PA), 2009.

(Editor with Andrew Fusek Peters) *Switching on the Moon: A Very First Book of Bedtime Poems,* illustrated by G. Brian Karas, Candlewick Press (Cambridge, MA), 2010.

FOR YOUNG ADULTS; FICTION

(With Anne Huston) *Trust a City Kid,* illustrated by J.C. Kocsis, Lothrop (New York, NY), 1966.

(Editor) *Zoo 2000: Twelve Stories of Science Fiction and Fantasy Beasts,* Seabury (New York, NY), 1973.

The Magic Three of Solatia, illustrated by Julia Noonan, Crowell (New York, NY), 1974.

(Editor and contributor) *Shape Shifters: Fantasy and Science Fiction Tales about Humans Who Can Change Their Shape,* Seabury (New York, NY), 1978.

The Gift of Sarah Barker, Viking (New York, NY), 1981.

Neptune Rising: Songs and Tales of the Undersea Folk (story collection), illustrated by David Wiesner, Philomel (New York, NY), 1982.

The Stone Silenus, Philomel (New York, NY), 1984.

Children of the Wolf, Viking (New York, NY), 1984.

(Editor and contributor with Martin H. Greenberg and Charles G. Waugh) *Dragons and Dreams,* Harper (New York, NY), 1986.

(Editor and contributor with Martin H. Greenberg and Charles G. Waugh) *Spaceships and Spells,* Harper (New York, NY), 1987.

The Devil's Arithmetic, Viking (New York, NY), 1988.

(Editor and contributor with Martin H. Greenberg) *Werewolves: A Collection of Original Stories,* Harper (New York, NY), 1988.

The Faery Flag: Stories and Poems of Fantasy and the Supernatural, Orchard Books (New York, NY), 1989.

(Editor and contributor with Martin H. Greenberg) *Things That Go Bump in the Night,* Harper (New York, NY), 1989.

(Editor and contributor) *2041 AD: Twelve Stories about the Future by Top Science-Fiction Writers* (anthology), Delacorte (New York, NY), 1990.

(Editor and contributor with Martin H. Greenberg) *Vampires,* HarperCollins (New York, NY), 1991.

Here There Be Dragons (stories and poetry), illustrated by David Wilgus, Harcourt (New York, NY), 1993.

Here There Be Unicorns (stories and poetry), illustrated by David Wilgus, Harcourt (New York, NY), 1994.

Here There Be Witches (stories and poetry), illustrated by David Wilgus, Harcourt (New York, NY), 1995.

(Editor and contributor) *Camelot: A Collection of Original Arthurian Tales,* illustrated by Winslow Pels, Putnam (New York, NY), 1995.

(Editor, with Martin H. Greenberg, and contributor) *The Haunted House: A Collection of Original Stories,* illustrated by Doron Ben-Ami, HarperCollins (New York, NY), 1995.

Here There Be Angels (stories and poetry), illustrated by David Wilgus, Harcourt (New York, NY), 1996.

Here There Be Ghosts (stories and poetry), illustrated by David Wilgus, Harcourt (New York, NY), 1998.

(With Bruce Coville) *Armageddon Summer,* Harcourt (New York, NY), 1998.

(With Adam Stemple) *Pay the Piper,* Tor (New York, NY), 2005.

(Editor, with Patrick Nielsen Hayden) *Year's Best Science Fiction and Fantasy for Teens,* Tor (New York, NY), 2005.

Foiled (graphic novel), illustrated by Michael Cavallaro, First Second (New York, NY), 2010.

(With Midori Snyder) *Except the Queen,* Roc (New York, NY), 2010.

Birds of a Feather, Wordsong (Honesdale, PA), 2011.

Snow in Summer, Philomel Books (New York, NY), 2011.

"PIT DRAGON CHRONICLES"; YOUNG-ADULT FICTION

Dragon's Blood: A Fantasy, Delacorte (New York, NY), 1982, reprinted, 2004.

Heart's Blood, Delacorte (New York, NY), 1984, reprinted, 2004.

A Sending of Dragons, illustrated by Tom McKeveny, Delacorte (New York, NY), 1987, reprinted, 2004.

Dragon's Heart, Harcourt (Boston, MA), 2009.

FOR ADULTS; FICTION

Merlin's Booke (short stories), illustrated by Thomas Canty, Ace Books (New York, NY), 1982.

Tales of Wonder (short stories), Schocken (New York, NY), 1983.

Cards of Grief (science fiction), Ace Books (New York, NY), 1984.

Dragonfield and Other Stories, Ace Books (New York, NY), 1985.

(Editor) *Favorite Folktales from around the World,* Pantheon (New York, NY), 1986.

Sword and the Stone, Pulphouse (Eugene, OR), 1991.

Briar Rose, Tor (New York, NY), 1992.

Storyteller, illustrated by Merle Insinga, New England Science Fiction Association Press (Cambridge, MA), 1992.

(Editor and contributor with Martin H. Greenberg) *Xanadu,* Tor (New York, NY), 1993.

(Editor and contributor with Martin H. Greenberg) *Xanadu Two,* Tor (New York, NY), 1994.

(Editor and contributor with Martin H. Greenberg) *Xanadu Three,* Tor (New York, NY), 1995.

The Books of Great Alta, St. Martin's Press (New York, NY), 1997.

(Editor) *Gray Heroes: Elder Tales from around the World,* Viking Penguin (New York, NY), 1998.

Not One Damsel in Distress, Harcourt (New York, NY), 2000.

(With Heidi E.Y. Stemple) *Mirror, Mirror,* Viking (New York, NY), 2000.

(Editor and contributor) *Sherwood: A Collection of Original Robin Hood Stories,* illustrated by Dennis Nolan, Philomel (New York, NY), 2000.

(With Robert J. Harris) *Queen's Own Fool,* Philomel (New York, NY), 2000.

"WHITE JENNA" ADULT NOVEL SERIES

Sister Light, Sister Dark, Tor (New York, NY), 1988.

White Jenna, Tor (New York, NY), 1989.

The One-armed Queen, with music by Adam Stemple, Tor (New York, NY), 1998.

COOKBOOKS

(Reteller) *Fairy Tale Feasts: A Literary Cookbook for Young Readers and Eaters,* recipes by Heidi E.Y. Stemple, illustrated by Philippe Beïcha, Crocodile Books (Northampton, MA), 2006.

(Reteller) *Fairy Tale Breakfasts: A Cookbook for Young Readers and Eaters,* recipes by Heidi E.Y. Stemple, illustrations by Philippe Béha, Alphabet Soup (New York, NY), 2010.

(Reteller) *Fairy Tale Desserts: A Cookbook for Young Readers and Eaters,* recipes by Heidi E.Y. Stemple, illustrations by Philippe Béha, Alphabet Soup (New York, NY), 2010.

(Reteller) *Fairy Tale Dinners: A Cookbook for Young Readers and Eaters,* recipes by Heidi E.Y. Stemple, illustrations by Philippe Béha, Alphabet Soup (New York, NY), 2010.

(Reteller) *Fairy Tale Lunches: A Cookbook for Young Readers and Eaters,* recipes by Heidi E.Y. Stemple, illustrations by Philippe Béha, Alphabet Soup (New York, NY), 2010.

OTHER

Writing Books for Children, Writer (Boston, MA), 1973, revised edition, 1983.

Touch Magic: Fantasy, Faerie, and Folklore in the Literature of Childhood, Philomel (New York, NY), 1981, revised edition, August House, 2000.

Guide to Writing for Children, Writer (Boston, MA), 1989.

(Author of introduction) Robert D. San Souci, reteller, *Cut from the Same Cloth: American Women of Myth, Legend, and Tall Tale,* Philomel (New York, NY), 1993.

(Author of introduction) *Best-Loved Stories Told at the National Storytelling Festival,* National Storytelling Association, 1996.

(Author of introduction) Kathleen Ragan, *Fearless Girls, Wise Women, and Beloved Sisters: Heroines in Folktales from around the World,* Norton (New York, NY), 1998.

Take Joy: A Book for Writers, Writers Books (Waukesha, WI), 2003, published as *Take Joy: A Writer's Guide to Loving the Craft,* Writer's Digest Books (Cincinnati, OH), 2006.

Also author of musical *Robin Hood,* music by Barbara Greene, produced in Boston, MA, 1967. Author of chapbook *The Whitethorn Wood.* Ghostwriter of books for Rutledge Press. Contributor to books, including *Dragons of Light,* edited by Orson Scott Card, Ace Books, 1981; *Elsewhere,* 2 volumes, edited by Terri Windling and Mark Alan Arnold, Ace Books, 1981-82; *Hecate's Cauldron,* edited by Susan Schwartz, DAW Books, 1982; *Heroic Visions,* edited by Jessica Amanda Salmonson, Ace Books, 1983; *Faery!,* edited by Windling, Ace Books, 1985; *Liavek,* edited by Will Shetterly and Emma Bull, Ace Books, 1985; *Moonsinger's Friends,* edited by Schwartz, Bluejay, 1985; *Imaginary Lands,* edited by Robin McKinley, Greenwillow, 1985; *Don't Bet on the Prince: Contemporary Feminist Fairy Tales in North America and England,* edited by Jack Zipes, Methuen, 1986; *Liavek: Players of Luck,* edited by Shetterly and Bull, Ace Books, 1986; *Liavek: Wizard's Row,* edited by Shetterly and Bull, Ace Books, 1987; *Visions,* edited by Donald R. Gallo, Delacorte, 1987; *Liavek: Spells of Binding,* edited by Shetterly and Bull, Ace Books, 1988; *Invitation to Camelot,* edited by Parke Godwin, Ace Books, 1988; *The Unicorn Treasury,* edited by Bruce Coville, Doubleday, 1988; and *Hamsters,*

Shells, and Spelling Bees: School Poems, edited by Lee Bennett Hopkins, HarperCollins, 2008. Author of folk songs and lyrics.

Author of column "Children's Bookfare" for *Daily Hampshire Gazette,* c. 1970s. Contributor of articles, reviews, poems, and short stories to periodicals, including *Chicago Jewish Forum, Horn Book, Isaac Asimov's Science Fiction Magazine, Language Arts, Los Angeles Times, Magazine of Fantasy and Science Fiction, New Advocate, New York Times, Parabola, Parents' Choice, Washington Post Book World, Wilson Library Bulletin,* and *Writer.* Member of editorial board, *Advocate* (now *New Advocate*) and *National Storytelling Journal,* until 1989.

Yolen's books have been translated into numerous languages, including Afrikaans, Chinese, Danish, French, German, Greek, Japanese, Korean, Spanish, Swedish, Russian, and Thai.

Yolen's papers are housed at the Kerlan Collection, University of Minnesota.

Adaptations

The Seventh Mandarin was produced as a motion picture by Xerox Films, 1973; *The Emperor and the Kite* was produced as a filmstrip with cassette by Listening Library, 1976; *The Bird of Time* was adapted into a play

Yolen's picture book **Beneath the Ghost Moon** ***features detailed artwork by Laurel Molk.*** (Little, Brown & Company, 1994. Illustration copyright © 1994 by Laurel Molk. Reproduced by permission of Hachette Book Group and Curtis Brown, Ltd.)

and produced in Northampton, MA, 1982; *The Girl Who Cried Flowers and Other Tales* was released on audio cassette by Weston Woods, 1983; *Dragon's Blood* was produced as an animated television movie by Columbia Broadcasting System (CBS), 1985; *Commander Toad in Space* was released on audio cassette by Listening Library, 1986; *Touch Magic . . . Pass It On,* a selection of Yolen's short stories, was released on audio cassette by Weston Woods, 1987; *Owl Moon* was produced as a filmstrip with cassette by Weston Woods, 1988, and as both a read-along cassette and a video, 1990; *Owl Moon* was also adapted as part of the video *Owl Moon and Other Stories,* produced by Children's Circle; *Piggins* and *Picnic with Piggins* were released on audio cassette by Caedmon, 1988; *Best of Science Fiction and Fantasy* was released on audio cassette by New Star Media, 1991; *Merlin and the Dragons* was released on audio cassette by Lightyear Entertainment, 1991, produced as a video by Coronet, 1991, and released with commentary by Yolen as *What's a Good Story? Merlin and the Dragon; Greyling* was released on audio cassette by Spoken Arts, 1993; *Hands* was released on audio cassette by Sundance Publishing, 1993; *Beneath the Ghost Moon* was produced as a video by Spoken Arts, 1996; *Wizard's Hall* was released on audio cassette by "Words Take Wings," narrated by Yolen, 1997; *How Do Dinosaurs Say Good Night?* was produced as a video, Weston Woods, 2002. Recorded Books issued audio cassettes of *Briar Rose, The Devil's Arithmetic,* and *Good Griselle.*

Sidelights

A prolific and highly esteemed author, Jane Yolen is the creator of hundreds of books for children, teens, and adults. In her work Yolen spans genres from fiction and poetry to biography, criticism, and books on the art of writing and is particularly well known for her history-based fiction, fantasy novels such as her "Pit Dragon" series, nature-themed picture books such as *An Egret's Day,* and standalone novels such as *The Devil's Arithmetic* and *Armageddon Summer.* A folksinger and storyteller, she creates works that reflect her love of music and oral folklore; others are autobiographical or incorporate elements from her life or the lives of her family. Now grown, Yolen's three children also contribute to her works: daughter Heidi E.Y. Stemple as a writer and sons Adam and Jason Stemple as musical arranger and photographer, respectively. She has also moved into the graphic-novel format at the urging of granddaughter Maddison, teaming up with artist Michael Cavallaro to produce *Foiled.*

Yolen's original folk tales and fables contain a surprising twist and a strong moral core, and her literary fairy tales mix familiar fantasy motifs with contemporary elements and philosophical themes. As a fantasist, she includes dragons, unicorns, witches, and mermaids as characters, and her stories often feature shape-shifters: animals that have the ability to transform into humans or vice versa. As a writer, Yolen invests her works with images, symbols, and allusions as well as with wordplay—especially puns—and metaphors. In *Twentieth-Century Children's Writers,* Marcia G. Fuchs commented: "Faerie, fiction, fact, or horrible fantasy, Yolen's lyrical and magical tales are indeed tales to read and to listen to, to share, to remember, and to pass on."

Born in New York City in 1939, Yolen bloomed as a writer early on. A voracious reader as well as a tomboy, she played games in Central Park while being encouraged in her reading and writing by her teachers. "I was," she later recalled in *Something about the Author Autobiography Series* (SAAS), "the gold star star. And I was also pretty impossibly full of myself. In first or second grade, I wrote the school musical, lyrics and music, in which everyone was some kind of vegetable. I played the lead carrot. Our finale was a salad. Another gold star."

Yolen's favorite books as a child included the stories collected by British folklorist Andrew Lang in his colored fairy books, "as well as by *Treasure Island* [by Robert Louis Stevenson] and the Louisa May Alcott books," as she once told *SATA.* "I read *The Wind in the Willows* and the Mowgli stories. We didn't have 'young adult' fiction, so I skipped right into adult books which tended to be very morose Russian novels—my Dostoevsky phase—then I got hooked on Joseph Conrad. Adventure novels or lugubrious emotional books are what I preferred. Then I went back into my fairy tale and fantasy stage. Tolkien and C.S. Lewis, metaphysical and folkloric fantasy."

In sixth grade, Yolen was accepted by Hunter, a girls' school for what were called "intelligently gifted" students. While navigating the academic challenges at Hunter, music—especially folk songs, an interest she shared with her father—became Yolen's new focus. In addition to starring as Hansel in the school production of Engelbert Humperdinck's opera *Hansel and Gretel,* she now played the piano and wrote songs; she also became the lead dancer in her class at Balanchine's American School of Ballet.

In addition to her other achievements, Yolen developed an interest in writing during her early teens, and in eighth grade she penned her first two books: a nonfiction work about pirates and a novel about a trip across the American West by covered wagon. She eventually described this latter work, which is seventeen pages long and includes a plague of locusts, death by snake bite, and the birth of a baby on the trail, as "a masterpiece of economy"; in fact, short stories and poetry continue to be her favored genres.

At age thirteen the high-achieving Yolen moved with her family to Westport, Connecticut, where she became captain of her high school girls' basketball team; news editor of the school paper; head of the Jewish Youth Group; vice president of the Spanish, Latin, and jazz

Yolen's picture book Off We Go! *pairs her engaging story with Laurel Molk's delightful watercolor art.* (Little, Brown & Company 2000. Illustration copyright © 2000 by Laurel Molk. Reproduced by permission of Hachette Book Group.)

clubs; a member of the school's top singing group; and a contributor to the school literary magazine. She also won a Scholastic essay contest called "I Speak for Democracy" as well as her school's English prize. Before graduation, her class named Yolen's voice to be a composite part of "The Perfect Senior." She also became close to her cousin-in-law, Honey Knopp, who sparked Yolen's lifelong interest in the Quaker faith.

After graduating from high school, Yolen attended Smith College where she majored in English and Russian literature and minored in religion. In addition to continuing her involvement in campus activities, she also continued her writing and saw poems published in *Poetry Digest* as well as in small literary magazines. Deciding to pursue a career in journalism due to its practicality, Yolen worked as a cub reporter for a Connecticut newspaper the summer before her sophomore year. Although she continued to intern for newspapers during the next few years, she dismissed the idea of being a journalist when she found herself making up facts and writing stories off the top of her head.

After graduating from Smith College, Yolen moved to New York City and worked briefly for *This Week* magazine and the *Saturday Review* before launching her career as a freelance writer by helping her father write his book *The Young Sportsman's Guide to Kite Flying.* While living in Greenwich Village in the summer of 1960, she met her future husband, David Stemple, who was a friend of one of her roommates; the couple was married in 1962.

Several years spent working for New York City publishers followed, and then Yolen's father introduced her to the vice president of David McKay Publishing

Company. Yolen's first book for children, the nonfiction title *Pirates in Petticoats,* was published by McKay in 1963; the publisher also bought Yolen's second work, *See This Little Line?,* a picture book in rhyme that was published the same year. While continuing to work in publishing, she became a ghostwriter for Rutledge Press, authoring concept and activity books published under different names. In 1963 she became an assistant editor in the children's department at Knopf, where she met authors and illustrators such as Roald Dahl and Roger Duvoisin and learned about juvenile literature.

In 1965 Yolen and her husband spent nine months traveling in Europe, Israel, and Greece. Their daughter Heidi was born in 1966, shortly after her parents returned to America. When David Stemple took a job at the University of Massachusetts Computer Center in Amherst, he and Yolen moved to western Massachusetts, where son Adam was born in 1968 and Jason two years later. While raising her children, Yolen began her writing career in earnest.

The picture book *The Emperor and the Kite* was the first of Yolen's books to receive a major award. The story outlines how Djeow Seow, the youngest and smallest daughter of an ancient Chinese emperor, saves her father after he is kidnapped by sending him a kite trailing a long rope made of grass, vines, and strands of her hair. As a reviewer in *Children's Book News* commented, "Here is a writer who delights in words and can use them in a controlled way to beautiful effect." In 1968, *The Emperor and the Kite* earned Yolen her first Lewis Carroll Shelf Award; the second would come for *The Girl Who Loved the Wind,* in 1972.

Another early award winner, *The Girl Who Cried Flowers and Other Tales* earned Yolen a Golden Kite Award and was also nominated for the National Book Award in 1975. The book collects five stories that, according to a reviewer in *Publishers Weekly,* "could be called modern folk or fairy tales, since they boast all the usual ingredients—supernatural beings, inexplicable happenings, the struggle between good and evil forces." The critic concluded that Yolen's "artistry with words . . . makes a striking book," while a critic in *Kirkus Reviews* called *The Girl Who Cried Flowers and Other Tales* a "showpiece, for those who can forego the tough wisdom of traditional fairy tales for a masterful imitation of the manner."

All in the Woodland Early: An ABC Book, one of several song books authored by Yolen, teaches the alphabet through rhyming verses. The book outlines a little boy's hunting expedition in the woods; each letter represents the animal, bird, or insect—both familiar and unfamiliar—for which he is searching. At the end of the final verse readers discover that the boy is gathering the animals to play with him and a little girl. Yolen also provides music to go with her words. Writing in the *Washington Post Book World,* Jerome Beatty, Jr., asserted: "Count on versatile Jane Yolen to invent something special and intriguing," while a reviewer for *Publishers Weekly* called *All in the Woodland Early* "an outstanding alphabet book." Other song books by Yolen include *Apple for the Teacher: Thirty Songs for Singing while You Work* and *Jane Yolen's Songs of Summer*, both of which feature music by Adam Stemple.

Other highly praised picture books by Yolen include *Harvest Home*, a story about a farm family's wheat harvest that *School Library Journal* contributor Catherine Threadgill praised as a "reflective and respectful tribute to a bygone era." Illustrated by Laura Regan, *Welcome to the River of Grass* introduces young children to the Florida Everglades ecosystem, while *Naming Liberty* tells the story of the creation of the Statue of Liberty through the story of an immigrant family's arrival in New York Harbor. Another young immigrant is the focus of *Elsie's Bird*, which finds Elsie joining her widowed father on his trek from Boston to Nebraska, where the flat lands and rudimentary living conditions eventually reveal their unique beauty. While "Yolen's prose moves gracefully from solemn to euphoric" as Elsie accepts the prairie as her home, David Small's illustrations for *Elsie's Bird* reveal a "keen sensitivity to the emotional pull of place," according to a *Publishers Weekly* contributor.

Yolen turns to nature in picture books such as *An Egret's Day*, which photographs by Jason Stemple are paired with fact-filled prose and poems in various forms, all which focus on the American egret. Reviewing *An Egret's Day*, a *Kirkus Reviews* writer deemed it "a stunning combination of scientific and ecological knowledge offered through a graceful fusion of lyrical and visual media."

Many of Yolen's picture books reflect her fascination with folk stories, among them *The Flying Witch*, a Baba Yaga story about an old woman who uses young children as a main ingredient in her evening meal, and *The Firebird*, a unique retelling of a classic Eastern-European fable. Another fascination—the life stories of inspiring people—reveals itself in books such as *My Brothers' Flying Machine: Wilbur, Orville, and Me*, which introduces readers to the fathers of flight through the eyes of younger sister, Katherine; and *Johnny Appleseed: The Legend and the Truth*, about nineteenth-century farmer and roving apple-planter John Chapman. *All Star!: Honus Wagner and the Most Famous Baseball Card Ever* focuses on a star baseball player for the fledgling Pittsburgh Pirates whose renown increased when it was found that the collectible card bearing his name was perhaps the rarest and most valuable ever printed. Praising Jim Burke's illustrations for *All Star!*, a *Publishers Weekly* critic added that, in Yolen's care, Wagner's story "becomes an eloquently understated tribute to that archetypal American combination of stoicism, decency, drive, and sheer talent."

Illustrated by Steve Adams, Yolen's picture-book biography *Lost Boy: The Story of the Man Who Created Peter Pan* focuses on Scottish-born playwright J.M. Barrie

and comprises what Mary Landrum dubbed "a beautiful tribute" in *School Library Journal*. The author also focuses on a literary figure in *My Uncle Emily*, which describes the life of noted nineteenth-century poet and Amherst, Massachusetts, resident Emily Dickinson and features Nancy Carpenter's pastel-and-ink art. According to a *Kirkus Reviews* writer, Yolen's story, which is based on an actual incident involving Dickinson and her six-year-old nephew Thomas, "artfully" presents examples of the poet's work that "give readers an inside look at the enigmatic ['Belle of Amherst']."

More fanciful picture books by Yolen include *How Do Dinosaurs Get Well Soon?*, part of a series of books that finds large, bulky, and often naughty dinosaurs dealing with common, child-sized problems while attempting to fit into a tiny, child-sized world. Other volumes in the "How Do Dinosaurs . . . ?" series include *How Do Dinosaurs Say Good Night?*, *How Do Dinosaurs Eat Their Food?*, *How Do Dinosaurs Laugh Out Loud?*, *How Do Dinosaurs Love Their Dogs?*, and *How Do Dinosaurs Say Happy Birthday?*, all which feature colorful comic artwork by Mark Teague. With its focus on an average day at school for Silvasaurus, Herrasau-

A powerful retelling of *Sleeping Beauty* that is "heartbreaking and heartwarming."

BRIAR ROSE

JANE YOLEN

Cover of Yolen's young-adult novel Briar Rose, *a retelling of the story of Snow White from an unusual perspective.* (Copyright © 1992 by TOR Books. Reproduced by permission.)

rus, and Centrosaurus, *How Do Dinosaurs Go to School?* pairs Yolen's "easy rhymes" with Teague's "positively pop-off-the-page paintings," according to a *Kirkus Reviews* writer. *Booklist* critic Gillian Engberg noted of the "Dinosaurs" series that "kids will see themselves in the familiar scenarios and emotions."

Throughout her career Yolen has balanced her prose work with poetry, some of which has been collected in anthologies. The companion volumes *Color Me a Rhyme: Nature Poems for Young Children, Count Me a Rhyme: Animal Poems by the Numbers,* and *Shape Me a Rhyme: Nature's Forms in Poetry*—as well as *Water Music: Poems for Children, Wild Wings: Poems for Young People,* and *A Mirror to Nature: Poems about Reflection*—all feature stunning nature photography by son Jason Stemple. Reviewing *A Mirror to Nature,* winner of the John Burroughs Society Award, *Booklist* critic Hazel Rochman wrote noted that Yolen's use of water as a way to isolate the beauty in nature will help "kids . . . see reflections, strange and beautiful, in the natural world." A *Publishers Weekly* critic dubbed the anthology "a gem" in which "Stemple's photographs startle the readers with the extraordinary beauty of . . . ordinary things," while *School Library Journal* contributor Marilyn Taniguchi recommended *A Mirror to Nature* as a "thoughtful combination of wordplay, nature factoids, and photographs."

Yolen's historical novels often focus on an unusual subject, as in *The Gift of Sarah Barker.* Set in a Shaker community, this story features teens Abel and Sarah. The two friends have grown up in the Society of Believers, a celibate religious community, and now find that they are sexually attracted to each other. As the young people struggle with their feelings, Yolen depicts the contradiction between the religious ecstasy of the Shakers—whose dances and celebrations gave the group their nickname—and the repressive quality of the sect's lifestyle. Sarah and Abel decide to leave the community, but not before Sister Agatha, Sarah's abusive mother, commits suicide.

Before writing *The Gift of Sarah Barker*, Yolen interviewed some of the few remaining Shakers for background information. She also used her daughter, Heidi, who was then becoming interested in boys, as the prototype for Sarah. As the author once explained to *SATA,* "I kept wondering how, in a Shaker community, you could keep the boys away from a girl like Heidi or keep Heidi away from the boys. I imagined a Romeo and Juliet story within the Shaker setting." Writing in *Children's Book Review Service,* Barbara Baker called *The Gift of Sarah Barker* "an absorbing tale" and a "jewel of a[n] historical novel," while Stephanie Zvirin noted in *Booklist:* "Into the fabric of a teenage romance [Yolen] weaves complicated and disturbing—at times violent—undercurrents that add a dimension both powerful and provocative."

Working in collaboration with Scots writer Robert J. Harris, Yolen has penned a number of novels based on Scottish history, one of Yolen's abiding interests (she makes her home in that part of Great Britain for part of each year). The first of these, *Queen's Own Fool,* recounts the tragic reign of the ill-fated Mary, queen of Scots, from the viewpoint of her fool, Nicola. A French-born orphan, Nicola follows Mary from France to Scotland as the young queen—half-sister to Elizabeth I of England—tries to gain her place as queen of Scotland while political power is fought over by a variety of Scottish nobles. In the historical novel *Girl in a Cage* the eleven-year-old daughter of Robert the Bruce becomes a captive to the English troops her father hopes to keep out of his beloved Scotland at the turn of the fourteenth century. In *The Rogues,* a collaborative novel, Yolen and Harris set their history-based tale against the backdrop of the Highland clearances, a time when the Scottish lords evicted their clansmen in favor transitioning clan homelands to the more lucrative use of grazing sheep.

Praising *Queen's Own Fool* in *Kliatt,* Claire Rosser wrote that Yolen "knows how to appeal to young people and keep a story moving swiftly," while in *Booklist* Anne O'Malley concluded of *The Rogues* that the story's "plot races along flawlessly in this excellent historical adventure."

The story of Bonny Prince Charlie is told by Yolen from the point of view of a young recruit in *Prince across the Water,* as thirteen-year-old Highlander Duncan joins the rebels hoping to place the Scottish prince on the throne of England in the mid-1700s. Duncan loyally follows the call of clan and king until the massacre of Charlie's followers by British forces at the Battle of Culloden Field dashes Scots hopes. In *Booklist,* Carolyn Phelan praised *Prince across the Water* for its "convincing depictions of people and relationships," while in *Horn Book* Anita L. Burkham dubbed it a "well-told story set in an intriguing era that will leave readers mulling over thoughts of war and peace."

Several of Yolen's historical works have been in the area of nonfiction, as in the "Mystery from History" series, written with daughter Heidi E.Y. Stemple. In *The Wolf Girls: An Unsolved Mystery from History,* as in other volumes in the series, a fictional story is built around an actual incident that left many questions unanswered. The novel focuses on two orphaned girls living in India who, in the 1920s, were reported to have been raised among wolves by missionary Joseph Singh, who ultimately gave the children a home. Noting the authors' inclusion of expert scientific evidence and a number of possible explanations for the girls' feral condition, *School Library Journal* reviewer Anne Chapman dubbed *The Wolf Girls* "tasty fodder for emerging detectives."

Other mother-daughter collaborations in the "Mystery from History" series include *Mary Celeste: An Unsolved Mystery from History,* about a ghost ship; *Roanoke, the Lost Colony: An Unsolved Mystery from History;* and

Yolen shares a poignant and inspiring story about setting down new roots in her picture book **Elsie's Bird,** *featuring artwork by David Small.*

The Salem Witch Trials: An Unsolved Mystery from History, the last about the hysteria that gripped the Massachusetts Bay colony during its early days. Although many books have been published that detail the frenzy caused by two girls over a supposed witch in their community, *The Salem Witch Trials* "gives a different perspective" by presenting the facts in an organized and impartial manner, lets young sleuths "evaluate the evidence and draw their own conclusions," according to *School Library Journal* contributor Elaine Fort Weischedel.

Dragon's Blood is the first volume in Yolen's "Pit Dragon Chronicles." High fantasy for young adults that incorporates elements of science fiction, the series presents a completely realized imaginary world. *Dragon's Blood* introduces Jakkin, a fifteen-year-old slave boy. Jakkin's master is the best dragon breeder on planet Austar IV, a former penal colony where inhabitants train and fight dragons that were domesticated by early

colonists. Jakkin steals a female dragon hatchling to train in secret for the gaming pits, a cockfighting ritual that contributes largely to the planet's economy. He intends to win his freedom by raising a superior fighting dragon, until he establishes a psychic link with his "snatchling," which he names Heart's Blood. Along with the dragon's first win, Jakkin—now free—learns that his master knew about his theft and that Akki, a bond girl training in medicine who Jakkin loves, is actually his former master's illegitimate daughter. Writing in *Horn Book,* Ann A. Flowers called *Dragon's Blood* an "original and engrossing fantasy," while *School Library Journal* critic Patricia Manning asserted that the novel provides a "fascinating glimpse of a brand new world."

In *Heart's Blood* Jakkin is the new Dragon Master and Heart's Blood has given birth to five hatchlings. Jakkin becomes involved in Austarian politics when he is asked to infiltrate rebel forces and rescue Akki. Becoming pawns in a deadly game, he and Akki flee with Heart's Blood into the freezing cold of night, called Dark After. Cornered by the authorities after inadvertently blowing up a major city, the trio fights for its life. In the battle, Heart's Blood is killed. In order to survive the freezing temperatures, Jakkin and Akki enter her carcass; when they emerge, they have been given the gift of dragon's sight—telepathy—and the ability to withstand the cold of Dark After.

A Sending of Dragons finds Jakkin and Akki avoiding capture by fleeing into the wilderness with Heart's Blood's five babies. When they enter a hidden tunnel, the group encounters an underground tribe of primitives who have discovered a way to extract metals on Austar IV. Jakkin and Akki also learn that these people, who, like them, are bonded to dragons, have developed a bloody, terrifying ritual of dragon sacrifice. At the end of the novel, Akki, Jakkin, and the fledglings escape with two of the primitive community's dragons. Confronted by their pursuers from above ground, they decide to return to the city and use their new knowledge to bring about an end to the feudalism and enslavement on Austar IV. Jakkin and Akki return to their people in *Dragon's Heart,* their purpose to slowly begin teaching other how to tap their own physical and psychic abilities until Akki is kidnaped by a relentless foe.

Writing in *School Library Journal,* Michael Cart noted that, like the two volumes preceding it, *A Sending of Dragons* benefits from "the almost encyclopedic detail which Yolen has lavished upon her fully realized alternative world of Austar IV, in her sympathetic portrayal of the dragons as both victims and telepathic partners, and in the symbolic sub-text which enriches her narrative and reinforces her universal theme of the interdependency and unique value of all life forms." Appraising *Dragon's Heart,* a *Kirkus Reviews* writer praised Yolen's story as "well supplied with danger and action," while Jonathan Hunt cited the "accomplished" world-building and "engaging and sympathetic" characters as attributes of a novel that marks "a welcome return to one of the best sci-fi fantasies of the previous generation." A *Publishers Weekly* critic noted of the "Pit Dragon Chronicles" that "Yolen's tightly plotted, adventurous trilogy constitutes superb storytelling. She incorporates elements of freedom and rebellion, power and control, love and friendship in a masterfully crafted context."

One of Yolen's most highly acclaimed books combines history and fantasy. *The Devil's Arithmetic,* a young-adult novel, is a time-travel fantasy that is rooted in one of the darkest episodes of history. The novel features Hannah Stern, a twelve-year-old Jewish girl who is transported from contemporary New York City to rural Poland in 1942 when she opens the door for Elijah during her family's Seder celebration. Captured by the Nazis, Hannah—now called Chaya—is taken to a death camp, where she meets Rivka, a spirited young girl who teaches her to fight against the dehumanization of

the camp wherein some must live to bear witness. When Rivka is chosen to be taken to the gas chamber, Chaya, in an act of self-sacrifice, goes in her place; as the doors of the gas chamber close, another transformation takes place and Hannah realizes that her Aunt Eva played a central role in her time-travel experience.

"Yolen is the author of a hundred books, many of which have been praised for their originality, humor, or poetic vision," wrote a *Kirkus Reviews* critic, in appraising *The Devil's Arithmetic,* "but this thoughtful, compelling novel is unique among them." In the *Bulletin of the Center for Children's Books,* Roger Sutton noted that Yolen's depiction of the horrors in the Nazi death camp "is more graphic than any we've seen in holocaust fiction for children before." Confirming that Yolen has brought the "time travel convention to a new and ambitious level," Cynthia Samuels concluded in the *New York Times Book Review* that "sooner or later, all our children must know what happened in the days of the Holocaust. *The Devil's Arithmetic* offers an affecting way to begin."

Yolen wrote *The Devil's Arithmetic* for her own children. As she stated in her acceptance speech for the Sydney Taylor Book Award, "There are books one writes because they are a delight. There are books one writes because one is asked to. There are books one writes because . . . they are there. And there are books one writes simply because the book has to be written."

With *Encounter,* a picture book published to coincide with the 500th anniversary of the discovery of America, Yolen presented readers with what has been seen as is her most controversial work. Written as the remembrance of an elderly Taino man, *Encounter* describes the first meeting between Native Americans and Christopher Columbus. Then a small boy, the narrator awakens from a terrifying dream about three predatory birds riding the waves to see three anchored Spanish ships. Frightened yet fascinated by the strangely garbed strangers who now come ashore, he tells his chief not to welcome the men, but he is ignored. The boy and several others in his tribe are taken aboard the ships as slaves. After he escapes by jumping overboard, the boy tries to warn other tribes, but to no avail; the Taino are wiped out.

Calling *Encounter* an "unusual picture book," Carolyn Phelan noted in *Booklist* that "while the portrayal of Columbus as evil may strike traditionalists as heresy, he did hunger for gold, abduct native people, and ultimately (though unintentionally), destroy the Taino. This book effectively presents their point of view." Writing in the *New Advocate,* James C. Junhke called *Encounter* "among the most powerful and disturbing publications of the Columbus Quincentennial." Noting the "pioneering brilliance" of the book, the critic cited its "reversal of perspective" as a means of allowing "readers to confront what a disaster it was for the Taino people to be discovered and destroyed by Europeans.;"

"We cannot change history," Yolen responded in the same periodical. "But we—and most especially our children—can learn from it so that the next encounters, be they at home, abroad, or in space, may be gentler and mutually respectful."

Throughout her career, Yolen has woven bits and pieces of her personal history—and that of her family and friends—into her works. Several of the author's books are directly autobiographical. For example, *All Those Secrets of the World,* a picture book published in 1991, is set during the two years the author's father was away at war. Yolen recalls how, as a four year old, she watched her father depart by ship. The next day, the fictional Janie and her five-year-old cousin Michael see some tiny specks on the horizon while they are playing on the beach; the specks are ships. Michael teaches Janie a secret of the world, that as he moves farther away, he gets smaller. Two years later, when her father returns, Janie whispers Michael's secret after he tells her that she seems bigger: that when he was so far away, everything seemed smaller, but now that he is here, she is big. A reviewer in *Publishers Weekly* wrote that "Yolen here relates a bittersweet memory from an important period in her childhood. . . . This timely nostalgic story is told with simple grace, and Janie's thoughts and experiences are believably childlike." Phyllis G. Sidorsky, in *School Library Journal,* called *All Those Secrets of the World* an "affecting piece without an extraneous word and one that is particularly timely today."

And Twelve Chinese Acrobats is a tale for middle graders that is based on family stories about Yolen's father's older brother. Set in a Russian village in 1910, the book features Lou the Rascal, a charming troublemaker who keeps getting into scrapes. When Lou is sent to a military school in Kiev, the family—especially narrator Wolf, Lou's youngest brother (and Yolen's father)—is sad. Lou is eventually expelled from military school, and months later he surprises everyone by bringing home a troupe of twelve Chinese acrobats he met while working in a Moscow circus. The acrobats fascinate the locals with their descriptions of an exotic world far removed from the little village. When the acrobats leave the shtel in the spring, Lou's father recognizes his son's managerial ability and sends him to America to find a place for the family.

Reviewing *And Twelve Chinese Acrobats* for the *Bulletin of the Center for Children's Books,* Betsy Hearne noted that "the relationship between the two brothers . . . lends an immediate dynamic to the historical setting," and concluded that the compressed narrative, brief chapters, spacious format, large print, and Jean Gralley's "vivaciously detailed pen-and-ink illustrations dancing across almost every page make this a prime choice for young readers venturing into historical fiction for the first time, or, for that matter, considering a probe into their own family stories." A critic in *Kirkus Reviews* called *And Twelve Chinese Acrobats* a book "radiating family warmth, in words, art, and remembrance."

In the fall of 2010 Yolen's 300th published work reached bookstore shelves. Although such an amazing output was labelled by the media as prolific—especially when one also considers the works she submitted that were rejected by editors—the author herself takes a different view. "'Prolific' carries with it a sneer, a sense of the pejorative," Yolen noted to *School Library Journal* online interviewer Donna Liquori. "Critics use it to mean a hack, someone who is not careful about what they write. I prefer the word 'versatile,' which is an admiring word, as in 'Gosh, she's so versatile. I'm amazed!'" To achieve such versatility has been no simple feat; in addition to being talented Yolen is also amazingly hard working. As she told Liquori: "To write 30 books or 300 books or 3 books? BIC. Butt in chair. Every day."

Biographical and Critical Sources

BOOKS

Children's Books and Their Creators, edited by Anita Silvey, Houghton Mifflin (Boston, MA), 1995, pp. 700-701.
Children's Literature Review, Gale (Detroit, MI), Volume 4, 1982, pp. 255-269, Volume 44, 1997, pp. 167-211.
Dictionary of Literary Biography, Volume 52: *American Writers for Children since 1960: Fiction,* Gale (Detroit, MI), 1986, pp. 398-405.
Drew, Bernard A., *The One Hundred Most Popular Young Adult Authors,* Libraries Unlimited, 1996.
Roginski, Jim, *Behind the Covers: Interviews with Authors and Illustrators of Books for Children and Young Adults,* Libraries Unlimited, 1985.
St. James Guide to Fantasy Writers, St. James Press (Detroit, MI), 1996.
St. James Guide to Young-Adult Writers, St. James Press (Detroit, MI), 1999.
Something about the Author Autobiography Series, Volume 4, Gale (Detroit, MI), 1987, pp. 327-346.
Twentieth-Century Children's Writers, 3rd edition, St. James Press (Detroit, MI), 1989, pp. 1075-1078.
Yolen, Jane, *Guide to Writing for Children,* Writer, 1989.
Yolen, Jane, *Touch Magic: Fantasy, Faerie, and Folktale in the Literature of Childhood,* Philomel (New York, NY), 1981.

PERIODICALS

Booklist, November 15, 1980, Judith Goldberger, review of *Commander Toad in Space,* p. 464; May 15, 1981, Stephanie Zvirin, review of *The Gift of Sarah Barker,* p. 1250; March 1, 1992, Carolyn Phelan, review of *Encounter,* p. 1281; March 15, 2001, Hazel Rochman, review of *Dear Mother, Dear Daughter: Poems for Young People,* p. 1393; April 15, 2001, Gillian Engberg, review of *Odysseus in the Serpent Maze,* p 1561; July, 2001, Ilene Cooper, review of *The Wolf Girls: An Unsolved Mystery from History,* p. 2007; October 1, 2001, Connie Fletcher, review of *Welcome to the River of Grass,* p. 321; November 15, 2001, Todd Morning, review of *The Fish Prince and Other Stories: Mermen Folk Tales,* p. 562; April 15, 2002, Sally Estes, review of *Wizard's Hall,* p. 1416, and Catherine Andronik, review of *The Bagpiper's Ghost,* p. 1418; May 15, 2992, Susan Dove Lempke, review of *Wild Wings: Poems for Young People,* p. 1596; June 1, 2002, Gillian Engberg, review of *The Firebird,* p. 1732; October 15, 2002, Shelley Townsend-Hudson, review of *Harvest Home,* p. 413; January 1, 2003, Ilene Cooper, review of *How Do Dinosaurs Get Well Soon?,* p. 881; February, 1, 2003, John Peters, review of *Atalanta and the Arcadian Beast,* p. 996; March 1, 2003, Carolyn Phelan, review of *My Brothers' Flying Machine,* p. 1208; April 15, 2003, Carolyn Phelan, review of *Sword of the Rightful King: A Novel of King Arthur,* p. 1464; May 15, 2003, Karin Snelson, review of *Hoptoad,* p. 1674; July, 2003, Carolyn Phelan, review of *Roanoke, the Lost Colony: An Unsolved Mystery from History,* p. 1888; September 15, 2003, Ray Olson, review of *The Radiation Sonnets,* p. 195; October 1, 2003, Linda Perkins, review of *The Flying Witch,* p. 325; February 15, 2004, John Peters, review of *Jason and the Gorgon's Blood,* p. 1060; September 1, 2004, Ilene Cooper, review of *The Salem Witch Trials,* p. 118; November 1, 2004, GraceAnne A. DeCandido, review of *Fine Feathered Friends,* p. 478, and Ilene Cooper, review of *Barefoot Book of Ballet Stories,* p. 498; November 15, 2004, Carolyn Phelan, review of *Prince across the Water,* p. 585; July, 2005, Jennifer Mattson, review of *How Do Dinosaurs Eat Their Food?,* p. 1931; August, 2005, Jennifer Locke, review of *Meow: Cat Stories from around the World,* p. 2033; October 1, 2005, Candace Smith, review of *How Do Dinosaurs Get Well Soon?,* p. 74; October 1, 2005, Kay Weisman, review of *Apple for the Teacher: Thirty Songs for Singing While You Work,* p. 56; November 1, 2005, Jennifer Mattson, review of *Soft House,* p. 55; April 1, 2006, Carolyn Phelan, review of *Count Me a Rhyme: Animal Poems by the Numbers,* p. 38; June 1, 2006, Carolyn Phelan, review of *Dimity Duck,* p. 90; September 1, 2006, Diana Tixier Herald, review of *Trollbridge: A Rock 'n' Roll Fairy Tale,* p. 114; November 15, 2006, GraceAnne A. DeCandido, review of *Sleep, Black Bear, Sleep,* p. 56; April 1, 2007, Randall Enos, review of *How Do Dinosaurs Go to School?,* p. 61; April 1, 2007, Hazel Rochman, review of *Here's a Little Poem,* p. 50; August, 2007, Carolyn Phelan, review of *Baby Bear's Big Dreams,* p. 81; September 15, 2007, Anne O'Malley, review of *The Rogues,* p. 63; April 15, 2008, Kay Weisman, review of *Naming Liberty,* p. 58; June 1, 2008, Gillian Engberg, review of *Sea Queens: Women Pirates around the World,* p. 10, and Thom Barthelmess, review of *Johnny Appleseed: The Legend and the Truth,* p. 104; December 15, 2008, Daniel Kraus, review of *Mama's Kiss,* p. 54; March 15, 2009, Hazel

Rochman, review of *A Mirror to Nature: Poems about Reflection,* p. 57; July 1, 2009, Gillian Engberg, review of *The Scarecrow's Dance,* p. 69; November 1, 2009, Gillian Engberg, review of *How Do Dinosaurs Say I Love You?,* p. 53; January 1, 2010, Carolyn Phelan, review of *An Egret's Day,* p. 76; March 15, 2010, Courtney Jones, review of *Foiled,* p. 51; June 1, 2010, Carolyn Phelan, review of *Lost Boys: The Story of the Man Who Created Peter Pan,* p. 96; October 1, 2010, Hazel Rochman, review of *Switching On the Moon: A Very First Book of Bedtime Poems,* p. 45.

Book Report, January-February, 2002, Anne Hanson, review of *The Fish Prince and Other Stories,* p. 74.

Bulletin of the Center for Children's Books, October, 1988, Roger Sutton, review of *The Devil's Arithmetic,* pp. 23-24; June, 1995, Betsy Hearne, review of *And Twelve Chinese Acrobats,* p. 365; September, 2003, Elizabeth Bush, review of *Roanoke, the Lost Colony,* p. 40; September, 2005, Hope Morrison, review of *Meow,* p. 58.

Children's Book News, January-February, 1970, review of *The Emperor and the Kite,* pp. 23-24.

Children's Book Review Service, December, 1973, Eleanor Von Schweinitz, review of *The Girl Who Loved the Wind,* pp. 172-173; June, 1981, Barbara Baker, review of *The Gift of Sarah Barker,* p. 100.

Horn Book, August, 1982, Ann A. Flowers, review of *Dragon's Blood,* pp. 418-419; April, 1984, Charlotte W. Draper, review of *Heart's Blood,* p. 206; November-December, 1994, Jane Yolen, "An Empress of Thieves," pp. 702-705; January-February, 2003, Anita L. Burkam, review of *Girl in a Cage,* p. 86; March-April, 2003, Christine M. Hepperman, review of *How Do Dinosaurs Get Well Soon?,* p. 208; May-June, 2003, Anita L. Burkham, review of *Sword of the Rightful King,* p. 359, and Susan Dove Lempke, review of *Mightier than the Sword,* p. 362; November-December, 2004, Anita L. Burkam, review of *Prince across the Water,* p. 720; September-October, 2005, Christine M. Heppermann, review of *How Do Dinosaurs Eat Their Food?,* p. 571; July-August, 2007, Martha V. Parravano, review of *How Do Dinosaurs Go to School?,* p. 388; July-August, 2009, Joanna Rudge Long, review of *My Uncle Emily,* p. 415; July-August, 2009, Jonathan Hunt, review of *Dragon's Heart,* p. 435; July-August, 2010, Tanya D. Auger, review of *Foiled,* p. 127; September-October, 2010, Joanna Rudge Long, review of *Elsie's Bird,* p. 69.

Judaica Librarianship, spring, 1989-winter, 1990, Jane Yolen, transcript of acceptance speech for Sydney Taylor Book Award, pp. 52-53.

Kirkus Reviews, July 15, 1974, review of *The Girl Who Cried Flowers and Other Tales,* p. 741; August 15, 1988, review of *The Devil's Arithmetic,* p. 1248; April 15, 1995, review of *And Twelve Chinese Acrobats,* p. 564; September 15, 2991, review of *Welcome to the River of Grass,* p. 1372; January 1, 2002, review of *Hippolyta and the Curse of the Amazons,* p. 54; March 1, 2002, reviews of *Wild Wings* and *The Bagpiper's Ghost,* both p. 349; May 1, 2002, review of *The Firebird,* p. 670; August 15, 2002, reviews of *Girl in a Cage* and *Harvest Home,* both p. 1240; December 1,

2002, reviews of *How Do Dinosaurs Get Well Soon?* and *The Sea King,* both p. 1776; March 15, 2003, review of *My Brothers' Flying Machine,* p. 482; April 15, 2003, review of *Mightier than the Sword,* p. 614; May 1, 2003, review of *Sword of the Rightful King,* p. 686; May 15, 2003, review of *Hoptoad,* p. 758; June 15, 2003, review of *Roanoke, the Lost Colony,* p. 865; July 1, 2003, review of *The Flying Witch,* p. 917; September 1, 2003, review of *Least Things,* p. 1133; August 15, 2004, review of *The Salem Witch Trials,* p. 815; September 15, 2004, review of *Prince across the Water,* p. 923; January 1, 2005, review of *The Perfect Wizard: Hans Christian Andersen,* p. 175; July 1, 2005, review of *Meow,* p. 745; July 15, 2005, review of *Soft House,* p. 797; April 15, 2006, review of *Dimity Duck,* p. 419; June 15, 2007, review of *How Do Dinosaurs Go to School?;* April 15, 2008, review of *Naming Liberty;* June 1, 2008, review of *Sea Queens;* March 1, 2009, review of *A Mirror to Nature;* April 1, 2009, review of *Dragon's Heart;* April 15, 2009, review of *My Uncle Emily;* September 1, 2009, review of *Come to the Fairies' Ball;* December 1, 2009, review of *An Egret's Day;* March 1, 2010, review of *Foiled.*

Kliatt, March, 2002, Claire Rosser, review of *Queen's Own Fool,* p. 20; May, 2003, Claire Rosser, review of *Sword of the Rightful King,* p. 15; September, 2003, Stacey Conrad, review of *Boots and the Seven Leaguers,* p. 29.

Library Journal, June 15, 1972, Janet G. Polacheck, review of *Friend: The Story of George Fox and the Quakers,* p. 2245.

New Advocate, spring, 1993, James C. Juhnke and Jane Yolen, "An Exchange on *Encounter,*" pp. 94-96.

New York Times Book Review, November 20, 1977, Jane Langton, review of *The Hundredth Dove and Other Tales,* p. 30; November 13, 1988, Cynthia Samuels, "Hannah Learns to Remember," p. 62; November 8, 1992, Noel Perrin, "Bulldozer Blues," p. 54; July 12, 2009, "A Mirror to Nature," p. 20; October 11, 2009, Julie Just, review of *My Uncle Emily,* p. 13.

Publishers Weekly, August 14, 1967, review of *The Emperor and the Kite,* p. 50; July 22, 1974, review of *The Girl Who Cried Flowers and Other Tales,* p. 70; January 11, 1980, review of *All in the Woodland Early: An ABC Book,* p. 88; October 9, 1987, review of *A Sending of Dragons,* p. 90; March 22, 1991, review of *All Those Secrets of the World,* p. 80; April 29, 2002, review of *The Firebird,* p. 68; February, 2003, Angela J. Reynolds, review of *Atalanta and the Arcadian Beast,* p. 150; March 24, 2003, review of *My Brothers' Flying Machine,* p. 75; April 14, 2003, review of *Sword of the Rightful King,* p. 72; July 7, 2003, review of *The Radiation Sonnets,* p. 60; August 4, 2003, review of *The Flying Witch,* p. 78; November 29, 2004, review of *The Book of Ballads,* p. 24; February 21, 2005, review of *The Perfect Wizard,* p. 175; July 25, 2005, review of *How Do Dinosaurs Eat Their Food?,* p. 74; December 19, 2005, reviews of *Baby Bear's Chairs,* p. 62, and *Soft House,* p. 64; December 18, 2006, review of *Sleep, Black Bear, Sleep,* p. 61; October 20, 2008, review of *Mama's Kiss,* p. 49; April 20, 2009, review of *A Mirror to Nature,* p. 49; May 4, 2009, review of *My Uncle Emily,* p. 50; July 20, 2009, review of *The Scarecrow's Dance,* p. 139; February 8, 2010, review of *All Star! Honus Wagner and the Most Famous Baseball Card Ever,* p. 50; April 5, 2010, review of *Foiled,* p. 64; May 24, 2010, review of *Not All Princesses Dress in Pink,* p. 50; September 9, 2010, review of *Flying High,* p. 100; November 22, 2010, review of *Tales, Tongue-Twister, and More,* p. 56.

School Librarian, December, 1983, Pauline Thomas, review of *Dragon's Blood,* p. 384.

School Library Journal, March, 1973, Marilyn R. Singer, review of *The Girl Who Loved the Wind,* p. 102; December, 1980, review of *Commander Toad in Space,* p. 66; September, 1982, Patricia Manning, review of *Dragon's Blood,* p. 146; January, 1988, Michael Cart, review of *A Sending of Dragons,* pp. 87-88; July, 1991, Phyllis G. Sidorsky, review of *All Those Secrets of the World,* p. 66; December, 2000, review of *Color Me a Rhyme,* p. 167; May, 2001, Cynthia J. Rieben, review of *Mirror, Mirror,* p. 178; July, 2001, Angela J. Reynolds, review of *Odysseus in the Serpent Maze,* p. 116; August, 2001, Anne Chapman, review of *The Wolf Girls,* p. 174; November, 2001, Margaret Bush, review of *Welcome to the River of Grass,* p. 153; March, 2002, Beth L. Meister, review of *Hippolyta and the Curse of the Amazons,* and Cherie Estes, review of *The Bagpiper's Ghost,* both p. 240; June, 2002, Sharon Korbeck, review of *Wild Wings,* and Ellen Heath, review of *The Firebird,* both p. 127; October, 2002, Nina Lindsay, review of *Poems as Far as the Eye Can See,* p. 152, and Starr E. Smith, review of *Girl in a Cage,* p. 178; November, 2002, Catherine Threadgill, review of *Harvest Home,* p. 140, and Jessica Snow, review of *Time for Naps,* p. 142; February, 2003, Jody McCoy, review of *How Do Dinosaurs Get Well Soon?,* p. 126; March, 2003, Harriett Fargnoli, review of *My Brothers' Flying Machine,* p. 225; May, 2003, Miriam Lang Budin, review of *Mightier than the Sword,* p. 143; July, 2003, Margaret A. Chang, review of *Sword of the Rightful King,* p. 135; September, 2003, James K. Irwin, review of *The Flying Witch,* p. 208; October, 2003, Nancy Palmer, review of *Roanoke, the Lost Colony,* and Donna Cardon, review of *Least Things,* both p. 157; February, 2004, Angela J. Reynolds, review of *Jason and the Gorgon's Blood,* p. 154; November, 2004, Elaine Fort Weischedel, review of *The Salem Witch Trials,* p. 174; December, 2004, Kimberly Monaghan, review of *Prince across the Water,* p. 154, and Susan Scheps, review of *Fine Feathered Friends,* and Carol Schene, review of *The Barefoot Book of Ballet Stories,* both p. 172; August, 2005, Roxanne Burg, review of *How Dinosaurs Eat Their Food?,* p. 110, and Kathleen Whalin, review of *Meow,* p. 120; June, 2006, Joy Fleishacker, review of *Dimity Duck,* p. 130; February, 2007, Susan Weitz, review of *Sleep, Black Bear, Sleep,* p. 98; June, 2007, Neala Arnold, review of *How Do Dinosaurs Go to School?,* p. 128; July, 2008, Carol S. Surges, review of *Sea Queens,* p. 118; October, 2008, Susan Scheps, review of *Johnny Appleseed: the Legend and the Truth,* p. 137; June, 2009, Marilyn Taniguchi, review of *A*

Mirror to Nature, p. 113; October, 2009, Debbie S. Hoskins, review of *How Do Dinosaurs Say I Love You?,* p. 108; December, 2009, Adrienne Wilson, review of *Come to the Fairies' Ball,* p. 94; March, 2010, Marilyn Taniguchi, review of *All Star!,* p. 146, and Karen Alexander, review of *Foiled,* p. 187; June, 2010, Lauralyn Persson, review of *Not All Princesses Dress in Pink,* p. 86; July, 2010, Mary Landrum, review of *Lost Boy: The Story of the Man Who Created Peter Pan,* p. 76; September, 2010, Barbara Ellman, review of *Elsie's Bird,* p. 136; October, 2010, Julie Roach, review of *Switching on the Moon,* p. 105.

Teaching and Learning Literature, November-December, 1996, Lee Bennett Hopkins, "O Yolen: A Look at the Poetry of Jane Yolen," pp. 66-68.

Washington Post Book World, April 13, 1980, Jerome Beatty Jr., "Herds of Hungry Hogs Hurrying Home," p. 10.

Writer, March, 1997, John Koch, interview with Yolen, p. 20.

Writer's Journal, January-February, 2011, Dorit Sasson, interview with Yolen, p. 41.

ONLINE

Jane Yolen Home Page, http://www.janeyolen.com (May 15, 2011).

School Library Journal Online, http://www.schoollibrary journal.com/ (September 9, 2010), Donna Liquori, interview with Yolen.

Writers Write Web site, http://www.writerswrite.com/ (June 1, 2002), Claire E. White, interview with Yolen.

OTHER

Children's Writer at Work: Jane Yolen (film), Reel Life, 1997.*